James Osmond / Alamy

PHILIP'S ROAD ATLAS

2017 COMPLETE BRITAIN & IRELAND

www.philips-maps.co.uk

First published in 2009 by Philip's
a division of Octopus Publishing Group Ltd
www.octopusbooks.co.uk
Carmelite House, 50 Victoria Embankment
London EC4Y 0DZ
An Hachette UK Company
www.hachette.co.uk

Eighth edition 2016
First impression 2016

ISBN 978-1-84907-412-4 (spiral)
ISBN 978-1-84907-413-1 (hardback)

Cartography by Philip's
Copyright © 2016 Philip's

This product includes mapping data licensed from Ordnance Survey®, with the permission of the Controller of Her Majesty's Stationery Office. © Crown copyright 2016. All rights reserved. Licence number 100011710.

The map of Ireland on pages XVIII-XIX is based upon the Crown Copyright and is reproduced with the permission of Land & Property Services under delegated authority from the Controller of Her Majesty's Stationery Office, © Crown Copyright and database right 2016, PMLPA number 100503, and on Ordnance Survey Ireland by permission of the Government © Ordnance Survey Ireland / Government of Ireland Permit number 9040.

Inside back cover: **County and unitary authority boundaries**

Road map symbols

M6 — Motorway, toll motorway

4 5 — Motorway junction – full, restricted access

S S — Motorway service area – full, restricted access

Motorway under construction

A453 — Primary route – dual, single carriageway

S ⊕ ○ — Service area, roundabout, multi-level junction

4 5 — Numbered junction – full, restricted access

Primary route under construction

Narrow primary route

Derby — Primary destination

A34 — A road – dual, single carriageway

A road under construction, narrow A road

B2135 — B road – dual, single carriageway

B road under construction, narrow B road

Minor road – over 4 metres, under 4 metres wide

Minor road with restricted access

2 — Distance in miles

Scenic route

TOLL — Toll, steep gradient – arrow points downhill

Tunnel

National trail – England and Wales

Long distance footpath – Scotland

Railway with station

Level crossing, tunnel

Preserved railway with station

National boundary

County / unitary authority boundary

Car ferry, catamaran

Passenger ferry, catamaran

Hovercraft

CALAIS — Ferry destination

Ferry — Car ferry – river crossing

✈ ✈ — Principal airport, other airport

National park

Area of Outstanding Natural Beauty – England and Wales National Scenic Area – Scotland

forest park / regional park / national forest

Woodland

Beach

Linear antiquity

Roman road

⊡ ⚔ 1066 — Hillfort, battlefield – with date

🔆 🍁 ▲795 — Viewpoint, nature reserve, spot height – in metres

⚑ ▲ ◎ — Golf course, youth hostel, sporting venue

⚎ 🚐 🏕 — Camp site, caravan site, camping and caravan site

🛒 ▲ P&R — Shopping village, park and ride

29 — Adjoining page number – road maps

Approach map symbols

M6 — Motorway

Toll motorway

6 5 — Motorway junction – full, restricted access

S — Service area

Under construction

A6 — Primary route – dual, single carriageway

S — Service area

○ — Multi-level junction

◉ — roundabout

Under construction

A195 — A road – dual, single carriageway

B1288 — B road – dual, single carriageway

Minor road – dual, single carriageway

Ring road

3 — Distance in miles

Congestion charge area

COSELEY — Railway with station

LOXDALE — Tramway with station

M ⊖ ⊖ ● — Underground or metro station

Town plan symbols

Motorway

Primary route – dual, single carriageway

A road – dual, single carriageway

B road – dual, single carriageway

Minor through road

→ One-way street

Pedestrian roads

Shopping streets

Railway with station

City Hall — Tramway with station

Bus or railway station building

Shopping precinct or retail park

Park

🏛 — Building of public interest

🎭 🎥 — Theatre, cinema

P ♿ — Parking, shopmobility

Bank ⊖ — Underground station

West St ● — Metro station

H ▣ — Hospital, Police station

PO — Post office

Tourist information

✝ Abbey, cathedral or priory

🏛 Ancient monument

🐟 Aquarium

🖼 Art gallery

🦜 Bird collection or aviary

🏰 Castle

⛪ Church

Country park
🏛 England and Wales
🏛 Scotland

🐎 Farm park

❀ Garden

⛵ Historic ship

🏠 House

🏠 House and garden

▨ Motor racing circuit

🏛 Museum

Ⓐ Picnic area

🚂 Preserved railway

🏇 Race course

🦅 Roman antiquity

🦌 Safari park

🎡 Theme park

Tourist information centre
i open all year
i open seasonally

🐘 Zoo

✦ Other place of interest

Relief

Feet	metres
3000	914
2600	792
2200	671
1800	549
1400	427
1000	305
0	0

Road map scales

3·15 miles to 1 inch • 1:200 000

0 1 2 3 4 5 6 miles

0 1 2 3 4 5 6 7 8 9 10 km

Parts of Scotland

4.18 miles to 1 inch • 1:265 000

0 1 2 3 4 5 6 miles

0 2 4 6 8 10 km

Scottish Highlands and Islands

5.24 miles to 1 inch • 1:332 000

0 1 2 3 4 5 6 7 8 miles

0 2 4 6 8 10 12 km

Orkney and Shetland Islands 1:400 000, 6.31 miles to 1 inch

Motorway service areas

Restricted motorway junctions

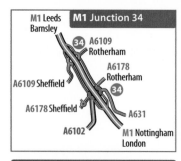

M1 Junction 34

M1 Leeds Barnsley
34 A6109 Rotherham
A6109 Sheffield
A6178 Rotherham
34
A6178 Sheffield
A631
A6102
M1 Nottingham London

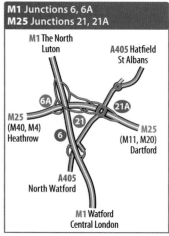

M1 Junctions 6, 6A
M25 Junctions 21, 21A

M1 The North Luton
A405 Hatfield St Albans
6A
21A
M25 (M40, M4) Heathrow
21
6
M25 (M11, M20) Dartford
A405 North Watford
M1 Watford Central London

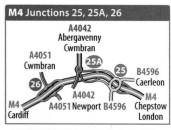

M4 Junctions 25, 25A, 26

A4042 Abergavenny Cwmbran
A4051 Cwmbran
25A
25
B4596 Caerleon
26
A4042
A4051 Newport
B4596
M4 Chepstow London
M4 Cardiff

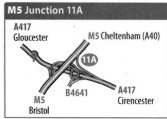

M5 Junction 11A

A417 Gloucester
M5 Cheltenham (A40)
11A
M5 Bristol
B4641
A417 Cirencester

M8 Junctions 8, 9 · M73 Junctions 1, 2
M74 Junctions 2A, 3, 3A, 4

M8 Glasgow
9
M73 Stirling
8
A89 Coatbridge
2
A8 Edinburgh
B7058
A74
B765
A74
1/4
M73
M74 Glasgow
2A
3
M74
3A
B7001
A763
B758
A721
B7071
M74 Carlisle

M1	Northbound	Southbound
2	No exit	No access
4	No exit	No access
6A	No exit. Access from M25 only	No access. Exit to M25 only
7	No exit. Access from A414 only	No access. Exit to A414 only
17	No access. Exit to M45 only	No exit. Access from M45 only
19	No exit to A14	No access from A14
21A	No access	No exit
23A		Exit to A42 only
24A	No exit	No access
35A	No access	No exit
43	No access. Exit to M621 only	No exit. Access from M621 only
48	No exit to A1(M) southbound	

M3	Eastbound	Westbound
8	No exit	No access
10	No access	No exit
13	No access to M27 eastbound	
14	No exit	No access

M4	Eastbound	Westbound
1	Exit to A4 eastbound only	Access from A4 westbound only
2	Access from A4 eastbound only	Access to A4 westbound only
21	No exit	No access
23	No access	No exit
25	No exit	No access
25A	No exit	No access
29	No exit	No access
38		No access
39	No exit or access	No exit
41	No access	No exit
41A	No exit	No access
42	Access from A483 only	Exit to A483 only

M5	Northbound	Southbound
10	No exit	No access
11A	No access from A417 eastbound	No exit to A417 westbound

M6	Northbound	Southbound
3A	No access. Exit to M42 northbound only	No exit. Access from M6 eastbound only
4A	No exit. Access from M42 southbound only	No access. Exit to M42 only
5	No access	No exit
10A	No access. Exit to M54 only	No exit. Access from M54 only
11A	No exit. Access from M6 Toll only	No access. Exit to M6 Toll only
20	No exit to M56 eastbound	No access from M56 westbound
24	No exit	No access
25	No access	No exit
30	No exit. Access from M61 northbound only	No access. Exit to M61 southbound only
31A	No access	No exit
45	No access	No exit

M6 Toll	Northbound	Southbound
T1		No exit
T2	No exit, no access	No access
T5	No exit	No access
T7	No access	No exit
T8	No access	No exit

M8	Eastbound	Westbound
8	No exit to M73 northbound	No access from M73 southbound
9	No access	No exit
13	No exit southbound	Access from M73 southbound only
14	No access	No exit
16	No exit	No access
17	No exit	No access
18		No exit
19	No exit to A814 eastbound	No access from A814 westbound
20	No exit	No access
21	No access from M74	No exit
22	No exit. Access from M77 only	No access. Exit to M77 only
23	No exit	No access
25	Exit to A739 northbound only. Access from A739 southbound only	Access from A739 southbound only
25A	No exit	No access
28	No exit	No access
28A	No exit	No access

M9	Eastbound	Westbound
1A	No exit	No access
2	No access	No exit
3	No exit	No access
6	No access	No exit
8	No exit	No access

M11	Northbound	Southbound
4	No exit. Access from A406 only	No access. Exit to A406 only
5	No access	No exit
9	No access	No exit
13	No access	No exit
14	No exit to A428 westbound	No exit. Access from A14 westbound only

M20	Eastbound	Westbound
2	No access	No access
3	No exit Access from M26 eastbound only	No access Exit to M26 westbound only
11A	No access	No exit

M23	Northbound	Southbound
7	No exit to A23 southbound	No access from A23 northbound
10A	No exit	No access

M25	Clockwise	Anticlockwise
5	No exit to M26 eastbound	No access from M26 westbound
19	No access	No exit
21	No exit to M1 southbound. Access from M1 southbound only	No exit to M1 southbound. Access from M1 southbound only
31	No exit	No access

M27	Eastbound	Westbound
10	No exit	No access
12	No access	No exit

M40	Eastbound	Westbound
3	No exit	No access
7	No exit	No access
8	No exit	No access
13	No exit	No access
14	No access	No exit
16	No access	No exit

M42	Northbound	Southbound
1	No exit	No access
7	No access Exit to M6 northbound only	No exit Access from M6 northbound only
7A	No access. Exit to M6 southbound only	No exit
8	No exit. Access from M6 southbound only	Exit to M6 northbound only. Access from M6 southbound only

M45	Eastbound	Westbound
M1 J17	Access to M1 southbound only	No access from M1 southbound
With A45	No access	No exit

M48	Eastbound	Westbound
M4 J21	No exit to M4 westbound	No access from M4 eastbound
M4 J23	No access from M4 westbound	No exit to M4 eastbound

M49	Southbound	Northbound
18A	No exit to M5 northbound	No access from M5 southbound

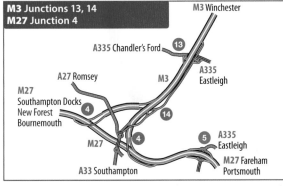

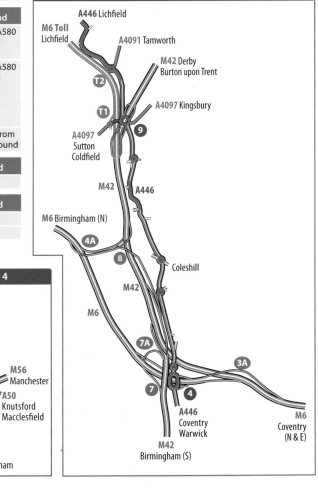

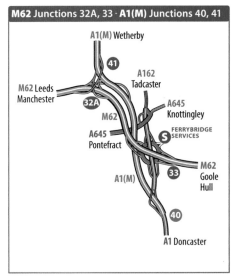

M53	Northbound	Southbound
11	Exit to M56 eastbound only. Access from M56 westbound only	Exit to M56 eastbnd only. Access from M56 westbound only

M56	Eastbound	Westbound
2	No exit	No access
3	No access	No exit
4	No exit	No access
7		No access
8	No exit or access	No exit
9	No access from M6 northbound	No access to M6 southbound
15	No exit to M53	No access from M53 northbound

M57	Northbound	Southbound
3	No exit	No access
5	No exit	No access

M58	Eastbound	Westbound
1	No exit	No access

M60	Clockwise	Anticlockwise
2	No exit	
3	No exit to A34 northbound	No exit to A34 northbound
4	No access from M56	No exit to M56
5	No exit to A5103 southbound	No exit to A5103 northbound
14	No exit	No access
16	No exit	No access
20	No access	No exit
22		No access
25	No access	
26		No exit or access
27	No exit	No access

M61	Northbound	Southbound
2	No access from A580 eastbound	No exit to A580 westbound
3	No access from A580 eastbound. No access from A666 southbound	No exit to A580 westbound
M6 J30	No exit to M6 southbound	No access from M6 northbound

M62	Eastbound	Westbound
23	No access	No exit

M65	Eastbound	Westbound
9	No access	No exit
11	No exit	No access

M66	Northbound	Southbound
1	No access	No exit

M67	Eastbound	Westbound
1A	No access	No exit
2	No exit	No access

M69	Northbound	Southbound
2	No exit	No access

M73	Northbound	Southbound
2	No access from M8 or A89 eastbound. No exit to A89	No exit to M8 or A89 westbound. No access from A89

M74	Northbound	Southbound
3	No access	No exit
3A	No exit	No access
7	No exit	No access
9	No exit or access	No access
10		No exit
11	No exit	No access
12	No access	No exit

M77	Northbound	Southbound
4	No exit	No access
6	No exit	No access
7	No exit or access	
8	No access	No access

M80	Northbound	Southbound
4A	No access	No exit
6A	No access	
8	Exit to M876 northbound only. No access	Access from M876 southbound only. No exit

M90	Northbound	Southbound
2A	No access	No exit
7	No exit	No access
8	No access	No exit
10	No access from A912	No exit to A912

M180	Eastbound	Westbound
1	No access	No exit

M621	Eastbound	Westbound
2A	No exit	No access
4	No exit	
5	No exit	No access
6	No access	No exit

M876	Northbound	Southbound
2	No access	No exit

A1(M)	Northbound	Southbound
2	No access	No exit
3		No access
5	No exit	No access
14	No exit	No access
40	No access	No exit
43	No exit. Access from M1 only	No access. Exit to M1 only
57	No access	No exit
65	No access	No exit

A3(M)	Northbound	Southbound
1	No access	No access
4	No exit	No exit

A38(M)	Northbound	Southbound
With Victoria Rd, (Park Circus) Birmingham	No exit	No access

A48(M)	Northbound	Southbound
M4 Junc 29	Exit to M4 eastbound only	Access from M4 westbound only
29A	Access from A48 eastbound only	Exit to A48 westbound only

A57(M)	Eastbound	Westbound
With A5103	No access	No exit
With A34	No access	No exit

A58(M)		Southbound
With Park Lane and Westgate, Leeds		No access

A64(M)	Eastbound	Westbound
With A58 Clay Pit Lane, Leeds	No access	No exit
With Regent Street, Leeds	No access	No access

A74(M)	Northbound	Southbound
18	No access	No exit
22		No exit

A194(M)	Northbound	Southbound
A1(M) J65 Gateshead Western Bypass	Access from A1(M) northbound only	Exit to A1(M) southbound only

M3 Junctions 13, 14
M27 Junction 4

M3 Winchester
A335 Chandler's Ford — 13
A335 Eastleigh
A27 Romsey
M3
M27 Southampton Docks New Forest Bournemouth
4
14
5 A335 Eastleigh
M27
A33 Southampton
M27 Fareham Portsmouth

M6 Junctions 3A, 4A · M42 Junctions 7, 7A, 8, 9
M6 Toll Junctions T1, T2

A446 Lichfield
M6 Toll Lichfield
A4091 Tamworth
M42 Derby Burton upon Trent
T2
A4097 Kingsbury
T1
9
A4097 Sutton Coldfield
M42
A446
M6 Birmingham (N)
4A
8
Coleshill
M42
M6
7A
3A
7
4
A446 Coventry Warwick
M6 Coventry (N & E)
M42 Birmingham (S)

M6 Junction 20 · M56 Junction 4

M6 Preston Liverpool
A50 Warrington
B5158 Lymm
LYMM SERVICES
S
M56 Manchester
A50 Knutsford Macclesfield
20
9
M56 Runcorn Chester
M6 Birmingham

M62 Junctions 32A, 33 · A1(M) Junctions 40, 41

A1(M) Wetherby
41
A162 Tadcaster
M62 Leeds Manchester
32A
M62
A645 Knottingley
FERRYBRIDGE SERVICES
A645 Pontefract
S
M62 Goole Hull
33
A1(M)
40
A1 Doncaster

Mobile Layby Cafés – gourmet or gruesome?

Do you drive on by?

**Stephen Mesquita,
Philip's On the Road Correspondent**

▲ A roadside snack van sign in Herefordshire *Jeff Morgan / Alamy*

Have you ever done this? You're driving along on one of Britain's A-Roads. It's sometime between 6am and 2pm. You're feeling a bit peckish. You see a layby coming up. There's a notice by the road. Something about hot food. There's a van flying a Union Jack. There are a couple of truck drivers there, queueing up. You might even catch a tempting whiff of something frying.

And you drive straight past. Not really for you? You've never eaten in a layby so you'll wait for a place you know and recognise. Or buy a sandwich at the next petrol station.

Well, that's what I've always done. Up until yesterday. That's when I set out, with my trusty accomplice (and Philip's Sales Supremo) Stuart, to see if my lifelong prejudices were justified.

Butty Vans

A quick word about terminology first. We're going to drop the 'Mobile Layby Cafés' and go with 'Butty Vans'. Stuart and I were out to beat The Breakfast Buns from Butty Vans in One Morning Record.

And so it was with some trepidation that we set off from Northampton and headed for our first Butty Van. Here's confession number one: as soon as we'd photographed the bacon roll that we'd ordered, we polished it off.

This was a good start – and in stark contrast to our Motorway Service Area research, where the fare was so unappetising that we tried only a tiny portion of each item and left the rest.

And as the day started, so it went on. Of the eight buns, only one really disappointed. The other seven were tasty, hot, great value and came with friendly chat. Stuart and I polished almost all of them off – and two especially good ones were down the gullets of Philip's intrepid breakfast critics before you could say 'another bacon roll please'.

▼ **Roadside snack van, Perthshire** *Mar Photographics / Alamy*

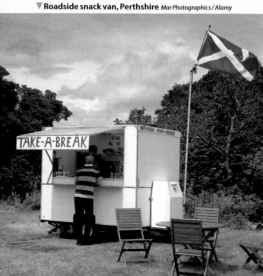

▲ The first bacon butty of the day in a layby alongside the A43

Eight in a Day

Would I recommend eight in a day? As a gastronomic experience, no. It's too much salt intake (my car was littered with empty bottles of water by the end of the day). And I did long for a freshly made flat white by the end of the day.

But a Butty Van breakfast or snack every now and again? Absolutely. Now I've done it once, I'll be very happy to do it again. In fact, I'm rather ashamed I hadn't managed to overcome my prejudices before now.

So to answer my question. Gourmet: no. Gruesome: certainly not. A tasty roadside snack, piping hot, cooked to order and served with a smile – definitely. I'll have one of those.

Butty Vans – what you need to know

- **Layby cafes are licensed by the local authority**, normally annually, to do business in a particular layby.

- **Food Hygiene is an important part of their credibility** – most of them display their certificates prominently.

- **You can't go there for dinner.** Most open early (often around 6am) and shut up around 2pm (sometimes 3pm).

- **They aren't just found in laybys on A Roads.** Some are on industrial estates and business parks.

- **The good ones are there come rain or shine** (bad weather can be good for business) most days of the year.

- **Most of them have a name:** we sampled the fare at Dom's Doorsteps, Taste Buds Snacks, Sizzlers, Delicias and Smell the Bacon.

Butty Vans vs. Motorway Service Areas– how they compare

If you're expecting Butty Vans to serve up the fare you get at your local deli, you probably don't need to read on. The buns are not made of artisanal sourdough ciabatta. The butter isn't Danish unsalted. The bacon didn't cost £15 a kilo. The eggs probably aren't fresh from the farm that morning. Butty Vans aren't posh.

But the point is this – all the Butty Vans we ate at were owned by people who took great pride in what they did. We met one real foody proprietor who told us he'd been to a burger fair the weekend before and always offered specials ('Codfinger'; 'Blue Burger Special'). All of them were aware that, to compete against the big brands, they had to offer good food at good prices.

The ingredients were perfectly decent. The bacon was almost universally of a better quality than we tasted last year in our Full English Breakfast campaign in Motorway Service Areas. And it was all cooked to order in front of you, which gave it one spectacular advantage over the Motorway Service Areas. It was hot.

And it was a fraction of the price.

The only disappointment was the tea and coffee. But at £0.70–£0.80 a cup, you should know what you're getting and you get what you pay for – although at one Butty Van, the teabags were Yorkshire Tea.

You can compare further in our **Butty Van vs. Motorway Service Area checklist:**

	Butty Vans	Motorway Services
Good Value for Money	✔	✗
Proud of what they do	✔	✗
Cooked to Order	✔	rarely
Meal Hot	✔	✗
Quality of ingredients	See above	See above
Quality of hot drinks	✗	✗
Friendly Service	✔	✗
Parking	✔	✔
Easy to find	✗	✔

- **It's a competitive business** – and their regulars (mostly truck drivers and white van men on A Roads) are discerning customers who expect tasty food at reasonable prices. We heard one van driver say he draws the line at paying £1 for a cup of tea.

- **We were made very welcome**, even though it was obvious we weren't their usual clientele.

Our thanks to all the proprietors who answered our questions about their businesses so openly.

Eight Meals in a Bun between 9am and 2pm – how was it for me?

Meal in a Bun One

Location	A43 West of Northampton
Meal	Bacon roll plus tea
Price	£2.50 plus £0.60

Verdict Generous helping of tasty bacon, cooked in front of us and piping hot. The tea was wet and warm.

Meal in a Bun Two

Location	A43 Brackley
Meal	Sausage and Bacon roll plus tea
Price	£3.20 plus £0.50

Verdict A breakfast on its own served with a smile and lots of chat. The ingredients were nothing special but all tasty.

Meal in a Bun Three

Location	A422 between Buckingham and Milton Keynes
Meal	Bacon and Egg roll plus coffee
Price	£3.00 plus £0.80

Verdict Another very decent breakfast in a bun, with the egg cooked to order. Yorkshire Tea teabags spurned for instant coffee. Should have had the tea.

Meal in a Bun Four

Location	Harding Road, Milton Keynes
Meal:	Sausage and Egg roll plus tea
Price:	£2.25 plus £0.50

Verdict Sausage and egg: not expensive ingredients but properly cooked, nice and hot and at a nugatory price.

Meal in a Bun Five

Location	Yardley Road Industrial Estate, Olney
Meal	Double egg roll
Price	£2.50

Verdict I was stupid. I had a double egg sandwich (which was tasty) but I was rightly berated by Mr Sizzler for not being more adventurous and having one of his speciality burgers or chicken dishes. The things I sacrifice to make these surveys fair.

Meal in a Bun Six

Location	A505 West of Royston
Meal	Bacon Roll
Price	£2.00

Verdict The best bread (slightly toasted) and loads of decent bacon for £2.00. I rest my case. I should have added: cooked by Italians. They know how to cook, the Italians. Even good old English Bacon butties. Buonissimo!

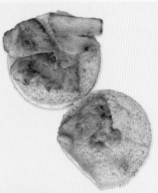

Meal in a Bun Seven

Location	A505 West of Royston
Meal	Bacon Roll
Price	£2.50

Verdict A bit disappointing. Bread tough, bacon tough. Our only below par experience of the day.

Meal in a Bun Eight

Location:	A505 East of Royston
Meal:	Sausage roll
Price:	£3.00

Verdict This café was called *Smell the Bacon* but the sausages were from *Musks* of Newmarket. They were delicious! They seemed to disappear remarkably quickly, Stuart.

How to find Butty Vans

Most Butty Vans are either an 'impulse buy' (you see them as you pass by) or have their regular customers who know where they are. But say you are planning a journey and you want to know for sure there's a Butty Van at a point on your route. Then you need the free app from Butty Van Finder (go to buttyvan.com). We don't even need to describe it: these screen grabs say it all.

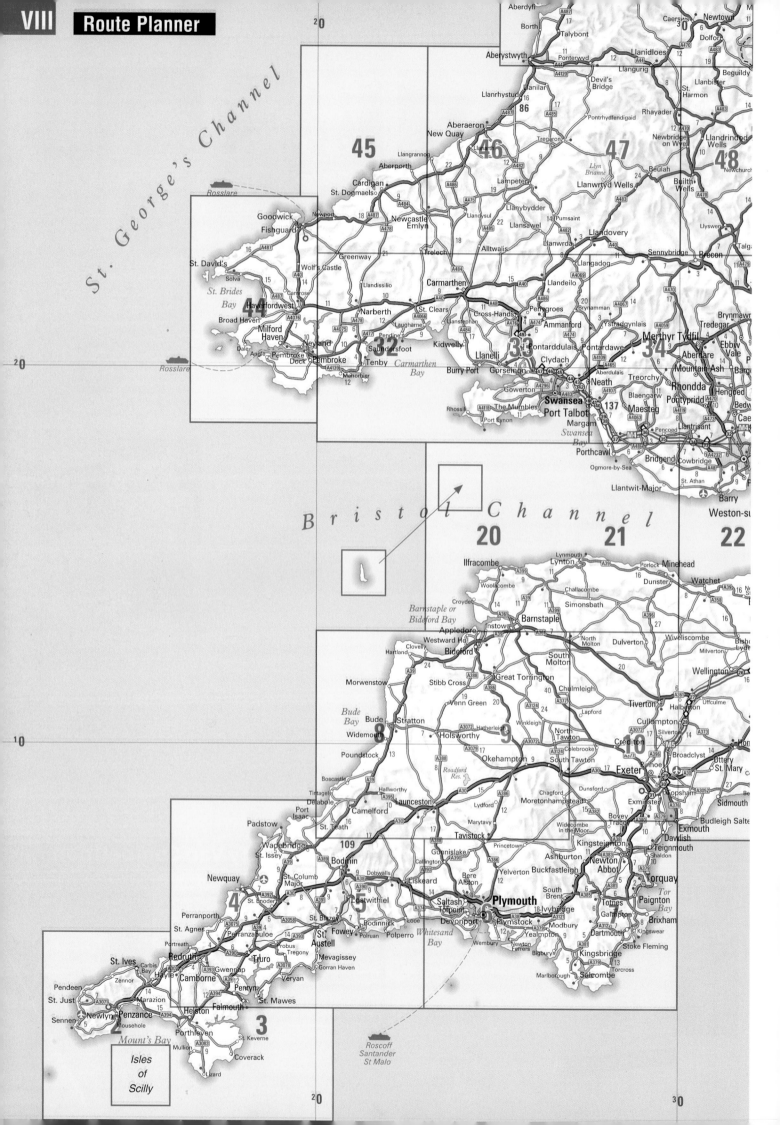

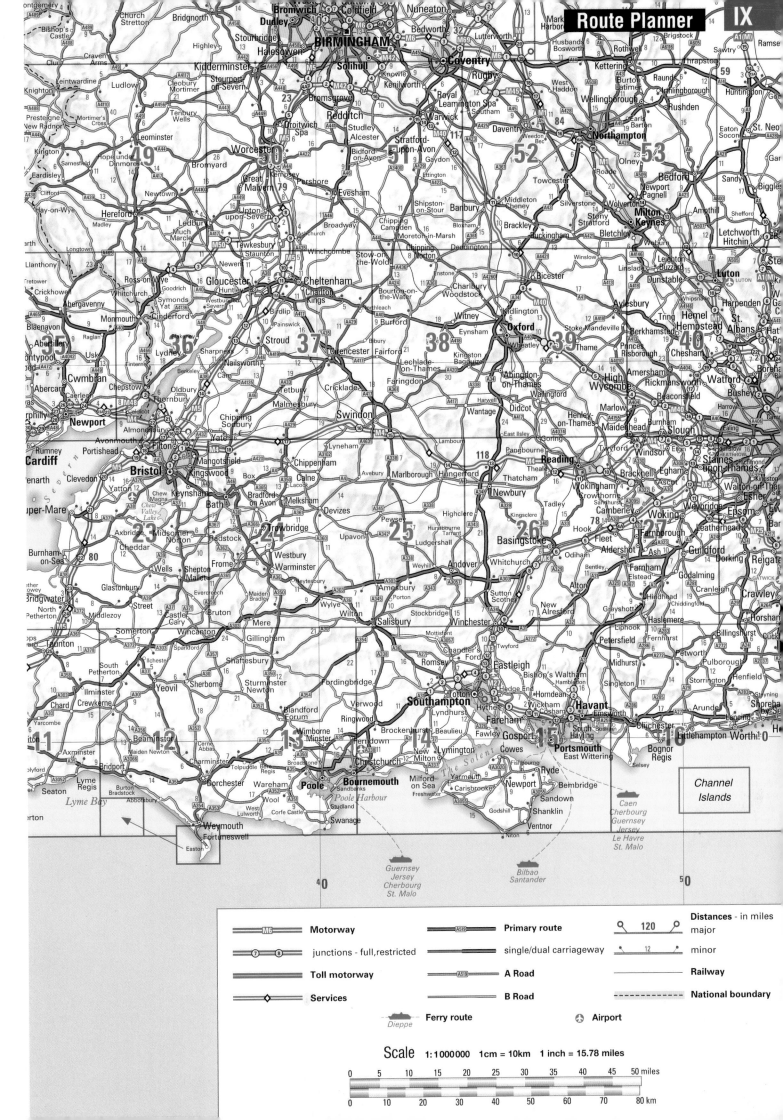

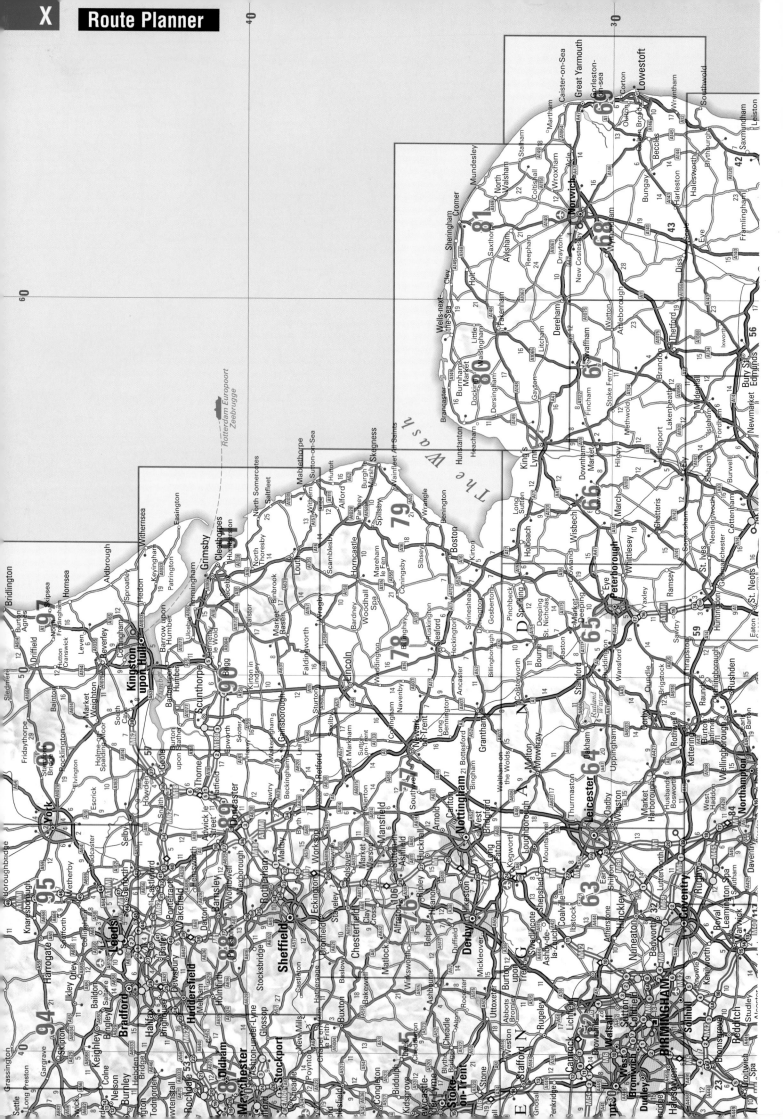

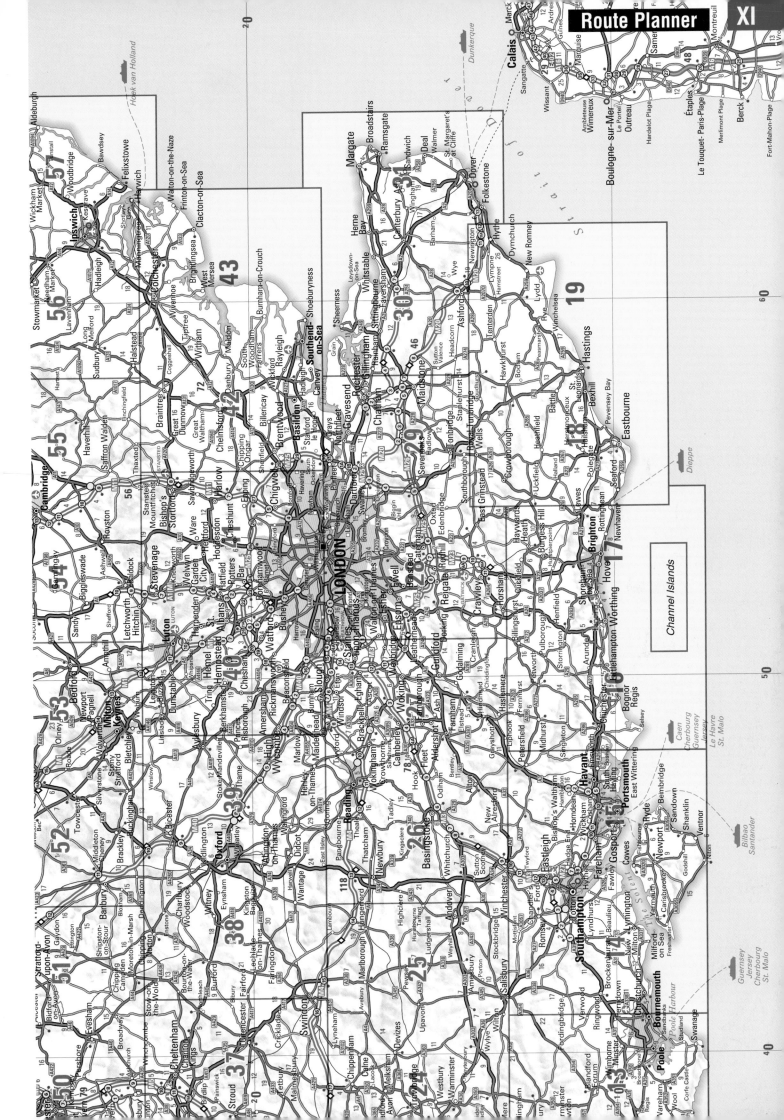

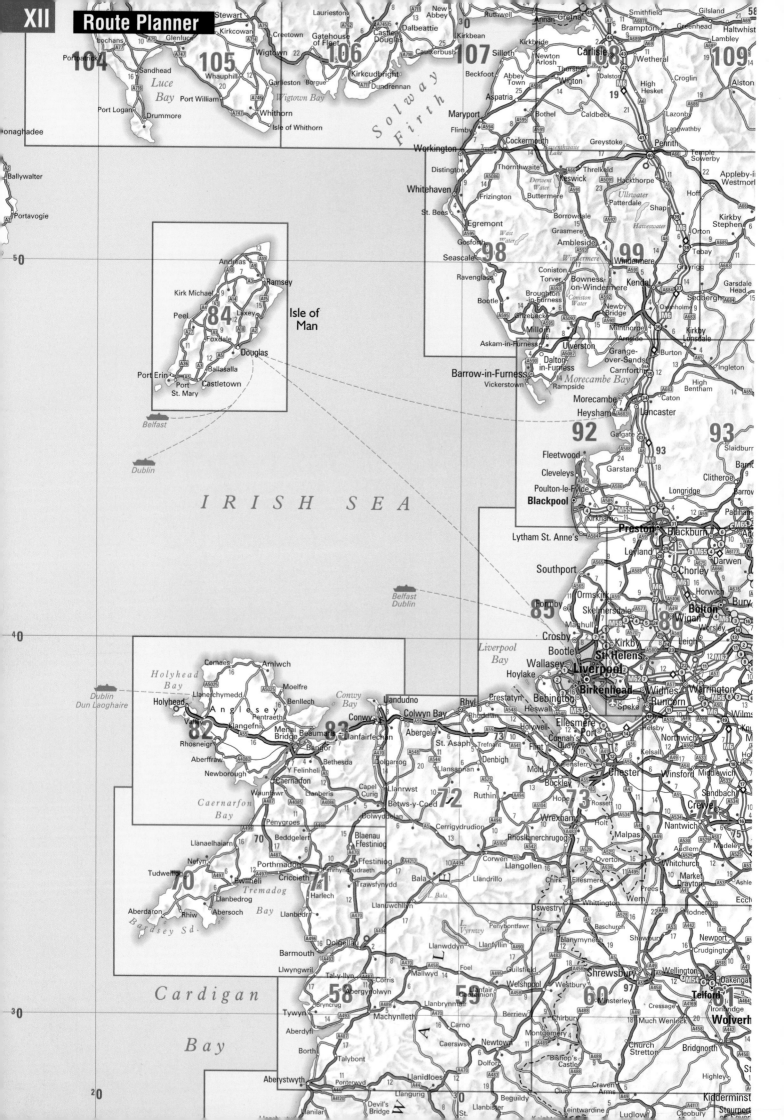

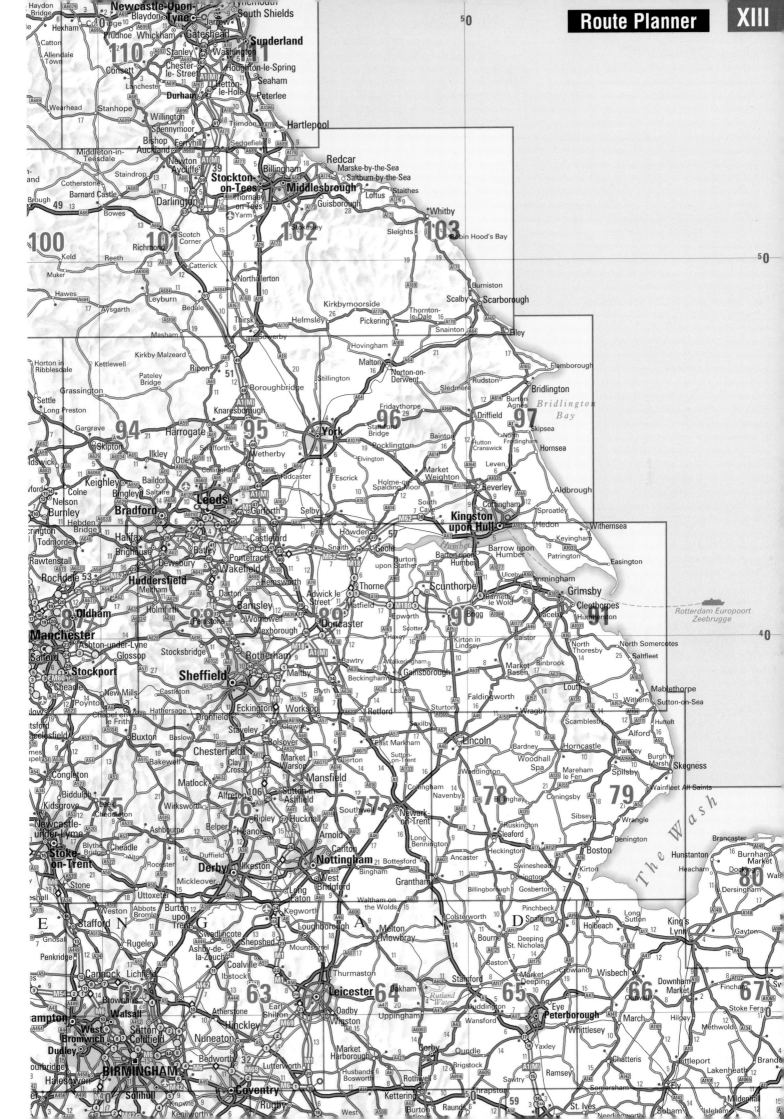

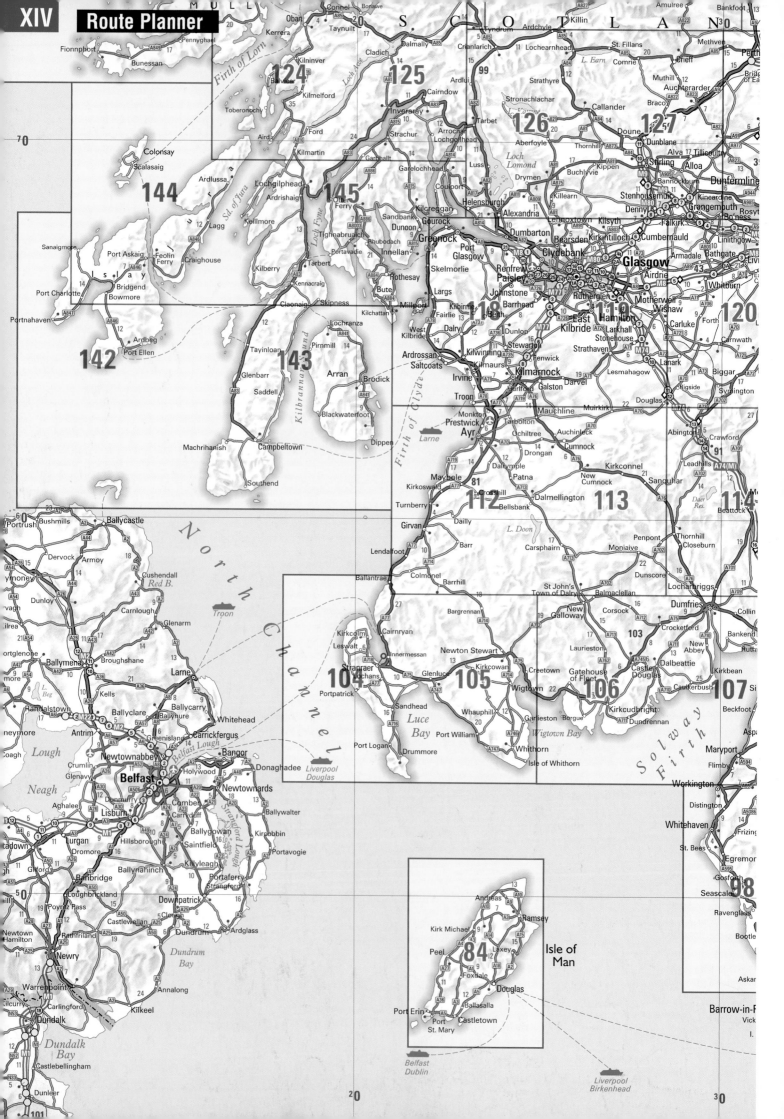

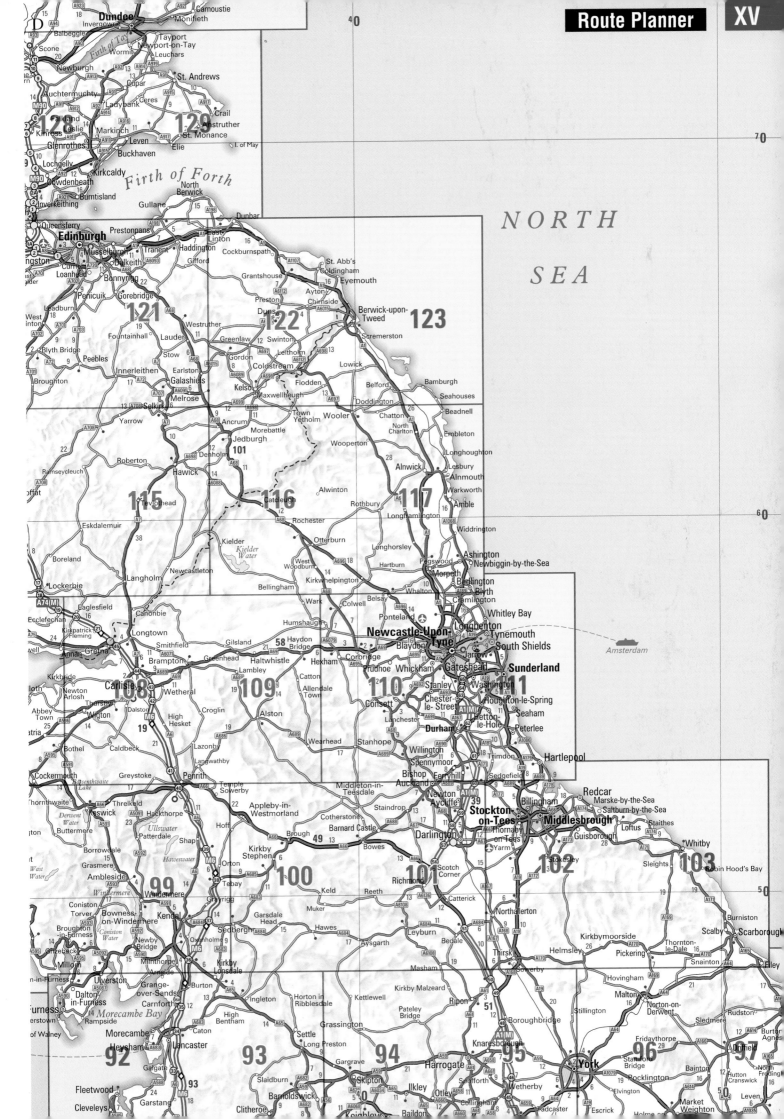

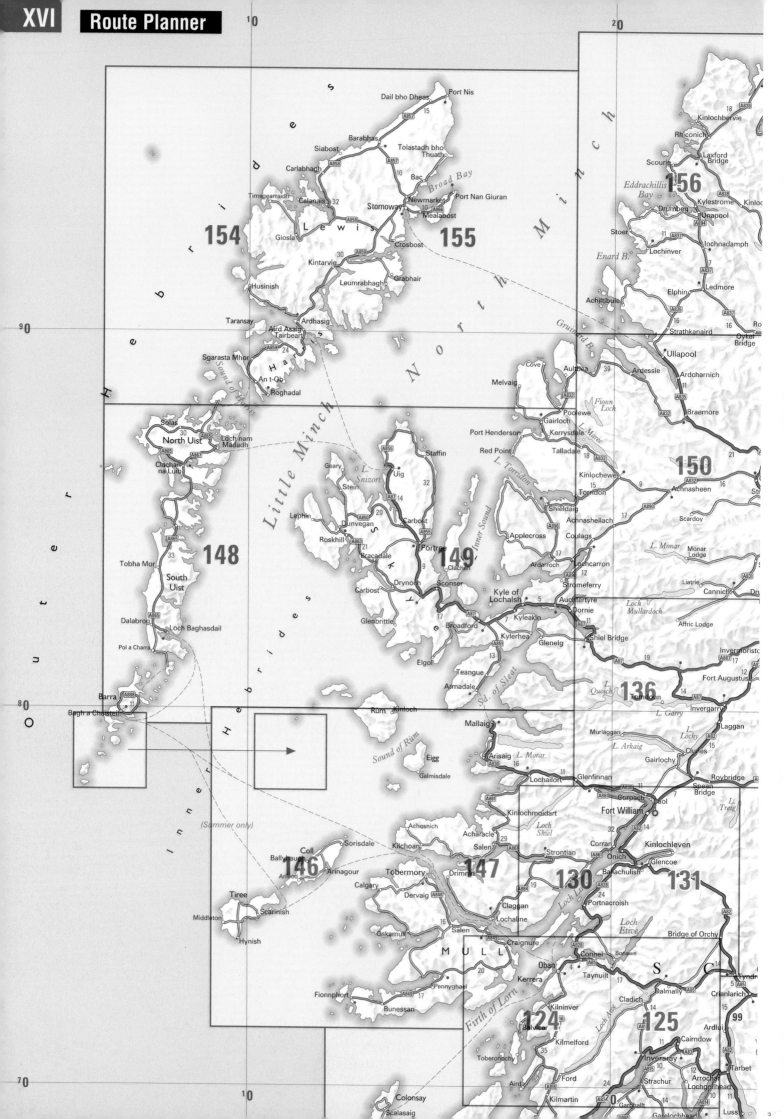

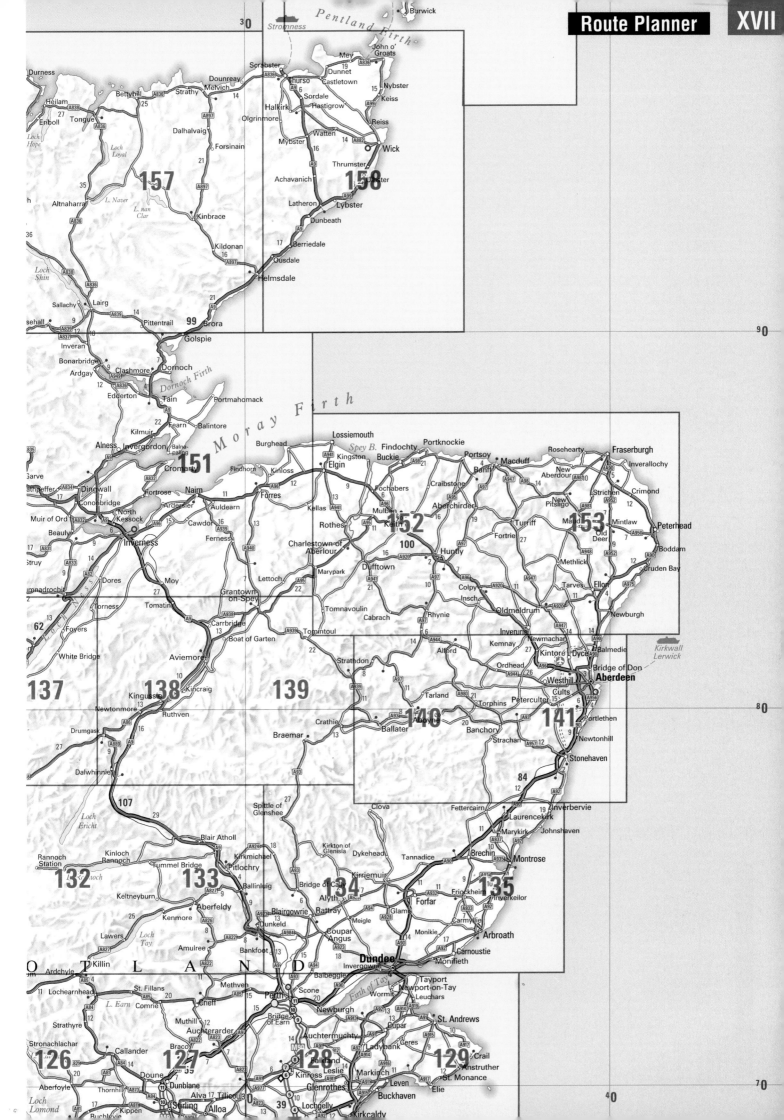

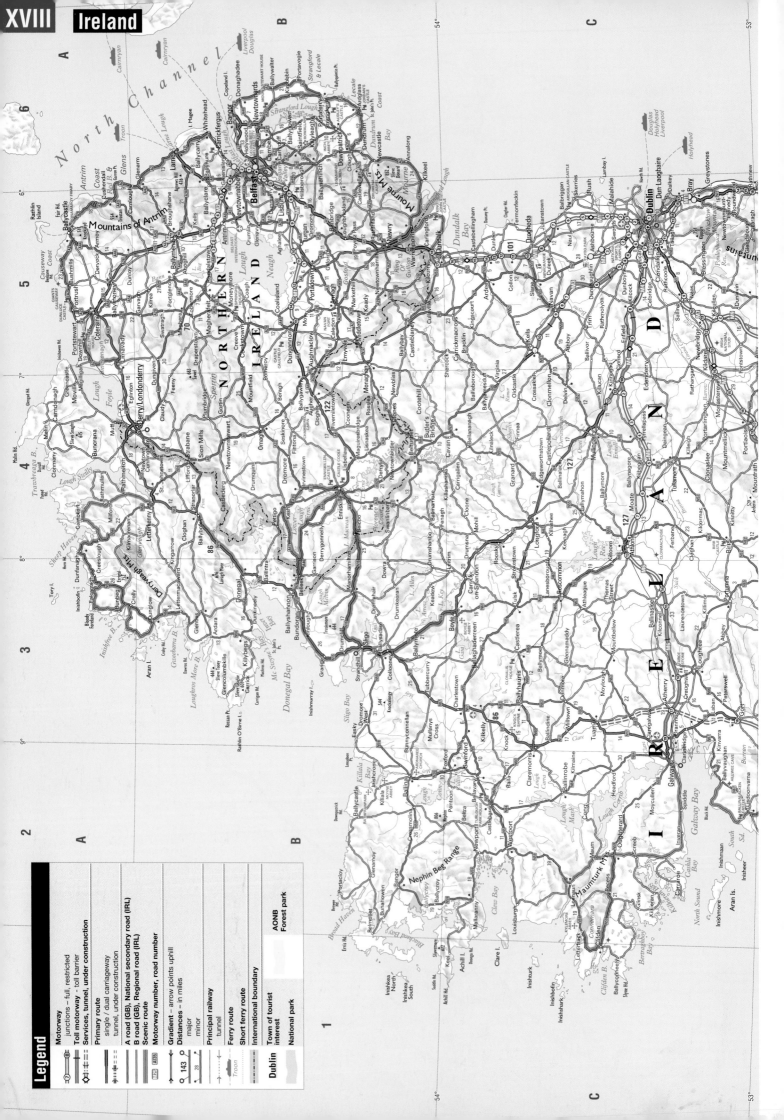

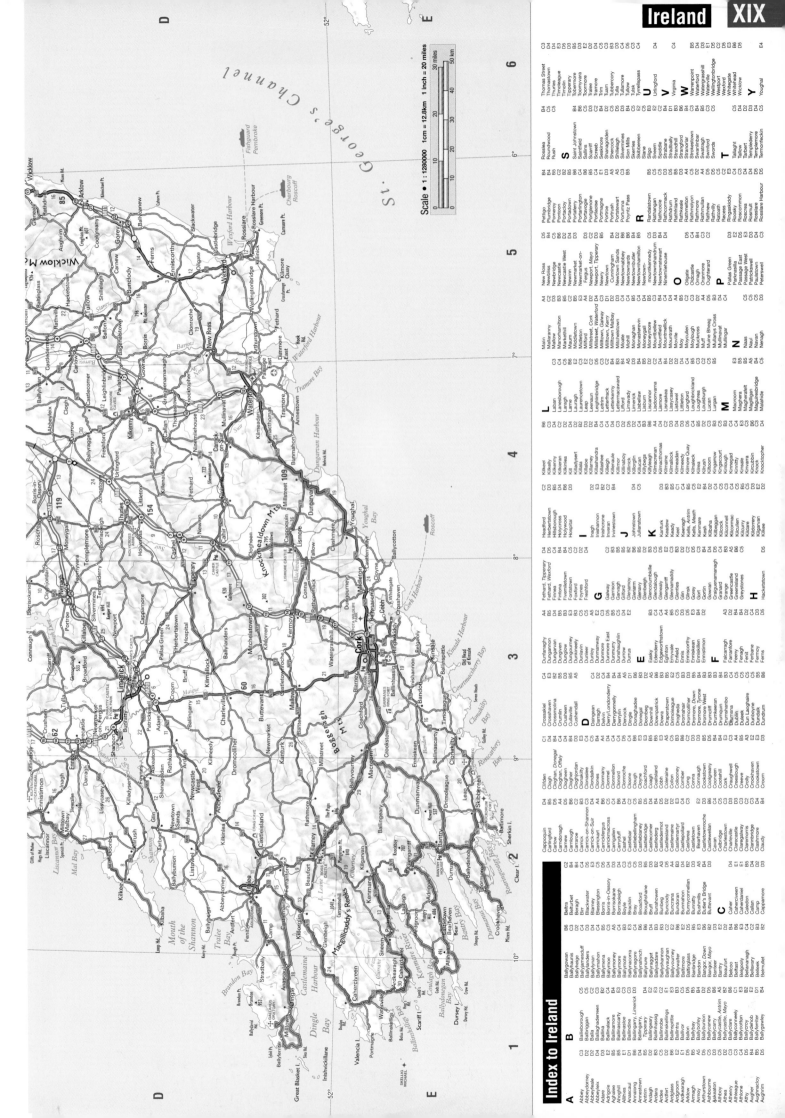

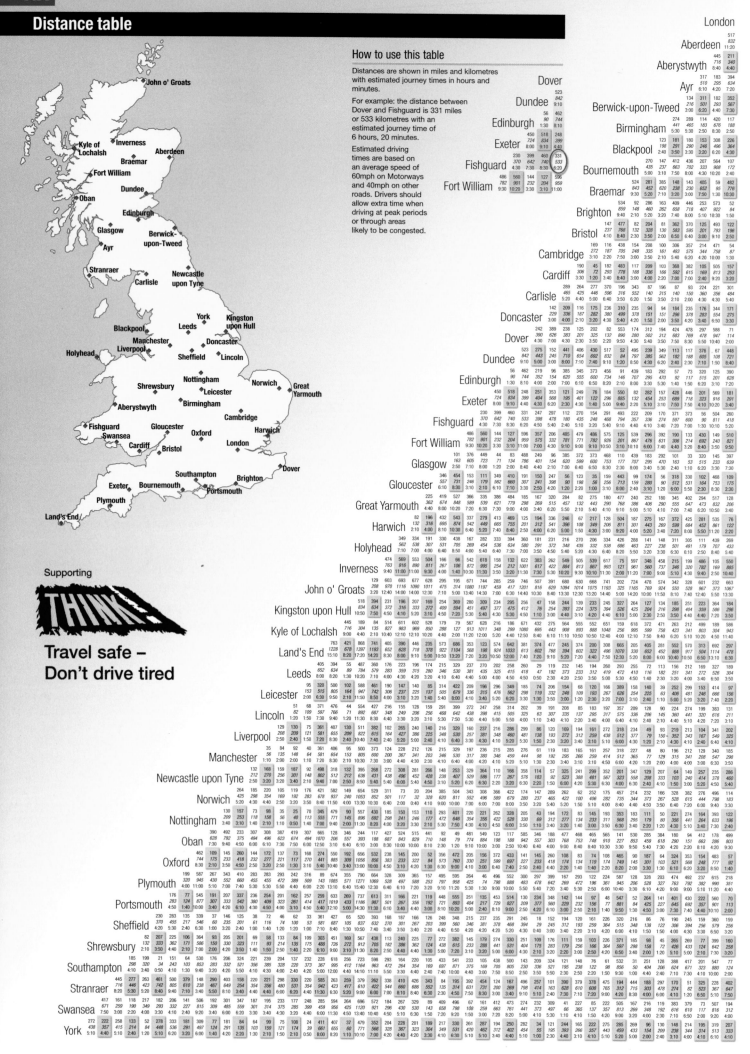

How to use this table

Distances are shown in miles and kilometres with estimated journey times in hours and minutes.

For example: the distance between Dover and Fishguard is 331 miles or 533 kilometres with an estimated journey time of 6 hours, 20 minutes.

Estimated driving times are based on an average speed of 60mph on Motorways and 40mph on other roads. Drivers should allow extra time when driving at peak periods or through areas likely to be congested.

Supporting

THINK!

Travel safe –
Don't drive tired

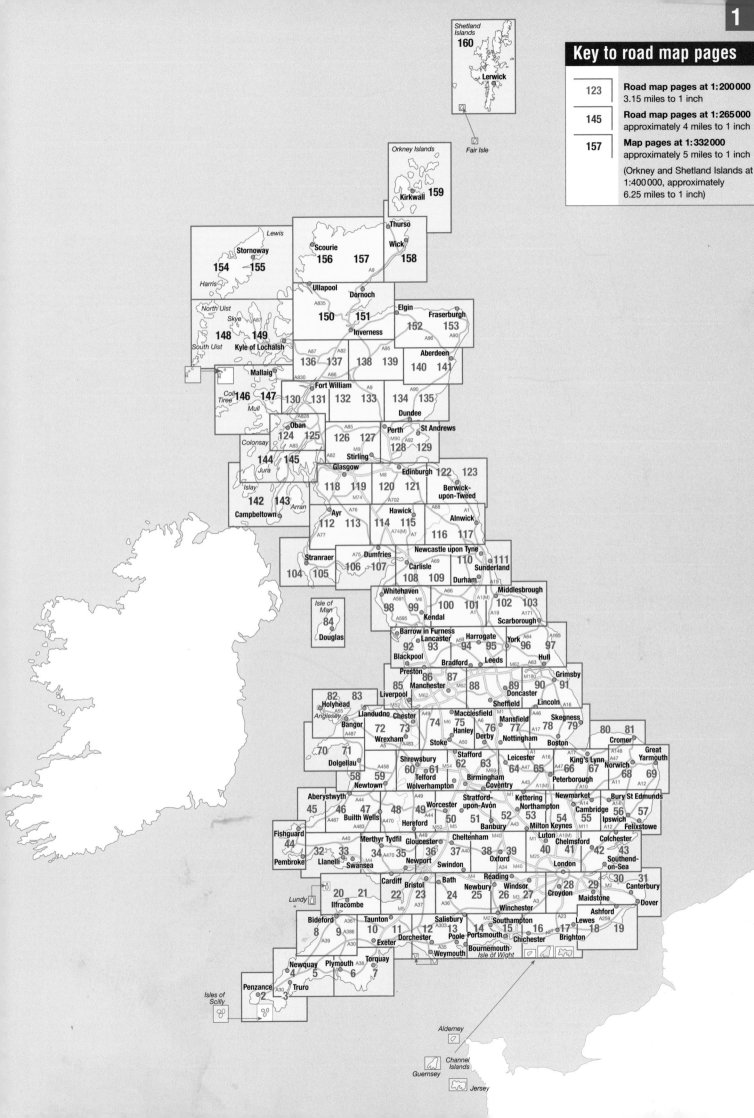

Key to road map pages

123	**Road map pages at 1:200 000** 3.15 miles to 1 inch
145	**Road map pages at 1:265 000** approximately 4 miles to 1 inch
157	**Map pages at 1:332 000** approximately 5 miles to 1 inch

(Orkney and Shetland Islands at 1:400 000, approximately 6.25 miles to 1 inch)

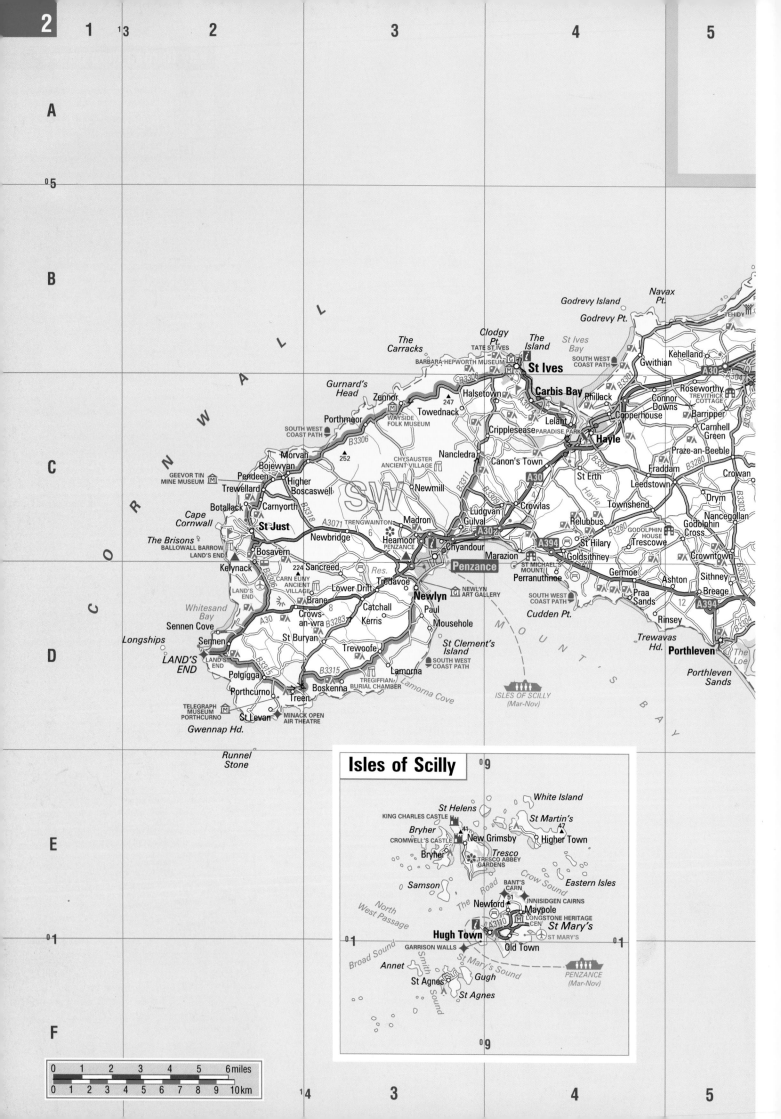

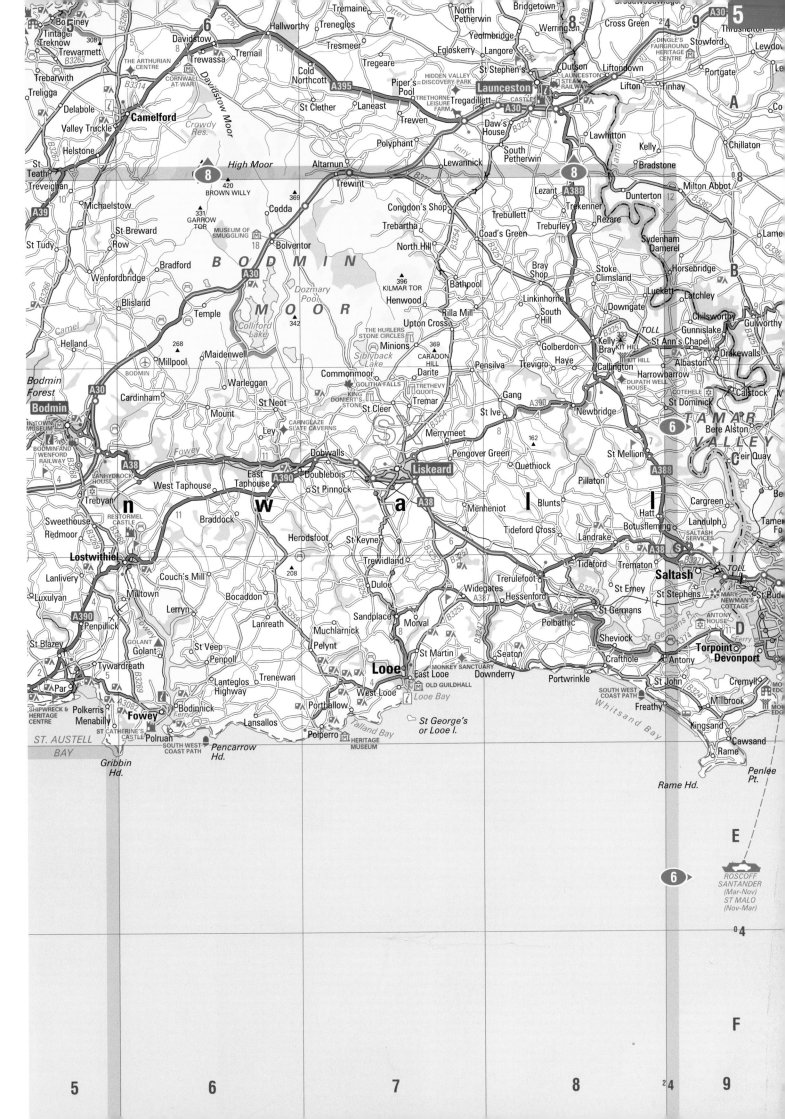

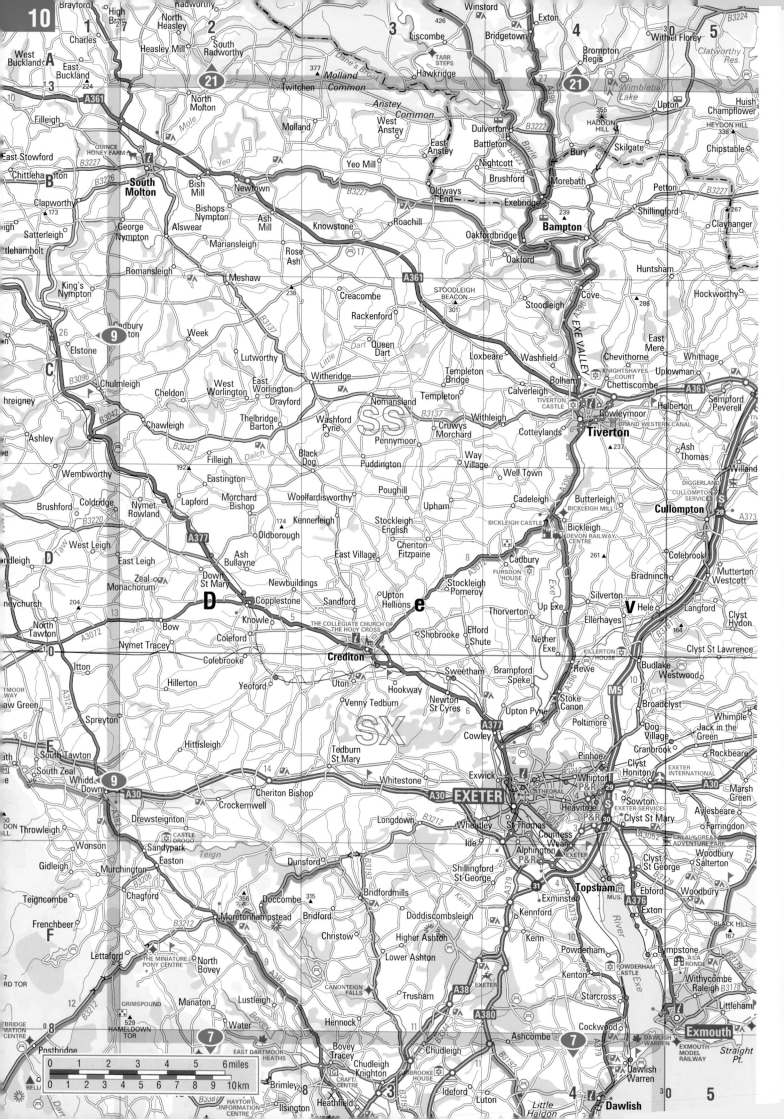

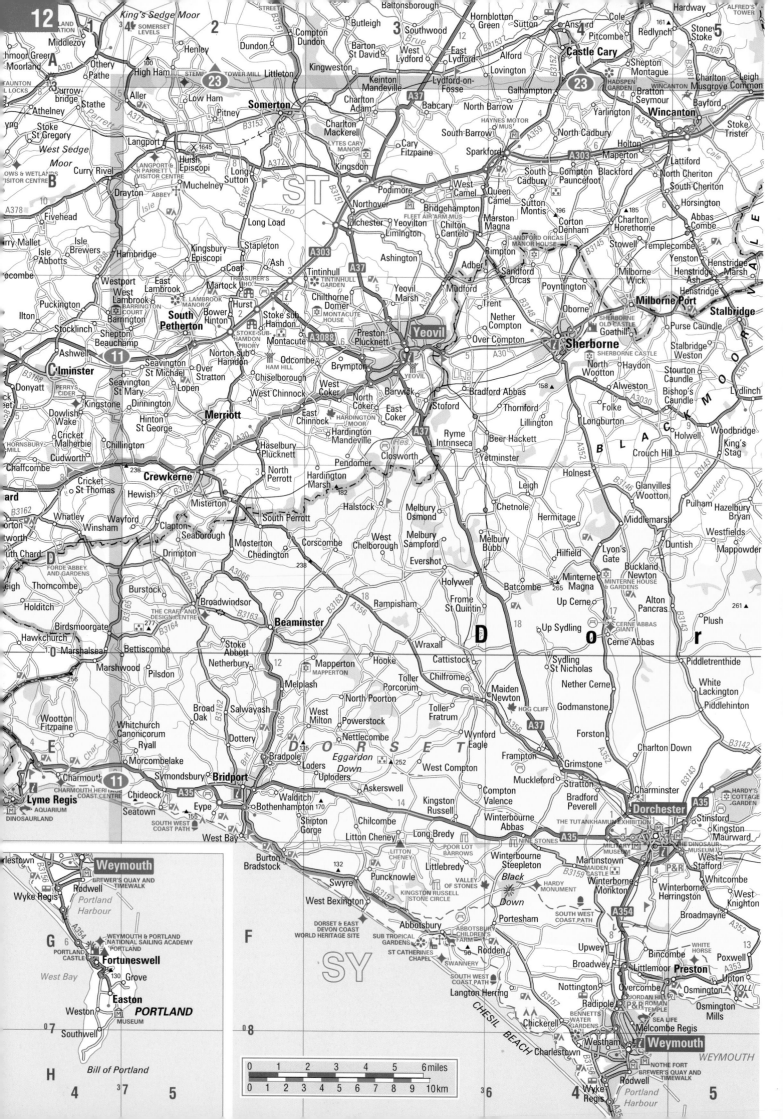

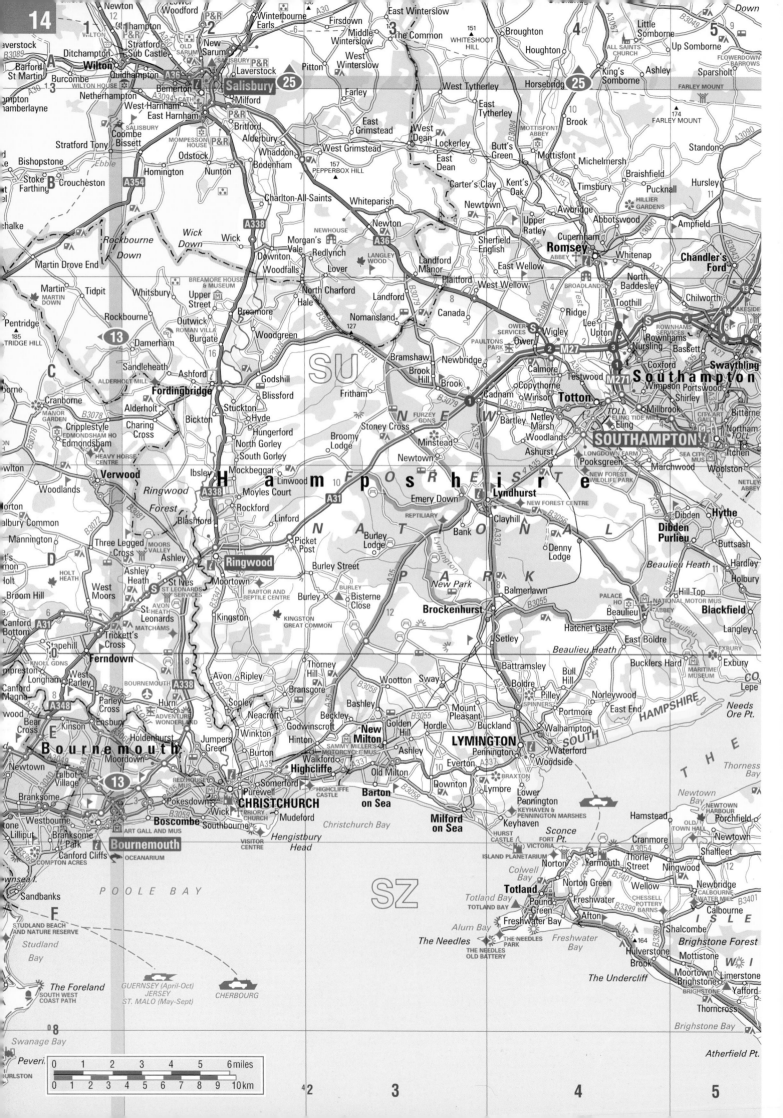

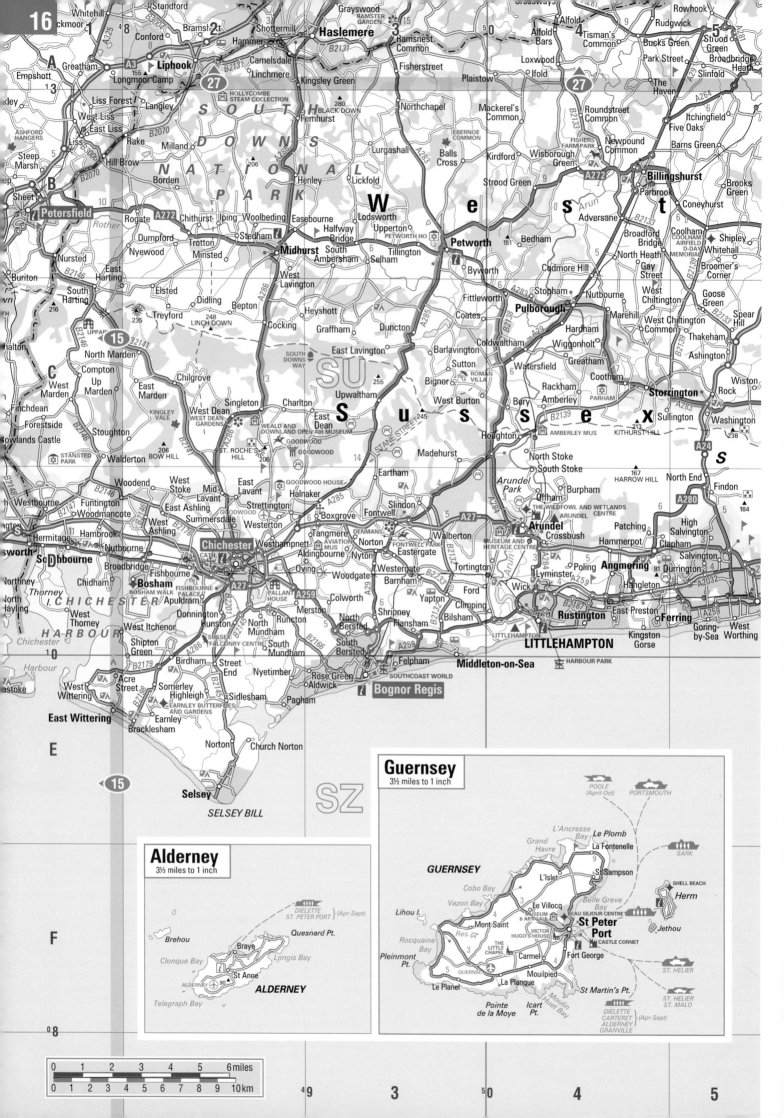

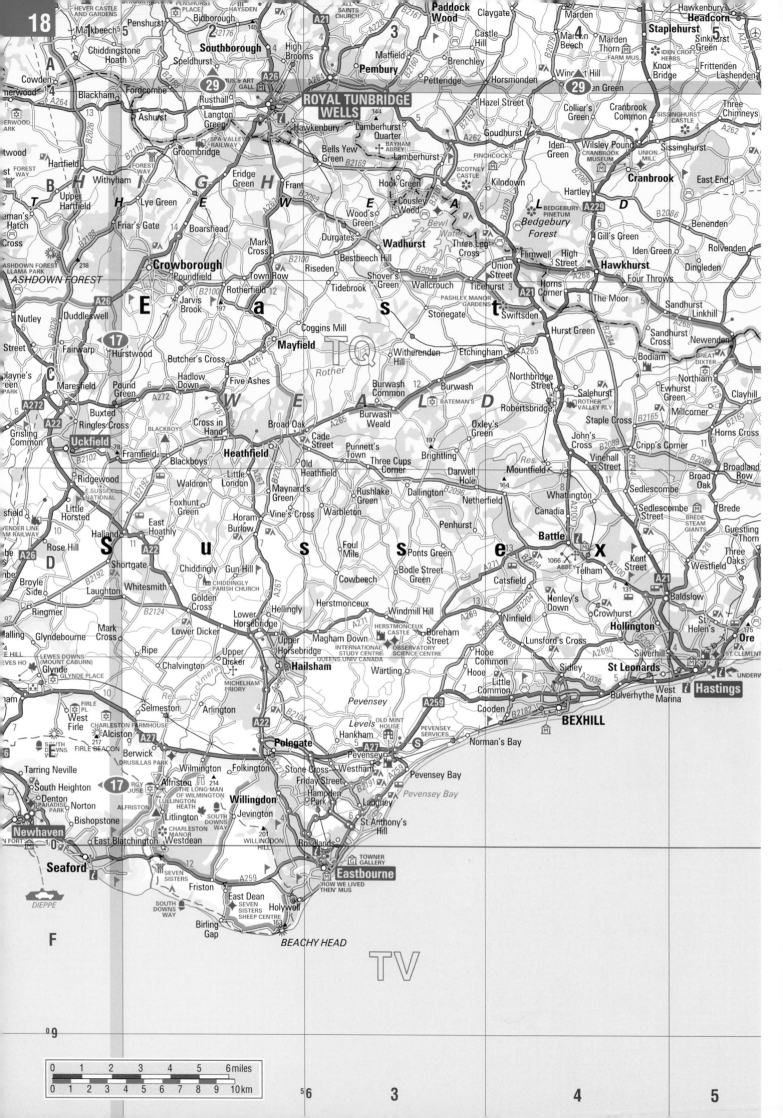

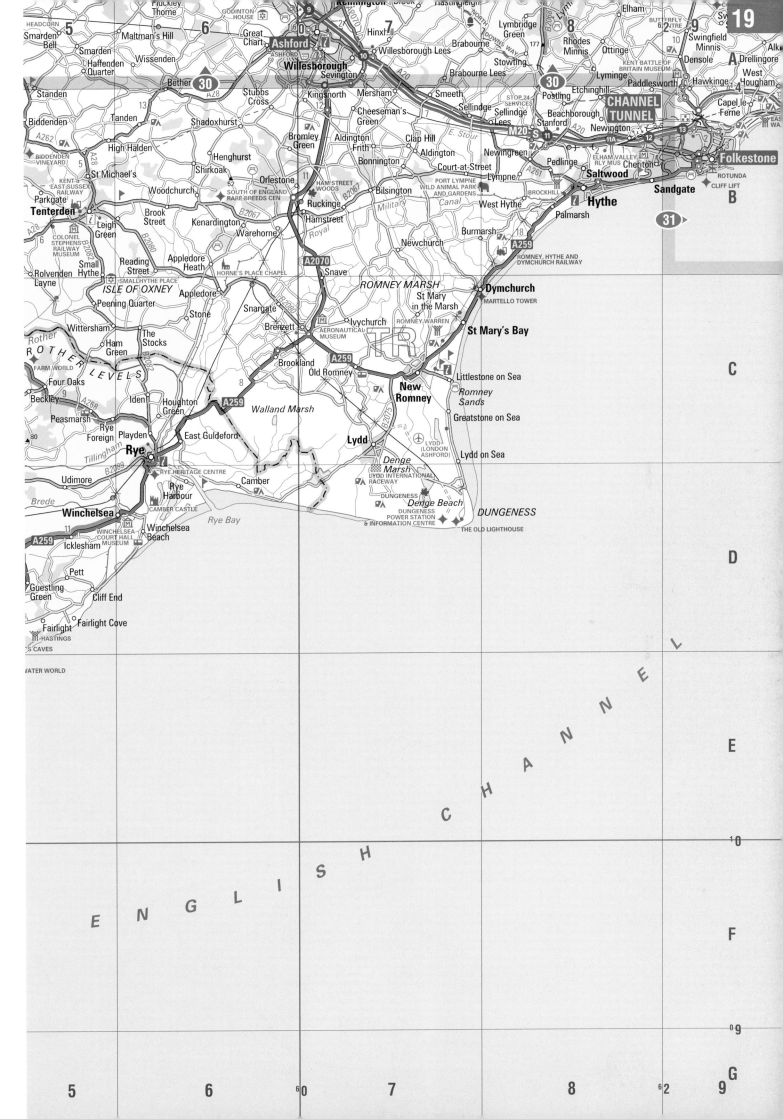

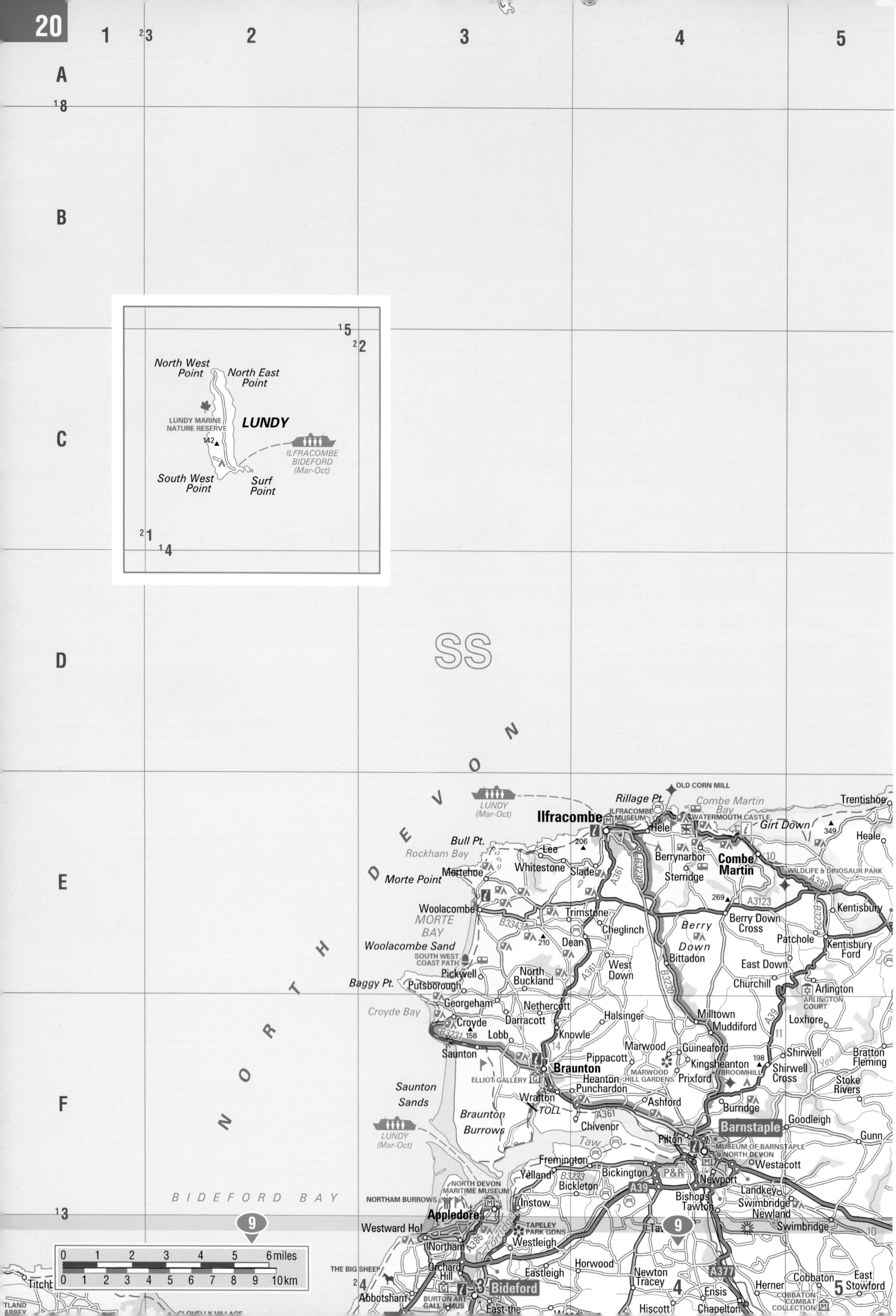

1   2 3   2   3   4   5

A

18

B

5
2 2

North West
Point   North East
Point

LUNDY MARINE
NATURE RESERVE   **LUNDY**

C

142

*ILFRACOMBE
BIDEFORD
(Mar-Oct)*

South West
Point   Surf
Point

2 1
1 4

SS

D

E

*LUNDY
(Mar-Oct)*   Rillage Pt.   *Combe Martin
Bay*   Trentishoe

OLD CORN MILL

Ilfracombe   ILFRACOMBE
MUSEUM   WATERMOUTH CASTLE   Girt Down

Bull Pt.   Hele   349   Heale

Rockham Bay   Lee   206   Berrynarbor   **Combe
Martin**   10

Mortehoe   Whitestone   Slade   Sterridge   WILDLIFE & DINOSAUR PARK

Morte Point   269   A3123   Kentisbury

Woolacombe   Trimstone   *Berry*   Berry Down
Cross

*MORTE
BAY*   B3343   Cheglinch   *Down*   Patchole   Kentisbury
Ford

Woolacombe Sand   210   Dean   Bittadon   East Down

SOUTH WEST
COAST PATH   Pickwell   North   West
Buckland   Down   Churchill   Arlington

Baggy Pt.   Putsborough   ARLINGTON
COURT

F

Croyde Bay   Georgeham   Nethercott   Halsinger   Milltown   Loxhore

Croyde   Darracott   Muddiford   11

158   Lobb   Knowle   Marwood   Guineaford   198   Shirwell   Bratton
Fleming

Saunton   14   Pippacott   Kingsheanton   Shirwell
Cross   Stoke
Rivers

Braunton   Heanton   MARWOOD   Prixford
HILL GARDENS

ELLIOT GALLERY   Punchardon   Burridge   Goodleigh

*Saunton
Sands*   Wrafton   Ashford   Gunn

TOLL   A361   Chivenor   Taw   Pilton   **Barnstaple**

*Braunton
Burrows*   MUSEUM OF BARNSTAPLE
& NORTH DEVON   Westacott

*LUNDY
(Mar-Oct)*   Fremington   Newport   Landkey

Yelland   Bickington   P&R   Bishops
Tawton   Swimbridge
Newland

BIDEFORD BAY   Instow   Bickleton   Swimbridge

NORTH DEVON
MARITIME MUSEUM   Newton
Tracey   10

G

13

9

NORTHAM BURROWS   TAPELEY
PARK GDNS   Herner   Cobbaton   East
Stowford

Appledore   Westleigh   9   A377

Westward Ho!   Horwood   Ensis   COBBATON
COMBAT
COLLECTION

0 1 2 3 4 5 6miles   Northam   Tapeley   Chapelton
0 1 2 3 4 5 6 7 8 9 10km

THE BIG SHEEP   Orchard
Hill   Eastleigh   **Bideford**   4

TLAND
ABBEY   Titch   Abbotsham   BURTON ART
GALL & MUS   East-the   Hiscott   Chapelton

CLOVELLY VILLAGE

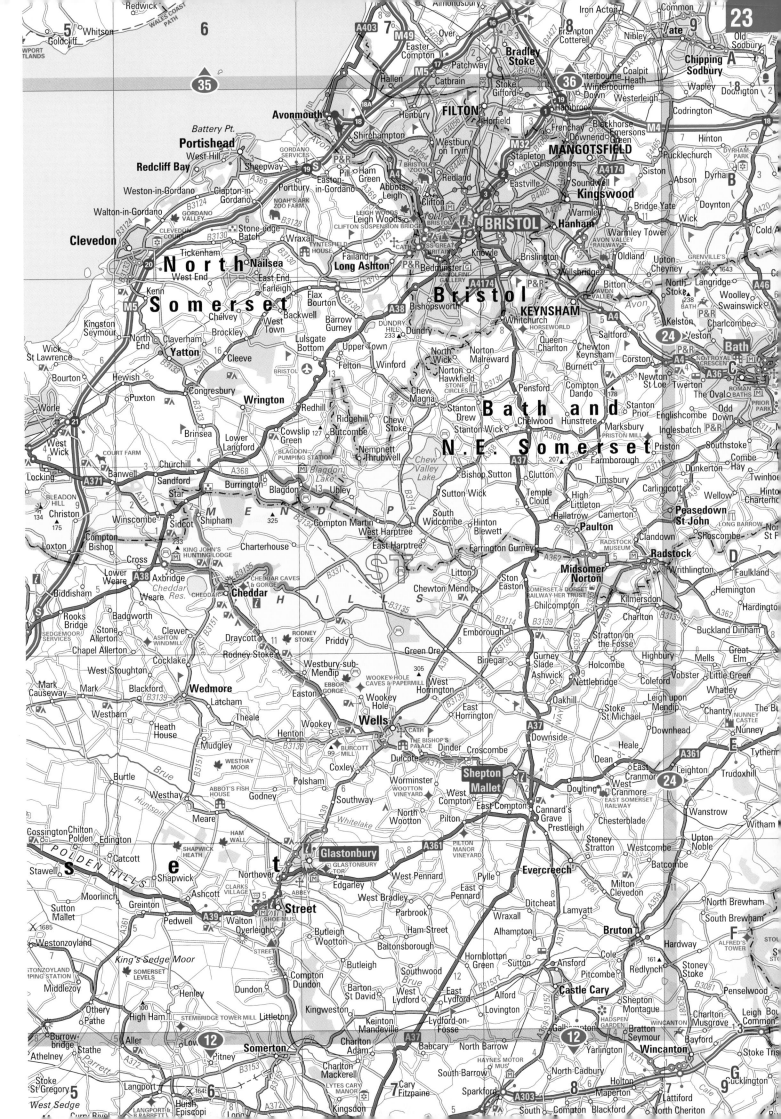

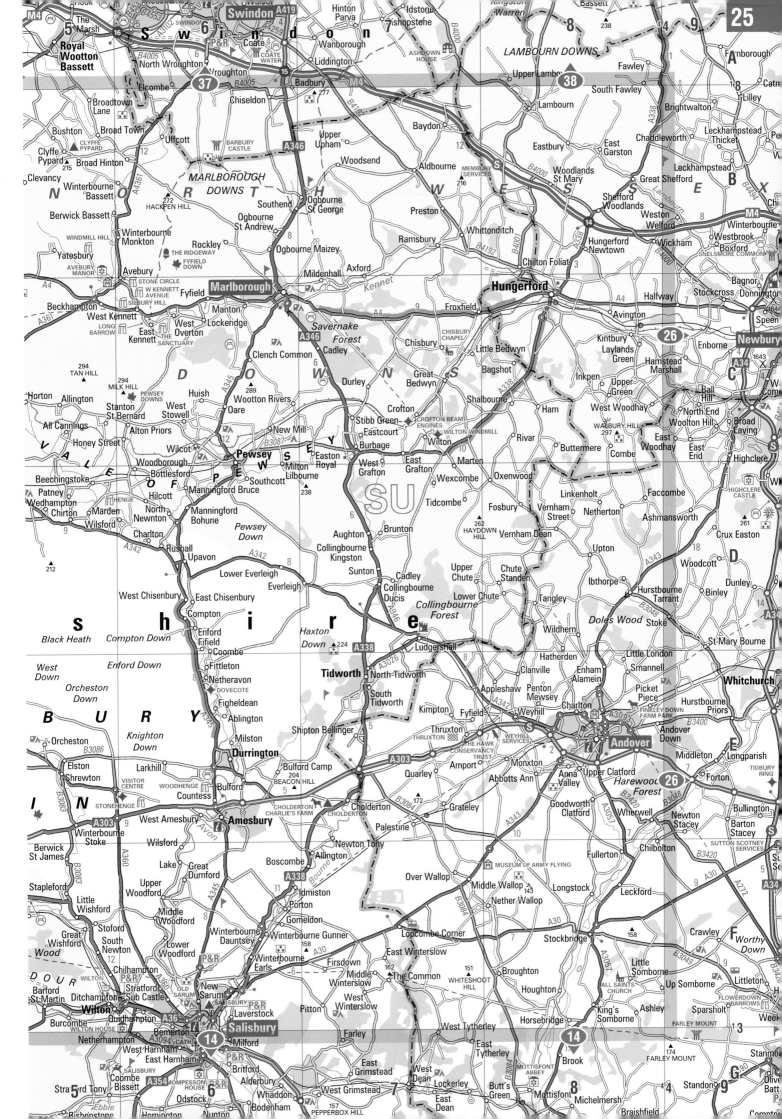

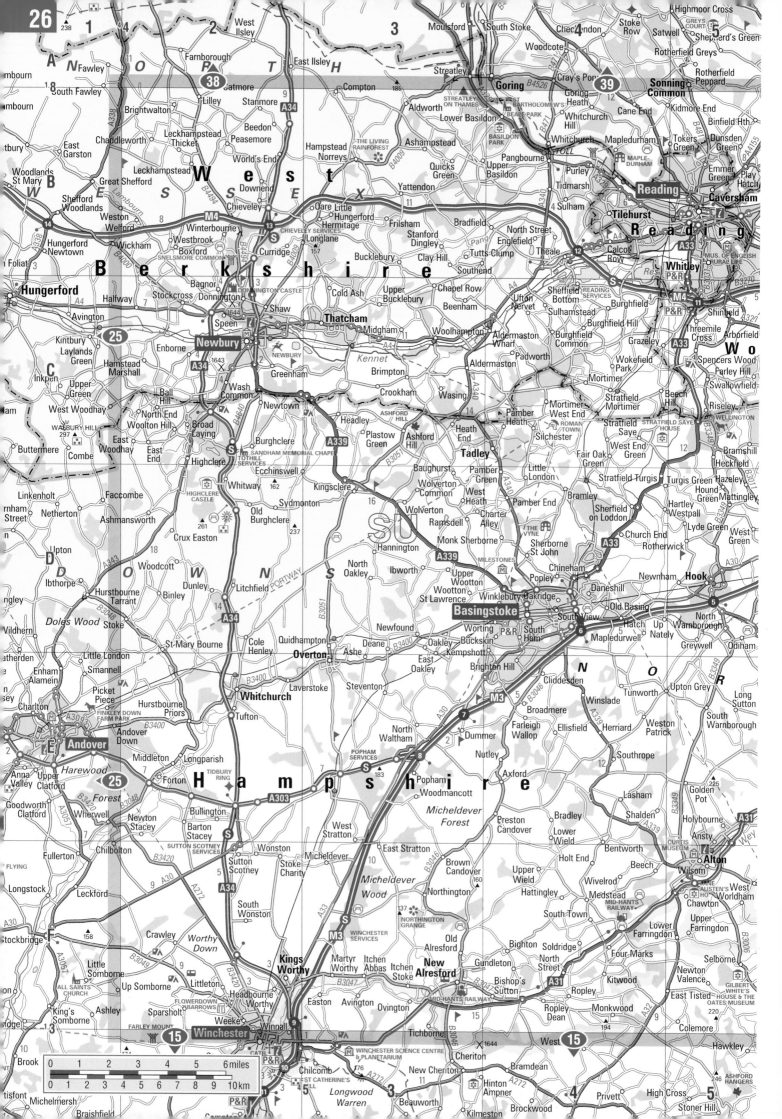

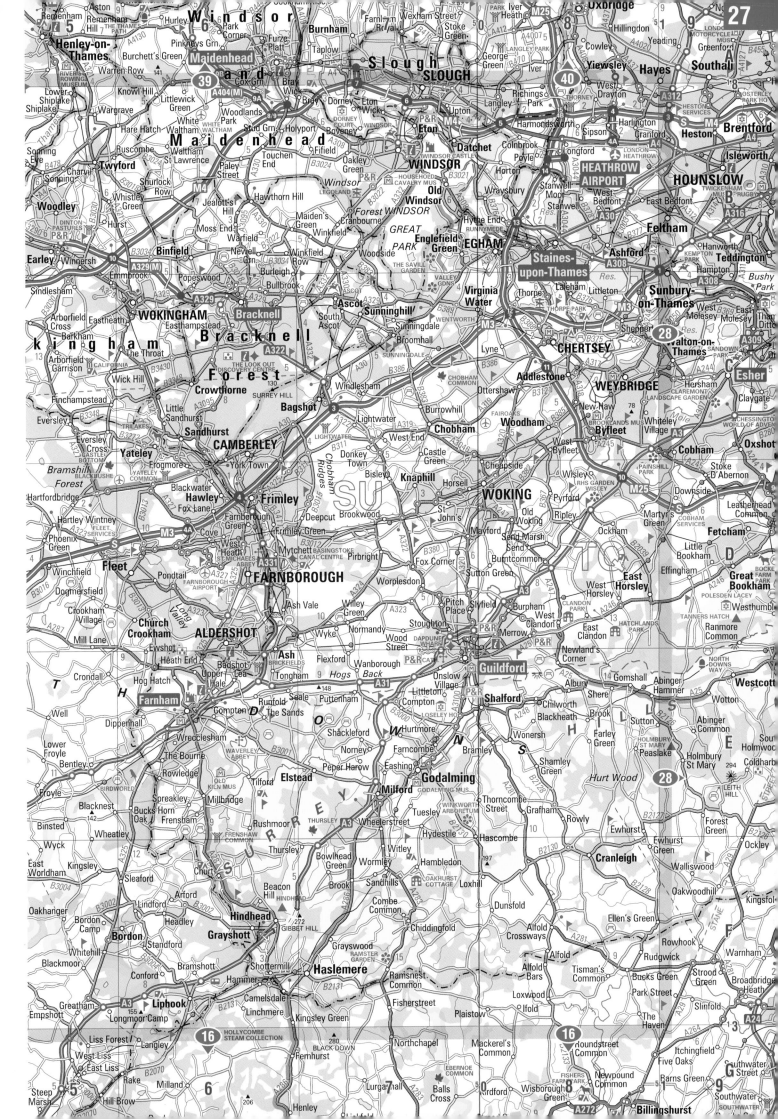

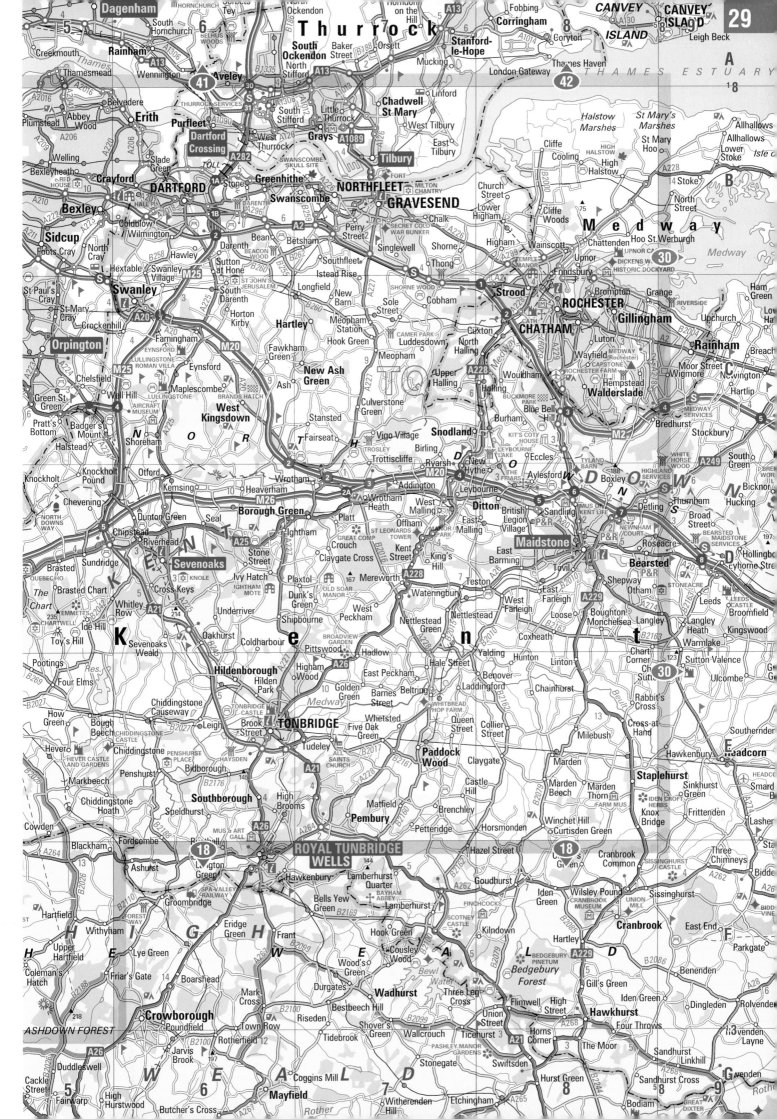

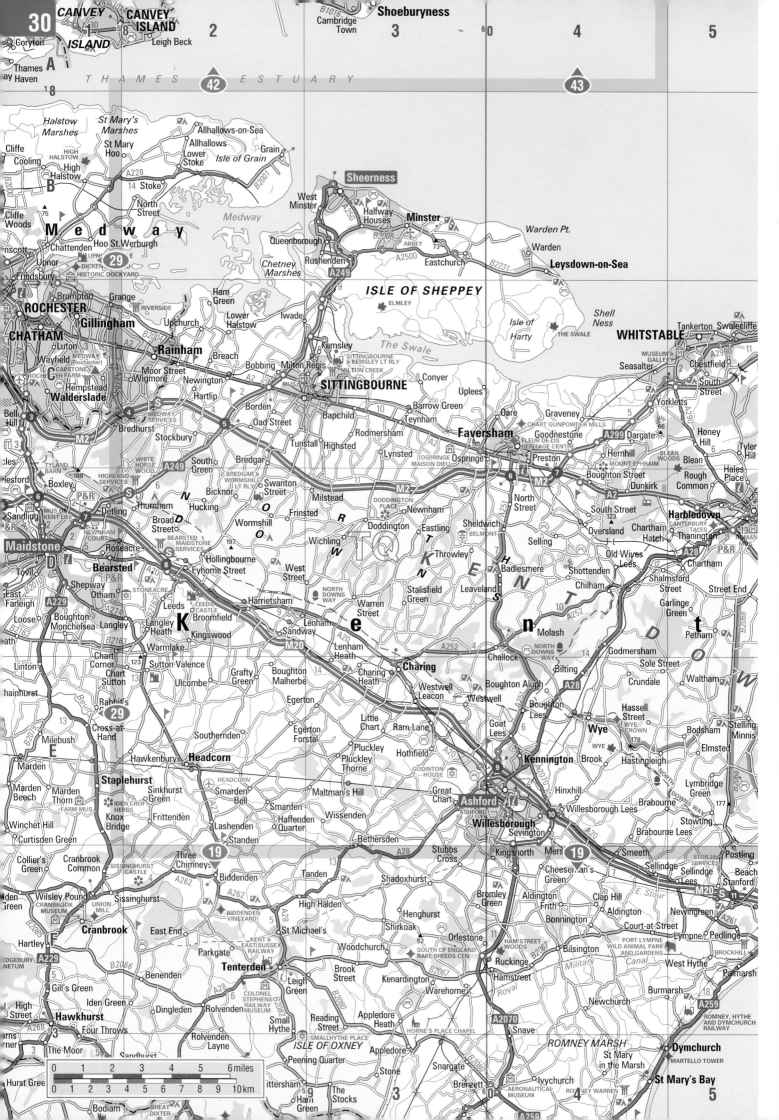

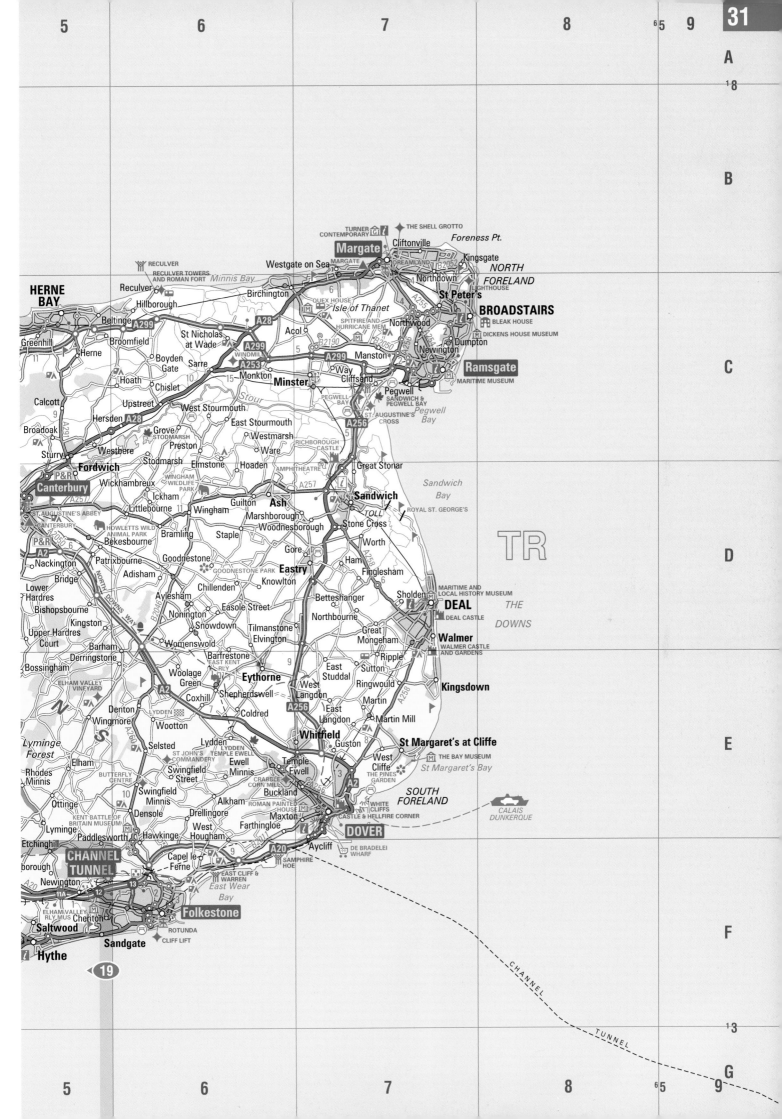

A

B

C

D

E

F

G

5 6 7 8 9

TURNER CONTEMPORARY

THE SHELL GROTTO

Margate

Foreness Pt.

Cliftonville

MARGATE

Westgate on Sea

DREAMLAND

Kingsgate

NORTH FORELAND LIGHTHOUSE

Northdown

St Peter's

BROADSTAIRS

RECULVER

RECULVER TOWERS AND ROMAN FORT

Minnis Bay

HERNE BAY

Reculver

Birchington

QUEX HOUSE

Isle of Thanet

SPITFIRE AND HURRICANE MEM.

Northwood

BLEAK HOUSE

DICKENS HOUSE MUSEUM

Hillborough

Beltinge

Greenhill

Herne

A299

St Nicholas at Wade

Broomfield

Acol

WINDMILL

A299

A28

A253

Way

Cliffsend

Newington

Dumpton

Boyden Gate

Sarre

Monkton

Minster

Manston

A299

Ramsgate

Hoath

Chislet

10

15

MARITIME MUSEUM

Calcott

Upstreet

West Stourmouth

Pegwell

SANDWICH & PEGWELL BAY

Broadoak

Hersden

A28

Grove

STODMARSH

East Stourmouth

Westmarsh

Pegwell Bay

ST AUGUSTINE'S CROSS

A256

Sturry

Westbere

Stodmarsh

Elmstone

Ware

RICHBOROUGH CASTLE

Preston

Hoaden

AMPHITHEATRE

Fordwich

Wickhambreux

WINGHAM WILDLIFE PARK

Ickham

A257

Great Stonar

Sandwich

Sandwich Bay

P&R

Canterbury

A257

Littlebourne

Wingham

Ash

TOLL

Royal St. George's

ST AUGUSTINE'S ABBEY

HOWLETTS WILD ANIMAL PARK

Marshborough

Stone Cross

TR

P&R

A2

Bekesbourne

Bramling

Staple

Woodnesborough

Worth

Nackington

Patrixbourne

Goodnestone

Gore

Ham

Finglesham

Bridge

Adisham

GOODNESTONE PARK

Eastry

MARITIME AND LOCAL HISTORY MUSEUM

Lower Hardres

Chillenden

Knowlton

Sholden

DEAL

Bishopsbourne

Aylesham

Easole Street

Betteshanger

Northbourne

DEAL CASTLE

Kingston

Nonington

Snowdown

Tilmanstone

Elvington

Great Mongeham

THE DOWNS

Upper Hardres Court

Womenswold

Walmer

Barham

EAST KENT RLY

Barfrestone

WALMER CASTLE AND GARDENS

Derringstone

Woolage Green

Eythorne

West Studdal

Sutton

Ripple

Bossingham

ELHAM VALLEY VINEYARD

Coxhill

Shepherdswell

9

East Studdal

Ringwould

Kingsdown

A2

West Langdon

Martin

ELHAM VALLEY

Coldred

A256

East Langdon

Martin Mill

A258

Denton

Wingmore

Wootton

LYDDEN

Whitfield

Guston

West Cliffe

St Margaret's at Cliffe

Selsted

Lydden

THE BAY MUSEUM

Elham

ST JOHN'S COMMANDERY

LYDDEN TEMPLE EWELL

Ewell Minnis

Temple Ewell

West Cliffe

St Margaret's Bay

Rhodes Minnis

BUTTERFLY CENTRE

Swingfield Street

CRABBLE CORN MILL

THE PINES GARDEN

SOUTH FORELAND

CALAIS DUNKERQUE

Ottinge

Swingfield Minnis

Alkham

Buckland

WHITE CLIFFS

10

Densole

Drellingore

ROMAN PAINTED HOUSE

Maxton

CASTLE & HELLFIRE CORNER

Lyminge

Lyminge Forest

Hawkinge

West Hougham

Farthingloe

DOVER

Etchinghill

Paddlesworth

A20

Aycliff

DE BRADELEI WHARF

CHANNEL TUNNEL

Capel le Ferne

EAST CLIFF & WARREN

SAMPHIRE HOE

Newington

A20

11A

12

13

East Wear Bay

ELHAM VALLEY RLY MUS

Cheriton

Saltwood

ROTUNDA

Folkestone

Sandgate

CLIFF LIFT

Hythe

19

CHANNEL TUNNEL

8 65 9 G

5 6 7 8 65 9

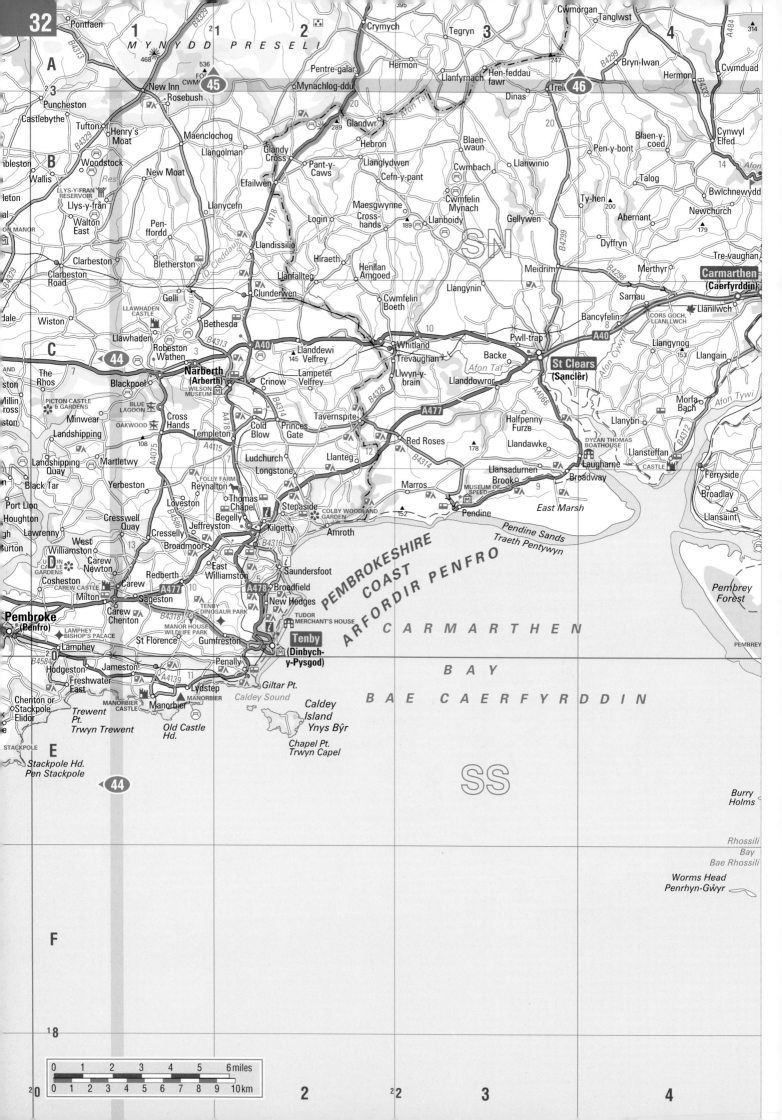

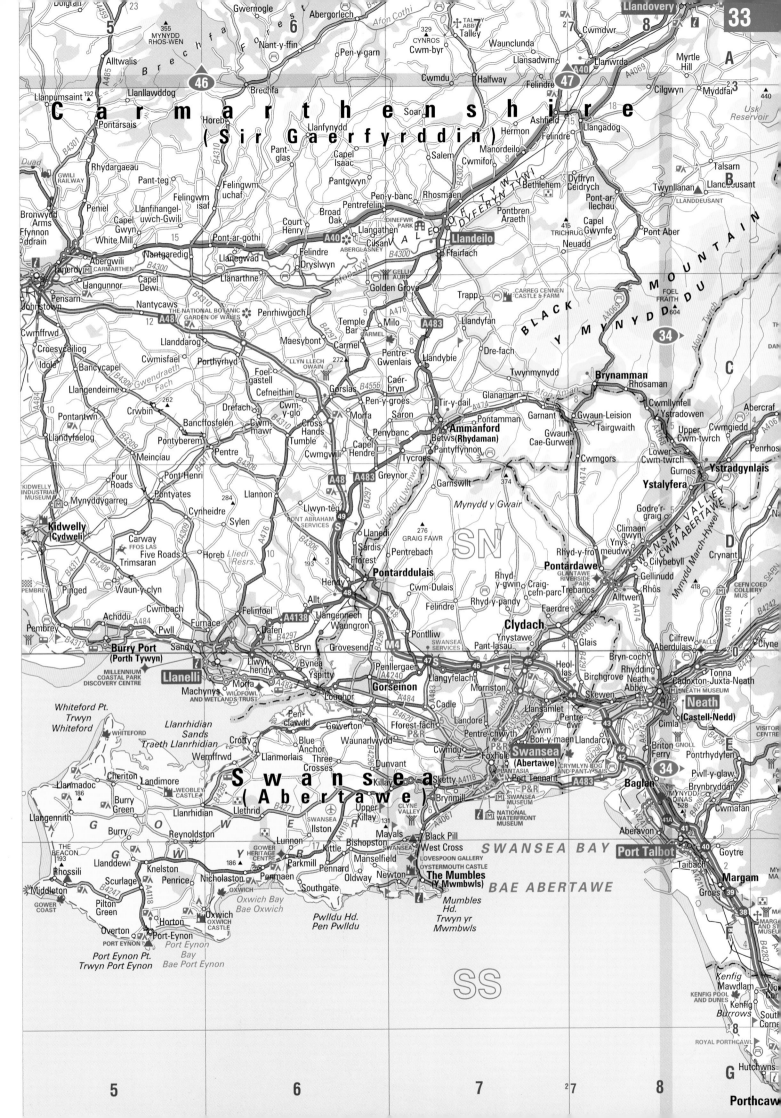

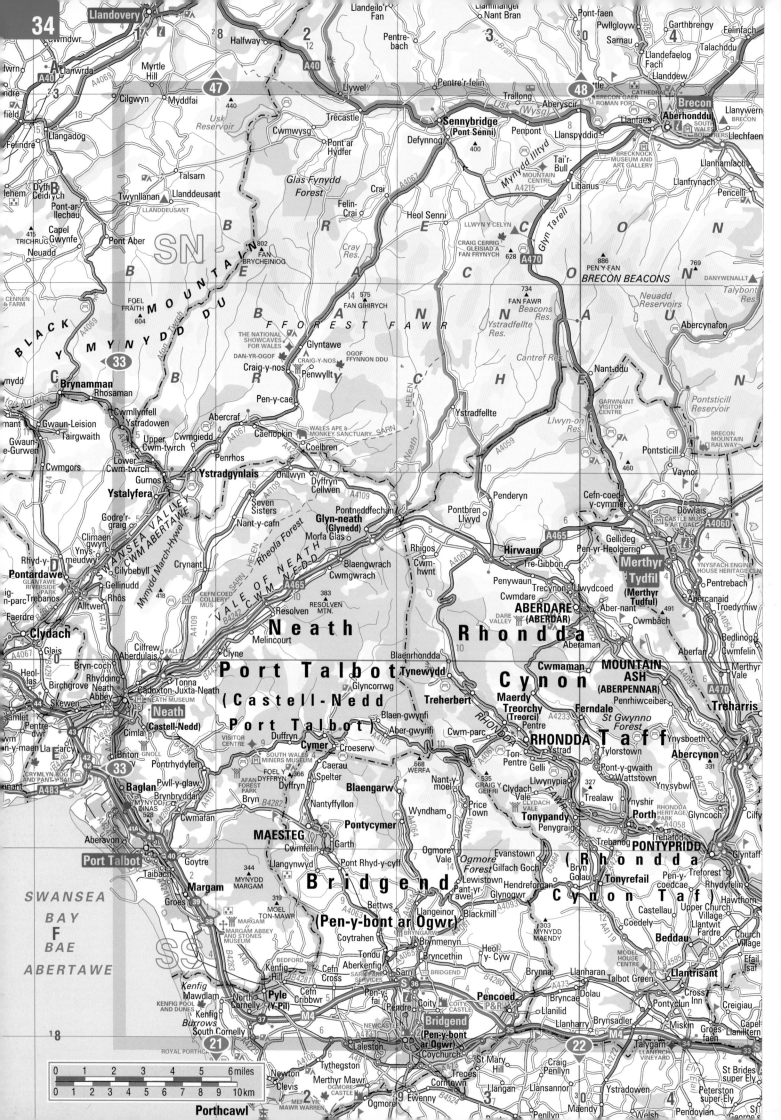

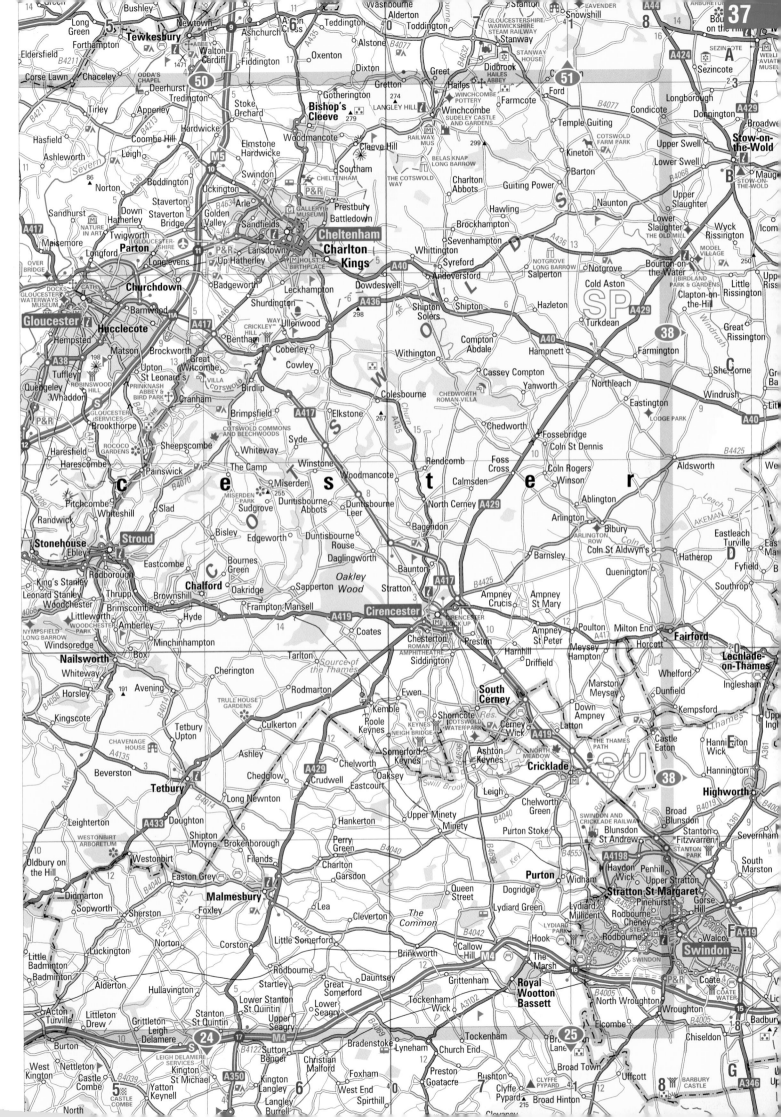

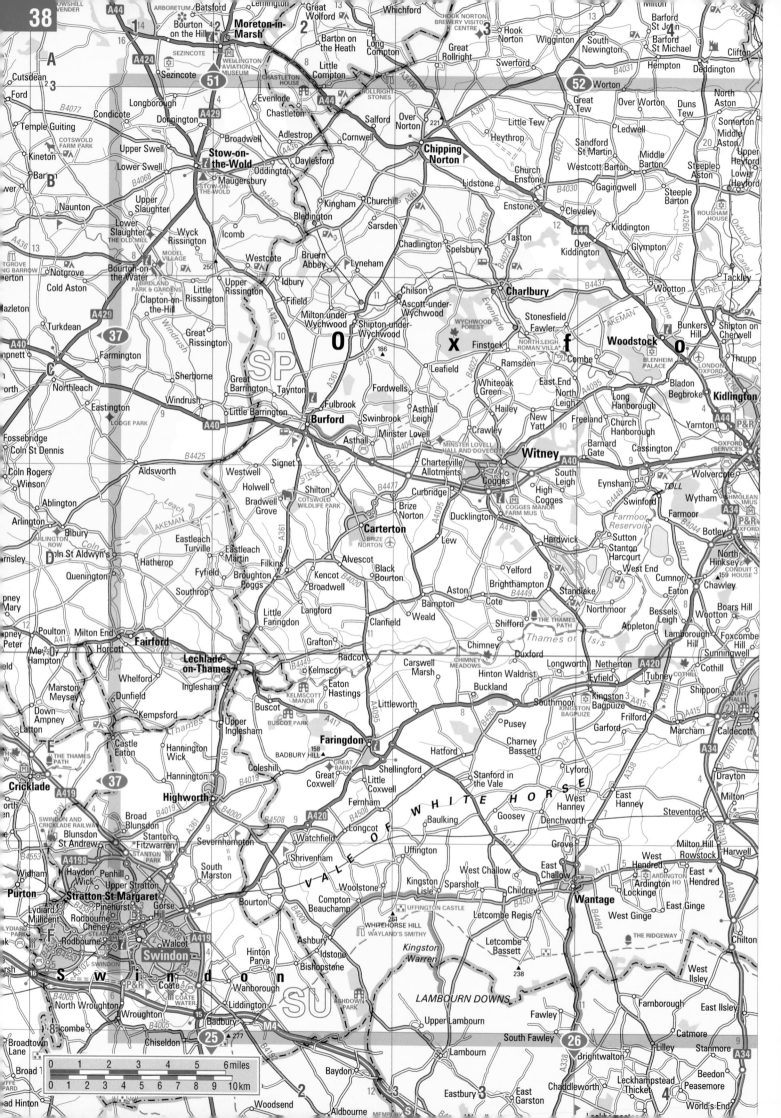

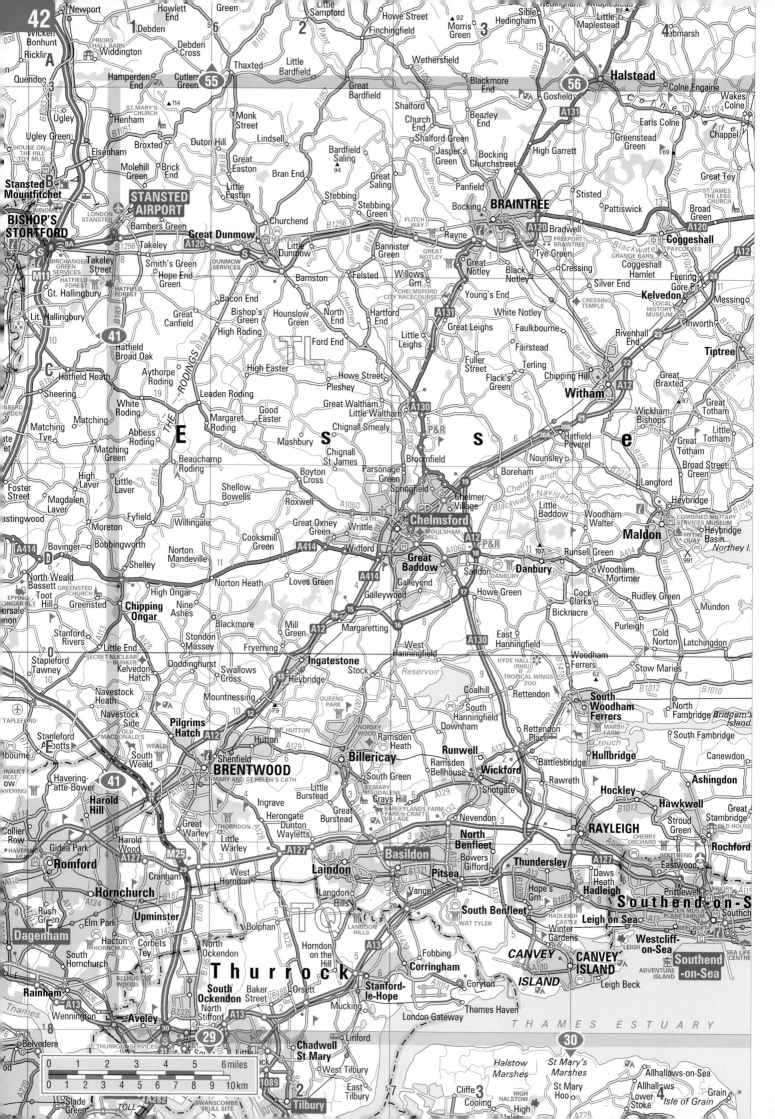

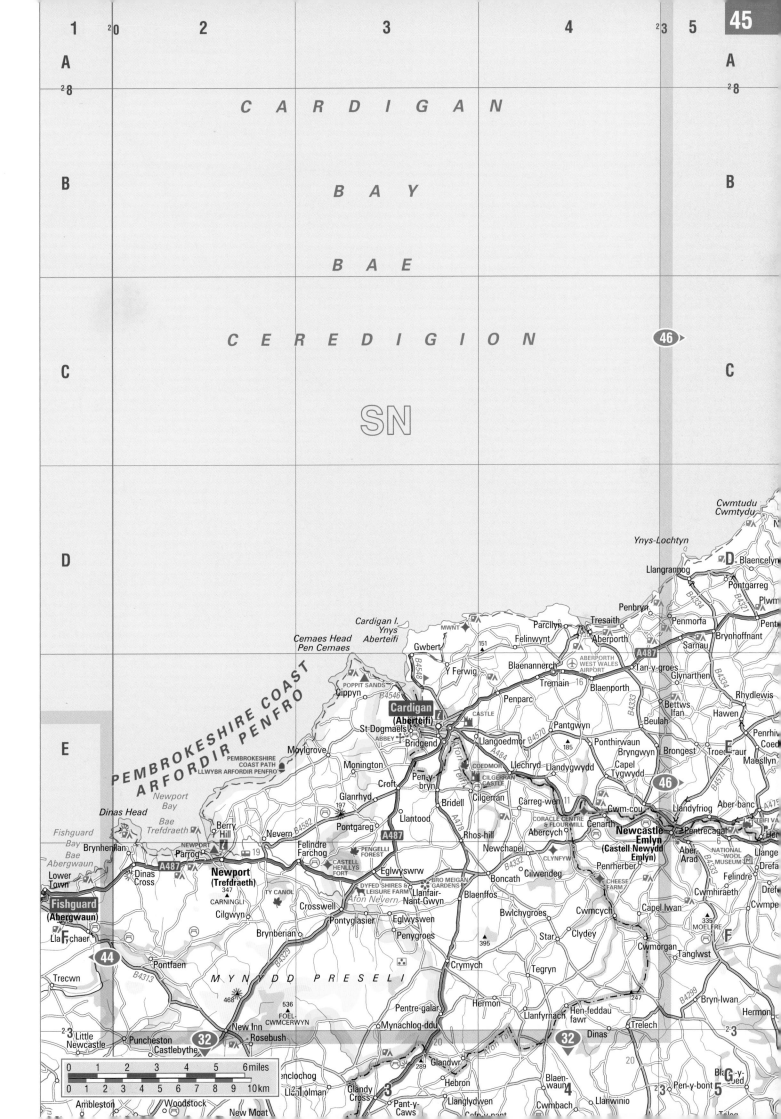

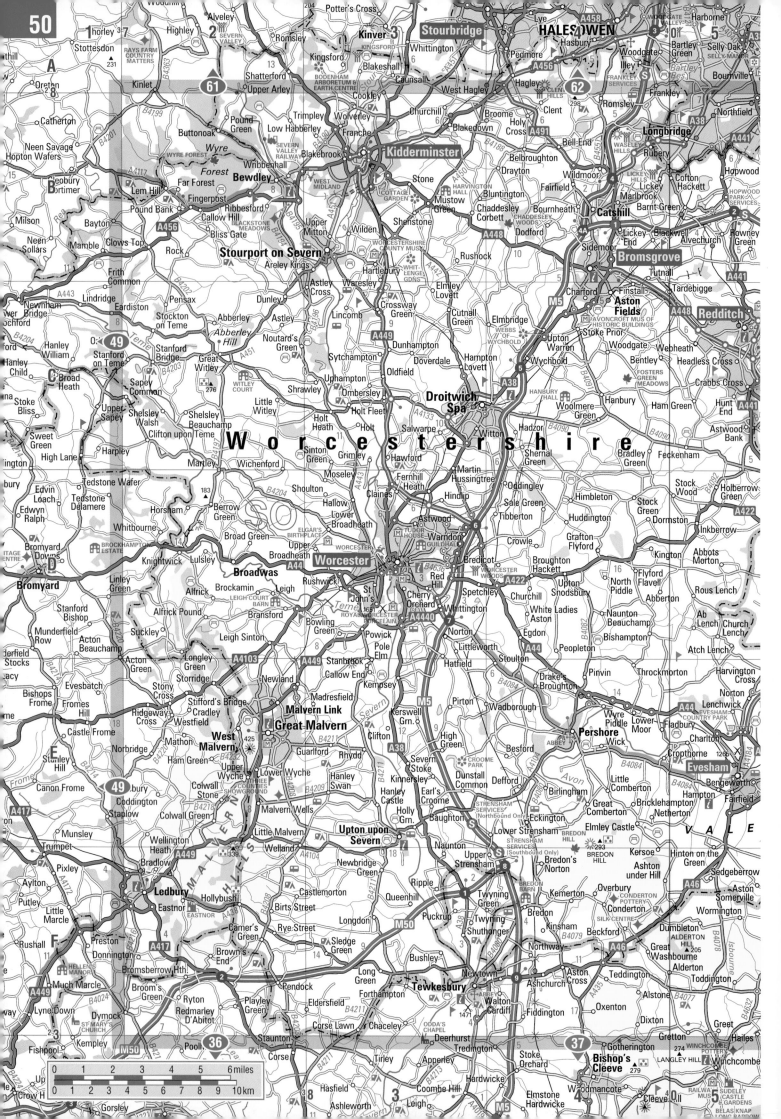

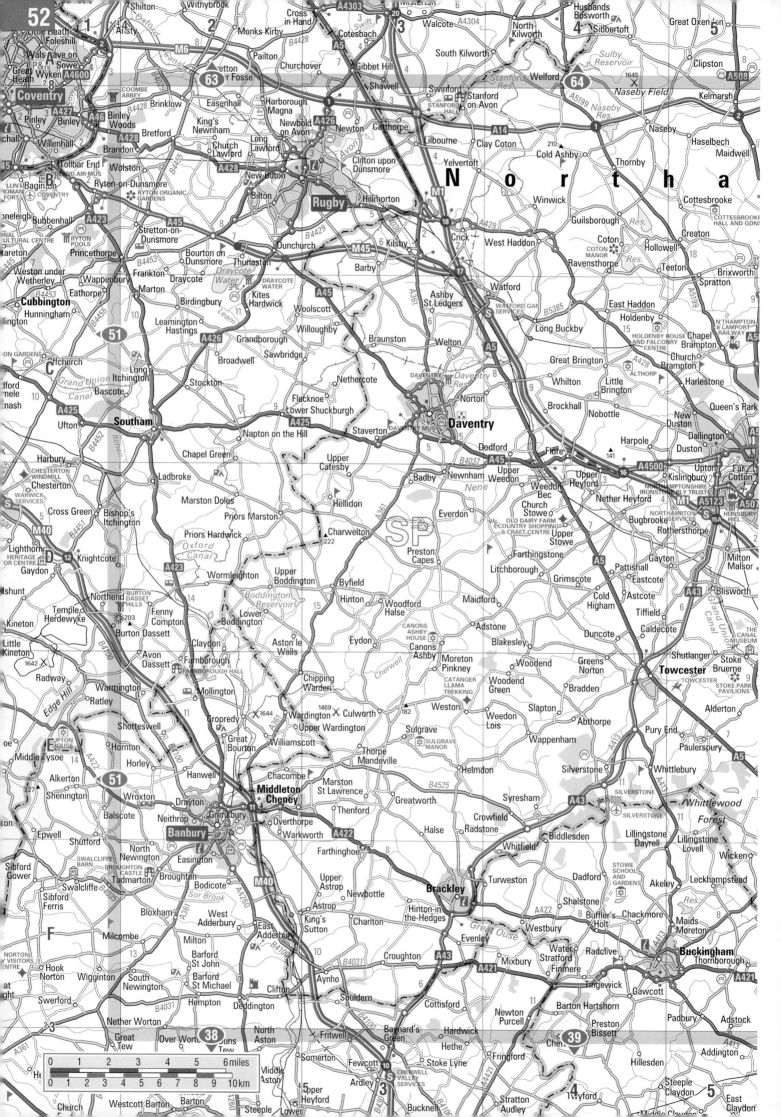

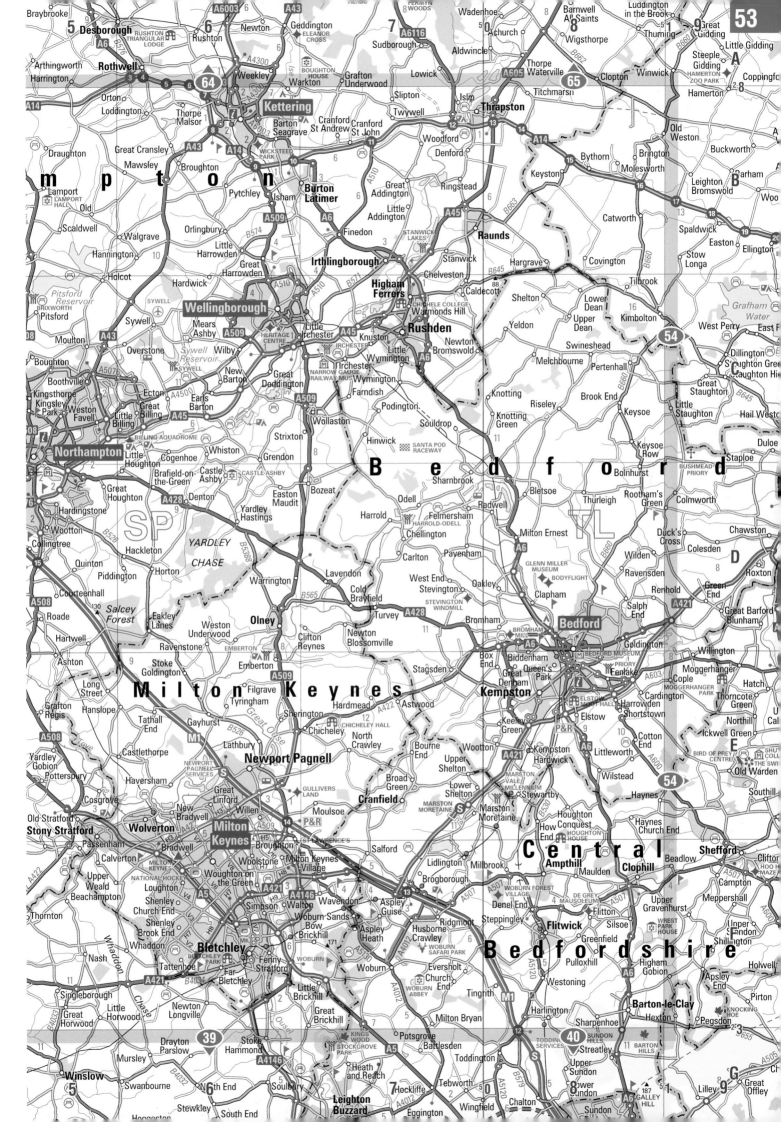

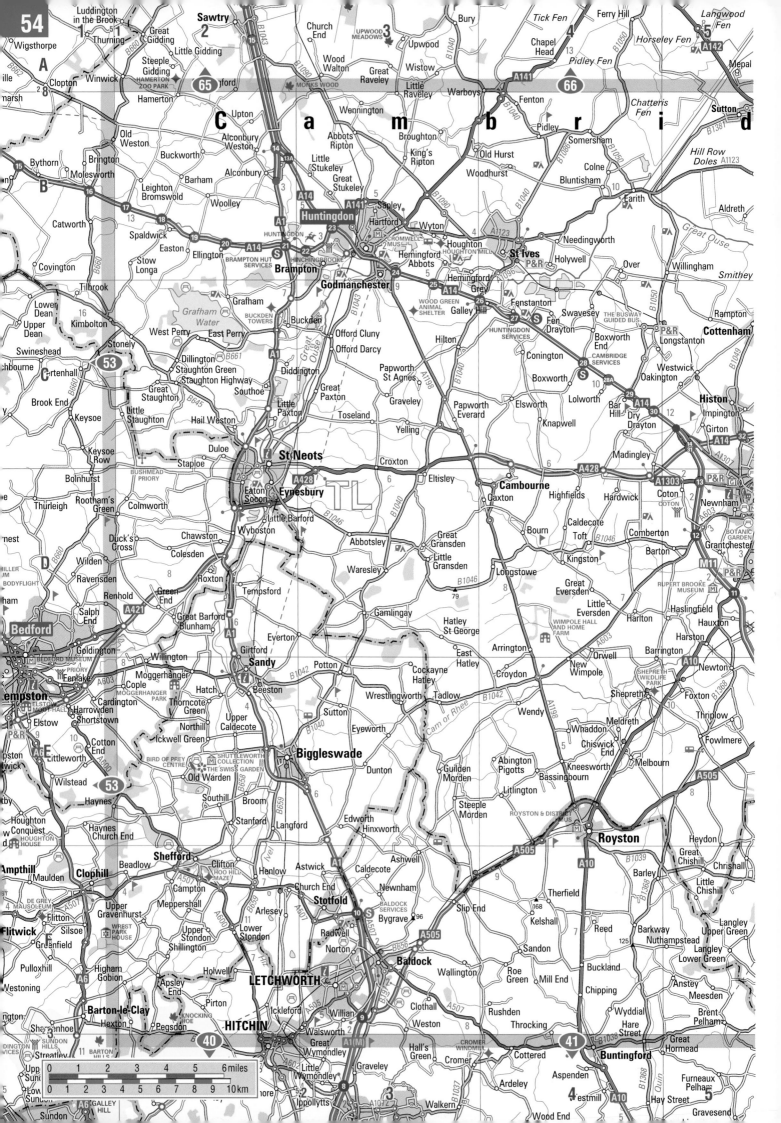

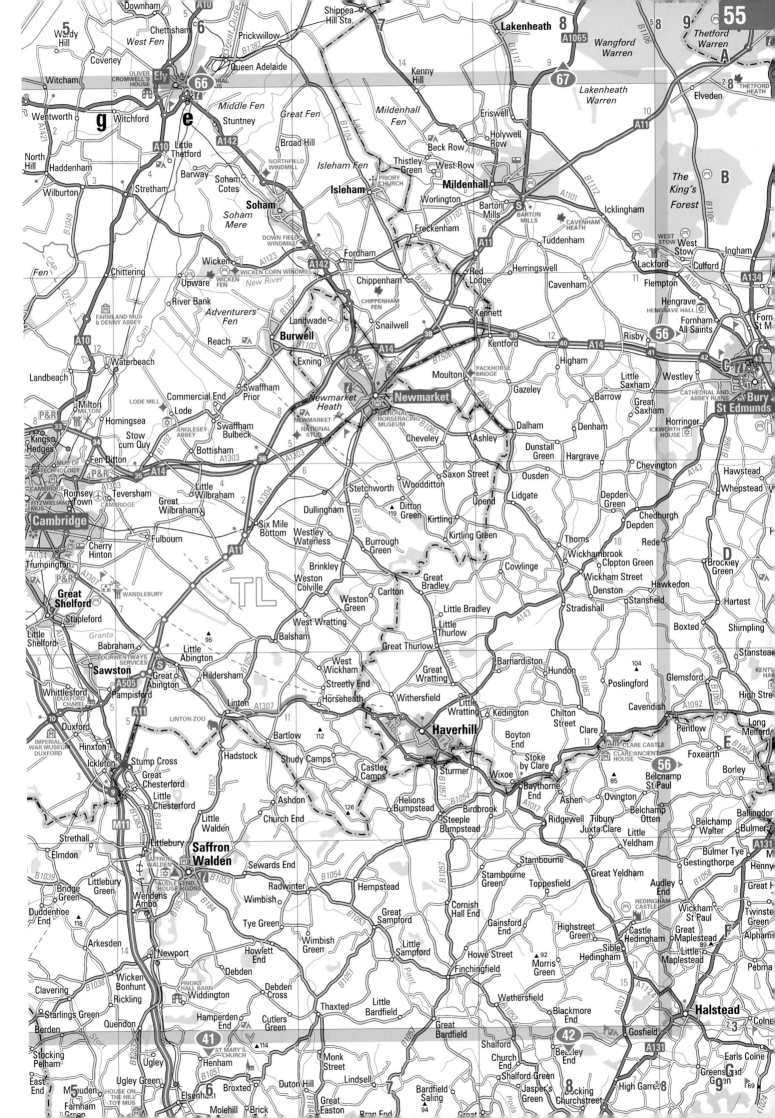

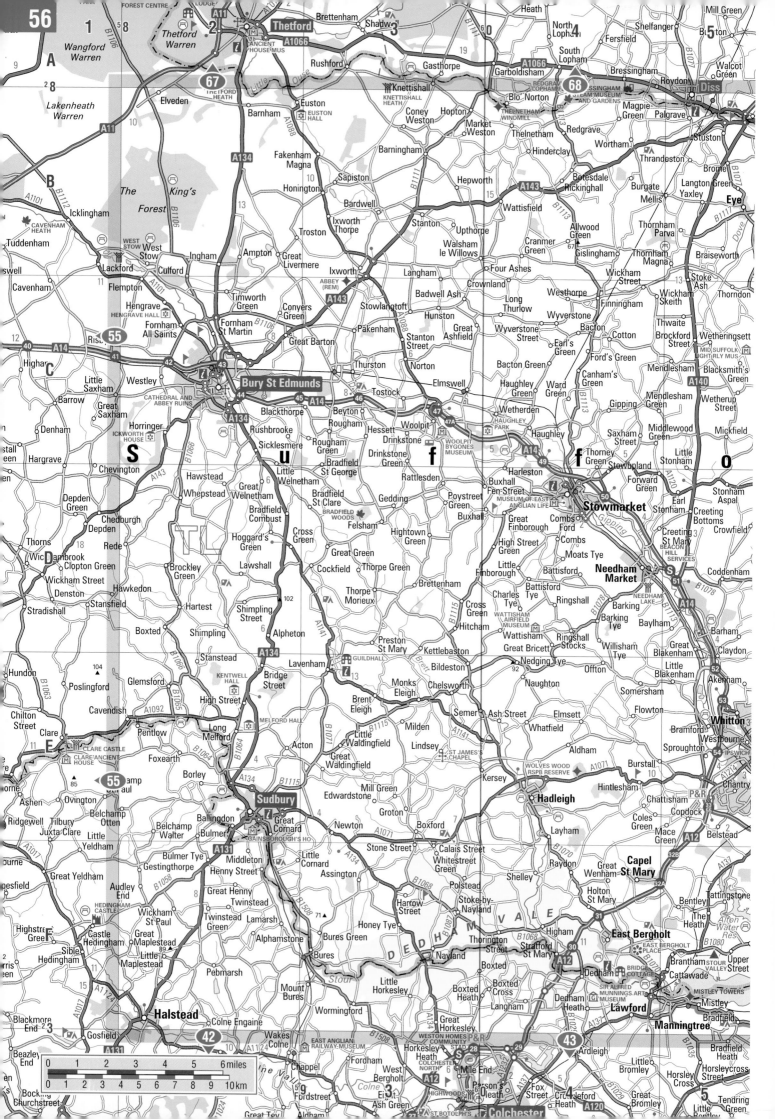

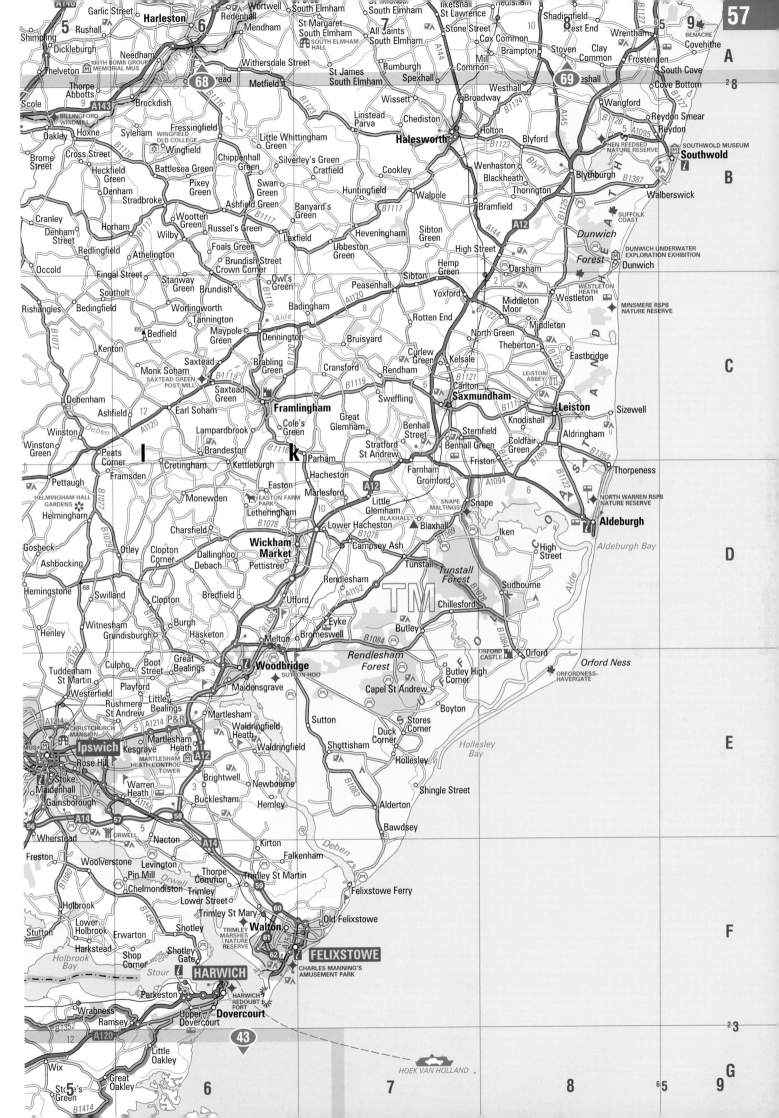

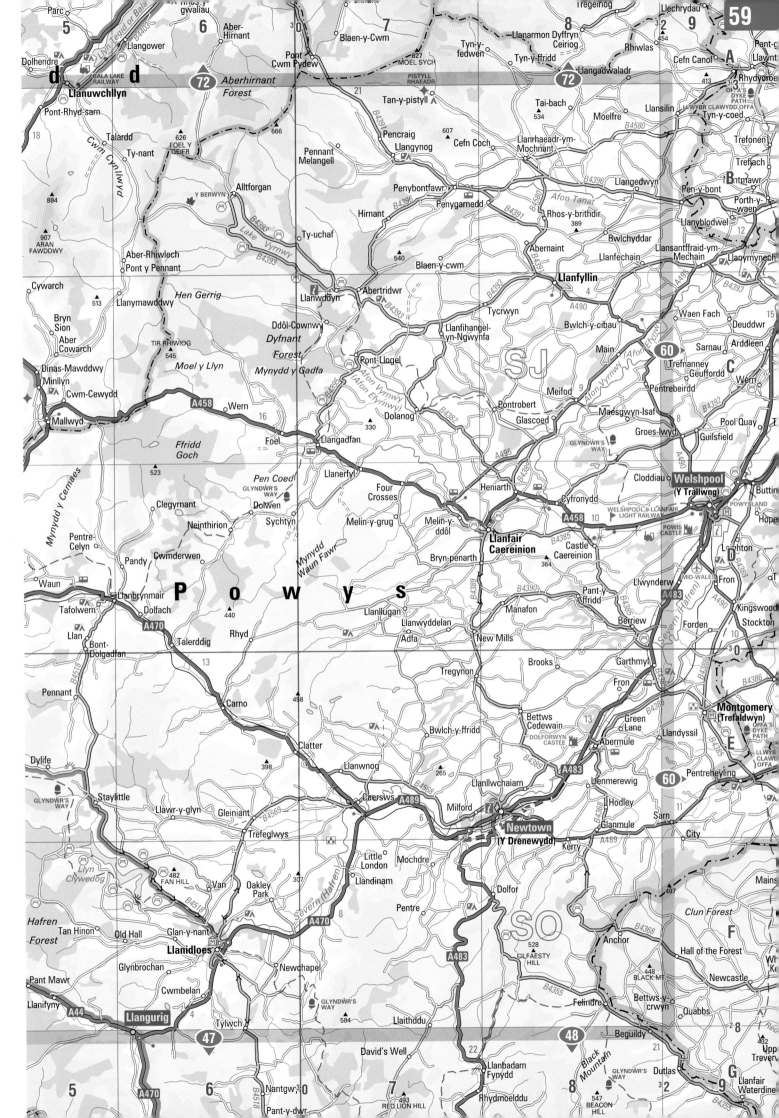

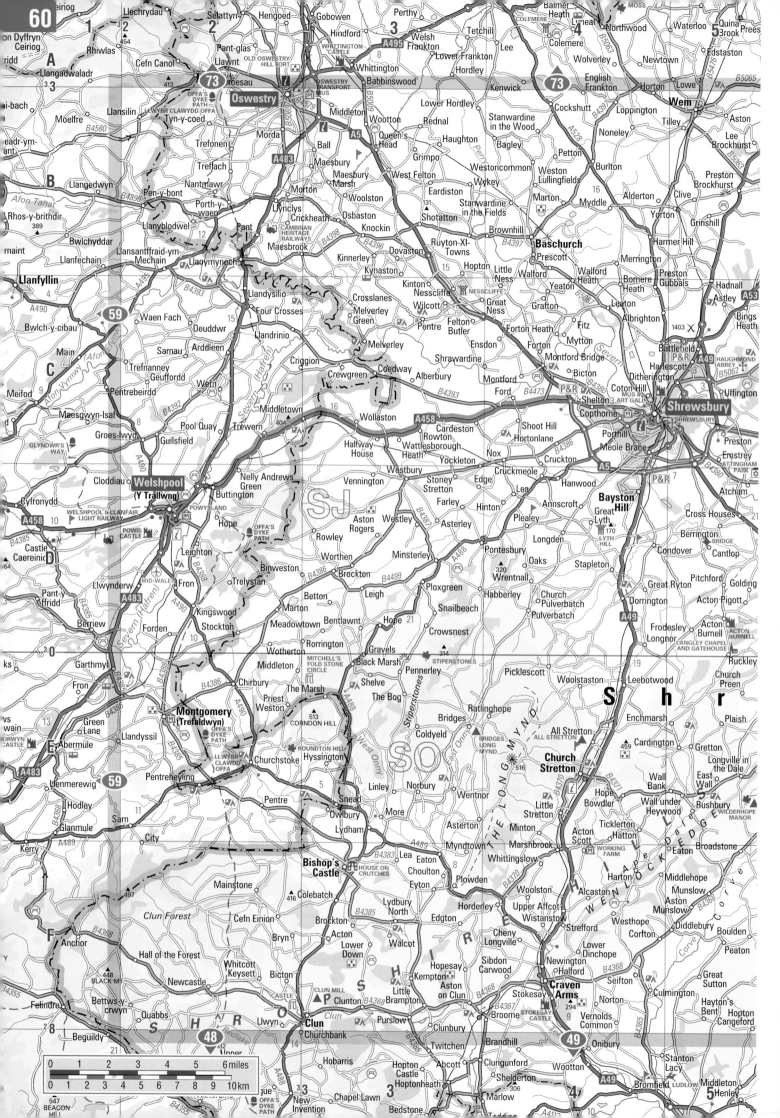

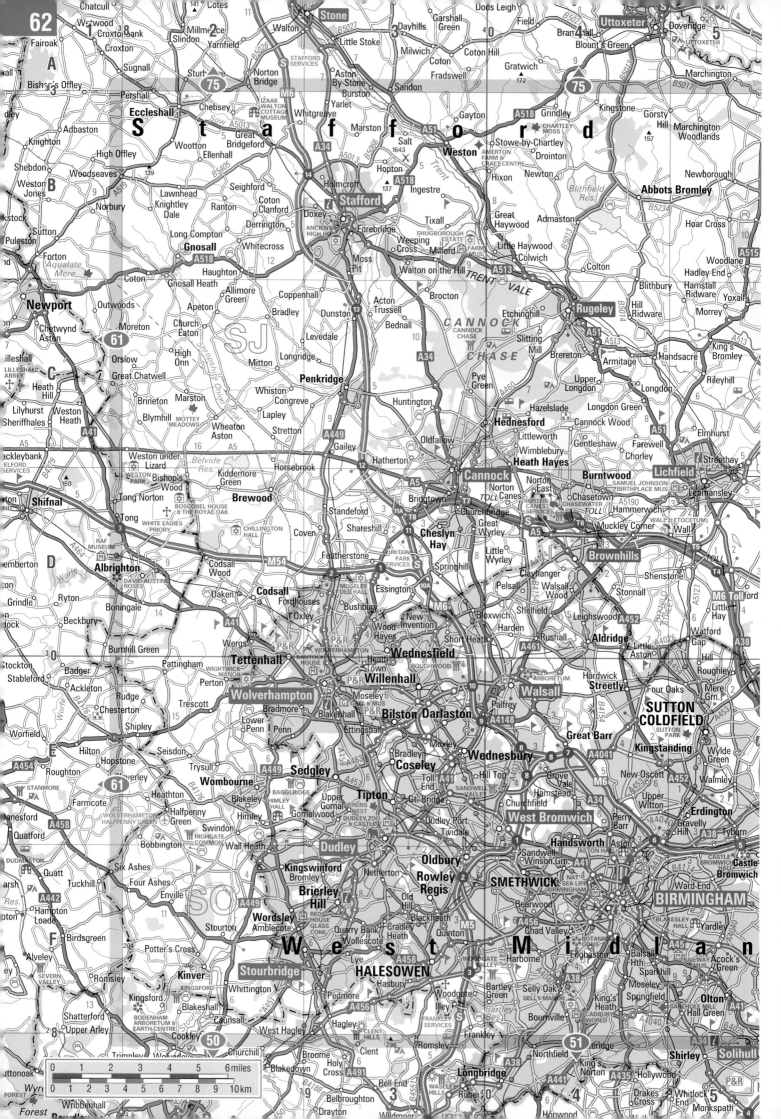

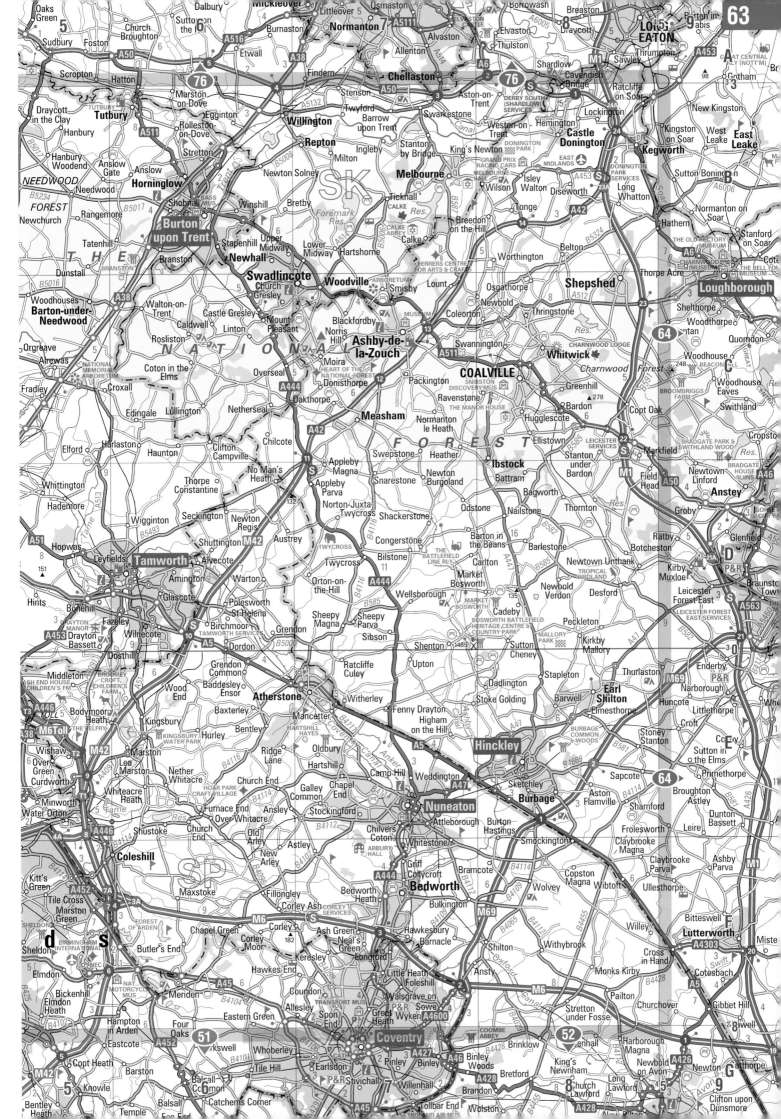

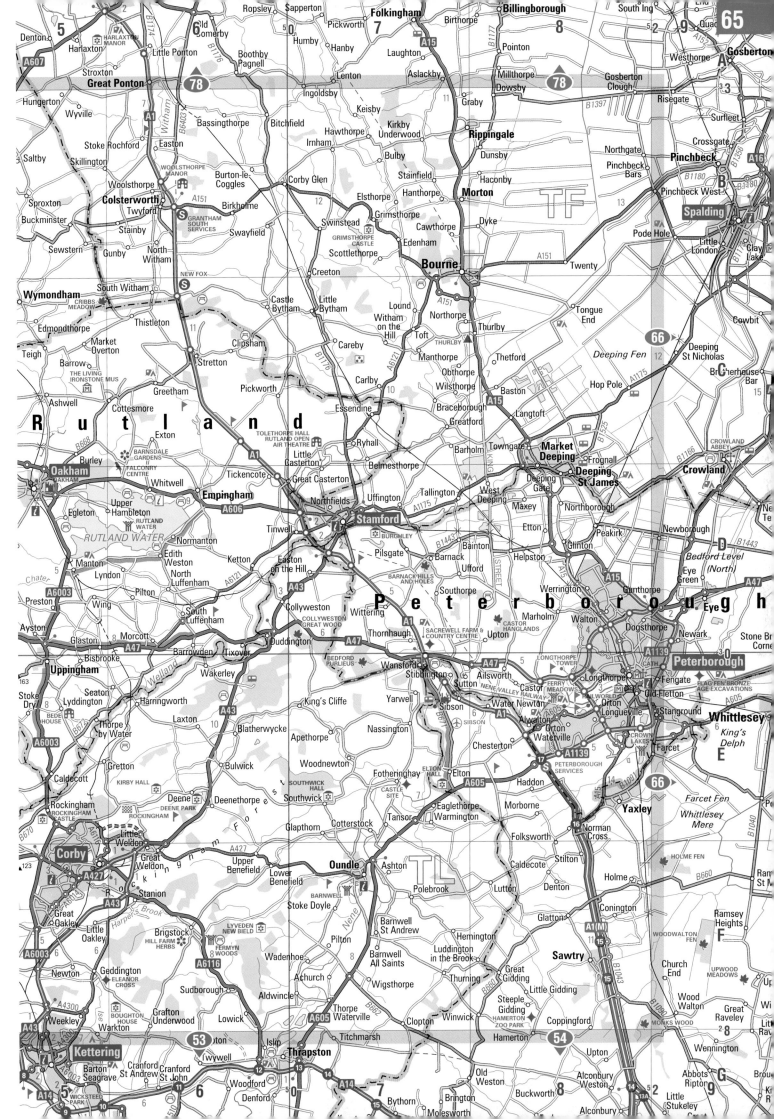

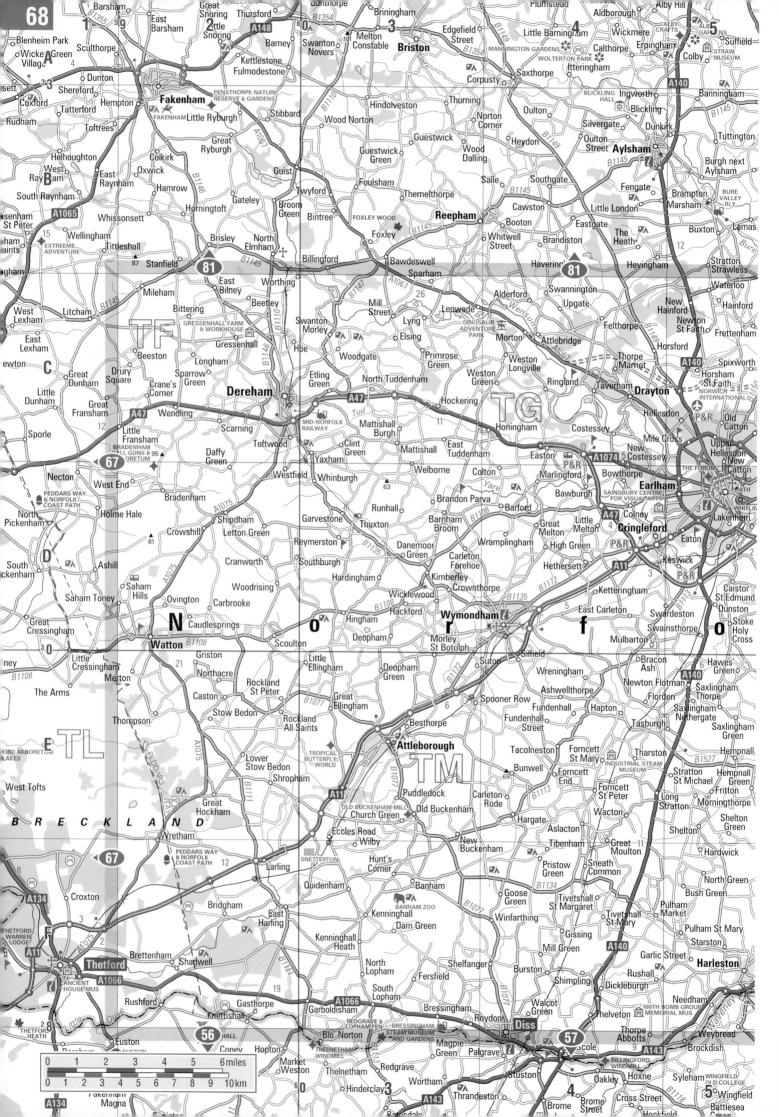

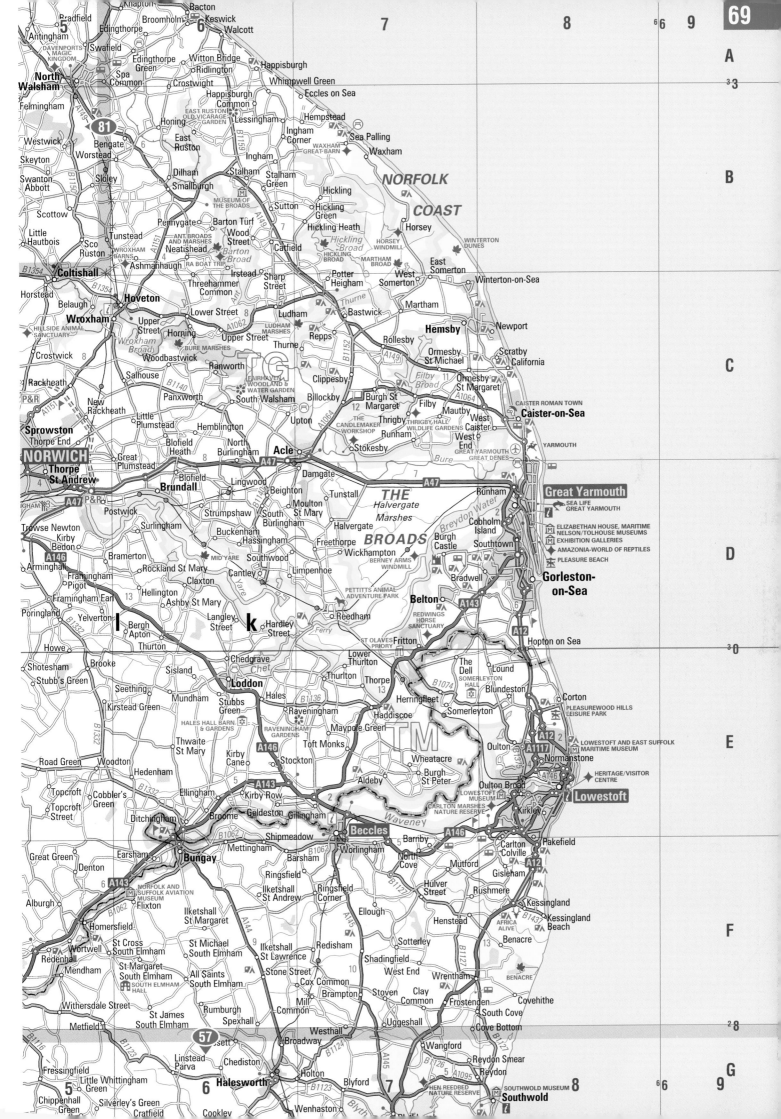

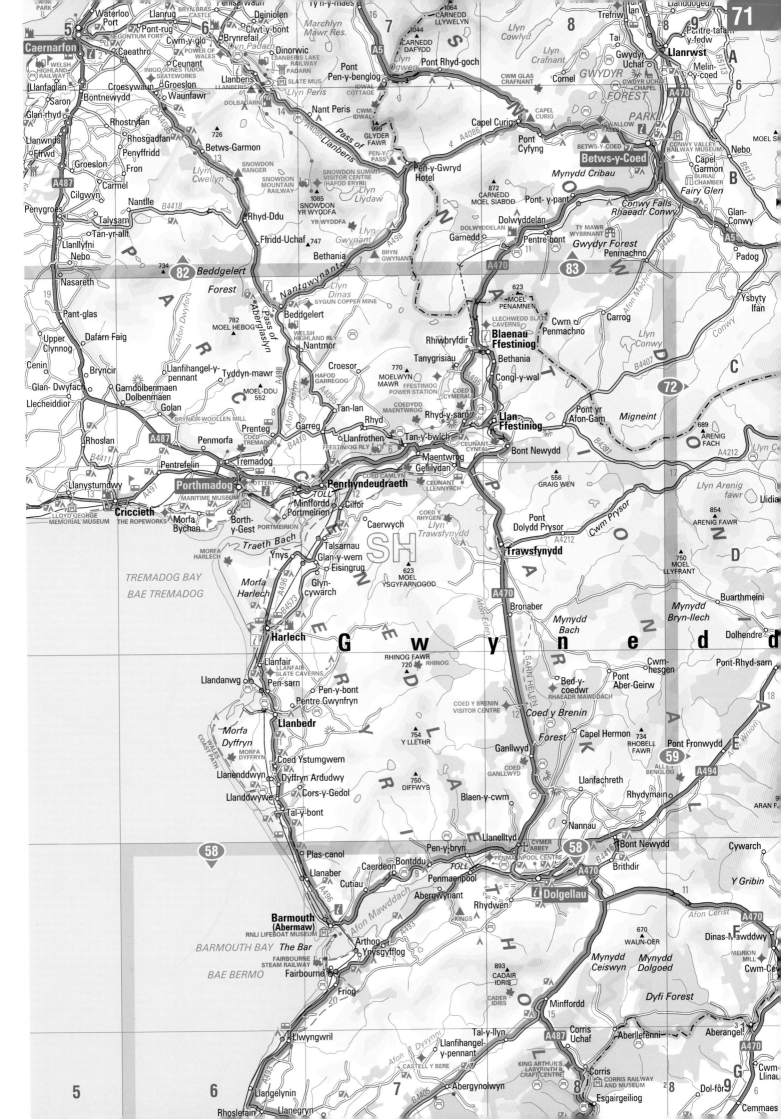

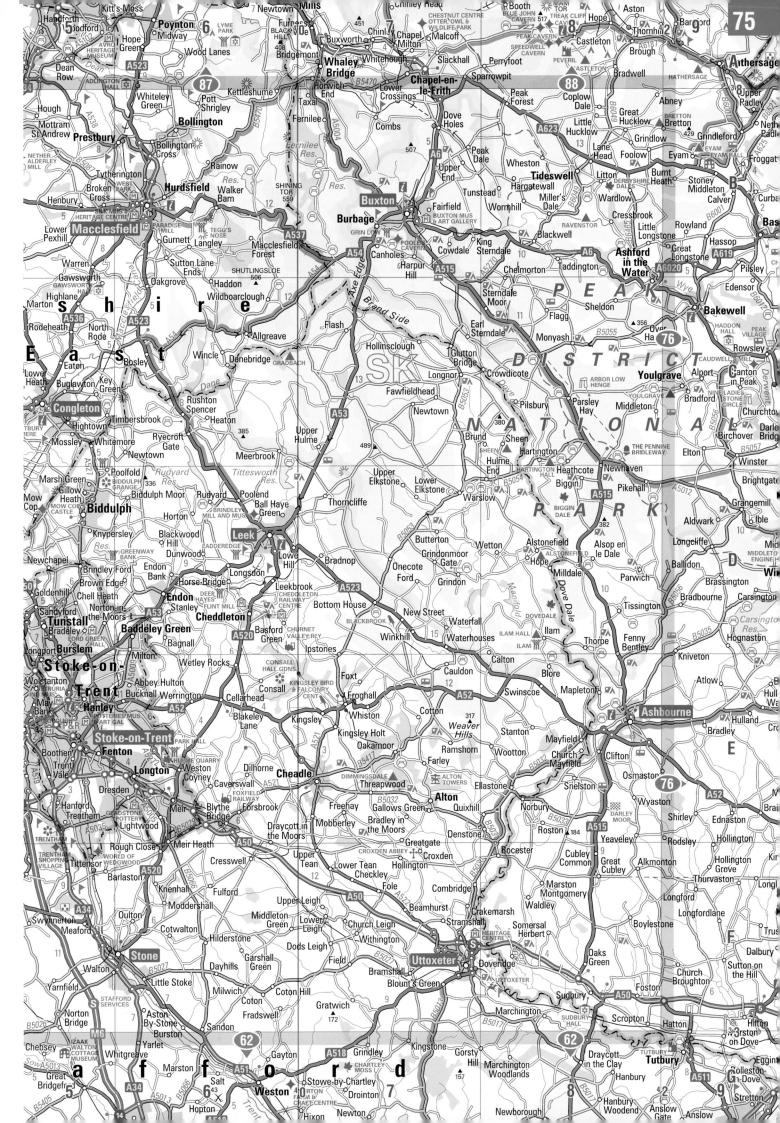

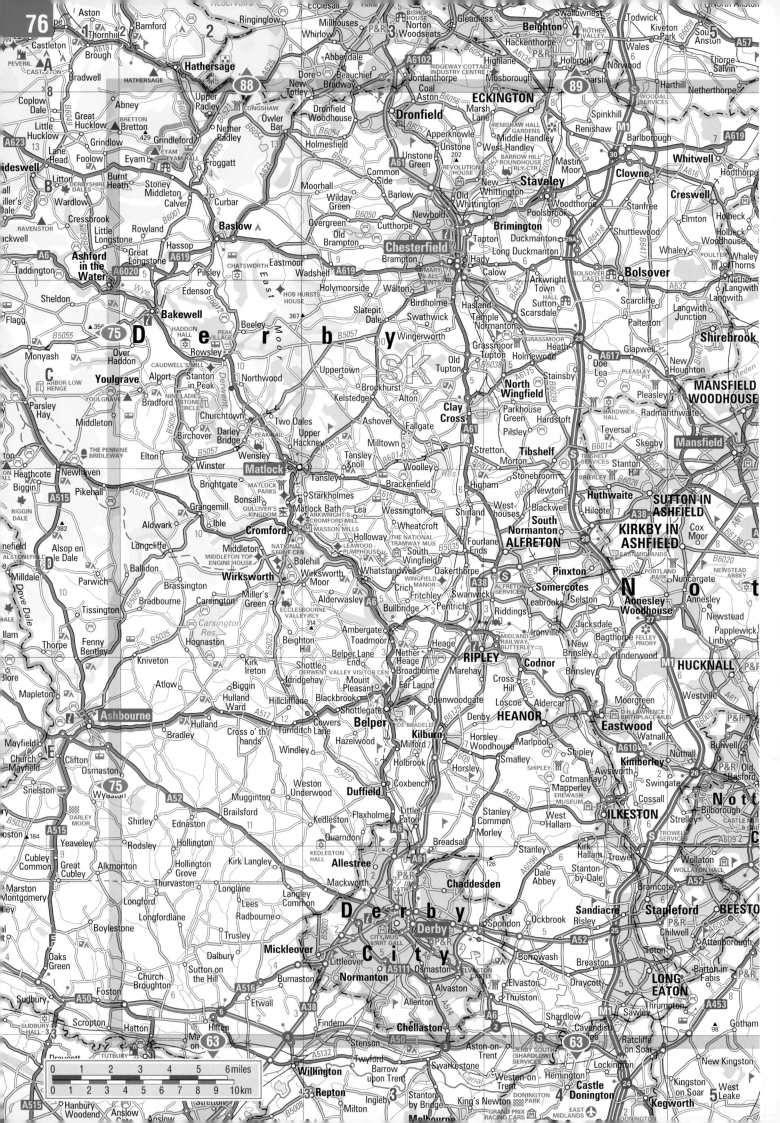

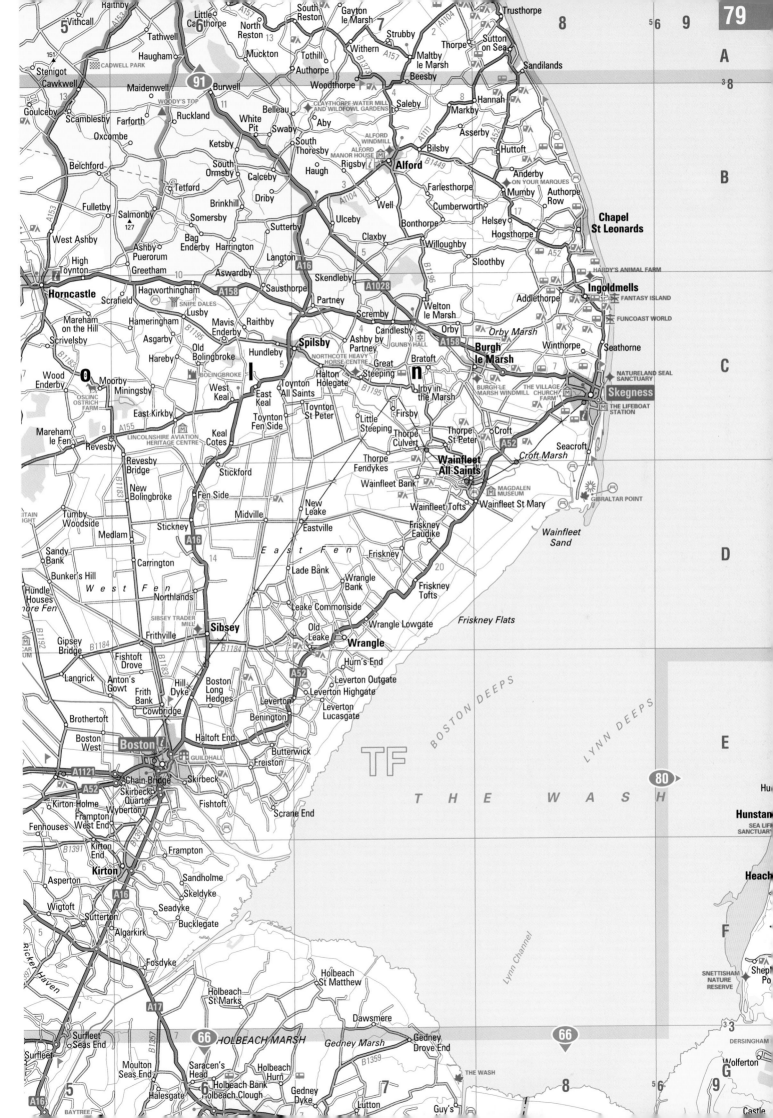

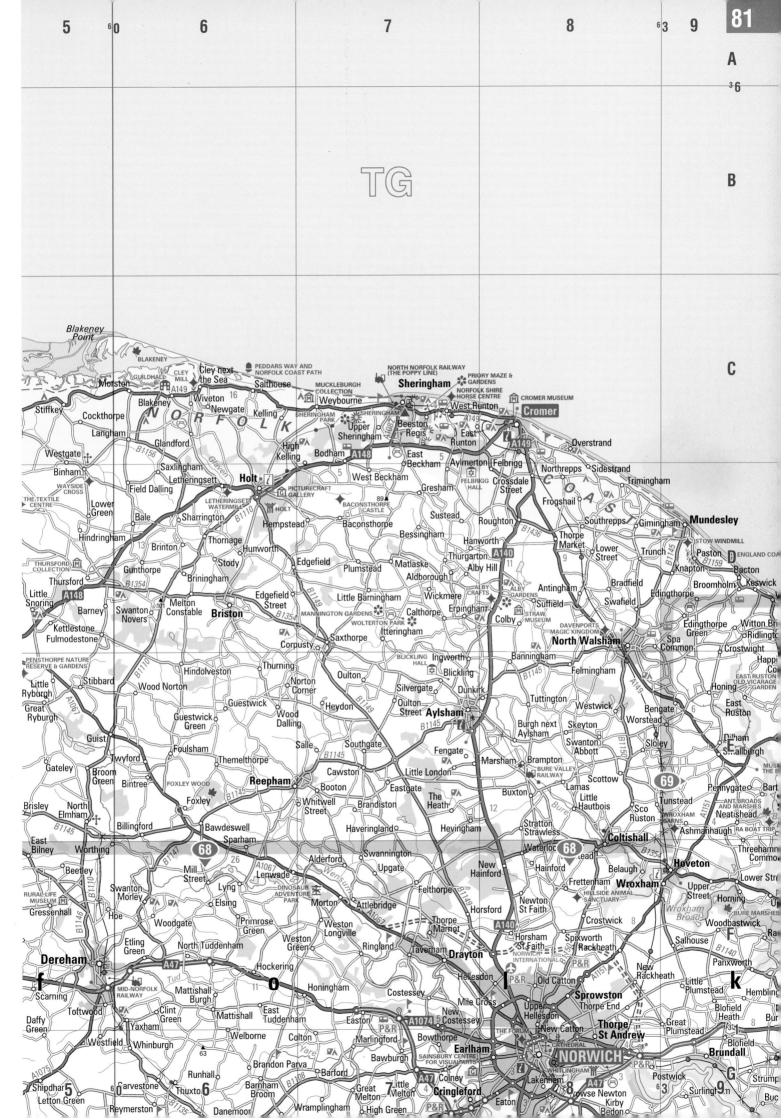

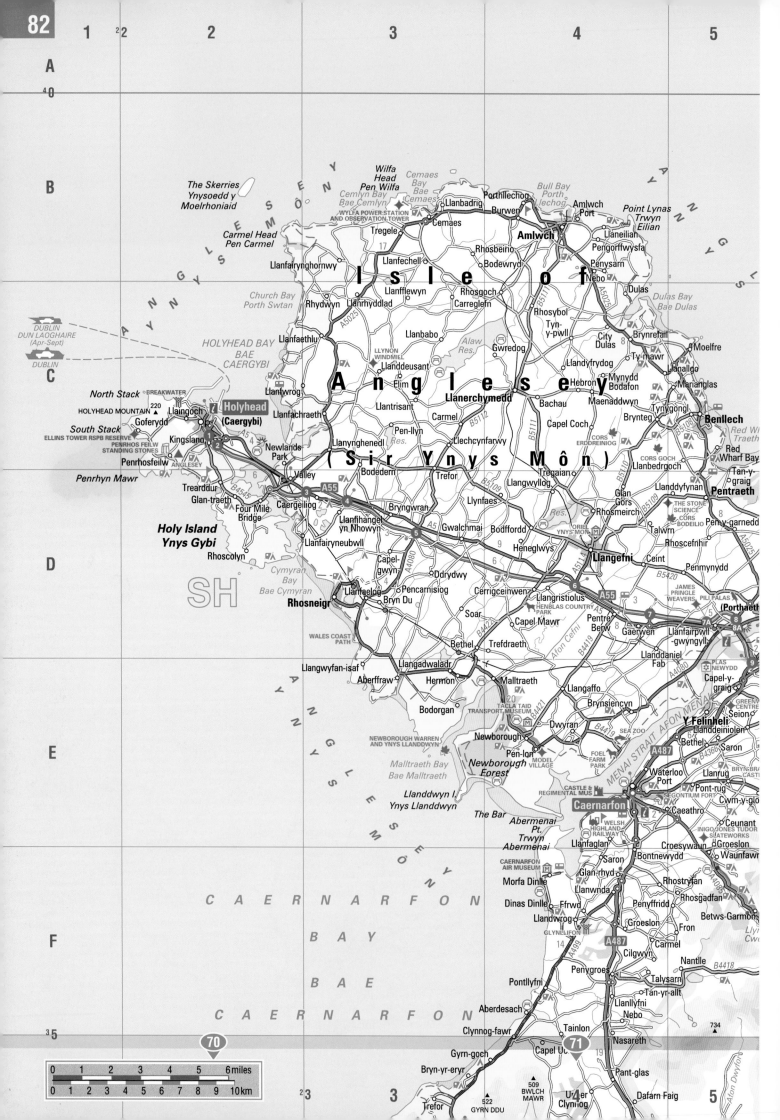

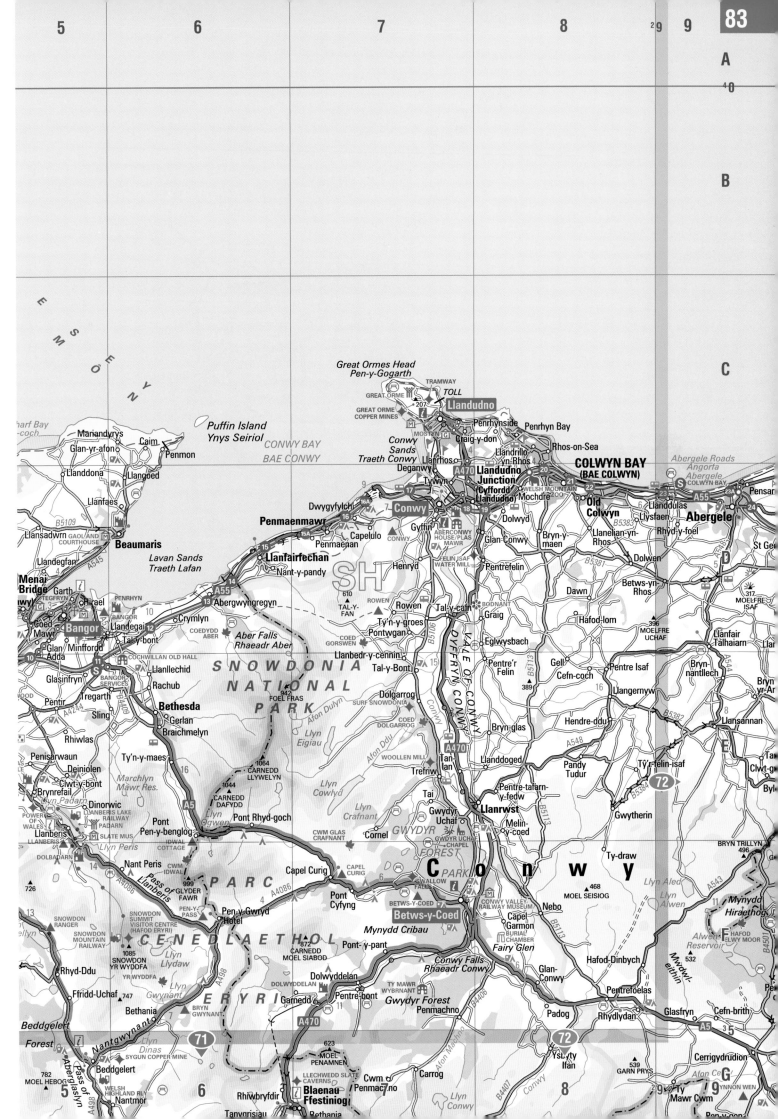

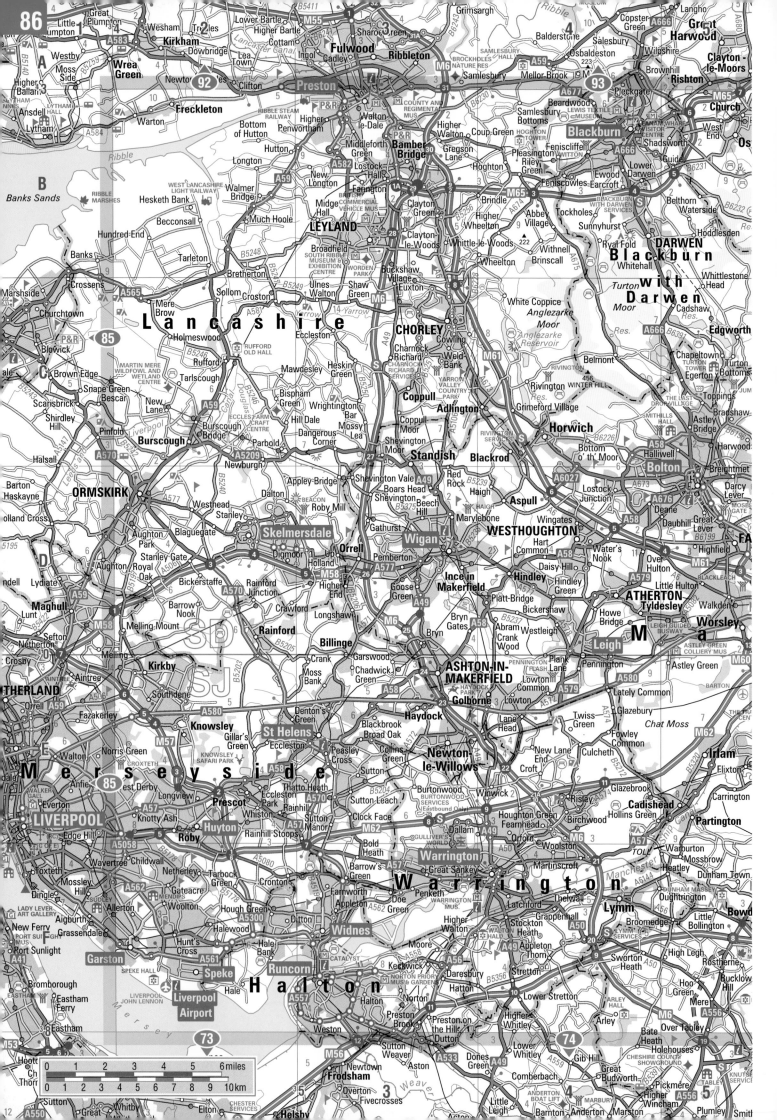

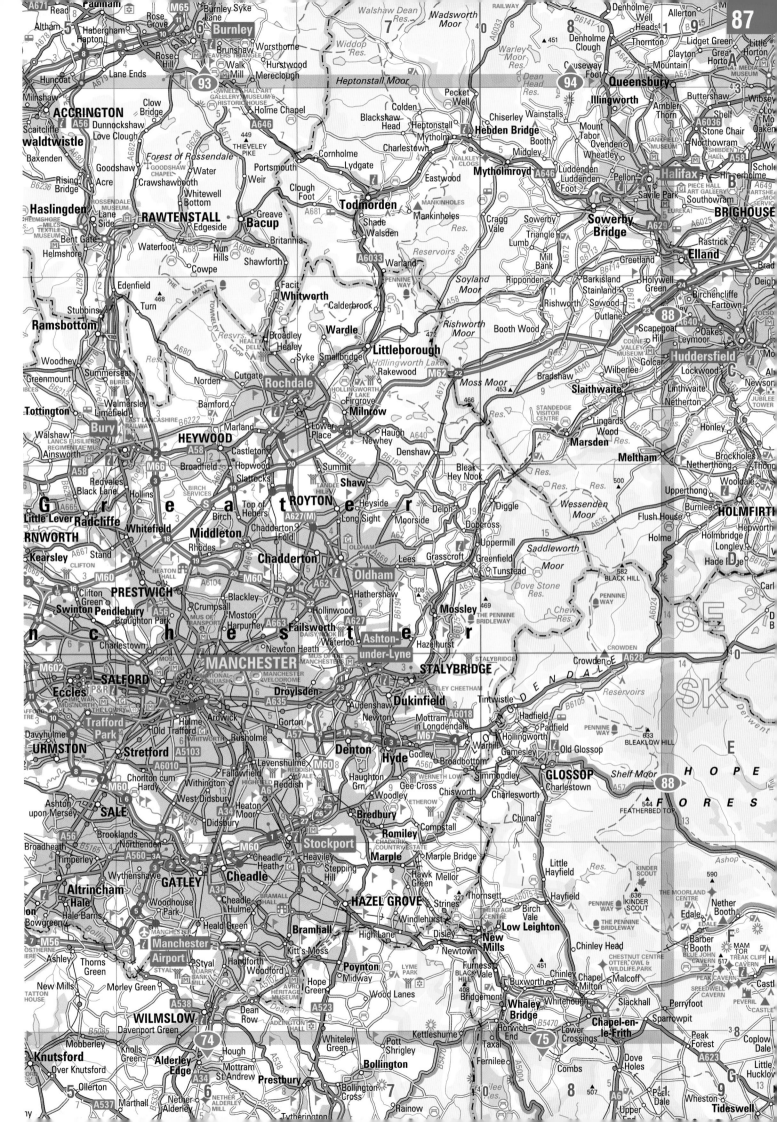

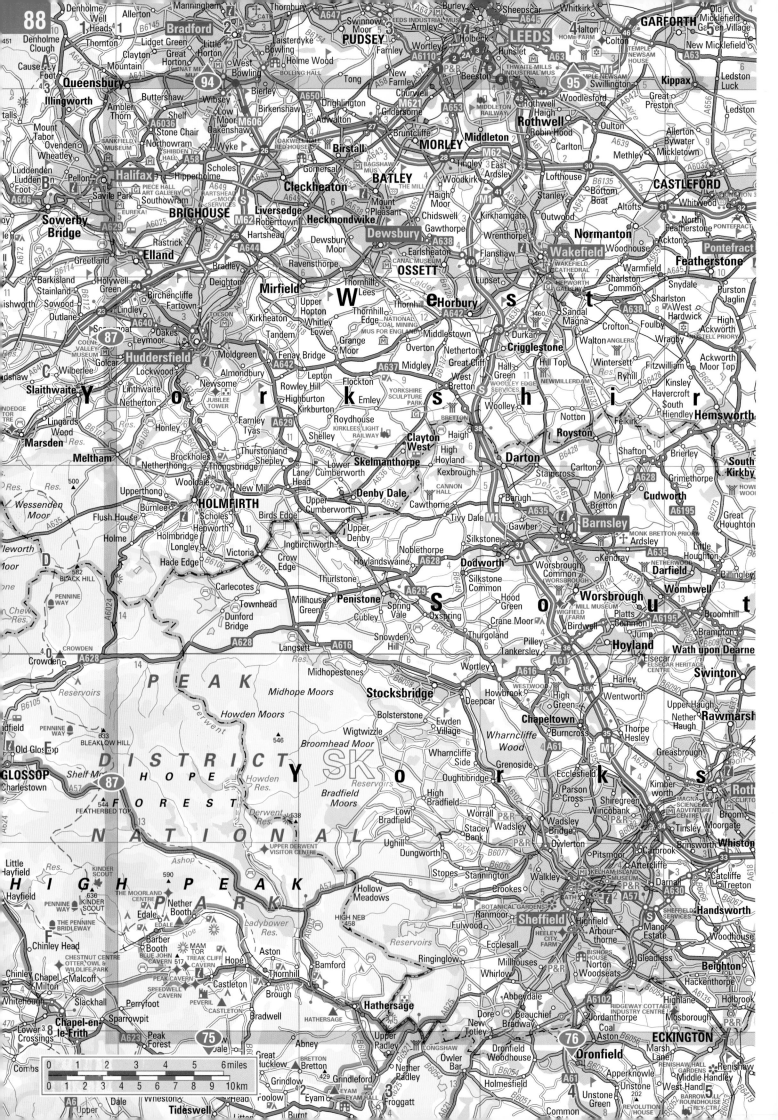

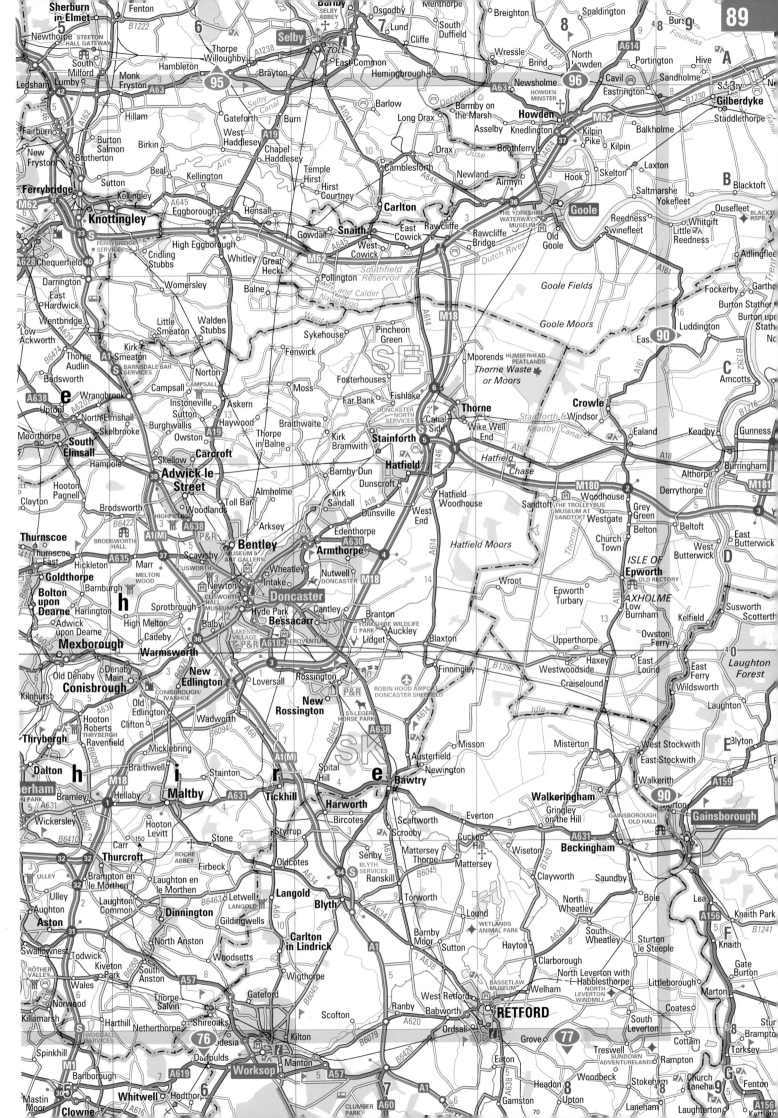

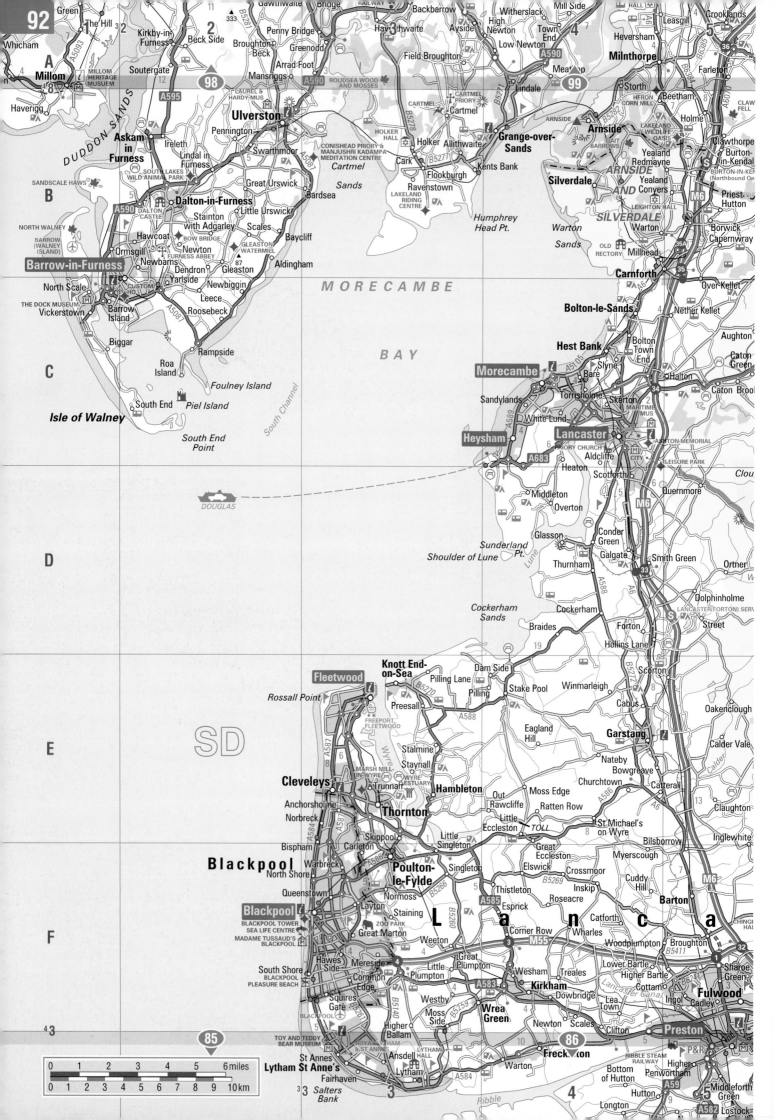

MORECAMBE

BAY

Isle of Walney

DUDDON SANDS

Millom
Haverigg
Whicham
Green
The Hill
Kirkby-in-Furness
Beck Side
Soutergate
Penny Bridge
Broughton Beck
Greenodd
Arrad Foot
Mansriggs
Pennington
Ulverston
Swarthmoor
Lindal in Furness
Great Urswick
Little Urswick
Scales
Bardsea
Bayliff
Aldingham
Newbiggin
Leece
Roosebeck
Rampside
Biggar
Roa Island
Foulney Island
Piel Island
South End
South End Point

Askam in Furness
Ireleth
Dalton-in-Furness
Stainton with Adgarley
Hawcoat
Newton
Gleaston
Yarlside
Dendron
Ormsgill
Newbarns
Barrow-in-Furness
North Scale
Vickerstown
Barrow Island
North Walney
Sandscale Haws
Barrow (Walney Island)
The Dock Museum

Gawthwaite
Backbarrow
Haverthwaite
Ayside
Field Broughton
Cartmel
Holker
Cark
Flookburgh
Ravenstown
Allithwaite
Kents Bank
Humphrey Head Pt.
Warton Sands

Bridge
Penny Bridge
Low Newton
High Newton
Lindale
Meathop
Grange-over-Sands
Silverdale
Arnside
Warton

Mill Side
Witherslack
Town End
Milnthorpe
Storth
Beetham
Holme
Heversham
Farleton
Clawthorpe
Burton-in-Kendal
Priest Hutton
Borwick
Capernwray
Millhead
Carnforth
Over-Kellet
Nether Kellet
Bolton-le-Sands
Aughton
Caton Green
Hest Bank
Bolton Town End
Slyne
Halton
Caton Brook
Morecambe
Bare
Torrisholme
Skerton
Sandylands
White Lund
Heysham
Lancaster
Aldcliffe
Heaton
Scotforth
Middleton
Overton
Glasson
Conder Green
Galgate
Smith Green
Quernmore
Sunderland Pt.
Shoulder of Lune
Thurnham
Cockerham
Cockerham Sands
Braides
Forton
Hollins Lane
Scorton
Dolphinholme
Street
Ortner

DOUGLAS

Knott End-on-Sea
Fleetwood
Rossall Point
Preesall
Pilling
Dam Side
Stake Pool
Winmarleigh
Cabus
Oakenclough
Garstang
Calder Vale
Nateby
Bowgreave
Churchtown
Catterall
Claughton
Inglewhite
Barton
Woodplumpton
Broughton
Fulwood
Preston

SD

Cleveleys
Anchorsholme
Thornton
Trunnah
Hambleton
Stalmine
Staynall
Out Rawcliffe
Little Eccleston
Moss Edge
Ratten Row
St Michael's on Wyre
Bilsborrow
Myerscough
Cuddy Hill
Crossmoor
Inskip
Roseacre
Catforth
Higher Bartle
Lower Bartle
Cottam
Ingol
Cadley

Blackpool
North Shore
Norbreck
Bispham
Warbreck
Queenstown
Poulton-le-Fylde
Carleton
Skippool
Singleton
Little Singleton
Great Eccleston
Elswick
Thistleton
Wesham
Treales
Dowbridge
Kirkham
Wrea Green
Newton
Clifton
Freckleton
Warton
Lea Town
Cottam

Blackpool Tower
Sea Life Centre
Madame Tussaud's Blackpool
South Shore
Blackpool Pleasure Beach
Squires Gate
Hawes Side
Mereside
Common Edge
Great Marton
Layton
Staining
Weeton
Great Plumpton
Little Plumpton
Westby
Moss Side
Wrea Green
Newton Scales
Corner Row
Wharles
Esprick
Roseacre
Singleton

St Annes
Lytham St Anne's
Fairhaven
Ansdell
Lytham
Salters Bank
Toy and Teddy Bear Museum
Royal Lytham & St Anne's

L a n c a

| 0 | 1 | 2 | 3 | 4 | 5 | 6 miles |
| 0 | 1 2 3 4 5 6 7 8 9 | 10km |

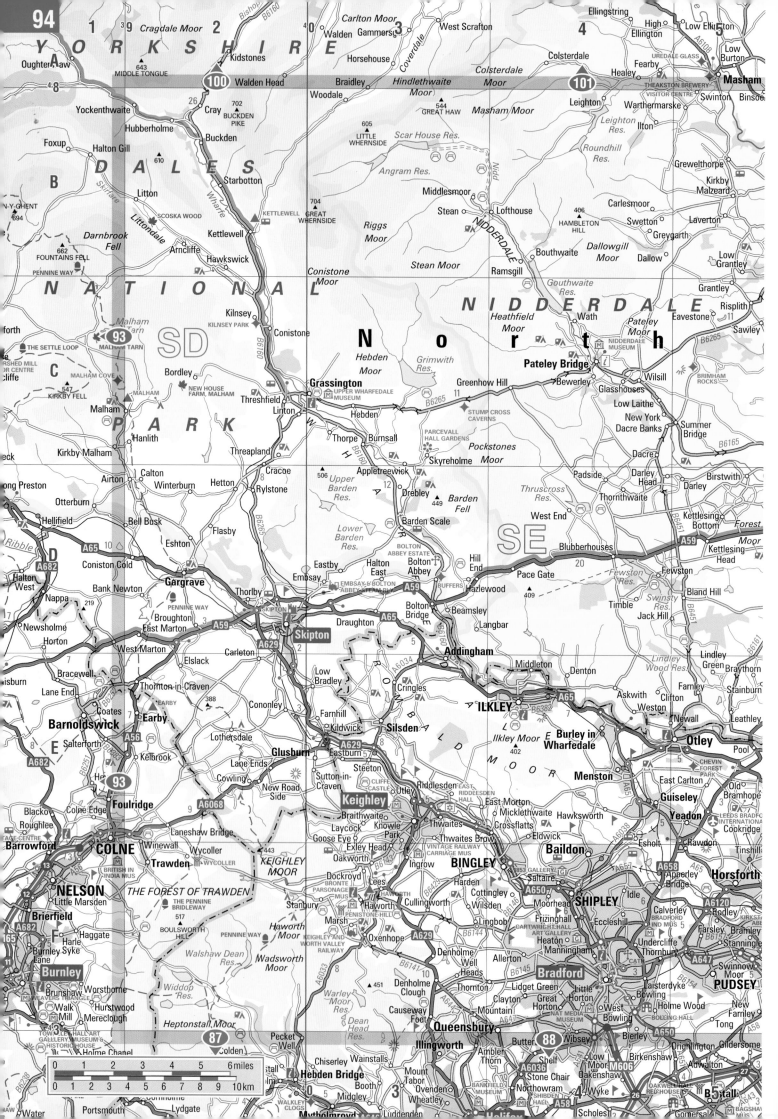

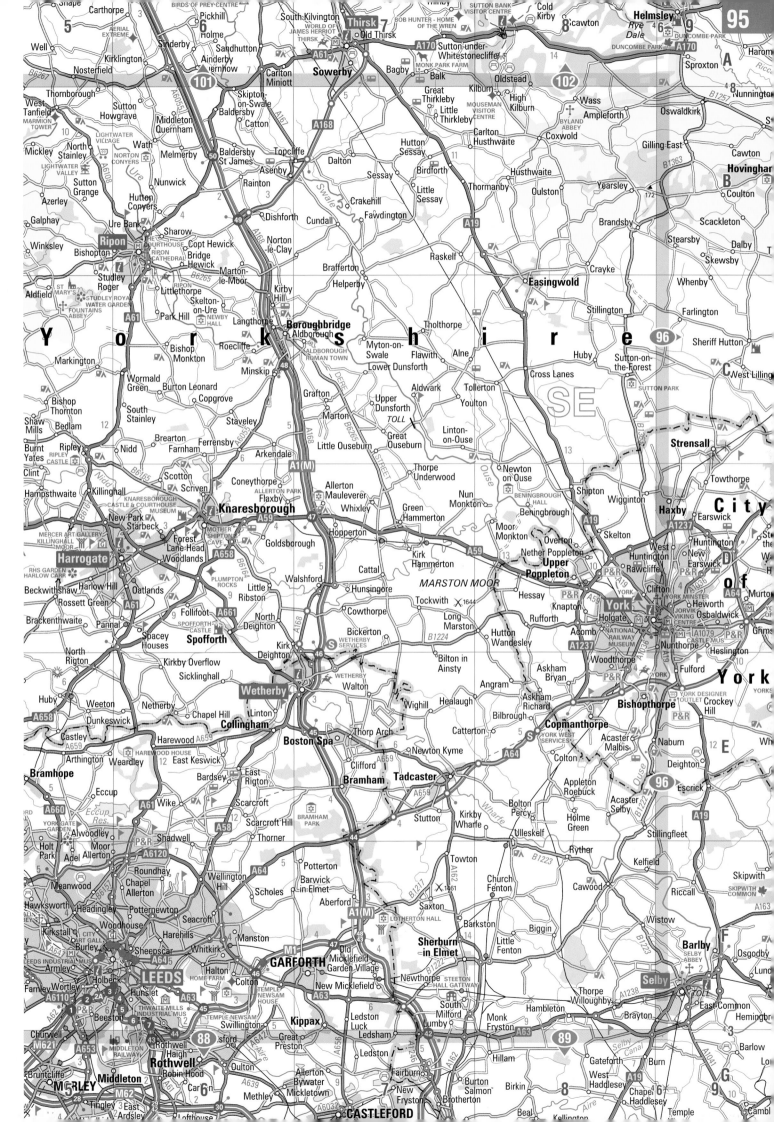

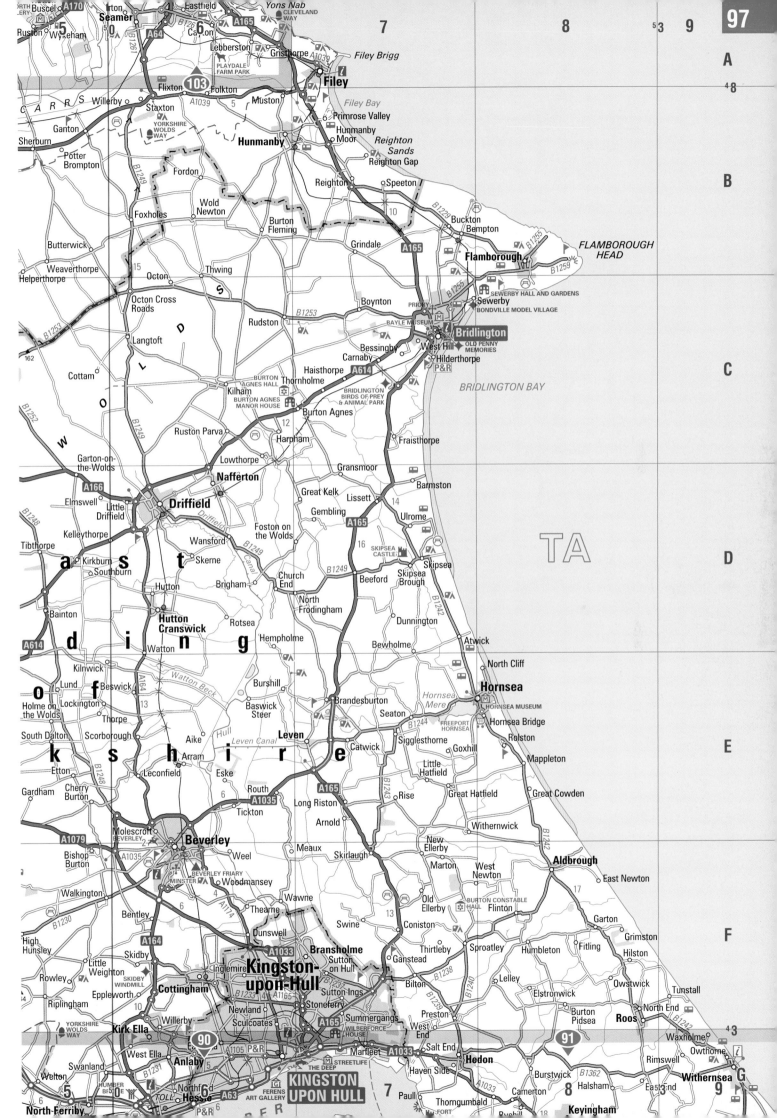

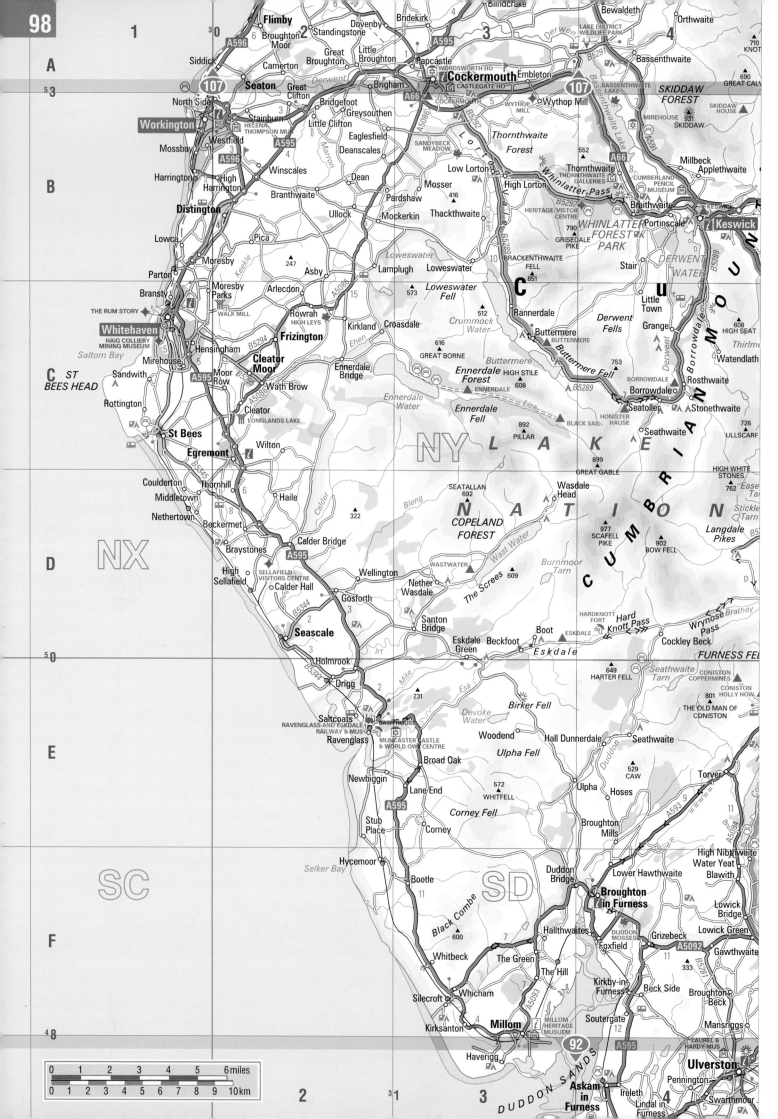

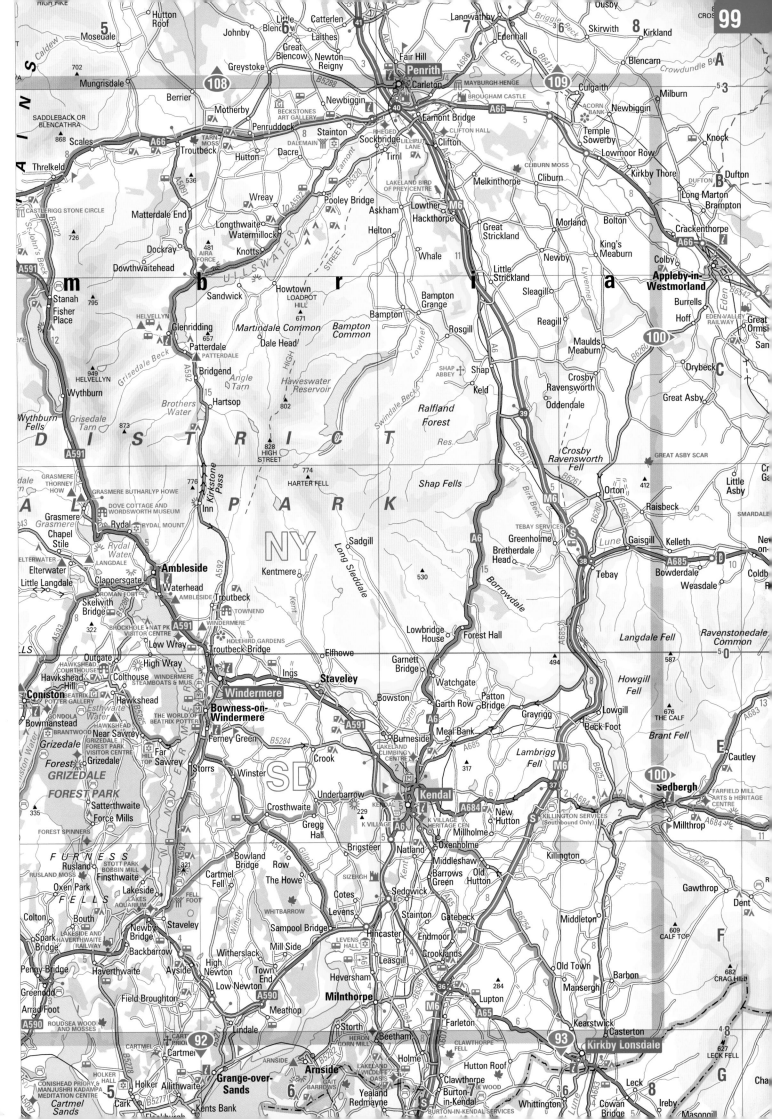

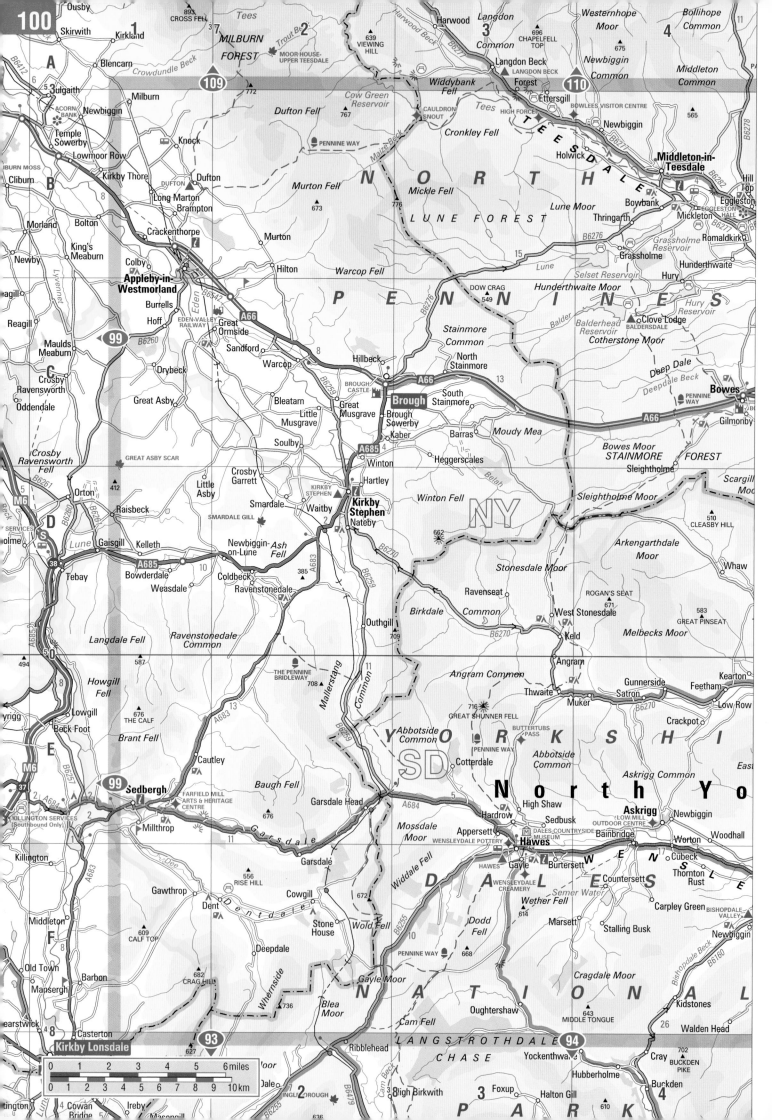

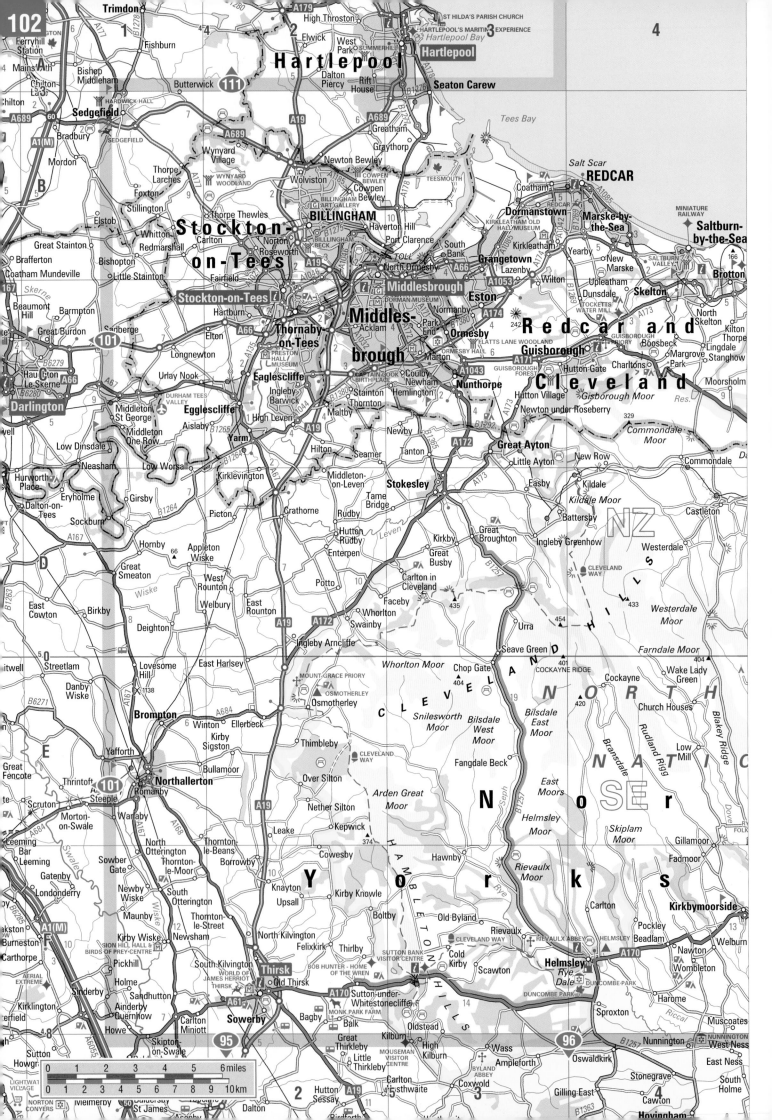

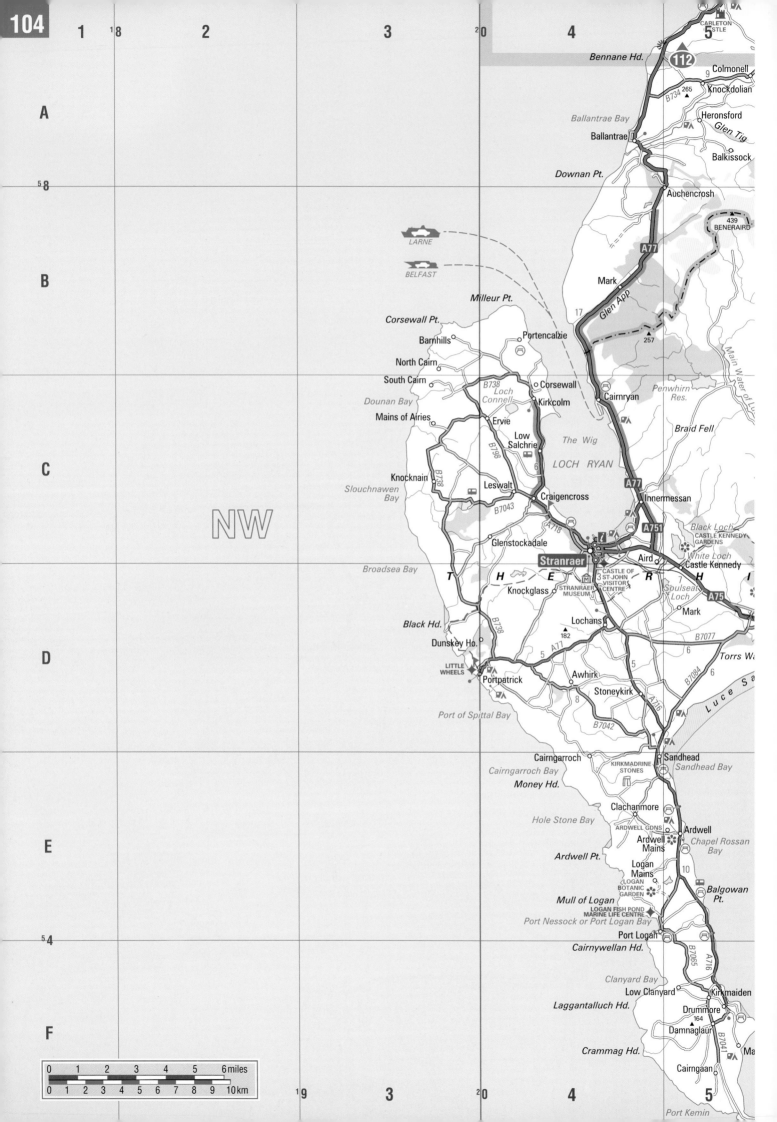

1   2   3   4

A

B

C

NW

D

E

F

Stranraer

CARLETON CSTLE
Bennane Hd.
112
Colmonell
B734   265   Knockdolian
Heronsford
Glen Tig
Ballantrae Bay
Ballantrae
Balkissock
Downan Pt.
Auchencrosh
439 BENERAIRD
A77
Mark
17   Glen App
257
Corsewall Pt.
Milleur Pt.
Portencalzie
Barnhills
North Cairn
South Cairn
B738   Loch Connell
Corsewall
Kirkcolm
Cairnryan
Penwhirn Res.
Braid Fell
Dounan Bay
Mains of Airies
Ervie
B798
Low Salchrie
The Wig
LOCH RYAN
Knocknain
Leswalt
A77
Slouchnawen Bay
B738
B7043
Craigencross
Innermessan
A718
Black Loch
CASTLE KENNEDY GARDENS
A751
Glenstockadale
Stranraer
Aird
White Loch
Castle Kennedy
Broadsea Bay
THE
CASTLE OF ST. JOHN VISITOR CENTRE
STRANRAER MUSEUM
R
H
I
Soulseat Loch
A75
Knockglass
Mark
Black Hd.
Lochans
182
A77
B7077
Dunskey Ho.
5
6
Torrs Wa
LITTLE WHEELS
Awhirk
5
B7084
Portpatrick
Stoneykirk
A716
6
Port of Spittal Bay
8
B7042
Cairngarroch
KIRKMADRINE STONES
Sandhead
Cairngarroch Bay
Sandhead Bay
Money Hd.
Clachanmore
Hole Stone Bay
ARDWELL GDNS
Ardwell
Ardwell Mains
Chapel Rossan Bay
Ardwell Pt.
Logan Mains
10
LOGAN BOTANIC GARDEN
Balgowan Pt.
Mull of Logan
LOGAN FISH POND MARINE LIFE CENTRE
Port Nessock or Port Logan Bay
Port Logan
Cairnywellan Hd.
B7065
A716
Clanyard Bay
Low Clanyard
Kirkmaiden
Laggantalluch Hd.
Drummore
164
Crammag Hd.
Damnaglaur
B7041
Cairngaan
Port Kemin

LARNE
BELFAST

0   1   2   3   4   5   6 miles
0   1   2   3   4   5   6   7   8   9   10km

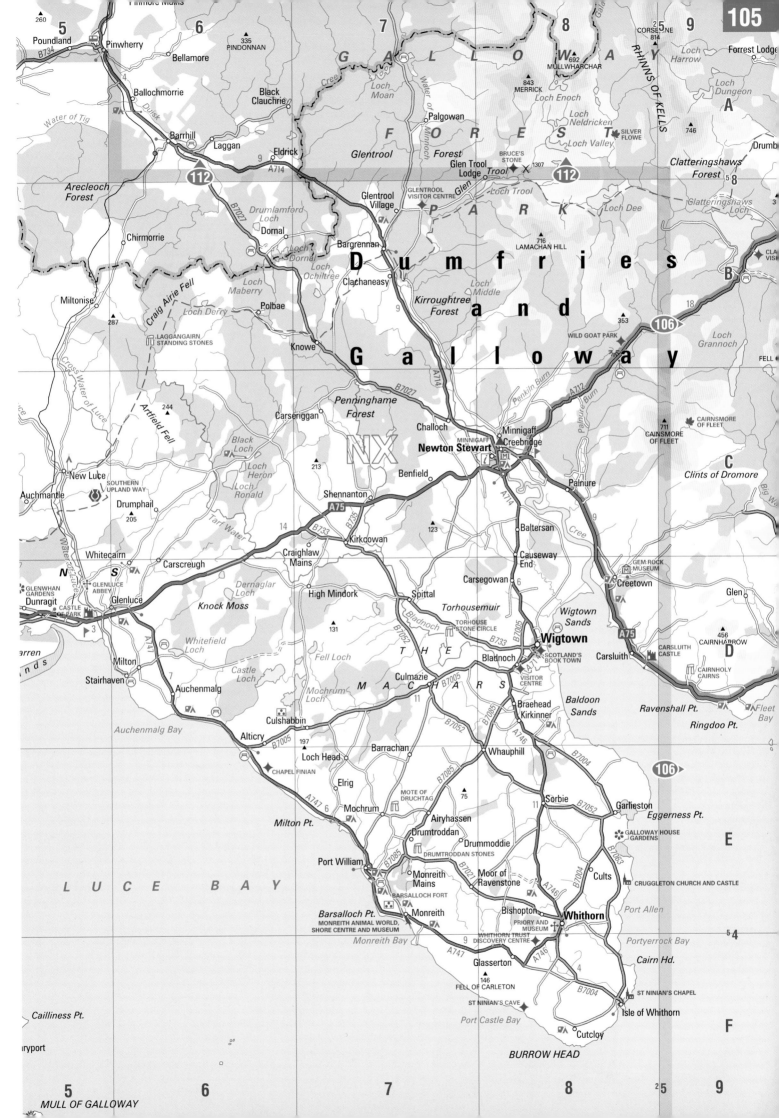

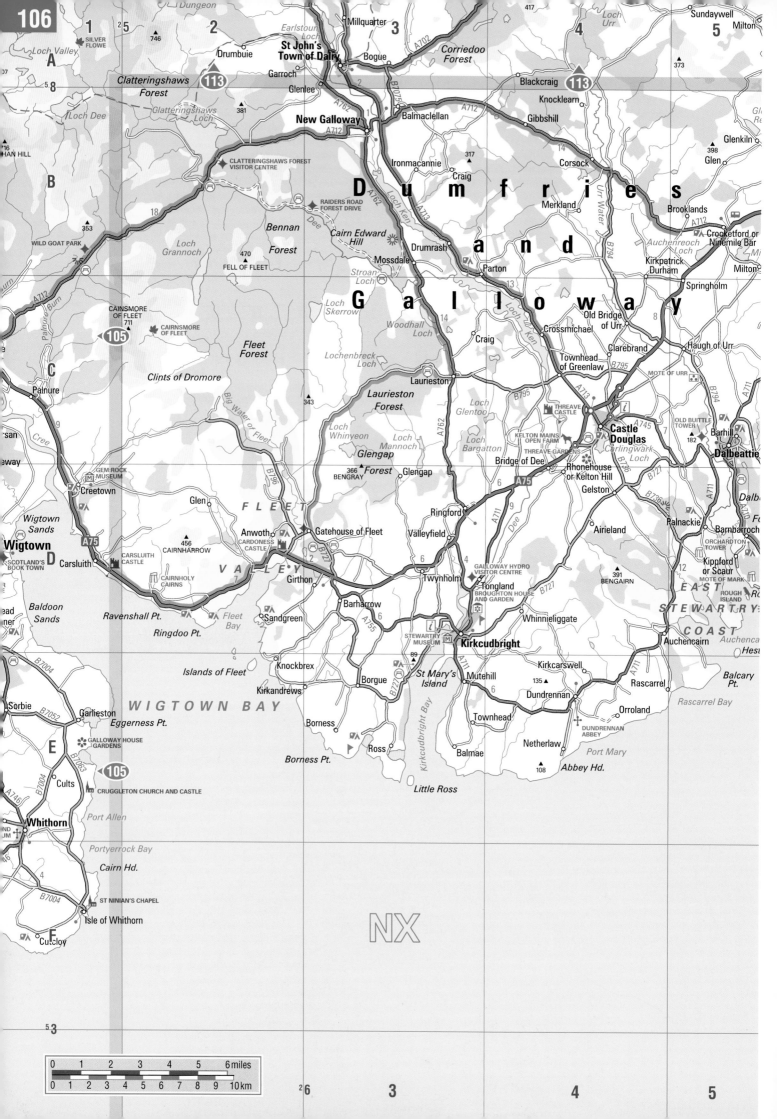

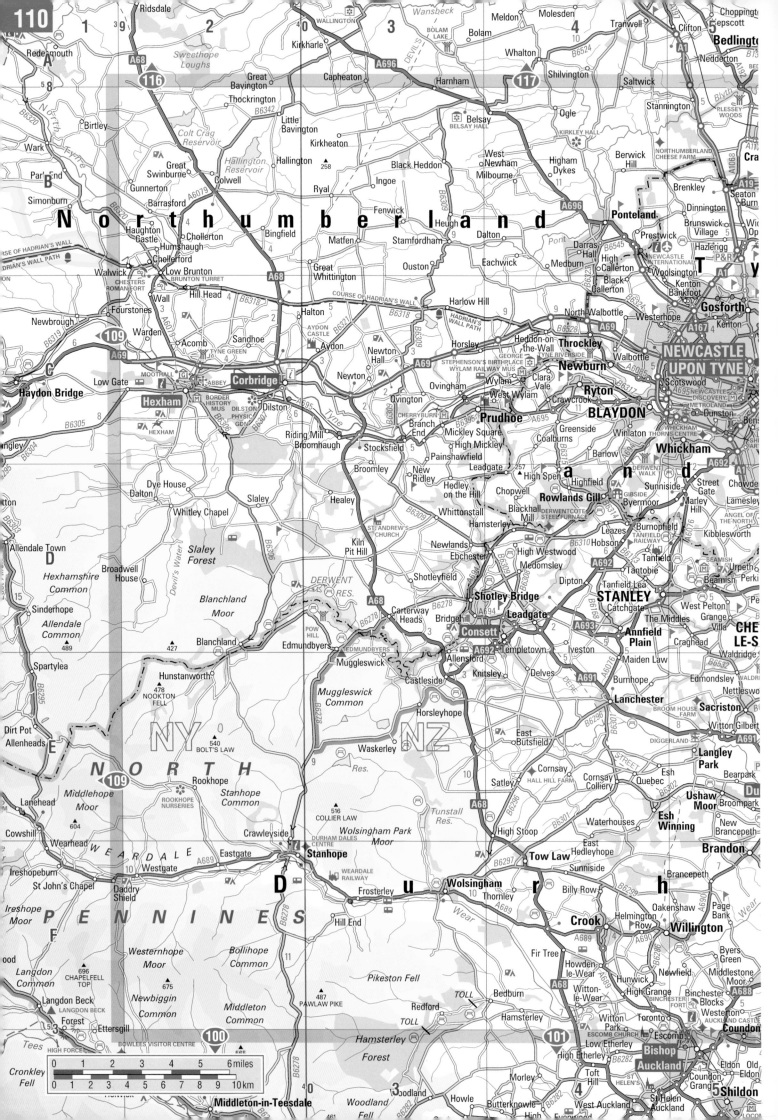

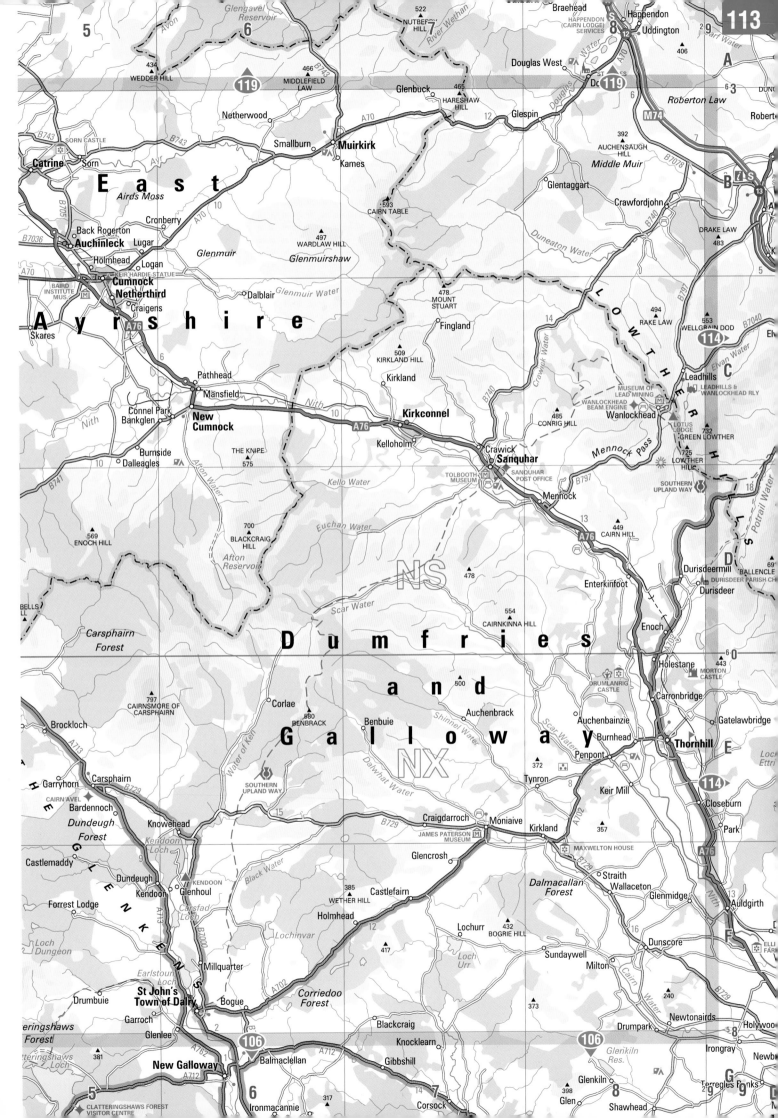

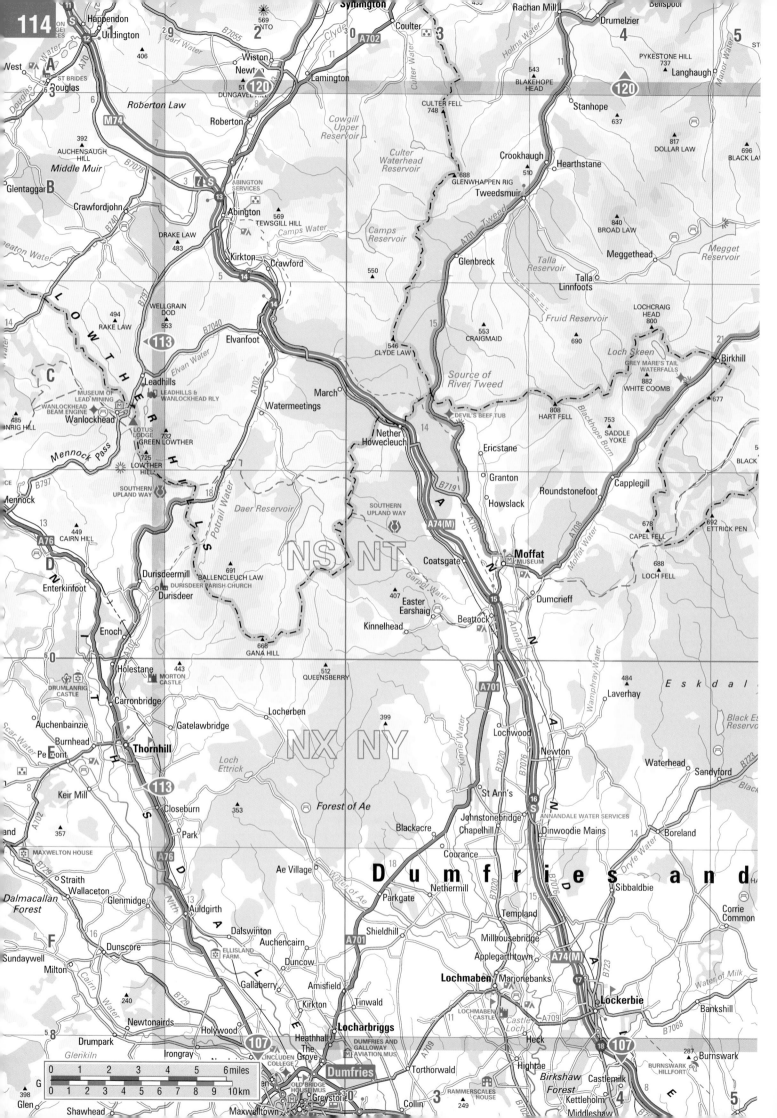

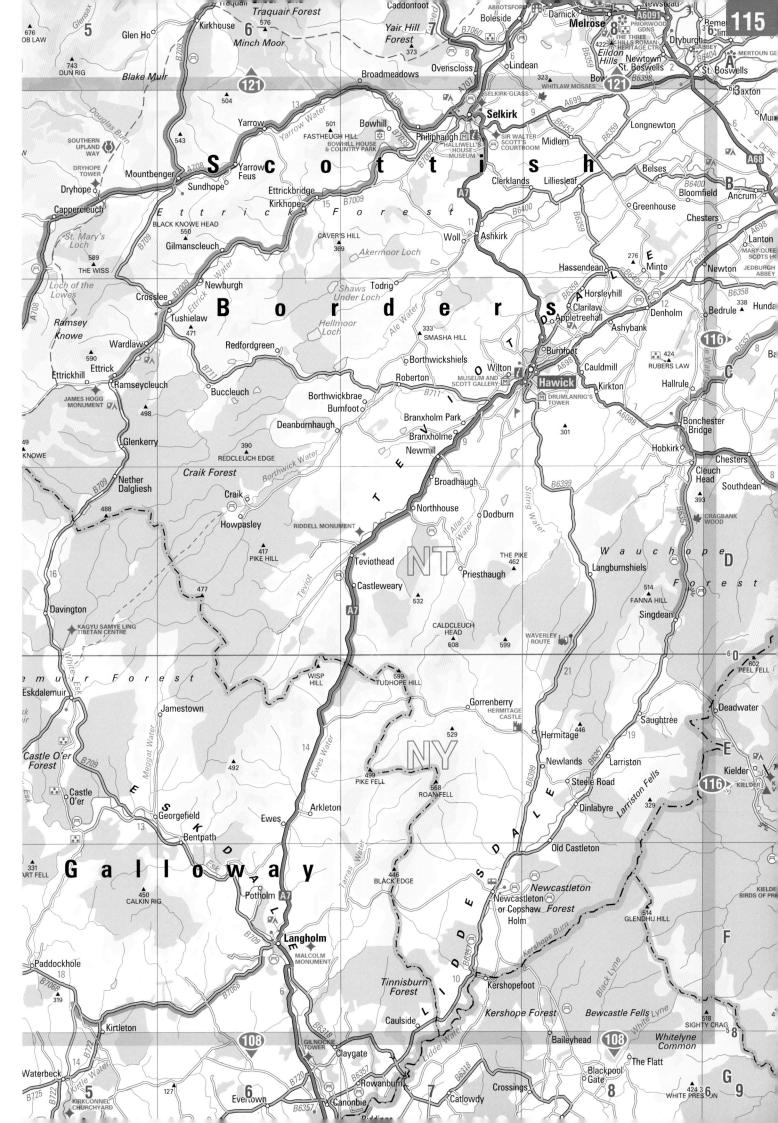

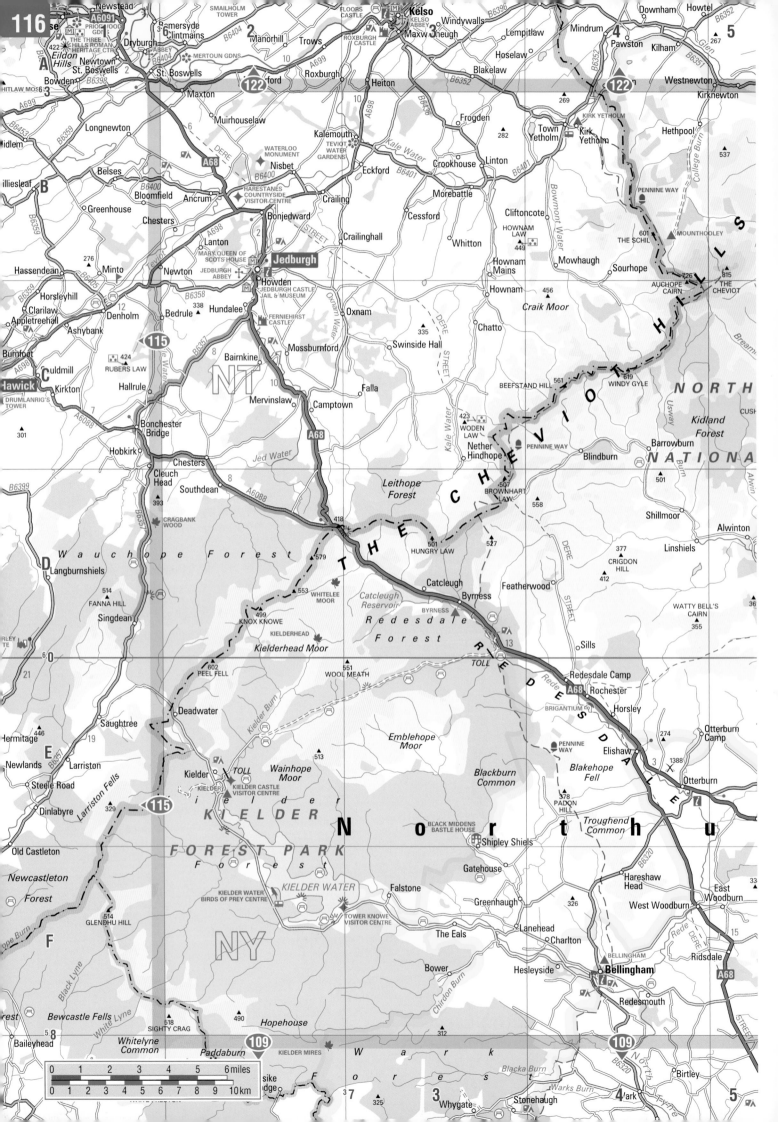

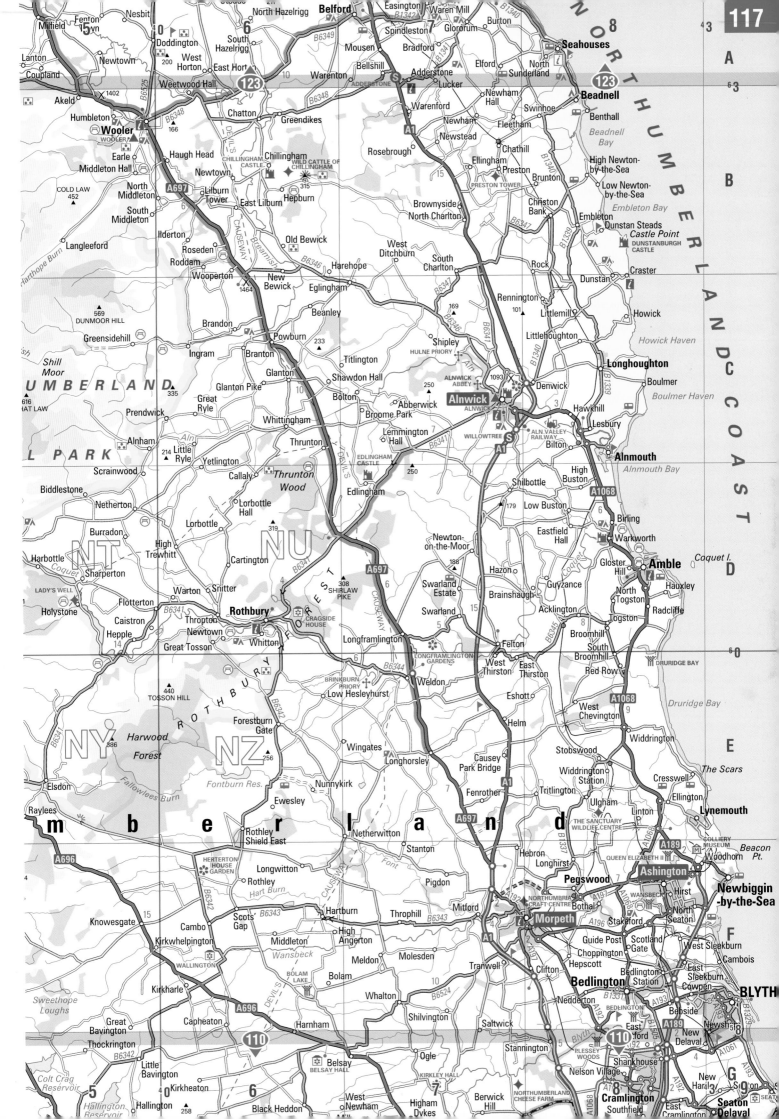

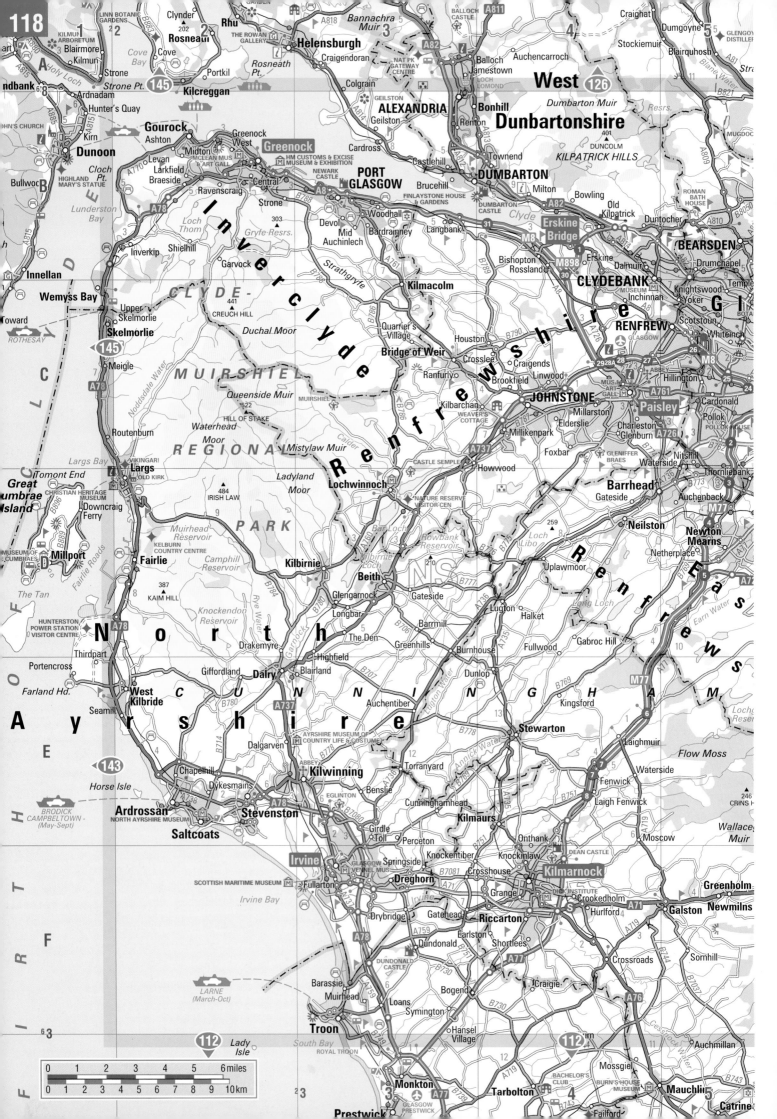

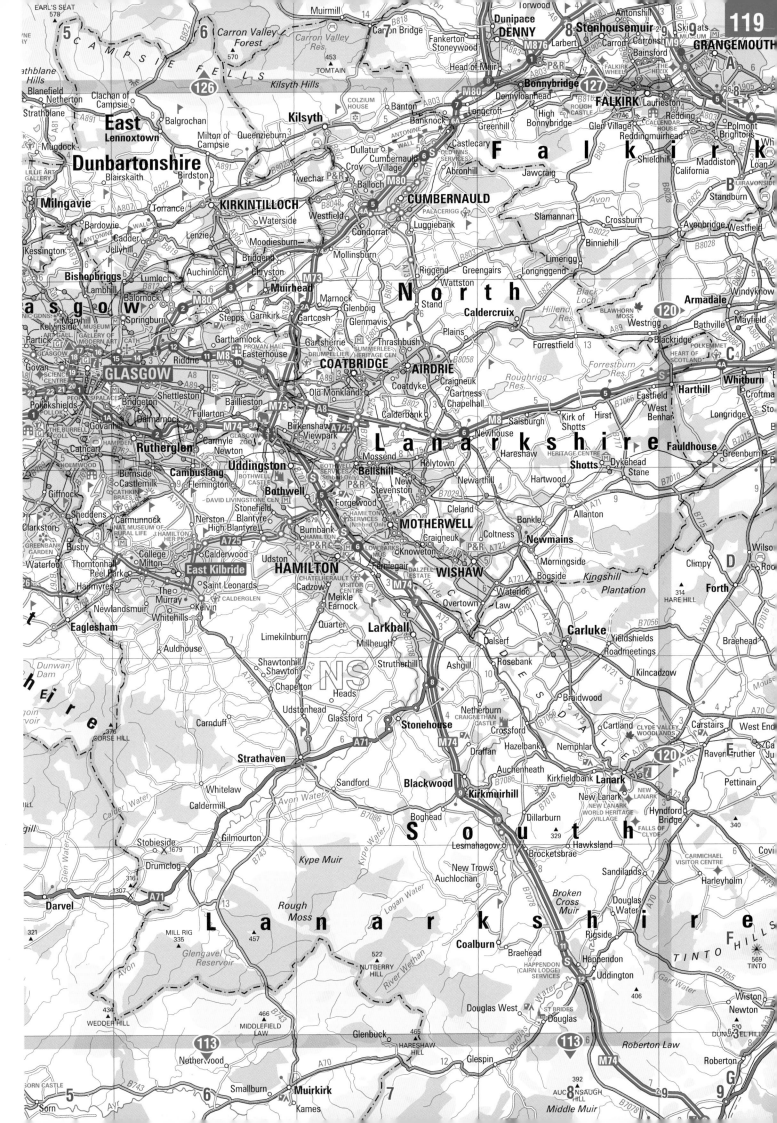

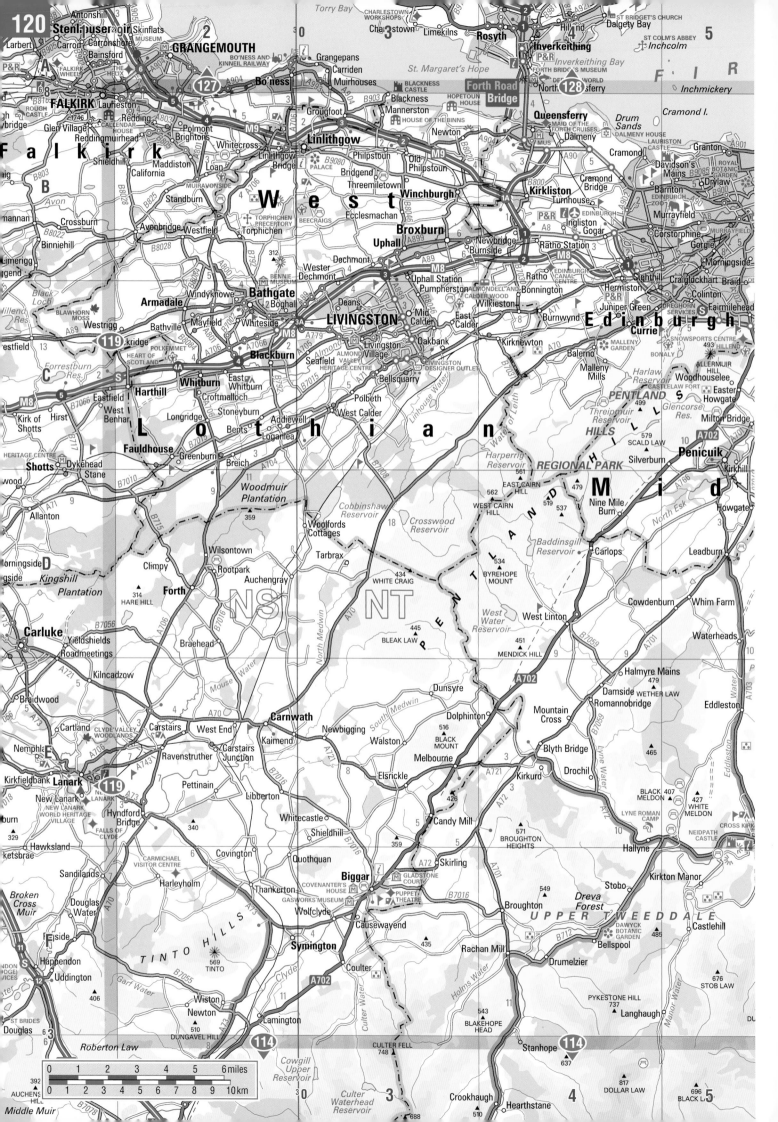

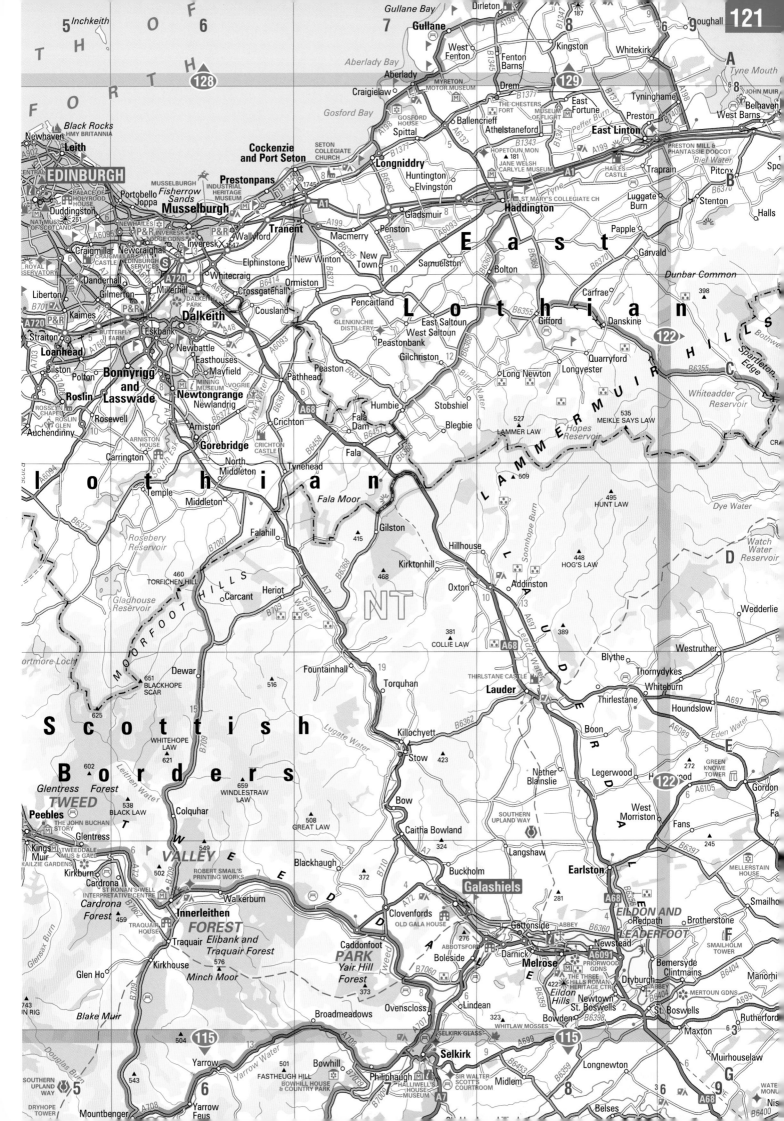

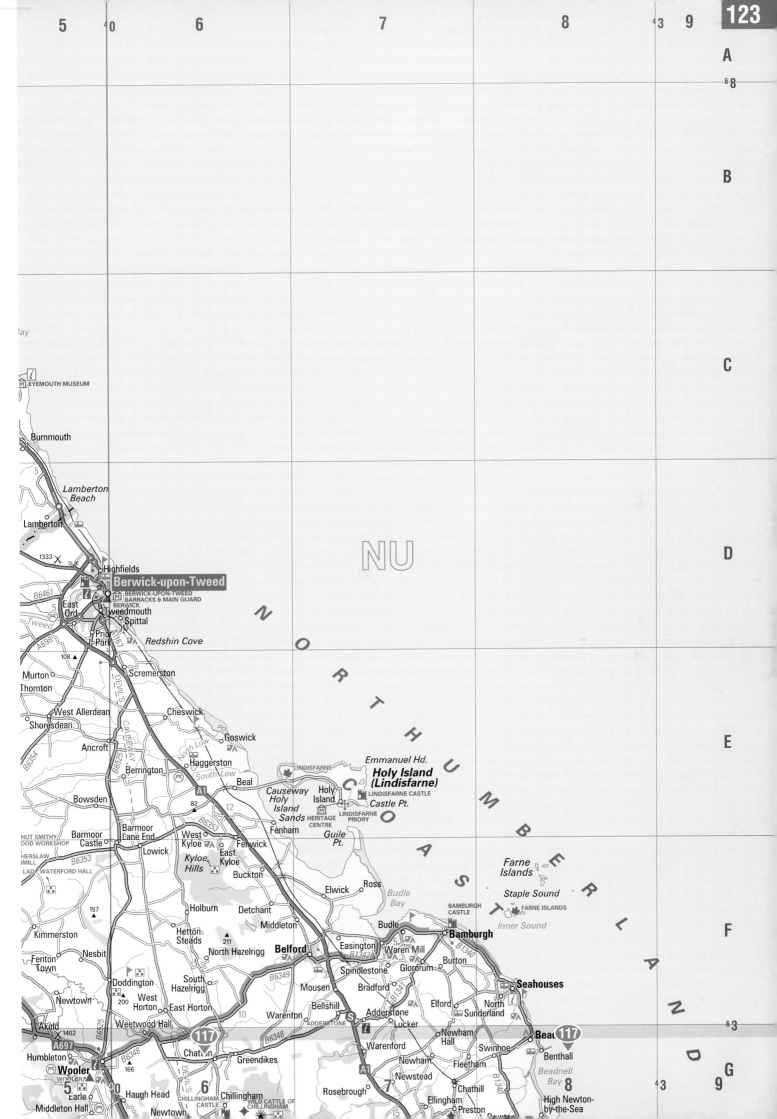

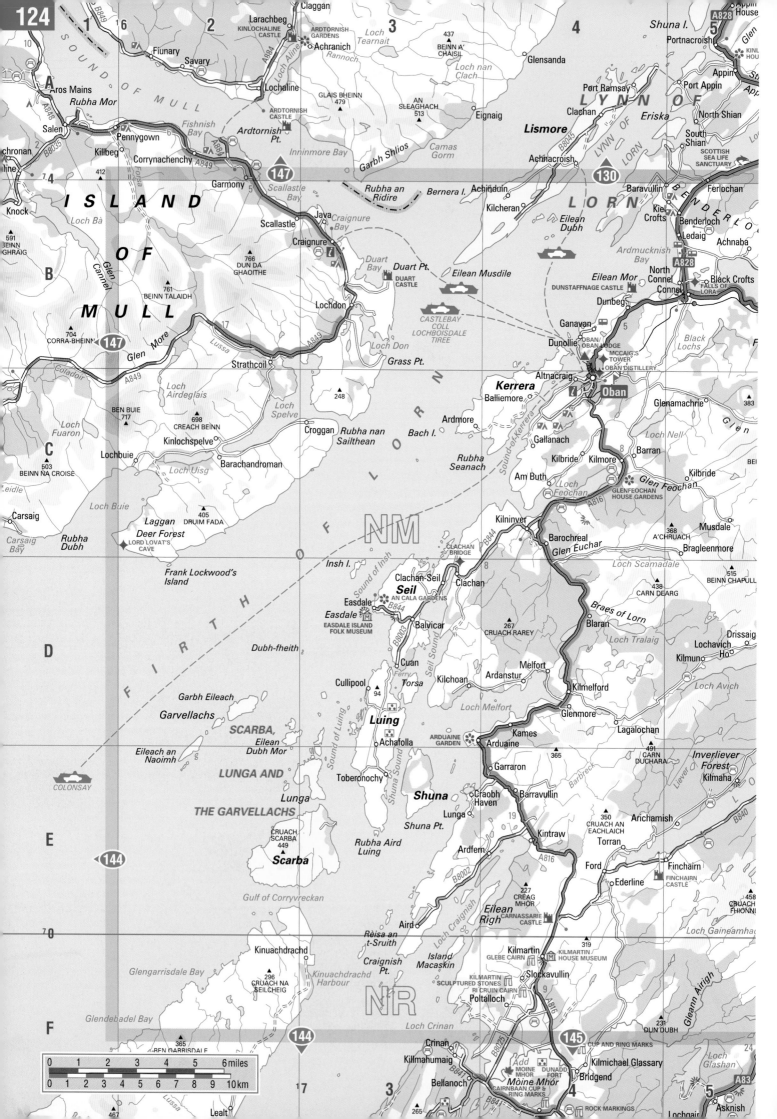

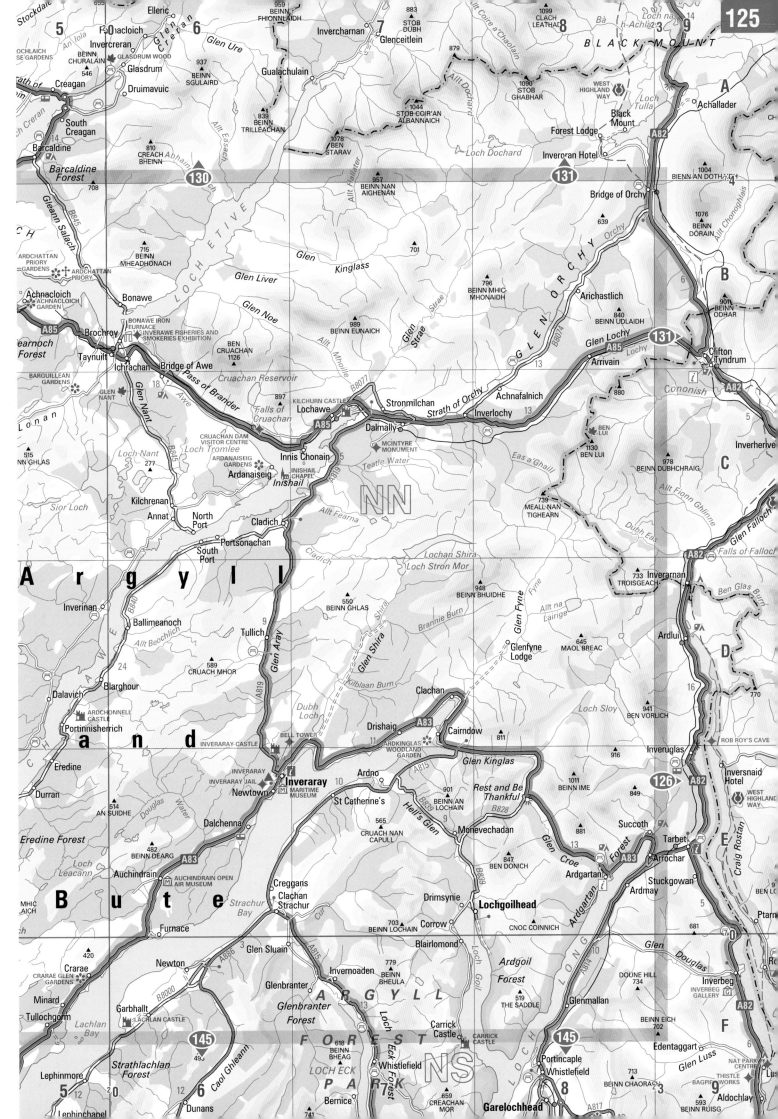

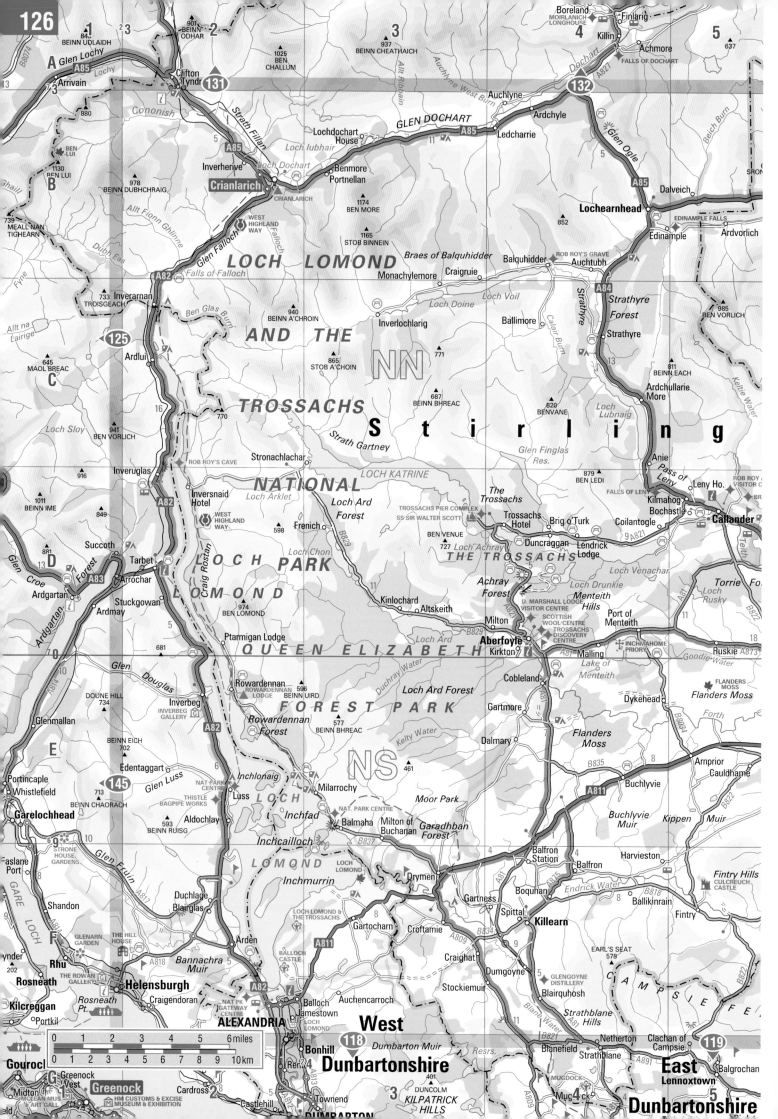

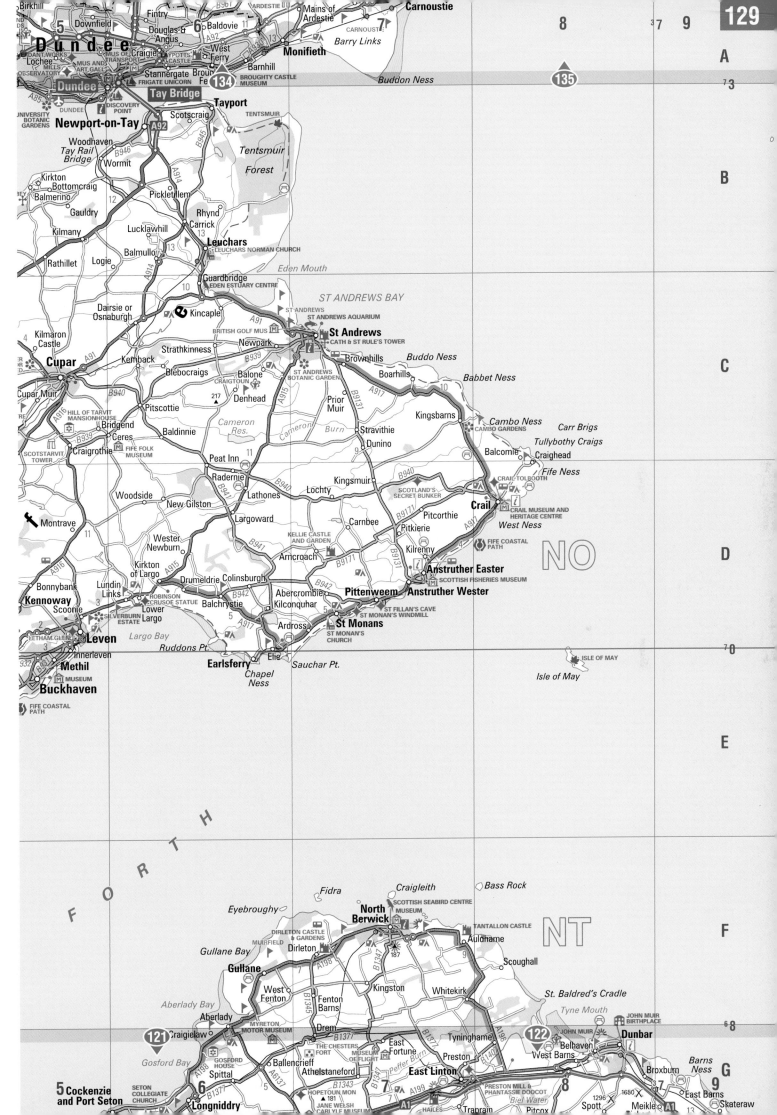

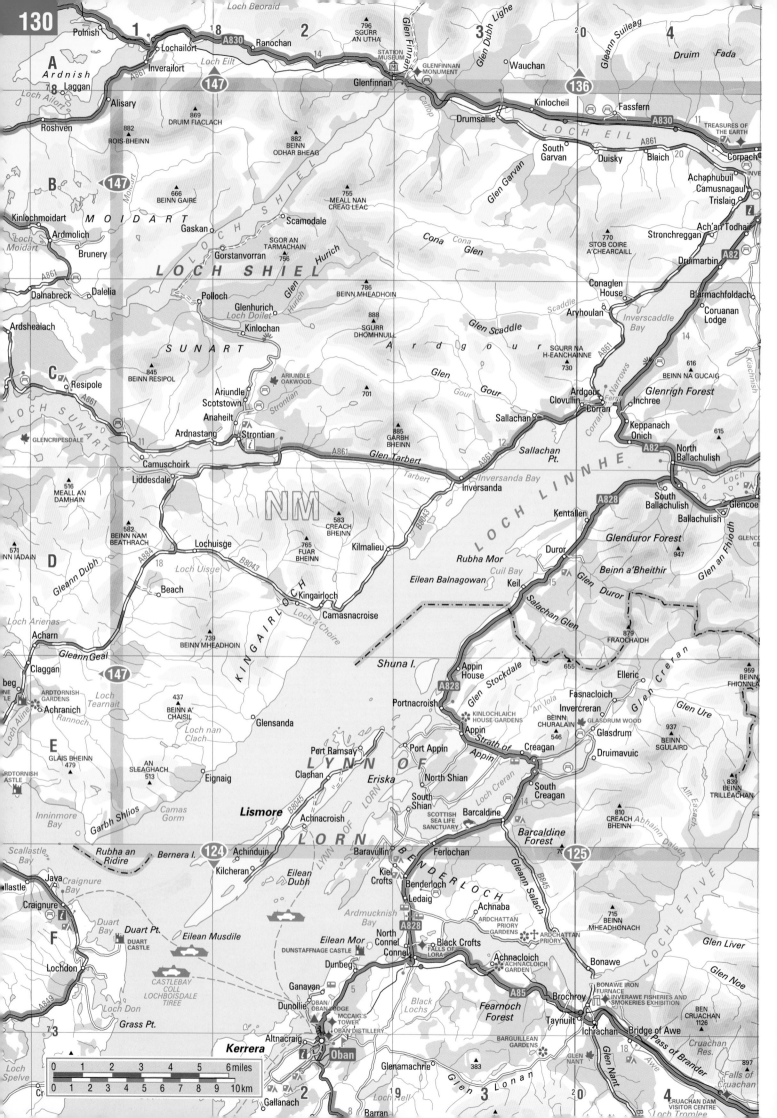

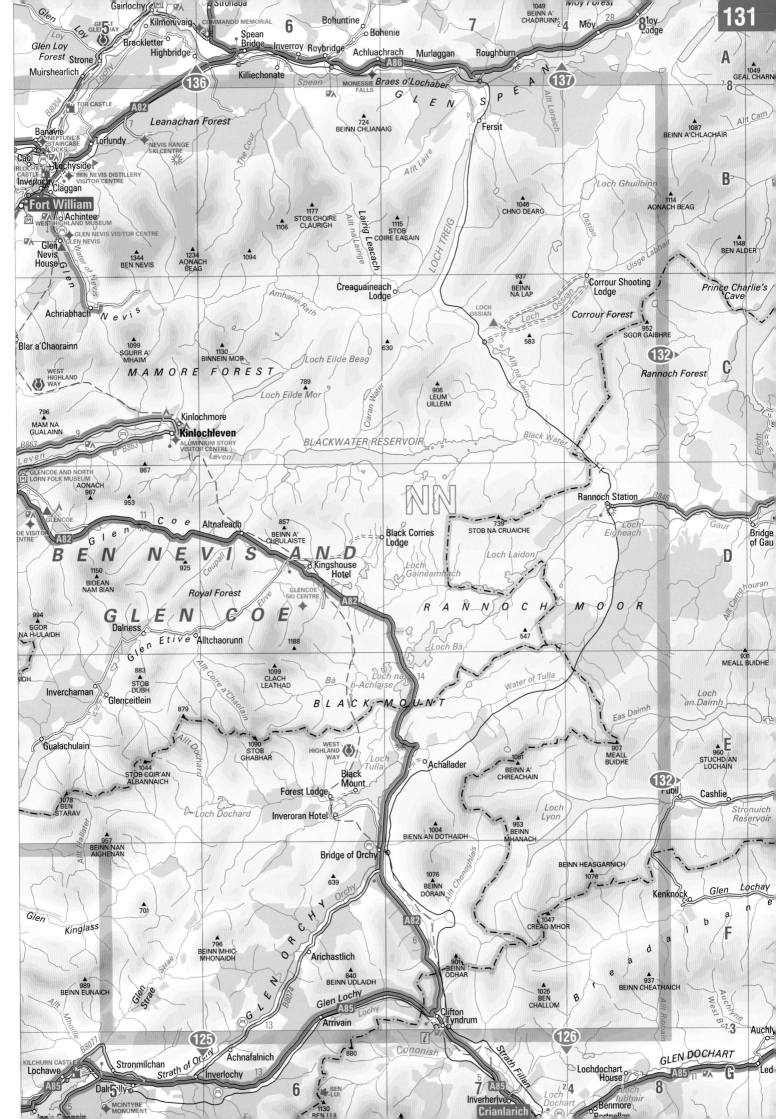

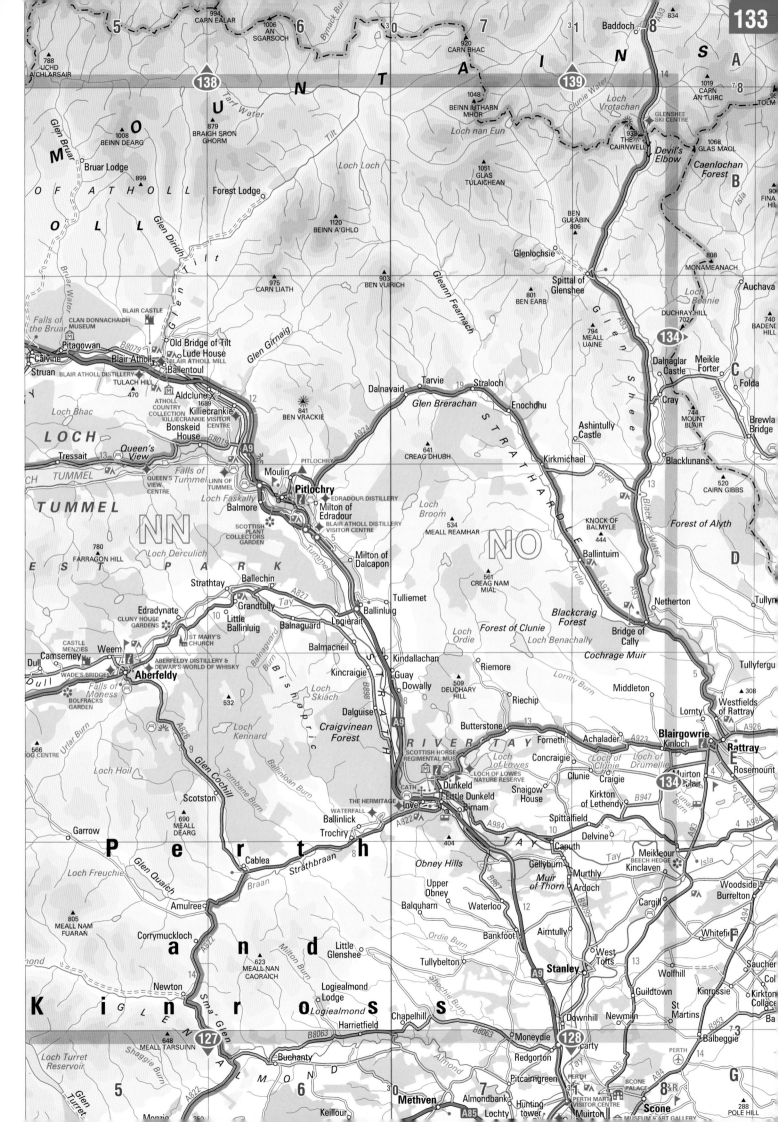

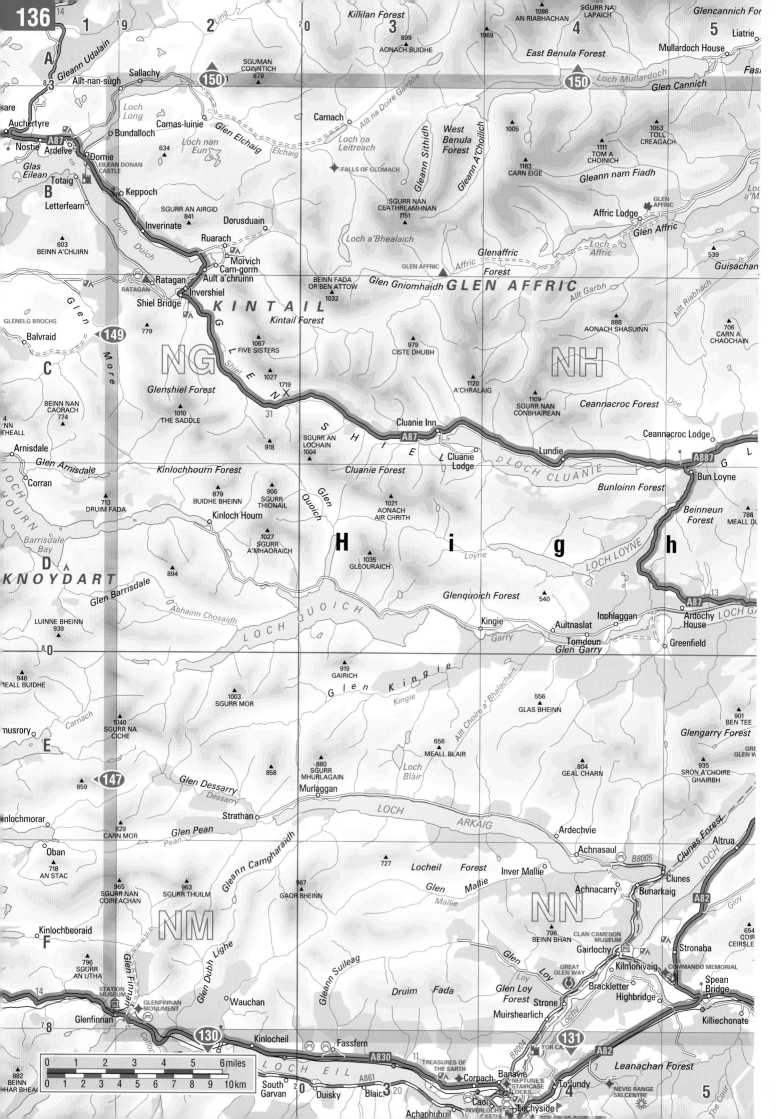

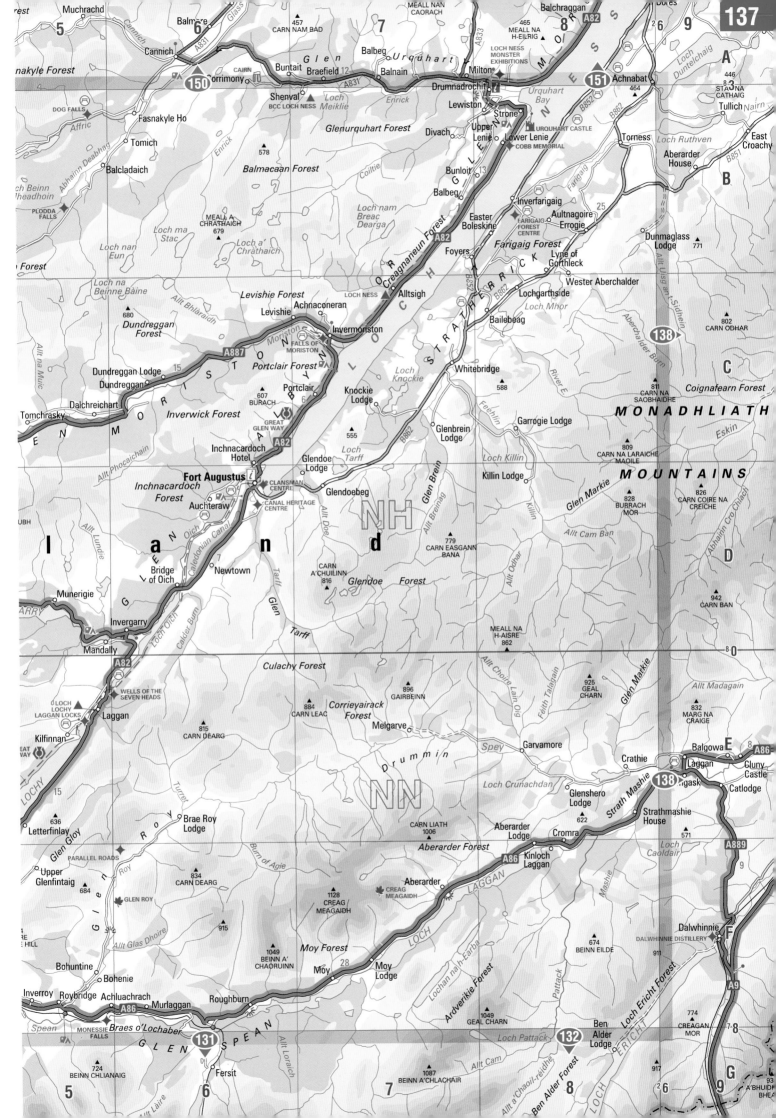

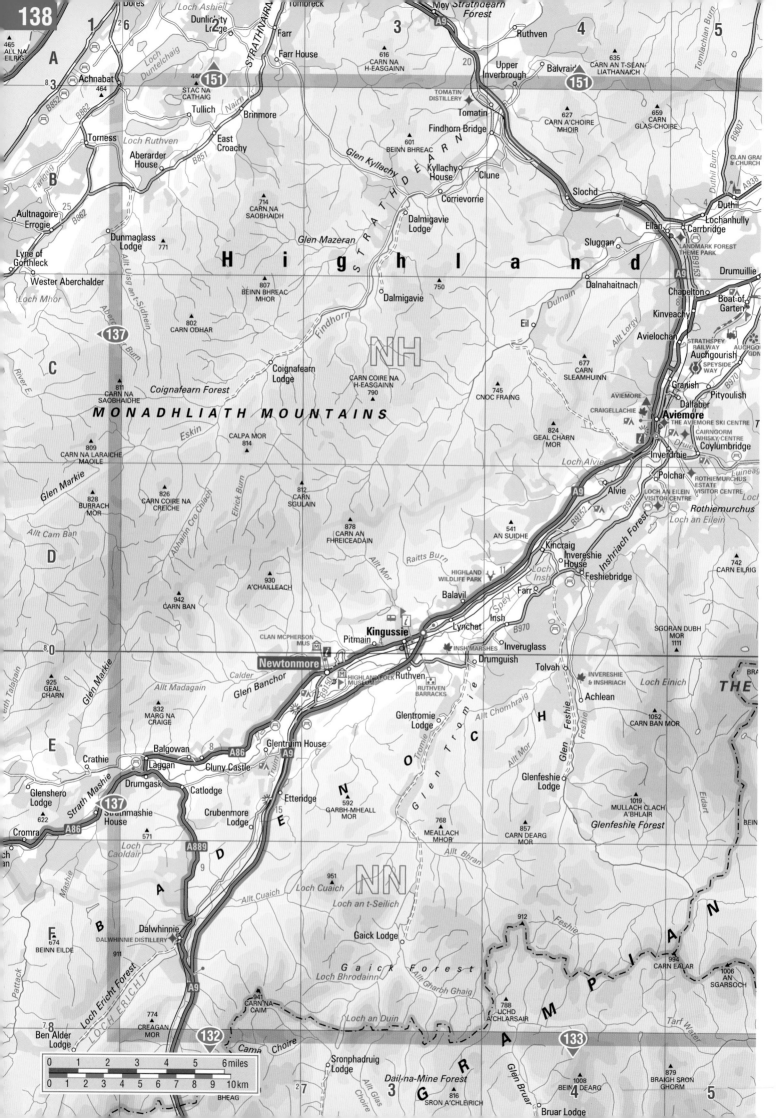

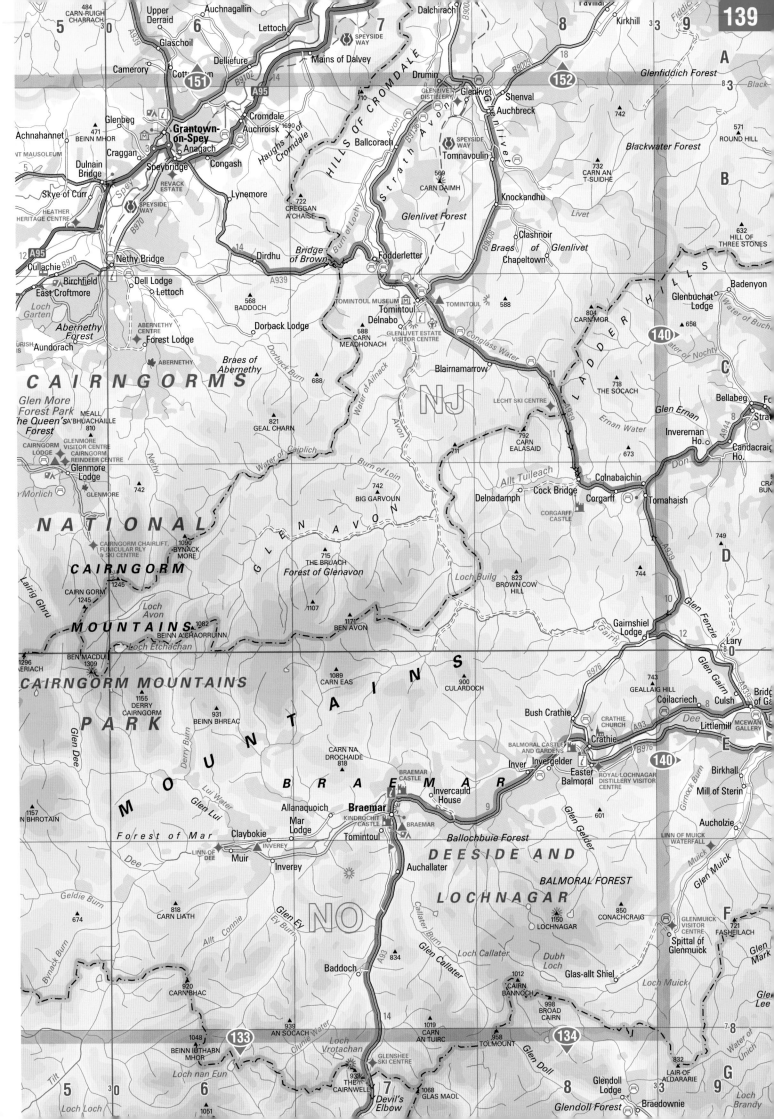

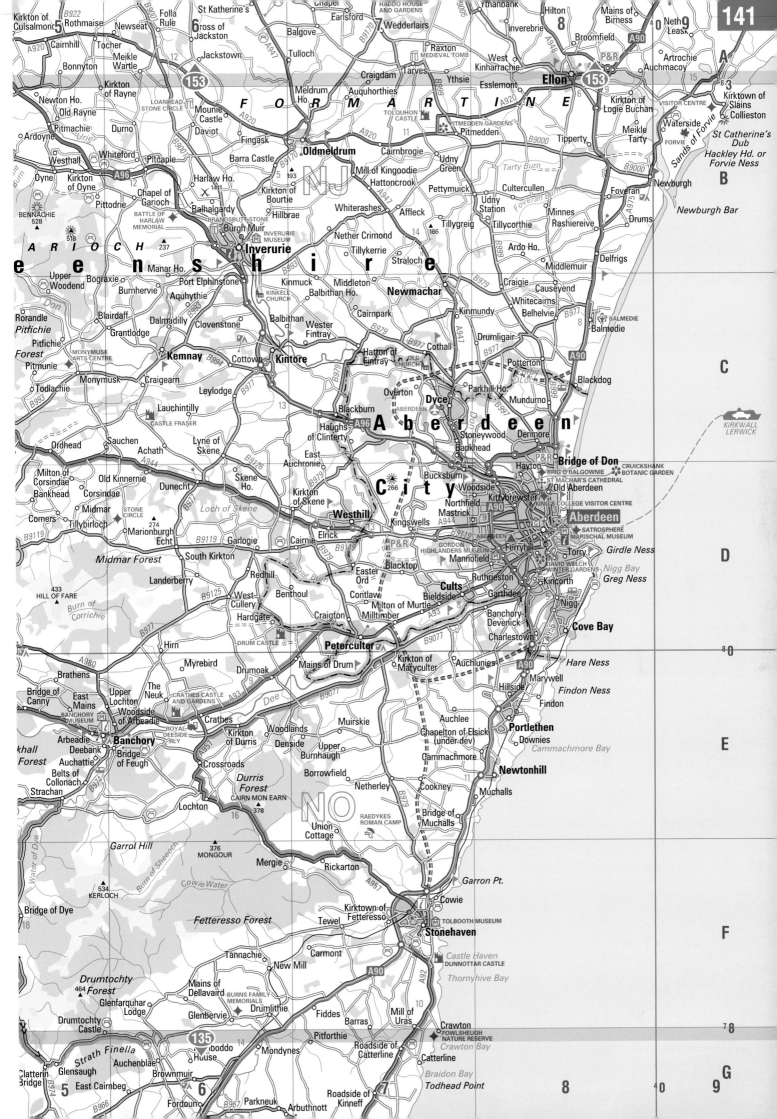

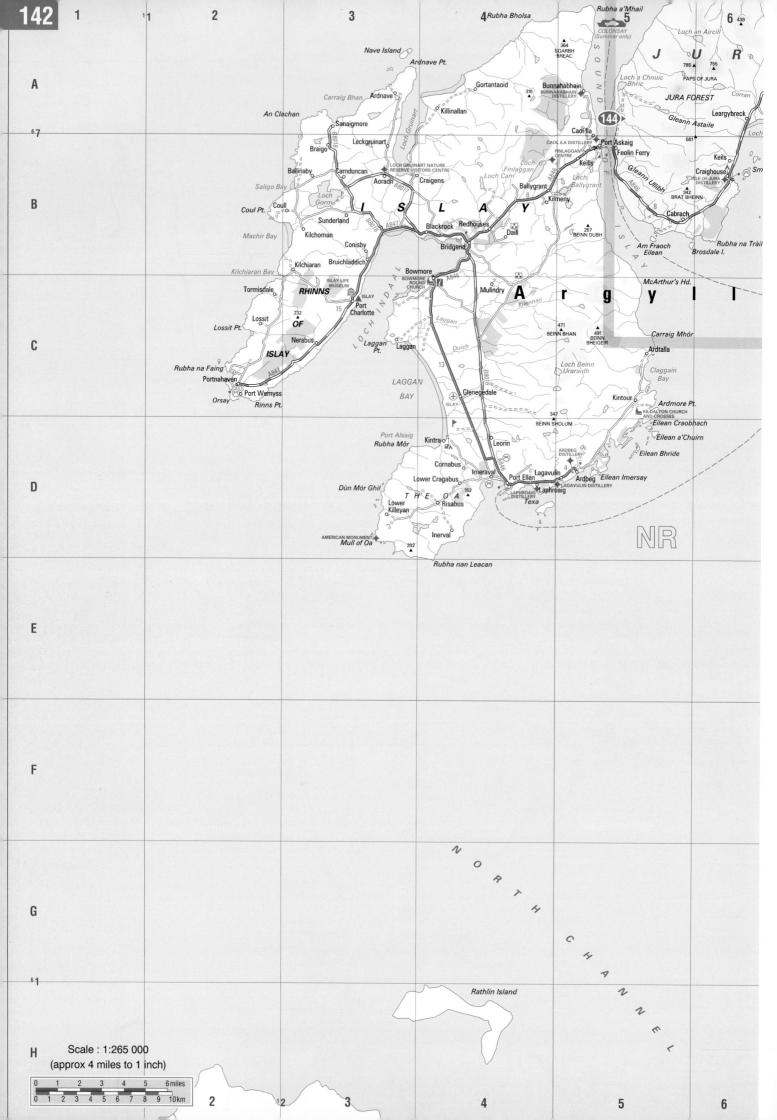

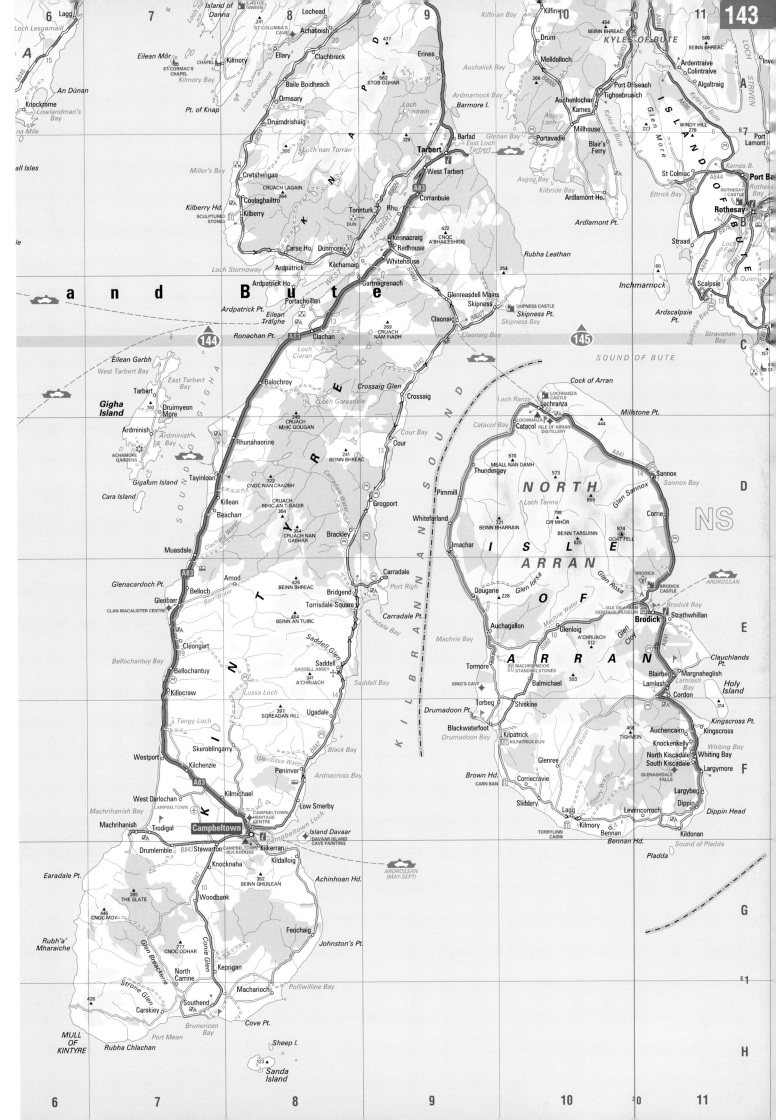

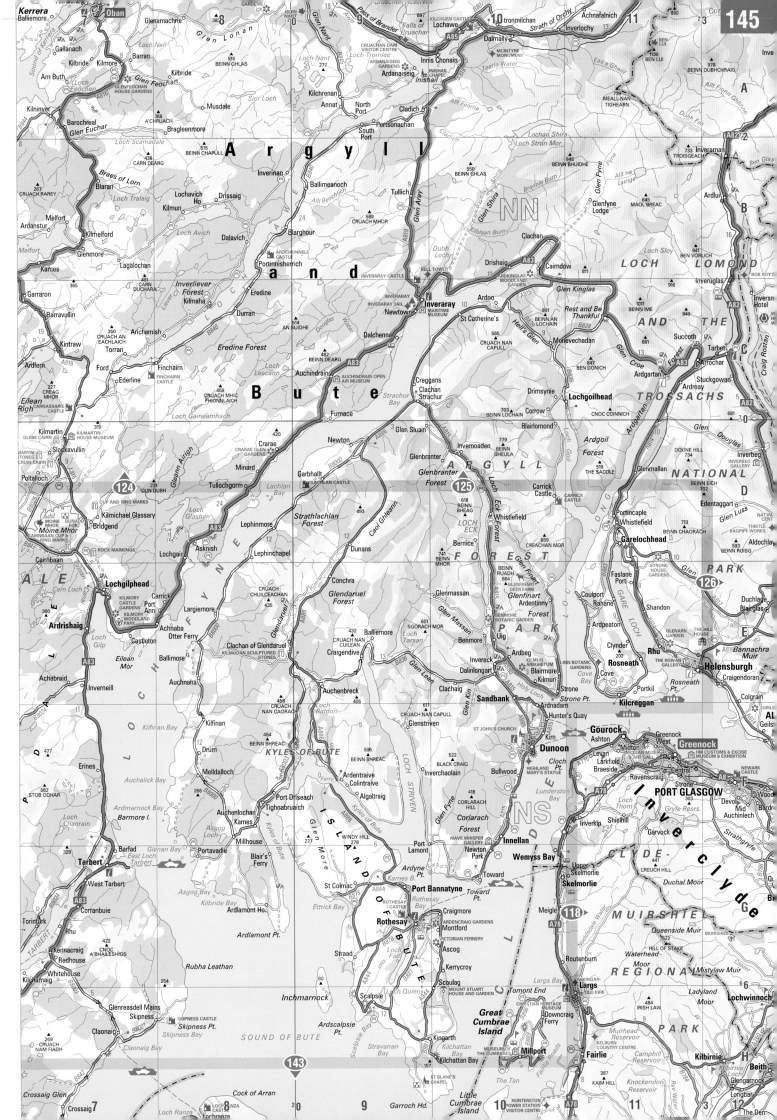

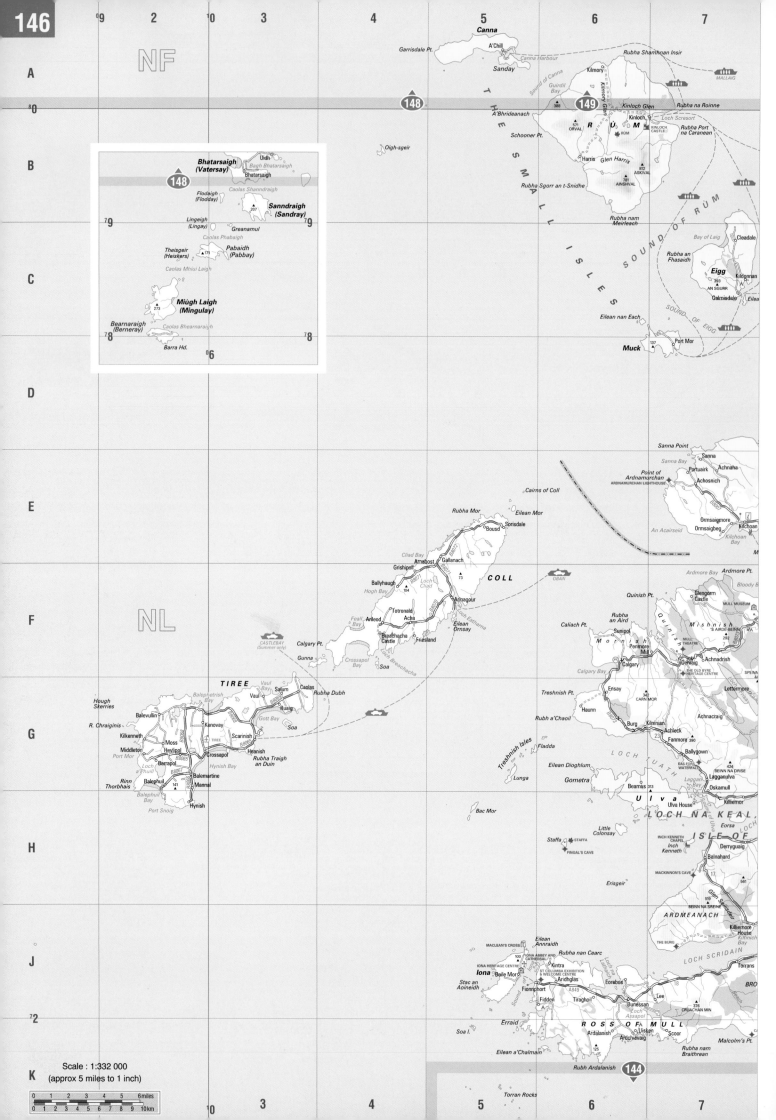

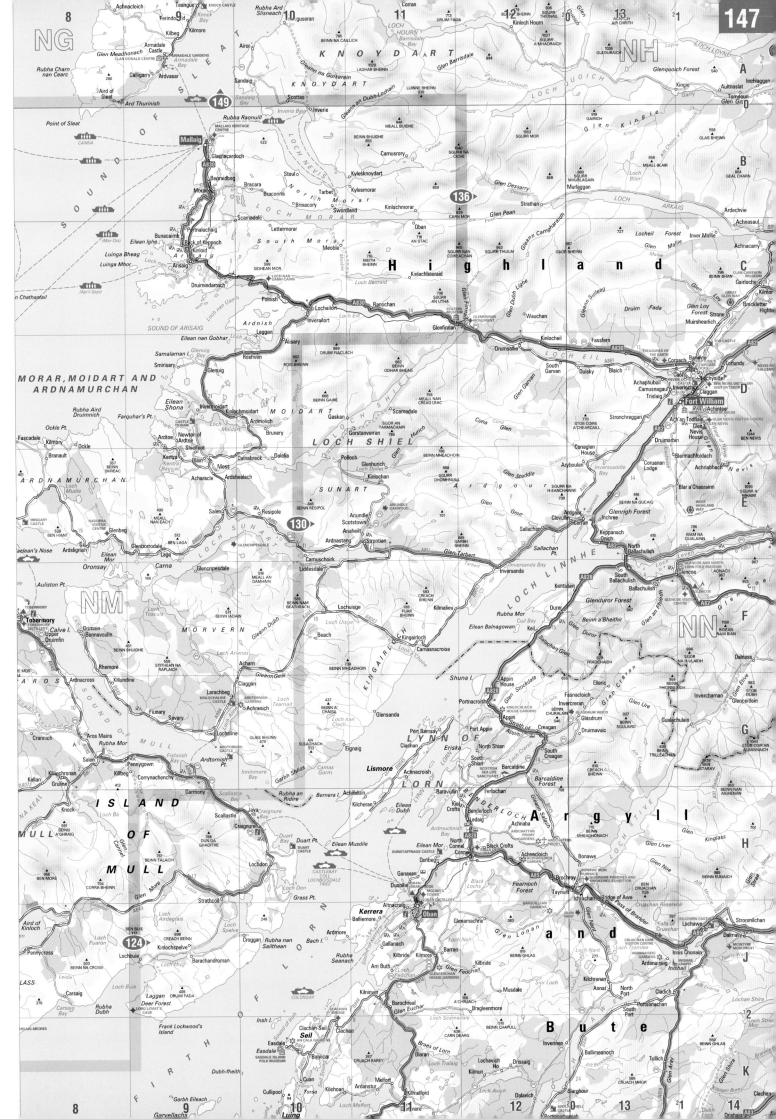

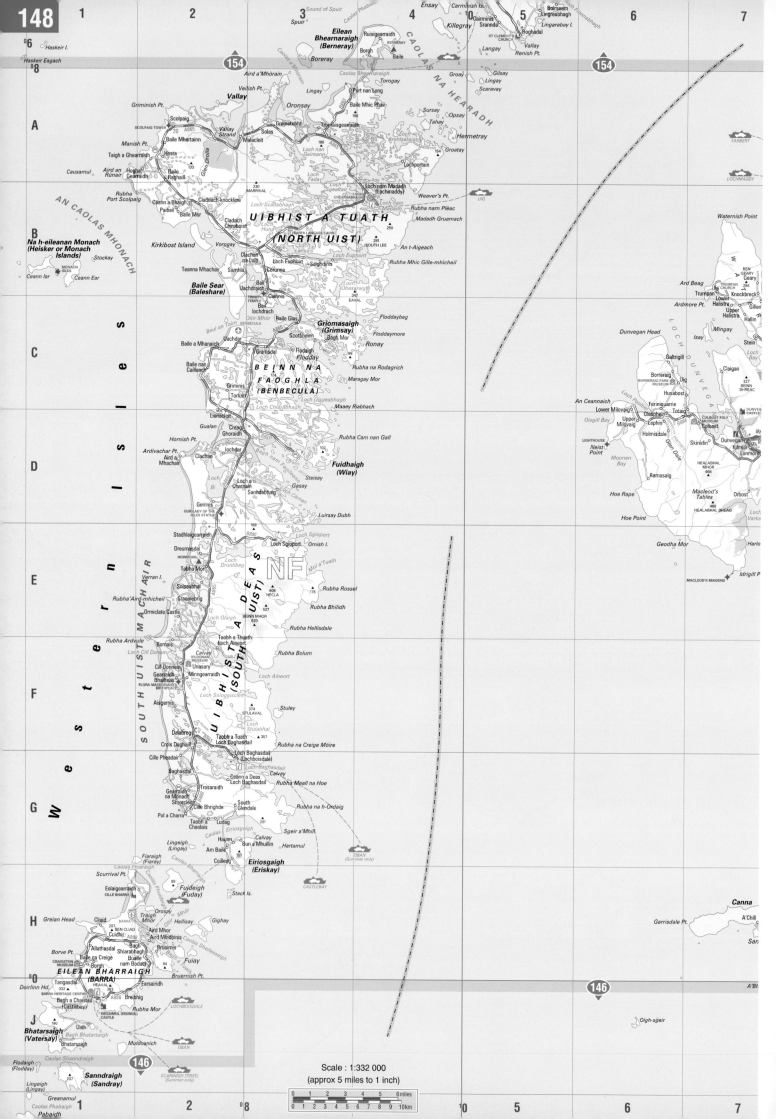

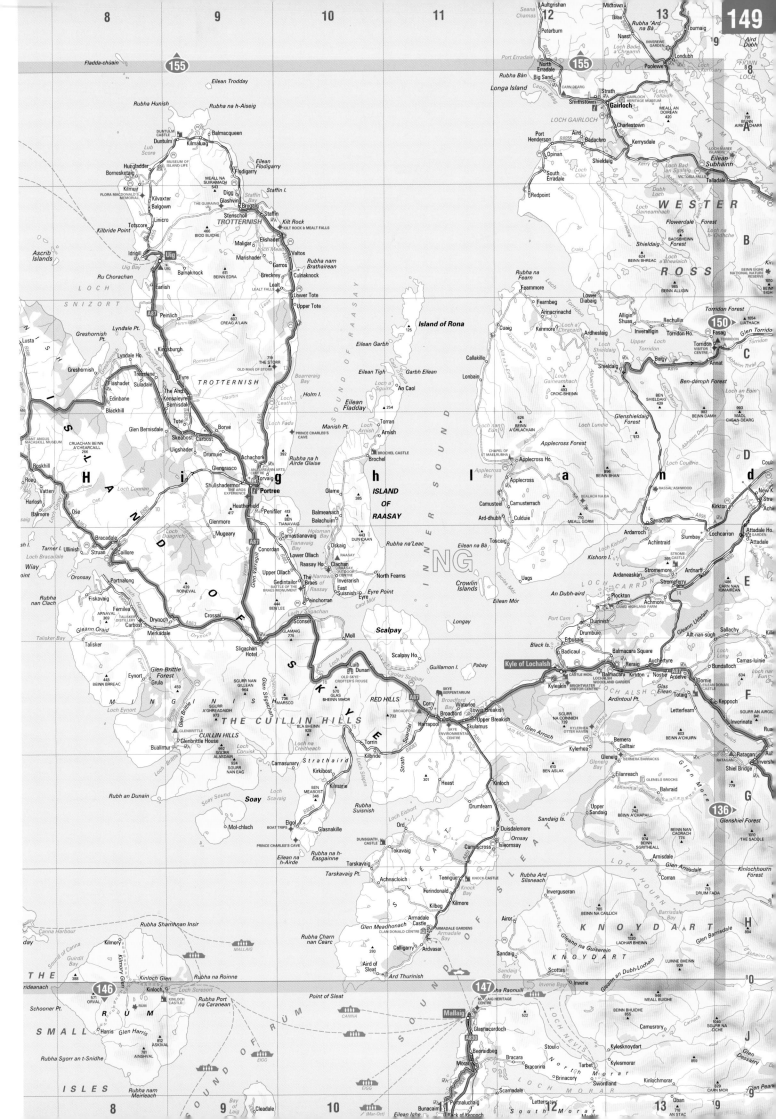

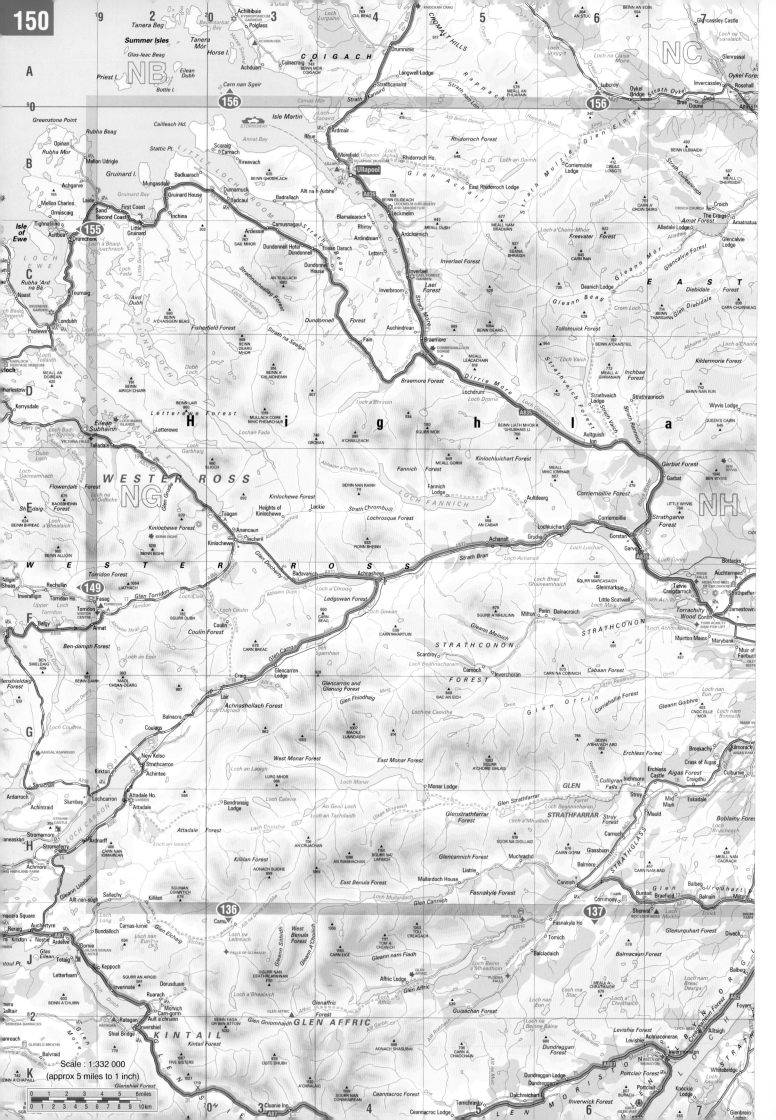

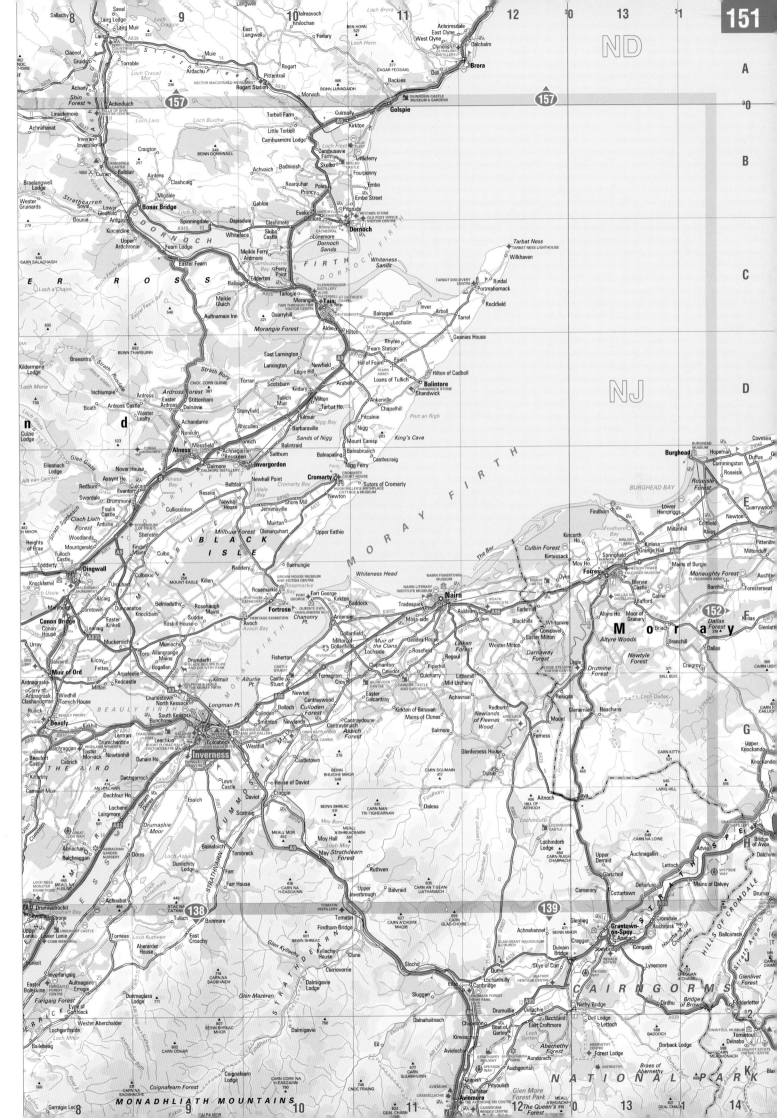

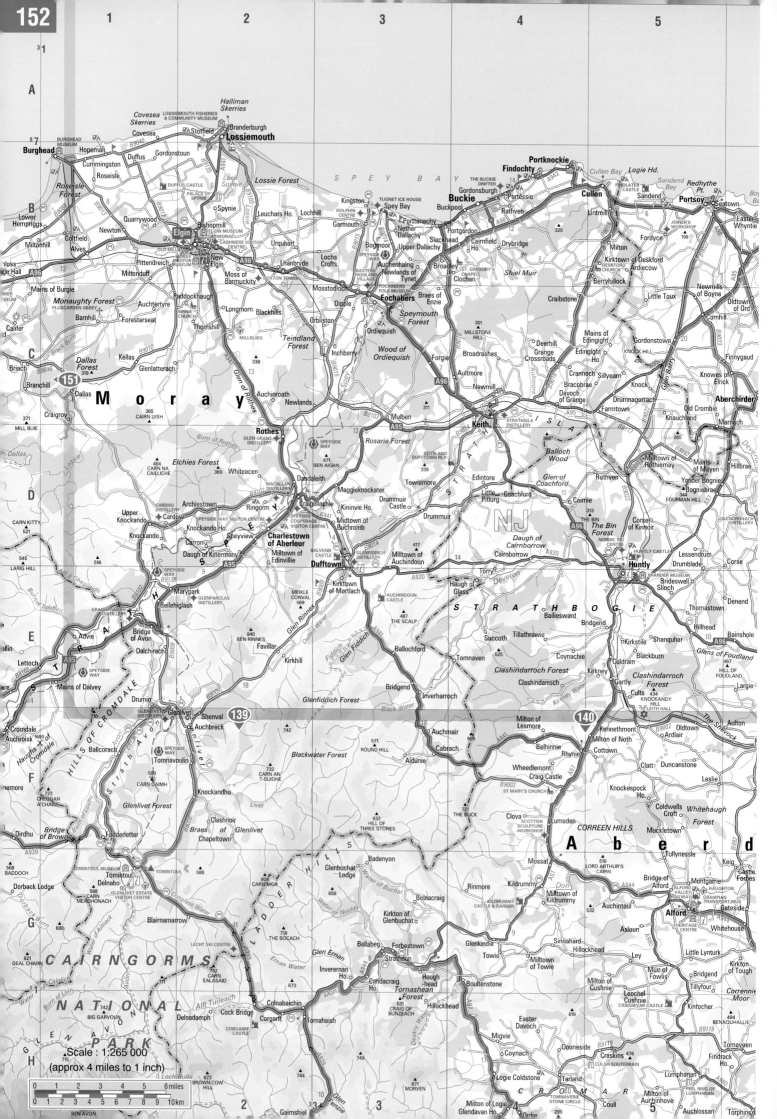

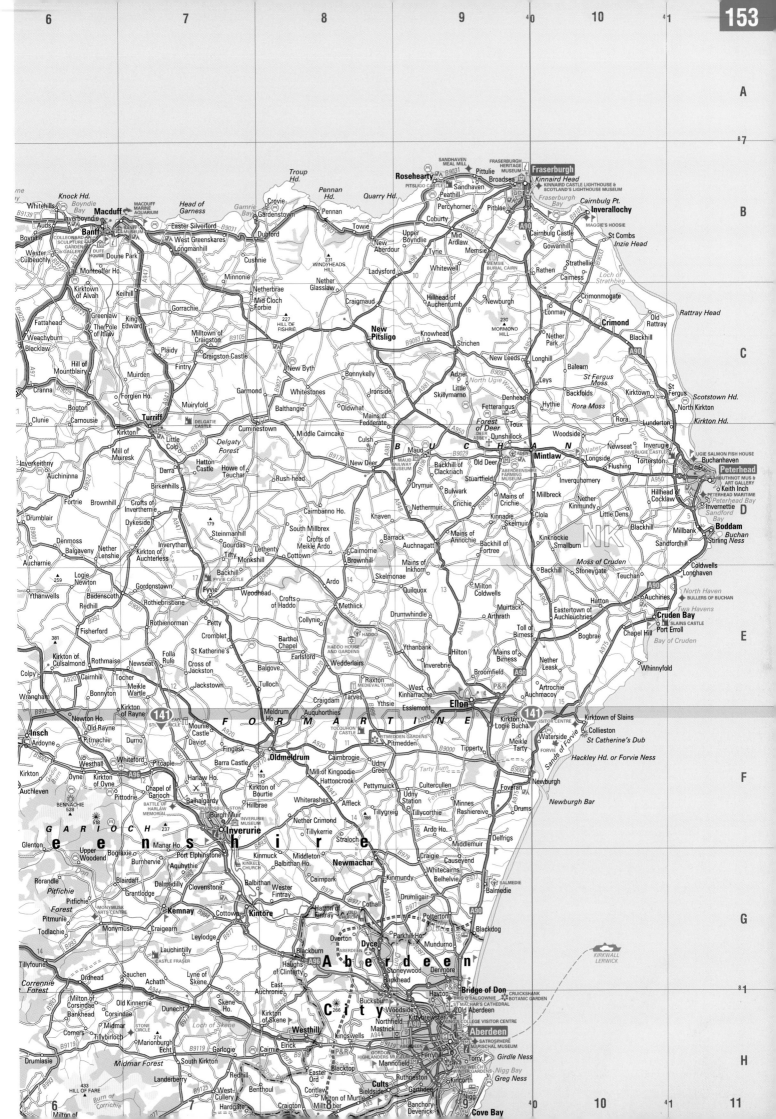

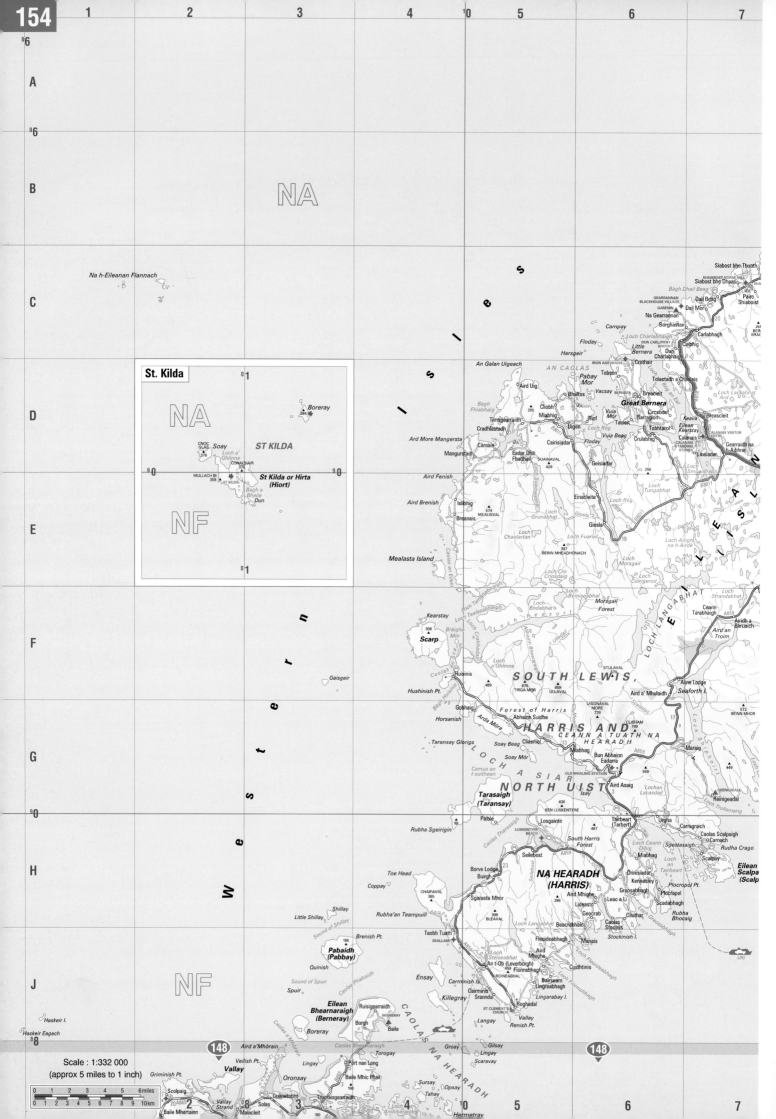

St. Kilda

NA

NF

ST KILDA

Boreray

CNOC GLAS · Soay · Loch a' Ghlinne · CONACHAIR
MULLACH BI · ST KILDA · St Kilda or Hirta (Hiort)
Bàgh a Bhaille · Dun

NA

NF

WESTERN ISLES

Na h-Eileanan Flannach

Na h-Eileanan Flannach

Gàisgeir

Scarp

Kearstay
Bràighe Mòr

SOUTH LEWIS,
Huisinis
TIRGA MOR · ULLAVAL

Hushinish Pt.
Hushinish

Gobhaig
Horsanish
Arda Mòra

Forest of Harris
Abhainn Suidhe

HARRIS AND
CEANN A TUATH NA HEARADH

Taransay Glorigs
Soay Beag
Soay Mòr

Cliasmol
Miabhag · Bun Abhainn Eadarra

Tarasaigh (Taransay)

NORTH UIST
Isay
Aird Asaig

Camus an t-suthean

OLD WHALING STATION

BEN LUSKENTYRE

Paible
Rubha Sgeirigin

Losgaintir

LUSKENTYRE BEACH

South Harris Forest

Tàirbeart (Tarbert)
Urgha
Carragraich

Caolas Scalpaigh

Seilebost

NA HEARADH (HARRIS)

Miabhag

Rubha Crago
Scalpay

Eilean Scalpa (Scalp

Toe Head
Coppay

Borve Lodge
Buirgh

CHAIPAVAL

Sgarasta Mhor

Aird Mhighe

Greosabhagh
Plocropol Pt.

Kennacley
Liceasto
Leac a Li
Geocrab
BLEAVAL

Caolas Stocinis
Ciuthat

Rubha Bhocaig
Scadabhagh

Little Shillay
Shillay
Sound of Shillay

Rubha'an Teampuill

Brenish Pt.
Taobh Tuath

SEALLAM!

Manais
Fleoideabhagh
Aird Mhighe

Stockinish I.

UIG

Pabaidh (Pabbay)
Quinish

An-t-Ob (Leverburgh)
Fionnsbhagh
ROINEABHAL

Boirseam
Lingreabhagh
Lingarabay I.

Sound of Spuir
Spuir

Ensay
Carminish

Cuidhtinis

Eilean Bhearnaraigh (Berneray)
Boreray

Ruisigearraidh
Borgh
Baile

Killegray
Cairinis
Srannda

ST CLEMENT'S CHURCH

Roghadal

Valley
Renish Pt.

Haskeir I.

Haskeir Eagach

Aird a'Mhòrain

Veilish Pt.
Griminish Pt.

Torogay
Port nan Long

Gilsay
Groay
Scaravay

Scale : 1:332 000
(approx 5 miles to 1 inch)

0 1 2 3 4 5 6miles
0 1 2 3 4 5 6 7 8 9 10km

Valley
Scolpaig

Baile Mhartainn
Valley Strand
Solas · Malaclete
Griminish

Oronsay
Baile Mhic Phail
Sursay
Opsay
Tahay

Lingay

Hermetray

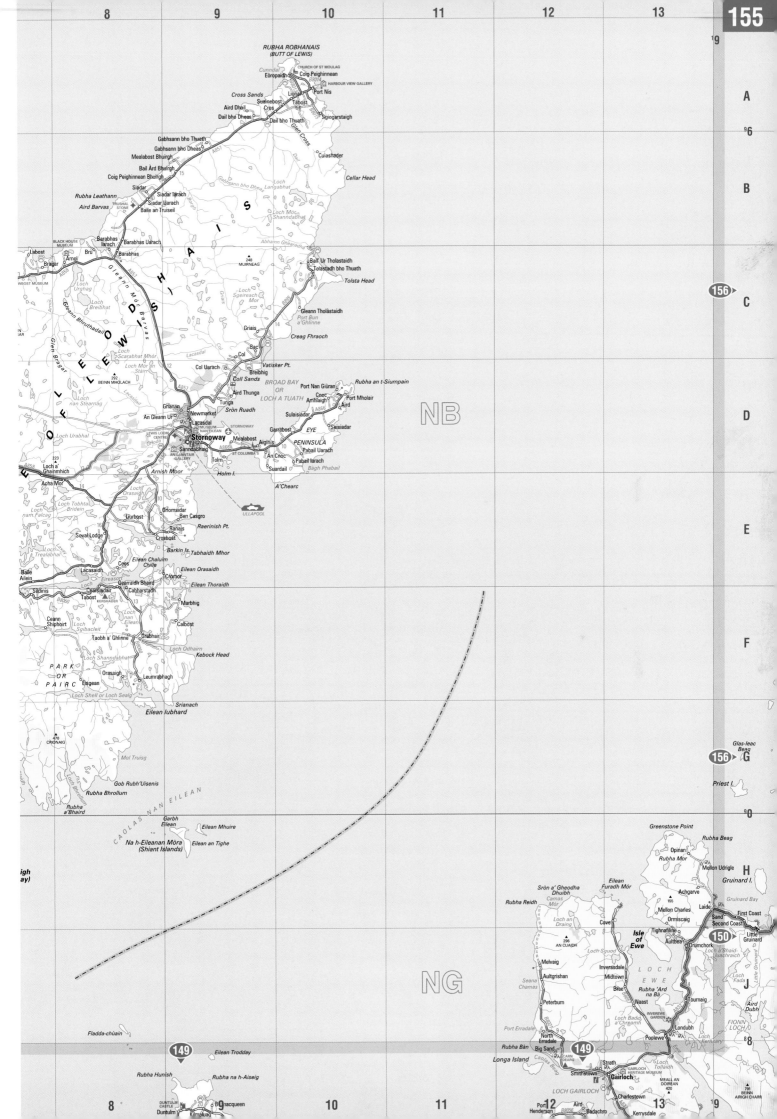

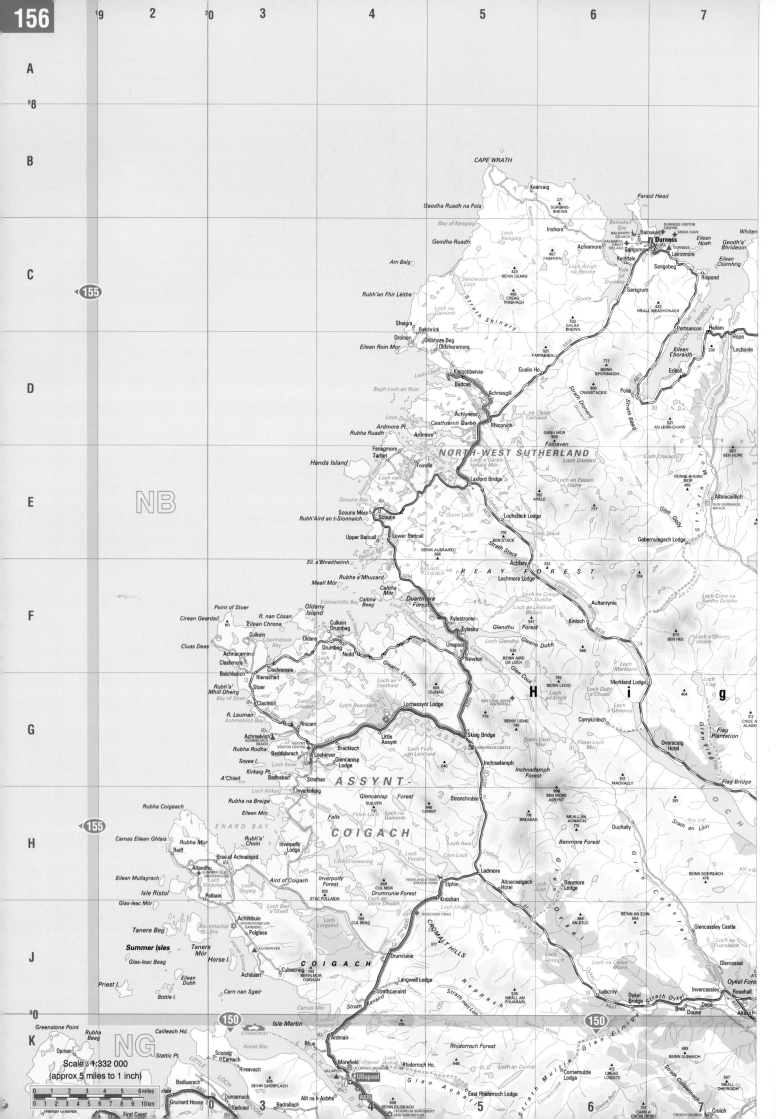

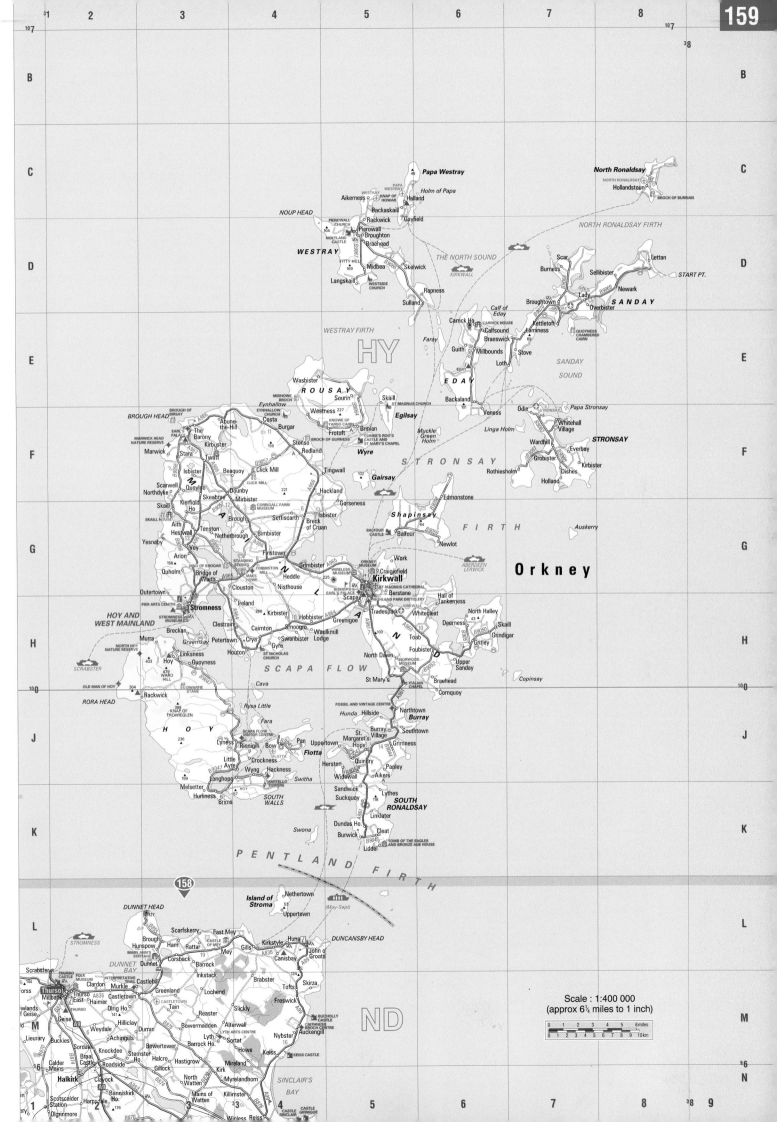

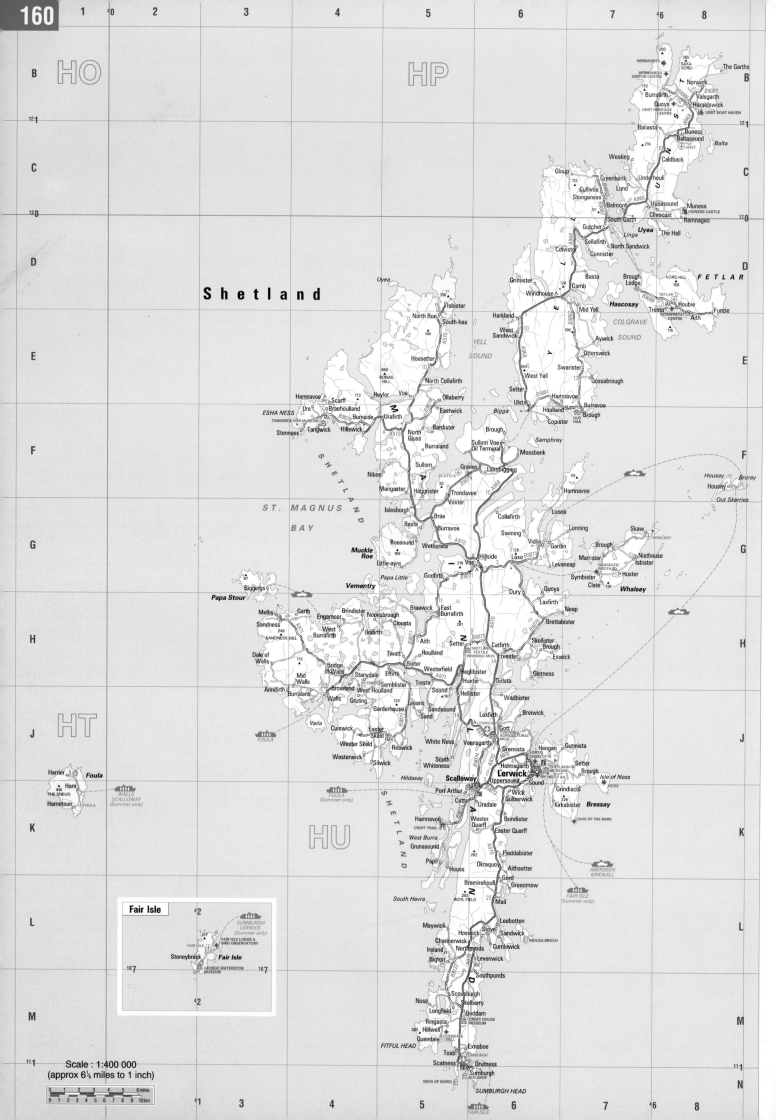

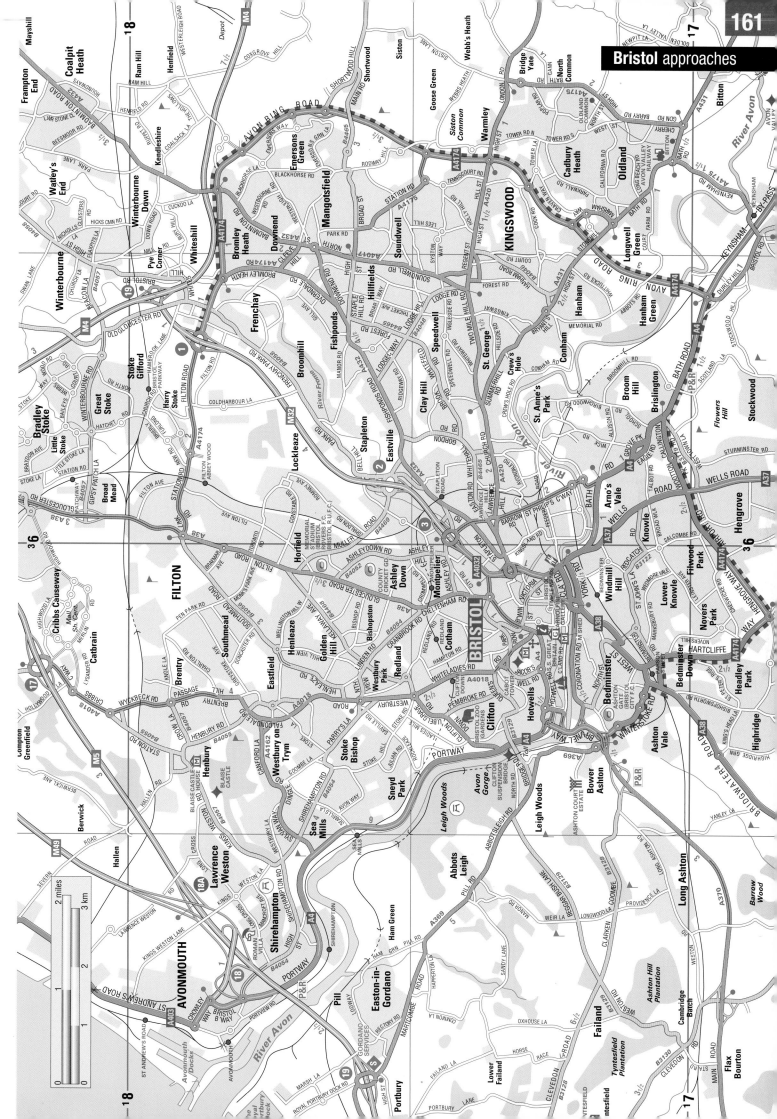

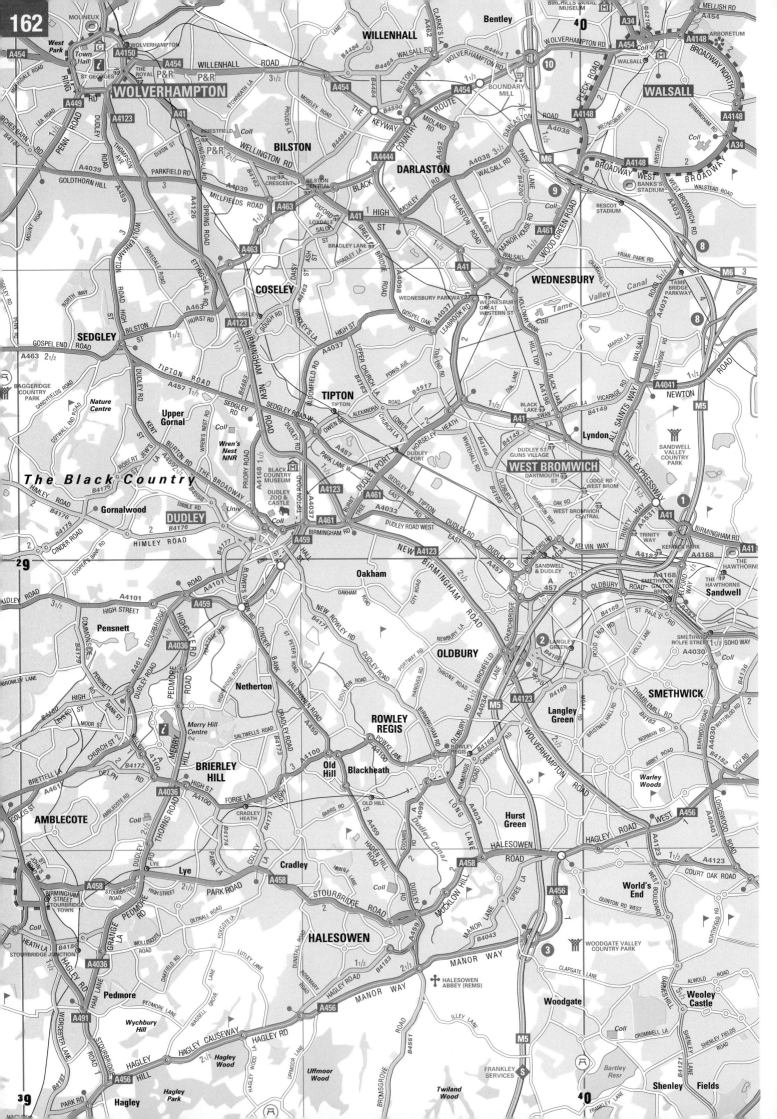

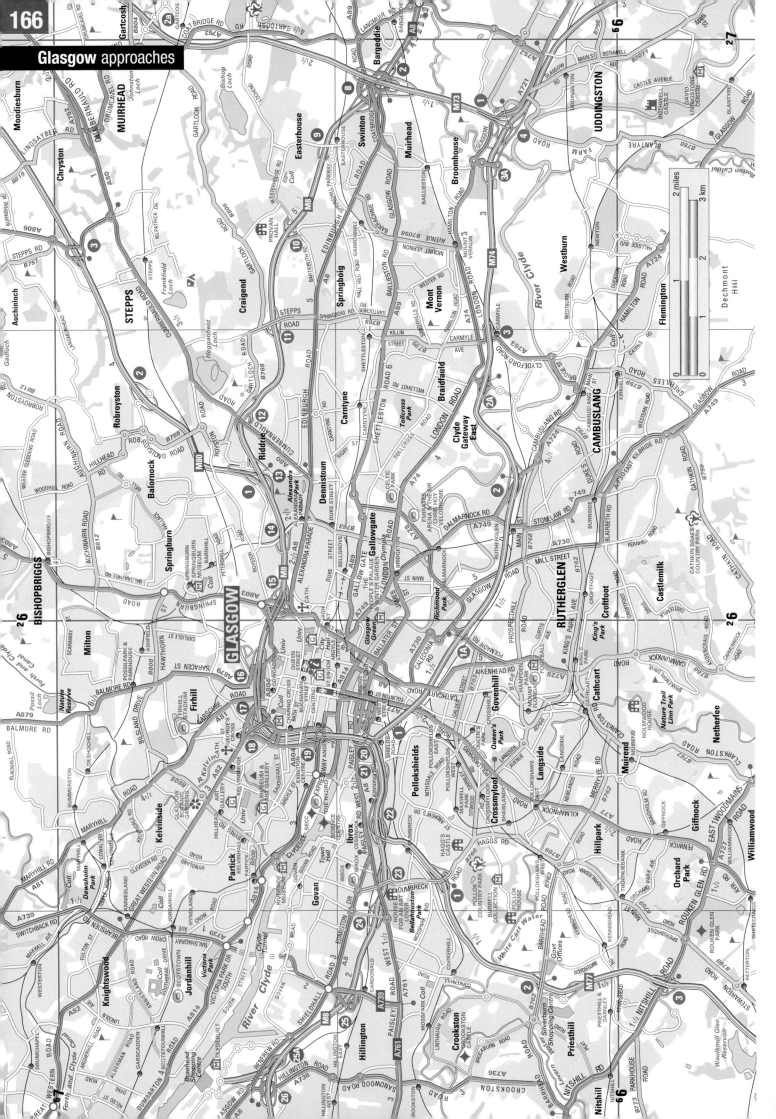

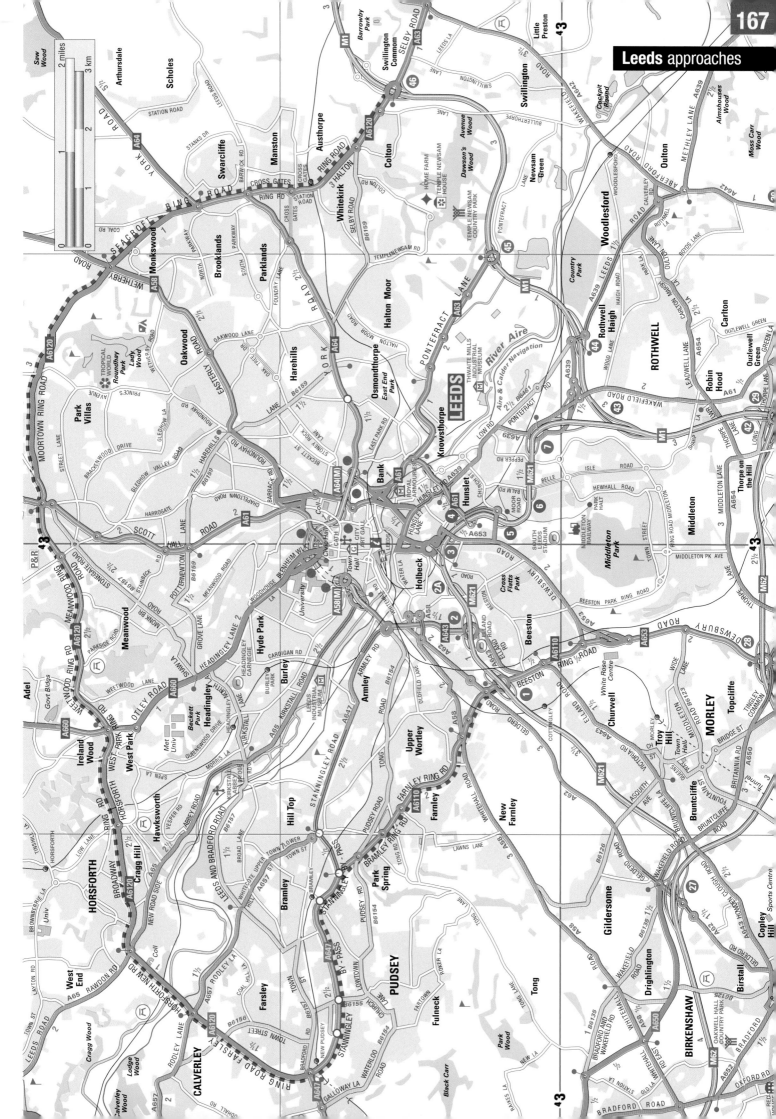

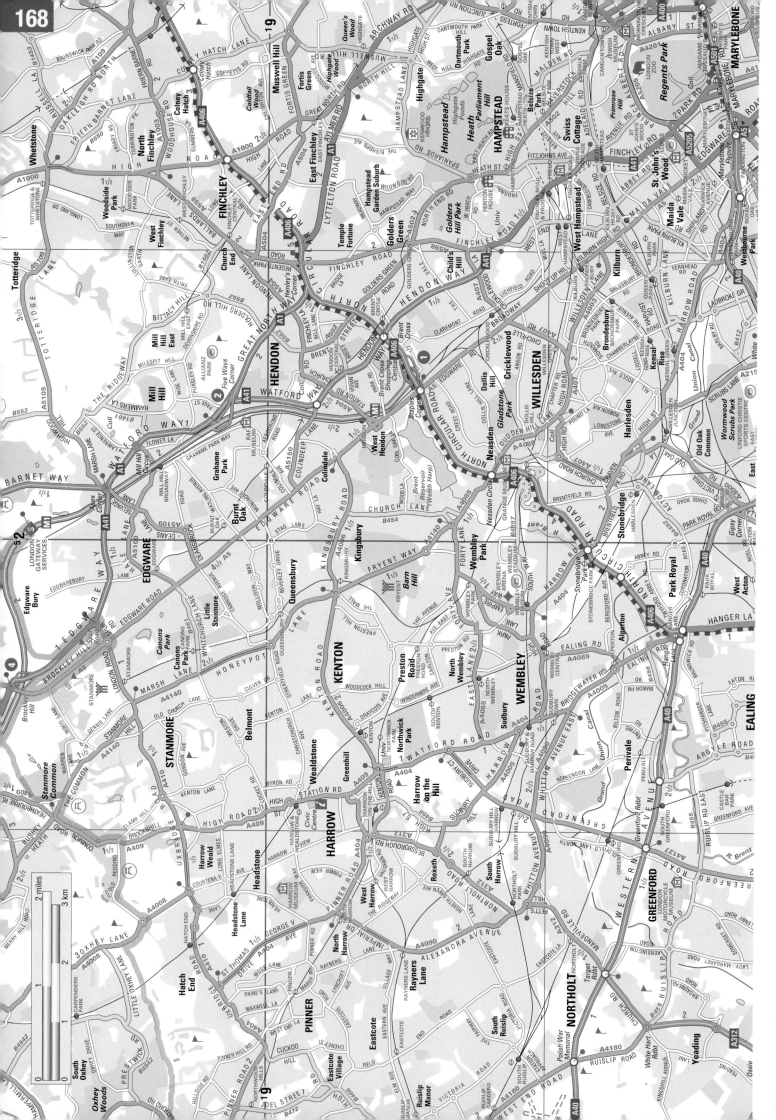

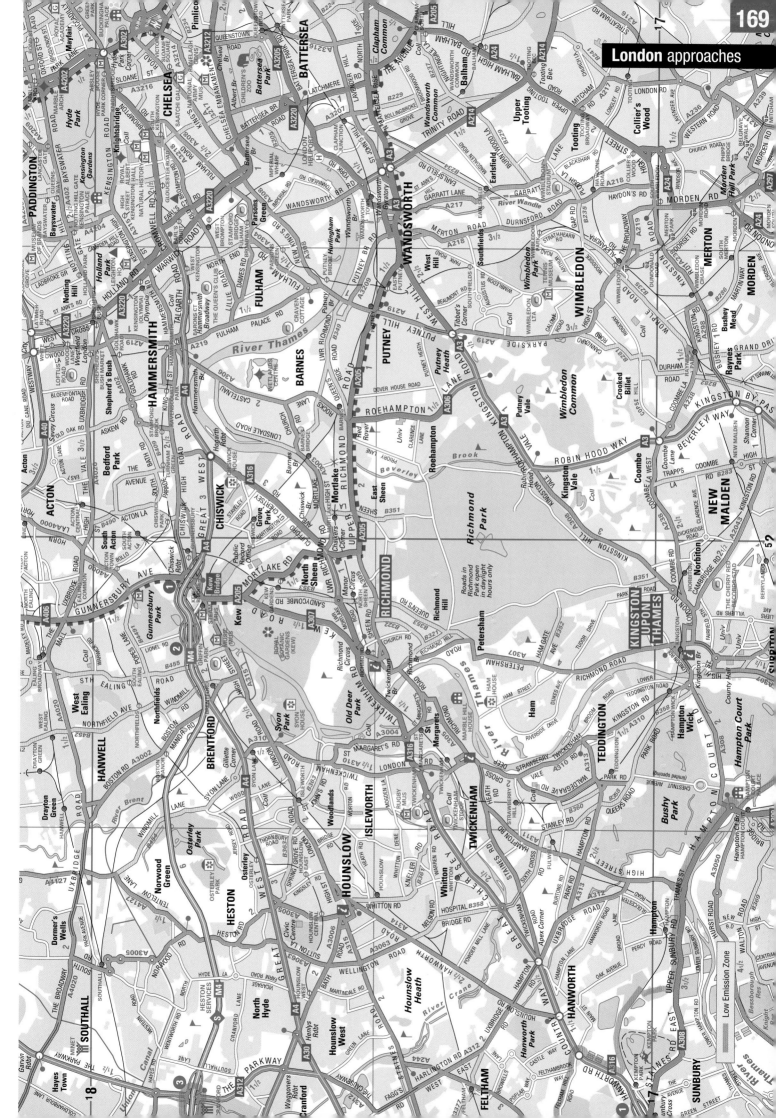

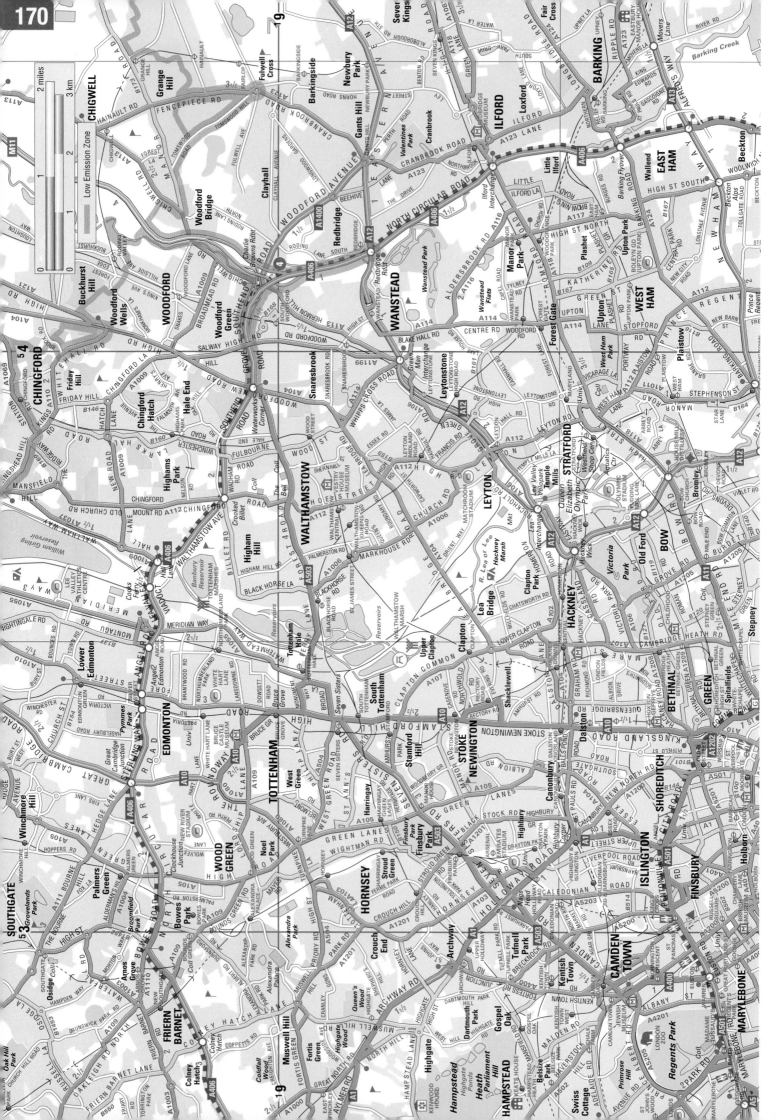

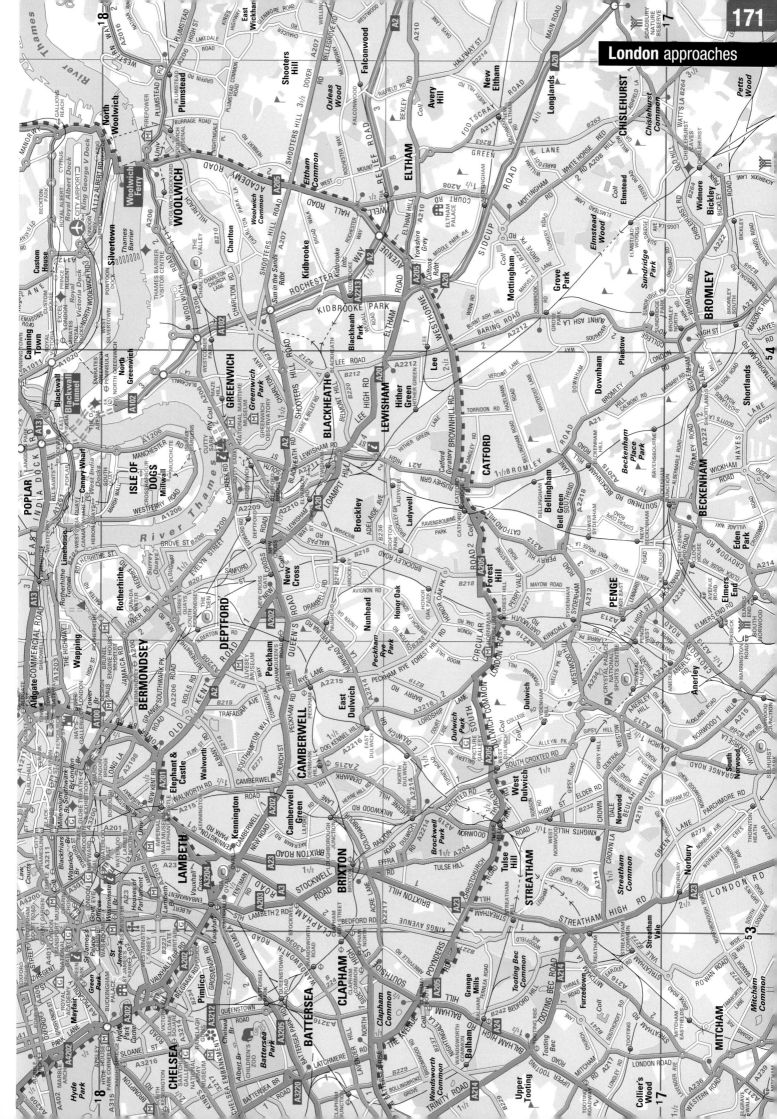

Liverpool approaches

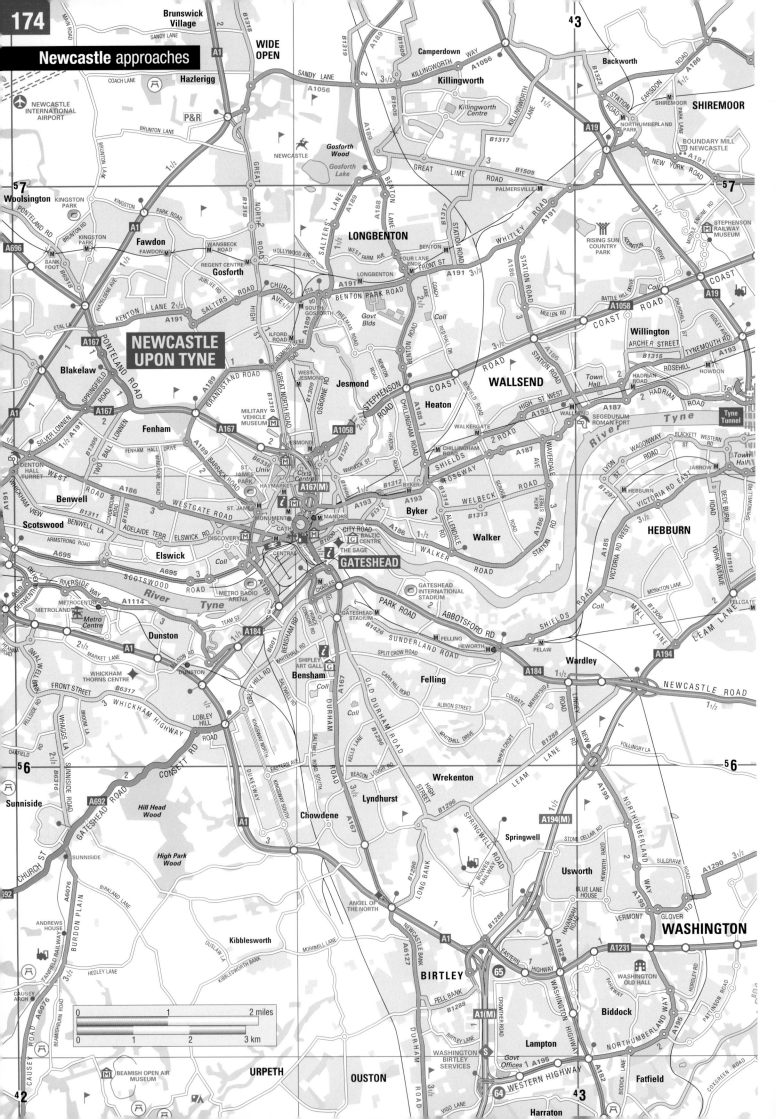

Town plan symbols

Motorway	
Primary route – dual, single carriageway	
A road – dual, single carriageway	
B road – dual, single carriageway	

Minor through road
One-way street
Pedestrian roads
Shopping streets

Railway with station
Tramway with station
Underground or Metro station

H Hospital
P Parking
Police, Post Office
Shopmobility
▲ Youth hostel

Bus or railway station building
Shopping precinct or retail park
Park
Congestion charge zone

✝ Abbey or cathedral
Ancient monument
Aquarium
Art gallery
Bird collection or aviary
Building of interest
Castle
Church of interest
Cinema
Garden
Historic ship
House
House and garden
Museum
Preserved railway
Roman antiquity
Safari park
Theatre
ℹ Tourist information centre
Zoo
◆ Other place of interest

Aberdeen

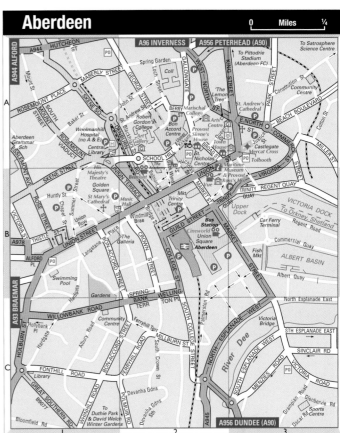

Bath

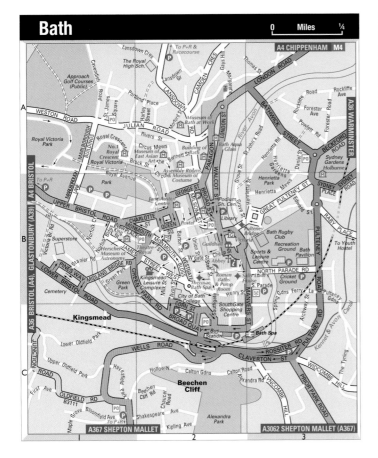

Blackpool

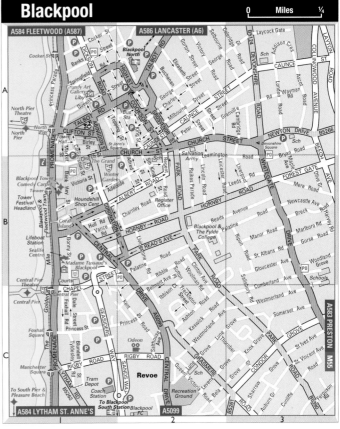

Birmingham

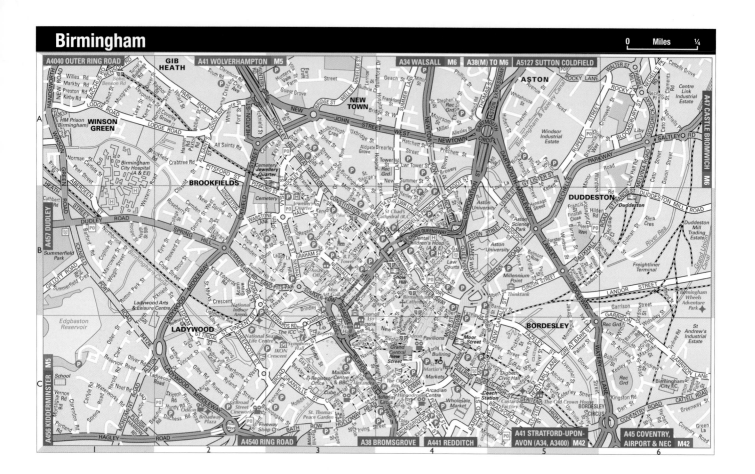

Bournemouth

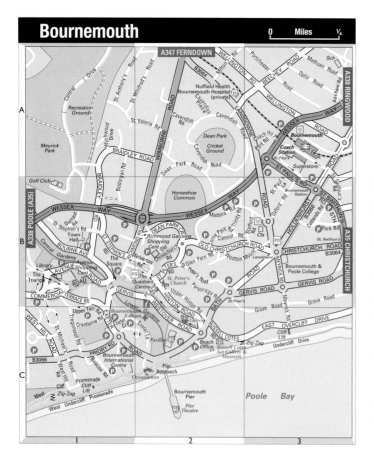

Bradford

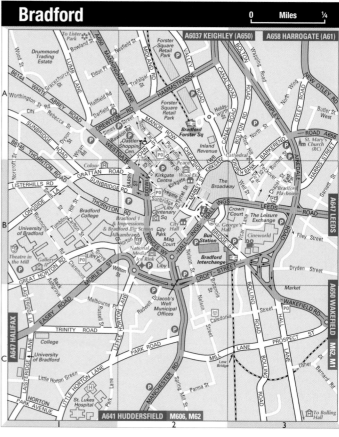

Bristol

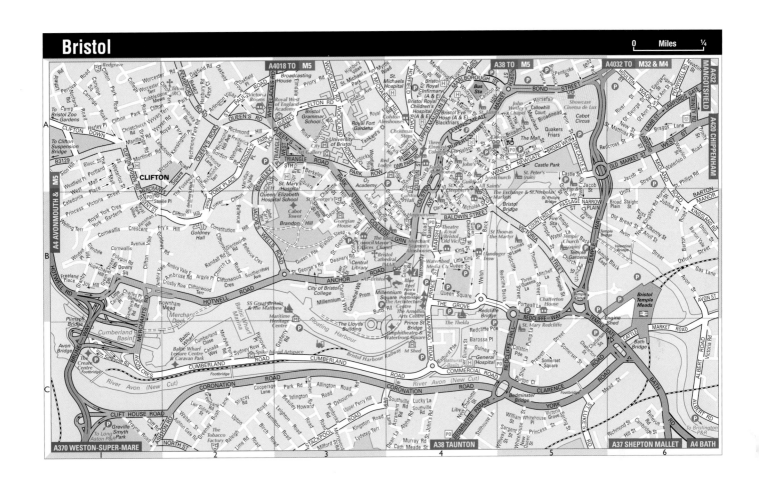

Brighton

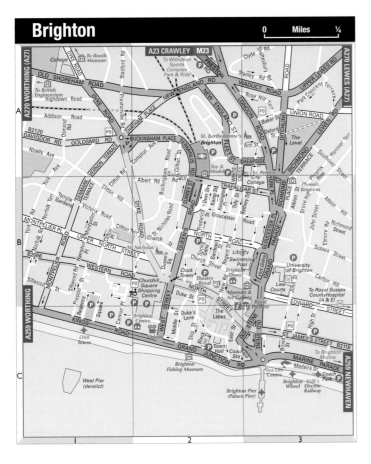

Cambridge

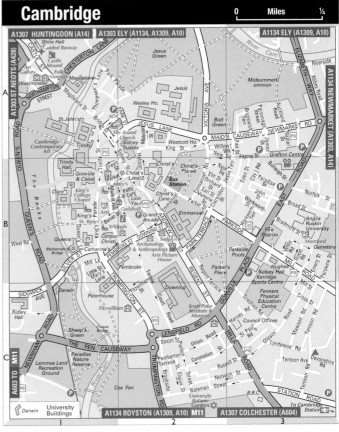

Canterbury

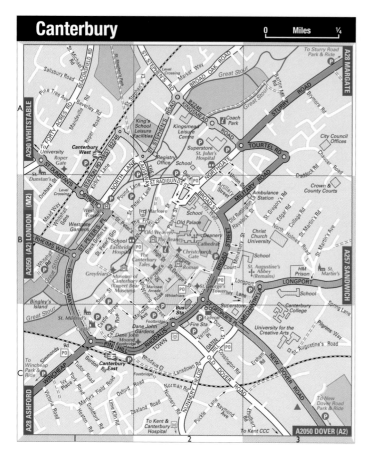

Cardiff / Caerdydd

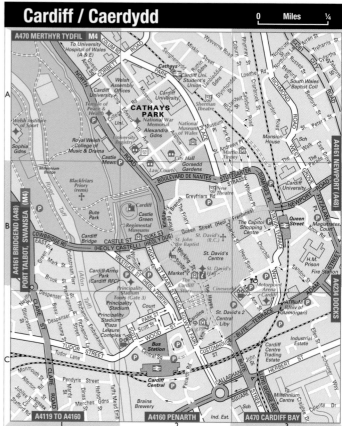

Cheltenham

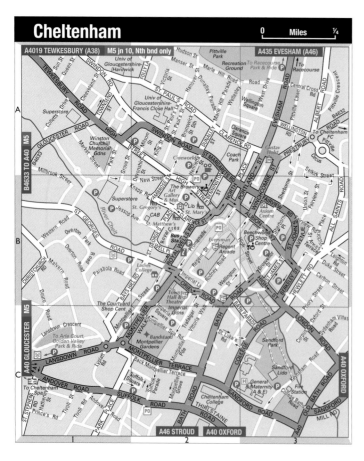

Chester

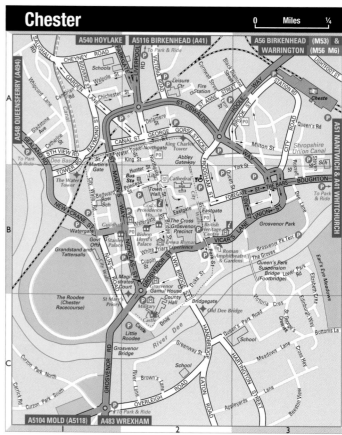

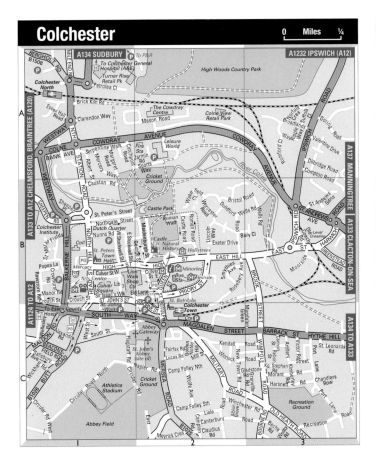

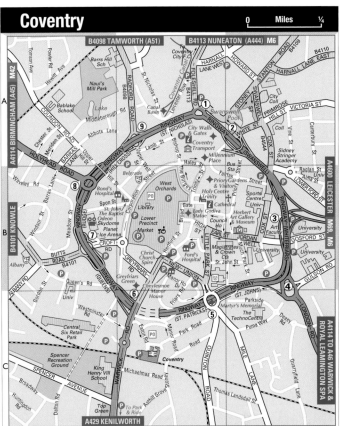

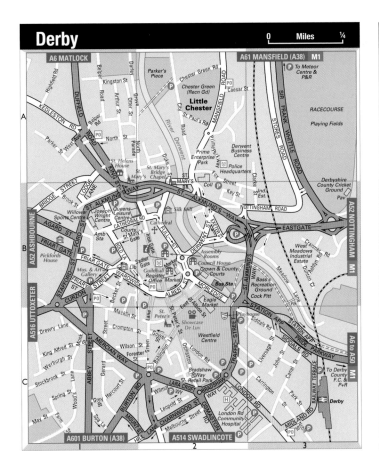

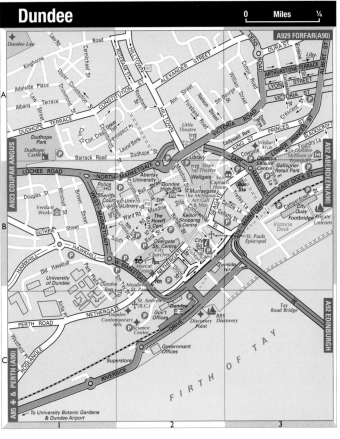

Edinburgh

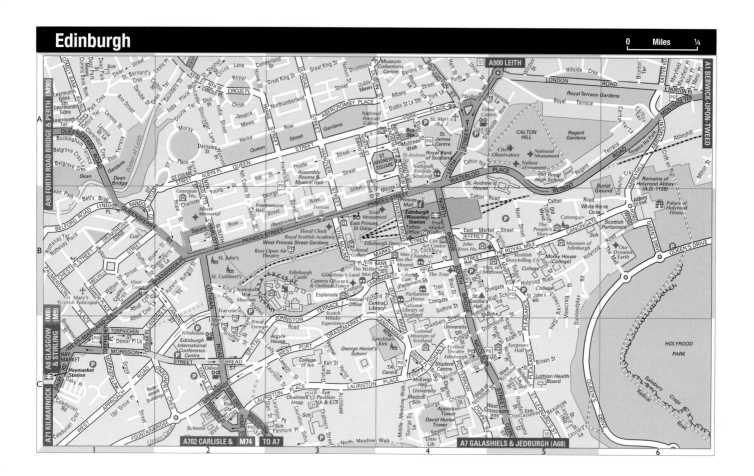

Durham

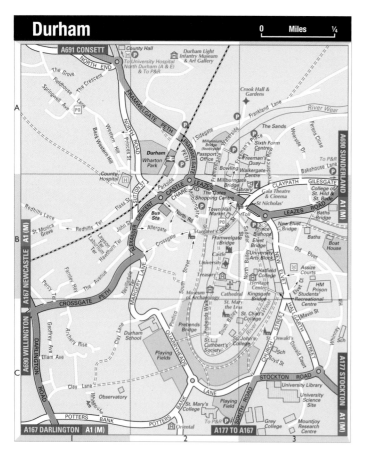

Exeter

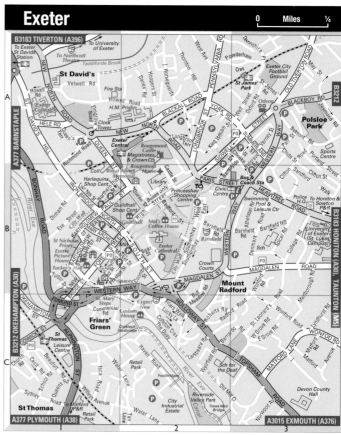

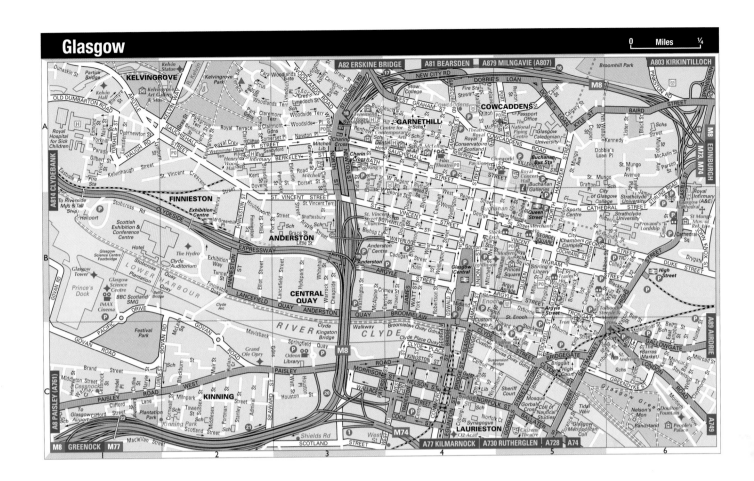

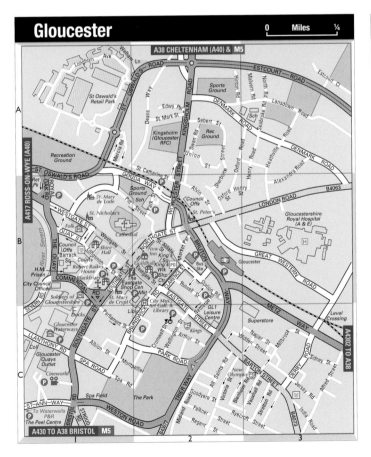

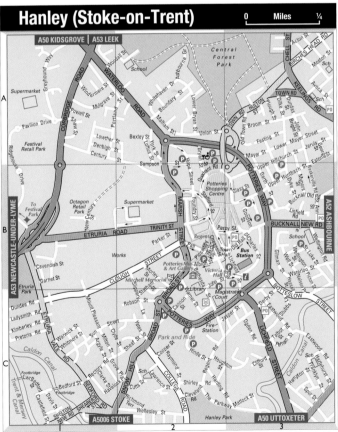

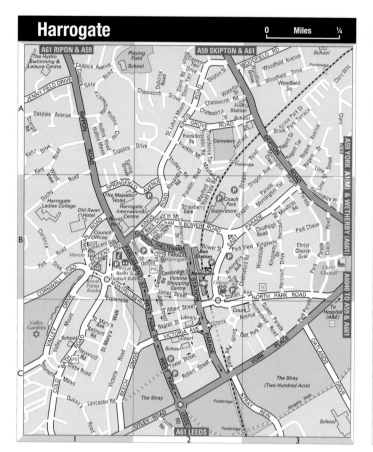

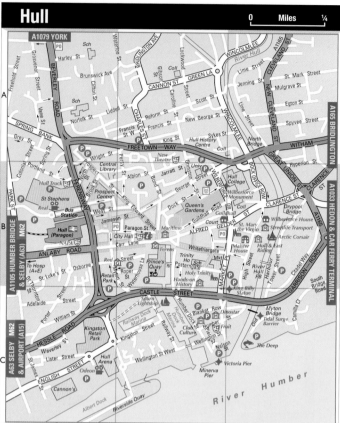

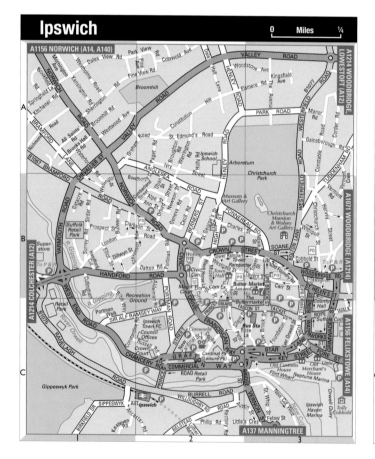

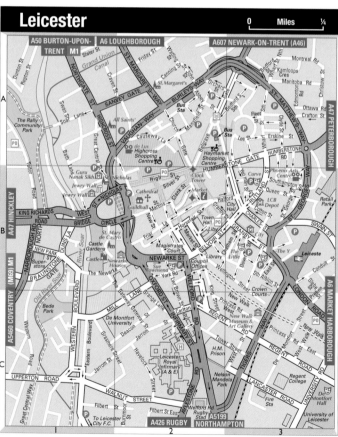

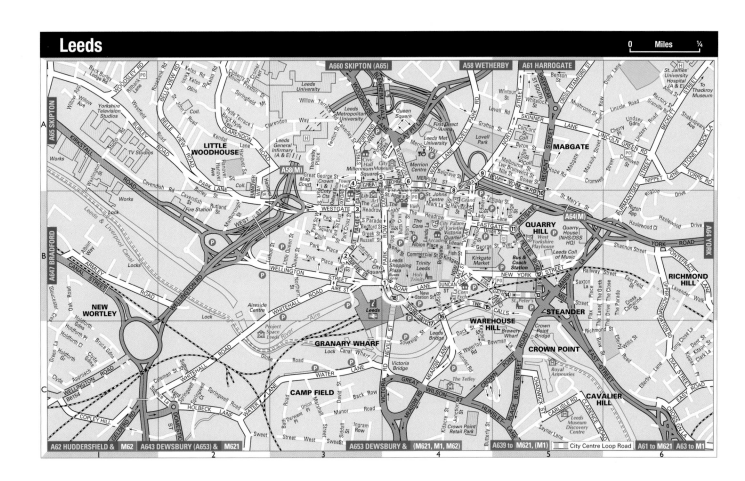

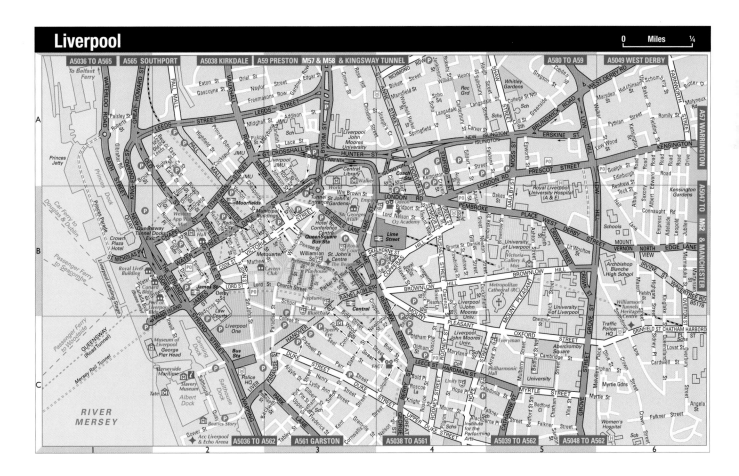

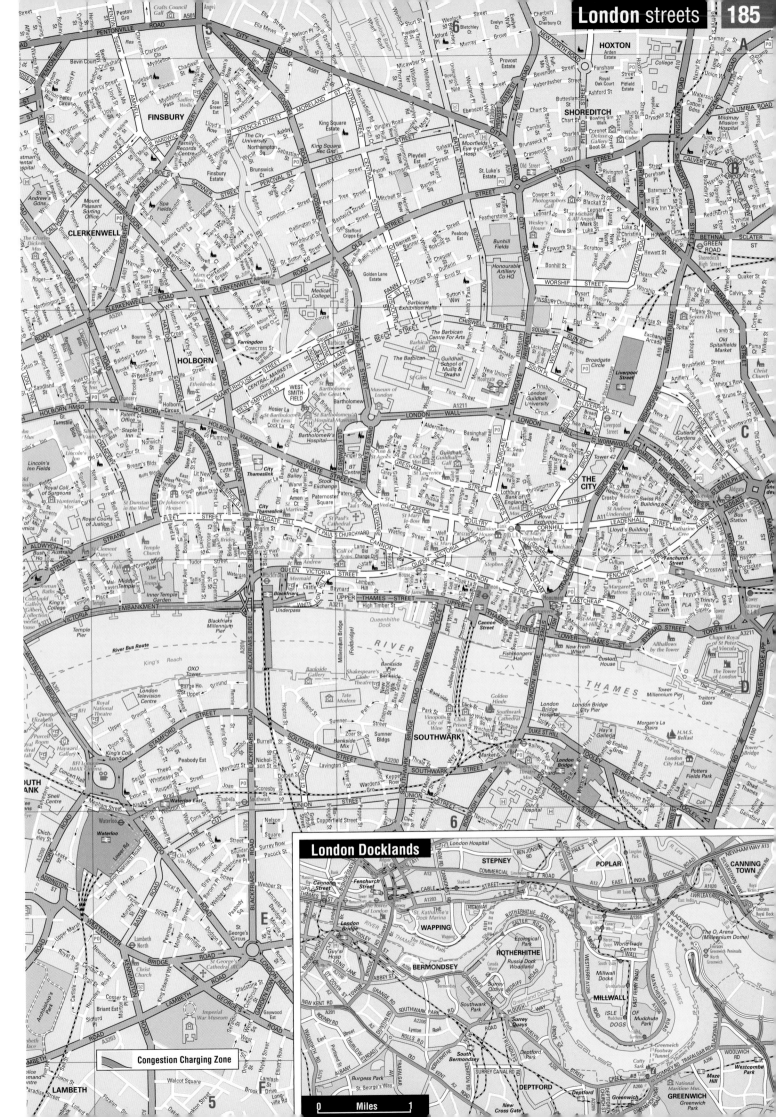

London Docklands

Congestion Charging Zone

0   Miles   1

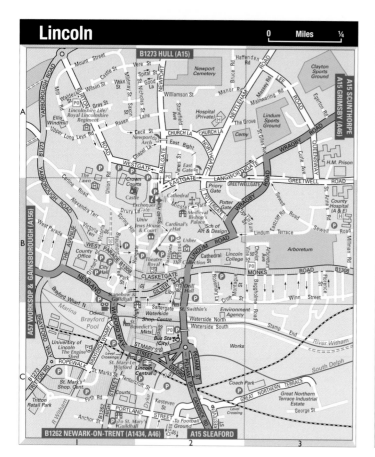

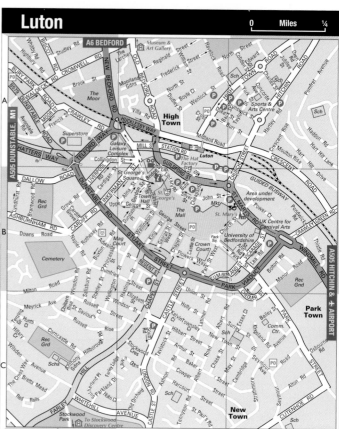

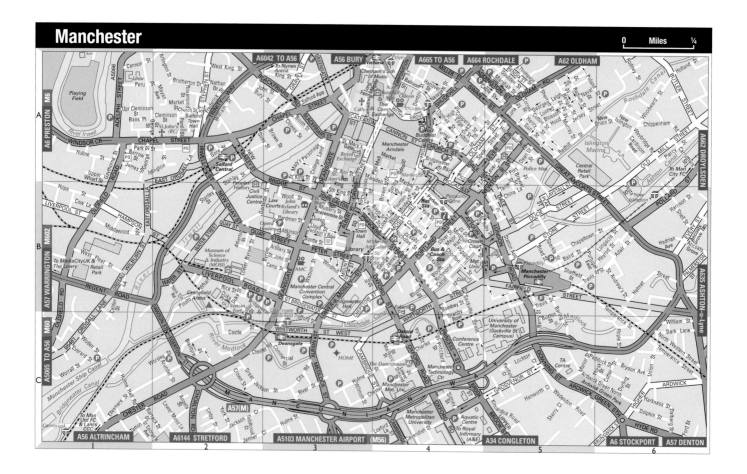

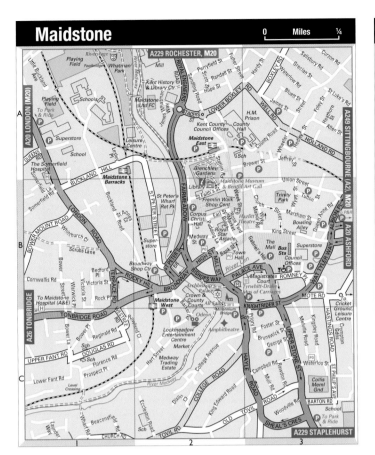

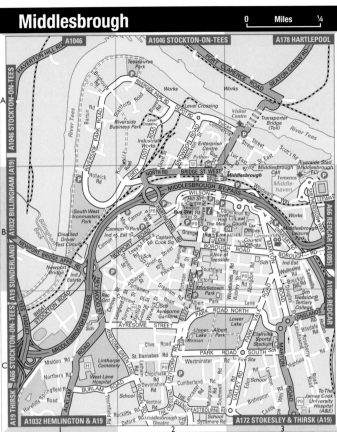

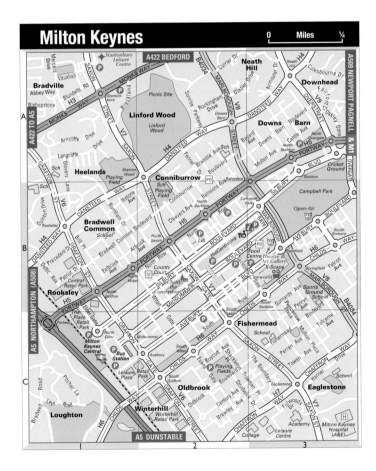

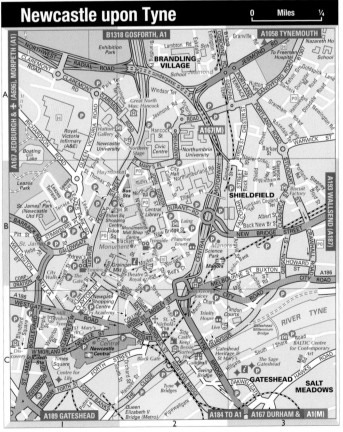

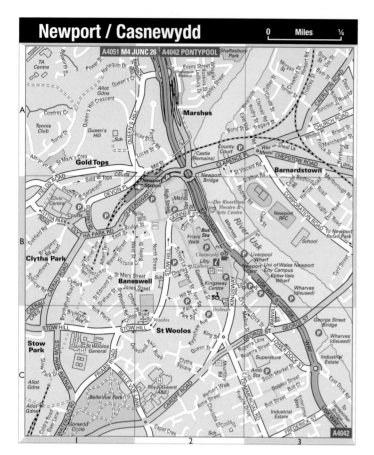

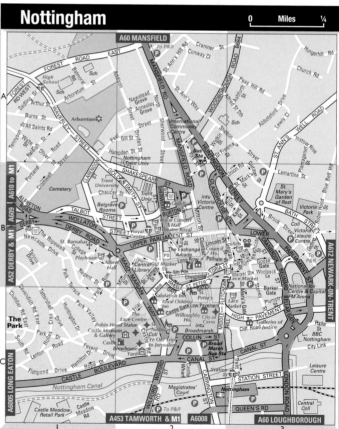

Oxford

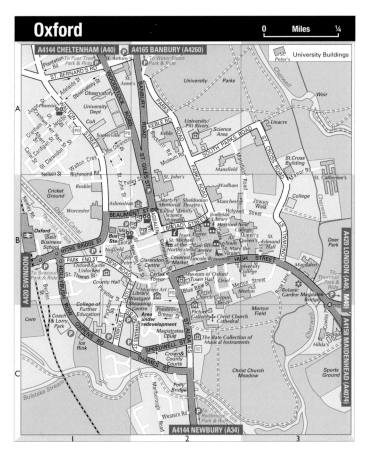

Peterborough

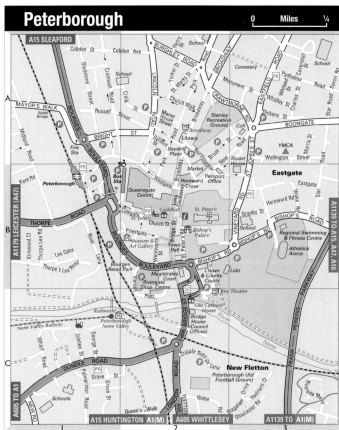

Plymouth

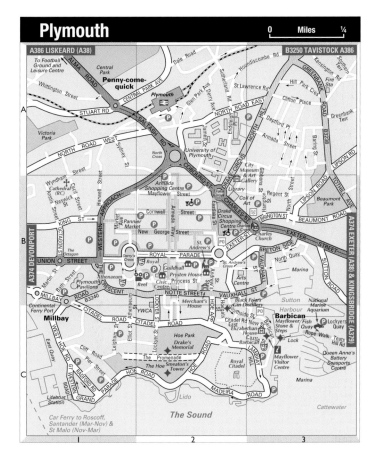

Portsmouth

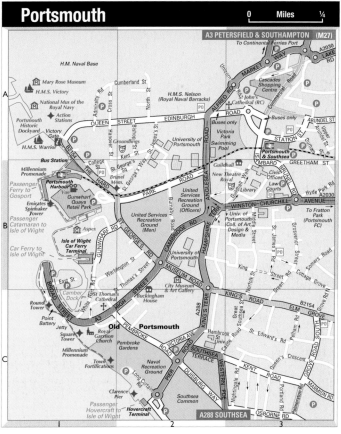

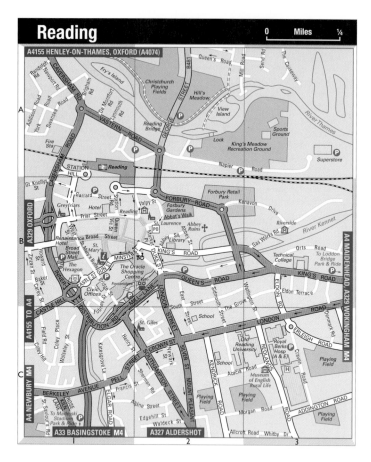

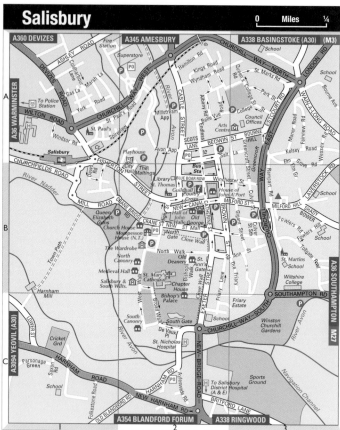

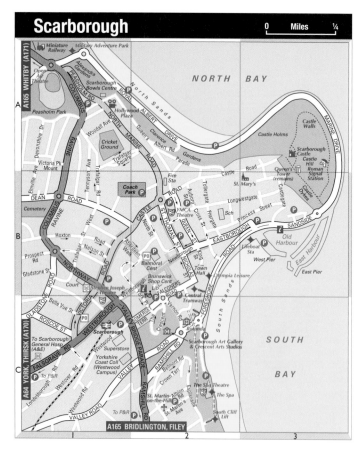

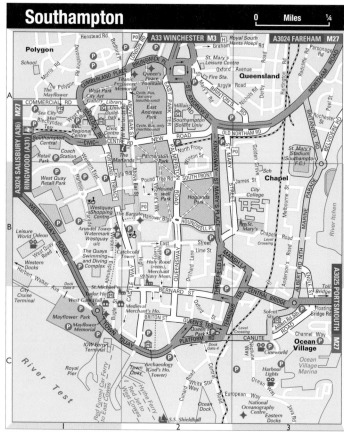

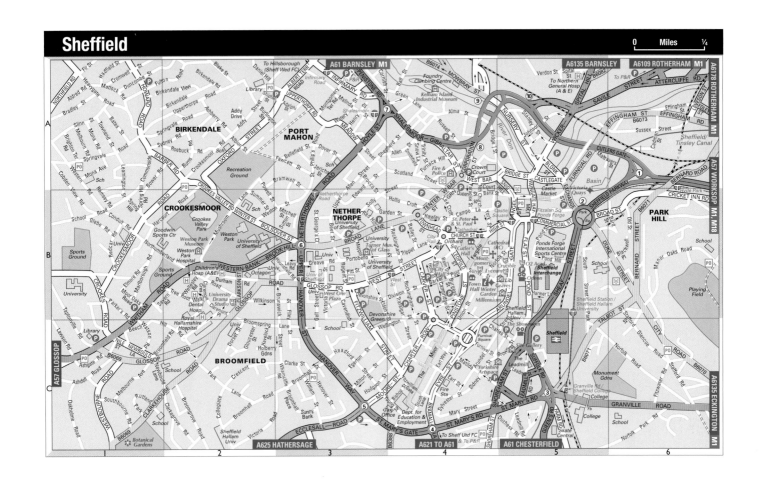

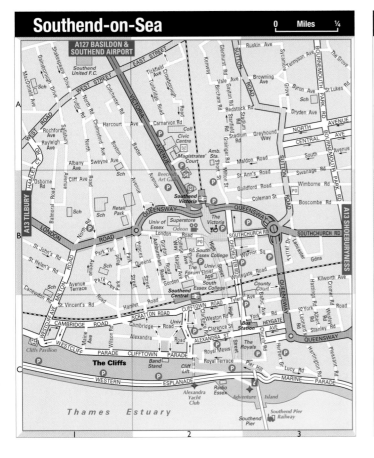

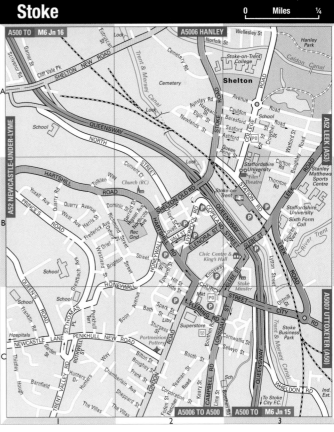

Stratford-upon-Avon

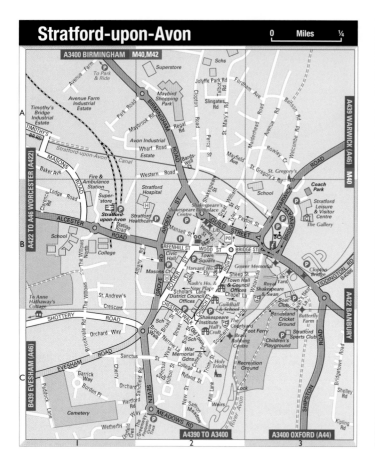

Sunderland

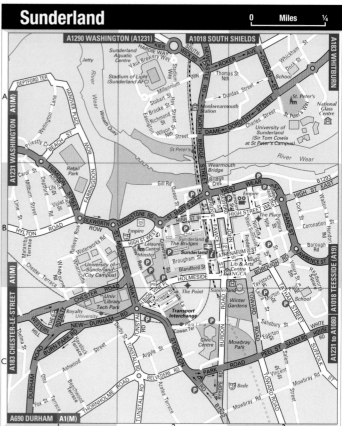

Swansea / Abertawe

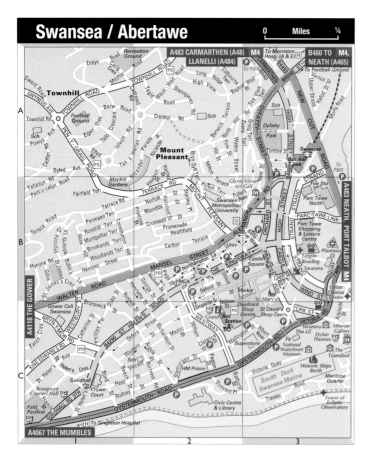

Swindon

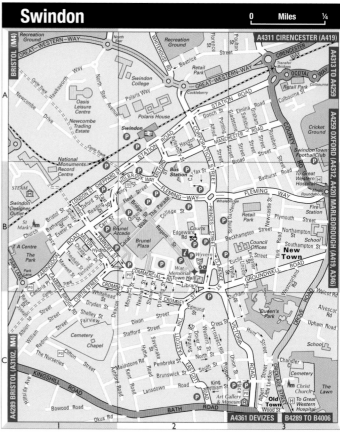

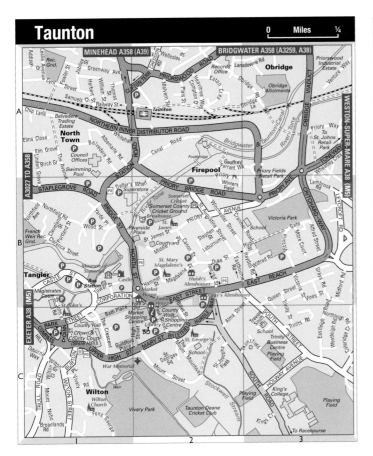

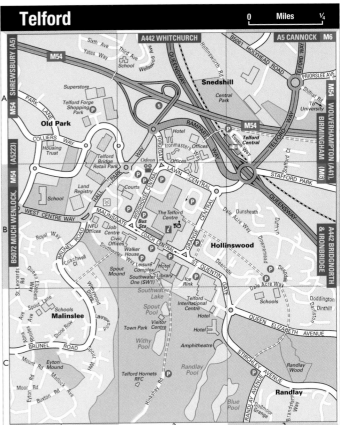

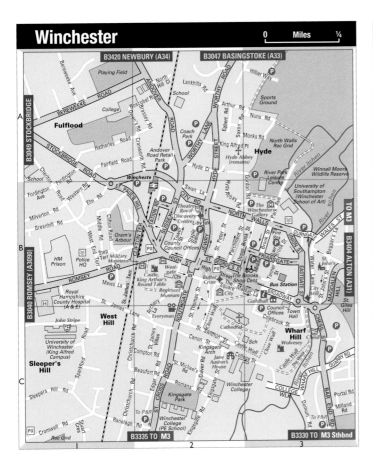

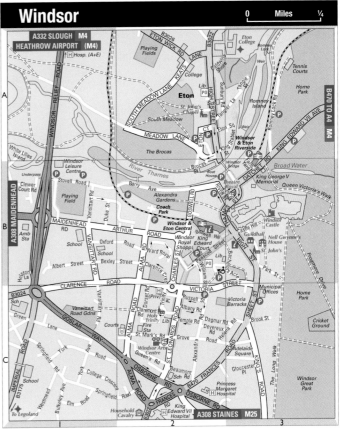

Wolverhampton

0 Miles ¼

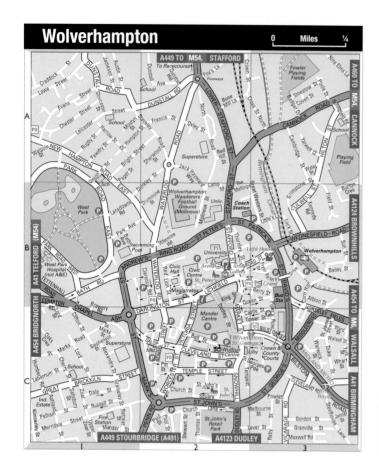

Worcester

0 Miles ¼

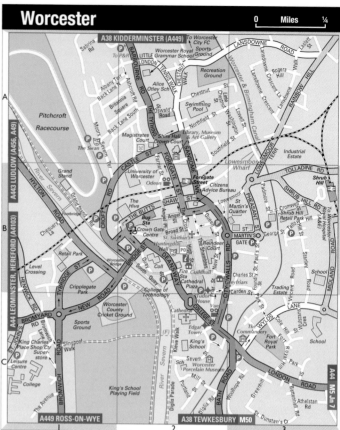

Wrexham

0 Miles ¼

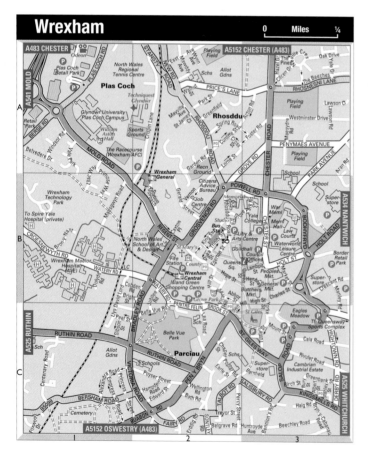

York

0 Miles ¼

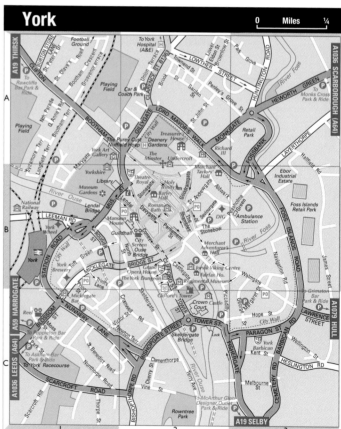

Aberdeen • Bath • Birmingham • Blackpool • Bournemouth • Bradford • Brighton 195

Town plan indexes

Aberdeen 175
Aberdeen B2
Aberdeen Grammar School A1
Academy, The B2
Albert Basin B3
Albert Quay B3
Albury Rd C1
Alford Pl B1
Art Gallery A2
Arts Centre A2
Back Wynd A2
Baker St A1
Beach Blvd A3
Belmont B2
Belmont St B2
Berry St A2
Blackfriars St A2
Bloomfield Rd C1
Bon Accord Centre A2
Bon-Accord St B1/C1
Bridge St B2
Broad St A2
Bus Station B2
Car Ferry Terminal B3
Castlegate A3
Central Library A1
Chapel St B1
Cineworld B2
College A2
College St B2
Commerce St A3
Commercial Quay B3
Com Centre A3/C1
Constitution St A3
Cotton St A3
Crown St B2
Denburn Rd A2
Devanha Gardens C2
Devanha Gardens South C2
East North St A3
Esslemont Ave A1
Ferryhill Rd C2
Ferryhill Terr C2
Fish Market B3
Fonthill Rd C1
Galleria, The B1
Gallowgate A2
George St A2
Glenbervie Rd C3
Golden Sq B1
Grampian Rd C3
Great Southern Rd C1
Guild St B2
Hardgate B1/C1
His Majesty's Theatre A1
Holburn St C1
Hollybank Pl C1
Huntly St B1
Hutcheon St A1
Information Ctr B2
John St A2
Justice St A3
King St A2
Langstane Pl B1
Lemon Tree, The A2
Library C1
Loch St A2
Maberly St A1
Marischal College A2
Maritime Museum and Provost Ross's House B2
Market B2
Market St B2/B3
Menzies Rd C3
Mercat Cross ✦ A3
Millburn St C2
Miller St A3
Mount St A1
Music Hall B1
North Esp East C3
North Esp West C2
Oscar Rd C3
Palmerston Rd C2
Park St A3
Police Station A2
Polmuir Rd C2
Post Office A1/A2/A3/B1/C3
Provost Skene's House A2
Queen St A2
Regent Quay B3
Regent Road B3
Robert Gordon's College A2
Rose St B1
Rosemount Pl A1
Rosemount Viaduct A1
St Andrew St A2
St Andrew's Cathedral † A3
St Mary's Cathedral † B1
St Nicholas Centre A2
St Nicholas St A2
School Hill A2
Sinclair Rd C3
Skene Sq A1
Skene St B1
South College St C2
South Crown St C2
South Esp East C3
South Esp West C3
South Mount St A1
Sports Centre C3
Spring Garden A2
Springbank Terr C2
Summer St B1
Swimming Pool B1
Thistle St B1
Tolbooth A3
Town House A2
Trinity Centre B2
Trinity Quay B3
Union Row B1
Union Square B2
Union St B1/B2
Upper Dock B3
Upper Kirkgate A2
Victoria Bridge C3
Victoria Dock B3
Victoria Rd C3
Victoria St B2
Virginia St A3
Vue B2
Wellington Pl B2
West North St A2
Whinhill Rd C1
Willowbank Rd C1
Windmill Brae B2
Woolmanhill Hospital A1

Bath 175
Alexandra Park C2
Alexandra Rd C2
Approach Golf Courses (Public) A1
Archway St C3
Assembly Rooms & Mus of Costume A2
Avon St B2
Barton St B2
Bath Abbey † B2
Bath Aqua Glass A2
Bath City College B2
Bath Pavilion B3
Bath Rugby Club B3
Bath Spa Station C3
Bathwick St A3
Beckford Road A3
Beechen Cliff Rd C2
Bennett St A2
Bloomfield Ave C1
Broad Quay C2
Broad St B2
Brock St A1
Building of Bath Museum A2
Bus Station C2
Calton Gdns C2
Calton Rd C2
Camden Cr A2
Cavendish Rd A1
Cemetery B1
Charlotte St B2
Chaucer Rd C2
Cheap St B2
Circus Mews A2
Claverton St C2
Corn St C2
Cricket Ground B3
Daniel St A3
Edward St B3
Ferry La B3
First Ave C1
Forester Ave A3
Forester Rd A3
Gays Hill A2
George St B2
Great Pulteney St B3
Green Park B1
Green Park Rd B2
Grove St B2
Guildhall B2
Harley St A2
Hayesfield Park C1
Henrietta Gdns A3
Henrietta Mews B3
Henrietta Park B3
Henrietta Rd A3
Henrietta St B3
Henry St B2
Herschel Museum of Astronomy B1
Holburne Mus B3
Holloway C2
Information Ctr B2
James St West B1/B2
Jane Austen Ctr B2
Julian Rd A1
Junction Rd C1
Kingsmead Leisure Complex B2
Kipling Ave C2
Lansdown Cr A1
Lansdown Gr A2
Lansdown Rd A2
Library B2
London Rd A3
London St A2
Lower Bristol Rd B1
Lower Oldfield Park C1
Lyncombe Hill C3
Manvers St B3
Maple Gr C1
Margaret's Hill A2
Marlborough Bldgs A1
Marlborough La B1
Midland Bridge Rd B1
Milk St B2
Milsom St B2
Monmouth St B2
Morford St A2
Museum of Bath at Work A2
Museum of East Asian Art A2
New King St B1
No 1 Royal Cres A1
Norfolk Bldgs B1
Norfolk Cr B1
North Parade Rd B3
Oldfield Rd C1
Paragon A2
Pines Way B1
Podium Shopping Ctr B2
Police Station B3
Portland Pl A2
Post Office A1/A3/B2/C1/C2
Postal Museum B2
Powlett Rd A3
Prior Park Rd C3
Pulteney Bridge ✦ B2
Pulteney Gdns B3
Pulteney Rd B3/C3
Queen Sq B2
Raby Pl B3
Recreation Ground B3
Rivers St A2
Rockliffe Ave A3
Rockliffe Rd A3
Roman Baths & Pump Room B2
Rossiter Rd C3
Royal Ave A1
Royal Cr A1
Royal High School, The A2
Royal Victoria Park A1
St James Sq A1
St John's Rd A3
Sally Lunn's House ✦ B2
Shakespeare Ave C2
South Pde B3
Southgate C2
Sports & Leisure Ctr B3
Spring Gdns C3
Stall St B2
Stanier Rd B1
Superstore B1
Sydney Gdns A3
Sydney Pl B3
Sydney Rd B3
Theatre Royal B2
Thermae Bath Spa ✦ B2
Thomas St A3
Tyning, The C3
Union St B2
Upper Bristol Rd B1
Upper Oldfield Park C1
Victoria Art Gallery B2
Victoria Bridge Rd B1
Walcot St B2
Wells Rd C1
Westgate Buildings B2
Westgate St B2
Weston Rd A1
Widcombe Hill C3

Birmingham 176
Abbey St A2
Aberdeen St A1
Acorn Gr B2
Adams St A5
Adderley St C5
Albert St B4/B5
Albion St B2
Alcester St C5
Aldgate Gr A3
All Saint's St A2
All Saints Rd A2
Allcock St C5
Allesley St A4
Allison St C4
Alma Cr B6
Alston Rd C1
Arcadian Centre C4
Arthur St C6
Assay Office B3
Aston Expressway A5
Aston Science Park B5
Aston St B4
Aston University B4/B5
Avenue Rd A5
Bacchus Rd A1
Bagot St B4
Banbury St B5
Barford Rd B1
Barford St C4
Barn St C5
Barnwell Rd C6
Barr St A3
Barrack St B5
Bartholomew St C4
Barwick St B4
Bath Row C3
Beaufort Rd C1
Belmont Row B5
Benson Rd A1
Berkley St C3
Bexhill Gr C3
Birchall St C5
Birmingham City FC C6
Birmingham City Hospital (A&E) A1
Birmingham Wheels Adventure Pk ✦ B6
Bishopsgate St C3
Blews St A4
Bloomsbury St A6
Blucher St C3
Bordesley St C4
Bowyer St C5
Bradburne Way A5
Bradford St C5
Branston St A3
Brearley St A4
Brewery St A4
Bridge St A3
Bridge St C3
Bridge St West A4
Brindley Dr B3
Broad St C3
Broad Street Cineworld C2
Broadway Plaza ✦ C2
Bromley St C5
Bromsgrove St C4
Brookfield Rd A2
Browning St C2
Bryant St A1
BT Tower ✦ B3
Buckingham St A3
Bull St B4
Bull St B4
Bullring C4
Cambridge St C3
Camden Dr B3
Camden St B2
Cannon St C4
Cardigan St B5
Carlisle St A1
Carlyle Rd C1
Caroline St B3
Carver St B2
Cato St A6
Cattell Rd C6
Cattells Gr A6
Cawdor Cr C1
Cecil St B4
Cemetery A2/B2
Cemetery La A2
Ctr Link Ind Est A6
Charlotte St B3
Cheapside C4
Chester St A5
Children's Hospital (A&E) B4
Church St B4
Claremont Rd A2
Clarendon Rd C1
Clark St C1
Clement St B3
Clissold St B2
Cliveland St B4
Coach Station C5
College St B2
Colmore Circus B4
Colmore Row B4
Commercial St C3
Constitution Hill B3
Convention Ctr, The C3
Cope St B2
Coplow St B1
Corporation St C4
Corporation St B4
Council House B3
County Court B4
Coveley Gr A2
Coventry Rd C6
Coventry St C5
Cox St B3
Crabtree Rd A2
Cregoe St C3
Crescent Ave A2
Crescent Theatre C3
Crescent, The A2
Cromwell St A6
Cromwell St B3
Cube, The C3
Curzon St B5
Custard Factory ✦ C5
Cuthbert Rd B1
Dale End B4
Dart St C6
Dartmouth Circus A4
Dartmouth Middleway A5
Dental Hospital B4
Deritend C5
Devon St A6
Devonshire St A1
Digbeth Civic Hall C5
Digbeth High St C4
Dolman St B6
Dover St A1
Duchess Rd C2
Duddeston B6
Duddeston Manor Rd B5
Duddeston Mill Rd B6
Duddeston Mill Trading Estate B6
Dudley Rd B1
Edgbaston Sh Ctr C2
Edmund St B3
Edward St B3
Elkington St A4
Ellen St B2
Ellis St C3
Erskine St B6
Essex St C4
Eyre St B2
Farm Croft A3
Farm St A3
Fazeley St B4/C5
Felstead Way B5
Finstall Cl B5
Five Ways C2
Fiveway Sh Ctr C2
Fleet St B3
Floodgate St C5
Ford St A2
Fore St C4
Forster St B5
Francis Rd C2
Francis St B5
Frankfort St A4
Frederick St B3
Freeth St C1
Freightliner Terminal B6
Garrison La C6
Garrison St B6
Gas St C3
Geach St A4
George St B3
George St West B2
Gibb St C5
Gilby Rd C2
Gillott Rd B1
Glover St C5
Goode Ave A2
Goodrick Way A6
Gordon St B6
Graham St B3
Grand Central C4
Granville St C3
Gray St C6
Great Barr St C5
Great Charles St B3
Great Francis St B6
Great Hampton Row A3
Great Hampton St A3
Great King St A3
Great Lister St A5
Great Tindal St C2
Green La C6
Green St C5
Greenway St C6
Grosvenor St West C2
Guest Gr A3
Guild Cl C2
Guildford Dr A4
Guthrie Cl A3
Hagley Rd C1
Hall St B3
Hampton St A3
Handsworth New Rd A1
Hanley St B4
Harford St A3
Harmer Rd A2
Harold Rd C1
Hatchett St A4
Heath Mill La C5
Heath St B1
Heath St South B1
Heaton St A2
Heneage St B5
Henrietta St B4
Herbert Rd C6
High St C4
High St C5
Hilden Rd B5
Hill St C3/C4
Hindlow Cl B6
Hingeston St B2
Hippodrome Theatre C4
HM Prison A1
Hockley Circus A2
Hockley Hill A3
Hockley St A3
Holliday St C3
Holloway Circus C4
Holloway Head C3
Holt St B5
Hooper St B1
Horse Fair C4
Hospital St A4
Howard St B3
Howe St B5
Hubert St A5
Hunters Rd A2
Hunters Vale A3
Huntly Rd C2
Hurst St C4
Icknield Port Rd B1
Icknield Sq B2
Icknield St A2/B2
IKON C3
Information Ctr C4
Inge St C4
Irving St C3
Ivy La C5
James Watt Queensway B4
Jennens Rd B5
Jewellery Quarter A3
Jewellery Quarter Museum B3
John Bright St C4
Keeley St C6
Kellett Rd B5
Kent St C4
Kenyon St B3
Key Hill A3
Kilby Ave C2
King Edwards Rd B2
King Edwards Rd C3
Kingston Rd C6
Kirby Rd A1
Ladywood Arts & Leisure Centre B1
Ladywood Middleway C2/C3
Ladywood Rd C1
Lancaster St B4
Landor St B6
Law Courts B4
Lawford Cl B5
Lawley Middleway B5
Ledbury Cl C2
Ledsam St B2
Lees St A1
Legge La B3
Lennox St A3
Library A6/C3
Library Walk B2
Lighthorne Ave B2
Link Rd B1
Lionel St B3
Lister St B5
Little Ann St C5
Little Hall Rd A6
Liverpool St C5
Livery St B3/B4
Lodge Rd A1
Lord St A5
Love La A5
Loveday St B4
Lower Dartmouth St C6
Lower Loveday St B4
Lower Tower St A4
Lower Trinity St C5
Ludgate Hill B3
Mailbox Ctr & BBC C3
Margaret St B3
Markby Rd A1
Marroway St B1
Maxstoke St C6
Melvina Rd A6
Meriden St C4
Metropolitan (RC) † B4
Midland St B6
Milk St C5
Mill St A5
Millennium Point B5
Miller St A4
Milton St A4
Moat La C4
Montague Rd C1
Montague St C5
Monument Rd C1
Moor St Queensway C4
Moor Street C4
Moorsom St A4
Morville St C2
Mosborough Cr A3
Moseley St C4
Mott St B3
Mus & Art Gallery B3
Musgrave Rd A1
National Indoor Arena ✦ C2
National Sea Life Centre C3
Navigation St C3
Nechell's Park Rd A6
Nechells Parkway B5
Nechells Pl A6
New Alexandra C3
New Bartholomew St C4
New Canal St C5
New John St West A3
New Spring St B2
New St C4
New Street C4
New Summer St A4
New Town Row A4
Newhall Hill B3
Newhall St B3
Newton St B4
Newtown A4
Noel Rd C1
Norman St A1
Northbrook St B1
Northwood St B3
Norton St A2
Odeon C2
Old Crown House C5
Old Rep Theatre, The C4
Old Snow Hill B4
Oliver Rd C1
Oliver St A5
Osler St C1
Oxford St C5
Palmer St C5
Paradise Circus C3
Paradise St C3
Park Rd A2
Park St C4
Pavilions C4
Paxton Rd A2
Peel St A1
Penn St B5
Pershore St C4
Phillips St A4
Pickford St C5
Pinfold St C4
Pitsford St A2
Plough & Harrow Rd C1
Police Station A4/B1/B4/C2/C4
Pope St B2
Portland Rd C1
Post Office A3/A5/B1/B3/B4/B5/C2/C3/C5
Preston Rd A1
Price St B4
Princip St B4
Printing House St B4
Priory Queensway B4
Pritchett St A4
Proctor St A5
Queensway B3
Radnor St A2
Rea St C4
Regent Pl B3
Register Office C3
Repertory Theatre C3
Reservoir Rd C1
Richard St A5
River St C5
Rocky La A5/A6
Rodney Cl C2
Roseberry St B2
Rotton Park St B1
Rupert St A5
Ruston St C2
Ryland St C2
St Andrew's Ind Est C6
St Andrew's Rd C6
St Andrew's St C6
St Bolton St C6
St Chads Queensway B4
St Clements Rd A6
St George's St A3
St James Pl B5
St Marks Cr B2
St Martin's C4
St Paul's B3
St Paul's B3
St Paul's Sq B3
St Philip's † B4
St Stephen's St A4
St Thomas' Peace Garden C3
St Vincent St C2
Saltley Rd A6
Sand Pits Pde B3
Severn St C3
Shadwell St B4
Sheepcote St C2
Shefford Rd A4
Sherborne St C2
Shylton's Croft C2
Skipton Rd C2
Smallbrook Queensway C4
Smith St A3
Snow Hill B4
Snow Hill Queensway B4
Soho, Benson Rd A1
South Rd A2
Spencer St B3
Spring Hill B2
Staniforth St B4
Station St C4
Steelhouse La B4
Stephenson St C4
Steward St B2
Stirling Rd C1
Stour St B2
Suffolk St C3
Summer Hill Rd B2
Summer Hill St B2
Summer Hill Terr B2
Summer La A4
Summer Row B3
Summerfield Cr B1
Summerfield Park B1
Sutton St C3
Swallow St C3
Sydney Rd C6
Symphony Hall C3
Talbot St A1
Temple Row C4
Temple St C4
Templefield St C6
Tenby St B3
Tenby St North B2
Tennant St C2/C3
Thimble Mill La A6
Thinktank (Science & Discovery) B5
Thomas St A4
Thorpe St C4
Tilton Rd C6
Tower St A4
Town Hall C3
Trent St C5
Turner's Buildings A1
Unett St A3
Union Terr B5
Upper Trinity St C5
Uxbridge St A3
Vauxhall Gr B5
Vauxhall Rd B5
Vernon Rd C1
Vesey St B4
Viaduct St B5
Victoria Sq C3
Villa St A3
Vittoria St B3
Vyse St B3
Walter St A6
Wardlow Rd A5
Warstone La B2
Washington St C3
Water St B3
Waterworks Rd C1
Watery La C5
Well St A3
Western Rd B1
Wharf St A2
Wheeler St A3
Whitehouse St A5
Whitmore St A2
Whittall St B4
Wholesale Market C4
Wiggin St B1
Willes Rd A1
Windsor Ind Est A5
Windsor St A5
Windsor St B5
Winson Green Rd A1
Witton St C6
Wolseley St C6
Woodcock St B5

Blackpool 175
Abingdon St A1
Addison Cr A3
Adelaide St B1
Albert Rd B2
Alfred St B2
Ascot Rd A3
Ashton Rd C2
Auburn Gr C3
Bank Hey St B1
Banks St A1
Beech Ave A3
Bela Gr C2
Belmont Ave B2
Birley St A1
Blackpool & Fleetwood Tram B1
Blackpool & The Fylde College B2
Blackpool FC C2
Blackpool North A2
Blackpool Tower ✦ B1
Blundell St C1
Bonny St B1
Breck Rd B3
Bryan Rd A3
Buchanan St A2
Bus Station A2
Cambridge Rd A3
Caunce St A2/A3
Central Dr B1/C2
Central Pier ✦ C1
Central Pier C1
Central Pier Theatre C1
Chapel St C1
Charles St A2
Charnley Rd B2
Church St A1/A2
Clinton Ave B2
Coach Station A2/C1
Cocker St A1
Cocker St A1
Coleridge Rd A3
Collingwood Ave A3
Comedy Carpet ✦ B1
Condor Gr C3
Cookson St A2
Coronation St B1
Corporation St A1
Courts B1
Cumberland Ave B3
Cunliffe Rd C3
Dale St C1
Devonshire Rd A3
Devonshire Sq A3
Dickson Rd A1
Elizabeth St A2
Ferguson Rd C3
Forest Gate B3
Foxhall Rd C1
Foxhall Sq C1
Freckleton St C2
George St A2
Gloucester Ave B3
Golden Mile, The C1
Gorse Rd B3
Gorton St A2
Grand Theatre, The B1
Granville Rd A2
Grasmere Rd C2
Grosvenor St A2
Grundy Art Gallery A1
Harvey Rd B3
Hornby Rd B2
Houndshill Sh Ctr B1
Hull Rd B1
Ibbison Ct C2
Information Ctr A1
Kent Rd C2
Keswick Rd C2
King St A2
Knox Gr C3
Laycock Gate A3
Layton Rd A3
Leamington Rd B2
Leeds Rd B3
Leicester Rd B2
Levens Gr C2
Library A1
Lifeboat Station B1
Lincoln Rd B2
Liverpool Rd B3
Livingstone Rd B2
London Rd A3
Lune Gr C2
Lytham Rd C1
Madame Tussaud's Blackpool B1
Manchester Sq C1
Manor Rd B3
Maple Ave B3
Market St A1
Marlboro Rd B3
Mere Rd B3
Milbourne St A2
Newcastle Ave B3
Newton Dr A3
North Pier ✦ A1
North Pier A1
North Pier Theatre A1
Odeon C2
Olive Gr B3
Palatine Rd B2
Park Rd B2/C3
Peter St A2
Police Station B1
Post Office A1/A3/B1/B2/B3
Princess Parade A1
Princess St C1/C2
Promenade A1/C1
Queen St A1
Queen Victoria Rd C2
Raikes Pde B2
Reads Ave B2
Regent Rd B2
Register Office B2
Ribble Rd B2
Rigby Rd C1/C2
Ripon Rd B3
St Albans Rd B3
St Ives Ave C3
St John's Square A1
St Vincent Ave C3
Salisbury Rd B3
Salthouse Ave C2
Salvation Army Ctr A2
Sands Way C2
Sealife Centre B1
Seasiders Way C1
Selbourne Rd A2
Sharrow Gr C3
Somerset Ave C3
South King St B2
Springfield Rd A1
Sutton Pl B2
Talbot Rd A1/A2
Thornber Gr C2
Topping St A1
Tower B1
Town Hall A1
Tram Depot C1
Tyldesley Rd C1
Vance Rd B1
Victoria St B1
Victory Rd A2
Wayman Rd A3
Westmorland Ave C2/C3
Whitegate Dr B3
Winter Gardens Theatre B1
Woodland Gr B3
Woolman Rd B2

Bournemouth 176
Ascham Rd A3
Avenue Rd B1
Ave Shopping Centre B1
Bath Rd C2
Beach Office C2
Beacon Rd C1
Beechey Rd A3
Bodorgan Rd B1
Bourne Ave B1
Bournemouth A3
Bournemouth & Poole College B3
Bournemouth Balloon ✦ C2
Bournemouth Int Ctr C1
Bournemouth Pier C2
Bournemouth Sta A3
Bradley Rd B1
Cavendish Place A2
Cavendish Rd A2
Central Drive A1
Central Gdns B1
Christchurch Rd B3
Cliff Lift C1/C3
Coach House Pl A3
Coach Station A3
Commercial Rd B1
Cotlands Rd B3
Courts B3
Cranborne Rd C1
Cricket Ground A2
Cumnor Rd B2
Dean Park A2
Dean Park Cr B2
Dean Park Rd A2
Durrant Rd B1
East Overcliff Dr C3
Exeter Cr C1
Exeter La C2
Exeter Rd C1
Gervis Place B1
Gervis Rd B3
Glen Fern Rd B2
Golf Club B1
Grove Rd B3
Hinton Rd C2
Holdenhurst Rd B3
Horseshoe Common B2
Information Ctr B2
Lansdowne B3
Lansdowne Rd A2
Lorne Park Rd B2
Lower Gdns B1/C2
Madeira Rd B2
Methuen Rd A3
Meyrick Park A1
Meyrick Rd B3
Milton Rd A2
Nuffield Health Bournemouth Hospital (private) A2
Oceanarium C2
Odeon Cinema C2
Old Christchurch Rd B2
Ophir Rd A3
Oxford Rd B3
Park Rd A3
Parsonage Rd B2
Pavilion C2
Pier Approach C2
Pier Theatre C2
Police Station A3/B3
Portchester Rd A3
Post Office B1/B3
Priory Rd C1
Quadrant, The B2
Recreation Ground A1
Richmond Gardens Shopping Centre B2
Richmond Hill Rd B1
Russell Cotes Art Gallery & Mus C2
Russell Cotes Rd C2
St Anthony's Rd A1
St Michael's Rd C1
St Paul's A3
St Paul's La B3
St Paul's Rd A3
St Peter's B2
St Peter's B2
St Peter's Rd B2
St Stephen's Rd B1/B2
St Swithun's B3
St Swithun's Rd B3
St Swithun's Rd South B3
St Valerie Rd A2
St Winifred's Rd A2
Square, The B1
Stafford Rd B3
Terrace Rd B1
Town Hall B1
Tregonwell Rd C1
Triangle, The B1
Trinity Rd B2
Undercliff Drive C3
Upper Hinton Rd B2
Upper Terr Rd C1
Wellington Rd A2/A3
Wessex Way A3/B1/B2
West Cliff Prom C1
West Hill Rd C1
West Undercliff Promenade C1
Westover Rd B2
Wimborne Rd A2
Wootton Mount B2
Wychwood Dr A1
Yelverton Rd B2
York Rd B3
Zig-Zag Walks C1/C3

Bradford 176
Alhambra B2
Back Ashgrove B1
Barkerend Rd A3
Barnard Rd C3
Barry St B2
Bolling Rd C3
Bolton Rd A3
Bowland St A1
Bradford 1 B2
Bradford College B1
Bradford Forster Square A2
Bradford Interchange B3
Bradford Playhouse B3
Bridge St B2
Britannia St B2
Broadway, The B2
Burnett St B3
Bus Station B2
Butler St West A3
Caledonia St C2
Canal Rd A2
Carlton St B1
Cathedral † A3
Centenary Sq B2
Chapel St B3
Cheapside A2
Church Bank B3
Cineworld B3
City Hall B2
City Rd A1
Claremont B1
Colour Museum B1
Croft St B2
Crown Court B3
Darfield St A1
Darley St A2
Drewton Rd A1
Drummond Trading Estate A1
Dryden St B3
Dyson St A1
Easby Rd C1
East Parade B3
Eldon Pl A1
Filey St B3
Forster Sq Ret Pk A2
Gallery II B1
Garnett St B3
Godwin St B2
Gracechurch St A1
Grattan Rd B1
Great Horton Rd B1/B2
Grove Terr B1
Hall Ings B2
Hall La C3
Hallfield Rd A1
Hammstrasse A2
Harris St B3
Holdsworth St A2
Ice Rink ✦ B2
Impressions B2
Information Ctr B2
Inland Revenue A2
Ivegate B2
Jacob's Well Municipal Offices B2
James St A2
John St A2
Kirkgate B2
Kirkgate Centre B2
Laisteridge La C1
Leeds Rd B3
Leisure Exchange, The B3
Library B1/B2
Listerhills Rd B1
Little Horton Gn C1
Little Horton La C1
Longside La B1
Lower Kirkgate B2
Lumb La A1
Magistrates Court B2
Manchester Rd C2
Manningham La A1
Manor Row A2
Market C3
Market St B2
Melbourne Place C1
Midland Rd A2
Mill La C2
Morley St B1
National Media B2
Nelson St B2/C2
Nesfield St A2
New Otley Rd A3
Norcroft St B1
North Parade A2
North St A3
North Wing A3
Oastler Shopping Ctr A2
Otley Rd A3
Park Ave C1
Park La C1
Park Rd C2
Parma St C2
Peace Museum B2
Peckover St B3
Piccadilly A2
Police Station B2/C2
Post Office A2/B1/B2/C3
Princes Way B2
Prospect St C3
Radwell Drive C2
Rawson Rd A1
Rebecca St A1
Richmond Rd B1
Russell St C1
St George's Hall B2
St Lukes Hospital C1
St Mary's A3
Shipley Airedale Rd A3/B3
Simes St A1
Smith St B1
Spring Mill St C2
Stott Hill A3
Sunbridge Rd A1/B1/B2
Theatre in the Mill B1
Thornton Rd A1/B1
Trafalgar St A2
Trinity Rd C1
Tumbling Hill St B1
Tyrrel St B2
Univ of Bradford B1/C1
Usher St C3
Valley Rd A2
Vicar La B3
Wakefield Rd C3
Wapping Rd A3
Well St B3
Westgate A1
White Abbey Rd A1
Wigan Rd A1
Wilton St B1
Wood St A1
Wool Exchange B2
Worthington St A1

Brighton 177
Addison Rd A1
Albert Rd B2
Albion Hill B3
Albion St B3
Ann St A3
Baker St A3
Black Lion St C2
Brighton A2
Brighton Centre C2
Brighton Fishing Museum C2
Brighton Pier (Palace Pier) ✦ C3
Brighton Wheel ✦ C3
Broad St C3
Buckingham Pl A2
Buckingham Rd B2
Cannon Pl C1
Carlton Hill B3
Chatham Pl A1
Cheapside A3
Church St B2
Churchill Sq Sh Ctr B2
Clifton Hill B1
Clifton Pl B1

Clifton Rd B1
Clifton St A2
Clifton Terr B1
Clock Tower B2
Clyde Rd A3
Coach Park C3
Coach Station C3
Compton Ave A2
Davigdor Rd A1
Denmark Terr B1
Ditchling Rd A3
Dome 🏛 B2
Duke St B2
Duke's La C2
Dyke Rd A1/B2
East St C2
Edward St B3
Elmore Rd B3
Fleet St A2
Frederick St B2
Gardner St B2
Gloucester Pl B3
Gloucester Rd B2
Goldsmid Rd A1
Grand Junction Rd C2
Grand Pde B3
Grove Hill B3
Guildford St A2
Hampton Pl B1
Hanover Terr A3
High St C3
Highdown Rd A1
i360 Tower ✦ C1
Information Ctr ℹ C2
John St B3
Kemp St B2
Kensington Pl B2
Kings Rd C1
Lanes, The C2
Law Courts B3
Lewes Rd A3
Library B2
London Rd A3
Madeira Dr C3
Marine Pde C3
Middle St C2
Montpelier Pl B1
Montpelier Rd B1
Montpelier St B1
Mus & Art Gallery 🏛 B3
New England Rd A2
New England St A2
New Rd B2
Nizells Ave A1
Norfolk Rd B1
Norfolk Terr B1
North Rd B2
North St B2
Odeon 🎦 C2
Old Shoreham Rd A1
Old Steine C3
Osmond Rd A1
Over St B2
Oxford St A3
Park Crescent Terr A3
Phoenix Brighton 🏛 B3
Phoenix Rise A3
Police Station 🚓 B3
Post Office ✉ A1/A3/B2/C3
Preston Rd A2
Preston St B1
Prestonville Rd A1
Queen's Rd B2
Queen's Sq B2
Regency Sq C1
Regent St B2
Richmond Pl B3
Richmond St B3
Richmond Terr A3
Rose Hill Terr A3
Royal Alexandra Hospital Ⓗ B1
Royal Pavilion 🏛 B2
St Bartholomew's ⛪ A3
St James's St C3
St Nicholas Rd B2
St Nicholas' ⛪ B2
St Peter's ⛪ A3
Sea Life Centre 🐟 C3
Shaftesbury Rd A3
Ship St C2
Sillwood Rd B1
Sillwood St B1
Southover St A3
Spring Gdns B2
Stanford Rd A1
Stanley Rd A3
Surrey St B2
Sussex St B3
Swimming Pool B3
Sydney St B3
Temple Gdns B1
Terminus Rd A2
Theatre Royal 🎭 B2
Tidy St B2
Town Hall C2
Toy & Model Mus 🏛 A2
Trafalgar St B2
Union Rd A3
Univ of Brighton B3
Upper Lewes Rd A3
Upper North St B1
Viaduct Rd A3
Victoria Gdns B3
Victoria Rd B1
Volk's Electric Railway ✦ C3
West Pier (derelict) C1
West St C2
Western Rd B1
Whitecross St B2
York Ave B1
York Pl B3
York Rd B1

Bristol 177

Acramans Rd C4
Albert Rd C6
Alfred Hill A4
All Saint's St A4
All Saints' ⛪ B4
Allington Rd C3
Alpha Rd C4
Ambra Vale B1
Ambra Vale East B2
Ambrose Rd B2
Amphitheatre & Waterfront Sq ✦ C4
Anchor Rd B3
Anvil St B6
Arcade, The A5
Architecture Centre, The ✦ B4
Argyle Pl B2
Arlington Villas A2
Arnolfini Arts Centre, The ✦ B4
Art Gallery 🏛 A3
Ashton Gate Rd C2
Ashton Rd C1
At-Bristol ✦ B3
Avon Bridge C1
Avon Cr C1
Avon St B6
Baldwin St B4
Baltic Wharf C2
Baltic Wharf L Ctr & Caravan Pk ✦ C2
Baltic Wharf Marina C2
Barossa Pl C4
Barton Manor B6
Barton Rd B6
Barton Vale B6
Bath Rd C6
Bathurst Basin C4
Bathurst Parade C4
Beauley Rd C3
Bedminster Bridge C5
Bedminster Parade C4
Bellevue B2
Bellevue Cr B2
Bellevue Rd C6
Berkeley Pl A2
Berkeley Sq A3
Birch Rd C2
Blackfriars A4
Bond St A5
Braggs La A6
Brandon Hill B3
Brandon Steep B3
Bristol Bridge B5
Bristol Cath (CE) ✝ B3
Bristol Eye Hospital (A&E) A4
Bristol Grammar School A3
Bristol Harbour Railway 🚂 C3
Bristol Royal Children's Hospital Ⓗ A4
Bristol Royal Infirmary (A&E) Ⓗ A4
Bristol Temple Meads Station ⇌ B6
Broad Plain B6
Broad Quay B4
Broad St A4
Broad Weir A5
Broadcasting House A3
Broadmead A5
Brunel Way C1
Brunswick Sq A5
Burton Cl C5
Bus Station A4
Butts Rd B3
Cabot Circus A5
Cabot Tower ✦ B3
Caledonia Pl B1
Callowhill Ct A5
Cambridge St C6
Camden Rd C3
Camp Rd A1
Canada Way C2
Cannon St A4
Canon's Way B3
Cantock's Cl A3
Canynge Rd A1
Canynge Sq A1
Castle Park A5
Castle St A5
Cathedral Walk B3
Catherine Meade St C4
Cattle Market Rd C6
Central Library B3
Charles Pl B1
Charlotte St B3
Charlotte St South B3
Chatterton House 🏛 B5
Chatterton Sq C5
Chatterton St C5
Cheese La B5
Christchurch ⛪ A4
Christchurch Rd A1
Christmas Steps ✦ A4
Church La B2/B5
Church St B5
City Museum 🏛 A3
City of Bristol College B3
Clare St B4
Clarence Rd C5
Cliff Rd C1
Clift House Rd C1
Clifton Cathedral (RC) ✝ A2
Clifton Down A1
Clifton Down Rd A1
Clifton Hill B2
Clifton Park A1/A2
Clifton Park Rd A1
Clifton Rd A2
Clifton Vale B1
Cliftonwood Cr B2
Cliftonwood Rd B2
Cliftonwood Terr B2
Cobblestone Mews A1
College Green B3
College Rd A1
College St B3
Colston Almshouses 🏛 A4
Colston Ave B4
Colston Hall 🎭 B4
Colston Parade C5
Colston St A4
Commercial Rd C4
Constitution Hill B2
Cooperage La C2
Corn St B4
Cornwallis Ave B1
Cornwallis Cr B1
Coronation Rd C2/C4
Council House 🏛 B3
Counterslip B5
Courts A4
Create Centre, The ✦ C1
Crosby Row B2
Culver St B3
Cumberland Basin C1
Cumberland Cl C2
Cumberland Rd C2/C3
Dean La C4
Deanery Rd B3
Denmark St B4
Dowry Sq B1
Eaton Cr A2
Elmdale Rd A3
Elton Rd A3
Eugene St A4/A6
Exchange, The and St Nicholas' Mkts 🏛 B4
Fairfax St A4
Fire Station B5
Floating Harbour C3
Fosseway, The A2
Foster Almshouses 🏛 A4
Frayne Rd C1
Frederick Pl A2
Freeland Pl B1
Frogmore St B3
Fry's Hill B2
Gas La B6
Gasferry Rd C3
General Hospital Ⓗ C4
Georgian House 🏛 B3
Glendale B1
Glentworth Rd B2
Gloucester St A1
Goldney Hall B2
Goldney Rd B1
Gordon Rd A2
Granby Hill B1
Grange Rd A1
Great Ann St A6
Great George Rd B3
Great George St A6/B3
Green St North B1
Green St South B1
Greenay Bush La C2
Greenbank Rd C2
Greville Smyth Park C1
Grove, The B4
Guildhall 🏛 A4
Guinea St C4
Hamilton Rd C3
Hanbury Rd A2
Hanover Pl C2
Harley Pl A1
Haymarket A5
Hensman's Hill B1
High St B4
Highbury Villas A3
Hill St B3
Hill St C6
Hippodrome 🎭 B4
Hopechapel Hill B1
Horfield Rd A4
Horsefair, The A5
Horton St B6
Host St A4
Hotwell Rd B1/B2
Houlton St A6
Howard Rd C3
IMAX Cinema 🎦 B4
Information Ctr ℹ B4
Islington Rd C3
Jacob St A5/A6
Jacob's Wells Rd B2
John Carr's Terr B2
John Wesley's Chapel ⛪ A5
Joy Hill B1
Jubilee St B6
Kensington Pl A2
Kilkenny St B6
King St B4
Kingsland Rd B6
Kingston Rd C3
Lamb St A6
Lansdown Rd A2
Lawford St A6
Lawfords Gate A6
Leighton Rd C3
Lewins Mead A4
Lime Rd C2
Litfield Rd A1
Little Ann St A6
Little Caroline Pl B1
Little George St A6
Little King St B4
Llandoger Trow 🏛 B4
Lloyds' Building, The C3
Lodge St A4
Lord Mayor's Chapel, The ⛪ B4
Lower Castle St A5
Lower Church La A4
Lower Clifton Hill B2
Lower Guinea St C4
Lower Lamb St B3
Lower Maudlin St A4
Lower Park Rd A4
Lower Sidney St C2
Lucky La C4
Lydstep Terr C3
M Shed 🏛 C4
Mall (Galleries Shopping Ctr), The A5
Mall, The A1
Manilla Rd A1
Mardyke Ferry Rd C2
Maritime Heritage Centre 🏛 B3
Marlborough Hill A4
Marlborough St A4
Marsh St B4
Mead St C5
Merchant Dock B2
Merchant Seamen's Almshouses 🏛 B4
Merchant St A5
Merchants Rd A1
Merchants Rd C1
Meridian Pl A2
Meridian Vale A2
Merrywood Rd C3
Midland Rd A6
Milford St C3
Millennium Prom B3
Millennium Sq B3
Mitchell La B5
Mortimer Rd A1
Murray Rd C4
Myrtle Rd A3
Narrow Plain B5
Narrow Quay B4
Nelson St A4
New Charlotte St C4
New Kingsley Rd B6
New Queen St C5
New St A6
Newgate A5
Newton St A6
Norland Rd A1
North St C2
O2 Academy B3
Oakfield Gr A2
Oakfield Pl A2
Oakfield Rd A2
Old Bread St B6
Old Market St A6
Old Park Hill A4
Oldfield Rd B1
Orchard Ave B4
Orchard La B4
Orchard St B4
Osbourne Rd C3
Oxford St B6
Park Pl A2
Park Rd C3
Park Row A3
Park St A3
Passage St B5
Pembroke Gr A2
Pembroke Rd A2
Pembroke Rd C3
Pembroke St A5
Penn St A5
Pennywell Rd A6
Percival Rd A1
Pero's Bridge B4
Perry Rd A4
Pip & Jay ⛪ A5
Plimsoll Bridge B1
Police Sta 🚓 A4/A6
Polygon Rd B1
Portland St A1
Portwall La B5
Post Office ✉ A1/A3/A5/B1/B4/C4/C5
Prewett St C5
Prince St B4
Prince St Bridge C4
Princess St C5
Princess Victoria St B1
Priory Rd A3
Pump La C5
QEH Theatre 🎭 A2
Quakers Friars A5
Quay St A4
Queen Charlotte St B4
Queen Elizabeth Hospital School B2
Queen Sq B4
Queen St A5
Queen's Ave A3
Queen's Parade B3
Queen's Rd A2/A3
Raleigh Rd C2
Randall Rd B2
Red Lodge 🏛 A4
Redcliffe Backs B5
Redcliffe Bridge B4
Redcliffe Hill C5
Redcliffe Parade C4
Redcliffe St B5
Redcliffe Way B5
Redcross St A6
Redgrave Theatre 🎭 A1
Regent St B1
Richmond Hill A2
Richmond Hill Ave A2
Richmond La A2
Richmond Park Rd A2
Richmond St C6
Richmond Terr A2
River St A6
Rownham Mead B2
Royal Fort Rd A3
Royal Park A2
Royal West of England Academy 🏛 A3
Royal York Cr B1
Royal York Villas B1
Rupert St A4
Russ St B6
St Andrew's Walk B2
St George's 🎭 B3
St George's Rd B3
St James ⛪ A4
St John's ⛪ A4
St John's Rd C4
St Luke's Rd C5
St Mary Redcliffe ⛪ C5
St Mary's Hospital Ⓗ A3
St Matthias Park A6
St Michael's Hill A3
St Michael's Hospl Ⓗ A4
St Michael's Park A3
St Nicholas St B4
St Paul St A5
St Paul's Rd A2
St Peter's (ruin) ⛪ A5
St Philip's Bridge B5
St Philips Rd A6
St Stephen's ⛪ B4
St Stephen's St B4
St Thomas St B5
St Thomas the Martyr ⛪ B5
Sandford Rd B1
Sargent St C5
Saville Pl B1
Ship La C5
Showcase Cinema de Lux 🎦 A5
Silver St A4
Sion Hill A1
Small St A4
Smeaton Rd C1
Somerset Sq C5
Somerset St C5
Southernhay Ave B2
Southville Rd C4
Spike Island Artspace 🏛 C2
Spring St C5
SS Great Britain and The Matthew ⛵ B2
Stackpool Rd C3
Staight St B6
Stillhouse La C4
Stracey Rd C2
Sydney Row C2
Tankard's Cl A3
Temple Back B5
Temple Back East B5
Temple Bridge B5
Temple Church ⛪ B5
Temple Circus B5
Temple Gate C5
Temple St B5
Temple Way B5
Terrell St A4
Theatre Royal (Bristol Old Vic) 🎭 B4
Thekla ⛵ B4
Thomas La B5
Three Kings of Cologne ⛪ A4
Three Queens La B5
Tobacco Factory, The 🎭 C2
Tower Hill B5
Tower La A4
Trenchard St A4
Triangle South A3
Triangle West A3
Trinity Rd A6
Trinity St A6
Tyndall Ave A3
Union St A5
Union St B6
Unity St A6
Unity St B3
University of Bristol A3
University Rd A3
Upper Byron Pl A3
Upper Maudlin St A4
Upper Perry Hill C3
Upton Rd C2
Valentine Bridge B6
Victoria Gr C5
Victoria Rd C6
Victoria Rooms 🏛 A2
Victoria Sq A2
Victoria St B5
Vyvyan Rd A1
Vyvyan Terr A1
Wade St A6
Walter St C2
Wapping Rd C4
Water La B5
Waterloo Rd A6
Waterloo St A1
Waterloo St A6
Watershed Media Centre ✦ B4
Welling Terr B1
Welsh Back B4
West Mall A1
West St A6
Westfield Pl A1
Wetherell Pl A2
Whitehouse Pl C5
Whitehouse St C5
Whiteladies Rd A2
Whitson St A4
William St C5
Willway St C5
Windsor Pl B1
Wine St A4
Woodland Rd A3
Woodland Rise A3
Worcester Rd A1
Worcester Terr A1
YHA ▲ B4
York Gdns B1
York Pl A2
York Rd C5

Cambridge 177

Abbey Rd A3
ADC 🎭 A2
Anglia Ruskin Univ B3
Archaeology & Anthropology 🏛 B2
Art Gallery 🏛 A1
Arts Picture House 🎦 B2
Arts Theatre 🎭 B1
Auckland Rd A3
Backs, The B1
Bateman St C2
BBC C3
Benet St B1
Bradmore St B3
Bridge St A1
Broad St B3
Brookside C2
Brunswick Terr A3
Burleigh St B3
Bus Station B2
Butt Green A2
Cambridge Contemporary Art Gallery 🏛 B1
Castle Mound 🏰 A1
Castle St A1
Cemetery B3
Chesterton La A1
Christ's (Coll) B2
Christ's Lane B2
Christ's Pieces B2
City Rd B3
Clare (Coll) B1
Clarendon St B2
Coe Fen C2
Coronation St C2
Corpus Christi (Coll) B1
Council Offices C3
Cross St C3
Crusoe Bridge C1
Darwin (Coll) C1
Devonshire Rd C3
Downing (Coll) C2
Downing St B2
Earl St B2
East Rd B3
Eden St B3
Elizabeth Way A3
Elm St B2
Emery St B3
Emmanuel (Coll) B2
Emmanuel Rd B2
Emmanuel St B2
Fair St A3
Fen Causeway, The C1
Fenners Physical Education Centre C3
Fire Station B3
Fitzroy St A3
Fitzwilliam Mus 🏛 C2
Fitzwilliam St C2
Folk Museum 🏛 A1
Glisson Rd C3
Gonville & Caius (Coll) B1
Gonville Place C2
Grafton Centre A3
Grand Arcade B2
Green St B1
Gresham Rd C3
Guest Rd B3
Guildhall 🏛 B2
Harvey Rd C3
Hills Rd C3
Hobson St B2
Hughes Hall (Coll) B3
Information Ctr ℹ B2
James St A3
Jesus (Coll) A2
Jesus Green A2
Jesus La A2
Jesus Terr B3
John St B3
Kelsey Kerridge Sports Centre B3
King St A2
King's (Coll) B1
King's Coll Chapel ⛪ B1
King's Parade B1
Lammas Land Rec Gd C1
Lensfield Rd C2
Library B2
Lion Yard B2
Little St Mary's La B1
Lyndewod Rd C3
Magdalene (Coll) A1
Magdalene St A1
Maid's Causeway A3
Malcolm St A2
Market Hill B1
Market St B1
Mathematical Bridge B1
Mawson Rd C3
Midsummer Common A3
Mill La B1
Mill Rd B3
Mill St C3
Mumford 🎭 B3
Napier St A3
New Square A2
Newmarket Rd A3
Newnham Rd C1
Norfolk St B3
Northampton St A1
Norwich St C2
Orchard St B2
Panton St C2
Paradise Nature Reserve C1
Paradise St B3
Park Parade A1
Park St A2
Park Terr B2
Parker St B2
Parker's Piece B2
Parkside B3
Parkside Pools B3
Parsonage St A3
Pemberton Terr C2
Pembroke (Coll) B2
Pembroke St B1
Perowne St B3
Peterhouse (Coll) C1
Petty Cury B2
Police Station 🚓 B3
Post Office ✉ A1/A3/B2/B3/C1/C2/C3
Queen's La B1
Queen's Rd B1
Queens' (Coll) B1
Regent St B2
Regent Terr B2
Ridley Hall (Coll) C1
Riverside A3
Round Church, The ⛪ A1
Russell St C2
St Andrew's St B2
St Benet's ⛪ B1
St Catharine's (Coll) B1
St Eligius St C2
St John's (Coll) A1
St Mary's ⛪ B1
St Paul's Rd C3
Saxon St C2
Scott Polar Institute & Museum 🏛 C2
Sedgwick Museum 🏛 B2
Sheep's Green C1
Shire Hall A1
Sidgwick Ave C1
Sidney St A2
Sidney Sussex (Coll) A2
Silver St B1
Station Rd C3
Tenison Ave C3
Tenison Rd C3
Tennis Court Rd B2
Thompson's La A1
Trinity (Coll) A1
Trinity Hall (Coll) B1
Trinity St B1
Trumpington Rd C2
Trumpington St B1
Union Rd C2
University Botanic Gardens ✿ C2
Victoria Ave A2
Victoria St B2
Warkworth St B3
Warkworth Terr B3
Wesley House (Coll) A2
West Rd B1
Westcott Ho (Coll) A2
Westminster (Coll) A1
Whipple 🏛 A2
Willis Rd B3
Willow Walk A2

Canterbury 178

Artillery St B2
Barton Mill Rd A3
Beaconsfield Rd A1
Beaney, The 🏛 B2
Beverley Rd A1
Bingley's Island B1
Black Griffin La B1
Broad Oak Rd A2
Broad St B2
Brymore Rd A3
Burgate B2
Bus Station C2
Canterbury College C3
Canterbury East ⇌ C1
Canterbury Tales, The ✦ B2
Canterbury West ⇌ A1
Castle 🏰 C1
Castle Row C1
Castle St C1
Cathedral ✝ B2
Causeway, The A2
Chaucer Rd A3
Christ Church Univ B3
Christchurch Gate ✦ B2
City Council Offices A3
City Wall B2
Coach Park A2
College Rd B3
Cossington Rd C2
Court B2
Craddock Rd A3
Crown & County Courts B3
Dane John Gdns C2
Dane John Mound ✦ C1
Deanery B2
Dover St C2
Duck La B2
Eastbridge Hospl 🏛 B1
Edgar Rd B3
Ersham Rd C3
Ethelbert Rd C3
Fire Station C2
Forty Acres Rd A1
Friars, The B2
Gordon Rd C1
Greyfriars ✦ B1
Guildford Rd C1
Havelock St B2
Heaton Rd C1
High St B2
HM Prison B3
Information Ctr ℹ A2/B2
Ivy La B2
Ivy Pl C1
King St B2
King's School B2/B3
King's School Leisure Facilities A2
Kingsmead L Ctr A2
Kingsmead Rd A2
Kirby's La B1
Lansdown Rd C2
Lime Kiln Rd C1
Longport B3
Lower Chantry La C3
Mandeville Rd A1
Market Way A2
Marlowe Arcade B2
Marlowe Ave C2
Marlowe Theatre 🎭 B2
Martyrs Field Rd C1
Mead Way B1
Military Rd B2
Monastery St B2
Museum of Canterbury (Rupert Bear Museum) 🏛 B1
New Dover Rd C3
Norman Rd C2
North Holmes Rd B3
North La B1
Northgate A2
Nunnery Fields C2
Nunnery Rd C2
Oaten Hill C2
Odeon Cinema 🎦 C2
Old Dover Rd C2
Old Palace B2
Old Ruttington La B2
Old Weavers 🏛 B2
Orchard St B1
Oxford Rd C1
Palace St B2
Pilgrims Way C3
Pin Hill C1
Pine Tree Ave A1
Police Station 🚓 C2
Post Office ✉ B2/C1/C2
Pound La B1
Puckle La C2
Raymond Ave C2
Registry Office A2
Rheims Way B1
Rhodaus Cl C2
Rhodaus Town C2
Roman Museum 🏛 B2
Roper Gateway A1
Roper Rd A1
Rose La B2
St Augustine's Abbey (remains) ✝ B3
St Augustine's Rd C3
St Dunstan's ⛪ A1
St Dunstan's St A1
St George's Pl C2
St George's St B2
St George's Tower ✦ B2
St Gregory's Rd B3
St John's Hospital 🏛 A2
St Margaret's St B2
St Martin's ⛪ B3
St Martin's Ave B3
St Martin's Rd B3
St Michael's Rd A1
St Mildred's ⛪ C1
St Peter's Gr B1
St Peter's La B2
St Peter's Pl B1
St Peter's St B1
St Radigunds St B2
St Stephen's Ct A1
St Stephen's Path A1
St Stephen's Rd A2
Salisbury Rd A1
Simmonds Rd C1
Spring La C3
Station Rd West B1
Stour St B1
Sturry Rd A3
Tourtel Rd A3
Tudor Rd C1
Union St B2
University for the Creative Arts C3
Vernon Pl C2
Victoria Rd C1
Watling St B2
Westgate Gdns B1
Westgate Towers 🏛 B1
Whitefriars B2
Whitehall Gdns B1
Whitehall Rd B1
Wincheap C1
York Rd C1
Zealand Rd C2

Cardiff Caerdydd 178

Adam St B3
Alexandra Gdns A2
Allerton St C1
Arran St A3
ATRiuM (Univ of Glamorgan) C3
Beauchamp St C1
Bedford St A3
Blackfriars Priory (rems) ✝ B1
Boulevard De Nantes B2
Brains Brewery C2
Brook St B1
Bus Station C2
Bute Park B1
Bute St C2
Bute Terr C3
Callaghan Sq C2/C3
Capitol Sh Ctr, The B3
Cardiff Arms Park (Cardiff RFC) B1
Cardiff Bridge B1
Cardiff Castle 🏰 B2
Cardiff Central ⇌ C2
Cardiff Centre Trading Estate C3
Cardiff Story, The 🏛 B2
Cardiff Univ A1/A2/B3
Cardiff University Student's Union A2
Caroline St C2
Castle Green B2
Castle Mews A1
Castle St (Heol y Castell) B1
Cathays Station ⇌ A2
Celerity Drive C3
Central Library C2
Central Sq C2
Charles St (Heol Siarl) B3
Churchill Way B3
City Hall 🏛 A2
City Rd A3
Clare Rd C1
Clare St C1
Coburn St A3
Coldstream Terr B1
College Rd A1
Colum Rd A1
Court C2
Court Rd C1
Craiglee Drive C3
Cranbrook St A3
Customhouse St C2
Cyfartha St A3
Despenser Place C1
Despenser St C1
Dinas St C1
Duke St (Heol y Dug) B2
Dumfries Place B3
East Grove A3
Ellen St C3
Fire Station B3
Fitzalan Place B3
Fitzhamon Emb C1
Fitzhamon La C1
Friary, The B2
g39 🏛 B2
Gloucester St C1
Glynrhondda St A2
Gordon Rd A3
Gorsedd Gdns B2
Green St B1
Greyfriars Rd B2
Hafod St C1
Hayes, The B2
Herbert St C3
High St B2
HM Prison B3
Industrial Estate C3
John St C3
Jubilee St C1
King Edward VII Ave A1
Kingsway (Ffordd y Brenin) B2
Knox Rd B3
Law Courts B2
Llanbleddian Gdns A2
Llantwit St A2
Lloyd George Ave C3
Lower Cathedral Rd B1
Lowther Rd A3
Magistrates Court B3
Mansion House A3
Mardy St C1
Mark St B1
Market B2
Mary Ann St C3
Merches Gdns C1
Mill La C2
Millennium Bridge B1
Miskin St A2
Monmouth St C1
Motorpoint Arena Cardiff ✦ C3
Museum Ave A2
Museum Place A2
National Museum of Wales 🏛 A2
National War Memorial ✦ A2
Neville Place C1
New Theatre 🎭 B2
Newport Rd B3
Northcote La A3
Northcote St A3
Parade, The A3
Park Grove A4
Park Place A2
Park St C2
Penarth Rd C2
Pendyris St C1
Plantaganet St C1
Principality Plaza Leisure Complex 🎦 C1
Principality Stadium C1
Principality Stadium Tours (Gate 3) ✦ B2
Quay St B2
Queen Anne Sq A1
Queen St (Heol y Frenhines) B2
Queen St Station ⇌ B3
Regimental Museums 🏛 B2
Rhymney St A3
Richmond Rd A3
Royal Welsh College of Music and Drama A1
Russell St A3
Ruthin Gdns A2
St Andrews Place A2
St David's ✝ B2
St David's 2 C2
St David's Centre B2
St David's Hall ✦ B2
St John The Baptist ⛪ B2
St Mary St (Heol Eglwys Fair) B2
St Peter's St A3
Salisbury Rd A3
Sandon St B3
Schooner Way C3
Scott Rd C2
Scott St C2
Senghennydd Rd A2
Sherman Theatre 🎭 A2
Sophia Gardens A1
South Wales Baptist College A3
Stafford Rd C1
Station Terr B3
Stuttgarter Strasse B2
Sussex St C1
Taffs Mead Emb C1
Talworth St A3
Temple of Peace & Health ✦ A1
Treharris St A3
Trinity St B2
Tudor La C1
Tudor St C1
Walk, The A3
Welsh Assembly Offices A1
Welsh Inst of Sport ✦ A1
West Grove A3
Westgate St (Heol y Porth) B2
Windsor Place B3
Womanby St B2
Wood St C2
Working St B2
Wyeverne Rd A2

Cheltenham 178

Albert Rd A3
Albion St B3
All Saints Rd B3
Ambrose St B2
Andover Rd C1
Art Gallery & Mus 🏛 B2
Axiom Centre 🏛 B3
Back Montpellier Terr C2
Bandstand ✦ C2
Bath Pde B2
Bath Rd C2
Bays Hill Rd C1
Beechwood Sh Ctr B3
Bennington St B2
Berkeley St B3
Brewery, The A2
Brunswick St South A2
Bus Station B2
CAB B2
Carlton St B3
Central Cross Road A3
Cheltenham College C2
Cheltenham FC A3
Cheltenham General (A&E) Ⓗ C3
Christchurch Rd B1
Cineworld 🎦 A2
Clarence Rd A2
Clarence Sq A2
Clarence St B2
Cleeveland St A1
Coach Park A2
College Baths Road C3
College Rd C2
Colletts Dr A1
Corpus St C3
Devonshire St A2
Douro Rd B1
Duke St B3
Dunalley Pde A2
Dunalley St A2
Everyman 🎭 B2
Evesham Rd A3
Fairview Rd B3
Fairview St B3
Fire Station C3
Folly La A2
Gloucester Rd A1
Grosvenor St B3
Grove St A1
Gustav Holst 🏛 A3
Hanover St A2
Hatherley St C1
Henrietta St A2
Hewlett Rd B3
High St B2/B3
Hudson St A2
Imperial Gdns C2
Imperial La B2
Imperial Sq C2
Information Ctr ℹ B2
Keynsham Rd C3
King St A2
Knapp Rd B2
Ladies College 🏛 B2
Lansdown Cr C1
Lansdown Rd C1
Leighton Rd B3
Library B2
London Rd C3
Lypiatt Rd C1
Malvern Rd B1
Manser St A2
Market St A1
Marle Hill Pde A2
Marle Hill Rd A2
Millbrook St A1
Milsom St A2
Montpellier Gdns C2
Montpellier Gr C2
Montpellier Pde C2
Montpellier Spa Rd C2
Montpellier St C1
Montpellier Terr C2
Montpellier Walk C2
New St B2
North Pl B2
Old Bath Rd C3
Oriel Rd B2
Overton Park Rd B1
Overton Rd B1
Oxford St C3
Parabola Rd B1
Park Pl C1
Park St A1
Pittville Circus A3
Pittville Cr A3
Pittville Lawn A3
Pittville Park A2
Playhouse 🎭 B2
Police Station 🚓 B1/C1
Portland St B3
Post Office ✉ B2/C2
Prestbury Rd A3
Prince's Rd C1
Priory St B3
Promenade B2
Queen St A1
Recreation Ground A2
Regent Arcade B2
Regent St B2
Rodney Rd B2
Royal Cr B2
Royal Wells Rd B2
St George's Pl B2
St Georges Rd B1
St Gregory's ⛪ B2
St James St B3
St John's Ave B3
St Luke's Rd C2
St Margarets Rd A2
St Mary's ⛪ B2
St Matthew's ⛪ B2
St Paul's La A2
St Paul's Rd A2
St Paul's St A2
St Stephen's Rd C1
Sandford Lido C3
Sandford Mill Road C3
Sandford Park C3
Sandford Rd C2
Selkirk St A3
Sherborne Pl B3
Sherborne St B3
Suffolk Pde C2
Suffolk Rd C1
Suffolk Sq C1
Sun St A1
Swindon Rd B2
Sydenham Villas Rd C3
Tewkesbury Rd A1
The Courtyard B1
Thirlstaine Rd C2
Tivoli Rd C1

Tivoli St C1
Town Hall &
  Theatre B2
Townsend St A1
Trafalgar St C2
Union St B3
Univ of Gloucestershire
  (Francis Cl Hall) . A2
Univ of Gloucestershire
  (Hardwick) B1
Victoria Pl B3
Victoria St A1
Vittoria Walk C2
Wel Pl B3
Wellesley Rd A2
Wellington Rd A3
Wellington Sq A3
Wellington St A3
West Drive A3
Western Rd B1
Winchcombe St B2
Winston Churchill
  Meml Gardens ❋ ... A1

Chester 178

Abbey Gateway A2
Appleyards La C1
Bars, The B3
Bedward Row B1
Beeston View C3
Bishop Lloyd's Pal 🏛 B2
Black Diamond St .. A1
Bottoms La C3
Boughton B3
Bouverie St A1
Bridge St B2
Bridgegate C2
British Heritage
  Centre B2
Brook St A3
Brown's La C3
Bus Station B2
Cambrian Rd A1
Canal St B1
Carrick Rd C1
Castle ◆ C2
Castle Dr C2
Cathedral † B2
Catherine St A3
Chester ⭑ A3
Cheyney Rd A1
Chichester St A1
City Rd A3
City Walls B1/B2
City Walls Rd B1
Cornwall St A2
County Hall C2
Cross Hey C3
Cross, The B2
Cuppin St B2
Curzon Park North . C1
Curzon Park South . C1
Dee Basin A1/A2
Dee La B3
Delamere St A2
Dewa Roman
  Experience 🏛 B2
Duke St B2
Eastgate B2
Eastgate St B2
Eaton Rd C3
Edinburgh Way C3
Elizabeth Cr B3
Fire Station A2
Foregate St B2
Frodsham St B2
Gamul House B2
Garden La A1
George St A2
Gladstone Ave A1
God's Providence
  House 🏛 B2
Gorse Stacks A2
Greenway St C2
Grosvenor Bridge .. C1
Grosvenor Mus 🏛 ... B2
Grosvenor Park B3
Grosvenor Park Terr C1
Grosvenor Precinct B2
Grosvenor St B2
Groves Rd B3
Groves, The B3
Guildhall Museum 🏛 B1
Handbridge C2
Hartington St C3
Hoole Way A2
Hunter St B2
Information Ctr ℹ .. B2
King Charles'
  Tower ◆ A2
King St B2
Leisure Centre B2
Library A3
Lightfoot St A3
Little Roodee C2
Liverpool Rd A1
Love St B3
Lower Bridge St ... B2
Lower Park Rd B3
Lyon St A2
Magistrates Court . B2
Meadows La C3
Meadows, The B3
Military Museum 🏛 . A3
Milton St A3
New Crane St B1
Nicholas St B2
Northgate A2
Northgate St A2
Nun's Rd C1
Old Dee Bridge ◆ .. C2
Overleigh Rd C2
Park St B2
Police Station ▣ .. B2
Post Office ⊠ .. A2/A3/B2
Princess St B2
Queen St B2
Queen's Park Rd ... C3
Queen's Rd A3
Race Course B1
Raymond St A1
River La C1
Roman Amphitheatre
  & Gardens 🏛 B2
Roodee, The (Chester
  Racecourse) B1
Russell St A3
St Anne St A2
St George's Cr C1
St Martin's Gate .. B1
St Martin's Way ... B1
St Mary's Priory ◆ B2
St Oswalds Way A2
Saughall Rd A1
Sealand Rd A1
South View Rd A1

Stanley Palace 🏛 .. B1
Station Rd A3
Steven St A3
Tower Rd B1
Town Hall B2
Union St B3
Vicar's La B2
Victoria Cr C3
Victoria Rd A2
Walpole St A1
Water Tower St B1
Water Tower, The ◆ B1
Watergate B2
Watergate St B2
Whipcord La A1
White Friars B2
York St B3

Colchester 179

Abbey Gateway † ... C2
Albert St C1
Albion Grove C1
Alexandra Rd C1
Artillery St B2
Arts Centre 🏛 B1
Balkerne Hill B1
Barrack St C3
Beaconsfield Rd ... C1
Beche Rd C3
Bergholt Rd A1
Bourne Rd C3
Brick Kiln Rd A1
Bristol Rd B2
Broadlands Way A3
Brook St B2
Bury Cl B2
Bus Sta B2
Butt Rd C2
Camp Folley North . C2
Camp Folley South . C2
Campion Rd C2
Cannon St C2
Canterbury Rd C2
Castle ◆ B2
Castle Park B2
Castle Rd B2
Catchpool Rd A1
Causton Rd B1
Chandlers Row C2
Circular Rd East .. C2
Circular Rd North . C1
Circular Rd West .. C1
Clarendon Way A1
Claudius Rd C2
Colchester ⭑ A1
Colchester Camp
  Abbey Field C1
Colchester Institute B1
Colchester Town ⭑ . C2
Colne Bank Ave A1
Colne View Retail Pk A2
Compton Rd A3
Cowdray Ave A1/A2
Cowdray Ctr, The .. A2
Crouch St B1
Crowhurst Rd B1
Culver Square Sh Ctr B2
Culver St East B2
Culver St West B2
Dilbridge Rd A3
East Hill B2
East St B3
East Stockwell St . B1
Eld La B1
Essex Hall Rd B1
Exeter Dr B2
Fairfax Rd B2
Fire Station A2
Firstsite 🏛 B2
George St B2
Gladstone Rd C2
Golden Noble Hill . C2
Goring Rd A3
Granville Rd B2
Greenstead Rd B3
Guildford Rd A2
Harsnett Rd C3
Harwich Rd A3
Head St B1
High St B1/B2
High Woods Ctry Pk A2
Hollytrees 🏛 B2
Hythe Hill C3
Information Ctr ℹ . A2
Ipswich Rd A3
Jarmin Rd A2
Kendall Rd C3
Kimberley Rd C3
King Stephen Rd ... C3
Leisure World A2
Library B1
Lincoln Way A3
Lion Walk Sh Ctr .. B2
Lisle Rd C2
Lucas Rd C2
Magdalen Green C3
Magdalen St C2
Maidenburgh St B2
Maldon Rd B1
Manor Rd B1
Margaret Rd A1
Mason Rd A2
Mercers Way A1
Mersea Rd C2
Meyrick Cr C2
Mile End Rd A1
Military Rd C2
Mill St C2
Minories 🏛 B2
Moorside B3
Morant Rd C2
Napier Rd C2
Natural History 🏛 B2
New Town Rd C2
Norfolk Ave A3
North Hill B1
North Station Rd .. A1
Northgate St B1
Nunns Rd B1
Odeon 🎬 B1
Old Coach Rd B3
Old Heath Rd C3
Osborne St B2
Petrolea Cl A1
Police Station ▣ .. B1
Popes La C1
Port La C2
Post Office ⊠ ... B2/C1
Priory St B2
Queen St B2
Rawstorn Rd B1
Rebon St C2
Recreation Rd C2
Ripple Way A3

Roman Rd B2
Roman Wall B2
Romford Cl B2
Rosebery Ave B2
St Andrews Ave B3
St Andrews Gdns ... B3
St Botolph St B2
St Botolphs B2
St John's Abbey
  (site of) † C2
St John's St C2
St Johns Walk Sh Ctr B1
St Leonards Rd C3
St Marys Fields ... B1
St Peter's St B1
St Peters B1
Salisbury Ave C1
Serpentine Walk ... A1
Sheepen Pl B1
Sheepen Rd B1
Sir Isaac's Walk .. B2
Smythies Ave B2
South St C1
South Way C1
Sports Way A3
Suffolk Cl A3
Town Hall B1
Turner Rise Retail Pk A1
Valentine Dr A3
Victor Rd C3
Wakefield Cl B2
Wellesley Rd B2
Wells Rd B2/B3
West St B2
West Stockwell St . B1
Weston Rd C3
Westway A1
Wickham Rd C1
Wimpole Rd C2
Winchester Rd C2
Winnock Rd C2
Wolfe Ave C2
Worcester Rd B2

Coventry 179

Abbots La A1
Albany 🎭 B1
Albany Rd B1
Alma St B3
Art Faculty C2
Asthill Grove C2
Bablake School A1
Barras La A1/B1
Barrs Hill School . A1
Belgrade 🎭 B2
Bishop St A2
Bond's Hospital 🏛 B1
Broad Gate B2
Broadway C1
Burges, The B2
Bus Station A3
Butts Radial B1
Canal Basin ◆ A2
Canterbury St A3
Cathedral † B3
Central Six Retail Pk C1
Chester St A1
Cheylesmore Manor
  House 🏛 B2
Christ Church
  Spire † B2
City Coll B1
City Walls & Gates ◆ B2
Corporation St B2
Council House B2
Coundon Rd A1
Coventry Station ⭑ C2
Coventry Transport
  Museum 🏛 B2
Cox St A3
Croft Rd B1
Dalton Rd C1
Deasy Rd C3
Earl St B2
Eaton Rd C2
Fairfax St B2
Foleshill Rd A2
Ford's Hospital 🏛 B2
Fowler Rd C1
Friars Rd C2
Gordon St C1
Gosford St B3
Greyfriars Green ◆ B2
Greyfriars Rd B2
Gulson Rd B3
Hales St A3
Harnall Lane East . A3
Harnall Lane West . A2
Herbert Art Gallery &
  Museum 🏛 B3
Hertford St B2
Hewitt Ave A1
High St B1
Hill St B1
Holy Trinity ⛪ ... B2
Holyhead Rd A1
Howard St A3
Huntingdon Rd C1
Information Ctr ℹ . B2
Jordan Well B3
King Henry VIII
  School C1
Lady Godiva
  Statue ◆ B2
Lamb St B2
Leicester Row A2
Library B2
Little Park St B2
London Rd C2
Lower Ford St B3
Lower Prec Shop Ctr B2
Magistrates &
  Crown Courts B2
Manor House Drive . C2
Manor Rd C2
Market B2
Martyr's Memorial ◆ C2
Meadow St B1
Meriden St A1
Michaelmas Rd C2
Middleborough Rd .. A1
Mile La C3
Millennium Place ◆ A2
Much Park St B3
Naul's Mill Park .. A1
New Union B2
Odeon 🎬 B1
Park Rd C2
Parkside C3
Planet Ice Arena .. C3
Post Office ⊠ ... B2/C2
Priory Gardens &
  Visitor Centre ... B2
Priory St B2
Puma Way C3

Quarryfield La C3
Queen's Rd B1
Quinton Rd C2
Radford Rd A2
Raglan St B3
Ringway (Hill Cross) A1
Ringway (Queens) .. B1
Ringway (Rudge) ... B1
Ringway (St Johns) B2
Ringway
  (St Nicholas) A2
Ringway (St Patricks) C2
Ringway (Swanswell) A2
Ringway
  (Whitefriars) B3
St John St B2
St John The Baptist
  ⛪ B2
St Nicholas St A2
Sidney Stringer
  Academy A3
Skydome B1
Spencer Ave C1
Spencer Rec Gnd ... C1
Spon St B1
Sports Centre B3
Stoney Rd C2
Stoney Stanton Rd . A3
Swanswell Pool A3
Technocentre, The . C3
Thomas Landsdail St C2
Tomson Ave A3
Top Green B1
Trinity St B2
University B3
University Sports Ctr B3
Upper Hill St A1
Upper Well St A2
Victoria St A3
Vine St A3
Warwick Rd C2
Waveley Rd B1
West Orchards Sh Ctr B2
Westminster Rd C1
White St A3
Windsor St B1

Derby 179

Abbey St C1
Agard St B1
Albert St B2
Albion St B2
Ambulance Station . B1
Arthur St A1
Ashlyn Rd B3
Assembly Rooms 🏛 B2
Babington La C2
Becket St B1
Belper Rd A1
Bold La B1
Bradshaw Way C2
Bradshaw Way Ret Pk C2
Bridge St B1
Brook St B1
Burton Rd C1
Bus Station B2
Caesar St A2
Canal St C3
Carrington St C3
Cathedral † B1
Cathedral Rd B1
Charnwood St C2
Chester Green Rd .. A2
City Rd A2
Clarke St A3
Cock Pitt B3
Council House 🏛 .. B2
Courts B2
Cranmer Rd B3
Crompton St C1
Crown & County
  Courts B2
Curzon St B1
Darley Grove A1
Derby ⭑ C3
Derbyshire County
  Cricket Ground ... B3
Derwent Bsns Ctr .. B2
Derwent St B2
Drewry La C1
Duffield Rd A1
Duke St A2
Dunton Cl B3
Eagle Market C2
East St B2
Eastgate B2
Exeter St B2
Farm St C1
Ford St B1
Forester St C1
Fox St A2
Friar Gate B1
Friary St B1
Full St B2
Gerard St C1
Gower St C2
Green La C2
Grey St C1
Guildhall 🏛 B2
Harcourt St C1
Highfield Rd A1
Hill La A1
Information Ctr ℹ . B2
Iron Gate B2
John St C2
Joseph Wright Ctr . B2
Kedleston Rd A1
Key St B2
King Alfred St C1
King St A1
Kingston St A2
Lara Croft Way C2
Leopold St C2
Library A2
Liversage St C3
Lodge La A1
London Rd C3
London Rd Community
  Hospital H C3
Macklin St C1
Mansfield Rd A2
Market B2
Market Pl B2
May St C1
Meadow La B3
Melbourne St C2
Mercian Way C1
Midland Rd C3
Monk St C1
Morledge B2
Mount St C1
Mus & Art Gallery 🏛 B1
Noble St C1
North Parade A2
North St A1
Nottingham Rd B3

Osmaston Rd C2
Otter St A1
Park St C3
Parker St A1
Pickfords House 🏛 B1
Playhouse 🎭 A2
Police HQ ⊞ A2
Police Station ▣ . B2
Post Office ⊠
  A1/A2/B1/B2/C2/C3
Pride Parkway C3
Prime Enterprise Pk A2
Prime Parkway A2
Queens Leisure Ctr B2
Racecourse A3
Railway Terr C3
Register Office ... B2
Sadler Gate B2
St Alkmund's Way B1/B2
St Helens House 🏛 A1
St Mary's Bridge .. A2
St Mary's Bridge
  Chapel 🏛 A2
St Mary's Gate B1
St Paul's Rd A1
St Peter's St B2
St Peter's † B2
Showcase De Lux 🎬 B2
Siddals Rd B3
Silk Mill 🏛 B2
Sir Frank Whittle Rd A3
Spa La B3
Spring St C1
Stafford St B1
Station Approach .. C3
Stockbrook St C1
Stores Rd A3
Traffic St B2
Vernon St B1
Vine St A3
Wardwick B1
Werburgh St C1
West Ave A1
West Meadows
  Industrial Estate B3
Westfield Centre .. C2
Wharf Rd A2
Wilmot St C1
Wilson St C1
Wood's La C1

Dundee 179

Abertay University B2
Adelaide Pl A1
Airlie Pl C1
Albany Terr A1
Albert St A3
Alexander St A2
Ann St A2
Arthurstone Terr .. A3
Bank St B2
Barrack Rd A1
Barrack St B2
Bell St B2
Blackscroft B3
Blinshall St B1
Brown St B1
Bus Station B3
Caird Hall B2
Camperdown St B3
Candle La B2
Carmichael St A1
City Churches B2
City Quay B3
City Sq B2
Commercial St B2
Constable St A3
Constitution Cres A1
Constitution Ct ... A1
Constitution St A1/B2
Cotton Rd A3
Courthouse Sq B2
Cowgate B3
Crescent St A1
Crichton St B2
Dens Brae A3
Dens Rd A3
Discovery Point ◆ C2
Douglas St B1
Drummond St A1
Dudhope Castle 🏰 A1
Dudhope St A2
Dudhope Terr A1
Dundee ⭑ C2
Dundee Contemporary
  Arts ◆ C1
Dundee High School B2
Dundee Law ▲ A1
Dundee Repertory 🎭 C2
Dunhope Park A1
Dura St A3
East Dock St B3
East Marketgait ... B3
East Whale La B3
Erskine St A3
Euclid Cr B2
Forebank Rd A2
Foundry La A3
Frigate Unicorn ◆ B3
Gallagher Retail Park B3
Gellatly St B2
Government Offices B1
Guthrie St B1
Hawkhill B1
Hilltown A2
Howff Cemetery, The B2
Information Ctr ℹ . B2
Keiller Shopping Ctr B2
Keillor Ctr, The .. B2
King St A3
Kinghorne Rd A1
Ladywell Ave A2
Laurel Bank A2
Law Rd A1
Law St A1
Library A2/A3
Library and Steps
  Theatre 🎭 B2
Lochee Rd B1
Lower Princes St .. A3
Lyon St A3
McManus Museum &
  Art Gallery, The 🏛 B2
Meadow Side B2
Meadowside
  St Pauls ⛪ B2
Mercat Cross ◆ ... B2
Mid Wynd B1
Nelson St A2
Nethergate B2/C1
North Lindsay St .. B2
North Marketgait .. B2
Old Hawkhill B1
Olympia Leisure Ctr B3
Overgate Sh Ctr ... B2
Park Pl B1

Perth Rd C1
Police Station ▣ A2/B1
Post Office ⊠ A3
Princes St A3
Prospect Pl A2
Reform St B2
Riverside Dr C2
Roseangle C1
Rosebank St A2
RRS Discovery ⚓ .. C2
St Andrew's ⭑ C2
St Pauls Episcopal † B2
Science Centre ◆ . C2
Seagate B2
Sheriffs Court A2
Shopmobility B2
South George St ... A2
South Marketgait .. B2
South Tay St B2
South Ward Rd B2
Tay Road Bridge ◆ C3
Tayside House B2
Trades La B3
Union St B2
Union Terr A1
University ⊞ C1
University Library B1
University of Dundee C1
Upper Constitution
  St A1
Verdant Works 🏛 .. B1
Victoria Dock B3
Victoria Rd B2
Victoria St A3
Ward Rd B1
Wellgate B2
West Bell St B1
West Marketgait B1/B2
Westfield Pl C1
William St A3
Wishart Arch ◆ ... A3

Durham 180

Alexander Cr B2
Allergate B1
Archery Rise C1
Assize Courts B2
Avenue, The B1
Back Western Hill . A1
Bakehouse La A3
Baths B3
Baths Bridge B3
Boat House A2
Bowling A2
Boyd St C2
Bus Station B2
Castle Chare B2
Cathedral † C2
Church St C3
Clay La C3
Claypath B2
College of St Hild &
  St Bede B3
County Hall A1
County Hospital H . B1
Crescent, The A3
Crook Hall &
  Gardens ◆ B2
Crossgate B2
Crossgate Peth C1
Darlington Rd C1
Durham ⭑ B2
Durham Light Infantry
  Museum & Arts
  Gallery 🏛 A2
Durham School C2
Ellam Ave C1
Elvet Bridge B2
Elvet Court B3
Farnley Hey C1
Ferens Cl A3
Fieldhouse La A1
Flass St B1
Framwellgate
  Bridge B2
Framwellgate B2
Framwellgate Peth . A1
Framwellgate
  Waterside B2
Frankland La A2
Freeman's Pl A3
Freeman's Quay L Ctr A3
Gala Theatre &
  Cinema 🎭 B2
Gates Sh Ctr, The . B2
Geoffrey Ave C1
Gilesgate B3
Grey College C3
Grove, The A1
Hallgarth St C3
Hatfield College .. B2
Hawthorn Terr B1
HM Prison A3
Information Ctr ℹ . B2
John St B1
Kingsgate Bridge .. B3
Laburnum Terr B1
Lawson Terr B1
Leazes Rd B2/B3
Library B2
Margery La C1
Market B2
Mavin St C3
Millburngate B2
Millburngate Bridge B2
Millennium Bridge
  (foot/cycle) B2
Mountjoy Research
  Centre C2
Museum of
  Archaeology 🏛 ... B2
Nevilledale Terr .. B1
New Elvet B3
New Elvet Bridge .. B2
North Bailey C2
North End A1
North Rd A1/B2
Observatory C1
Old Elvet B3
Oriental Museum 🏛 C2
Oswald Court C3
Parkside C3
Passport Office ... B2
Percy Terr B1
Pimlico C2
Police Station ▣ . B2
Post Office ⊠ ... A1/B2
Potters Bank C1/C2
Prebends Bridge ... C2
Prebends Walk C2
Prince Bishops Sh Ctr B3
Princes St A2
Providence Row A3
Quarryheads La C2
Redhills La B1

Redhills Terr B1
Saddler St B2
St Chad's College . C3
St Cuthbert's Society C2
St John's College . C2
St Margaret's ⛪ .. B2
St Mary The Less ⛪ C2
St Mary's College . C2
St Monica Grove ... B1
St Nicholas' ⛪ ... B2
St Oswald's ⛪ C3
Sands, The A3
Sidegate A2
Silver St B2
South Bailey C2
South Rd C2
South St B1
Springwell Ave A1
Stockton Rd C3
Students' Rec Ctr . B3
Sutton St B1
Town Hall B2
Treasury Museum 🏛 B2
University ⊞ B2
University Arts Block B3
University Library B2
Univ Science Site . C3
Walkergate Centre . B2
Wearside Dr A1
Western Hill A1
Wharton Park A2
Whinney Hill C3
Whitehouse Ave C1

Edinburgh 180

Abbey Strand B6
Abbeyhill A6
Abbeyhill Cr A6
Abbeymount A6
Abercromby Pl A2
Adam St C5
Albany La A2
Albany St A2
Albert Memorial ◆ A2
Albyn Pl A2
Alva Pl A6
Alva St B1
Ann St A1
Appleton Tower ... C4
Archibald Pl C3
Argyle House C3
Assembly Rooms &
  Musical Hall A3
Atholl Cr B1
Atholl Crescent La B1
Bank St B4
Barony St A4
Beaumont Pl C5
Belford Rd B1
Belgrave Cr A1
Belgrave Crescent La A1
Bell's Brae B1
Blackfriars St B4
Blair St B4
Bread St C2
Bristo Pl C4
Bristo St C4
Brougham St C2
Broughton St A4
Brown St C5
Brunton Terr A6
Buckingham Terr .. A1
Burial Ground A4
Bus Station A4
Caledonian Cr C1
Caledonian Rd C1
Calton Hill A5
Calton Hill A4
Calton Rd B4
Camera Obscura &
  Outlook Tower ◆ . B4
Candlemaker Row ... C4
Canning St B2
Canongate B5
Canongate ⛪ B5
Carlton St A1
Carlton Terr A6
Carlton Terrace La A6
Castle ◆ B3
Castle Terr B3
Castlehill B3
Central Library ... B4
Chalmers Hospital H C3
Chalmers St C3
Chambers St C4
Chapel St C4
Charles St C4
Charlotte Sq B2
Chester St B1
Circus La A2
Circus Pl A2
City Art Centre 🏛 B4
City Chambers 🏛 . B4
City Observatory ◆ A5
Clarendon Cr A1
Clerk St C5
Coates Cr B1
Cockburn St B4
College of Art C3
Comely Bank Ave ... A1
Comely Bank Row ... A1
Cornwall St C2
Cowans Cl C5
Cowgate B4
Cranston St B5
Crichton St C4
Croft-An-Righ A6
Cumberland St A2
Dalry Pl C1
Dalry Rd C1
Danube St A1
Darnaway St A2
David Hume Tower .. C4
Davie St C5
Dean Bridge A1
Dean Gdns A1
Dean Park Cr A1
Dean Park Mews A1
Dean Park St A1
Dean Path B1
Dean St A1
Dean Terr A1
Dewar Pl C1
Dewar Pl La C1
Doune Terr A2
Drummond Pl A3
Drummond St C5
Drumsheugh Gdns ... B1
Dublin Mews A2
Dublin St A3
Dublin St La South A3
Dumbiedykes Rd C5
Dundas St A2
Earl Grey St C2
East Crosscauseway C5

East Market St B4
East Norton Pl A6
East Princes St Gdns B3
Easter Rd A6
Edinburgh
  (Waverley) ⭑ B3
Edinburgh Castle 🏰 B3
Edinburgh
  Dungeon ◆ B4
Edinburgh Int
  Conference Ctr ... C1
Elder St A4
Esplanade B3
Eton Terr A1
Eye Pavilion H ... C4
Festival Office ... B4
Festival Theatre
  Edinburgh 🎭 C4
Filmhouse 🎬 C2
Fire Station B2
Floral Clock ◆ ... B3
Forres St A2
Forth St A4
Fountainbridge C2
Frederick St A3
Freemasons' Hall . B2
Fruit Market 🏛 ... B4
Gardner's Cr C2
George Heriot's
  School C3
George IV Bridge .. B4
George Sq C4
George Sq La C4
George St A2
Georgian House 🏛 B2
Gladstone's Land 🏛 B3
Glen St C3
Gloucester La A2
Gloucester Pl A2
Gloucester St A2
Graham St C3
Grassmarket B3
Great King St A3
Great Stuart B1
Greenside La A5
Greenside Row A5
Greyfriars Kirk ⛪ C4
Grindlay St C2
Grosvenor Cr B1
Grove St C1
Gullan's Cl B5
Guthrie St B4
Hanover St A3
Hart St A4
Haymarket C1
Haymarket Sta ⭑ .. C1
Heriot Pl C3
Heriot Row A2
High School Yard .. B5
High St B4
Hill Pl C5
Hill St A2
Hillside Cr A5
Holyrood Abbey
  (remains of) A6
Holyrood Park C6
Holyrood Rd B5
Home St C2
Hope St B2
Horse Wynd B6
Howden St C5
Howe St A2
India Pl A2
India St A2
Infirmary St B4
Information Ctr ℹ B4
Jamaica Mews A2
Jeffrey St B4
John Knox House 🏛 B4
Johnston Terr C3
Keir St C3
Kerr St A2
King's Stables Rd . B2
Lady Lawson St C3
Lauriston Gdns C3
Lauriston Park C3
Lauriston Pl C3
Lauriston St C3
Lawnmarket B3
Learmonth Gdns A1
Learmonth Terr A1
Leith St A4
Lennox St A1
Lennox St La A1
Leslie Pl A1
London Rd A5
Lothian Health Board C5
Lothian Rd B2
Lothian St C4
Lower Menz Pl B1
Lynedoch Pl B1
Mall, The B6
Manor Pl B1
Market St B4
Marshall St C4
Maryfield A6
Maryfield Pl A6
McEwan Hall C4
Medical School C4
Melville St B1
Meuse La B4
Middle Meadow Walk C4
Milton St A6
Montrose Terr A6
Moray House (Coll) B5
Moray Place A2
Morrison Link C1
Morrison St C1
Mound Pl B3
Mound, The B3
Multrees Walk A4
Mus Collections Ctr C4
Museum of
  Childhood 🏛 B5
Museum of
  Edinburgh 🏛 B5
Museum on the
  Mound 🏛 B4
National Museum
  of Scotland 🏛 ... C4
National Gallery 🏛 B3
National Library of
  Scotland 🏛 B4
National
  Monument ◆ A5
National Portrait
  Gallery 🏛 A4
National Records of
  Scotland 🏛 A4
Nelson Monument ◆ A5
Nelson St A3
New St B5
Nicolson Sq C5
Nicolson St C5
Niddry St B4
North Bank St B4
North Bridge B4

North Castle St ... A2
North Charlotte St A2
North Meadow Walk . C3
North St Andrew St A4
North St David St . A3
North West Circus Pl A2
Northumberland St . A3
Odeon 🎬 C2
Old Royal
  High School A5
Old Tolbooth Wynd . B5
Omni Centre ◆ A4
Our Dynamic Earth ◆ B6
Oxford Terr A1
Palace of Holyrood
  House 🏰 B6
Palmerston Pl B1
Panmure Pl C3
Parliament House 🏛 B4
Parliament Sq B4
People's Story,
  The 🏛 B5
Playhouse Theatre 🎭 A4
Pleasance C5
Police Station ▣ . A4
Ponton St C2
Post Office ⊠ .. A3/A4/
  B5/C1/C2/C4/C5
Potterrow C4
Princes Mall B4
Princes St B3
Princes St ⭑ B3
Queen St A2
Queen Street Gdns A2
Queen's Dr B6/C6
Queensferry Rd A1
Queensferry St B1
Queensferry St La . B1
Radical Rd C6
Randolph Cr B1
Regent Gdns A5
Regent Rd A5
Regent Rd Park A6
Regent Terr A5
Richmond La C5
Richmond Pl C5
Rose St B2
Rosemount Bldgs .. C1
Ross Open Air
  Theatre 🎭 B3
Rothesay Pl B1
Rothesay Terr B1
Roxburgh Pl C5
Roxburgh St C5
Royal Bank of
  Scotland A4
Royal Circus A2
Royal Lyceum 🎭 .. C2
Royal Mile, The .. B5
Royal Scottish
  Academy 🏛 B3
Royal Terr A5
Royal Terrace Gdns A5
Rutland Sq B2
Rutland St B2
St Andrew Sq A4
St Andrew Sq ⭑ ... A4
St Andrew's House A5
St Bernard's Cr .. A1
St Cecilia's Hall . B4
St Colme St A2
St Cuthbert's ⛪ .. B2
St Giles' † B4
St James Centre .. B5
St John St B5
St John's ⛪ B2
St John's Hill C5
St Leonard's La .. C5
St Leonard's St .. C5
St Mary's
  Episcopal † B1
St Mary's St B5
St Stephen St A2
Salisbury Crags .. C6
Saunders St A2
Scotch Whisky
  Experience ◆ B3
Scott Monument ◆ B4
Scottish Parliament B6
Scottish Storytelling
  Centre ◆ B5
Semple St C2
Shandwick Pl B2
South Bridge B4
South Charlotte St B2
South College St .. C4
South Learmonth
  Gdns A1
South St Andrew St A4
South St David St . B3
Spittal St C2
Stafford St B1
Student Centre C4
Surgeons' Hall 🏛 C5
TA Centre C4
Tattoo Office B4
Teviot Pl C4
Thistle St A2
Torphichen Pl C1
Torphichen St C1
Traverse Theatre 🎭 B2
Tron, The ◆ B4
Tron Sq B4
Union St A4
University C4
University Library C4
Upper Grove Pl .. C1
Usher Hall 🎭 C2
Vennel C3
Victoria St B3
VUE 🎬 A4
Walker St B1
Waterloo Pl A4
Waverley Bridge .. B4
Wemyss Pl A2
West Approach Rd .. C1
West Crosscauseway C5
West End ⭑ C1
West Maitland St .. C1
West of Nicholson St C5
West Port C2
West Princes St
  Gdns B3
West Richmond St .. C5
West Tollcross C2
White Horse Cl ... B5
William St B1
Windsor St A5
York La A4
York Pl A4
York Pl ⭑ B2
Young St B2

Exeter 180

Alphington St	C1
Athelstan Rd	B3
Bampfylde St	B2
Barnardo Rd	C3
Barnfield Hill	B3
Barnfield Rd	B2/B3
Barnfield Theatre	B3
Bartholomew St East	B1
Bartholomew St West	B1
Bear St	C2
Beaufort Rd	C1
Bedford St	B2
Belgrave Rd	A3
Belmont Rd	A3
Blackall Rd	A2
Blackboy Rd	A3
Bonhay Rd	B1
Bull Meadow Rd	C2
Bus & Coach Sta	B1
Castle St	B2
Cecil Rd	C1
Cheeke St	A3
Church Rd	C1
Chute St	A3
City Industrial Estate	B1/B2
City Wall	B1/B2
Civic Centre	B2
Clifton Rd	A3
Clifton St	A3
Clock Tower	A1
College Rd	B3
Colleton Cr	C1
Commercial Rd	C1
Coombe St	C2
Cowick St	C1
Crown Courts	B2
Custom House	C2
Cygnet New Theatre	C2
Danes' Rd	A2
Denmark Rd	B3
Devon County Hall	B3
Devonshire Pl	A3
Dinham Rd	B1
East Grove Rd	C3
Edmund St	C1
Elmgrove Rd	A1
Exe St	B1
Exeter Cathedral †	B2
Exeter Central Sta ≷	A1
Exeter City Football Ground	A3
Exeter College	A2
Exeter Picture Ho	B1
Fire Station	A1
Fore St	B1
Friars Walk	C2
Guildhall	B2
Guildhall Sh Ctr	B2
Harlequins Sh Ctr	B1
Haven Rd	C2
Heavitree Rd	B3
Hele Rd	A1
High St	A2
HM Prison	A2
Holloway St	C2
Hoopern St	A2
Horseguards	A2
Howell Rd	A1
Information Ctr	B3
Iron Bridge	B1
Isca Rd	C1
Jesmond Rd	A3
King St	B1
King William Rd	A2
Larkbeare Rd	C2
Leisure Centre	C1
Library	A2
Longbrook St	A2
Longbrook Terr	B1
Lower North St	B1
Lucky La	C2
Lyndhurst Rd	C3
Magdalen Rd	B3
Magdalen St	B2
Magistrates & Crown Courts	A2
Market	A2
Market St	B2
Marlborough Rd	C3
Mary Arches St	B1
Matford Ave	C3
Matford La	C3
Matford Rd	C3
May St	A3
Mol's Coffee Ho	B2
New Bridge St	B1
New North Rd	A1/A2
North St	B1
Northernhay St	B1
Norwood Ave	C3
Odeon	A3
Okehampton St	C1
Old Mill Cl	C2
Old Tiverton Rd	A3
Oxford Rd	A3
Paris St	B2
Parr St	B3
Paul St	B1
Pennsylvania Rd	A2
Police HQ	A3
Portland Street	B3
Post Office	A3/B2/B3/C1
Powderham Cr	A3
Preston St	B1
Princesshay Sh Ctr	B2
Quay, The	C2
Queen St	A1
Queen's Terr	A1
Queens Rd	C1
Radford Rd	C2
Richmond Rd	A1
Roberts Rd	C3
Rougemont Castle	B2
Rougemont House ◆	B2
Royal Albert Memorial Museum	B2
St David's Hill	A1
St James' Pk Sta ≷	A3
St James' Rd	A3
St Leonard's Rd	C3
St Mary Steps	B1
St Nicholas Priory	B1
St Thomas Station	B1
Sandford Walk	B3
School for the Deaf	C2
School Rd	C1
Sidwell St	A3
Smythen St	B1
South St	B2
Southernhay East	B2
Southernhay West	B2
Spacex Gallery	B2
Spicer Rd	B3

Sports Centre	A3
Summerland St	A3
Swimming Pool & Leisure Centre	A3
Sydney Rd	C1
Tan La	A3
Thornton Hill	A2
Topsham Rd	C2
Tucker's Hall	B1
Tudor St	B1
University of Exeter (St Luke's Campus)	A3
Velwell Rd	A1
Verney St	A3
Water La	C1/C2
Weirfield Rd	C2
Well St	A3
West Ave	A3
West Grove Rd	C3
Western Way	A3/B1/B2
Willeys Ave	C1
Wonford St	B3/C3
York Rd	A2

Glasgow 181

Admiral St	C2
Albert Bridge	C5
Albion St	B5
Anderston ≷	B3
Anderston Centre	B3
Anderston Quay	B3
Argyle St	A1/A2/B3/B4/B5
Argyle Street ≷	B5
Argyll Arcade	B5
Arlington St	A3
Arts Centre ◆	A4
Ashley St	A3
Bain St	C6
Baird St	A6
Baliol St	A3
Ballater St	C5
Barras, The (Market)	C6
Bath St	A3
BBC Scotland/SMG	A2
Bell St	C5
Bell's Bridge	B1
Bentinck St	A2
Berkeley St	A3
Bishop La	A1
Black St	A6
Blackburn St	C2
Blackfriars St	B6
Blantyre St	A1
Blythswood Sq	A4
Blythswood St	B4
Bothwell St	B4
Brand St	C1
Breadalbane St	A2
Bridge St	C4
Bridge St Ⓜ	C4
Bridgegate	C5
Briggait	C5
Broomhill Park	A6
Broomielaw	B3
Broomielaw Quay Gdns	B3
Brown St	B3
Brunswick St	B5
Buccleuch St	A3
Buchanan Bus Sta	A5
Buchanan Galleries	A5
Buchanan St	B5
Buchanan St Ⓜ	B5
Cadogan St	B4
Caledonian Univ	A5
Calgary St	A5
Cambridge St	A4
Canal St	A5
Candleriggs	B5
Carlton Pl	C4
Carnarvon St	A3
Carrick St	B4
Castle St	B6
Cathedral Sq	B6
Cathedral St	B5
Ctr for Contemporary Arts ◆	A4
Centre St	C4
Cessnock Ⓜ	C1
Cessnock St	C1
Charing Cross ≷	A3
Charlotte St	C6
Cheapside St	B3
Cineworld	A5
Citizens' Theatre	C5
City Chambers	B5
City Halls	B5
City of Glasgow Coll	B6
Clairmont Gdns	A2
Claremont St	A2
Claremont Terr	A2
Claythorne St	C6
Cleveland St	A3
Clifford La	C1
Clifford St	C1
Clifton Pl	A2
Clifton St	A2
Clutha St	C1
Clyde Arc	B2
Clyde Auditorium	B1
Clyde Pl	C4
Clyde Place Quay	C4
Clyde St	C5
Clyde Walkway	C4
Clydeside Expressway	B2
Coburg St	C4
Cochrane St	B5
College of Nautical Studies	C6
College St	B6
Collins St	B6
Commerce St	C4
Cook St	C4
Cornwall St	A1
Couper St	A5
Cowcaddens Ⓜ	A4
Cowcaddens Rd	A4
Crimea St	B3
Custom House	C5
Custom House Quay Gdns	C4
Dalhousie St	A4
Dental Hospital	A4
Derby St	A2
Dobbie's Loan	A4/A5
Dobbie's Loan Pl	A5
Dorset St	A3
Douglas St	B4
Doulton Fountain ◆	C6
Dover St	A2
Drury St	B5
Drygate	B6
Duke St	B6

Dunaskin St	A1
Dunblane St	A4
Dundas St	B5
Dunlop St	C5
East Campbell St	C6
Eastvale Pl	A1
Eglinton St	C4
Elderslie St	A3
Elliot St	B2
Elmbank St	A3
Esmond St	A1
Exhibition Centre ≷	B2
Exhibition Way	B1
Eye Infirmary	A2
Festival Park	C1
Film Theatre	A4
Finnieston Quay	B2
Finnieston Sq	A2
Finnieston St	B2
Fitzroy Pl	A2
Florence St	C5
Fox St	C5
Gallowgate	C6
Garnet St	A3
Garnethill St	A4
Garscube Rd	A4
George Sq	B5
George St	B5
George V Bridge	C4
Gilbert St	A1
Glasgow Bridge	C4
Glasgow Cathedral †	B6
Glasgow Central ≷	B5
Glasgow Green	C6
Glasgow Science Centre ◆	B1
Glasgow Science Centre Footbridge	B1
Glasgow Tower ◆	B1
Glassford St	B5
Glebe St	A6
Gorbals Cross	C5
Gorbals St	C5
Gordon St	B4
Govan Rd	B1/C1/C2
Grace St	B3
Grafton Pl	A5
Grand Ole Opry ◆	C2
Grant St	A3
Granville St	A3
Gray St	A2
Greendyke St	C6
Grey Eagle St	B7
Harley St	C1
Harvie St	C1
Haugh Rd	A1
Heliport	A1
Henry Wood Hall	A2
High Court	C5
High St	B6
High Street ≷	B6
Hill St	A3
Holland St	A3
Holm St	B4
Hope St	A5
Houldsworth St	B2
Houston Pl	C3
Houston St	C3
Howard St	C5
Hunter St	C6
Hutcheson St	B5
Hydepark St	B3
Hydro, The	B2
Imax Cinema	B1
India St	A3
Information Ctr	B5
Ingram St	B5
Jamaica St	B4
James Watt St	B4
John Knox St	B6
John St	B5
Kelvin Hall ◆	A1
Kelvin Statue ◆	A2
Kelvin Way	A2
Kelvingrove Art Gallery & Museum ◆	A1
Kelvingrove Park	A2
Kelvingrove St	A2
Kelvinhaugh St	A1
Kennedy St	A6
Kent Rd	A2
Killermont St	A5
King St	B5
King's	A3
Kingston Bridge	C3
Kingston St	C4
Kinning Park Ⓜ	C2
Kyle St	A5
Lancefield Quay	B2
Lancefield St	B3
Langshot St	C1
Lendel Pl	C1
Lighthouse ◆	B4
Lister St	A6
Little St	B3
London Rd	C6
Lorne St	C1
Lower Harbour	B1
Lumsden St	A1
Lymburn St	A1
Lyndoch Cr	A3
Lynedoch Pl	A3
Lynedoch St	A3
Maclellan St	C1
Mair St	C2
Maitland St	A4
Mansell St	C7
Mavisbank Gdns	C2
Mcalpine St	B3
Mcaslin St	A6
McLean Sq	C2
McLellan Gallery	A4
McPhater St	A4
Merchants' House	B5
Middlesex St	C1
Middleton St	C1
Midland St	B4
Miller St	B5
Millroad St	C6
Milnpark St	C1
Milton St	A4
Minerva St	A2
Mitchell Library	A3
Mitchell St West	B4
Mitchell Theatre	A3
Modern Art Gallery	B5
Moir St	C6
Molendinar St	C6
Moncur St	C6
Montieth Row	C6
Montrose St	B5
Morrison St	C3
Mosque	C5
Nairn St	A1
Nelson Mandela Sq	B5
Nelson St	C4

Nelson's Monument	C6
New City Rd	A4
Newton Pl	A3
Newton St	A3
Nicholson St	C4
Nile St	B5
Norfolk Court	C4
Norfolk St	C4
North Frederick St	B5
North Hanover St	B5
North Portland St	B6
North St	A3
North Wallace St	A5
O2 Academy	C4
Odeon	A4
Old Dumbarton Rd	A1
Osborne St	B5/C5
Oswald St	B4
Overnewton St	A1
Oxford St	C4
Pacific Dr	B1
Paisley Rd	C3
Paisley Rd West	C1
Park Circus	A2
Park Gdns	A2
Park St South	A2
Park Terr	A2
Parkgrove Terr	A2
Parnie St	C5
Parson St	A6
Partick Bridge	A1
Passport Office	A5
Pavilion Theatre	A4
Pembroke St	A3
People's Palace	C6
Pinkston Rd	A6
Piping Centre, The National ◆	A5
Pitt St	A4/B4
Plantation Park	C1
Plantation Sq	B2
Police Sta	A4/A6/B5
Port Dundas Rd	A5
Port St	B2
Portman St	C2
Prince's Dock	B1
Princes Sq	B5
Provand's Lordship	B6
Queen St	B5
Queen Street ≷	B5
Renfrew St	A3/A4
Renton St	A5
Richmond St	B5
Robertson St	B4
Rose St	A4
Rottenrow	B5
Royal Concert Hall	A5
Royal Conservatoire of Scotland	A5
Royal Cr	C1
Royal Exchange Sq	B5
Royal Highland Fusiliers Mus	A3
Royal Hospital for Sick Children	C1
Royal Infirmary	B6
Royal Terr	A2
Rutland Cr	C2
St Andrew's	C5
St Andrew's (RC) †	B5
St Enoch	B5
St Enoch Sh Ctr	B5
St Enoch Sq	B4
St George's Rd	A3
St James Rd	B6
St Kent St	A3
St Mungo Ave	A5
St Mungo Museum of Religious Life	B6
St Mungo Pl	A6
St Vincent Cr	A2
St Vincent Pl	B5
St Vincent St	A2/B4
St Vincent Street Church	B4
St Vincent Terr	A2
Saltmarket	C5
Sandyford Pl	A3
Sauchiehall St	A2/A4
School of Art	A4
Sclater St	B7
Scotland St	C2
Scott St	A4
Scottish Exhibition & Conference Centre	B1
Seaward St	C2
Shaftesbury St	A3
Sheriff Court	C5
Shields Rd Ⓜ	C2
Shuttle St	B6
Somerset Pl	A2
South Portland St	C4
Springburn Rd	A6
Springfield Quay	C3
Stanley St	C2
Stevenson St	C6
Stewart St	A4
Stirling Rd	B6
Stirling's Library	B5
Stobcross Quay	B1
Stobcross Rd	B1
Stock Exchange	B5
Stockwell Pl	C5
Stockwell St	C5
Stow College	A4
Strathclyde Univ	B6
Sussex St	C1
Synagogues	A3/C4
Taylor Pl	A6
Tenement House	A3
Teviot St	A1
Theatre Royal	A4
Tolbooth Steeple & Mercat Cross ◆	C6
Tower St	C2
Trades House	B5
Tradeston St	C4
Transport Mus	A1
Tron	C5
Trongate	C5
Tunnel St	B2
Turnbull St	C5
Union St	B4
Victoria Bridge	C5
Virginia St	B5
Wallace St	C3
Walls St	B6
Walmer Cr	C1
Warrock St	B3
Washington St	B3
Waterloo St	B4
Watson St	C6
Watt St	C2
Wellington St	B4
West Campbell St	B4

West George St	B4
West Graham St	A4
West Greenhill Pl	B2
West Regent St	A4
West Regent St	B4
West St	C4
West St Ⓜ	C4
Westminster Terr	A2
Whitehall St	B3
Wilkes St	C7
Wilson St	B5
Woodlands Gate	A3
Woodlands Rd	A3
Woodlands Terr	A2
Woodside Cr	A3
Woodside Pl	A3
Woodside Terr	A3
York St	B4
Yorkhill Pde	A1
Yorkhill St	A1

Gloucester 181

Albion St	C1
Alexandra Rd	B3
Alfred St	C2
All Saints Rd	C2
Alvin St	A2
Arthur St	C2
Barrack Square	C2
Barton St	C2
Blenheim Rd	C2
Bristol Rd	C1
Brunswick Rd	C2
Bruton Way	B2
Bus Station	B2
Cineworld	B2
City Council Offices	B2
City Museum, Art Gallery & Library	B2
Clarence St	B2
Commercial Rd	B1
Council Offices	B1
Courts	C2
Cromwell St	C2
Deans Way	A2
Denmark Rd	A3
Derby Rd	C3
Docks	C1
Eastgate St	B2
Eastgate, The	B2
Edwy Parade	A2
Estcourt Cl	A3
Estcourt Rd	A3
Falkner St	C2
GL1 Leisure Centre	C2
Gloucester Cath †	B1
Gloucester Quays Outlet	C1
Gloucester Sta ≷	B2
Gloucester Waterways	C1
Gloucestershire Royal Hospital (A&E)	B3
Goodyere St	C2
Gouda Way	A1
Great Western Rd	B3
Guildhall	B2
Heathville Rd	A3
Henry Rd	A3
Henry St	A2
Hinton Rd	A2
HM Prison	B1
India Rd	C3
Jersey Rd	C3
King's	B2
King's Walk Sh Ctr	B2
Kingsholm (Gloucester RFC)	A2
Kingsholm Rd	A2
Lansdown Rd	A3
Library	B2
Llanthony Rd	C1
London Rd	B3
Longhorn Ave	A1
Longsmith St	B1
Malvern Rd	A3
Market	B2
Market Pde	B2
Mercia Rd	A2
Metz Way	C3
Midland Rd	C2
Millbrook St	C3
Montpellier	C1
Napier St	C3
Nettleton Rd	C2
New Inn	B2
New Olympus	B2
North Rd	A3
Northgate St	B2
Oxford Rd	A2
Oxford St	C2
Pk & Ride Gloucester	A1
Park Rd	C2
Park St	B2
Park, The	C2
Parliament St	C2
Peel Centre, The	C3
Pitt St	B1
Police Station	B1/C3
Post Office	A3/C3
Quay St	B1
Quay, The	B1
Recreation Gd	A1/A2
Regent St	C2
Robert Raikes House ◆	B1
Royal Oak Rd	A1
Russell St	B2
Ryecroft St	C2
St Aldate St	B2
St Ann Way	C1
St Catherine St	A2
St Mark St	A2
St Mary de Crypt †	B1
St Mary de Lode †	B1
St Nicholas's †	B1
St Oswald's Rd	A1
St Oswald's Retail Pk	A1
St Peter's	B2
Seabroke Rd	A3
Sebert St	A2
Severn Rd	C1
Sherborne St	A2
Shire Hall	B2
Sidney St	C3
Soldiers of Gloucestershire Museum	B1
Southgate St	B1/C1
Spa Field	C1
Spa Rd	C1
Sports Ground	A2/B2
Station Rd	B2
Stratton Rd	C3

Stroud Rd	C1
Superstore	A1
Swan Rd	A2
Trier Way	C1/C2
Union St	A2
Vauxhall Rd	C3
Victoria St	C2
Walham Lane	A1
Wellington St	C2
Westgate Retail Park	B1
Westgate St	B1
Weston Rd	C1
Widden St	C2
Worcester St	A2

Hanley (Stoke-on-Trent) 181

Acton St	A3
Albion St	B2
Argyle St	C1
Ashbourne Gr	A3
Avoca St	A3
Baskerville Rd	B3
Bedford Rd	B3
Bedford St	C1
Bethesda St	B2
Bexley St	A3
Birches Head Rd	A3
Botteslow St	C3
Boundary St	A1
Broad St	A3
Broom St	A3
Bryan St	A2
Bucknall New Rd	B3
Bucknall Old Rd	B3
Bus Station	B2
Cannon St	C2
Castlefield St	C1
Cavendish St	A1
Central Forest Pk	A2
Charles St	B3
Cheapside	B2
Chell St	A3
Clarke St	C1
Cleveland Rd	C2
Clifford St	C2
Clough St	A1
Clyde St	C1
College Rd	C2
Cooper St	C2
Corbridge Rd	A1
Cutts St	C2
Davis St	C2
Denbigh St	A1
Derby St	C3
Dilke St	A3
Dundas St	A3
Dundee Rd	C1
Dyke St	B3
Eastwood Rd	C3
Eaton St	A2
Etruria Park	B1
Etruria Rd	B1
Etruria Vale Rd	C1
Festing St	A3
Festival Retail Park	A1
Fire Station	B2
Foundry St	B2
Franklyn St	C2
Garnet St	C1
Garth St	B2
George St	A3
Gilman St	A3
Glass St	A3
Goodson St	B3
Greyhound Way	A1
Grove Pl	C1
Hampton St	C2
Hanley Park	C2
Hanley Park	B2
Harding Rd	C2
Hassall St	C3
Havelock Pl	A3
Hazlehurst St	C3
Hinde St	C2
Hope St	B2
Houghton St	A2
Hulton St	A3
Information Ctr	B3
Jasper St	C1
Jervis St	A3
John Bright St	A3
John St	B2
Keelings Rd	A3
Kimberley Rd	C1
Ladysmith Rd	C1
Lawrence St	C2
Leek Rd	C2
Library	B2
Lichfield St	C2
Linfield Rd	B3
Loftus St	C1
Lower Bedford St	C1
Lower Bryan St	A2
Lower Mayer St	A3
Lowther St	A1
Magistrates Court	C2
Malham St	A2
Marsh St	B2
Matlock St	C1
Mayer St	A3
Milton St	C1
Mitchell Memorial Theatre	B2
Morley St	A3
Moston St	A3
Mount Pleasant	C1
Mulgrave St	A1
Mynors St	B3
Nelson Pl	A3
New Century St	B1
Octagon Retail Park	B1
Ogden Rd	C2
Old Hall St	B3
Old Town Rd	A3
Pall Mall	B2
Palmerston St	C2
Park and Ride	A2
Parker St	A2
Parkway, The	C1
Pavilion Dr	A1
Pelham St	C2
Percy St	B2
Piccadilly	B2
Picton St	A3
Plough St	A2
Police Station	B2
Portland St	A3
Post Office	A3/C3
Potteries Museum & Art Gallery	B2
Potteries Sh Ctr	B2
Potteries Way	C1
Powell St	A1
Pretoria Rd	C1
Quadrant Rd	B2

Ranelagh St	C2
Raymond St	C1
Rectory Rd	C1
Regent Rd	C2
Regent Theatre	B2
Richmond Terr	A1
Ridgehouse Dr	A1
Robson St	A1
St Ann St	B2
St Luke St	B3
Sampson St	B2
Shaw St	A1
Sheaf St	C2
Shearer St	C1
Shelton New Rd	C1
Shirley Rd	C2
Slippery La	B2
Snow Hill	C2
Spur St	C3
Stafford St	B2
Statham St	B3
Stubbs La	C3
Sun St	C1
Supermarket	A1/B2
Talbot St	C2
Town Hall	B2
Town Rd	A3
Trinity St	B2
Union St	A2
Upper Hillchurch St	A3
Upper Huntbach St	B3
Victoria Hall Theatre	B3
Warner St	A1
Warwick St	C1
Waterloo Rd	B3
Waterloo St	B3
Well St	A3
Wellesley St	C2
Wellington Rd	B3
Wellington St	B3
Whitehaven Dr	C1
Whitmore St	C1
Windermere St	A1
Woodall St	A1
Yates St	C2
York St	A2

Harrogate 182

Albert St	C2
Alexandra Rd	C1
Arthington Ave	B2
Ashfield Rd	A2
Back Cheltenham Mount	B1
Beech Grove	C1
Belmont Rd	C1
Bilton Dr	A2
Bower Rd	A2
Bower St	A2
Bus Station	B2
Cambridge Rd	B2
Cambridge St	B2
Cemetery	A3
Chatsworth Grove	A2
Chatsworth Pl	A2
Chatsworth Rd	A2
Chelmsford Rd	B2
Cheltenham Cr	B2
Cheltenham Mt	B2
Cheltenham Pde	B2
Christ Church	B3
Christ Church Oval	B3
Chudleigh Rd	B3
Clarence Dr	B1
Claro Rd	A3
Claro Way	A3
Coach Park	B2
Coach Rd	A3
Cold Bath Rd	C1
Commercial St	B2
Coppice Ave	A1
Coppice Dr	A1
Coppice Gate	A1
Cornwall Rd	B1
Council Offices	B1
Court	C2
Crescent Gdns	B1
Crescent Rd	B1
Dawson Terr	A2
Devonshire Pl	B3
Diamond Mews	A2
Dixon Rd	A2
Dixon Terr	A2
Dragon Ave	A3
Dragon Parade	A2
Dragon Rd	B2
Duchy Rd	B1
East Parade	B2
East Park Rd	C2
Esplanade	B1
Fire Station	A2
Franklin Mount	A2
Franklin Rd	A2
Franklin Square	A2
Glebe Rd	C1
Grove Park Ct	A3
Grove Park Terr	A3
Grove Rd	A2
Hampswaite Rd	A1
Harcourt Dr	B2
Harcourt Rd	B2
Harrogate	B2
Harrogate Int Ctr	B1
Harrogate Ladies College	B1
Harrogate Theatre	B2
Heywood Rd	C1
Hollins Cr	A1
Hollins Mews	A1
Hollins Rd	A1
Homestead Rd	C2
Hydro L Ctr, The	A1
Information Ctr	B1
James St	B2
Jenny Field Dr	A1
John St	B2
Kent Dr	A1
Kent Rd	A1
Kings Rd	A2
Kingsway	B3
Kingsway Dr	A3
Lancaster St	C2
Leeds Rd	C2
Lime Grove	A3
Lime St	A3
Mayfield Grove	A2
Mayfield Pl	A2
Mercer	B2
Montpellier Hill	C1
Mornington Cr	A3
Mornington Terr	A3
Mowbray Sq	A3
North Park Rd	B3
Nydd Vale Rd	A2
Oakdale Ave	A1

Hull 182

Adelaide St	C1
Albert Dock	C1
Albion St	B2
Alfred Gelder St	B2
Anlaby Rd	B1
Arctic Corsair ◆	B3
Beverley Rd	A1
Blanket Row	C2
Bond St	B2
Bridlington Ave	A2
Brook St	B1
Brunswick Ave	A1
Bus Station	B1
Camilla Cl	C3
Cannon St	A2
Cannon's	A1
Caroline St	A2
Carr La	B2
Castle St	C2
Central Library	B1
Charles St	A2
Citadel Way	B3
City Hall	B2
City Hall Theatre	B2
Clarence St	B3
Cleveland St	A3
Clifton St	A1
Club Culture	B2
Colonial St	B1
Court	C2
Deep, The ◆	C3
Dinostar ◆	B2
Dock Office Row	B3
Drypool Bridge	B3
Egton St	A3
English St	C1
Ferens Gallery	B2
Ferensway	B1
Francis St	B1
Francis St West	A1
Freehold St	A1
Freetown Way	A2
Fruit Theatre ◆	C2
Garrison Rd	B3
George St	B2
Gibson St	A2
Great Thornton St	B1
Great Union St	A3
Green La	A2
Grey St	A1
Grimston St	B2
Grosvenor St	A1
Guildhall	B2
Guildhall Rd	B2
Hands-on History ◆	B2
Harley St	A1
Hessle Rd	C1
High St	B3
Holy Trinity ◆	B2
Hull (Paragon) Sta ≷	B1
Hull & East Riding Museum ◆	B3
Hull Arena	C1
Hull College	B3
Hull History Centre	A1
Hull Truck Theatre	B1
Humber Dock Marina	C2
Humber Dock St	C2
Humber St	C2
Hyperion St	A3
Information Ctr	B2
Jameson St	B1
Jarratt St	B2
Jenning St	A3
King Billy Statue ◆	C2
King Edward St	B2

King St	A2
Kingston Retail Park	C1
Kingston St	C2
Liddell St	A1
Lime St	A3
Lister St	C1
Lockwood St	A2
Maister House	B3
Maritime Mus	B2
Market	B2
Market Place	B2
Minerva Pier	C2
Mulgrave St	A3
Myton Bridge	C3
Myton St	B1
NAPA (Northern Academy of Performing Arts)	B1
Nelson St	C2
New Cleveland St	A3
New George St	A2
New Theatre	A2
Norfolk St	A1
North Bridge	A3
North St	B1
Odeon	C1
Old Harbour	C3
Osborne St	B1
Paragon St	B2
Park St	B1
Percy St	A2
Pier St	C2
Police Station	B3
Porter St	C1
Portland St	A1
Post Office	A1/B1/B2
Posterngate	B2
Prince's Quay	C2
Prospect Centre	B1
Prospect St	A2
Queen's Gdns	B2
Railway Dock Marina	C2
Railway St	C1
Real	B1
Red Gallery	A2
Reform St	A2
Retail Park	B1
River Hull Footbridge	B3
Riverside Quay	C2
Roper St	A2
St James St	C1
St Luke's St	B1
St Mark St	A3
St Mary the Virgin	B3
St Stephens Shr Ctr	B1
Scott St	A2
South Bridge Rd	C3
Spring Bank	A1
Spring St	B1
Spurn Lightship ◆	C2
Spyvee St	A3
Streetlife Transport Museum ◆	B3
Sykes St	A2
Tidal Surge Barrier ◆	C3
Tower St	B3
Trinity House	B2
University	A1
Vane St	A1
Victoria Pier ◆	C2
Waterhouse La	B1
Waterloo St	A1
Waverley St	C1
Wellington St	B2
Wellington St West	C2
West St	B1
Whitefriargate	B2
Wilberforce Dr	B2
Wilberforce Ho ◆	B3
Wilberforce Monument ◆	B3
William St	C1
Wincolmlee	A3
Witham	A3
Wright St	A1

Ipswich 182

Alderman Rd	B2
All Saints' Rd	A1
Alpe St	B2
Ancaster Rd	C1
Ancient House	B3
Anglesea Rd	A2
Ann St	B2
Arboretum	A2
Austin St	C2
Avenue, The	A3
Belstead Rd	C1
Berners St	B2
Bibb Way	B1
Birkfield Dr	C1
Black Horse La	B2
Bolton La	B3
Bond St	B3
Bowthorpe Cl	B1
Bramford La	A1
Bramford Rd	A1
Bridge St	C2
Brookfield Rd	A1
Brooks Hall Rd	A1
Broomhill	A1
Broomhill Rd	A1
Broughton Rd	B2
Bulwer Rd	C1
Burrell Rd	C2
Butter Market	B2
Buttermarket Shopping Ctr, The	B3
Cardinal Park L Park	C2
Carr St	B3
Cecil Rd	B2
Cecilia St	C2
Chancery Rd	C2
Chevallier St	A1
Christchurch Mansion & Wolsey Art Gallery ◆	A3
Christchurch Park	A3
Christchurch St	B3
Cineworld	B2
Civic Centre	B2
Civic Dr	B2
Clarkson St	B1
Cobbold St	A3
Commercial Rd	C2
Constable Rd	A3
Constantine Rd	C1
Constitution Hill	A2
Corder Rd	A2
Corn Exchange	B2
Cotswold Ave	A1
Council Offices	C1
County Hall	B3

Buckingham Pal Rd F2
Bunhill Row B6
Byward St D7
Cabinet War Rooms & Churchill Mus E3
Cadogan La E2
Cadogan Pl E1
Cadogan Sq F1
Caledonian Rd A4
Calshot St A4
Calthorpe St B4
Calvert Ave B7
Cambridge Circus C3
Camomile St C7
Cannon St D6
Cannon St D6
Carey St C4
Carlisle La E4
Carlisle Pl E3
Carlton House Terr D3
Carmelite St D5
Carnaby St C3
Carter La C5
Carthusian St C6
Cartwright Gdns B4
Castle Baynard St D5
Cavendish Pl C2
Cavendish Sq C2
Caxton Hall E3
Caxton St E3
Central St B6
Chalton St B3
Chancery Lane C5
Chapel St E2
Charing Cross D4
Charing Cross Rd C3
Charles II St D3
Charles Sq B6
Charles St D2
Charlotte Rd B7
Charlotte St C3
Chart St B6
Charterhouse Sq C5
Charterhouse St C5
Cheapside C6
Chenies St C3
Chesham St E2
Chester Sq F2
Chesterfield Hill D2
Chiltern St C2
Chiswell St C6
City Garden Row A5
City Rd B6
City Thameslink C5
City University, The B5
Claremont Sq A5
Clarges St D2
Clerkenwell Cl B5
Clerkenwell Green B5
Clerkenwell Rd B5
Cleveland St C3
Clifford St D3
Clink Prison Mus D6
Clock Museum C6
Club Row B7
Cockspur St D3
Coleman St C6
Columbia Rd B7
Commercial St C7
Compton St B5
Conduit St D2
Constitution Hill E2
Copperfield St E5
Coptic St C4
Cornhill C6
Cornwall Rd D5
Coronet St B7
Courtauld Gallery D4
Covent Garden D4
Covent Garden D4
Cowcross St C5
Cowper St B6
Cranbourn St D3
Craven St D4
Crawford St C1
Creechurch La C7
Cremer St A7
Cromer St B4
Cumberland Gate D1
Cumberland Terr A2
Curtain Rd B7
Curzon St D2
Cut, The E5
D'arblay St C3
Davies St C2
Dean St C3
Deluxe Gallery B7
Denmark St C3
Dering St C2
Devonshire St C2
Diana, Princess of Wales Meml Wlk E3
Dingley Rd B6
Dorset St C1
Doughty St B4
Dover St D2
Downing St E4
Druid St E7
Drummond St B3
Drury La C4
Drysdale St B7
Duchess St C2
Dufferin St B6
Duke of Wellington Pl E2
Duke St C2
Duke St D3
Duke St Hill D6
Duke's Pl C7
Duncannon St D4
East Rd B6
Eastcastle St C3
Eastcheap D7
Eastman Dental Hospital B4
Eaton Pl E2
Eaton Sq E2
Eccleston St E2
Edgware Rd C1
Eldon St C6
Embankment D4
Endell St C4
Endsleigh Pl B3
Euston B3
Euston Rd B3
Euston Square B3
Evelina Children's Hospital E4
Eversholt St A3
Exmouth Market B5
Fann St B6
Farringdon C5
Farringdon Rd C5
Farringdon St C5
Featherstone St B6
Fenchurch St D7
Fenchurch St D7
Fetter La C5
Finsbury Circus C6
Finsbury Pavement C6
Finsbury Sq B6
Fitzalan St F5
Fitzmaurice Pl D2
Fleet St C5
Floral St D4
Florence Nightingale Museum E4
Folgate St C7
Foot Hospital B3
Fore St C6
Foster La C6
Francis St F3
Frazier St E5
Freemason's Hall C4
Friday St C6
Gainsford St E7
Garden Row E5
Gee St B6
George St C1
Gerrard St D3
Giltspur St C5
Glasshouse St D3
Gloucester Pl C1
Golden Hinde D6
Golden La B6
Golden Sq D3
Goodge St C3
Goodge St C3
Gordon Sq B3
Goswell Rd B5
Gough St B4
Goulston St C7
Gower St B3
Gracechurch St D6
Grafton Way B3
Gray's Inn Rd B4
Great College St E4
Great Cumberland Pl C1
Great Eastern St B7
Great Guildford St D6
Great Marlborough St C3
Great Ormond St B4
Great Ormond St Children's Hospl B4
Great Percy St B4
Great Peter St E3
Great Portland St B2
Great Portland St C2
Great Queen St C4
Great Russell St C3
Great Scotland Yd D4
Great Smith St E3
Great Suffolk St D5
Great Titchfield St C3
Great Tower St D7
Great Windmill St D3
Greek St C3
Green Park D3
Green St D2
Greencoat Pl F3
Gresham St C6
Greville St B4/C5
Greycoat Hosp Sch E3
Greycoat Pl E3
Grosvenor Cres E2
Grosvenor Gdns E2
Grosvenor Pl E2
Grosvenor Sq D2
Grosvenor St D2
Guards Museum and Chapel E3
Guildhall Art Gallery C6
Guilford St B4
Guy's Hospital D6
Haberdasher St B6
Hackney Rd B7
Half Moon St D2
Halkin St E2
Hall St B5
Hallam St C2
Hampstead Rd B3
Hanover Sq C2
Hans Cres E1
Hanway St C3
Hardwick St B5
Harley St C2
Harrison St B4
Hastings St B4
Hatfields D5
Hay's Galleria D7
Hay's Mews D2
Hayles St F5
Haymarket D3
Hayne St C5
Hayward Gallery D4
Helmet Row B6
Herbrand St B4
Hercules Rd E4
Hertford St D2
High Holborn C4
Hill St D2
HMS Belfast D7
Hobart Pl E2
Holborn C4
Holborn C5
Holborn Viaduct C5
Holland St D5
Holmes Mus B1
Holywell La B7
Horse Guards' Rd D3
Houndsditch C7
Houses of Parliament E4
Howland St C3
Hoxton Sq B7
Hoxton St B7
Hunter St B4
Hunterian Mus C4
Hyde Park D1
Hyde Park Cnr E2
Imperial War Mus E5
Inner Circle B2
Inst of Archaeology (London Univ) B2
Ironmonger Row B6
James St C2
James St D4
Jermyn St D3
Jockey's Fields C4
John Carpenter St D5
John St B4
Judd St B4
Kennington Rd E5
King Charles St E4
King St D3
King St D4
King William St C6
King's Coll London D5
King's Cross A4
King's Cross Rd B4
King's Cross St Pancras A4
King's Rd E2
Kingley St C3
Kingsland Rd B7
Kingsway C4
Kinnerton St E2
Knightsbridge E1
Lamb St C7
Lamb's Conduit St C4
Lambeth Bridge F4
Lambeth High St F4
Lambeth North E5
Lambeth Palace E4
Lambeth Palace Rd E4
Lambeth Rd E5
Lambeth Walk F4
Lancaster Pl D4
Langham Pl C2
Leadenhall St C7
Leake St E4
Leather La C5
Leicester Sq D3
Leicester St D3
Leonard St B6
Lever St B6
Lexington St D3
Lidlington Pl A3
Lime St D7
Lincoln's Inn Fields C4
Lindsey St C5
Lisle St D3
Liverpool St C7
Liverpool St C7
Lloyd Baker St B5
Lloyd Sq B5
Lombard St C6
London Aquarium E4
London Bridge D6
London Bridge Hospital D6
London City Hall D7
London Dungeon, The E4
London Film Mus E4
London Guildhall University C6
London Rd E5
London Transport Museum D4
London Wall C6
London-Eye E4
Long Acre D4
Long La C5
Longford St B2
Lower Belgrave St E2
Lower Grosvenor Pl E2
Lower Marsh E5
Lower Thames St D6
Lowndes St E1
Ludgate Circus C5
Ludgate Hill C5
Luxborough St C2
Lyall St E2
Macclesfield Rd B6
Madame Tussaud's B2
Maddox St D2
Malet St C3
Mall, The E3
Manchester Sq C2
Manchester St C2
Mandeville Pl C2
Mansell St D7
Mansion House C6
Mansion House D6
Maple St C3
Marble Arch C1
Marble Arch D1
Marchmont St B4
Margaret St C3
Margery St B5
Mark La D7
Marlborough Rd D3
Marshall St C3
Marsham St E3
Marylebone High St C2
Marylebone La C2
Marylebone Rd B2
Marylebone St C2
Mecklenburgh Sq B4
Middle Temple La C5
Middlesex St (Petticoat La) C7
Midland Rd A3
Minories C7
Monck St E3
Monmouth St C4
Montagu Pl C1
Montagu Sq C1
Montagu St C4
Montague Pl C3
Monument D6
Monument St D6
Monument, The D6
Moor La C6
Moorfields C6
Moorfields Eye Hospital B6
Moorgate C6
Moorgate C6
Moreland St B5
Morley St E5
Mortimer St C3
Mount Pleasant B5
Mount St D2
Murray Gr A6
Mus of Garden History E4
Mus of London C6
Museum St C4
Myddelton Sq B5
Myddelton St B5
National Gallery D3
National Hospital B4
National Portrait Gallery D3
Neal St C4
Nelson's Column D4
New Bond St C2/D2
New Bridge St C5
New Cavendish St C2
New Change C6
New Fetter La C5
New Inn Yard B7
New North Rd A6
New Oxford St C3
New Scotland Yard E3
New Sq C4
Newgate St C5
Newton St C4
Nile St B6
Noble St C6
Noel St C3
North Audley St D2
North Cres C3
North Row D2
Northampton Sq B5
Northington St B4
Northumberland Ave D4
Norton Folgate C7
Nottingham Pl C2
Obstetric Hosp B3
Old Bailey C5
Old Broad St C6
Old Compton St C3
Old County Hall E4
Old Gloucester St C4
Old King Edward St C6
Old Nichol St B7
Old Paradise St F4
Old Spitalfields Mkt C7
Old St B6
Old St B6
Old Vic E5
Open Air Theatre B2
Operating Theatre Museum D6
Orange St D3
Orchard St C2
Ossulston St A3
Outer Circle B1
Oxford Circus C3
Oxford St C2/C3
Paddington St C2
Palace St E3
Pall Mall D3
Pall Mall East D3
Pancras Rd A4
Panton St D3
Paris Gdn D5
Park Cres B2
Park La D2
Park Rd B1
Park St D2
Park St D6
Parker St C4
Parliament Sq E4
Parliament St E4
Paternoster Sq C5
Paul St B6
Pear Tree St B5
Penton Rise B4
Penton St A5
Pentonville Rd A4/A5
Percival St B5
Petticoat La (Middlesex St) C7
Petty France E3
Phoenix Pl B4
Phoenix Rd A3
Photo Gallery D3
Piccadilly D2
Piccadilly Circus D3
Pitfield St B7
Pollock's Toy Mus C3
Polygon Rd A3
Pont St E1
Portland Pl C2
Portman Mews C2
Portman Sq C2
Portman St C1
Portugal St C4
Poultry C6
Primrose St C7
Princes St C6
Procter St C4
Provost St B6
Quaker St B7
Queen Anne St C2
Queen Elizabeth Hall D4
Queen Sq B4
Queen St D6
Queen Street Pl D6
Queen Victoria St D5
Queens Gallery E3
Radnor St B6
Rathbone Pl C3
Rawstorne St B5
Red Lion Sq C4
Red Lion St C4
Redchurch St B7
Redcross Way D6
Regency St F3
Regent Sq B4
Regent St C3
Regent's Park B2
Richmond Terr E4
Ridgmount St C3
Rivington St B7
Robert St B2
Rochester Row F3
Ropemaker St C6
Rosebery Ave B5
Roupell St D5
Royal Acad of Arts D3
Royal Academy of Dramatic Art B3
Royal Acad of Music B2
Royal Artillery Memorial E2
Royal Coll of Nursing C2
Royal College of Surgeons C4
Royal Festival Hall D4
Royal London Hospital for Integrated Medicine C4
Royal National Theatre D5
Royal National Throat, Nose and Ear Hospital B4
Royal Opera House D4
Russell Sq B3
Russell Square B4
Sackville St D3
Sadlers Wells B5
Saffron Hill C5
St Alban's St D3
St Andrew St C5
St Bartholomew's Hospital C5
St Botolph St C7
St Bride St C5
St George's Circus E5
St George's Rd E5
St Giles High St C3
St James's Palace D3
St James's Park E3
St James's St D3
St John St B5
St Margaret St E4
St Mark's Hosp B5
St Martin's La D4
St Martin's Le Grand C6
St Mary Axe C7
St Pancras Int A4
St Paul's C6
St Paul's Cath C6
St Paul's Churchyard C5
St Peter's Hosp D4
St Thomas St D6
St Thomas' Hosp E4
Savile Row D3
Savoy Pl D4
Savoy St D4
School of Hygiene & Tropical Medicine C3
Scrutton St B7
Sekforde St B5
Serpentine Rd D1
Seven Dials C4
Seward St B5
Seymour St C1
Shad Thames D7
Shaftesbury Ave D3
Shakespeare's Globe Theatre D6
Shepherd Market D2
Sherwood St D3
Shoe La C5
Shoreditch High St B7
Shoreditch High St B7
Shorts Gdns C4
Sidmouth St B4
Silk St C6
Sir John Soane's Museum C4
Skinner St B5
Sloane St E1
Snow Hill C5
Soho Sq C3
Somerset House D4
South Audley St D2
South Carriage Dr E1
South Molton St C2
South Pl C6
South St D2
Southampton Row C4
Southampton St D4
Southwark D5
Southwark Bridge D6
Southwark Bridge Rd D6
Southwark Cath D6
Southwark St D6
Speakers' Corner D1
Spencer St B5
Spital Sq C7
Stamford St D5
Stanhope St B3
Stephenson Way B3
Stock Exchange C5
Stoney St D6
Strand C5
Stratton St D2
Sumner St D5
Sutton's Way B6
Swanfield St B7
Swinton St B4
Tabernacle St B6
Tate Modern D6
Tavistock Pl B4
Tavistock Sq B3
Tea & Coffee Mus D6
Temple D5
Temple Ave D5
Temple Pl D4
Terminus Pl E2
Thayer St C2
Theobald's Rd C4
Thorney St F4
Threadneedle St C6
Throgmorton St C6
Tonbridge St B4
Tooley St D7
Torrington Pl B3
Tothill St E3
Tottenham Court Rd B3
Tottenham Ct Rd C3
Tottenham St C3
Tower Bridge D7
Tower Bridge App D7
Tower Bridge Rd E7
Tower Hill D7
Tower Hill D7
Tower of London, The D7
Toynbee St C7
Trafalgar Square D3
Trinity Sq D7
Trocadero Centre D3
Tudor St D5
Turnmill St C5
Ufford St E5
Union St D5
Univ Coll Hospl B3
University of London C3
Univ of Westminster C2
University St B3
Upper Belgrave St E2
Upper Berkeley St C1
Upper Brook St D2
Upper Grosvenor St D2
Upper Ground D5
Upper Montague St C1
Upper St Martin's La D4
Upper Thames St D6
Upper Wimpole St C2
Upper Woburn Pl B3
Vere St C2
Vernon Pl C4
Vestry St B6
Victoria E2
Victoria Emb D4
Victoria Pl Sh Ctr F2
Victoria St E3
Villiers St D4
Vincent Sq F3
Vinopolis City of Wine D6
Virginia Rd B7
Wakley St B5
Walbrook C6
Wallace Collection C2
Wardour St C3/D3
Warner St B5
Warren St B3
Warren St B3
Waterloo E5
Waterloo Bridge D4
Waterloo East D5
Waterloo Rd E5
Watling St C6
Webber St E5
Welbeck St C2
Wellington Arch E2
Wellington Mus E2
Wells St C3
Wenlock St A6
Wentworth St C7
West Smithfield C5
West Sq E5
Westminster E4
Westminster Abbey E4
Westminster Bridge E4
Westminster Bridge Rd E5
Westminster Cathedral (RC) E3
Westminster City Hall E3
Westminster Hall E4
Weymouth St C2
Wharf Rd A6
Wharton St B4
Whitcomb St D3
White Cube B7
White Lion Hill D5
White Lion St A5
Whitecross St B6
Whitefriars St C5
Whitehall D4
Whitehall Pl D4
Wigmore Hall C2
Wigmore St C2
William IV St D4
Wilmington Sq B5
Wilson St C6
Wilton Cres E2
Wimpole St C2
Windmill Walk D5
Woburn Pl B4
Woburn Sq B3
Women's Hosp C3
Wood St C6
Woodbridge St B5
Wootton St D5
Wormwood St C7
Worship St B6
Wren St B4
Wynyatt St B5
York Rd E4
York St C1
York Terrace East B2
York Terrace West B2
York Way A4

Luton 186

Adelaide St B1
Albert Rd C2
Alma St B2
Alton Rd C3
Anthony Gdns C1
Arthur St C2
Ashburnham Rd B1
Ashton Rd C2
Avondale Rd A1
Back St A2
Bailey St C3
Baker St C2
Biscot Rd A1
Bolton Rd B3
Boyle Cl A2
Brantwood Rd B1
Bretts Mead C1
Bridge St B2
Brook St A1
Brunswick St A3
Burr St A3
Bury Park Rd A1
Bute St B2
Buxton Rd B2
Cambridge St C3
Cardiff Grove B1
Cardiff Rd B1
Cardigan St A2
Castle St B2/C2
Chapel St C2
Charles St A3
Chase St C2
Cheapside B2
Chequer St C3
Chiltern Rise C1
Church St B2/B3
Cinema A2
Cobden St A3
Collingdon St A1
Community Centre C3
Concorde Ave A3
Corncastle Rd C1
Cowper St C2
Crawley Green Rd B3
Crawley Rd A1
Crescent Rd A3
Crescent Rise A3
Cromwell Rd A1
Cross St A2
Cross Way, The C1
Crown Court B2
Cumberland St B2
Cutenhoe Rd C3
Dallow Rd B1
Downs Rd B1
Dudley St A2
Duke St A2
Dumfries St B1
Dunstable Place B2
Dunstable Rd A1/B1
Edward St A3
Elizabeth St C2
Essex Cl C3
Farley Hill C1
Farley Lodge C1
Flowers Way B2
Francis St A1
Frederick St A2
Galaxy Leisure Complex A2
George St B2
George St West B2
Gordon St B2
Grove Rd B1
Guildford St A2
Haddon Rd A3
Harcourt St C2
Hart Hill Drive A3
Hart Hill Lane A3
Hartley Rd A3
Hastings St B2
Hat Factory, The B2
Hatters Way A1
Havelock Rd A2
Hibbert St C2
High Town Rd A3
Highbury Rd A1
Hightown Community Sports & Arts Ctr A3
Hillary Cres C1
Hillborough Rd C1
Hitchin Rd A3
Holly St C2
Holm C1
Hucklesby Way A2
Hunts Cl C1
Information Ctr B2
Inkerman St A2
John St B2
Jubilee St A3
Kelvin Cl C2
King St B2
Kingsland Rd C3
Larches, The A2
Latimer Rd C2
Lawn Gdns C2
Lea Rd B3
Library B2
Library Rd B2
Liverpool Rd B1
London Rd C2
Luton Station A2
Lyndhurst Rd B1
Magistrates Court B2
Mall, The B2
Manchester St B2
Manor Rd B3
May St C3
Meyrick Ave C1
Midland Rd A2
Mill St A2
Milton Rd B1
Moor St A1
Moor, The A1
Moorland Gdns A2
Moulton Rise A3
Museum & Art Gallery A2
Napier Rd B1
New Bedford Rd A1
New Town St C2
North St A3
Old Bedford Rd A2
Old Orchard C2
Osbourne Rd C3
Oxen Rd A3
Park Sq B2
Park St B3/C3
Park St West B2
Park Viaduct B3
Parkland Drive C1
Police Station B1
Pomfret Ave A3
Pondwicks Rd B3
Post Office A1/A2/B2/C3
Power Court B3
Princess St B1
Red Rails C1
Regent St B2
Reginald St A2
Rothesay Rd B1
Russell Rise C1
Russell St C1
St Ann's Rd B3
St George's B2
St George's Square B2
St Mary's B3
St Marys Rd B3
St Paul's Rd C2
St Saviour's Cres C1
Salisbury Rd B1
Seymour Ave C3
Seymour Rd C3
Silver St B2
South Rd C2
Stanley St B1
Station Rd A2
Stockwood Cres C2
Stockwood Park C1
Strathmore Ave C2
Stuart St B2
Studley Rd A1
Surrey St C3
Sutherland Place C1
Tavistock St C2
Taylor St A3
Telford Way A1
Tennyson Rd C2
Tenzing Grove C1
Thistle Rd B3
Town Hall B2
Townsley Cl C2
UK Centre for Carnival Arts B3
Union St B2
Univ of Bedfordshire B3
Upper George St B2
Vicarage St B3
Villa Rd A2
Waldeck Rd A1
Wellington St B1/B2
Wenlock St A2
Whitby Rd A1
Whitehill Ave C1
William St A2
Wilsden Ave C1
Windmill Rd B3
Windsor St C2
Winsdon Rd B1
York St A3

Maidstone 187

Albion Pl B3
All Saints B2
Allen St A3
Amphitheatre C2
Archbishop's Palace B2
Bank St B2
Barker Rd C2
Barton Rd C3
Beaconsfield Rd C1
Bedford Pl B1
Bishops Way B2
Bluett St A3
Bower La C1
Bower Mount Rd B1
Bower Pl C1
Bower St B1
Bowling Alley B3
Boxley Rd A3
Brenchley Gardens A2
Brewer St A3
Broadway B2
Broadway Sh Ctr B2
Brunswick St C3
Buckland Hill A1
Buckland Rd B1
Bus Station B3
Campbell Rd C3
Church Rd C1
Church St B3
Cinema C2
College Ave C2
College Rd C2
Collis Memorial Gdn C3
Cornwallis Rd B1
Corpus Christi Hall B2
Council Offices B3
County Hall A2
County Rd A3
Crompton Gdns C3
Crown & County Courts B2
Curzon Rd A3
Dixon Cl C2
Douglas Rd C1
Earl St B2
Eccleston Rd C2
Fairmeadow B2
Fisher St A2
Florence Rd C1
Foley St A3
Foster St C3
Fremlin Walk Sh Ctr B2
Gabriel's Hill B3
George St C3
Grecian St A3
Hardy St A3
Hart St C2
Hastings Rd C3
Hayle Rd C3
Hazlitt Theatre B2
Heathorn St A3
Hedley St A3
High St B2
HM Prison A3
Holland Rd A3
Hope St A2
Information Ctr B2
James St A3
James Whatman Way A2
Jeffrey St A3
Kent County Council Offices A2
Kent History & Library Centre A2
King Edward Rd C2
King St B3
Kingsley Rd C3
Knightrider St B3
Launder Way C1
Leisure Ctr A1
Lesley Pl A1
Library B2
Little Buckland Ave A1
Lockmeadow Leisure Complex C2
London Rd B1
Lower Boxley Rd A2
Lower Fant Rd C1
Magistrates Court B3
Maidstone Barracks Station A1
Maidstone East Station A2
Maidstone Museum & Bentlif Art Gall B2
Maidstone Utd FC A2
Maidstone West Station B2
Mall, The B3
Market C2
Market Buildings B2
Marsham St B3
Medway St B2
Medway Trading Est C2
Melville Rd C3
Mill St B2
Millennium Bridge C2
Mote Rd B3
Muir Rd C3
Old Tovil Rd C2
Palace Ave B3
Perryfield St A2
Police Station B3
Post Office B2/C3
Priory Rd C3
Prospect Pl C1
Pudding La B2
Queen Anne Rd B3
Queens Rd A1
Randall St A2
Rawdon Rd C3
Reginald Rd C1
Riverstage A1
Rock Pl B1
Rocky Hill B1
Romney Pl B3
Rose Yard B2
Rowland Cl C1
Royal Engineers' Rd A2
Royal Star Arcade B2
St Annes Ct B1
St Faith's St B2
St Luke's Rd A3
St Peter St B2
St Peter's Br B2
St Peter's Wharf Retail Park B2
St Philip's Ave C3
Salisbury Rd A3
Sandling Rd A2
Scott St A2
Scrubs La B1
Sheal's Cres C3
Somerfield Hospital, The A1
Somerfield La B1
Somerfield Rd B1
Staceys St A2
Station Rd A2
Superstore A1/B2/B3
Terrace Rd B1
Tonbridge Rd C1
Tovil Rd C2
Town Hall B2
Trinity Park B3
Tufton St B3
Tyrwhitt-Drake Museum of Carriages B2
Union St B3
Upper Fant Rd C1
Upper Stone St C3
Victoria St B1
Warwick Pl B1
Wat Tyler Way B3
Waterloo St C3
Waterlow Rd A3
Week St B2
Well Rd A3
Westree Rd C1
Wharf Rd C1
Whatman Park A1
Wheeler St A3
Whitchurch Cl B1
Woodville Rd C3
Wyatt St B3
Wyke Manor Rd B3

Manchester 186

Adair St B6
Addington St A5
Adelphi St A1
Albert Sq B3
Albion St C3
AMC Great Northern B3
Ancoats Gr B6
Ancoats Gr North B6
Angela St C2
Aquatic Centre C4
Ardwick Green North C5
Ardwick Green Park C5
Ardwick Green South C5
Arlington St A2
Artillery St B3
Arundel St C2
Atherton St B2
Atkinson St B3
Aytoun St B4
Back Piccadilly A4
Baird St B5
Balloon St A4
Bank Pl A1
Baring St B5
Barrack St C1
Barrow St A1
Bendix St A5
Bengal St A5
Berry St C5
Blackfriars Rd A3
Blackfriars St A3
Blantyre St C2
Bloom St B4
Blossom St A5
Boad St B5
Bombay St B4
Booth St A3
Booth St B4
Bootle St B3
Brazennose St B3
Brewer St A5
Bridge St A3
Bridgewater Hall B3
Bridgewater Pl A4
Bridgewater St B2
Brook St C4
Brotherton Dr A2
Brown St A3
Brown St B4
Brunswick St C6
Brydon Ave C6
Buddhist Centre A4
Bury St A2
Bus & Coach Station B4
Bus Station B4
Butler St A6
Buxton St C5
Byrom St B3
Cable St A5
Calder St B1
Cambridge St C3/C4
Camp St B3
Canal St B4
Cannon St A1
Cannon St A4
Cardroom Rd A6
Carruthers St A6
Castle St C2
Castlefield Arena B2
Cateaton St A3
Cathedral A3
Cathedral St A3
Cavendish St C4
Central Retail Pk A5
Chapel St A1/A3
Chapeltown St B5
Charles St C4
Charlotte St B4
Chatham St B4
Cheapside A3
Chepstow St B3
Chester Rd C1/C2
Chester St C4
Chetham's School of Music A3
China La B5
Chippenham Rd A6
Chorlton Rd C2
Chorlton St B4
Church St A2
Church St A4
City Park A4
City Rd C3
Civil Justice Centre B2
Cleminson St A2
Clowes St A3
College Land A3
Collier St B2
Commercial St C3
Conference Centre C4
Cooper St B4
Copperas St A4
Corn Exchange, The A4
Cornbrook C1
Cornell St A5
Corporation St A4
Cotter St C6
Cotton St A5
Cow La B1
Cross St B3
Crown Court B4
Crown St C2
Dalberg St C6
Dale St A4/B5
Dancehouse, The C4
Dantzic St A4
Dark La C6
Dawson St C2
Dean St A5
Deansgate A3/B3
Deansgate Castlefield C3
Deansgate Sta C3
Dolphin St C6
Downing St C5
Ducie St B5
Duke Pl B2
Duke St B2
Durling St C6
East Ordsall La A2/B1
Edge St A4
Egerton St C2
Ellesmere St C1
Everard St C1
Every St B6
Fairfield St B5
Faulkner St B4
Fennel St A3
Ford St A2
Ford St C6
Fountain St B4
Frederick St A2
Gartside St B2
Gaythorne St A1
George Leigh St A5
George St A1
George St B4
Gore St A2
Goulden St A5
Granby Row B4
Gravel St A3
Great Ancoats St A5
Great Bridgewater St B3
Great George St A1
Great Jackson St C2
Great Marlborough St C4
Greengate A3
Grosvenor St C5
Gun St A5
Hadrian Ave B6
Hall St B3
Hampson St B1
Hanover St A4

202 Oxford • Peterborough • Plymouth • Portsmouth • Reading • Salisbury • Scarborough • Sheffield

Burton St B2
Bus Station A2
Canal St C2
Carlton St B3
Carrington St C2
Castle C2
Castle Blvd C1
Castle Gate C2
Castle Meadow Rd C1
Castle Mdw Retail Pk C1
Castle Museum & Gallery C2
Castle Rd C2
Castle Wharf C2
Cavendish Rd East C1
Cemetery B1
Chaucer St B1
Cheapside B2
Church Rd A3
City Link C3
City of Caves ✦ C2
Clarendon St B1
Cliff Rd C3
Clumber Rd East C1
Clumber St B2
College St B1
Collin St C2
Conway Cl A2
Council House B2
Cranbrook St B3
Cranmer St A2
Cromwell St B1
Curzon St B3
Derby Rd B1
Dryden St A2
Exchange Ctr, The B2
Fishpond Dr C1
Fletcher Gate B3
Forest Rd East A1
Forest Rd West A1
Friar La C2
Galleries of Justice C3
Gedling Gr A1
Gedling St B3
George St B3
Gill St A2
Glasshouse St B2
Goldsmith St B2
Goose Gate B3
Great Freeman St A2
Guildhall B2
Hamilton Dr C1
Hampden St A1
Heathcote St B3
High Pavement C3
High School A1
Holles Cr C1
Hope Dr C1
Hungerhill Rd A3
Huntingdon Dr C1
Huntingdon St A2
Information Ctr B2
Instow Rise A3
Int Com Ctr A2
intu Broadmarsh C2
intu Victoria Centre B2
Kent St B3
King St B2
Lace Centre, The C2
Lace Market B3
Lace Mkt Theatre C3
Lamartine St B3
Leisure Ctr C3
Lenton Rd C1
Lewis Cl A3
Lincoln St B2
London Rd C3
Long Row B2
Low Pavement C2
Lower Parliament St B3
Magistrates' Court C2
Maid Marian Way B2
Mansfield Rd A2/B2
Middle Hill C2
Milton St B2
Mount St B2
National Ice Centre C3
Newcastle Dr B1
Newstead Gr A2
North Sherwood St A2
Nottingham Arena C3
Nottingham Sta C3
Nottingham Trent University A2/B2
Old Market Sq B2
Oliver St A1
Park Dr C1
Park Row C1
Park Terr B1
Park Valley C1
Park, The C1
Peas Hill Rd A3
Peel St A1
Pelham St B2
Peveril Dr C1
Plantagenet St A3
Playhouse Theatre B1
Plumptre St C3
Police Station B1/B2
Poplar St C3
Portland Rd B1
Post Office B2
Queen's Rd C3
Raleigh St A1
Regent St B1
Rick St B3
Robin Hood St B3
Robin Hood Statue ✦ C2
Ropewalk, The B1
Royal Centre B2
Royal Children Inn C2
Royal Concert Hall B2
St Ann's Hill Rd A2
St Ann's Way A2
St Ann's Well Rd A3
St Barnabas ✝ B1
St James' St B2
St Mark's St B3
St Mary's Gdn of Rest B3
St Mary's Gate B3
St Nicholas C2
St Peter's C2
St Peter's Gate B2
Salutation Inn C2
Shakespeare St B2
Shelton St A2
Shopmobility A2
South Pde B2
South Rd C1
South Sherwood St B2
Station St C3
Station Street C3
Stoney St B3
Talbot St B1
Tattershall Dr C1
Tennis Dr B1
Tennyson St A1
Theatre Royal B2
Trent St C3
Trent University B2
Union Rd B3
Upper Parliament St B2
Victoria Leisure Ctr B3
Victoria Park B3
Victoria St B2
Walter St A1
Warser Gate B3
Watkin St A2
Waverley St A1
Wheeler Gate B2
Wilford Rd C2
Wilford St C2
Willoughby House C2
Wollaton St B1
Woodborough Rd A2
Woolpack La B3
Ye Old Trip to Jerusalem ✦ C2
York St A2

Oxford 189

Adelaide St A1
Albert St A1
All Souls (Coll) B2
Ashmolean Mus B2
Balliol (Coll) B2
Banbury Rd A2
Bate Collection of Musical Instruments C2
Beaumont St B1
Becket St B1
Blackhall Rd A2
Blue Boar St B2
Bodleian Library B2
Botanic Garden B3
Brasenose (Coll) B2
Brewer St C2
Broad St B2
Burton-Taylor Theatre B2
Bus Station B1
Canal St A1
Cardigan St A1
Carfax Tower B2
Castle B1
Castle St B1
Catte St B2
Cemetery C1
Christ Church (Coll) B2
Christ Church Cath ✝ C2
Christ Church Mdw C2
Clarendon Centre B2
Coach & Lorry Park C1
College B3
Coll of Further Ed C1
Cornmarket St B2
Corpus Christi (Coll) B2
County Hall B1
Covered Market B2
Cowley Pl C3
Cranham St A1
Cranham Terr A1
Cricket Ground B1
Crown & County Courts C2
Deer Park B3
Exeter (Coll) B2
Folly Bridge C2
George St B1
Great Clarendon St A1
Hart St A1
Hertford (Coll) B2
High St B3
Hollybush Row B1
Holywell St B2
Hythe Bridge St B1
Ice Rink C1
Information Ctr B2
Jericho St A1
Jesus (Coll) B2
Jowett Walk B3
Juxon St A1
Keble (Coll) A2
Keble Rd A2
Library B2
Linacre (Coll) A3
Lincoln (Coll) B2
Little Clarendon St A1
Longwall St B3
Magdalen (Coll) B3
Magdalen Bridge B2
Magdalen St B2
Magistrate's Court C2
Manchester (Coll) B2
Manor Rd B3
Mansfield (Coll) A2
Mansfield Rd A3
Market B1
Marlborough Rd C2
Martyrs' Memorial ✦ B2
Merton (Coll) B3
Merton Field B3
Merton St B2
Mus of Modern Art B2
Museum of Oxford B2
Museum Rd A2
New College (Coll) B3
New Inn Hall St B2
New Rd B1
New Theatre B2
Norfolk St C1
Nuffield (Coll) B1
Observatory A1
Observatory St A1
Odeon B1/B2
Old Fire Station B1
Old Greyfriars St C2
Oriel (Coll) B2
Oxford Station B1
Oxford Story, The ✦ B2
Oxford University Research Centres A1
Oxpens Rd C1
Paradise Sq C1
Paradise St B1
Park End St B1
Parks Rd A2/B2
Pembroke (Coll) C2
Phoenix A1
Picture Gallery C2
Plantation Rd A1
Playhouse B2
Police Station C2
Post Office A1/B2
Pusey St B1
Queen's (Coll) B3
Queen's La B3
Radcliffe Camera B2
Rewley Rd B1
Richmond Rd A1
Rose La B3
Ruskin (Coll) B1
Said Business School B1
St Aldates C2
St Anne's (Coll) A1
St Antony's (Coll) A1
St Bernard's Rd A1
St Catherine's (Coll) B3
St Cross Building A3
St Cross Rd A3
St Edmund Hall (Coll) B3
St Giles St A2
St Hilda's (Coll) C3
St John St B2
St John's (Coll) B2
St Mary the Virgin B2
St Michael at the Northgate B2
St Peter's (Coll) B1
St Thomas St B1
Science Area A2
Science Museum B2
Sheldonian Theatre B2
Somerville (Coll) A1
South Parks Rd A2
Speedwell St C2
Sports Ground C3
Thames St C2
Town Hall B2
Trinity (Coll) B2
Turl St B2
University Coll (Coll) B3
Univ Mus & Pitt Rivers Mus A2
University Parks A2
Wadham (Coll) B2
Walton Cr A1
Walton St A1
Western Rd C2
Westgate Sh Ctr B2
Woodstock Rd A1
Worcester (Coll) B1

Peterborough 189

Athletics Arena B3
Bishop's Palace B2
Bishop's Rd B2/B3
Boongate A3
Bourges Boulevard A1
Bourges Retail Pk B1/B2
Bridge House (Council Offices) C2
Bridge St B2
Bright St A1
Broadway A2
Broadway A2
Brook St A2
Burghley Rd A2
Bus Station B2
Cavendish St A3
Charles St A3
Church St B2
Church Walk A2
Cobden Ave A1
Cobden St A1
Cowgate B2
Craig St A2
Crawthorne Rd A2
Cripple Sidings La C2
Cromwell Rd A1
Dickens St A3
Eastfield Rd A3
Eastgate B3
Fire Station A1
Fletton Ave C2
Frank Perkins Parkway C3
Geneva St A2
George St C2
Gladstone St A1
Glebe Rd C2
Gloucester Rd C3
Granby St B3
Grove St C1
Guildhall B2
Hadrians Ct C3
Henry St A2
Hereward Cross (Sh) B2
Hereward Rd B3
Information Ctr B2
Jubilee St C1
Kent Rd B1
Key Theatre C2
Kirkwood Cl B1
Lea Gdns B1
Library A2
Lincoln Rd A2
London Rd C2
Long Causeway B2
Lower Bridge St C2
Magistrates Court B2
Manor House St A2
Mayor's Walk A1
Midland Rd A1
Monument St A2
Morris St A3
Mus & Art Gallery B2
Nene Valley Railway C1
New Rd A2
New Rd C1
Northminster A2
Old Customs Ho C2
Oundle Rd C1
Padholme Rd A3
Palmerston Rd C1
Park Rd A2
Passport Office B2
Peterborough Nene Valley C1
Peterborough Sta B1
Peterborough United FC C2
Police Station B2
Post Office A3/B1/B2/B3/C1
Priestgate B2
Queen's Walk C2
Queensgate Centre B2
Railworld C1
Regional Swimming & Fitness Centre B3
River La B1
Rivergate Sh Ctr B2
Riverside Mead C3
Russell St A1
St John's B2
St John's St A3
St Marks St A2
St Peter's ✝ B2
St Peter's Rd B2
Saxon Rd A3
Spital Bridge A1
Stagshaw Dr C3
Star Rd B3
Thorpe Lea Rd B1
Thorpe Rd B1
Thorpe's Lea Rd B1
Tower St A2
Town Hall B2
Viersen Platz B2
Vineyard Rd B3
Wake Rd B3
Wellington St A3
Wentworth St B2
Westgate B2
Whalley St A3
Wharf Rd C1
Whitsed St A3
YMCA A3

Plymouth 189

Alma Rd A1
Anstis St B1
Armada Shop Ctr B2
Armada St A3
Armada Way B2
Arts Centre B2
Athenaeum B1
Athenaeum St C1
Barbican C3
Barbican C3
Baring St A3
Bath St B1
Beaumont Park B3
Beaumont Rd B3
Black Friars Gin Distillery ✦ C2
Breton Side B3
Castle St C3
Cathedral (RC) ✝ B1
Cecil St B1
Central Park A1
Central Park Ave A2
Charles Church B3
Charles Cross B3
Charles St B2
Citadel Rd C2
Citadel Rd East C2
City Museum & Art Gallery B2
Civic Centre B2
Cliff Rd C1
Clifton Pl A3
Cobourg St A2
College of Art B2
Continental Ferry Port B1
Cornwall St B2
Crescent, The B1
Dale Rd A2
Deptford Pl A3
Derry Ave A2
Derry's Cross B1
Drake Circus B2
Drake Cir Sh Ctr B2
Drake's Memorial ✦ C2
Eastlake St B2
Ebrington St B3
Elizabethan House C3
Elliot St C1
Endsleigh Pl A2
Exeter St B3
Fire Station A3
Fish Quay C3
Gibbons St A3
Glen Park Ave A2
Grand Pde C1
Great Western Rd C1
Greenbank Rd A3
Greenbank Terr A3
Guildhall B2
Hampton St B3
Harwell St B1
Hill Park Cr A3
Hoe Approach B2
Hoe Rd C2
Hoe, The C2
Hoegate St C2
Houndiscombe Rd A2
Information Ctr C3
James St A2
Kensington Rd A3
King St B1
Lambhay Hill C3
Leigham St C1
Library B2
Lipson Rd A3/B3
Lockyer St C2
Lockyers Quay C3
Madeira Rd C2
Marina B3
Market Ave B1
Martin St B1
Mayflower St B2
Mayflower Stone & Steps C3
Mayflower Visitor Centre ✦ C3
Merchant's House B2
Millbay Rd B1
National Marine Aquarium C3
Neswick St B1
New George St B2
New St C3
North Cross A2
North Hill A3
North Quay B2
North Rd East A2
North Rd West A1
North St B3
Notte St B2
Octagon, The B1
Octagon St B1
Pannier Market B1
Pennycomequick A1
Pier St C1
Plymouth Pavilions B1
Plymouth Station A2
Police Station B3
Post Office C2
Princess St B2
Promenade, The C2
Prysten House B2
Queen Anne's Battery Seasports Centre C3
Radford Rd C1
Reel B2
Regent St B3
Rope Walk C3
Royal Citadel C2
Royal Pde B2
Royal Theatre B2
St Andrew's B2
St Andrew's Cross B2
St Andrew's St B2
St Lawrence Rd A2
Saltash Rd A2
Shopmobility B2
Smeaton's Tower ✦ C2
Southern Terr A3
Southside St C2
Stuart Rd A1
Sutherland Rd A2
Sutton Rd B3
Sydney St A1
Teats Hill Rd C3
Tothill Ave B3
Union St B1
Univ of Plymouth A2
Vauxhall St B2/3
Victoria Park A1
West Hoe Rd C1
Western Approach B1
Whittington St A1
Wyndham St B1
YMCA B2
YWCA C2

Portsmouth 189

Action Stations ✦ C1
Admiralty Rd A1
Alfred Rd A2
Anglesea Rd B2
Arundel St B3
Aspex B1
Bishop St A2
Broad St C1
Buckingham Ho C2
Burnaby Rd B2
Bus Station B1
Camber Dock C1
Cambridge Rd B2
Car Ferry to Isle of Wight B1
Cascades Sh Ctr A3
Castle Rd C3
City Museum & Art Gallery B2
Civic Offices B3
Clarence Pier C2
College St B1
Commercial Rd A3
Cottage Gr B3
Cross St A1
Cumberland St A2
Duisburg Way C2
Durham St A3
East St B1
Edinburgh Rd A2
Elm Gr C3
Emirates Spinnaker Tower ✦ B1
Great Southsea St C3
Green Rd B3
Greetham St B3
Grosvenor St B3
Groundlings A2
Grove Rd North C3
Grove Rd South C3
Guildhall B3
Guildhall Walk B3
Gunwharf Quays Retail Park B1
Gunwharf Rd B1
Hambrook St C2
Hampshire Terr B2
Hanover St A1
Hard, The B1
High St C2
HM Naval Base A1
HMS Nelson (Royal Naval Barracks) A2
HMS Victory A1
HMS Warrior A1
Hovercraft Terminal C2
Hyde Park Rd B3
Information Ctr A1/B3
Isambard Brunel Rd B3
Isle of Wight Car Ferry Terminal B1
Kent Rd C3
Kent St A2
King St C3
King's Rd C3
King's Terr C2
Lake Rd A3
Law Courts B3
Library B3
Long Curtain Rd C2
Market Way A3
Marmion Rd C3
Mary Rose Mus A1
Middle St B3
Millennium Prom B1/C1
Museum Rd B2
National Museum of the Royal Navy A1
Naval Recreation Gd C2
Nightingale Rd C3
Norfolk St B3
North St A2
Osborne Rd C3
Park Rd B2
Passenger Catamaran to Isle of Wight B1
Passenger Ferry to Gosport B1
Pelham Rd C3
Pembroke Gdns C2
Pier Rd C2
Point Battery C1
Police Station B3
Portsmouth & Southsea A3
Portsmouth Harbour B1
Portsmouth Historic Dockyard A1
Post Office A2/A3/B1/B3/C3
Queen St A1
Queen's Cr C3
Round Tower ✦ C1
Royal Garrison Church C1
St Edward's Rd C3
St George's Rd B2
St George's Sq B1
St George's Way B2
St James's Rd B3
St James's St A2
St John's Cath (RC) ✝ A3
St Thomas's Cath ✝ C1
St Thomas's St B2
Somers Rd B3
Southsea Common C2
Southsea Terr C2
Square Tower ✦ C1
Station St A3
Swimming Pool A2
Town Fortifications ✦ C1
Unicorn Rd A2
United Services Recreation Ground B2
University of Portsmouth A2/B2
Univ of Portsmouth – Coll of Art, Design & Media B3
Upper Arundel St A3
Victoria Ave C2
Victoria Park A2
Victory Gate A1
Vue B1
Warblington St B1
Western Pde C2
White Hart Rd C1
Winston Churchill Ave B3

Reading 190

Abbey Ruins ✝ B2
Abbey Sq B2
Abbey St B2
Abbot's Walk B2
Acacia Rd C2
Addington Rd C3
Addison Rd A1
Allcroft Rd C3
Alpine St C2
Baker St B1
Berkeley Ave C1
Bridge St B1
Brigham Rd A1
Broad St B1
Broad Street Mall B1
Carey St B1
Castle Hill C1
Castle St B1
Causeway, The A3
Caversham Rd A1
Christchurch Playing Fields A2
Civic Offices B1
Coley Hill C1
Coley Pl C1
Craven Rd C3
Crown St C2
De Montfort Rd A1
Denmark Rd C3
Duke St B2
East St B2
Edgehill St C2
Eldon Rd B3
Eldon Terr B3
Elgar Rd C1
Erleigh Rd C3
Field Rd C1
Fire Station A1
Fobney St B1
Forbury Gdns B2
Forbury Rd B2
Forbury Retail Park B2
Francis St C1
Friar St B1
Garrard St B1
Gas Works Rd B3
George St A2
Great Knollys St B1
Greyfriars B1
Grove, The B2
Gun St B1
Henry St C1
Hexagon Theatre, The B1
Hill's Meadow A2
Howard St B1
Information Ctr B1
Inner Distribution Rd B1
Katesgrove La C1
Kenavon Dr B2
Kendrick Rd C2
King's Mdw Rec Gd A2
King's Rd B2
Library B2
London Rd C3
London St B2
Lynmouth Rd A1
Magistrate's Court B1
Market Pl B2
Mill La B2
Mill Rd A2
Minster St B1
Morgan Rd C3
Mount Pleasant C2
Museum of English Rural Life C3
Napier Rd A2
Newark St C2
Newport Rd A1
Old Reading Univ C3
Oracle Sh Ctr, The B1
Orts Rd B3
Pell St C1
Police Station B1
Post Office B2
Queen Victoria St B1
Queen's Rd A2
Queen's Rd B2
Randolph Rd A1
Reading Bridge A2
Reading Station A1
Redlands Rd C3
Renaissance Hotel B1
Riverside Museum B3
Rose Kiln La C1
Royal Berks Hospital (A&E) C3
St Giles C2
St Laurence B2
St Mary's B1
St Mary's Butts B1
St Saviour's Rd C1
Send Rd A3
Sherman Rd C2
Sidmouth St B2
Silver St C2
South St B2
Southampton St C2
Station Hill A1
Station Rd B1
Superstore A3
Swansea Rd A1
Technical College B3
Valpy St B2
Vastern Rd A1
Vue B2
Waldeck St C2
Watlington St B3
West St B1
Whitby Dr C3
Wolseley St C1
York Rd A1
Zinzan St B1

Salisbury 190

Albany Rd A2
Arts Centre A3
Ashley Rd A1
Avon Approach A2
Ayleswade Rd C2
Bedwin St A2
Belle Vue A2
Bishop's Palace C2
Bishops Walk B2
Blue Boar Row B2
Bourne Ave A3
Bourne Hill A3
Britford La C2
Broad Walk C2
Brown St B2
Bus Station B2
Castle St A2
Catherine St B2
Chapter House B2
Church House B2
Churchfields Rd B1
Churchill Way East B3
Churchill Way North A3
Churchill Way South C2
Churchill Way West A1
City Hall B2
Close Wall B2
Coldharbour La A1
College St A3
Council Offices A3
Court A1
Crane Bridge Rd B2
Crane St B2
Cricket Ground C1
Culver St South B3
De Vaux Pl C2
Devizes Rd A1
Dews Rd B1
Elm Grove B3
Elm Grove Rd A3
Endless St A2
Estcourt Rd A3
Exeter St C2
Fairview Rd A3
Fire Station A1
Fisherton St A1
Folkestone Rd C1
Fowlers Hill B3
Fowlers Rd B3
Friary Estate C3
Friary La B2
Friary, The B3
Gas La A1
Gigant St B3
Greencroft B3
Greencroft St A3
Guildhall B2
Hall of John Halle B2
Hamilton Rd A2
Harnham Mill B1
Harnham Rd C1/C2
High St B2
Hospital A1
Ho of John A'Port B2
Information Ctr B2
Kelsey Rd A3
King's Rd A2
Laverstock Rd B3
Library B2
London Rd A3
Lower St C1
Maltings, The B2
Manor Rd A3
Marsh La A1
Medieval Hall B2
Milford Hill B3
Milford St B3
Mill Rd B1
Millstream Approach A2
Mompesson House (NT) B2
New Bridge Rd C2
New Canal B2
New Harnham Rd C2
New St B2
North Canonry B2
North Gate B2
North Walk B2
Old Blandford Rd C1
Old Deanery B2
Old George Hall B2
Park St A3
Parsonage Green C1
Playhouse Theatre A2
Post Office A2/B2/C2
Poultry Cross B2
Queen Elizabeth Gdns B1
Queen's Rd A3
Rampart Rd B3
St Ann St B2
St Ann's Gate B2
St Marks Rd A3
St Martins B3
St Mary's Cath ✝ B2
St Nicholas Hospl C2
St Paul's A1
St Paul's Rd A1
St Thomas B2
Salisbury & South Wiltshire Mus B2
Salisbury General Hospital (A&E) C2
Salisbury Station A1
Salt La A3
Saxon Rd C1
Scots La A2
Shady Bower B3
South Canonry C2
South Gate C2
Southampton Rd B2
Spire View A1
Sports Ground C3
Tollgate Rd B3
Town Path B1
Wain-a-Long Rd A3
Wardrobe, The B2
Wessex Rd A3
West Walk C2
Wilton Rd A1
Wiltshire College B3
Winchester St B3
Windsor Rd A1
Winston Churchill Gdns C3
Wyndham Rd A2
YHA B3
York Rd A1

Scarborough 190

Aberdeen Walk B2
Albert Rd A2
Albion Rd C2
Alexandra Gardens A1
Auborough St B2
Balmoral Ctr B2
Belle Vue St C1
Belmont Rd C2
Brunswick Shop Ctr B2
Castle Dykes B3
Castle Hill A3
Castle Holms A3
Castle Rd A2
Castle Walls A3
Castlegate B3
Cemetery B1
Central Tramway ✦ B2
Clarence Gardens A2
Coach Park B1
Columbus Ravine A1
Court B1
Crescent, The C2
Cricket Ground A1
Cross St B2
Crown Terr C2
Dean Rd B1
Devonshire Dr A1
East Harbour B3
East Pier B3
Eastborough B2
Elmville Ave B1
Esplanade C2
Falconers Rd B2
Falsgrave Rd C1
Fire Station B2
Foreshore Rd B2
Friargate B2
Gladstone Rd B1
Gladstone St B1
Hollywood Plaza A1
Hoxton Rd B1
Information Ctr B2/B3
King St B2
Library B2
Lifeboat Station ✦ B3
Londesborough Rd C1
Longwestgate B3
Marine Dr A3
Military Adventure Park A1
Miniature Railway A1
Nelson St B1
Newborough B2
Nicolas St B2
North Marine Rd A1
North St B2
Northway B1
Old Harbour B3
Olympia Leisure ✦ B2
Peasholm Park A1
Peasholm Rd A1
Police Station B1
Post Office B2/C1
Princess St B3
Prospect Rd B1
Queen St B2
Queen's Parade A2
Queen's Tower (Remains) A3
Ramshill Rd C2
Roman Signal Sta A3
Roscoe St C1
Rotunda Museum C2
Royal Albert Dr A2
St Martin-on-the-Hill C2
St Martin's Ave C2
St Mary's B3
St Thomas St B2
Sandside B3
Scarborough C1
Scarborough Art Gallery and Crescent Art Studios C2
Scarborough Bowls Centre A1
Scarborough Castle A3
Shopmobility C2
Somerset Terr C2
South Cliff Lift ✦ C2
Spa Theatre, The C2
Spa, The ✦ C2
Stephen Joseph Theatre B1
Tennyson Ave B1
Tollergate B2
Town Hall B2
Trafalgar Rd B1
Trafalgar Square A1
Trafalgar St West B1
Valley Bridge Parade C2
Valley Rd C1
Vernon Rd C2
Victoria Park Mount A1
Victoria Rd B1
West Pier B3
Westborough C1
Westover Rd C1
Westwood C1
Woodall Ave A1
YMCA Theatre B2
York Pl B2
Yorkshire Coast College (Westwood Campus) C1

Sheffield 191

Addy Dr A2
Addy St A2
Adelphi St A3
Albert Terrace Rd A3
Albion St A2
Aldred Rd A1
Allen St A4
Alma St A4
Angel St B5
Arundel Gate B5
Arundel St C4
Ashberry Rd A2
Ashdell Rd C1
Ashgate Rd C1
Athletics Centre B2
Attercliffe Rd A6
Bailey St B4
Ball St A4
Balm Green B4
Bank St B4
Barber Rd A2
Bard St B5
Barker's Pool B4
Bates St A1
Beech Hill Rd C1
Beet St B3
Bellefield St A3
Bernard Rd A6
Bernard St B6
Birkendale A2
Birkendale Rd A2
Birkendale View A1
Bishop St C4
Blackwell Pl B6
Blake St A2
Blonk St A5
Bolsover St B2
Botanical Gdns C1
Bower Rd A1
Bradley St A1
Bramall La C4
Bramwell St A3
Bridge St A4/A5
Brighton Terrace Rd A1
Broad La B3
Broad St B6
Brocco St A3
Brook Hill B3
Broomfield Rd C1
Broomgrove Rd C2
Broomhall Pl C3
Broomhall Rd C2
Broomhall St C3
Broomspring La C2
Brown St C5
Brunswick St B3
Burgess St B4
Burlington St A2
Burns Rd A2
Cadman St A6
Cambridge St B4
Campo La B4
Carver St B4
Castle Market B5
Castle Square B5
Castlegate A5
Cathedral B4
Cathedral (RC) ✝ B4
Cavendish St B3
Charles St C4
Charter Row C4
Children's Hospital (A&E) B2
Church St B4
City Hall B4
City Hall B4
City Rd C6
Claremont Cr B2
Claremont Pl B2
Clarke St C3
Clarkegrove Rd C2
Clarkehouse Rd C1
Clarkson St B2
Cobden View Rd A1
Collegiate Cr C2
Commercial St B5
Commonside A1
Conduit Rd B1
Cornish St A3
Corporation St A4
Court B4
Cricket Inn Rd B6
Cromwell St A1
Crookes Rd B1
Crookes Valley Park B2
Crookes Valley Rd B2
Crookesmoor Rd A2
Crown Court A4
Crucible Theatre B5
Cutler's Hall B4
Cutlers Gate A6
Daniel Hill A2
Dental Hospital B2
Dept for Education & Employment C4
Devonshire Green B3
Devonshire St B3
Division St B4
Dorset St C2
Dover St A3
Duchess Rd C5
Duke St B5
Duncombe St A1
Durham Rd B2
Earl St C4
Earl Way C4
Ecclesall Rd C3
Edward St B3
Effingham Rd A6
Effingham St A6
Egerton St C3
Eldon St B3
Elmore Rd B1
Exchange St B5
Eyre St C4
Fargate B4
Farm Rd C5
Fawcett St A3
Filey St B3
Fir St A1
Fire & Police Mus A4
Fire Station C4
Fitzalan Sq/Ponds Forge B5
Fitzwater Rd C6
Fitzwilliam Gate C4
Fitzwilliam St B3
Flat St B5
Foley St A6
Foundry Climbing Centre A4
Fulton Rd A1
Furnace Hill A4
Furnival Rd A5
Furnival Sq C4
Furnival St C4
Garden St B3
Gell St B3
Gibraltar St A4
Glebe Rd B1
Glencoe Rd C6
Glossop Rd B2/B3/C1
Gloucester St C2
Granville Rd C6
Granville Rd/Sheffield College C5
Graves Gallery B5
Greave Rd B3
Green La A4
Hadfield St A1
Hanover St C3
Hanover Way C3
Harcourt Rd B1
Harmer La B5
Havelock St C2
Hawley St B4
Haymarket B5
Headford St C3
Heavygate Rd A1
Henry St A3
High St B4
Hodgson St C3
Holberry Gdns C2
Hollis Croft B4
Holly St B4
Hounsfield Rd B3
Howard Rd A1
Hoyle St A3
Hyde Park A6
Infirmary Rd A3
Infirmary Rd A3
Information Ctr B4
Jericho St A3
Johnson St A5

Southampton • Southend-on-Sea • Stoke • Stratford-upon-Avon • Sunderland • Swansea • Swindon 203

Kelham Island Ind Mus A4
Lawson Rd C1
Leadmill Rd C5
Leadmill St C5
Leadmill, The C5
Leamington St A1
Leavy Rd B3
Lee Croft B4
Leopold St B4
Leveson St A6
Library A2
Library B5
Library C1
Lyceum Theatre B5
Malinda St A3
Maltravers St A5
Manor Oaks Rd B6
Mappin St B3
Marlborough Rd B1
Mary St C4
Matilda St C4
Matlock Rd A1
Meadow St A3
Melbourn Rd A1
Melbourne Ave C1
Millennium Galleries B5
Milton St C3
Mitchell St B3
Mona Ave A1
Mona Rd A1
Montgomery Terr Rd A3
Montgomery Theatre B4
Monument Gdns C6
Moor Oaks Rd B1
Moor, The C4
Moore St C3
Mowbray St A4
Mushroom La B2
Netherthorpe Rd B3
Netherthorpe Rd B3
Newbould La C1
Nile St C1
Norfolk Park Rd C6
Norfolk Rd C6
Norfolk St B4
North Church St B4
Northfield Rd A1
Northumberland Rd B1
Nursery St A5
O2 Academy B5
Oakholme Rd C1
Octagon B2
Odeon B5
Old St B6
Orchard Square B4
Oxford St A2
Paradise St B4
Park La C2
Park Sq B5
Parker's Rd B1
Pearson Building (Univ) C2
Penistone Rd A3
Pinstone St B4
Pitt St B3
Police Station A4/B5
Pond Hill B5
Pond St B5
Ponds Forge Int Sports Ctr B5
Portobello St B3
Post Office A1/A2/B3/B4/B5/B6/C1/C3/C4/C6
Powell St A2
Queen St B4
Queen's Rd C5
Ramsey Rd B1
Red Hill B3
Redcar Rd B1
Regent St B3
Rockingham St B4
Roebuck Rd A2
Royal Hallamshire Hospital C2
Russell St A4
Rutland Park C1
St George's Cl B3
St Mary's Gate C3
St Mary's Rd C4/C5
St Peter & St Paul Cathedral B4
St Philip's Rd A3
Savile St A5
School Rd B1
Scotland St A4
Severn Rd B1
Shalesmoor A4
Shalesmoor A3
Sheaf St B5
Sheffield Hallam Univ B5
Sheffield Ice Sports Ctr – Skate Central C5
Sheffield Interchange B5
Sheffield Parkway A6
Sheffield Station C5
Sheffield Sta/Sheffield Hallam Univ B5
Sheffield University B2
Shepherd St A3
Shipton St A2
Shoreham St C4
Showroom, The C5
Shrewsbury Rd C5
Sidney St C4
Site Gallery C5
Slinn St A1
Smithfield A4
Snig Hill A5
Snow La A4
Solly St B3
South La C4
South Street Park B5
Southbourne Rd C1
Spital Hill A5
Spital St A5
Spring Hill B1
Spring Hill Rd B1
Springvale Rd A1
Stafford Rd C6
Stafford St B6
Stanley St A5
Suffolk Rd C5
Summer St B2
Sunny Bank C3
Surrey St B4
Sussex St A6
Sutton St B3
Sydney Rd A2
Sylvester St C4
Talbot St B5
Taptonville Rd B1
Tax Office C4
Tenter St B4
Town Hall B4
Townend St A1
Townhead St B4
Trafalgar St B4
Tree Root Walk B2
Trinity St A4
Trippet La B4
Turner Museum of Glass B3
Union St B4
Univ Drama Studio B2
Univ of Sheffield B3
Upper Allen St A3
Upper Hanover St B3
Upperthorpe Rd A2/A3
Verdon St A5
Victoria Quays B5
Victoria Rd C2
Victoria St B3
Waingate B5
Watery St A3
Watson Rd C1
Wellesley Rd B2
Wellington St C3
West Bar A4
West Bar Green A4
West One Plaza B3
West St B3
West St B4
Westbourne Rd C1
Western Bank B2
Western Rd A1
Weston Park B2
Weston Park Hospl B2
Weston Park Mus B2
Weston St B2
Wharncliffe Rd C3
Whitham Rd B1
Wicker A5
Wilkinson St B2
William St C3
Winter Garden B4
Winter St B2
York St B4
Yorkshire Artspace C5
Young St C4

Southampton 190

Above Bar St A2
Albert Rd North B3
Albert Rd South C3
Anderson's Rd B3
Archaeology Mus (God's Ho Tower) C2
Argyle Rd A2
Arundel Tower B1
Bargate, The B2
BBC Regional Centre A1
Bedford Pl A1
Belvidere Rd A3
Bernard St C2
Blechynden Terr A1
Brinton's Rd A2
Britannia Rd A3
Briton St C2
Brunswick Pl A1
Bugle St C1
Canute Rd C3
Castle Way C2
Catchcold Tower B1
Central Bridge C3
Central Rd C2
Channel Way C3
Chapel Rd B3
Cineworld C3
City Art Gallery A1
City College B3
City Cruise Terminal C1
Civic Centre A1
Civic Centre Rd A1
Coach Station B1
Commercial Rd A1
Cumberland Pl A1
Cunard Rd C2
Derby Rd A3
Devonshire Rd A1
Dock Gate 4 C2
Dock Gate 8 B1
East Andrews Park A2
East Park Terr A2
East St B2
Endle St B3
European Way C2
Fire Station A2
Floating Bridge Rd C3
Golden Gr A3
Graham Rd A2
Guildhall A1
Hanover Bldgs B2
Harbour Lights C3
Harbour Pde B1
Hartington Rd A3
Havelock Rd A1
Henstead Rd A1
Herbert Walker Ave B1
High St B2
Hoglands Park B2
Holy Rood (Rems), Merchant Navy Memorial B2
Houndwell Park B2
Houndwell Pl B2
Hythe Ferry C2
Information Ctr A1
Isle of Wight Ferry Terminal C1
James St B3
Java Rd C2
Kingsway A2
Leisure World B1
Library A1
Lime St B2
London Rd A2
Marine Pde B3
Marlands Shopping Centre, The A1
Marsh La B2
Mayflower Meml C1
Mayflower Park C1
Mayflower Theatre, The A1
Medieval Merchant's House C1
Melbourne St B3
Millais A2
Morris Rd A1
National Oceanography Centre C3
Neptune Way C3
New Rd A2
Nichols Rd A3
North Front A2
Northam Rd A3
Ocean Dock C2
Ocean Village Marina C3
Ocean Way C3
Odeon B1
Ogle Rd B1
Old Northam Rd A2
Orchard La B2
Oxford Ave A2
Oxford St C2
Palmerston Park A2
Palmerston Rd A2
Parsonage Rd A3
Peel St A3
Platform Rd C2
Polygon, The A1
Portland Terr B1
Post Office A2/A3/B2
Pound Tree Rd B2
Quays Swimming and Diving Complex, The B1
Queen's Park C2
Queen's Peace Fountain A2
Queen's Terr C2
Queensway B2
Radcliffe Rd A3
Rochester St A3
Royal Pier C1
Royal South Hants Hospital A2
St Andrew's Rd A2
St Mary St A2
St Mary's B3
St Mary's Leisure Ctr A2
St Mary's Pl B2
St Mary's Rd A2
St Mary's Stadium (Southampton FC) A3
St Michael's C1
Sea City Mus A1
Solent Sky C3
South Front B2
Southampton Central Station A1
Southampton Solent University A2
SS Shieldhall C2
Terminus Terr C2
Threefield La B2
Titanic Engineers' Memorial A2
Town Quay C1
Town Walls B2
Tudor House C1
Vincent's Walk B2
West Gate Hall C1
West Marlands Rd A1
West Park A1
West Park Rd A1
West Quay Rd B1
West Quay Retail Pk B1
Western Esplanade B1
Westquay Shop Ctr B1
White Star Way C2
Winton St A2

Southend-on-Sea 191

Adventure Island C3
Albany Ave A1
Albert Rd C3
Alexandra Rd C2
Alexandra St C2
Alexandra Yacht Club C2
Ashburnham Rd B2
Ave Rd B1
Avenue Terr B1
Balmoral Rd B1
Baltic Ave B3
Baxter Ave A2/B2
Beecroft Art Gallery B2
Bircham Rd A2
Boscombe Rd B3
Boston Ave A1/B2
Bournemouth Pk Rd A3
Browning Ave A3
Bus Station C3
Byron Ave A3
Cambridge Rd C1/C2
Canewdon Rd B1
Carnarvon Rd A2
Central Ave A3
Chelmsford Ave A1
Chichester Rd B2
Church Rd C3
Civic Centre A2
Clarence Rd C2
Clarence St C2
Cliff Ave B1
Cliffs Pavilion C1
Clifftown Parade C2
Clifftown Rd C2
Colchester Rd A1
Coleman St B3
College Way B2
County Court B3
Cromer Rd B3
Crowborough Rd A2
Dryden Ave A3
East St A2
Elmer App B2
Elmer Ave B2
Forum, The B2
Gainsborough Dr A1
Gayton Rd A2
Glenhurst Rd A2
Gordon Pl B2
Gordon Rd B2
Grainger Rd A2
Greyhound Way A3
Grove, The A3
Guildford Rd B3
Hamlet Ct Rd B1
Hamlet Rd C1
Harcourt Ave A1
Hartington Rd C3
Hastings Rd B3
Herbert Gr C3
Heygate Ave C3
High St B2/C2
Information Ctr C3
Kenway A2
Kilworth Ave B3
Lancaster Gdns B3
London Rd B1
Lucy Rd C3
MacDonald Ave A1
Magistrates' Court A2
Maine Ave C1
Maldon Rd A2
Marine Parade C3
Marine Rd C1
Milton Rd B1
Milton St B2
Napier Ave B2
North Ave A3
North Rd A1/B1
Odeon B2
Osborne Rd B1
Park Cres B1
Park Rd B1
Park St B1
Park Terr B1
Pier Hill C3
Pleasant Rd C3
Police Station A2
Post Office B2/B3
Princes St B2
Queens Rd B2
Queensway B2/B3/C3
Radio Essex C2
Rayleigh Ave A1
Redstock Rd A2
Rochford Ave A1
Royal Mews C2
Royal Terr C2
Royals Sh Ctr, The C3
Ruskin Ave A3
St Ann's Rd B3
St Helen's Rd B1
St John's Rd B1
St Leonard's Rd C3
St Lukes Rd A3
St Vincent's Rd C1
Salisbury Ave A1/B1
Scratton Rd C2
Shakespeare Dr A1
Shopmobility B2
Short St A2
South Ave A3
South Essex College B2
Southchurch Rd B3
Southend Central B2
Southend Pier Railway C3
Southend United FC A1
Southend Victoria B2
Stadium Rd A2
Stanfield Rd A2
Stanley Rd C3
Sutton Rd A3/B3
Swanage Rd B3
Sweyne Ave A1
Sycamore Gr A3
Tennyson Ave A3
Tickfield Ave A2
Tudor Rd A1
Tunbridge Rd A2
Tylers Ave B3
Tyrrel Dr B3
Univ of Essex B2/C2
Vale Ave A2
Victoria Ave A2
Victoria Sh Ctr, The B2
Warrior Sq B3
Wesley Rd C3
West Rd A1
West St A1
Westcliff Ave C1
Westcliff Parade C1
Western Esplanade C1
Weston Rd C2
Whitegate Rd B3
Wilson Rd C1
Wimborne Rd B3
York Rd C3

Stoke 191

Ashford St A3
Avenue Rd A3
Aynsley Rd A2
Barnfield C1
Bath St C2
Beresford St A3
Bilton St C2
Boon Ave C2
Booth St C2
Boothen Rd C2/C3
Boughey St C2
Boughley Rd B3
Brighton St B1
Campbell Rd C2
Carlton Rd B1
Cauldon Rd A3
Cemetery A2
Cemetery Rd A2
Chamberlain Ave C1
Church (RC) B2
Church St C2
City Rd C3
Civic Centre & King's Hall B3
Cliff Vale Pk A1
College Rd A2
Convent Cl B2
Copeland St B3
Cornwallis St C3
Corporation St A3
Crowther St A3
Dominic St B1
Elenora St B2
Elgin St B2
Epworth St A3
Etruscan St A1
Film Theatre B3
Fleming Rd C2
Fletcher Rd C2
Floyd St B2
Foden St C2
Frank St C2
Franklin Rd C1
Frederick Ave B1
Garden St C1
Garner St A1
Gerrard St B2
Glebe St B3
Greatbach Ave B1
Hanley Park A3
Harris St B1
Hartshill Rd B1
Hayward St A2
Hide St B2
Higson Ave B2
Hill St B2
Honeywall B2
Hunters Dr C1
Hunters Way C1
Keary St C2
Kingsway B2
Leek Rd B3
Library C2
Lime St C2
Liverpool Rd B2
London Rd C2
Lonsdale St C2
Lovatt St B2
Lytton St B3
Market C2
Newcastle La C1
Newlands St A2
Norfolk St A2
North St A1/B2
Northcote Ave B2
Oldmill St C3
Oriel St B1
Oxford St B1
Penkhull New Rd C1
Penkhull St C1
Police Station C2
Portmeirion Pottery C2
Post Office A3
Prince's Rd B1
Pump St B2
Quarry Ave B1
Quarry Rd B1
Queen Anne St A3
Queen's Rd C1
Queensway A1/B2/C3
Richmond St B1
Rothwell St C1
St Peter's B3
St Thomas Pl C1
Scrivenor Rd A1
Seaford St A3
Selwyn St C3
Shelton New Rd A1
Shelton Old Rd B2
Sheppard St C2
Spark St C2
Spencer Rd B3
Spode St C2
Squires View B3
Staffordshire Univ B3
Stanley Matthews Sports Centre B3
Station Rd B3
Stoke Business Park C3
Stoke Rd A2
Stoke-on-Trent Coll A3
Stoke-on-Trent Station B3
Sturgess St C2
Thistley Hough C1
Thornton Rd B3
Tolkien Way B1
Trent Valley Rd C1
Vale St B2
Villas, The C1
Watford St A3
Wellesley St A3
West Ave B1
Westland St B1
Yeaman St C2
Yoxall Ave B1

Stratford-upon-Avon 192

Albany Rd B1
Alcester Rd B1
Ambulance Station B1
Arden St B1
Avenue Farm A1
Ave Farm Ind Est A1
Avenue Rd A3
Avon Industrial Est A2
Baker Ave A1
Bandstand C3
Benson Rd A3
Birmingham Rd A2
Boat Club B3
Borden Pl C1
Brass Rubbing Ctr C2
Bridge St B2
Bridgetown Rd C3
Bridgeway B3
Broad St C2
Broad Walk C2
Brookvale Rd C1
Bull St C2
Butterfly Farm C3
Cemetery C1
Chapel La B2
Cherry Orchard C1
Chestnut Walk B2
Children's Playground C3
Church St C2
Civic Hall B2
Clarence Rd B1
Clopton Bridge B3
Clopton Rd A2
College B1
College La C2
College St C2
Com Sports Centre B1
Council Offices (District) B2
Courtyard, The C2
Cox's Yard B3
Cricket Ground C3
Ely Gdns B2
Ely St B2
Evesham Rd C1
Fire Station B1
Foot Ferry C3
Fordham Ave A2
Gallery, The B3
Garrick Way C1
Gower Memorial B3
Great William St B2
Greenhill St B2
Greenway, The C2
Grove Rd B2
Guild St B2
Guildhall & School B2
Hall's Croft C2
Hartford Rd C1
Harvard House B2
Henley St B2
High St B2
Holton St C2
Holy Trinity C2
Information Ctr B3
Jolyffe Park Rd A2
Kipling Rd C3
Library B2
Lodge Rd B1
Maidenhead Rd A3
Mansell St B2
Masons Court B2
Masons Rd A1
Maybird Shopping Pk A2
Maybrook Rd A1
Mayfield Ave A2
Meer St B2
Mill La C2
Moat House Hotel B3
Narrow La C2
Nash's Ho & New Pl B2
New St C2
Old Town C2
Orchard Way C1
Paddock La C1
Park Rd A1
Payton St B2
Percy St A2
Police Station B2
Post Office B2
Recreation Ground C2
Regal Road A2
Rother St B2
Rowley Cr A3
Royal Shakespeare Theatre B3
Ryland St C2
Saffron Meadow C2
St Andrew's Cr B1
St Gregory's A3
St Gregory's Rd A3
St Mary's Rd A2
Sanctus Dr C2
Sanctus St C1
Sandfield Rd C2
Scholars La B2
Seven Meadows Rd C2
Shakespeare Ctr B2
Shakespeare Inst C2
Shakespeare St B2
Shakespeare's Birthplace B2
Sheep St B2
Shelley Rd C3
Shipston Rd C3
Shottery Rd C1
Slingates Rd A2
Southern La C2
Station Rd B1
Stratford Healthcare B2
Stratford Hospital B2
Stratford Leisure & Visitor Centre B3
Stratford Sports Club B1
Stratford-upon-Avon Station B1
Swan Theatre B3
Swan's Nest La B3
Talbot Rd A2
Tiddington Rd B3
Timothy's Bridge Industrial Estate A1
Timothy's Bridge Rd A1
Town Hall & Council Offices B2
Town Sq B2
Trinity St C2
Tyler St B2
War Memorial Gdns B3
Warwick Rd B3
Waterside B3
Welcombe Rd A3
West St C2
Western Rd A2
Wharf Rd A2
Willows North, The B1
Willows, The B1
Wood St B2

Sunderland 192

Albion Pl C2
Alliance Pl B1
Argyle St C2
Ashwood St C1
Athenaeum St B2
Azalea Terr C2
Beach St A1
Bede Theatre C3
Bedford St B2
Beechwood Terr C1
Belvedere Rd C2
Blandford St B2
Borough Rd B3
Bridge Cr B2
Bridge St B2
Bridges, The B2
Brooke St A2
Brougham St B2
Burdon Rd C2
Burn Park C1
Burn Park Rd C1
Burn Park Tech Park C1
Carol St B1
Charles St A3
Chester Rd C1
Chester Terr B1
Church St A3
Civic Centre C2
Cork St B3
Coronation St B3
Cowan Terr C2
Crowtree Rd B2
Dame Dorothy St A2
Deptford Rd B1
Deptford Terr A1
Derby St C2
Derwent St C2
Dock St A3
Dundas St A2
Durham Rd C1
Easington St A2
Egerton St C3
Empire B2
Empire Theatre B2
Farringdon Row B1
Fawcett St B2
Fox St C1
Foyle St B3
Frederick St B3
Gill Rd B2
Hanover Pl A1
Havelock Terr C1
Hay St A2
Headworth Sq B3
Hendon Rd B3
High St East B3
High St West B2/B3
Holmeside B2
Hylton Rd B1
Information Ctr B2
John St B3
Kier Hardie Way A2
Lambton St B3
Laura St C3
Lawrence St B3
Leisure Centre B2
Library & Arts Ctr B3
Lily St B1
Lime St B1
Livingstone Rd B2
Low Row B2
Matamba Terr B1
Millburn St B1
Millennium Way A2
Minster B2
Monkwearmouth Station Museum A2
Mowbray Park C3
Mowbray Rd C3
Murton St C3
National Glass Ctr A3
New Durham Rd C1
Newcastle Rd A2
Nile St B3
Norfolk St B3
North Bridge St A2
Northern Gallery for Contemporary Art B3
Otto Terr C1
Park La C2
Park Lane C2
Park Rd C2
Paul's Rd B3
Peel St C3
Place, The B3
Police Station B2
Post Office B2
Priestly Cr A1
Queen St B2
Railway Row B1
Retail Park B1
Richmond St A2
Roker Ave A2
Royalty Theatre C1
Royalty, The C1
Ryhope Rd C2
St Mary's Way B2
St Michael's Way B2
St Peter's A3
St Peter's A2
St Peter's Way A3
St Vincent St C3
Salem Rd C3
Salem St C3
Salisbury St C3
Sans St B3
Silkworth Row B1
Southwick Rd A2
Stadium of Light (Sunderland AFC) A2
Stadium Way A2
Stobart St A2
Stockton Rd C2
Suffolk St C3
Sunderland B2
Sunderland Aquatic Centre A2
Sunderland Mus B3
Sunderland St B3
Sunderland Sta B2
Tatham St C3
Tavistock Pl B3
Thelma St C1
Thomas St North A2
Thornholme Rd C1
Toward Rd C3
Transport Interchange C2
Trimdon St Way B1
Tunstall Rd C2
University C1
University Library C1
Univ of Sunderland (City Campus) B1
Univ of Sunderland (Sir Tom Cowie at St Peter's Campus) A3
Vaux Brewery Way A2
Villiers St B3
Villiers St South B3
Vine Pl C2
Violet St B1
Walton La B3
Waterworks Rd B1
Wearmouth Bridge B2
Wellington La A1
West Sunniside B3
West Wear St B3
Westbourne Rd B1
Western Hill C1
Wharncliffe B1
Whickham St A3
White House Rd C3
Wilson St North A2
Winter Gdns C3
Wreath Quay A1

Swansea
Abertawe 192

Adelaide St C3
Albert Row C3
Alexandra Rd B3
Argyle St C1
Baptist Well Pl A2
Beach St C1
Belle Vue Way B3
Berw Rd A1
Berwick Terr A2
Bond St C1
Brangwyn Concert Hall C1
Bridge St A3
Brookands Terr B1
Brunswick St C1
Bryn-Syfi Terr A2
Bryn-y-Mor Rd C1
Bullins La B1
Burrows Rd C1
Bus Station C2
Bus/Rail link A3
Cadfan Rd A1
Cadrawd Rd A1
Caer St B3
Carig Cr A1
Carlton Terr B2
Carmarthen Rd A3
Castle Square B3
Castle St B3
Catherine St C1
Cinema C3
Civic Ctr & Library C2
Clarence St C2
Colbourne Terr A2
Constitution Hill B1
Court B3
Creidiol Rd A2
Cromwell St B2
Crown Courts C1
Duke St B1
Dunvant Pl C2
Dyfatty Park A3
Dyfatty St A3
Dyfed Ave A1
Dylan Thomas Ctr B3
Dylan Thomas Theatre C3
Eaton Cr C1
Eigen Cr A1
Elfed Rd A1
Emlyn Rd A1
Evans Terr A3
Fairfield Terr B1
Ffynone Dr B1
Ffynone Rd B1
Fire Station B3
Firm St A2
Fleet St C1
Francis St C1
Fullers Row B2
George St B2
Glamorgan St C2
Glynn Vivian Art Gallery B3
Gower Coll Swansea C1
Graig Terr A3
Grand Theatre C2
Granogwen Rd A2
Guildhall C1
Guildhall Rd South C1
Gwent Rd A1
Gwynedd Ave A1
Hafod St A3
Hanover St B1
Harcourt St B2
Harries St A2
Heathfield B2
Henrietta St B1
Hewson St B2
High St A3/B3
High View A2
Hill St A2
Historic Ships Berth C3
HM Prison C2
Information Ctr C2
Islwyn Rd A1
King Edward's Rd C1
Kingsway, The B2
LC, The C3
Long Ridge A2
Madoc St C2
Mansel St B2
Maritime Quarter C3
Market B3
Mayhill Gdns B1
Mayhill Rd A1
Milton Terr A2
Mission Gallery C3
Montpellier Terr B1
Morfa Rd A3
Mount Pleasant B2
National Waterfront Museum C3
Nelson St C2
New Cut Rd A3
New St A3
Nicander Pde A2
Nicander Pl A2
Nicholl St B2
Norfolk St B2
North Hill Rd A2
Northampton La B2
Orchard St B3
Oxford St B2
Oystermouth Rd C1
Page St B2
Pant-y-Celyn Rd B1
Parc Tawe Link B3
Parc Tawe North B3
Parc Tawe Sh & L Ctr B3
Patti Pavilion C1
Paxton St C2
Pen-y-Graig Rd A1
Penmaen Terr B1
Phillips Pde C1
Picton Terr B2
Plantasia B3
Police Station B2
Post Office A1/A2/C1/C2
Powys Ave A1
Primrose St B2
Princess Way B3
Promenade B2
Pryder Gdns A1
Quadrant Shop Ctr C2
Quay Park B3
Rhianfa La B1
Rhondda St B2
Richardson St C2
Rodney St C1
Rose Hill B1
Rosehill Terr B1
Russell St B1
St David's Shop Ctr C3
St Helen's Ave C1
St Helen's Cr C1
St Helen's Rd C1
St James Gdns B1
St James's Cr B1
St Mary's B3
Sea View Terr A3
Singleton St C2
South Dock C3
Stanley Pl B2
Strand B3
Swansea Castle B3
Swansea Metropolitan University B2
Swansea Museum C3
Swansea Station A3
Taliesyn Rd B1
Tan y Marian Rd A1
Tegid Rd A2
Teilo Cr A1
Tenpin Bowling B3
Terrace Rd B1/B2
Tontine St A3
Tower of Ecliptic Observatory C3
Townhill Rd A1
Tramshed, The C3
Trawler Rd C3
Union St B2
Upper Strand A3
Vernon St A3
Victoria Quay C3
Victoria Rd B3
Vincent St C1
Walter Rd B1
Watkin St A2
Waun-Wen Rd A2
Wellington St C2
Westbury St C1
Western St C1
Westway C2
William St C2
Wind St B3
Woodlands Terr B1
YMCA B2
York St C3

Swindon 192

Albert St C3
Albion St C1
Alfred St A2
Alvescot Rd C3
Art Gallery & Mus C3
Ashford Rd C1
Aylesbury St A2
Bath Rd C2
Bathampton St B1
Bathurst Rd B3
Beatrice St A2
Beckhampton St B3
Bowood Rd C1
Bristol St B1
Broad St A3
Brunel Arcade B2
Brunel Plaza B2
Brunswick St C2
Bus Station B2
Cambria Bridge Rd B1
Cambria Place B1
Canal Walk B2
Carfax St B2
Carr St B1
Cemetery C1/C3
Chandler Cl C3
Chapel C1
Chester St B1
Christ Church C3
Church Place B1
Cirencester Way A3
Clarence St B2
Clifton St C1
Cockleberry A2
Colbourne A3
Colbourne St A3
College St B2
Commercial Rd B2
Corporation St A2
Council Offices B3
County Rd A3
Courts B2
Cricket Ground A3
Cricklade Street C3
Crombey St B1/C2
Cross St C2
Curtis St B1
Deacon St C1
Designer Outlet (Great Western) B1
Dixon St C2
Dover St C2
Dowling St C2
Drove Rd C3
Dryden St C1
Durham St C3
East St B1
Eastcott Hill C2
Eastcott Rd C2
Edgeware Rd B2
Edmund St C2
Elmina Rd A3
Emlyn Square B1
Euclid St B3
Exeter St B1
Fairview C1
Faringdon Rd B1
Farnsby St B1
Fire Station B3
Fleet St B2
Fleming Way B2/B3
Florence St A2
Gladstone St A3
Gooch St A2
Graham St A3
Great Western Way A1/A2
Groundwell Rd B3
Hawksworth Way A1
Haydon St A2
Henry St B2
Hillside Ave C1
Holbrook Way B2
Hunt St C3
Hydro B1
Hythe Rd C2
Information Ctr B2
Joseph St C1
Kent Rd C2
King William St C2
Kingshill Rd C1
Lansdown Rd C2
Lawn, The C3
Leicester St B3
Library B2
Lincoln St B3
Little London C3
London St B1
Magic B3
Maidstone Rd C2
Manchester Rd A3
Maxwell St B1
Milford St B2
Milton Rd B1
Morse St C2
National Monuments Record Centre B1
Newcastle St B3
Newcombe Drive A1
Newcombe Trading Estate A1
Newhall St C2
North St C2
North Star A1
North Star Ave A1
Northampton St B3
Nurseries, The C1
Oasis Leisure Ctr A1
Ocotal Way A3
Okus Rd C1
Old Town C3
Oxford St B1
Parade, The B2
Park Lane B1
Park Lane B1
Park, The B1
Pembroke St C2
Plymouth St B3
Polaris House A2
Polaris Way A2
Police Station B2
Ponting St A2
Post Office B1/B2/C1/C3
Poulton St A3
Princes St B2
Prospect Hill C2
Prospect Place C2
Queen St B2
Queen's Park C3
Radnor St C1
Read St C1
Reading St B1
Regent St B2
Retail Park A2/A3/B3
Rosebery St A3
St Mark's B1
Salisbury St A3
Savernake St C2
Shelley St C1
Sheppard St B1
South St C2
Southampton St B3
Spring Gardens B3
Stafford Street C2
Stanier St C2
Station Road A2

Index to road maps of Britain

Abbreviations used in the index

Aberdeen Aberdeen City	E Loth East Lothian	NE Lincs North East Lincolnshire	Soton Southampton
Aberds Aberdeenshire	E Renf East Renfrewshire	Neath Neath Port Talbot	Staffs Staffordshire
Ald Alderney	E Sus East Sussex	Newport City and County of Newport	Southend Southend-on-Sea
Anglesey Isle of Anglesey	E Yorks East Riding of Yorkshire	Norf Norfolk	Stirling Stirling
Angus Angus	Edin City of Edinburgh	Northants Northamptonshire	Stockton Stockton-on-Tees
Argyll Argyll and Bute	Essex Essex	Northumb Northumberland	Stoke Stoke-on-Trent
Bath Bath and North East Somerset	Falk Falkirk	Nottingham City of Nottingham	Suff Suffolk
Bedford Bedford	Fife Fife	Notts Nottinghamshire	Sur Surrey
Bl Gwent Blaenau Gwent	Flint Flintshire	Orkney Orkney	Swansea Swansea
Blackburn Blackburn with Darwen	Glasgow City of Glasgow	Oxon Oxfordshire	Swindon Swindon
Blackpool Blackpool	Glos Gloucestershire	Pboro Peterborough	T&W Tyne and Wear
Borders Scottish Borders	Gtr Man Greater Manchester	Pembs Pembrokeshire	Telford Telford and Wrekin
Brack Bracknell	Guern Guernsey	Perth Perth and Kinross	Thurrock Thurrock
Bridgend Bridgend	Gwyn Gwynedd	Plym Plymouth	Torbay Torbay
Brighton City of Brighton and Hove	Halton Halton	Poole Poole	Torf Torfaen
Bristol City and County of Bristol	Hants Hampshire	Powys Powys	V Glam The Vale of Glamorgan
Bucks Buckinghamshire	Hereford Herefordshire	Ptsmth Portsmouth	W Berks West Berkshire
C Beds Central Bedfordshire	Herts Hertfordshire	Reading Reading	W Dunb West Dunbartonshire
Caerph Caerphilly	Highld Highland	Redcar Redcar and Cleveland	W Isles Western Isles
Cambs Cambridgeshire	Hrtlpl Hartlepool	Renfs Renfrewshire	W Loth West Lothian
Cardiff Cardiff	Hull Hull	Rhondda Rhondda Cynon Taff	W Mid West Midlands
Carms Carmarthenshire	IoM Isle of Man	Rutland Rutland	W Sus West Sussex
Ceredig Ceredigion	IoW Isle of Wight	S Ayrs South Ayrshire	W Yorks West Yorkshire
Ches E Cheshire East	Invclyd Inverclyde	S Glos South Gloucestershire	Warks Warwickshire
Ches W Cheshire West and Chester	Jersey Jersey	S Lanark South Lanarkshire	Warr Warrington
Clack Clackmannanshire	Kent Kent	S Yorks South Yorkshire	Wilts Wiltshire
Conwy Conwy	Lancs Lancashire	Scilly Scilly	Windsor Windsor and Maidenhead
Corn Cornwall	Leicester City of Leicester	Shetland Shetland	Wokingham Wokingham
Cumb Cumbria	Leics Leicestershire	Shrops Shropshire	Worcs Worcestershire
Darl Darlington	Lincs Lincolnshire	Slough Slough	Wrex Wrexham
Denb Denbighshire	London Greater London	Som Somerset	York City of York
Derby City of Derby	Luton Luton		
Derbys Derbyshire	M Keynes Milton Keynes		
Devon Devon	M Tydf Merthyr Tydfil		
Dorset Dorset	Mbro Middlesbrough		
Dumfries Dumfries and Galloway	Medway Medway		
Dundee Dundee City	Mers Merseyside		
Durham Durham	Midloth Midlothian		
E Ayrs East Ayrshire	Mon Monmouthshire		
E Dunb East Dunbartonshire	Moray Moray		
	N Ayrs North Ayrshire		
	N Lincs North Lincolnshire		
	N Lanark North Lanarkshire		
	N Som North Somerset		
	N Yorks North Yorkshire		

How to use the index

Example

Trudoxhill Som 24 E2

— grid square
— page number
— county or unitary authority

Map of Britain showing counties and unitary authorities.

A

Ab Kettleby Leics	64	B4
Ab Lench Worcs	50	D5
Abbas Combe Som	12	B5
Abberley Worcs	50	C2
Abberton Essex	43	C6
Abberton Worcs	50	D4
Abberwick Northumb	117	C7
Abbess Roding Essex	42	C1
Abbey Devon	11	C6
Abbey-cwm-hir Powys	48	B2
Abbey Dore Hereford	49	F5
Abbey Field Essex	43	B5
Abbey Hulton Stoke	75	E6
Abbey St Bathans Borders	122	C3
Abbey Town Cumb	107	D8
Abbey Village Lancs	86	B4
Abbey Wood London	29	B5
Abbeydale S Yorks	88	F4
Abbeystead Lancs	93	D5
Abbots Bickington Devon	9	C5
Abbots Bromley Staffs	62	B4
Abbots Langley Herts	40	D3
Abbots Leigh N Som	23	B7
Abbots Morton Worcs	50	D5
Abbots Ripton Cambs	54	B3
Abbots Salford Warks	51	D5
Abbotsbury Dorset	12	F3
Abbotsham Devon	9	B6
Abbotskerswell Devon	7	C6
Abbotsley Cambs	54	D3
Abbotswood Hants	14	B4
Abbotts Ann Hants	25	E8
Abcott Shrops	49	B5
Abdon Shrops	61	F5
Aber Ceredig	46	E3
Aber-Arad Carms	46	E2
Aber-banc Ceredig	46	E2
Aber Cowarch Gwyn	59	C5
Aber-Giâr Carms	46	E4
Aber-gwynfi Neath	34	E2
Aber-Hirnant Gwyn	72	F3
Aber-nant Rhondda	34	D4
Aber-Rhiwlech Gwyn	59	B6
Aber-Village Powys	35	B5
Aberaeron Ceredig	46	C3
Aberaman Rhondda	34	D4
Aberangell Gwyn	58	C5
Aberarder Highld	137	F7
Aberarder House Highld	138	B2
Aberarder Lodge Highld	137	F8
Aberargie Perth	128	C3
Aberarth Ceredig	46	C3
Aberavon Neath	33	E8
Aberbeeg Bl Gwent	35	D6
Abercanaid M Tydf	34	D4
Abercarn Caerph	35	E6
Abercastle Pembs	44	B3
Abercegir Powys	58	D5
Aberchirder Aberds	152	C6
Abercraf Powys	34	C2
Abercrombie Fife	129	D7
Abercych Pembs	45	E4
Abercynafon Powys	34	C4
Abercynon Rhondda	34	E4
Aberdalgie Perth	128	B2
Aberdâr = Aberdare Rhondda	34	D3
Aberdare = Aberdâr Rhondda	34	D3
Aberdaron Gwyn	70	E2
Aberdaugleddau = Milford Haven Pembs	44	E4
Aberdeen Aberdeen	141	D8
Aberdesach Gwyn	82	F4
Aberdour Fife	128	F3
Aberdulais Neath	34	D1
Aberedw Powys	48	E2
Abereiddy Pembs	44	B2
Abererch Gwyn	70	D4
Aberfan M Tydf	34	D4
Aberfeldy Perth	133	E5
Aberffraw Anglesey	82	E3
Aberffrwd Ceredig	47	B5
Aberford W Yorks	95	F7
Aberfoyle Stirling	126	D4
Abergavenny = Y Fenni Mon	35	C6
Abergele Conwy	72	B3
Abergorlech Carms	46	F4
Abergwaun = Fishguard Pembs	44	B4
Abergwesyn Powys	47	D7
Abergwili Carms	33	B5
Abergwynant Gwyn	58	C3
Abergwyngregyn Gwyn	83	D6
Abergwynolwyn Gwyn	58	D3
Aberhonddu = Brecon Powys	34	B4
Aberhosan Powys	58	E5
Aberkenfig Bridgend	34	F2
Aberlady E Loth	129	F6
Aberlemno Angus	135	D5
Aberllefenni Gwyn	58	D4
Abermagwr Ceredig	47	B5
Abermaw = Barmouth Gwyn	58	C3
Abermeurig Ceredig	46	D4
Abermule Powys	59	E8
Abernaint Powys	59	B8
Abernant Carms	32	B4
Abernethy Perth	128	C3
Abernyte Perth	134	F2
Aberpennar = Mountain Ash Rhondda	34	E4
Aberporth Ceredig	45	D4
Abersoch Gwyn	70	E4
Abersychan Torf	35	D6
Abertawe = Swansea Swansea	33	E7
Aberteifi = Cardigan Ceredig	45	E3
Aberthin V Glam	22	B2
Abertillery = Abertyleri Bl Gwent	35	D6
Abertridwr Caerph	35	F5
Abertridwr Powys	59	C7
Abertyleri = Abertillery Bl Gwent	35	D6
Abertysswg Caerph	35	D5
Aberuthven Perth	127	C8
Aberyscir Powys	34	B3
Aberystwyth Ceredig	58	F2
Abhainn Suidhe W Isles	154	G5
Abingdon-on-Thames Oxon	38	E4
Abinger Common Sur	28	E2
Abinger Hammer Sur	27	E8
Abington S Lanark	114	B2
Abington Pigotts Cambs	54	E4
Ablington Glos	37	D8
Ablington Wilts	25	E6
Abney Derbys	75	B8
Aboyne Aberds	140	E4
Abram Gtr Man	86	D4
Abriachan Highld	151	H8
Abronhill N Lanark	119	B7
Abson S Glos	24	B2
Abthorpe Northants	52	E4
Abune-the-Hill Orkney	159	F3
Aby Lincs	79	B7
Acaster Malbis York	95	E8
Acaster Selby N Yorks	95	E8
Accrington Lancs	87	B5
Acha Argyll	146	F4
Acha Mor W Isles	155	E8
Achabraid Argyll	145	E7
Achachork Highld	149	D9
Achafolla Argyll	124	D3
Achagary Highld	157	D10
Achahoish Argyll	144	F6
Achalader Perth	133	E8
Achallader Argyll	131	E7
Ach'an Todhair Highld	130	B4
Achanalt Highld	150	E5
Achanamara Argyll	144	E6
Achandunie Highld	151	D9
Achany Highld	157	J8
Achaphubuil Highld	130	B4
Acharacle Highld	147	E9
Acharn Highld	147	F10
Acharn Perth	132	E4
Acharole Highld	158	E4
Achath Aberds	141	C6
Achavanich Highld	158	F3
Achavraat Highld	151	G12
Achddu Carms	33	D5
Achduart Highld	156	J3
Achentoul Highld	157	F11
Achfary Highld	156	F5
Achgarve Highld	155	H13
Achiemore Highld	156	C6
Achiemore Highld	157	D11
A'Chill Highld	148	H7
Achiltibuie Highld	156	J3
Achina Highld	157	C10
Achinduich Highld	157	J8
Achinduin Argyll	124	B4
Achingills Highld	158	D3
Achintee Highld	131	B5
Achintee Highld	150	G2
Achintraid Highld	149	E13
Achlean Highld	138	E4
Achleck Argyll	146	G7
Achluachrach Highld	137	F5
Achlyness Highld	156	D5
Achmelvich Highld	156	G3
Achmore Highld	149	E13
Achmore Stirling	132	F2
Achnaba Argyll	124	B5
Achnaba Argyll	145	E8
Achnabat Highld	151	H8
Achnacarnin Highld	156	F3
Achnacarry Highld	136	F4
Achnacloich Argyll	125	B5
Achnacloich Highld	149	H10
Achnaconeran Highld	137	C7
Achnacraig Argyll	146	G7
Achnacroish Argyll	130	E2
Achnadrish Argyll	146	F7
Achnafalnich Argyll	125	C8
Achnagarron Highld	151	E9
Achnaha Highld	146	E7
Achnahanat Highld	151	B8
Achnahannet Highld	139	B5
Achnairn Highld	157	H8
Achnaluachrach Highld	157	J9
Achnasaul Highld	136	F4
Achnasheen Highld	150	F4
Achosnich Highld	146	E7
Achranich Highld	147	G10
Achreamie Highld	157	C13
Achriabhach Highld	131	C5
Achriesgill Highld	156	D5
Achrimsdale Highld	157	J12
Achtoty Highld	157	C9
Achurch Northants	65	F7
Achuvoldrach Highld	157	D8
Achvaich Highld	151	B10
Achvarasdal Highld	157	C12
Ackergill Highld	158	E5
Acklam Mbro	102	C2
Acklam N Yorks	96	C3
Ackleton Shrops	61	E7
Acklington Northumb	117	D8
Ackton W Yorks	88	B5
Ackworth Moor Top W Yorks	88	C5
Acle Norf	69	C7
Acock's Green W Mid	62	F5
Acol Kent	31	C7
Acomb Northumb	110	C2
Acomb York	95	D8
Aconbury Hereford	49	F7
Acre Lancs	87	B5
Acre Street W Sus	15	E8
Acrefair Wrex	73	E6
Acton Ches E	74	D3
Acton Dorset	13	G7
Acton London	41	F5
Acton Shrops	60	F3
Acton Suff	56	E2
Acton Wrex	73	D7
Acton Beauchamp Hereford	49	D8
Acton Bridge Ches W	74	B2
Acton Green Hereford	49	D8
Acton Pigott Shrops	60	D5
Acton Round Shrops	61	E6
Acton Scott Shrops	60	F4
Acton Trussell Staffs	62	C3
Acton Turville S Glos	37	F5
Adbaston Staffs	61	B7
Adber Dorset	12	B3
Adderley Shrops	74	E3
Adderstone Northumb	123	F7
Addiewell W Loth	120	C2
Addingham W Yorks	94	E3
Addington Bucks	39	B7
Addington Kent	29	D7
Addington London	28	C4
Addinston Borders	121	D8
Addiscombe London	28	C4
Addlestone Sur	27	C8
Addlethorpe Lincs	79	C8
Adel W Yorks	95	F5
Adeney Telford	61	C7
Adfa Powys	59	D7
Adforton Hereford	49	B6
Adisham Kent	31	D6
Adlestrop Glos	38	B2
Adlingfleet E Yorks	90	B2
Adlington Lancs	86	C4
Admaston Staffs	62	C4
Admaston Telford	61	C6
Admington Warks	51	E7
Adstock Bucks	52	F5
Adstone Northants	52	D3
Adversane W Sus	16	B4
Advie Highld	152	E1
Adwalton W Yorks	88	B3
Adwell Oxon	39	E6
Adwick le Street S Yorks	89	D6
Adwick upon Dearne S Yorks	89	D5
Adziel Aberds	153	C9
Ae Village Dumfries	114	F2
Affleck Aberds	141	B7
Affpuddle Dorset	13	E6
Afon-wen Flint	72	B5
Afton IoW	14	F4
Agglethorpe N Yorks	101	F5
Agneash IoM	84	D4
Aigburth Mers	85	F4
Aiginis W Isles	155	D9
Aike E Yorks	97	E6
Aikerness Orkney	159	C5
Aikers Orkney	159	J5
Aiketgate Cumb	108	E4
Aikton Cumb	108	D2
Ailey Hereford	48	E5
Ailstone Warks	51	D7
Ailsworth Pboro	65	E8
Ainderby Quernhow N Yorks	102	F1
Ainderby Steeple N Yorks	101	E8
Aingers Green Essex	43	B7
Ainsdale Mers	85	C4
Ainsdale-on-Sea Mers	85	C4
Ainstable Cumb	108	E5
Ainsworth Gtr Man	87	C5
Ainthorpe N Yorks	103	D5
Aintree Mers	85	E4
Aird Argyll	124	E3
Aird Dumfries	104	C4
Aird Highld	149	A12
Aird W Isles	155	D10
Aird a Mhachair W Isles	148	D2
Aird a' Mhulaidh W Isles	154	F6
Aird Asaig W Isles	154	G6
Aird Dhail W Isles	155	A9
Aird Mhidhinis W Isles	148	H2
Aird Mhighe W Isles	154	H6
Aird Mhighe W Isles	154	J5
Aird Mhor W Isles	148	H2
Aird of Sleat Highld	149	H10
Aird Thunga W Isles	155	D9
Aird Uig W Isles	154	D5
Airdens Highld	151	B9
Airdrie N Lanark	119	C7
Airdtorrisdale Highld	157	C9
Airidh a Bhruaich W Isles	154	F7
Airieland Dumfries	106	D4
Airmyn E Yorks	89	B8
Airntully Perth	133	F7
Airor Highld	149	H12
Airth Falk	127	F7
Airton N Yorks	94	D2
Airyhassen Dumfries	105	E7
Aisby Lincs	78	F3
Aisby Lincs	90	E2
Aisgernis W Isles	148	F2
Aiskew N Yorks	101	F7
Aislaby N Yorks	103	D6
Aislaby N Yorks	103	F5
Aislaby Stockton	102	C2
Aisthorpe Lincs	78	A2
Aith Orkney	159	G3
Aith Shetland	160	D8
Aith Shetland	160	H5
Aithsetter Shetland	160	K6
Aitkenhead S Ayrs	112	D3
Aitnoch Highld	151	H12
Akeld Northumb	117	B5
Akeley Bucks	52	F5
Akenham Suff	56	E5
Albaston Corn	6	B2
Alberbury Shrops	60	C3
Albourne W Sus	17	C6
Albrighton Shrops	60	C4
Albrighton Shrops	62	D2
Alburgh Norf	69	F5
Albury Herts	41	B7
Albury Sur	27	E8
Albury End Herts	41	B7
Alby Hill Norf	81	D7
Alcaig Highld	151	F8
Alcaston Shrops	60	F4
Alcester Warks	51	D5
Alciston E Sus	18	E2
Alcombe Som	21	E8
Alcombe Wilts	24	C3
Alconbury Cambs	54	B2
Alconbury Weston Cambs	54	B2
Aldbar Castle Angus	135	D5
Aldborough Norf	81	D7
Aldborough N Yorks	95	C7
Aldbourne Wilts	25	B7
Aldbrough E Yorks	97	F8
Aldbrough St John N Yorks	101	C7
Aldbury Herts	40	C2
Aldcliffe Lancs	92	C4
Aldclune Perth	133	C6
Aldeburgh Suff	57	D8
Aldeby Norf	69	E7
Aldenham Herts	40	E4
Alderbury Wilts	14	B2
Aldercar Derbys	76	E4
Alderford Norf	68	C4
Alderholt Dorset	14	C2
Alderley Glos	36	E4
Alderley Edge Ches E	74	B5
Aldermaston W Berks	26	C3
Aldermaston Wharf W Berks	26	C4
Alderminster Warks	51	E7
Alder's End Hereford	49	E8
Aldersey Green Ches W	73	D8
Aldershot Hants	27	D6
Alderton Glos	50	F5
Alderton Northants	52	E5
Alderton Shrops	60	B4
Alderton Suff	57	E7
Alderton Wilts	37	F5
Alderwasley Derbys	76	D3
Aldfield N Yorks	95	C5
Aldford Ches W	73	D8
Aldham Essex	43	B5
Aldham Suff	56	E4
Aldie Highld	151	C10
Aldingbourne W Sus	16	D3
Aldingham Cumb	92	B2
Aldington Kent	19	B7
Aldington Worcs	51	E5
Aldington Frith Kent	19	B7
Aldochlay Argyll	126	E2
Aldreth Cambs	54	B5
Aldridge W Mid	62	D4
Aldringham Suff	57	C8
Aldsworth Glos	38	C1
Aldunie Moray	140	B2
Aldwark Derbys	76	D2
Aldwark N Yorks	95	C7
Aldwick W Sus	16	E3
Aldwincle Northants	65	F7
Aldworth W Berks	26	B3
Alexandria W Dunb	118	B3
Alfardisworthy Devon	8	C4
Alfington Devon	11	E6
Alfold Sur	27	F8
Alfold Bars W Sus	27	F8
Alfold Crossways Sur	27	F8
Alford Aberds	140	C4
Alford Lincs	79	B7
Alford Som	23	F8
Alfreton Derbys	76	D4
Alfrick Worcs	50	D2
Alfrick Pound Worcs	50	D2
Alfriston E Sus	18	E2
Algaltraig Argyll	145	F9
Algarkirk Lincs	79	F5
Alhampton Som	23	F8
Aline Lodge W Isles	154	F6
Alisary Highld	147	D10
Alkborough N Lincs	90	B2
Alkerton Oxon	51	E8
Alkham Kent	31	E6
Alkington Shrops	74	F2
Alkmonton Derbys	75	F8
Alladale Lodge Highld	150	C7
Allaleigh Devon	7	D6
Allanaquoich Aberds	139	E7
Allangrange Mains Highld	151	F9
Allanton Borders	122	D4
Allanton N Lanark	119	D8
Allathasdal W Isles	148	H1
Allendale Town Northumb	109	D8
Allenheads Northumb	109	E8
Allens Green Herts	41	C7
Allensford Durham	110	D3
Allensmore Hereford	49	F6
Allenton Derby	76	F3
Aller Som	12	B2
Allerby Cumb	107	F7
Allerford Som	21	E8
Allerston N Yorks	103	F6
Allerthorpe E Yorks	96	E3
Allerton Mers	86	F2
Allerton W Yorks	94	F4
Allerton Bywater W Yorks	88	B5
Allerton Mauleverer N Yorks	95	D7
Allesley W Mid	63	F7
Allestree Derby	76	F3
Allet Corn	3	B6
Allexton Leics	64	D5
Allgreave Ches E	75	C6
Allhallows Medway	30	B2
Allhallows-on-Sea Medway	30	B2
Alligin Shuas Highld	149	C13
Allimore Green Staffs	62	C2
Allington Lincs	77	E8
Allington Wilts	25	C5
Allington Wilts	25	F7
Allithwaite Cumb	92	B3
Alloa Clack	127	E7
Allonby Cumb	107	E7
Allostock Ches W	74	B4
Alloway S Ayrs	112	C3
Allt Carms	33	D6
Allt na h-Airbhe Highld	150	B4
Allt-nan-sùgh Highld	136	B2
Alltchaorunn Highld	131	D5
Alltforgan Powys	59	B6
Alltmawr Powys	48	E2
Alltnacaillich Highld	156	E7
Alltsigh Highld	137	C7
Alltwalis Carms	46	F3
Alltwen Neath	33	D8
Alltyblaca Ceredig	46	E4
Allwood Green Suff	56	B4
Almeley Hereford	48	D5
Almer Dorset	13	E7
Almholme S Yorks	89	D6
Almington Staffs	74	F4
Alminstone Cross Devon	8	B5
Almondbank Perth	128	B2
Almondbury W Yorks	88	C2
Almondsbury S Glos	36	F3
Alne N Yorks	95	C7
Alness Highld	151	E9
Alnham Northumb	117	C5
Alnmouth Northumb	117	C8
Alnwick Northumb	117	C7
Alperton London	40	F4
Alphamstone Essex	56	F2
Alpheton Suff	56	D2
Alphington Devon	10	E4
Alport Derbys	76	C2
Alpraham Ches E	74	D2
Alresford Essex	43	B6
Alrewas Staffs	63	C5
Alsager Ches E	74	D4
Alsagers Bank Staffs	74	E5
Alsop en le Dale Derbys	75	D8
Alston Cumb	109	E7
Alston Devon	11	D8
Alstone Glos	50	F4
Alstonefield Staffs	75	D8
Alswear Devon	10	B2
Altandhu Highld	156	H2
Altanduin Highld	157	G11
Altarnun Corn	8	F4
Altass Highld	156	J7
Alterwall Highld	158	D4
Altham Lancs	93	F7
Althorne Essex	43	E5
Althorpe N Lincs	90	D2
Alticry Dumfries	105	D6
Altnabreac Station Highld	157	E13
Altnacealgach Hotel Highld	156	H5
Altnacraig Argyll	124	C4
Altnafeadh Highld	131	D6
Altnaharra Highld	157	F8
Altofts W Yorks	88	B4
Alton Derbys	76	C3
Alton Hants	26	F5
Alton Staffs	75	E7
Alton Pancras Dorset	12	D5
Alton Priors Wilts	25	C6
Altrincham Gtr Man	87	F5
Altrua Highld	136	F5
Altskeith Stirling	126	D3
Altyre Ho. Moray	151	F13
Alva Clack	127	E7
Alvanley Ches W	73	B8
Alvaston Derby	76	F3
Alvechurch Worcs	50	B5
Alvecote Warks	63	D6
Alvediston Wilts	13	B7
Alveley Shrops	61	F7
Alverdiscott Devon	9	B7
Alverstoke Hants	15	E7
Alverstone IoW	15	F6
Alverton Notts	77	E7
Alves Moray	152	B1
Alvescot Oxon	38	D2
Alveston S Glos	36	F3
Alveston Warks	51	D7
Alvie Highld	138	D4
Alvingham Lincs	91	E7
Alvington Glos	36	D3
Alwalton Cambs	65	E8
Alweston Dorset	12	C4
Alwinton Northumb	117	D5
Alwoodley W Yorks	95	E5
Alyth Perth	134	E2
Amatnatua Highld	150	B7
Amber Hill Lincs	78	E5
Ambergate Derbys	76	D3
Amberley Glos	37	D5
Amberley W Sus	16	C4
Amble Northumb	117	D8
Amblecote W Mid	62	F2
Ambler Thorn W Yorks	87	B8
Ambleside Cumb	99	D5
Ambleston Pembs	44	C5
Ambrosden Oxon	39	C6
Amcotts N Lincs	90	C2
Amersham Bucks	40	E2
Amesbury Wilts	25	E6
Amington Staffs	63	D6
Amisfield Dumfries	114	F2
Amlwch Anglesey	82	B4
Amlwch Port Anglesey	82	B4
Ammanford = Rhydaman Carms	33	C7
Amod Argyll	143	E8
Amotherby N Yorks	96	B3
Ampfield Hants	14	B5
Ampleforth N Yorks	95	B8
Ampney Crucis Glos	37	D7
Ampney St Mary Glos	37	D7
Ampney St Peter Glos	37	D7
Amport Hants	25	E7
Ampthill C Beds	53	F8
Ampton Suff	56	B2
Amroth Pembs	32	D2
Amulree Perth	133	F5
An Caol Highld	149	C11
An Cnoc W Isles	155	D9
An Gleann Ur W Isles	155	D9
An t-Ob = Leverburgh W Isles	154	J5
Anagach Highld	139	B6
Anaheilt Highld	130	C2
Anancaun Highld	150	E3
Ancaster Lincs	78	E2
Anchor Shrops	59	F8
Anchorsholme Blackpool	92	E3
Ancroft Northumb	123	E5
Ancrum Borders	116	B2
Anderby Lincs	79	B8
Anderson Dorset	13	E6
Anderton Ches W	74	B3
Andover Hants	25	E8
Andover Down Hants	25	E8
Andoversford Glos	37	C7
Andreas IoM	84	C4
Anfield Mers	85	E4
Angersleigh Som	11	C6
Angle Pembs	44	E3
Angmering W Sus	16	D4
Angram N Yorks	95	E8
Angram N Yorks	100	E3
Anie Stirling	126	C4
Ankerville Highld	151	D11
Anlaby E Yorks	90	B4
Anmer Norf	80	E3
Anna Valley Hants	25	E8
Annan Dumfries	107	C8
Annat Argyll	125	C6
Annat Highld	149	C13
Annbank S Ayrs	112	B4
Annesley Notts	76	D5
Annesley Woodhouse Notts	76	D4
Annfield Plain Durham	110	D4
Annifirth Shetland	160	J3
Annitsford T&W	111	B5
Annscroft Shrops	60	D4
Ansdell Lancs	85	B4
Ansford Som	23	F8
Ansley Warks	63	E6
Anslow Staffs	63	B6
Anslow Gate Staffs	63	B6
Anstey Herts	54	F5
Anstey Leics	64	D2
Anstruther Easter Fife	129	D7
Anstruther Wester Fife	129	D7
Ansty Hants	26	E5
Ansty Warks	63	F7

Ansty Wilts 13 B7
Anthill Common Hants 15 C7
Anthorn Cumb 107 D8
Antingham Norf 81 D8
Anton's Gowt Lincs 79 E5
Antonshill Falk 127 F7
Antony Corn 5 D8
Anwick Lincs 78 D4
Anwoth Dumfries 106 D2
Aoradh Argyll 142 B3
Apes Hall Cambs 67 E5
Apethorpe Northants 65 E7
Apeton Staffs 62 C2
Apley Lincs 78 B4
Apperknowle Derbys 76 B3
Apperley Glos 37 B5
Apperley Bridge W Yorks 94 F4
Appersett N Yorks 100 E3
Appin Argyll 130 E3
Appin House Argyll 130 E3
Appleby N Lincs 90 C3
Appleby-in-Westmorland Cumb 100 B1
Appleby Magna Leics 63 D7
Appleby Parva Leics 63 D7
Applecross Highld 149 D12
Applecross Ho. Highld 149 D12
Appledore Devon 11 C5
Appledore Devon 20 F3
Appledore Kent 19 C6
Appledore Heath Kent 19 B6
Appleford Oxon 39 E5
Applegarthtown Dumfries 114 F4
Appleshaw Hants 25 E8
Applethwaite Cumb 98 B4
Appleton Halton 86 F3
Appleton Oxon 38 D4
Appleton-le-Moors N Yorks 103 F5
Appleton-le-Street N Yorks 96 B3
Appleton Roebuck N Yorks 95 E8
Appleton Thorn Warr 86 F4
Appleton Wiske N Yorks 102 D1
Appletreehall Borders 115 C8
Appletreewick N Yorks 94 C3
Appley Som 11 B5
Appley Bridge Lancs 86 D3
Apse Heath IoW 15 F6
Apsley End C Beds 54 F2
Apuldram W Sus 16 D2
Aquhythie Aberds 141 C6
Arabella Highld 151 D11
Arbeadie Aberds 141 E5
Arberth = Narberth Pembs 32 C2
Arbirlot Angus 135 E6
Arboll Highld 151 C11
Arborfield Wokingham 27 C5
Arborfield Cross Wokingham 27 C5
Arborfield Garrison Wokingham 27 C5
Arbour-thorne S Yorks 88 F4
Arbroath Angus 135 E6
Arbuthnott Aberds 135 B7
Archiestown Moray 152 D2
Arclid Ches E 74 C4
Ard-dhubh Highld 149 D12
Ardachu Highld 157 J9
Ardalanish Argyll 146 K6
Ardanaiseig Argyll 125 C6
Ardaneaskan Highld 149 E13
Ardanstur Argyll 124 D4
Ardargie House Hotel Perth 128 C2
Ardarroch Highld 149 E13
Ardbeg Argyll 142 D5
Ardbeg Argyll 145 E10
Ardcharnich Highld 150 C4
Ardchiavaig Argyll 146 K6
Ardchullarie More Stirling 126 C4
Ardchyle Stirling 126 B4
Arddleen Powys 60 C2
Ardechvie Highld 136 E4
Ardeley Herts 41 B6
Ardelve Highld 149 F13
Arden Argyll 126 F2
Ardens Grafton Warks 51 D6
Ardentinny Argyll 145 E10
Ardentraive Argyll 145 F9
Ardeonaig Stirling 132 F3
Ardersier Highld 151 F10
Ardessie Highld 150 C3
Ardfern Argyll 124 E4
Ardgartan Argyll 125 E8
Ardgay Highld 151 B8
Ardgour Highld 130 C4
Ardheslaig Highld 149 C12
Ardiecow Moray 152 B5
Ardindrean Highld 150 C4
Ardingly W Sus 17 B7
Ardington Oxon 38 F4
Ardlair Aberds 140 B4
Ardlamont Ho. Argyll 145 G8
Ardleigh Essex 43 B6
Ardler Perth 134 E2
Ardley Oxon 39 B5
Ardlui Argyll 126 C2
Ardlussa Argyll 144 E5
Ardmair Highld 150 B4
Ardmay Argyll 125 E8
Ardminish Argyll 143 D7
Ardmolich Highld 147 D10
Ardmore Argyll 124 C3
Ardmore Highld 151 C10
Ardmore Highld 156 D5
Ardnacross Argyll 147 G8
Ardnadam Argyll 145 F10
Ardnagrask Highld 151 G8
Ardnarff Highld 149 E13
Ardnastang Highld 130 C2
Ardnave Argyll 142 A3
Ardno Argyll 125 E7
Ardo Aberds 153 E8
Ardo Ho. Aberds 141 B8
Ardoch Perth 133 F7
Ardochy House Highld 136 D5
Ardoyne Aberds 141 B5
Ardpatrick Argyll 144 G6
Ardpatrick Ho. Argyll 144 H6
Ardpeaton Argyll 145 E11
Ardrishaig Argyll 145 E7
Ardross Fife 129 D7
Ardross Highld 151 D9
Ardross Castle Highld 151 D9
Ardrossan N Ayrs 118 E2
Ardshealach Highld 147 E9
Ardsley S Yorks 88 D4
Ardslignish Highld 147 E8
Ardtalla Argyll 142 C5
Ardtalnaig Perth 132 F4
Ardtoe Highld 147 D9
Ardtrostan Perth 127 B5
Arduaine Argyll 124 D3
Ardullie Highld 151 E8
Ardvasar Highld 149 H11
Ardvorlich Perth 126 B5
Ardwell Dumfries 104 E5
Ardwell Mains Dumfries 104 E5
Ardwick Gtr Man 87 E6
Areley Kings Worcs 50 B3
Arford Hants 27 F6
Argoed Caerph 35 E5
Argoed Mill Powys 47 C8
Arichamish Argyll 124 E5
Arichastlich Argyll 125 B8
Aridhglas Argyll 146 J6
Arileod Argyll 146 F4
Arinacrinachd Highld 149 C12
Arinagour Argyll 146 F5
Arion Orkney 159 G3
Arisaig Highld 147 C9
Ariundle Highld 130 C2
Arkendale N Yorks 95 C6
Arkesden Essex 55 F5
Arkholme Lancs 93 B5
Arkle Town N Yorks 101 D5
Arkleton Dumfries 115 E6
Arkley London 41 E5
Arksey S Yorks 89 D6
Arkwright Town Derbys 76 B4
Arle Glos 37 B6
Arlecdon Cumb 98 C2
Arlesey C Beds 54 F2
Arleston Telford 61 C6
Arley Ches E 86 F4
Arlingham Glos 36 C4
Arlington Devon 20 E5
Arlington E Sus 18 E2
Arlington Glos 37 D8
Armadale Highld 157 C10
Armadale W Loth 120 C2
Armadale Castle Highld 149 H11
Armathwaite Cumb 108 E5
Arminghall Norf 69 D5
Armitage Staffs 62 C4
Armley W Yorks 95 F5
Armscote Warks 51 E7
Armthorpe S Yorks 89 D7
Arnabost Argyll 146 F5
Arncliffe N Yorks 94 B2
Arncroach Fife 129 D7
Arne Dorset 13 F7
Arnesby Leics 64 E3
Arngask Perth 128 C3
Arnisdale Highld 149 G13
Arnish Highld 149 D10
Arniston Engine Midloth 121 C6
Arnol W Isles 155 C8
Arnold E Yorks 97 E7
Arnold Notts 77 E5
Arnprior Stirling 126 E5
Arnside Cumb 92 B4
Aros Mains Argyll 147 G8
Arowry Wrex 73 F8
Arpafeelie Highld 151 F9
Arrad Foot Cumb 99 F5
Arram E Yorks 97 E6
Arrathorne N Yorks 101 E7
Arreton IoW 15 F6
Arrington Cambs 54 D4
Arrivain Argyll 125 B8
Arrochar Argyll 125 E8
Arrow Warks 51 D5
Arthington W Yorks 95 E5
Arthingworth Northants 64 F4
Arthog Gwyn 58 C3
Arthrath Aberds 153 E9
Arthurstone Perth 134 E2
Artrochie Aberds 153 E10
Arundel W Sus 16 D4
Aryhoulan Highld 130 C4
Asby Cumb 98 B2
Ascog Argyll 145 G10
Ascot Windsor 27 C7
Ascott Warks 51 F8
Ascott-under-Wychwood Oxon 38 C3
Asenby N Yorks 95 B6
Asfordby Leics 64 C4
Asfordby Hill Leics 64 C4
Asgarby Lincs 78 E4
Asgarby Lincs 79 C6
Ash Kent 29 C6
Ash Kent 31 D6
Ash Som 12 B2
Ash Sur 27 D6
Ash Bullayne Devon 10 D2
Ash Green Warks 63 F7
Ash Magna Shrops 74 F2
Ash Mill Devon 10 B2
Ash Priors Som 11 B6
Ash Street Suff 56 E4
Ash Thomas Devon 10 C5
Ash Vale Sur 27 D6
Ashampstead W Berks 26 B3
Ashbocking Suff 57 D5
Ashbourne Derbys 75 E8
Ashbrittle Som 11 B5
Ashburton Devon 7 C5
Ashbury Devon 9 E7
Ashbury Oxon 38 F2
Ashby N Lincs 90 D3
Ashby by Partney Lincs 79 C7
Ashby cum Fenby NE Lincs 91 D6
Ashby de la Launde Lincs 78 D3
Ashby-de-la-Zouch Leics 63 C7
Ashby Folville Leics 64 C4
Ashby Magna Leics 64 E2
Ashby Parva Leics 64 F2
Ashby Puerorum Lincs 79 B6
Ashby St Ledgers Northants 52 C3
Ashby St Mary Norf 69 D6
Ashchurch Glos 50 F4
Ashcombe Devon 7 B7
Ashcott Som 23 F6
Ashdon Essex 55 E6
Ashe Hants 26 E3
Asheldham Essex 43 D5
Ashen Essex 55 E8
Ashendon Bucks 39 C7
Ashfield Carms 33 B7
Ashfield Stirling 127 D6
Ashfield Suff 57 C6
Ashfield Green Suff 57 B6
Ashfold Crossways W Sus 17 B6
Ashford Devon 20 F4
Ashford Hants 14 C2
Ashford Kent 30 E4
Ashford Sur 27 B8
Ashford Bowdler Shrops 49 B7
Ashford Carbonell Shrops 49 B7
Ashford Hill Hants 26 C3
Ashford in the Water Derbys 75 C8
Ashgill S Lanark 119 E7
Ashill Devon 11 C5
Ashill Norf 67 D8
Ashill Som 11 C8
Ashingdon Essex 42 E4
Ashington Northumb 117 F8
Ashington Som 12 B3
Ashington W Sus 16 C5
Ashintully Castle Perth 133 C8
Ashkirk Borders 115 B7
Ashlett Hants 15 D5
Ashleworth Glos 37 B5
Ashley Cambs 55 C7
Ashley Ches E 87 F5
Ashley Devon 9 C8
Ashley Dorset 14 D2
Ashley Glos 37 E6
Ashley Hants 14 E3
Ashley Hants 25 F8
Ashley Northants 64 E4
Ashley Staffs 74 F4
Ashley Green Bucks 40 D2
Ashley Heath Dorset 14 D2
Ashley Heath Staffs 74 F4
Ashmanhaugh Norf 69 B6
Ashmansworth Hants 26 D2
Ashmansworthy Devon 8 C5
Ashmore Dorset 13 C7
Ashorne Warks 51 D8
Ashover Derbys 76 C3
Ashow Warks 51 B8
Ashprington Devon 7 D6
Ashreigney Devon 9 C8
Ashtead Sur 28 D2
Ashton Ches W 74 C2
Ashton Corn 2 D5
Ashton Hants 15 C6
Ashton Hereford 49 C7
Ashton Invclyd 118 B2
Ashton Northants 53 E5
Ashton Northants 65 F7
Ashton Common Wilts 24 D3
Ashton-In-Makerfield Gtr Man 86 E3
Ashton Keynes Wilts 37 E7
Ashton under Hill Worcs 50 F4
Ashton-under-Lyne Gtr Man 87 E7
Ashton upon Mersey Gtr Man 87 E5
Ashurst Hants 14 C4
Ashurst Kent 18 B2
Ashurst W Sus 17 C5
Ashurstwood W Sus 28 F5
Ashwater Devon 9 E5
Ashwell Herts 54 F3
Ashwell Rutland 65 C5
Ashwell Som 11 C8
Ashwellthorpe Norf 68 E4
Ashwick Som 23 E8
Ashwicken Norf 67 C7
Ashybank Borders 115 C8
Askam in Furness Cumb 92 B2
Askern S Yorks 89 C6
Askerswell Dorset 12 E3
Askett Bucks 39 D8
Askham Cumb 99 B7
Askham Notts 77 B7
Askham Bryan York 95 E8
Askham Richard York 95 E8
Asknish Argyll 145 D8
Askrigg N Yorks 100 E4
Askwith N Yorks 94 E4
Aslackby Lincs 78 F3
Aslacton Norf 68 E4
Aslockton Notts 77 F7
Asloun Aberds 140 C4
Aspatria Cumb 107 E8
Aspenden Herts 41 B6
Asperton Lincs 79 F5
Aspley Guise C Beds 53 F7
Aspley Heath C Beds 53 F7
Aspull Gtr Man 86 D4
Asselby E Yorks 89 B8
Asserby Lincs 79 B7
Assington Suff 56 F3
Assynt Ho. Highld 151 E8
Astbury Ches E 74 C5
Astcote Northants 52 D4
Asterley Shrops 60 D3
Asterton Shrops 60 E3
Asthall Oxon 38 C2
Asthall Leigh Oxon 38 C3
Astley Shrops 60 C5
Astley Warks 63 F7
Astley Worcs 50 C2
Astley Abbotts Shrops 61 E7
Astley Bridge Gtr Man 86 C5
Astley Cross Worcs 50 C3
Astley Green Gtr Man 86 E5
Aston Ches E 74 E3
Aston Ches W 74 B2
Aston Derbys 88 F2
Aston Hereford 49 B6
Aston Herts 41 B5
Aston Oxon 38 D3
Aston S Yorks 89 F5
Aston Shrops 60 B5
Aston Staffs 74 E4
Aston Telford 61 D6
Aston W Mid 62 F4
Aston Wokingham 39 F7
Aston Abbotts Bucks 39 B8
Aston Botterell Shrops 61 F6
Aston-By-Stone Staffs 75 F6
Aston Cantlow Warks 51 D6
Aston Clinton Bucks 40 C1
Aston Crews Hereford 36 B3
Aston Cross Glos 50 F4
Aston End Herts 41 B5
Aston Eyre Shrops 61 E6
Aston Fields Worcs 50 C4
Aston Flamville Leics 63 E8
Aston Ingham Hereford 36 B3
Aston juxta Mondrum Ches E 74 D3
Aston le Walls Northants 52 D2
Aston Magna Glos 51 F6
Aston Munslow Shrops 60 F5
Aston on Clun Shrops 60 F3
Aston-on-Trent Derbys 63 B8
Aston Rogers Shrops 60 D3
Aston Rowant Oxon 39 E7
Aston Sandford Bucks 39 D7
Aston Somerville Worcs 50 F5
Aston Subedge Glos 51 E6
Aston Tirrold Oxon 39 F5
Aston Upthorpe Oxon 39 F5
Astrop Northants 52 F3
Astwick C Beds 54 F3
Astwood M Keynes 53 E7
Astwood Worcs 50 D3
Astwood Bank Worcs 50 C5
Aswarby Lincs 78 F3
Aswardby Lincs 79 B6
Atch Lench Worcs 50 D5
Atcham Shrops 60 D5
Athelhampton Dorset 13 E5
Athelington Suff 57 B6
Athelney Som 11 B8
Athelstaneford E Loth 121 B8
Atherington Devon 9 B7
Atherstone Warks 63 E7
Atherstone on Stour Warks 51 D7
Atherton Gtr Man 86 D4
Atley Hill N Yorks 101 D7
Atlow Derbys 76 E2
Attadale Highld 150 H2
Attadale Ho. Highld 150 H2
Attenborough Notts 76 F5
Atterby Lincs 90 E3
Attercliffe S Yorks 88 F4
Attleborough Norf 68 E3
Attleborough Warks 63 E7
Attlebridge Norf 68 C4
Atwick E Yorks 97 D7
Atworth Wilts 24 C3
Aubourn Lincs 78 C2
Auchagallon N Ayrs 143 E9
Auchallater Aberds 139 F7
Aucharnie Aberds 153 D6
Auchattie Aberds 141 E5
Auchavan Angus 134 C1
Auchbreck Moray 139 B8
Auchenback E Renf 118 D5
Auchenbainzie Dumfries 113 E8
Auchenblae Aberds 135 B7
Auchenbrack Dumfries 113 E7
Auchenbreck Argyll 145 E9
Auchencairn Dumfries 106 D4
Auchencairn Dumfries 114 F2
Auchencairn N Ayrs 143 F11
Auchencrosh S Ayrs 104 B5
Auchencrow Borders 122 C4
Auchendinny Midloth 121 C5
Auchengray S Lanark 120 D2
Auchenhalrig Moray 152 B3
Auchenheath S Lanark 119 E8
Auchenlochan Argyll 145 F8
Auchenmalg Dumfries 105 D6
Auchensoul S Ayrs 112 E2
Auchentiber N Ayrs 118 E3
Auchertyre Highld 149 F13
Auchgourish Highld 138 C5
Auchincarroch W Dunb 126 F3
Auchindrain Argyll 125 E6
Auchindrean Highld 150 C4
Auchininna Aberds 153 D6
Auchinleck E Ayrs 113 B5
Auchinloch N Lanark 119 B6
Auchinroath Moray 152 C2
Auchintoul Aberds 140 C4
Auchiries Aberds 153 E10
Auchlee Aberds 141 E7
Auchleven Aberds 140 B5
Auchlochan S Lanark 119 F8
Auchlossan Aberds 140 D4
Auchlunies Aberds 141 E7
Auchlyne Stirling 126 B4
Auchmacoy Aberds 153 E9
Auchmair Moray 140 B2
Auchmantle Dumfries 105 C5
Auchmillan E Ayrs 112 B5
Auchmithie Angus 135 E6
Auchmuirbridge Fife 128 D4
Auchmull Angus 135 B5
Auchnacree Angus 134 C4
Auchnagallin Highld 151 H13
Auchnagatt Aberds 153 D9
Auchnaha Argyll 145 E8
Auchnashelloch Perth 127 C6
Aucholzie Aberds 140 E2
Auchrannie Angus 134 D2
Auchroisk Highld 139 B6
Auchronie Angus 140 F3
Auchterarder Perth 127 C8
Auchteraw Highld 137 D6
Auchterderran Fife 128 E4
Auchterhouse Angus 134 F3
Auchtermuchty Fife 128 C4
Auchterneed Highld 150 F7
Auchtertool Fife 128 E4
Auchtertyre Moray 152 C1
Auchtubh Stirling 126 B4
Auckengill Highld 158 D5
Auckley S Yorks 89 D7
Audenshaw Gtr Man 87 E7
Audlem Ches E 74 E3
Audley Staffs 74 D4
Audley End Essex 56 F2
Auds Aberds 153 B6
Aughton E Yorks 96 F3
Aughton Lancs 85 D4
Aughton Lancs 93 C5
Aughton S Yorks 89 F5
Aughton Wilts 25 D7
Aughton Park Lancs 86 D2
Auldearn Highld 151 F12
Aulden Hereford 49 D6
Auldgirth Dumfries 114 F2
Auldhame E Loth 129 F7
Auldhouse S Lanark 119 D6
Ault a'chruinn Highld 136 B2
Aultanrynie Highld 156 F6
Aultbea Highld 155 J13
Aultdearg Highld 150 E5
Aultgrishan Highld 155 J12
Aultguish Inn Highld 150 D6
Aultibea Highld 157 G13
Aultiphurst Highld 157 C11
Aultmore Moray 152 C4
Aultnagoire Highld 137 B8
Aultnamain Inn Highld 151 C9
Aultnaslat Highld 136 D4
Aulton Aberds 140 B5
Aundorach Highld 139 C5
Aunsby Lincs 78 F3
Auquhorthies Aberds 141 B7
Aust S Glos 36 F2
Austendike Lincs 66 B2
Austerfield S Yorks 89 E7
Austrey Warks 63 D6
Austwick N Yorks 93 C7
Authorpe Lincs 91 F8
Authorpe Row Lincs 79 B8
Avebury Wilts 25 C6
Aveley Thurrock 42 F1
Avening Glos 37 E5
Averham Notts 77 D7
Aveton Gifford Devon 6 E4
Avielochan Highld 138 C5
Aviemore Highld 138 C4
Avington Hants 26 F3
Avington W Berks 25 C8
Avoch Highld 151 F10
Avon Hants 14 E2
Avon Dassett Warks 52 E2
Avonbridge Falk 120 B2
Avonmouth Bristol 23 B7
Avonwick Devon 6 D5
Awbridge Hants 14 B4
Awhirk Dumfries 104 D4
Awkley S Glos 36 F2
Awliscombe Devon 11 D6
Awre Glos 36 D4
Awsworth Notts 76 E4
Axbridge Som 23 D6
Axford Hants 26 E4
Axford Wilts 25 B7
Axminster Devon 11 E7
Axmouth Devon 11 E7
Axton Flint 85 F2
Aycliff Kent 31 E7
Aycliffe Durham 101 B7
Aydon Northumb 110 C3
Aylburton Glos 36 D3
Ayle Northumb 109 E7
Aylesbeare Devon 10 E5
Aylesbury Bucks 39 C8
Aylesby NE Lincs 91 D6
Aylesford Kent 29 D8
Aylesham Kent 31 D6
Aylestone Leicester 64 D2
Aylmerton Norf 81 D7
Aylsham Norf 81 E7
Aylton Hereford 49 F8
Aymestrey Hereford 49 C6
Aynho Northants 52 F3
Ayot St Lawrence Herts 40 C4
Ayot St Peter Herts 41 C5
Ayr S Ayrs 112 B3
Aysgarth N Yorks 101 F5
Ayside Cumb 99 F5
Ayston Rutland 65 D5
Aythorpe Roding Essex 42 C1
Ayton Borders 122 C5
Aywick Shetland 160 E7
Azerley N Yorks 95 B5

B

Babbacombe Torbay 7 C7
Babbinswood Shrops 73 F7
Babcary Som 12 B3
Babel Carms 47 F7
Babell Flint 73 B5
Babraham Cambs 55 D6
Babworth Notts 89 F7
Bac W Isles 155 C9
Bachau Anglesey 82 C4
Back of Keppoch Highld 147 C9
Back Rogerton E Ayrs 113 B5
Backaland Orkney 159 E6
Backaskaill Orkney 159 C5
Backbarrow Cumb 99 F5
Backe Carms 32 C3
Backfolds Aberds 153 C10
Backford Ches W 73 B8
Backford Cross Ches W 73 B7
Backhill Aberds 153 E7
Backhill Aberds 153 E10
Backhill of Clackriach Aberds 153 D9
Backhill of Fortree Aberds 153 D9
Backhill of Trustach Aberds 140 E5
Backies Highld 157 J11
Backlass Highld 158 E4
Backwell N Som 23 C6
Backworth T&W 111 B6
Bacon End Essex 42 C2
Baconsthorpe Norf 81 D7
Bacton Hereford 49 F5
Bacton Norf 81 D9
Bacton Suff 56 C4
Bacton Green Suff 56 C4
Bacup Lancs 87 B6
Badachro Highld 149 A12
Badanloch Lodge Highld 157 F10
Badavanich Highld 150 F4
Badbury Swindon 38 F1
Badby Northants 52 D3
Badcall Highld 156 D5
Badcaul Highld 150 B3
Baddeley Green Stoke 75 D6
Baddesley Clinton Warks 51 B7
Baddesley Ensor Warks 63 E6
Baddidarach Highld 156 G3
Baddoch Aberds 139 F7
Baddock Highld 151 F10
Badenscoth Aberds 153 E7
Badenyon Aberds 140 C2
Badger Shrops 61 E7
Badger's Mount Kent 29 C5
Badgeworth Glos 37 C6
Badgworth Som 23 D5
Badicaul Highld 149 F12
Badingham Suff 57 C7
Badlesmere Kent 30 D4
Badlipster Highld 158 F4
Badluarach Highld 150 B2
Badminton S Glos 37 F5
Badnaban Highld 156 G3
Badninish Highld 151 B10
Badrallach Highld 150 B3
Badsey Worcs 51 E5
Badshot Lea Sur 27 E6
Badsworth W Yorks 89 C5
Badwell Ash Suff 56 C3
Bae Colwyn = Colwyn Bay Conwy 83 D8
Bag Enderby Lincs 79 B6
Bagby N Yorks 102 F2
Bagendon Glos 37 D7
Bagh a Chaisteil = Castlebay W Isles 148 J1
Bagh Mor W Isles 148 C3
Bagh Shiarabhagh W Isles 148 H2
Baghasdal W Isles 148 G2
Bagillt Flint 73 B6
Baginton Warks 51 B8
Baglan Neath 33 E8
Bagley Shrops 60 B4
Bagnall Staffs 75 D6
Bagnor W Berks 26 C2
Bagshot Sur 27 C7
Bagshot Wilts 25 C8
Bagthorpe Norf 80 D3
Bagthorpe Notts 76 D4
Bagworth Leics 63 D8
Bagwy Llydiart Hereford 35 B8
Bail Àrd Bhuirgh W Isles 155 B9
Bail Uachdraich W Isles 148 B3
Baildon W Yorks 94 F4
Baile W Isles 154 J4
Baile a Mhanaich W Isles 148 C2
Baile Ailein W Isles 155 E7
Baile an Truiseil W Isles 155 B8
Baile Boidheach Argyll 144 F6
Baile Glas W Isles 148 C3
Baile Mhartainn W Isles 148 A2
Baile Mhic Phail W Isles 148 A3
Baile Mor Argyll 146 J5
Baile Mor W Isles 148 B2
Baile na Creige W Isles 148 H1
Baile nan Cailleach W Isles 148 C2
Baile Raghaill W Isles 148 A2
Bailebeag Highld 137 C8
Baileyhead Cumb 108 B5
Bailiesward Aberds 152 E4
Baillieston Glasgow 119 C6
Bail'lochdrach W Isles 148 C3
Bail'Ur Tholastaidh W Isles 155 C10
Bainbridge N Yorks 100 E4
Bainsford Falk 127 F7
Bainshole Aberds 152 E6
Bainton E Yorks 97 D5
Bainton Pboro 65 D7
Bairnkine Borders 116 C2
Baker Street Thurrock 42 F2
Baker's End Herts 41 C6
Bakewell Derbys 76 C2
Bala = Y Bala Gwyn 72 F3
Balachuirn Highld 149 D10
Balavil Highld 138 D3
Balbeg Highld 137 B7
Balbeg Highld 150 H7
Balbeggie Perth 128 B3
Balbithan Aberds 141 C6
Balbithan Ho. Aberds 141 C7
Balblair Highld 151 B8
Balblair Highld 151 E10
Balby S Yorks 89 D6
Balchladich Highld 156 F3
Balchraggan Highld 151 G8
Balchraggan Highld 151 H8
Balchrick Highld 156 D4
Balchrystie Fife 129 D6
Balcladaich Highld 137 B5
Balcombe W Sus 28 F4
Balcombe Lane W Sus 28 F4
Balcomie Fife 129 C8
Balcurvie Fife 128 D5
Baldersby N Yorks 95 B6
Baldersby St James N Yorks 95 B6
Balderstone Lancs 93 F6
Balderton Ches W 73 C7
Balderton Notts 77 D8
Baldhu Corn 3 B6
Baldinnie Fife 129 C6
Baldock Herts 54 F3
Baldovie Dundee 134 F4
Baldrine IoM 84 D4
Baldslow E Sus 18 D4
Baldwin IoM 84 D3
Baldwinholme Cumb 108 D3
Baldwin's Gate Staffs 74 E4
Bale Norf 81 D6
Balearn Aberds 153 C10
Balemartine Argyll 146 G2
Balephuil Argyll 146 G2
Balerno Edin 120 C4
Balevullin Argyll 146 G2
Balfield Angus 135 C5
Balfour Orkney 159 G5
Balfron Stirling 126 F4
Balfron Station Stirling 126 F4
Balgaveny Aberds 153 D6
Balgavies Angus 135 D5
Balgonar Fife 128 E2
Balgove Aberds 153 E8
Balgowan Highld 138 E2
Balgown Highld 149 B8
Balgrochan E Dunb 119 B6
Balgy Highld 149 C13
Balhaldie Stirling 127 D7
Balhalgardy Aberds 141 B6
Balham London 28 B3
Balhary Perth 134 E2
Baliasta Shetland 160 C8
Baligill Highld 157 C11
Balintore Angus 134 D2
Balintore Highld 151 D11
Balintraid Highld 151 D10
Balk N Yorks 102 F2
Balkeerie Angus 134 E3
Balkemback Angus 134 F3
Balkholme E Yorks 89 B8
Balkissock S Ayrs 104 A5
Ball Shrops 60 B3
Ball Haye Green Staffs 75 D6
Ball Hill Hants 26 C2
Ballabeg IoM 84 E2
Ballacannel IoM 84 D4
Ballachulish Highld 130 D4
Ballajora IoM 84 C4
Ballaleigh IoM 84 D3
Ballamodha IoM 84 E2
Ballantrae S Ayrs 104 A4
Ballaquine IoM 84 D4
Ballards Gore Essex 43 E5
Ballasalla IoM 84 C3
Ballasalla IoM 84 E2
Ballater Aberds 140 E2
Ballaugh IoM 84 C3
Ballaveare IoM 84 E3
Ballcorach Moray 139 B7
Ballechin Perth 133 D6
Balleigh Highld 151 C10
Ballencrieff E Loth 121 B7
Ballentoul Perth 133 C5
Ballidon Derbys 76 D2
Balliemore Argyll 124 C4
Balliemore Argyll 145 E9
Ballikinrain Stirling 126 F4
Ballimeanoch Argyll 125 D6
Ballimore Argyll 145 E8
Ballimore Stirling 126 C4
Ballinaby Argyll 142 B3
Ballindean Perth 128 B4
Ballingdon Suff 56 E2
Ballinger Common Bucks 40 D2
Ballingham Hereford 49 F7
Ballingry Fife 128 E3
Ballinlick Perth 133 E6
Ballinluig Perth 133 D6
Ballintuim Perth 133 D8
Balloch Angus 134 D3
Balloch Highld 151 G10
Balloch N Lanark 119 B7
Balloch W Dunb 126 F2
Ballochan Aberds 140 E4
Ballochford Moray 152 E3
Ballochmorrie S Ayrs 112 F2
Balls Cross W Sus 16 B3
Balls Green Essex 43 B6
Ballygown Argyll 146 G7
Ballygrant Argyll 142 B4
Ballyhaugh Argyll 146 F4
Balmacara Highld 149 F13
Balmacara Square Highld 149 F13
Balmaclellan Dumfries 106 B3
Balmacneil Perth 133 D6
Balmacqueen Highld 149 A9
Balmae Dumfries 106 E3
Balmaha Stirling 126 E3
Balmalcolm Fife 128 D5
Balmeanach Highld 149 D10
Balmedie Aberds 141 C8
Balmer Heath Shrops 73 F8
Balmerino Fife 129 B5
Balmerlawn Hants 14 D4
Balmichael N Ayrs 143 E10
Balmirmer Angus 135 F5
Balmore Highld 149 D7
Balmore Highld 150 H6
Balmore Highld 151 G11
Balmore Perth 133 D6
Balmule Fife 128 F4
Balmullo Fife 129 B6
Balmungie Highld 151 F10
Balnaboth Angus 134 C3
Balnabruaich Highld 151 E10
Balnabruich Highld 158 H3
Balnacoil Highld 157 H11
Balnacra Highld 150 G2
Balnafoich Highld 151 H9
Balnagall Highld 151 C11
Balnaguard Perth 133 D6
Balnahard Argyll 144 D3
Balnahard Argyll 146 H7
Balnain Highld 150 H7
Balnakeil Highld 156 C6
Balnaknock Highld 149 B9
Balnapaling Highld 151 E10
Balne N Yorks 89 C6
Balochroy Argyll 143 C8
Balone Fife 129 C6
Balornock Glasgow 119 C6
Balquharn Perth 133 F7
Balquhidder Stirling 126 B4
Balsall W Mid 51 B7
Balsall Common W Mid 51 B7
Balsall Heath W Mid 62 F4
Balscott Oxon 51 E8
Balsham Cambs 55 D6
Baltasound Shetland 160 C8
Balterley Staffs 74 D4
Baltersan Dumfries 105 C8
Balthangie Aberds 153 C8
Baltonsborough Som 23 F7
Balvaird Highld 151 F8
Balvicar Argyll 124 D3
Balvraid Highld 149 G13
Balvraid Highld 151 H11
Bamber Bridge Lancs 86 B3
Bambers Green Essex 42 B1
Bamburgh Northumb 123 F7
Bamff Perth 134 D2
Bamford Derbys 88 F3
Bamford Gtr Man 87 C6
Bampton Cumb 99 C7
Bampton Devon 10 B4
Bampton Oxon 38 D3
Bampton Grange Cumb 99 C7
Banavie Highld 131 B5
Banbury Oxon 52 E2
Bancffosfelen Carms 33 C5
Banchory Aberds 141 E5
Banchory-Devenick Aberds 141 D8
Bancycapel Carms 33 C5
Bancyfelin Carms 32 C4
Bancyffordd Carms 46 F3
Bandirran Perth 134 F2
Banff Aberds 153 B6
Bangor Gwyn 83 D5
Bangor-is-y-coed Wrex 73 E7
Banham Norf 68 F3
Bank Hants 14 D3
Bank Newton N Yorks 94 D2
Bank Street Worcs 49 C8
Bankend Dumfries 107 C7
Bankfoot Perth 133 F7
Bankglen E Ayrs 113 C6
Bankhead Aberdeen 141 C7
Bankhead Aberds 141 D5
Banknock Falk 119 B7
Banks Cumb 109 C5
Banks Lancs 85 B4
Bankshill Dumfries 114 F4
Banningham Norf 81 E8
Banniskirk Ho. Highld 158 E3
Bannister Green Essex 42 B2
Bannockburn Stirling 127 E7
Banstead Sur 28 D3
Bantham Devon 6 E4
Banton N Lanark 119 B7
Banwell N Som 23 D5
Banyard's Green Suff 57 B6
Bapchild Kent 30 C3
Bar Hill Cambs 54 C4
Barabhas W Isles 155 C8
Barabhas Iarach W Isles 155 C8
Barabhas Uarach W Isles 155 B8
Barachandroman Argyll 124 C2
Barassie S Ayrs 118 F3
Baravullin Argyll 124 E4
Barbaraville Highld 151 D10
Barber Booth Derbys 88 F2
Barbieston S Ayrs 112 C4
Barbon Cumb 99 F8
Barbridge Ches E 74 D3
Barbrook Devon 21 E6
Barby Northants 52 B3
Barcaldine Argyll 130 E3
Barcheston Warks 51 F7
Barcombe E Sus 17 C8
Barcombe Cross E Sus 17 C8
Barden N Yorks 101 E6
Barden Scale N Yorks 94 D3
Bardennoch Dumfries 113 E5
Bardfield Saling Essex 42 B2
Bardister Shetland 160 F5
Bardney Lincs 78 C4
Bardon Leics 63 C8
Bardon Mill Northumb 109 C7
Bardowie E Dunb 119 B5
Bardrainney Invclyd 118 B3
Bardsea Cumb 92 B3
Bardsey W Yorks 95 E6
Bardwell Suff 56 B3
Bare Lancs 92 C4
Barfad Argyll 145 G7
Barford Norf 68 D4
Barford Warks 51 C7
Barford St John Oxon 52 F2
Barford St Martin Wilts 25 F5
Barford St Michael Oxon 52 F2
Barfrestone Kent 31 D6
Bargod = Bargoed Caerph 35 E5
Bargoed = Bargod Caerph 35 E5
Bargrennan Dumfries 105 B7
Barham Cambs 54 B2
Barham Kent 31 D6
Barham Suff 56 D5
Barharrow Dumfries 106 D3
Barhill Dumfries 106 C5
Barholm Lincs 65 C7
Barkby Leics 64 D3
Barkestone-le-Vale Leics 77 F7
Barkham Wokingham 27 C5
Barking London 41 F7
Barking Suff 56 D4
Barking Tye Suff 56 D4
Barkingside London 41 F7
Barkisland W Yorks 87 C8
Barkston Lincs 78 E2
Barkston N Yorks 95 F7
Barkway Herts 54 F4
Barlaston Staffs 75 F5
Barlavington W Sus 16 C3
Barlborough Derbys 76 B4
Barlby N Yorks 96 F2
Barlestone Leics 63 D8
Barley Herts 54 F4
Barley Lancs 93 E8
Barley Mow T&W 111 D5
Barleythorpe Rutland 64 D5
Barling Essex 43 F5
Barlow Derbys 76 B3
Barlow N Yorks 89 B7
Barlow T&W 110 C4
Barmby Moor E Yorks 96 E3
Barmby on the Marsh E Yorks 89 B7
Barmer Norf 80 D4
Barmoor Castle Northumb 123 F5
Barmoor Lane End Northumb 123 F6
Barmouth = Abermaw Gwyn 58 C3
Barmpton Darl 101 C8
Barmston E Yorks 97 D7
Barnack Pboro 65 D7
Barnacle Warks 63 F7
Barnard Castle Durham 101 C5
Barnard Gate Oxon 38 C4
Barnardiston Suff 55 E8
Barnbarroch Dumfries 106 D5
Barnburgh S Yorks 89 D5
Barnby Suff 69 F7
Barnby Dun S Yorks 89 D7
Barnby in the Willows Notts 77 D8
Barnby Moor Notts 89 F7
Barnes Street Kent 29 E7
Barnet London 41 E5
Barnetby le Wold N Lincs 90 D4
Barney Norf 81 D5
Barnham Suff 56 B2
Barnham W Sus 16 D3
Barnham Broom Norf 68 D3
Barnhead Angus 135 D6
Barnhill Ches W 73 D8
Barnhill Dundee 134 F4
Barnhill Moray 152 C1
Barnhills Dumfries 104 B3
Barningham Durham 101 C5
Barningham Suff 56 B3
Barnoldby le Beck NE Lincs 91 D6
Barnoldswick Lancs 93 E8
Barns Green W Sus 16 B5
Barnsley Glos 37 D7
Barnsley S Yorks 88 D4
Barnstaple Devon 20 F4
Barnston Essex 42 C2
Barnston Mers 85 F3
Barnstone Notts 77 F7
Barnt Green Worcs 50 B5
Barnton Ches W 74 B3
Barnton Edin 120 B4
Barnwell All Saints Northants 65 F7
Barnwell St Andrew Northants 65 F7
Barnwood Glos 37 C5
Barochreal Argyll 124 C4
Barons Cross Hereford 49 D6
Barr S Ayrs 112 E2
Barra Castle Aberds 141 B6
Barrachan Dumfries 105 E7
Barrack Aberds 153 D8
Barraglom W Isles 154 D6
Barrahormid Argyll 144 E6
Barran Argyll 124 C4
Barrapol Argyll 146 G2
Barras Aberds 141 F7
Barras Cumb 100 C3
Barrasford Northumb 110 B2
Barravullin Argyll 124 E4
Barregarrow IoM 84 D3
Barrhead E Renf 118 D4
Barrhill S Ayrs 112 F2
Barrington Cambs 54 E4
Barrington Som 11 C8
Barripper Corn 2 C5
Barrmill N Ayrs 118 D3
Barrock Highld 158 C4
Barrock Ho. Highld 158 D4
Barrow Lancs 93 F7
Barrow Rutland 65 C5
Barrow Suff 55 C8
Barrow Green Kent 30 C3
Barrow Gurney N Som 23 C7
Barrow Haven N Lincs 90 B4
Barrow-in-Furness Cumb 92 C2
Barrow Island Cumb 92 C1
Barrow Nook Lancs 86 D2
Barrow Street Wilts 24 F3
Barrow upon Humber N Lincs 90 B4
Barrow upon Soar Leics 64 C2
Barrow upon Trent Derbys 63 B7
Barroway Drove Norf 67 D5
Barrowburn Northumb 116 C4
Barrowby Lincs 77 F8
Barrowcliff N Yorks 103 F8
Barrowden Rutland 65 D6
Barrowford Lancs 93 F8
Barrows Green Ches E 74 D3
Barrows Green Cumb 99 F7
Barrow's Green Mers 86 F3
Barry Angus 135 F5
Barry = Y Barri V Glam 22 C3
Barry Island V Glam 22 C3
Barsby Leics 64 C3
Barsham Suff 69 F6
Barston W Mid 51 B7
Bartestree Hereford 49 E7
Barthol Chapel Aberds 153 E8
Barthomley Ches E 74 D4
Bartley Hants 14 C4
Bartley Green W Mid 62 F4
Bartlow Cambs 55 E6
Barton Cambs 54 D5
Barton Ches W 73 D8
Barton Glos 37 B8
Barton Lancs 85 D4
Barton Lancs 92 F5
Barton N Yorks 101 D7
Barton Oxon 39 D5
Barton Torbay 7 C7
Barton Warks 51 D6
Barton Bendish Norf 67 D7
Barton Hartshorn Bucks 52 F4
Barton in Fabis Notts 76 F5
Barton in the Beans Leics 63 D7
Barton-le-Clay C Beds 53 F8
Barton-le-Street N Yorks 96 B3
Barton-le-Willows N Yorks 96 C3
Barton Mills Suff 55 B8
Barton on Sea Hants 14 E3
Barton on the Heath Warks 51 F7
Barton St David Som 23 F7
Barton Seagrave Northants 53 B6
Barton Stacey Hants 26 E2
Barton Turf Norf 69 B6
Barton-under-Needwood Staffs 63 C5
Barton-upon-Humber N Lincs 90 B4
Barton Waterside N Lincs 90 B4
Barugh S Yorks 88 D4
Barway Cambs 55 B6
Barwell Leics 63 E8
Barwick Herts 41 C6
Barwick Som 12 C3
Barwick in Elmet W Yorks 95 F6
Baschurch Shrops 60 B4
Bascote Warks 52 C2
Basford Green Staffs 75 D6
Bashall Eaves Lancs 93 E6
Bashley Hants 14 E3
Basildon Essex 42 F3
Basingstoke Hants 26 D4
Baslow Derbys 76 B2
Bason Bridge Som 22 E5
Bassaleg Newport 35 F6
Bassenthwaite Cumb 108 F2
Bassett Soton 14 C5
Bassingbourn Cambs 54 E4
Bassingfield Notts 77 F6
Bassingham Lincs 78 C2
Bassingthorpe Lincs 65 B6
Basta Shetland 160 D7
Baston Lincs 65 C8
Bastwick Norf 69 C7
Baswick Steer E Yorks 97 E6
Batchworth Heath Herts 40 E3
Batcombe Dorset 12 D4
Batcombe Som 23 F8
Bate Heath Ches E 74 B3
Batford Herts 40 C4
Bath Bath 24 C2
Bathampton Bath 24 C2
Bathealton Som 11 B5
Batheaston Bath 24 C2
Bathford Bath 24 C2
Bathgate W Loth 120 C2
Bathley Notts 77 D7
Bathpool Corn 5 B7
Bathpool Som 11 B7
Bathville W Loth 120 C2
Batley W Yorks 88 B3
Batsford Glos 51 F6
Battersby N Yorks 102 D3
Battersea London 28 B3
Battisborough Cross Devon 6 E3
Battisford Suff 56 D4
Battisford Tye Suff 56 D4
Battle E Sus 18 D4
Battle Powys 48 F2
Battledown Glos 37 B6
Battlefield Shrops 60 C5
Battlesbridge Essex 42 E3
Battlesden C Beds 40 B2
Battlesea Green Suff 57 B6
Battleton Som 10 B4
Battram Leics 63 D8
Battramsley Hants 14 E4
Baughton Worcs 50 E3
Baughurst Hants 26 D3

Braaid IoM 84 E3
Braal Castle Highld 158 D3
Brabling Green Suff 57 C6
Brabourne Kent 30 E4
Brabourne Lees Kent 30 E4
Brabster Highld 158 D5
Bracadale Highld 149 E8
Bracara Highld 147 B10
Braceborough Lincs 65 C7
Bracebridge Lincs 78 C2
Bracebridge Heath Lincs 78 C2
Bracebridge Low Fields Lincs 78 C2
Braceby Lincs 78 F3
Bracewell Lancs 93 E8
Brackenfield Derbys 76 D3
Brackenthwaite Cumb 108 E2
Brackenthwaite N Yorks 95 D5
Bracklesham W Sus 16 E2
Brackletter Highld 136 F4
Brackley Argyll 143 D8
Brackley Northants 52 F3
Brackloch Highld 156 G4
Bracknell Brack 27 C6
Braco Perth 127 D7
Bracobrae Moray 152 C5
Bracon Ash Norf 68 E4
Bracorina Highld 147 B10
Bradbourne Derbys 76 D2
Bradbury Durham 101 B8
Bradda IoM 84 F1
Bradden Northants 52 E4
Braddock Corn 5 C6
Bradeley Stoke 75 D5
Bradenham Bucks 39 E8
Bradenham Norf 68 D2
Bradenstoke Wilts 24 B5
Bradfield Essex 56 F5
Bradfield Norf 81 D8
Bradfield W Berks 26 B4
Bradfield Combust Suff 56 D2
Bradfield Green Ches E 74 D3
Bradfield Heath Essex 43 B7
Bradfield St Clare Suff 56 D3
Bradfield St George Suff 56 C3
Bradford Corn 5 B6
Bradford Derbys 76 C2
Bradford Devon 9 D6
Bradford Northumb 123 F7
Bradford W Yorks 94 F4
Bradford Abbas Dorset 12 C3
Bradford Leigh Wilts 24 C3
Bradford-on-Avon Wilts 24 C3
Bradford-on-Tone Som 11 B6
Bradford Peverell Dorset 12 E4
Brading IoW 15 F7
Bradley Derbys 76 E2
Bradley Hants 26 E4
Bradley NE Lincs 91 D6
Bradley Staffs 62 C2
Bradley W Mid 62 E3
Bradley W Yorks 88 B2
Bradley Green Worcs 50 C4
Bradley in the Moors Staffs 75 E7
Bradley Stoke S Glos 36 F3
Bradlow Hereford 50 F2
Bradmore Notts 77 F5
Bradmore W Mid 62 E2
Bradninch Devon 10 D5
Bradnop Staffs 75 D7
Bradpole Dorset 12 E2
Bradshaw Gtr Man 86 C5
Bradshaw W Yorks 87 C8
Bradstone Devon 9 F5
Bradwall Green Ches E 74 C4
Bradway S Yorks 88 F4
Bradwell Derbys 88 F2
Bradwell Essex 42 B4
Bradwell M Keynes 53 F6
Bradwell Norf 69 D8
Bradwell Staffs 74 E5
Bradwell Grove Oxon 38 D2
Bradwell on Sea Essex 43 D6
Bradwell Waterside Essex 43 D5
Bradworthy Devon 8 C5
Bradworthy Cross Devon 8 C5
Brae Dumfries 107 B5
Brae Highld 155 J13
Brae Highld 156 J7
Brae Shetland 160 G5
Brae of Achnahaird Highld 156 H3
Brae Roy Lodge Highld 137 E6
Braeantra Highld 151 D8
Braedownie Angus 134 B2
Braefield Highld 150 H7
Braegrum Perth 128 B2
Braehead Dumfries 105 D8
Braehead Orkney 159 D5
Braehead Orkney 159 H6
Braehead S Lanark 119 F8
Braehead S Lanark 120 D2
Braehead of Lunan Angus 135 D6
Braehoulland Shetland 160 F4
Braehungie Highld 158 G3
Braelangwell Lodge Highld 151 B8
Braemar Aberds 139 E7
Braemore Highld 150 D4
Braemore Highld 158 G2
Braes of Enzie Moray 152 C3
Braeside Invclyd 118 B2
Braeswick Orkney 159 E7
Braewick Shetland 160 H5
Brafferton Darl 101 B7
Brafferton N Yorks 95 B7
Brafield-on-the-Green Northants 53 D6
Bragar W Isles 155 C7
Bragbury End Herts 41 B5
Bragleenmore Argyll 124 C5
Braichmelyn Gwyn 83 E6
Braid Edin 120 C5
Braides Lancs 92 D4
Braidley N Yorks 101 F5
Braidwood S Lanark 119 E8
Braigo Argyll 142 B3
Brailsford Derbys 76 E2
Brainshaugh Northumb 117 D8
Braintree Essex 42 B3
Braiseworth Suff 56 B5
Braishfield Hants 14 B4
Braithwaite Cumb 98 B4
Braithwaite S Yorks 89 C7
Braithwaite W Yorks 94 E3
Braithwell S Yorks 89 E6
Bramber W Sus 17 C5
Bramcote Notts 76 F5
Bramcote Warks 63 F8
Bramdean Hants 15 B7
Bramerton Norf 69 D5
Bramfield Herts 41 C5
Bramfield Suff 57 B7
Bramford Suff 56 E5
Bramhall Gtr Man 87 F6
Bramham W Yorks 95 E7
Bramhope W Yorks 95 E5
Bramley Hants 26 D4
Bramley S Yorks 89 E5
Bramley Sur 27 E8
Bramley W Yorks 94 F5
Bramling Kent 31 D6
Brampford Speke Devon 10 E4
Brampton Cambs 54 B3
Brampton Cumb 100 B1
Brampton Cumb 108 C5
Brampton Derbys 76 B3
Brampton Hereford 49 F6
Brampton Lincs 77 B8
Brampton Norf 81 E8
Brampton S Yorks 88 D5
Brampton Suff 69 F7
Brampton Abbotts Hereford 36 B3
Brampton Ash Northants 64 F4
Brampton Bryan Hereford 49 B5
Brampton en le Morthen S Yorks 89 F5
Bramshall Staffs 75 F7
Bramshaw Hants 14 C3
Bramshill Hants 26 C5
Bramshott Hants 27 F6
Bran End Essex 42 B2
Branault Highld 147 E8
Brancaster Norf 80 C3
Brancaster Staithe Norf 80 C3
Brancepeth Durham 110 F5
Branch End Northumb 110 C3
Branchill Moray 151 F13
Brand Green Glos 36 B4
Branderburgh Moray 152 A2
Brandesburton E Yorks 97 E7
Brandeston Suff 57 C6
Brandhill Shrops 49 B6
Brandis Corner Devon 9 D6
Brandiston Norf 81 E7
Brandon Durham 110 F5
Brandon Lincs 78 E2
Brandon Northumb 117 C6
Brandon Suff 67 F7
Brandon Warks 52 B2
Brandon Bank Cambs 67 F6
Brandon Creek Norf 67 E6
Brandon Parva Norf 68 D3
Brandsby N Yorks 95 B8
Brandy Wharf Lincs 90 E4
Brane Corn 2 D3
Branksome Poole 13 E8
Branksome Park Poole 13 E8
Bransby Lincs 77 B8
Branscombe Devon 11 F6
Bransford Worcs 50 D2
Bransgore Hants 14 E2
Branshill Clack 127 E7
Bransholme Hull 97 F7
Branson's Cross Worcs 51 B5
Branston Leics 64 B5
Branston Lincs 78 C3
Branston Staffs 63 B6
Branston Booths Lincs 78 C3
Branstone IoW 15 F6
Bransty Cumb 98 C1
Brant Broughton Lincs 78 D2
Brantham Suff 56 F5
Branthwaite Cumb 98 B2
Branthwaite Cumb 108 F2
Brantingham E Yorks 90 B3
Branton Northumb 117 C6
Branton S Yorks 89 D7
Branxholm Park Borders 115 C7
Branxholme Borders 115 C7
Branxton Northumb 122 F4
Brassey Green Ches W 74 C2
Brassington Derbys 76 D2
Brasted Kent 29 D5
Brasted Chart Kent 29 D5
Brathens Aberds 141 E5
Bratoft Lincs 79 C7
Brattleby Lincs 90 F3
Bratton Telford 61 C6
Bratton Wilts 24 D4
Bratton Clovelly Devon 9 E6
Bratton Fleming Devon 20 F5
Bratton Seymour Som 12 B4
Braughing Herts 41 B6
Braunston Northants 52 C3
Braunston-in-Rutland Rutland 64 D5
Braunstone Town Leicester 64 D2
Braunton Devon 20 F3
Brawby N Yorks 96 B3
Brawl Highld 157 C11
Brawlbin Highld 158 E2
Bray Windsor 27 B7
Bray Shop Corn 5 B8
Bray Wick Windsor 27 B6
Braybrooke Northants 64 F4
Braye Ald 16
Brayford Devon 21 F5
Braystones Cumb 98 D2
Braythorn N Yorks 94 E5
Brayton N Yorks 95 F9
Brazacott Corn 8 E4
Breach Kent 30 C2
Breachacha Castle Argyll 146 F4
Breachwood Green Herts 40 B4
Breacleit W Isles 154 D6
Breaden Heath Shrops 73 F8
Breadsall Derbys 76 F3
Breadstone Glos 36 D4
Breage Corn 2 D5
Breakachy Highld 150 G7
Bream Glos 36 D3
Breamore Hants 14 C2
Brean Som 22 D4
Breanais W Isles 154 E4
Brearton N Yorks 95 C6
Breascleit W Isles 154 D7
Breaston Derbys 76 F4
Brechfa Carms 46 F4
Brechin Angus 135 C5
Breck of Cruan Orkney 159 G4
Breckan Orkney 159 H3
Breckrey Highld 149 B10
Brecon = Aberhonddu Powys 34 B4
Bredbury Gtr Man 87 E7
Brede E Sus 18 D5
Bredenbury Hereford 49 D8
Bredfield Suff 57 D6
Bredgar Kent 30 C2
Bredhurst Kent 29 C8
Bredicot Worcs 50 D4
Bredon Worcs 50 F4
Bredon's Norton Worcs 50 F4
Bredwardine Hereford 48 E5
Breedon on the Hill Leics 63 B8
Breibhig W Isles 148 J1
Breibhig W Isles 155 D9
Breich W Loth 120 C2
Breightmet Gtr Man 86 D5
Breighton E Yorks 96 F3
Breinton Hereford 49 F6
Breinton Common Hereford 49 E6
Breiwick Shetland 160 J6
Bremhill Wilts 24 B4
Bremirehoull Shetland 160 L6
Brenchley Kent 29 E7
Brendon Devon 21 E6
Brenkley T&W 110 B5
Brent Eleigh Suff 56 E3
Brent Knoll Som 22 D5
Brent Pelham Herts 54 F5
Brentford London 28 B2
Brentingby Leics 64 C4
Brentwood Essex 42 E1
Brenzett Kent 19 C7
Brereton Staffs 62 C4
Brereton Green Ches E 74 C4
Brereton Heath Ches E 74 C5
Bressingham Norf 68 F3
Bretby Derbys 63 B6
Bretford Warks 52 B2
Bretforton Worcs 51 E5
Bretherdale Head Cumb 99 D7
Bretherton Lancs 86 B2
Brettabister Shetland 160 H6
Brettenham Norf 68 F2
Brettenham Suff 56 D3
Bretton Derbys 76 B2
Bretton Flint 73 C7
Brewer Street Sur 28 D4
Brewlands Bridge Angus 134 C1
Brewood Staffs 62 D2
Briach Moray 151 F13
Briants Puddle Dorset 13 E6
Brick End Essex 42 B1
Brickendon Herts 41 D6
Bricket Wood Herts 40 D4
Bricklehampton Worcs 50 E4
Bride IoM 84 B4
Bridekirk Cumb 107 F8
Bridell Pembs 45 E3
Bridestowe Devon 9 F7
Brideswell Aberds 152 E5
Bridford Devon 10 F3
Bridfordmills Devon 10 F3
Bridge Kent 31 D5
Bridge End Lincs 78 F4
Bridge Green Essex 55 F5
Bridge Hewick N Yorks 95 B6
Bridge of Alford Aberds 140 C4
Bridge of Allan Stirling 127 E6
Bridge of Avon Moray 152 E1
Bridge of Awe Argyll 125 C6
Bridge of Balgie Perth 132 E2
Bridge of Cally Perth 133 D8
Bridge of Canny Aberds 141 E5
Bridge of Craigisla Angus 134 D2
Bridge of Dee Dumfries 106 D4
Bridge of Don Aberdeen 141 C8
Bridge of Dun Angus 135 D6
Bridge of Dye Aberds 141 F5
Bridge of Earn Perth 128 C3
Bridge of Ericht Perth 132 D2
Bridge of Feugh Aberds 141 E6
Bridge of Forss Highld 157 C13
Bridge of Gairn Aberds 140 E2
Bridge of Gaur Perth 132 D2
Bridge of Muchalls Aberds 141 E7
Bridge of Oich Highld 137 D6
Bridge of Orchy Argyll 125 B8
Bridge of Waith Orkney 159 G3
Bridge of Walls Shetland 160 H4
Bridge of Weir Renfs 118 C3
Bridge Sollers Hereford 49 E6
Bridge Street Suff 56 E2
Bridge Trafford Ches W 73 B8
Bridge Yate S Glos 23 B8
Bridgefoot Angus 134 F3
Bridgefoot Cumb 98 B2
Bridgehampton Som 12 B3
Bridgehill Durham 110 D3
Bridgemary Hants 15 D6
Bridgemont Derbys 87 F8
Bridgend Aberds 140 C4
Bridgend Aberds 152 E5
Bridgend Angus 135 C5
Bridgend Argyll 142 B4
Bridgend Argyll 143 E8
Bridgend Argyll 145 D7
Bridgend = Pen-Y-Bont Ar Ogwr Bridgend 21 B8
Bridgend Cumb 99 C5
Bridgend Fife 129 C5
Bridgend Moray 152 E3
Bridgend N Lanark 119 B6
Bridgend Pembs 45 E3
Bridgend W Loth 120 B3
Bridgend of Lintrathen Angus 134 D2
Bridgerule Devon 8 D4
Bridges Shrops 60 E3
Bridgeton Glasgow 119 C6
Bridgetown Corn 8 F5
Bridgetown Som 21 F8
Bridgham Norf 68 F2
Bridgnorth Shrops 61 E7
Bridgtown Staffs 62 D3
Bridgwater Som 22 F5
Bridlington E Yorks 97 C7
Bridport Dorset 12 E2
Bridstow Hereford 36 B2
Brierfield Lancs 93 F8
Brierley Glos 36 C3
Brierley Hereford 49 D6
Brierley S Yorks 88 C5
Brierley Hill W Mid 62 F3
Briery Hill Bl Gwent 35 D5
Brig o'Turk Stirling 126 D4
Brigg N Lincs 90 D4
Briggswath N Yorks 103 D6
Brigham Cumb 107 F7
Brigham E Yorks 97 D6
Brighouse W Yorks 88 B2
Brighstone IoW 14 F5
Brightgate Derbys 76 D2
Brighthampton Oxon 38 D3
Brightling E Sus 18 C3
Brightlingsea Essex 43 C6
Brighton Brighton 17 D7
Brighton Corn 4 D4
Brighton Hill Hants 26 E4
Brightons Falk 120 B2
Brightwalton W Berks 26 B2
Brightwell Suff 57 E6
Brightwell Baldwin Oxon 39 E6
Brightwell cum Sotwell Oxon 39 E5
Brignall Durham 101 C5
Brigsley NE Lincs 91 D6
Brigsteer Cumb 99 F6
Brigstock Northants 65 F6
Brill Bucks 39 C6
Brilley Hereford 48 E4
Brimaston Pembs 44 C4
Brimfield Hereford 49 C7
Brimington Derbys 76 B4
Brimley Devon 7 B5
Brimpsfield Glos 37 C6
Brimpton W Berks 26 C3
Brims Orkney 159 K3
Brimscombe Glos 37 D5
Brimstage Mers 85 F4
Brinacory Highld 147 B10
Brind E Yorks 96 F3
Brindister Shetland 160 H4
Brindister Shetland 160 K6
Brindle Lancs 86 B4
Brindley Ford Stoke 75 D5
Brineton Staffs 62 C2
Bringhurst Leics 64 E5
Brington Cambs 53 B8
Brinian Orkney 159 F5
Briningham Norf 81 D6
Brinkhill Lincs 79 B6
Brinkley Cambs 55 D7
Brinklow Warks 52 B2
Brinkworth Wilts 37 F7
Brinmore Highld 138 B2
Brinscall Lancs 86 B4
Brinsea N Som 23 C6
Brinsley Notts 76 E4
Brinsop Hereford 49 E6
Brinsworth S Yorks 88 F5
Brinton Norf 81 D6
Brisco Cumb 108 D4
Brisley Norf 81 E5
Brislington Bristol 23 B8
Bristol Bristol 23 B7
Briston Norf 81 D6
Britannia Lancs 87 B6
Britford Wilts 14 B2
Brithdir Gwyn 58 C4
British Legion Village Kent 29 D8
Briton Ferry Neath 33 E8
Britwell Salome Oxon 39 E6
Brixham Torbay 7 D7
Brixton Devon 6 D3
Brixton London 28 B4
Brixton Deverill Wilts 24 F3
Brixworth Northants 52 B5
Brize Norton Oxon 38 D3
Broad Blunsdon Swindon 38 E1
Broad Campden Glos 51 F6
Broad Chalke Wilts 13 B8
Broad Green C Beds 53 E7
Broad Green Essex 42 B4
Broad Green Worcs 50 D2
Broad Haven Pembs 44 D3
Broad Heath Worcs 49 C8
Broad Hill Cambs 55 B6
Broad Hinton Wilts 25 B6
Broad Laying Hants 26 C2
Broad Marston Worcs 51 E6
Broad Oak Carms 33 B6
Broad Oak Cumb 98 E3
Broad Oak Dorset 12 E2
Broad Oak Dorset 13 C5
Broad Oak E Sus 18 C3
Broad Oak E Sus 18 D5
Broad Oak Hereford 36 B1
Broad Oak Mers 86 E3
Broad Street Kent 30 D2
Broad Street Green Essex 42 D4
Broad Town Wilts 25 B5
Broadbottom Gtr Man 87 E7
Broadbridge W Sus 16 D2
Broadbridge Heath W Sus 28 F2
Broadclyst Devon 10 E4
Broadfield Gtr Man 87 C6
Broadfield Lancs 86 B3
Broadfield Pembs 32 D2
Broadfield W Sus 28 F3
Broadford Highld 149 F11
Broadford Bridge W Sus 16 B4
Broadhaugh Borders 115 D7
Broadhaven Highld 158 E5
Broadheath Gtr Man 87 F5
Broadhembury Devon 11 D6
Broadhempston Devon 7 C6
Broadholme Derbys 76 E3
Broadholme Lincs 77 B8
Broadland Row E Sus 18 D5
Broadlay Carms 32 D4
Broadley Lancs 87 C6
Broadley Moray 152 B3
Broadley Common Essex 41 D7
Broadmayne Dorset 12 F5
Broadmeadows Borders 121 F7
Broadmere Hants 26 E4
Broadmoor Pembs 32 D1
Broadoak Kent 31 C5
Broadrashes Moray 152 C4
Broadsea Aberds 153 B9
Broadstairs Kent 31 C7
Broadstone Poole 13 E8
Broadstone Shrops 60 F5
Broadtown Lane Wilts 25 B5
Broadwas Worcs 50 D2
Broadwater Herts 41 B5
Broadwater W Sus 17 D5
Broadway Carms 32 D3
Broadway Pembs 44 D3
Broadway Som 11 C8
Broadway Suff 57 B7
Broadway Worcs 51 F5
Broadwell Glos 36 C2
Broadwell Glos 38 B2
Broadwell Oxon 38 D2
Broadwell Warks 52 C2
Broadwell House Northumb 110 D2
Broadwey Dorset 12 F4
Broadwindsor Dorset 12 D2
Broadwood Kelly Devon 9 D8
Broadwoodwidger Devon 9 F6
Brobury Hereford 48 E5
Brochel Highld 149 D10
Brochloch Dumfries 113 E5
Brochroy Argyll 125 B6
Brockamin Worcs 50 D2
Brockbridge Hants 15 C7
Brockdam Northumb 117 B7
Brockdish Norf 57 B6
Brockenhurst Hants 14 D4
Brocketsbrae S Lanark 119 F8
Brockford Street Suff 56 C5
Brockhall Northants 52 C4
Brockham Sur 28 E2
Brockhampton Glos 37 B7
Brockhampton Hereford 49 F7
Brockholes W Yorks 88 C2
Brockhurst Derbys 76 C3
Brockhurst Hants 15 D7
Brocklebank Cumb 108 E3
Brocklesby Lincs 90 C5
Brockley N Som 23 C6
Brockley Green Suff 56 D2
Brockleymoor Cumb 108 F4
Brockton Shrops 60 D3
Brockton Shrops 60 F3
Brockton Shrops 61 D7
Brockton Shrops 61 E5
Brockton Telford 61 C7
Brockweir Glos 36 D2
Brockwood Hants 15 B7
Brockworth Glos 37 C5
Brocton Staffs 62 C3
Brodick N Ayrs 143 E11
Brodsworth S Yorks 89 D6
Brogaig Highld 149 B9
Brogborough C Beds 53 F7
Broken Cross Ches E 75 B5
Broken Cross Ches W 74 B3
Brokenborough Wilts 37 F6
Bromborough Mers 85 F4
Brome Suff 56 B5
Brome Street Suff 57 B5
Bromeswell Suff 57 D7
Bromfield Cumb 107 E8
Bromfield Shrops 49 B6
Bromham Bedford 53 D8
Bromham Wilts 24 C4
Bromley London 28 C5
Bromley W Mid 62 F3
Bromley Common London 28 C5
Bromley Green Kent 19 B6
Brompton Medway 29 C8
Brompton N Yorks 102 E1
Brompton N Yorks 103 F7
Brompton-on-Swale N Yorks 101 E7
Brompton Ralph Som 22 F2
Brompton Regis Som 21 F8
Bromsash Hereford 36 B3
Bromsberrow Heath Glos 50 F2
Bromsgrove Worcs 50 B4
Bromyard Hereford 49 D8
Bromyard Downs Hereford 49 D8
Bronaber Gwyn 71 D8
Brongest Ceredig 46 E2
Bronington Wrex 73 F8
Bronllys Powys 48 F3
Bronnant Ceredig 46 C5
Bronwydd Arms Carms 33 B5
Bronydd Powys 48 E4
Bronygarth Shrops 73 F6
Brook Carms 32 D3
Brook Hants 14 B4
Brook Hants 14 C3
Brook IoW 14 F4
Brook Kent 30 E4
Brook Sur 27 E8
Brook Sur 27 F7
Brook End Bedford 53 C8
Brook Hill Hants 14 C3
Brook Street Kent 19 B6
Brook Street Kent 29 E6
Brook Street W Sus 17 B7
Brooke Norf 69 E5
Brooke Rutland 64 D5
Brookenby Lincs 91 E6
Brookend Glos 36 E2
Brookfield Renfs 118 C4
Brookhouse Lancs 92 C5
Brookhouse Green Ches E 74 C5
Brookland Kent 19 C6
Brooklands Dumfries 106 B5
Brooklands Gtr Man 87 E5
Brooklands Shrops 74 E2
Brookmans Park Herts 41 D5
Brooks Powys 59 E8
Brooks Green W Sus 16 B5
Brookthorpe Glos 37 C5
Brookville Norf 67 E7
Brookwood Sur 27 D7
Broom C Beds 54 E2
Broom S Yorks 88 E5
Broom Warks 51 D5
Broom Worcs 50 B4
Broom Green Norf 81 E5
Broom Hill Dorset 13 D8
Broome Norf 69 E6
Broome Shrops 60 F4
Broome Park Northumb 117 C7
Broomedge Warr 86 F5
Broomer's Corner W Sus 16 B5
Broomfield Aberds 153 E9
Broomfield Essex 42 C3
Broomfield Kent 30 D2
Broomfield Kent 31 C5
Broomfield Som 22 F4
Broomfleet E Yorks 90 B2
Broomhall Ches E 74 E3
Broomhall Windsor 27 C7
Broomhaugh Northumb 110 C3
Broomhill Norf 67 D6
Broomhill Northumb 117 D8
Broomhill S Yorks 88 D5
Broomholm Norf 81 D9
Broomley Northumb 110 C3
Broompark Durham 110 E5
Broom's Green Glos 50 F2
Broomy Lodge Hants 14 C3
Brora Highld 157 J12
Broseley Shrops 61 D6
Brotherhouse Bar Lincs 66 C2
Brotherstone Borders 122 F2
Brothertoft Lincs 79 E5
Brotherton N Yorks 89 B5
Brotton Redcar 102 C4
Broubster Highld 157 C13
Brough Cumb 100 C2
Brough Derbys 88 F2
Brough E Yorks 90 B3
Brough Highld 158 C4
Brough Notts 77 D8
Brough Orkney 159 G4
Brough Shetland 160 F6
Brough Shetland 160 F7
Brough Shetland 160 G7
Brough Shetland 160 H6
Brough Shetland 160 J7
Brough Lodge Shetland 160 D7
Brough Sowerby Cumb 100 C2
Broughall Shrops 74 E2
Broughton Borders 120 F4
Broughton Cambs 54 B3
Broughton Flint 73 C7
Broughton Hants 25 F8
Broughton Lancs 92 F5
Broughton M Keynes 53 E6
Broughton N Lincs 90 D3
Broughton N Yorks 94 D2
Broughton N Yorks 96 B3
Broughton Northants 53 B6
Broughton Orkney 159 D5
Broughton Oxon 52 F2
Broughton V Glam 21 B8
Broughton Astley Leics 64 E2
Broughton Beck Cumb 98 F4
Broughton Common Wilts 24 C3
Broughton Gifford Wilts 24 C3
Broughton Hackett Worcs 50 D4
Broughton in Furness Cumb 98 F4
Broughton Mills Cumb 98 E4
Broughton Moor Cumb 107 F7
Broughton Park Gtr Man 87 D6
Broughton Poggs Oxon 38 D2
Broughtown Orkney 159 D7
Broughty Ferry Dundee 134 F4
Browhouses Dumfries 108 C2
Browland Shetland 160 H4
Brown Candover Hants 26 F3
Brown Edge Lancs 85 C4
Brown Edge Staffs 75 D6
Brown Heath Ches W 73 C8
Brownhill Aberds 153 D6
Brownhill Aberds 153 D8
Brownhill Blackburn 93 F6
Brownhill Shrops 60 B4
Brownhills Fife 129 C7
Brownhills W Mid 62 D4
Brownlow Ches E 74 C5
Brownlow Heath Ches E 74 C5
Brownmuir Aberds 135 B7
Brown's End Glos 50 F2
Brownshill Glos 37 D5
Brownston Devon 6 D4
Brownyside Northumb 117 B7
Broxa N Yorks 103 E7
Broxbourne Herts 41 D6
Broxburn E Loth 122 B2
Broxburn W Loth 120 B3
Broxholme Lincs 78 B2
Broxted Essex 42 B1
Broxton Ches W 73 D8
Broxwood Hereford 49 D5
Broyle Side E Sus 17 C8
Brù W Isles 155 C8
Bruairnis W Isles 148 H2
Bruan Highld 158 G5
Bruar Lodge Perth 133 B5
Brucehill W Dunb 118 B3
Bruera Ches W 73 C8
Bruern Abbey Oxon 38 B2
Bruichladdich Argyll 142 B3
Bruisyard Suff 57 C7
Brumby N Lincs 90 D2
Brund Staffs 75 C8
Brundall Norf 69 D6
Brundish Suff 57 C6
Brundish Street Suff 57 B6
Brunery Highld 147 D10
Brunshaw Lancs 93 F8
Brunswick Village T&W 110 B5
Bruntcliffe W Yorks 88 B3
Bruntingthorpe Leics 64 E3
Brunton Fife 128 B5
Brunton Northumb 117 B8
Brunton Wilts 25 D7
Brushford Devon 9 D8
Brushford Som 10 B4
Bruton Som 23 F8
Bryanston Dorset 13 D6
Brydekirk Dumfries 107 B8
Bryher Scilly 2 E3
Brymbo Wrex 73 D6
Brympton Som 12 C3
Bryn Carms 33 D6
Bryn Gtr Man 86 D3
Bryn Neath 34 E2
Bryn Shrops 60 F2
Bryn-coch Neath 33 E8
Bryn Du Anglesey 82 D3
Bryn Gates Gtr Man 86 D3
Bryn-glas Conwy 83 E8
Bryn Golau Rhondda 34 F3
Bryn-Iwan Carms 46 F2
Bryn-mawr Gwyn 70 D3
Bryn-nantllech Conwy 72 C3
Bryn-penarth Powys 59 D8
Bryn Rhyd-yr-Arian Conwy 72 C3
Bryn Saith Marchog Denb 72 D4
Bryn Sion Gwyn 59 C5
Bryn-y-gwenin Mon 35 C7
Bryn-y-maen Conwy 83 D8
Bryn-yr-eryr Gwyn 70 C4
Brynamman Carms 33 C8
Brynberian Pembs 45 F3
Brynbryddan Neath 34 E1
Brynbuga = Usk Mon 35 D7
Bryncae Rhondda 34 F3
Bryncethin Bridgend 34 F3
Bryncir Gwyn 71 C5
Bryncroes Gwyn 70 D3
Bryncrug Gwyn 58 D3
Bryneglwys Denb 72 E5
Brynford Flint 73 B5
Bryngwran Anglesey 82 D3
Bryngwyn Ceredig 45 E4
Bryngwyn Mon 35 D7
Bryngwyn Powys 48 E3
Brynhenllan Pembs 45 F2
Brynhoffnant Ceredig 46 D2
Brynithel Bl Gwent 35 D6
Brynmawr Bl Gwent 35 C5
Brynmenyn Bridgend 34 F3
Brynmill Swansea 33 E7
Brynna Rhondda 34 F3
Brynrefail Anglesey 82 C4
Brynrefail Gwyn 83 E5
Brynsadler Rhondda 34 F4
Brynsiencyn Anglesey 82 E4
Brynteg Anglesey 82 C4
Brynteg Ceredig 46 E3
Buaile nam Bodach W Isles 148 H2
Bualintur Highld 149 F9
Buarthmeini Gwyn 72 F2
Bubbenhall Warks 51 B8
Bubwith E Yorks 96 F3
Buccleuch Borders 115 C6
Buchanhaven Aberds 153 D11
Buchanty Perth 127 B8
Buchlyvie Stirling 126 E4
Buckabank Cumb 108 E3
Buckden Cambs 54 C2
Buckden N Yorks 94 B2
Buckenham Norf 69 D6
Buckerell Devon 11 D6
Buckfast Devon 6 C5
Buckfastleigh Devon 6 C5
Buckhaven Fife 129 E5
Buckholm Borders 121 F7
Buckholt Mon 36 C2
Buckhorn Weston Dorset 13 B5
Buckhurst Hill Essex 41 E7
Buckie Moray 152 B4
Buckies Highld 158 D3
Buckingham Bucks 52 F4
Buckland Bucks 40 C1
Buckland Devon 6 E4
Buckland Glos 51 F5
Buckland Hants 14 E4
Buckland Herts 54 F4
Buckland Kent 31 E7
Buckland Oxon 38 E3
Buckland Sur 28 D3
Buckland Brewer Devon 9 B6
Buckland Common Bucks 40 D2
Buckland Dinham Som 24 D2
Buckland Filleigh Devon 9 D6
Buckland in the Moor Devon 6 B5
Buckland Monachorum Devon 6 C2
Buckland Newton Dorset 12 D4
Buckland St Mary Som 11 C7
Bucklebury W Berks 26 B3
Bucklegate Lincs 79 F6
Bucklerheads Angus 134 F4
Bucklers Hard Hants 14 E5
Bucklesham Suff 57 E6
Buckley = Bwcle Flint 73 C6
Bucklow Hill Ches E 86 F5
Buckminster Leics 65 B5
Bucknall Lincs 78 C4
Bucknall Stoke 75 E6
Bucknell Oxon 39 B5
Bucknell Shrops 49 B5
Buckpool Moray 152 B4
Buck's Cross Devon 8 B5
Bucks Green W Sus 27 F8
Bucks Horn Oak Hants 27 E6
Buck's Mills Devon 9 B5
Bucksburn Aberdeen 141 D7
Buckshaw Village Lancs 86 B3
Buckskin Hants 26 D4
Buckton E Yorks 97 B7
Buckton Hereford 49 B5
Buckton Northumb 123 F6
Buckworth Cambs 54 B2
Budbrooke Warks 51 C7
Budby Notts 77 C6
Budd's Titson Corn 8 D4
Bude Corn 8 D4
Budlake Devon 10 E4
Budle Northumb 123 F7
Budleigh Salterton Devon 11 F5
Budock Water Corn 3 C6
Buerton Ches E 74 E3
Buffler's Holt Bucks 52 F4
Bugbrooke Northants 52 D4
Buglawton Ches E 75 C5
Bugle Corn 4 D5
Bugley Wilts 24 E3
Bugthorpe E Yorks 96 D3
Buildwas Shrops 61 D6
Builth Road Powys 48 D2
Builth Wells = Llanfair-Ym-Muallt Powys 48 D2
Buirgh W Isles 154 H5
Bulby Lincs 65 B7
Bulcote Notts 77 E6
Buldoo Highld 157 C12
Bulford Wilts 25 E6
Bulford Camp Wilts 25 E6
Bulkeley Ches E 74 D2
Bulkington Warks 63 F7
Bulkington Wilts 24 D4
Bulkworthy Devon 9 C5
Bull Hill Hants 14 E4
Bullamoor N Yorks 102 E1
Bullbridge Derbys 76 D3
Bullbrook Brack 27 C6
Bulley Glos 36 C4
Bullgill Cumb 107 F7
Bullington Hants 26 E2
Bullington Lincs 78 B3
Bull's Green Herts 41 C5
Bullwood Argyll 145 F10
Bulmer Essex 56 E2
Bulmer N Yorks 96 C2
Bulmer Tye Essex 56 F2
Bulphan Thurrock 42 F2
Bulverhythe E Sus 18 E4
Bulwark Aberds 153 D9
Bulwell Nottingham 76 E5
Bulwick Northants 65 E6
Bumble's Green Essex 41 D7
Bun a'Mhuillin W Isles 148 G2
Bun Abhainn Eadarra W Isles 154 G6
Bun Loyne Highld 136 D5
Bunacaimb Highld 147 C9
Bunarkaig Highld 136 F4
Bunbury Ches E 74 D2
Bunbury Heath Ches E 74 D2
Bunchrew Highld 151 G9
Bundalloch Highld 149 F13
Buness Shetland 160 C8
Bunessan Argyll 146 J6
Bungay Suff 69 F6
Bunker's Hill Lincs 78 B2
Bunker's Hill Lincs 79 D5
Bunkers Hill Oxon 38 C4
Bunloit Highld 137 B8
Bunnahabhain Argyll 142 A5
Bunny Notts 64 B2
Buntait Highld 150 H6
Buntingford Herts 41 B6
Bunwell Norf 68 E4
Burbage Derbys 75 B7
Burbage Leics 63 E8
Burbage Wilts 25 C7
Burchett's Green Windsor 39 F8
Burcombe Wilts 25 F5
Burcot Oxon 39 E5
Burcott Bucks 40 B1
Burdon T&W 111 D6
Bures Suff 56 F3
Bures Green Suff 56 F3
Burford Ches E 74 D3
Burford Oxon 38 C2
Burford Shrops 49 C7
Burg Argyll 146 G6
Burgar Orkney 159 F4
Burgate Hants 14 C2
Burgate Suff 56 B4
Burgess Hill W Sus 17 C7
Burgh Suff 57 D6
Burgh by Sands Cumb 108 D3
Burgh Castle Norf 69 D7
Burgh Heath Sur 28 D3
Burgh le Marsh Lincs 79 C8
Burgh Muir Aberds 141 B6
Burgh next Aylsham Norf 81 E8
Burgh on Bain Lincs 91 F6
Burgh St Margaret Norf 69 C7
Burgh St Peter Norf 69 E7
Burghclere Hants 26 C2
Burghead Moray 151 E14
Burghfield W Berks 26 C4
Burghfield Common W Berks 26 C4
Burghfield Hill W Berks 26 C4
Burghill Hereford 49 E6
Burghwallis S Yorks 89 C6
Burham Kent 29 C8
Buriton Hants 15 B8
Burland Ches E 74 D3
Burlawn Corn 4 B4
Burleigh Brack 27 C6
Burlescombe Devon 11 C5
Burleston Dorset 13 E5
Burley Hants 14 D3
Burley Rutland 65 C5
Burley W Yorks 95 F5
Burley Gate Hereford 49 E7
Burley in Wharfedale W Yorks 94 E4
Burley Lodge Hants 14 D3
Burley Street Hants 14 D3
Burleydam Ches E 74 E3
Burlingjobb Powys 48 D4
Burlow E Sus 18 D2
Burlton Shrops 60 B4
Burmarsh Kent 19 B7
Burmington Warks 51 F7
Burn N Yorks 89 B6
Burn of Cambus Stirling 127 D6
Burnaston Derbys 76 F2
Burnbank S Lanark 119 D7
Burnby E Yorks 96 E4
Burncross S Yorks 88 E4
Burneside Cumb 99 E7
Burness Orkney 159 D7
Burneston N Yorks 101 F8
Burnett Bath 23 C8
Burnfoot Borders 115 C7
Burnfoot Borders 115 C8
Burnfoot E Ayrs 112 D4
Burnfoot Perth 127 D8
Burnham Bucks 40 F2
Burnham N Lincs 90 C4
Burnham Deepdale Norf 80 C4
Burnham Green Herts 41 C5
Burnham Market Norf 80 C4
Burnham Norton Norf 80 C4
Burnham-on-Crouch Essex 43 E5
Burnham-on-Sea Som 22 E5
Burnham Overy Staithe Norf 80 C4
Burnham Overy Town Norf 80 C4
Burnham Thorpe Norf 80 C4
Burnhead Dumfries 113 E8
Burnhead S Ayrs 112 D2
Burnhervie Aberds 141 C6
Burnhill Green Staffs 61 D7
Burnhope Durham 110 E4
Burnhouse N Ayrs 118 D3
Burniston N Yorks 103 E8
Burnlee W Yorks 88 D2
Burnley Lancs 93 F8
Burnley Lane Lancs 93 F8
Burnmouth Borders 123 C5
Burnopfield Durham 110 D4
Burnsall N Yorks 94 C3
Burnside Angus 135 D5
Burnside E Ayrs 113 C5
Burnside Fife 128 D3
Burnside S Lanark 119 C6
Burnside Shetland 160 F4
Burnside W Loth 120 B3
Burnside of Duntrune Angus 134 F4
Burnswark Dumfries 107 B8
Burnt Heath Derbys 76 B2
Burnt Houses Durham 101 B6
Burnt Yates N Yorks 95 C5
Burntcommon Sur 27 D8
Burnthouse Corn 3 C6
Burntisland Fife 128 F4
Burnton E Ayrs 112 D4
Burntwood Staffs 62 D4
Burnwynd Edin 120 C4
Burpham Sur 27 D8
Burpham W Sus 16 D4
Burradon Northumb 117 D5
Burradon T&W 111 B5
Burrafirth Shetland 160 B8
Burraland Shetland 160 F5
Burraland Shetland 160 J4
Burras Corn 3 C5
Burravoe Shetland 160 F7
Burravoe Shetland 160 G5
Burray Village Orkney 159 J5
Burrells Cumb 100 C1
Burrelton Perth 134 F2
Burridge Devon 20 F4
Burridge Hants 15 C6
Burrill N Yorks 101 F7
Burringham N Lincs 90 D2
Burrington Devon 9 C8
Burrington Hereford 49 B6
Burrington N Som 23 D6
Burrough Green Cambs 55 D7
Burrough on the Hill Leics 64 C4
Burrow-bridge Som 11 B8
Burrowhill Sur 27 C7
Burry Swansea 33 E5
Burry Green Swansea 33 E5
Burry Port = Porth Tywyn Carms 33 D5
Burscough Lancs 86 C2
Burscough Bridge Lancs 86 C2
Bursea E Yorks 96 F4
Burshill E Yorks 97 E6
Bursledon Hants 15 D5
Burslem Stoke 75 E5
Burstall Suff 56 E4
Burstock Dorset 12 D2
Burston Norf 68 F4
Burston Staffs 75 F6
Burstow Sur 28 E4
Burstwick E Yorks 91 B6
Burtersett N Yorks 100 F3
Burtle Som 23 E5
Burton Ches W 73 B7
Burton Ches W 74 C2
Burton Dorset 14 E2
Burton Lincs 78 B2
Burton Northumb 123 F7
Burton Pembs 44 E4
Burton Som 22 E3
Burton Wilts 24 B3
Burton Agnes E Yorks 97 C7
Burton Bradstock Dorset 12 F2
Burton Dassett Warks 51 D8
Burton Fleming E Yorks 97 B6
Burton Green W Mid 51 B7
Burton Green Wrex 73 D7
Burton Hastings Warks 63 E8
Burton-in-Kendal Cumb 92 B5
Burton in Lonsdale N Yorks 93 B6
Burton Joyce Notts 77 E6
Burton Latimer Northants 53 B7
Burton Lazars Leics 64 C4
Burton-le-Coggles Lincs 65 B6
Burton Leonard N Yorks 95 C6
Burton on the Wolds Leics 64 B2
Burton Overy Leics 64 E3
Burton Pedwardine Lincs 78 E4
Burton Pidsea E Yorks 97 F8
Burton Salmon N Yorks 89 B5
Burton Stather N Lincs 90 C2
Burton upon Stather N Lincs 90 C2
Burton upon Trent Staffs 63 B6
Burtonwood Warr 86 E3
Burwardsley Ches W 74 D2
Burwarton Shrops 61 F6
Burwash E Sus 18 C3
Burwash Common E Sus 18 C3
Burwash Weald E Sus 18 C3
Burwell Cambs 55 C6
Burwell Lincs 79 B6
Burwen Anglesey 82 B4
Burwick Orkney 159 K5
Bury Cambs 66 F2
Bury Gtr Man 87 C6
Bury Som 10 B4
Bury W Sus 16 C4
Bury Green Herts 41 B7
Bury St Edmunds Suff 56 C2
Burythorpe N Yorks 96 C3
Busby E Renf 119 D5
Buscot Oxon 38 E2
Bush Bank Hereford 49 D6
Bush Crathie Aberds 139 E8
Bush Green Norf 68 F5
Bushbury W Mid 62 D3
Bushby Leics 64 D3
Bushey Herts 40 E4
Bushey Heath Herts 40 E4
Bushley Worcs 50 F3
Bushton Wilts 25 B5
Buslingthorpe Lincs 90 F4
Busta Shetland 160 G5
Butcher's Cross E Sus 18 C2
Butcombe N Som 23 C7
Butetown Cardiff 22 B3
Butleigh Som 23 F7
Butleigh Wootton Som 23 F7
Butler's Cross Bucks 39 D8
Butler's End Warks 63 F6
Butlers Marston Warks 51 E8
Butley Suff 57 D7
Butley High Corner Suff 57 E7
Butt Green Ches E 74 D3
Butterburn Cumb 109 B6
Buttercrambe N Yorks 96 D3
Butterknowle Durham 101 B6
Butterleigh Devon 10 D4
Buttermere Cumb 98 C3
Buttermere Wilts 25 C8
Buttershaw W Yorks 88 B2
Butterstone Perth 133 E7
Butterton Staffs 75 D7
Butterwick Durham 102 B1
Butterwick Lincs 79 E6
Butterwick N Yorks 96 B3
Butterwick N Yorks 97 B5
Buttington Powys 60 D2
Buttonoak Worcs 50 B2
Butt's Green Hants 14 B4
Buttsash Hants 14 D5
Buxhall Suff 56 D4
Buxhall Fen Street Suff 56 D4
Buxley Borders 122 D4
Buxted E Sus 17 B8
Buxton Derbys 75 B7

Buxton Norf 81 E8
Buxworth Derbys 87 F8
Bwcle = Buckley Flint 73 C6
Bwlch Powys 35 B5
Bwlch-Llan Ceredig 46 D4
Bwlch-y-cibau Powys 59 C8
Bwlch-y-fadfa Ceredig 46 E3
Bwlch-y-ffridd Powys 59 E7
Bwlch-y-sarnau Powys 48 B2
Bwlchgwyn Wrex 73 D6
Bwlchnewydd Carms 32 B4
Bwlchtocyn Gwyn 70 E4
Bwlchyddar Powys 59 B8
Bwlchygroes Pembs 45 F4
Byermoor T&W 110 D4
Byers Green Durham 110 F5
Byfield Northants 52 D3
Byfleet Sur 27 C8
Byford Hereford 49 E5
Bygrave Herts 54 F3
Byker T&W 111 C5
Bylchau Conwy 72 C3
Byley Ches W 74 C4
Bynea Carms 33 E6
Byrness Northumb 116 D3
Bythorn Cambs 53 B8
Byton Hereford 49 C5
Byworth W Sus 16 B3

C

Cabharstadh W Isles 155 E8
Cablea Perth 133 F6
Cabourne Lincs 90 D5
Cabrach Argyll 144 G3
Cabrach Moray 140 B2
Cabrich Highld 151 G8
Cabus Lancs 92 E4
Cackle Street E Sus 17 B8
Cadbury Devon 10 D4
Cadbury Barton Devon 9 C8
Cadder E Dunb 119 B6
Caddington C Beds 40 C3
Caddonfoot Borders 121 F7
Cade Street E Sus 18 C3
Cadeby Leics 63 D8
Cadeby S Yorks 89 D6
Cadeleigh Devon 10 D4
Cadgwith Corn 3 E6
Cadham Fife 128 D4
Cadishead Gtr Man 86 E5
Cadle Swansea 33 E7
Cadley Lancs 92 F5
Cadley Wilts 25 C7
Cadley Wilts 25 D7
Cadmore End Bucks 39 E7
Cadnam Hants 14 C3
Cadney N Lincs 90 D4
Cadole Flint 73 C6
Cadoxton V Glam 22 C3
Cadoxton-Juxta-Neath Neath 34 E1
Cadshaw Blackburn 86 C5
Cadzow S Lanark 119 D7
Caeathro Gwyn 82 E4
Caehopkin Powys 34 C2
Caenby Lincs 90 F4
Caenby Corner Lincs 90 F3
Caér-bryn Carms 33 C6
Caer Llan Mon 36 D1
Caerau Bridgend 34 E2
Caerau Cardiff 22 B3
Caerdeon Gwyn 58 C3
Caerdydd = Cardiff Cardiff 22 B3
Caerfarchell Pembs 44 C2
Caerffili = Caerphilly Caerph 35 F5
Caerfyrddin = Carmarthen Carms 33 B5
Caergeiliog Anglesey 82 D3
Caergwrle Flint 73 D7
Caergybi = Holyhead Anglesey 82 C2
Caerleon = Caerllion Newport 35 E7
Caerllion = Caerleon Newport 35 E7
Caernarfon Gwyn 82 E4
Caerphilly = Caerffili Caerph 35 F5
Caersws Powys 59 E7
Caerwedros Ceredig 46 D2
Caerwent Mon 36 E1
Caerwych Gwyn 71 D7
Caerwys Flint 72 B5
Caethle Gwyn 58 E3
Caim Anglesey 83 C6
Caio Carms 47 F5
Cairinis W Isles 148 B3
Cairisiadar W Isles 154 D5
Cairminis W Isles 154 J5
Cairnbaan Argyll 145 D7
Cairnbanno Ho. Aberds 153 D8
Cairnborrow Aberds 152 D4
Cairnbrogie Aberds 141 B7
Cairnbulg Castle Aberds 153 B10
Cairncross Angus 134 B4
Cairncross Borders 122 C4
Cairndow Argyll 125 D7
Cairness Aberds 153 B10
Cairneyhill Fife 128 F2
Cairnfield Ho. Moray 152 B4
Cairngaan Dumfries 104 F5
Cairngarroch Dumfries 104 E4
Cairnhill Aberds 153 E6
Cairnie Aberds 141 D7
Cairnie Aberds 152 D4
Cairnorrie Aberds 153 D8
Cairnpark Aberds 141 C7
Cairnryan Dumfries 104 C4
Cairnton Orkney 159 H4
Caister-on-Sea Norf 69 C8
Caistor Lincs 90 D5
Caistor St Edmund Norf 68 D5
Caistron Northumb 117 D5
Caitha Bowland Borders 121 E7
Calais Street Suff 56 F3
Calanais W Isles 154 D7
Calbost W Isles 155 F9
Calbourne IoW 14 F5
Calceby Lincs 79 B6
Calcot Row W Berks 26 B4
Calcott Kent 31 C5
Caldback Shetland 160 C8
Caldbeck Cumb 108 F3
Caldbergh N Yorks 101 F5
Caldecote Cambs 54 D4
Caldecote Cambs 65 F8
Caldecote Herts 54 F3
Caldecote Northants 52 D4
Caldecott Northants 53 C7
Caldecott Oxon 38 E4
Caldecott Rutland 65 E5
Calder Bridge Cumb 98 D2
Calder Hall Cumb 98 D2
Calder Mains Highld 158 E2
Calder Vale Lancs 92 E5
Calderbank N Lanark 119 C7
Calderbrook Gtr Man 87 C7
Caldercruix N Lanark 119 C8
Caldermill S Lanark 119 E6
Calderwood S Lanark 119 D6
Caldhame Angus 134 E4
Caldicot Mon 36 F1
Caldwell Derbys 63 C6
Caldwell N Yorks 101 C6
Caldy Mers 85 F3
Caledrhydiau Ceredig 46 D3
Calfsound Orkney 159 E6
Calgary Argyll 146 F6
Califer Moray 151 F13
California Falk 120 B2
California Norf 69 C8
Calke Derbys 63 B7
Callakille Highld 149 C11
Callaly Northumb 117 D6
Callander Stirling 126 D5
Callaughton Shrops 61 E6
Callestick Corn 4 D2
Calligarry Highld 149 H11
Callington Corn 5 C8
Callow Hereford 49 F6
Callow End Worcs 50 E3
Callow Hill Wilts 37 F7
Callow Hill Worcs 50 B2
Callows Grave Worcs 49 C7
Calmore Hants 14 C4
Calmsden Glos 37 D7
Calne Wilts 24 B5
Calow Derbys 76 B4
Calshot Hants 15 D5
Calstock Corn 6 C2
Calstone Wellington Wilts 24 C5
Calthorpe Norf 81 D7
Calthwaite Cumb 108 E4
Calton N Yorks 94 D2
Calton Staffs 75 D8
Calveley Ches E 74 D2
Calver Derbys 76 B2
Calver Hill Hereford 49 E5
Calverhall Shrops 74 F3
Calverleigh Devon 10 C4
Calverley W Yorks 94 F5
Calvert Bucks 39 B6
Calverton M Keynes 53 F5
Calverton Notts 77 E6
Calvine Perth 133 C5
Calvo Cumb 107 D8
Cam Glos 36 E4
Camas-luinie Highld 136 B2
Camasnacroise Highld 130 D2
Camastianavaig Highld 149 E10
Camasunary Highld 149 G10
Camault Muir Highld 151 G8
Camb Shetland 160 D7
Camber E Sus 19 D6
Camberley Sur 27 C6
Camberwell London 28 B4
Camblesforth N Yorks 89 B7
Cambo Northumb 117 F6
Cambois Northumb 117 F9
Camborne Corn 3 B5
Cambourne Cambs 54 D4
Cambridge Cambs 55 D5
Cambridge Glos 36 D4
Cambridge Town Southend 43 F5
Cambus Clack 127 E7
Cambusavie Farm Highld 151 B10
Cambusbarron Stirling 127 E6
Cambuskenneth Stirling 127 E7
Cambuslang S Lanark 119 C6
Cambusmore Lodge Highld 151 B10
Camden London 41 F5
Camelford Corn 8 F3
Camelsdale Sur 27 F6
Camerory Highld 151 H13
Camer's Green Worcs 50 F2
Camerton Bath 23 D8
Camerton Cumb 107 F7
Camerton E Yorks 91 B6
Camghouran Perth 132 D2
Cammachmore Aberds 141 E8
Cammeringham Lincs 90 F3
Camore Highld 151 B10
Camp Hill Warks 63 E7
Campbeltown Argyll 143 F8
Camperdown T&W 111 B5
Campmuir Perth 134 F2
Campsall S Yorks 89 C6
Campsey Ash Suff 57 D7
Campton C Beds 54 F2
Camptown Borders 116 C2
Camrose Pembs 44 C4
Camserney Perth 133 E5
Camster Highld 158 F4
Camuschoirk Highld 130 C1
Camuscross Highld 149 G11
Camusnagaul Highld 130 B4
Camusnagaul Highld 150 C3
Camusrory Highld 147 B11
Camusteel Highld 149 D12
Camusterrach Highld 149 D12
Camusvrachan Perth 132 E3
Canada Hants 14 C3
Canadia E Sus 18 D4
Canal Side S Yorks 89 C7
Candacraig Ho. Aberds 140 C2
Candlesby Lincs 79 C7
Candy Mill S Lanark 120 E3
Cane End Oxon 26 B4
Canewdon Essex 42 E4
Canford Bottom Dorset 13 D8
Canford Cliffs Poole 13 F8
Canford Magna Poole 13 E8
Canham's Green Suff 56 C4
Canholes Derbys 75 B7
Canisbay Highld 158 C5
Cann Dorset 13 B6
Cann Common Dorset 13 B6
Cannard's Grave Som 23 E8
Cannich Highld 150 H6
Cannington Som 22 F4
Cannock Staffs 62 D3
Cannock Wood Staffs 62 C4
Canon Bridge Hereford 49 E6
Canon Frome Hereford 49 E8
Canon Pyon Hereford 49 E6
Canonbie Dumfries 108 B3
Canons Ashby Northants 52 D3
Canonstown Corn 2 C4
Canterbury Kent 30 D5
Cantley Norf 69 D6
Cantley S Yorks 89 D7
Cantlop Shrops 60 D5
Canton Cardiff 22 B3
Cantraybruich Highld 151 G10
Cantraydoune Highld 151 G10
Cantraywood Highld 151 G10
Cantsfield Lancs 93 B6
Canvey Island Essex 42 F3
Canwick Lincs 78 C2
Canworthy Water Corn 8 E4
Caol Highld 131 B5
Caol Ila Argyll 142 A5
Caolas Argyll 146 G3
Caolas Scalpaigh W Isles 154 H7
Caolas Stocinis W Isles 154 H6
Capel Sur 28 E2
Capel Bangor Ceredig 58 F3
Capel Betws Lleucu Ceredig 46 D5
Capel Carmel Gwyn 70 E2
Capel Coch Anglesey 82 C4
Capel Curig Conwy 83 F7
Capel Cynon Ceredig 46 E2
Capel Dewi Carms 33 B5
Capel Dewi Ceredig 46 E3
Capel Dewi Ceredig 58 F3
Capel Garmon Conwy 83 F8
Capel-gwyn Anglesey 82 D3
Capel Gwyn Carms 33 B5
Capel Gwynfe Carms 33 B8
Capel Hendre Carms 33 C6
Capel Hermon Gwyn 71 E8
Capel Isaac Carms 33 B6
Capel Iwan Carms 45 F4
Capel le Ferne Kent 31 F6
Capel Llanilltern Cardiff 34 F4
Capel Mawr Anglesey 82 D4
Capel St Andrew Suff 57 E7
Capel St Mary Suff 56 F4
Capel Seion Ceredig 46 B5
Capel Tygwydd Ceredig 45 E4
Capel Uchaf Gwyn 70 C5
Capel-y-graig Gwyn 82 E5
Capelulo Conwy 83 D7
Capenhurst Ches W 73 B7
Capernwray Lancs 92 B5
Capheaton Northumb 117 F6
Cappercleuch Borders 115 B5
Capplegill Dumfries 114 D4
Capton Devon 7 D6
Caputh Perth 133 F7
Car Colston Notts 77 E7
Carbis Bay Corn 2 C4
Carbost Highld 149 D9
Carbost Highld 149 E8
Carbrook S Yorks 88 F4
Carbrooke Norf 68 D2
Carburton Notts 77 B6
Carcant Borders 121 D6
Carcary Angus 135 D6
Carclaze Corn 4 D5
Carcroft S Yorks 89 C6
Cardenden Fife 128 E4
Cardeston Shrops 60 C3
Cardiff = Caerdydd Cardiff 22 B3
Cardigan = Aberteifi Ceredig 45 E3
Cardington Bedford 53 E8
Cardington Shrops 60 E5
Cardinham Corn 5 C6
Cardonald Glasgow 118 C5
Cardow Moray 152 D1
Cardrona Borders 121 F6
Cardross Argyll 118 B3
Cardurnock Cumb 107 D8
Careby Lincs 65 C7
Careston Castle Angus 135 D5
Carew Pembs 32 D1
Carew Cheriton Pembs 32 D1
Carew Newton Pembs 32 D1
Carey Hereford 49 F7
Carfrae E Loth 121 C8
Cargenbridge Dumfries 107 B6
Cargill Perth 134 F1
Cargo Cumb 108 D3
Cargreen Corn 6 C2
Carham Northumb 122 F4
Carhampton Som 22 E2
Carharrack Corn 3 B6
Carie Perth 132 D3
Carie Perth 132 F3
Carines Corn 4 D2
Carisbrooke IoW 15 F5
Cark Cumb 92 B3
Carlabhagh W Isles 154 C7
Carland Cross Corn 4 D3
Carlby Lincs 65 C7
Carlecotes S Yorks 88 D2
Carlesmoor N Yorks 94 B4
Carleton Cumb 99 B7
Carleton Cumb 108 D4
Carleton Lancs 92 F3
Carleton N Yorks 94 E2
Carleton Forehoe Norf 68 D3
Carleton Rode Norf 68 E4
Carlin How Redcar 103 C5
Carlingcott Bath 23 D8
Carlisle Cumb 108 D4
Carlops Borders 120 D4
Carlton Bedford 53 D7
Carlton Cambs 55 D7
Carlton Leics 63 D7
Carlton N Yorks 89 B7
Carlton N Yorks 101 C6
Carlton N Yorks 101 F5
Carlton N Yorks 102 F4
Carlton Notts 77 E6
Carlton S Yorks 88 C4
Carlton Stockton 102 B1
Carlton Suff 57 C7
Carlton W Yorks 88 B4
Carlton Colville Suff 69 F8
Carlton Curlieu Leics 64 E3
Carlton Husthwaite N Yorks 95 B7
Carlton in Cleveland N Yorks 102 D3
Carlton in Lindrick Notts 89 F6
Carlton le Moorland Lincs 78 D2
Carlton Miniott N Yorks 102 F1
Carlton on Trent Notts 77 C7
Carlton Scroop Lincs 78 E2
Carluke S Lanark 119 D8
Carmarthen = Caerfyrddin Carms 33 B5
Carmel Anglesey 82 C3
Carmel Carms 33 C6
Carmel Flint 73 B5
Carmel Guern 16
Carmel Gwyn 82 F4
Carmont Aberds 141 F7
Carmunnock Glasgow 119 D6
Carmyle Glasgow 119 C6
Carmyllie Angus 135 E5
Carn-gorm Highld 136 B2
Carnaby E Yorks 97 C7
Carnach Highld 136 B3
Carnach Highld 150 B3
Carnach W Isles 154 H7
Carnachy Highld 157 D10
Càrnais W Isles 154 D5
Carnbee Fife 129 D7
Carnbo Perth 128 D2
Carnbrea Corn 3 B5
Carnduff S Lanark 119 E6
Carnduncan Argyll 142 B3
Carne Corn 3 C8
Carnforth Lancs 92 B4
Carnhedryn Pembs 44 C3
Carnhell Green Corn 2 C5
Carnkie Corn 3 C5
Carnkie Corn 3 C6
Carno Powys 59 E6
Carnoch Highld 150 F5
Carnoch Highld 150 H6
Carnock Fife 128 F2
Carnon Downs Corn 3 B6
Carnousie Aberds 153 C6
Carnoustie Angus 135 F5
Carnwath S Lanark 120 E2
Carnyorth Corn 2 C2
Carperby N Yorks 101 F5
Carpley Green N Yorks 100 F4
Carr S Yorks 89 E6
Carr Hill T&W 111 C5
Carradale Argyll 143 E9
Carragraich W Isles 154 H6
Carrbridge Highld 138 B5
Carrefour Selous Jersey 17
Carreg-wen Pembs 45 E4
Carreglefn Anglesey 82 C3
Carrick Argyll 145 E8
Carrick Fife 129 B6
Carrick Castle Argyll 145 D10
Carrick Ho. Orkney 159 E6
Carriden Falk 128 F2
Carrington Gtr Man 86 E5
Carrington Lincs 79 D6
Carrington Midloth 121 C6
Carrog Conwy 71 C8
Carrog Denb 72 E5
Carron Falk 127 F7
Carron Moray 152 D2
Carron Bridge Stirling 127 F6
Carronbridge Dumfries 113 E8
Carronshore Falk 127 F7
Carrshield Northumb 109 E8
Carrutherstown Dumfries 107 B8
Carrville Durham 111 E6
Carsaig Argyll 144 E6
Carsaig Argyll 147 J8
Carscreugh Dumfries 105 D6
Carse Gray Angus 134 D4
Carse Ho. Argyll 144 G6
Carsegowan Dumfries 105 D8
Carseriggan Dumfries 105 C7
Carsethorn Dumfries 107 D6
Carshalton London 28 C3
Carsington Derbys 76 D2
Carskiey Argyll 143 H7
Carsluith Dumfries 105 D8
Carsphairn Dumfries 113 E5
Carstairs S Lanark 120 E2
Carstairs Junction S Lanark 120 E2
Carswell Marsh Oxon 38 E3
Carter's Clay Hants 14 B4
Carterton Oxon 38 D2
Carterway Heads Northumb 110 D3
Carthew Corn 4 D5
Carthorpe N Yorks 101 F8
Cartington Northumb 117 D6
Cartland S Lanark 119 E8
Cartmel Cumb 92 B3
Cartmel Fell Cumb 99 F6
Carway Carms 33 D5
Cary Fitzpaine Som 12 B3
Cas-gwent = Chepstow Mon 36 E2
Cascob Powys 48 C4
Cashlie Perth 132 E1
Cashmoor Dorset 13 C7
Casnewydd = Newport Newport 35 F7
Cassey Compton Glos 37 C7
Cassington Oxon 38 C4
Cassop Durham 111 F6
Castell Denb 72 C5
Castell-Howell Ceredig 46 E3
Castell-Nedd = Neath Neath 33 E8
Castell Newydd Emlyn = Newcastle Emlyn Carms 46 E2
Castell-y-bwch Torf 35 E6
Castellau Rhondda 34 F4
Casterton Cumb 93 B6
Castle Acre Norf 67 C8
Castle Ashby Northants 53 D6
Castle Bolton N Yorks 101 E5
Castle Bromwich W Mid 62 F5
Castle Bytham Lincs 65 C6
Castle Caereinion Powys 59 D8
Castle Camps Cambs 55 E7
Castle Carrock Cumb 108 D5
Castle Cary Som 23 F8
Castle Combe Wilts 24 B3
Castle Donington Leics 63 B8
Castle Douglas Dumfries 106 C4
Castle Eaton Swindon 37 E8
Castle Eden Durham 111 F7
Castle Forbes Aberds 140 C5
Castle Frome Hereford 49 E8
Castle Green Sur 27 C7
Castle Gresley Derbys 63 C6
Castle Heaton Northumb 122 E5
Castle Hedingham Essex 55 F8
Castle Hill Kent 29 E7
Castle Huntly Perth 128 B5
Castle Kennedy Dumfries 104 D5
Castle O'er Dumfries 115 E5
Castle Pulverbatch Shrops 60 D4
Castle Rising Norf 67 B6
Castle Stuart Highld 151 G10
Castlebay = Bagh a Chaisteil W Isles 148 J1
Castlebythe Pembs 32 B1
Castlecary N Lanark 119 B7
Castlecraig Highld 151 E11
Castlefairn Dumfries 113 F7
Castleford W Yorks 88 B5
Castlehill Borders 120 F5
Castlehill Highld 158 D3
Castlehill W Dunb 118 B3
Castlemaddy Dumfries 113 F5
Castlemartin Pembs 44 F4
Castlemilk Dumfries 107 B8
Castlemilk Glasgow 119 D6
Castlemorris Pembs 44 B4
Castlemorton Worcs 50 F2
Castleside Durham 110 E3
Castlethorpe M Keynes 53 E6
Castleton Angus 134 E3
Castleton Argyll 145 E7
Castleton Derbys 88 F2
Castleton Gtr Man 87 C6
Castleton N Yorks 102 D4
Castleton Newport 35 F6
Castletown Ches W 73 D8
Castletown Highld 151 G10
Castletown Highld 158 D3
Castletown IoM 84 F2
Castletown T&W 111 D6
Castleweary Borders 115 D7
Castley N Yorks 95 E5
Caston Norf 68 E2
Castor Pboro 65 E8
Catacol N Ayrs 143 D10
Catbrain S Glos 36 F2
Catbrook Mon 36 D2
Catchall Corn 2 D3
Catchems Corner W Mid 51 B7
Catchgate Durham 110 D4
Catcleugh Northumb 116 D3
Catcliffe S Yorks 88 F5
Catcott Som 23 F5
Caterham Sur 28 D4
Catfield Norf 69 B6
Catfirth Shetland 160 H6
Catford London 28 B4
Catforth Lancs 92 F4
Cathays Cardiff 22 B3
Cathcart Glasgow 119 C5
Cathedine Powys 35 B5
Catherington Hants 15 C7
Catherton Shrops 49 B8
Catlodge Highld 138 E2
Catlowdy Cumb 108 B4
Catmore W Berks 38 F4
Caton Lancs 92 C5
Caton Green Lancs 92 C5
Catrine E Ayrs 113 B5
Cat's Ash Newport 35 E7
Catsfield E Sus 18 D4
Catshill Worcs 50 B4
Cattal N Yorks 95 D7
Cattawade Suff 56 F5
Catterall Lancs 92 E4
Catterick N Yorks 101 E7
Catterick Bridge N Yorks 101 E7
Catterick Garrison N Yorks 101 E6
Catterlen Cumb 108 F4
Catterline Aberds 135 B8
Catterton N Yorks 95 E8
Catthorpe Leics 52 B3
Cattistock Dorset 12 E3
Catton N Yorks 95 B6
Catton Northumb 109 D8
Catwick E Yorks 97 E7
Catworth Cambs 53 B8
Caudlesprings Norf 68 D2
Caulcott Oxon 39 B5
Cauldcots Angus 135 E6
Cauldhame Stirling 126 E5
Cauldmill Borders 115 C8
Cauldon Staffs 75 E7
Caulkerbush Dumfries 107 D6
Caulside Dumfries 115 F7
Caunsall Worcs 62 F2
Caunton Notts 77 D7
Causeway End Dumfries 105 C8
Causeway Foot W Yorks 94 F3
Causeway-head Stirling 127 E6
Causewayend S Lanark 120 F3
Causewayhead Cumb 107 D8
Causey Park Bridge Northumb 117 E7
Causeyend Aberds 141 C8
Cautley Cumb 100 E1
Cavendish Suff 56 E2
Cavendish Bridge Leics 63 B8
Cavenham Suff 55 C8
Caversfield Oxon 39 B5
Caversham Reading 26 B5
Caverswall Staffs 75 E6
Cavil E Yorks 96 F3
Cawdor Highld 151 F11
Cawkwell Lincs 79 B5
Cawood N Yorks 95 F8
Cawsand Corn 6 D2
Cawston Norf 81 E7
Cawthorne S Yorks 88 D3
Cawthorpe Lincs 65 B7
Cawton N Yorks 96 B2
Caxton Cambs 54 D4
Caynham Shrops 49 B7
Caythorpe Lincs 78 E2
Caythorpe Notts 77 E6
Cayton N Yorks 103 F8
Ceann a Bhaigh W Isles 148 B2
Ceann a Deas Loch Baghasdail W Isles 148 G2
Ceann Shiphoirt W Isles 155 F7
Ceann Tarabhaigh W Isles 154 F7
Ceannacroc Lodge Highld 136 C5
Cearsiadair W Isles 155 E8
Cefn Berain Conwy 72 C3
Cefn-brith Conwy 72 D3
Cefn Canol Powys 73 F6
Cefn-coch Conwy 83 E8
Cefn Coch Powys 59 B8
Cefn-coed-y-cymmer M Tydf 34 D4
Cefn Cribbwr Bridgend 34 F2
Cefn Cross Bridgend 34 F2
Cefn-ddwysarn Gwyn 72 F3
Cefn Einion Shrops 60 F2
Cefn-gorwydd Powys 47 E8
Cefn-mawr Wrex 73 E6
Cefn-y-bedd Flint 73 D7
Cefn-y-pant Carms 32 B2
Cefneithin Carms 33 C6
Cei-bach Ceredig 46 D3
Ceinewydd = New Quay Ceredig 46 D2
Ceint Anglesey 82 D4
Cellan Ceredig 46 E5
Cellarhead Staffs 75 E6
Cemaes Anglesey 82 B3
Cemmaes Powys 58 D5
Cemmaes Road Powys 58 D5
Cenarth Carms 45 E4
Cenin Gwyn 71 C5
Central Invclyd 118 B2
Ceos W Isles 155 E8
Ceres Fife 129 C6
Cerne Abbas Dorset 12 D4
Cerney Wick Glos 37 E7
Cerrigceinwen Anglesey 82 D4
Cerrigydrudion Conwy 72 E3
Cessford Borders 116 B3
Ceunant Gwyn 82 E5
Chaceley Glos 50 F3
Chacewater Corn 3 B6
Chackmore Bucks 52 F4
Chacombe Northants 52 E2
Chad Valley W Mid 62 F4
Chadderton Gtr Man 87 D7
Chadderton Fold Gtr Man 87 D6
Chaddesden Derby 76 F3
Chaddesley Corbett Worcs 50 B3
Chaddleworth W Berks 26 B2
Chadlington Oxon 38 B3
Chadshunt Warks 51 D8
Chadwell Leics 64 B4
Chadwell St Mary Thurrock 29 B7
Chadwick End W Mid 51 B7
Chadwick Green Mers 86 E3
Chaffcombe Som 11 C8
Chagford Devon 10 F2
Chailey E Sus 17 C7
Chain Bridge Lincs 79 E6
Chainbridge Cambs 66 D4
Chainhurst Kent 29 E8
Chalbury Dorset 13 D8
Chalbury Common Dorset 13 D8
Chaldon Sur 28 D4
Chaldon Herring Dorset 13 F5
Chale IoW 15 G5
Chale Green IoW 15 G5
Chalfont Common Bucks 40 E3
Chalfont St Giles Bucks 40 E2
Chalfont St Peter Bucks 40 E3
Chalford Glos 37 D5
Chalgrove Oxon 39 E6
Chalk Kent 29 B7
Challacombe Devon 21 E5
Challoch Dumfries 105 C7
Challock Kent 30 D4
Chalton C Beds 40 B3
Chalton Hants 15 C8
Chalvington E Sus 18 E2
Chancery Ceredig 46 B4
Chandler's Ford Hants 14 B5
Channel Tunnel Kent 19 B8
Channerwick Shetland 160 L6
Chantry Som 24 E2
Chantry Suff 56 E5
Chapel Fife 128 E4
Chapel Allerton Som 23 D6
Chapel Allerton W Yorks 95 F6
Chapel Amble Corn 4 B4
Chapel Brampton Northants 52 C5
Chapel Chorlton Staffs 74 F5
Chapel-en-le-Frith Derbys 87 F8
Chapel End Warks 63 E7
Chapel Green Warks 52 C2
Chapel Green Warks 63 F6
Chapel Haddlesey N Yorks 89 B6
Chapel Head Cambs 66 F3
Chapel Hill Aberds 153 E10
Chapel Hill Lincs 78 D5
Chapel Hill Mon 36 E2
Chapel Hill N Yorks 95 E6
Chapel Lawn Shrops 48 B5
Chapel-le-Dale N Yorks 93 B7
Chapel Milton Derbys 87 F8
Chapel of Garioch Aberds 141 B6
Chapel Row W Berks 26 C3
Chapel St Leonards Lincs 79 B8
Chapel Stile Cumb 99 D5
Chapelgate Lincs 66 B4
Chapelhall N Lanark 119 C7
Chapelhill Dumfries 114 E3
Chapelhill Highld 151 D11
Chapelhill N Ayrs 118 E2
Chapelhill Perth 128 B4
Chapelhill Perth 133 F7
Chapelknowe Dumfries 108 B3
Chapelton Angus 135 E6
Chapelton Devon 9 B7
Chapelton Highld 138 C5
Chapelton S Lanark 119 E6
Chapeltown Blackburn 86 C5
Chapeltown Moray 139 B8
Chapeltown S Yorks 88 E4
Chapmans Well Devon 9 E5
Chapmanslade Wilts 24 E3
Chapmore End Herts 41 C6
Chappel Essex 42 B4
Chard Som 11 D8
Chardstock Devon 11 D8
Charfield S Glos 36 E4
Charford Worcs 50 C4
Charing Kent 30 E3
Charing Cross Dorset 14 C2
Charing Heath Kent 30 E3
Charingworth Glos 51 F7
Charlbury Oxon 38 C3
Charlcombe Bath 24 C2
Charlecote Warks 51 D7
Charles Devon 21 F5
Charles Tye Suff 56 D4
Charlesfield Dumfries 107 C8
Charleston Angus 134 E3
Charleston Renfs 118 C4
Charlestown Aberdeen 141 D8
Charlestown Corn 4 D5
Charlestown Derbys 87 E8
Charlestown Dorset 12 G4
Charlestown Fife 128 F2
Charlestown Gtr Man 87 D6
Charlestown Highld 149 A13
Charlestown Highld 151 G9
Charlestown W Yorks 87 B7
Charlestown of Aberlour Moray 152 D2
Charlesworth Derbys 87 E8
Charleton Devon 7 E5
Charlton Hants 25 E8
Charlton Herts 40 B4
Charlton London 28 B5
Charlton Northants 52 F3
Charlton Northumb 116 F4
Charlton Som 23 D8
Charlton Telford 61 C5
Charlton W Sus 16 C2
Charlton Wilts 13 B7
Charlton Wilts 25 D6
Charlton Wilts 37 F6
Charlton Worcs 50 E5
Charlton Abbots Glos 37 B7
Charlton Adam Som 12 B3
Charlton-All-Saints Wilts 14 B2
Charlton Down Dorset 12 E4
Charlton Horethorne Som 12 B4
Charlton Kings Glos 37 B6
Charlton Mackerell Som 12 B3
Charlton Marshall Dorset 13 D6
Charlton Musgrove Som 12 B5
Charlton on Otmoor Oxon 39 C5
Charltons Redcar 102 C4
Charlwood Sur 28 E3
Charlynch Som 22 F4
Charminster Dorset 12 E4
Charmouth Dorset 11 E8
Charndon Bucks 39 B6
Charney Bassett Oxon 38 E3
Charnock Richard Lancs 86 C3
Charsfield Suff 57 D6
Chart Corner Kent 29 D8
Chart Sutton Kent 30 E2
Charter Alley Hants 26 D3
Charterhouse Som 23 D6
Charterville Allotments Oxon 38 C3
Chartham Kent 30 D5
Chartham Hatch Kent 30 D5
Chartridge Bucks 40 D2
Charvil Wokingham 27 B5
Charwelton Northants 52 D3
Chasetown Staffs 62 D4
Chastleton Oxon 38 B2
Chasty Devon 8 D5
Chatburn Lancs 93 E7
Chatcull Staffs 74 F4
Chatham Medway 29 C8
Chathill Northumb 117 B7
Chattenden Medway 29 B8
Chatteris Cambs 66 F3
Chattisham Suff 56 E4
Chatto Borders 116 C3
Chatton Northumb 117 B6
Chawleigh Devon 10 C2
Chawley Oxon 38 D4
Chawston Bedford 54 D2
Chawton Hants 26 F5
Cheadle Gtr Man 87 F6
Cheadle Staffs 75 E7
Cheadle Heath Gtr Man 87 F6
Cheadle Hulme Gtr Man 87 F6
Cheam London 28 C3
Cheapside Sur 27 D8
Chearsley Bucks 39 C7
Chebsey Staffs 62 B2
Checkendon Oxon 39 F6
Checkley Ches E 74 E4
Checkley Hereford 49 F7
Checkley Staffs 75 F7
Chedburgh Suff 55 D8
Cheddar Som 23 D6
Cheddington Bucks 40 C2
Cheddleton Staffs 75 D6
Cheddon Fitzpaine Som 11 B7
Chedglow Wilts 37 E6
Chedgrave Norf 69 E6
Chedington Dorset 12 D2
Chediston Suff 57 B7
Chedworth Glos 37 C7
Chedzoy Som 22 F5
Cheeklaw Borders 122 D3
Cheeseman's Green Kent 19 B7
Cheglinch Devon 20 E4
Cheldon Devon 10 C2
Chelford Ches E 74 B5
Chell Heath Stoke 75 D5
Chellaston Derby 76 F3
Chellington Bedford 53 D7
Chelmarsh Shrops 61 F7
Chelmer Village Essex 42 D3
Chelmondiston Suff 57 F6
Chelmorton Derbys 75 C8
Chelmsford Essex 42 D3
Chelsea London 28 B3
Chelsfield London 29 C5
Chelsworth Suff 56 E3
Cheltenham Glos 37 B6
Chelveston Northants 53 C7
Chelvey N Som 23 C6
Chelwood Bath 23 C8
Chelwood Common E Sus 17 B8
Chelwood Gate E Sus 17 B8
Chelworth Wilts 37 E6
Chelworth Green Wilts 37 E7
Chemistry Shrops 74 E2
Chenies Bucks 40 E3
Cheny Longville Shrops 60 F4
Chepstow = Cas-gwent Mon 36 E2
Chequerfield W Yorks 89 B5
Cherhill Wilts 24 B5
Cherington Glos 37 E6
Cherington Warks 51 F7
Cheriton Devon 21 E6
Cheriton Hants 15 B6
Cheriton Kent 19 B8
Cheriton Swansea 33 E5
Cheriton Bishop Devon 10 E2
Cheriton Fitzpaine Devon 10 D3
Cheriton or Stackpole Elidor Pembs 44 F4
Cherrington Telford 61 B6
Cherry Burton E Yorks 97 E5
Cherry Hinton Cambs 55 D5
Cherry Orchard Worcs 50 D3
Cherry Willingham Lincs 78 B3
Cherrybank Perth 128 B3
Chertsey Sur 27 C8
Cheselbourne Dorset 13 E5
Chesham Bucks 40 D2
Chesham Bois Bucks 40 E2
Cheshunt Herts 41 D6
Cheslyn Hay Staffs 62 D3
Chessington London 28 C2
Chester Ches W 73 C8
Chester-Le-Street Durham 111 D5
Chester Moor Durham 111 E5
Chesterblade Som 23 E8
Chesterfield Derbys 76 B3
Chesters Borders 116 B2
Chesters Borders 116 C2
Chesterton Cambs 55 C5
Chesterton Cambs 65 E8
Chesterton Glos 37 D7
Chesterton Oxon 39 B5
Chesterton Shrops 61 E7
Chesterton Staffs 74 E5
Chesterton Warks 51 D8
Chesterwood Northumb 109 C8
Chestfield Kent 30 C5
Cheston Devon 6 D4
Cheswardine Shrops 61 B7
Cheswick Northumb 123 E6
Chetnole Dorset 12 D4
Chettiscombe Devon 10 C4
Chettisham Cambs 66 F5
Chettle Dorset 13 C7
Chetton Shrops 61 E6
Chetwode Bucks 39 B6
Chetwynd Aston Telford 61 C7
Cheveley Cambs 55 C7
Chevening Kent 29 D5
Chevington Suff 55 D8
Chevithorne Devon 10 C4
Chew Magna Bath 23 C7
Chew Stoke Bath 23 C7
Chewton Keynsham Bath 23 C8
Chewton Mendip Som 23 D7
Chicheley M Keynes 53 E7
Chichester W Sus 16 D2
Chickerell Dorset 12 F4
Chicklade Wilts 24 F4
Chicksgrove Wilts 24 F4
Chidden Hants 15 C7
Chiddingfold Sur 27 F7
Chiddingly E Sus 18 D2
Chiddingstone Kent 29 E5
Chiddingstone Causeway Kent 29 E6
Chiddingstone Hoath Kent 29 E5
Chideock Dorset 12 E2
Chidham W Sus 15 D8
Chidswell W Yorks 88 B3
Chieveley W Berks 26 B2
Chignall Smealy Essex 42 C2
Chignall St James Essex 42 D2
Chigwell Essex 41 E7
Chigwell Row Essex 41 E7
Chilbolton Hants 25 F8
Chilcomb Hants 15 B6
Chilcombe Dorset 12 E3
Chilcompton Som 23 D8
Chilcote Leics 63 C6
Child Okeford Dorset 13 C6
Childer Thornton Ches W 73 B7
Childrey Oxon 38 F3
Child's Ercall Shrops 61 B6
Childswickham Worcs 51 F5
Childwall Mers 86 F2
Childwick Green Herts 40 C4
Chilfrome Dorset 12 E3
Chilgrove W Sus 16 C2
Chilham Kent 30 D4
Chilhampton Wilts 25 F5
Chilla Devon 9 D6
Chillaton Devon 9 F6
Chillenden Kent 31 D6
Chillerton IoW 15 F5
Chillesford Suff 57 D7
Chillingham Northumb 117 B6
Chillington Devon 7 E5
Chillington Som 11 C8
Chilmark Wilts 24 F4
Chilson Oxon 38 C3
Chilsworthy Corn 6 B2
Chilsworthy Devon 8 D5
Chilthorne Domer Som 12 C3
Chiltington E Sus 17 C7
Chilton Bucks 39 C6
Chilton Durham 101 B7
Chilton Oxon 38 F4
Chilton Cantelo Som 12 B3
Chilton Foliat Wilts 25 B8
Chilton Lane Durham 111 F6
Chilton Polden Som 23 F5
Chilton Street Suff 55 E8
Chilton Trinity Som 22 F4
Chilvers Coton Warks 63 E7
Chilwell Notts 76 F5
Chilworth Hants 14 C5
Chilworth Sur 27 E8
Chimney Oxon 38 D3
Chineham Hants 26 D4
Chingford London 41 E6
Chinley Derbys 87 F8
Chinley Head Derbys 87 F8
Chinnor Oxon 39 D7
Chipnall Shrops 74 F4
Chippenhall Green Suff 57 B6
Chippenham Cambs 55 C7
Chippenham Wilts 24 B4
Chipperfield Herts 40 D3
Chipping Herts 54 F4
Chipping Lancs 93 E6
Chipping Campden Glos 51 F6
Chipping Hill Essex 42 C4
Chipping Norton Oxon 38 B3
Chipping Ongar Essex 42 D1
Chipping Sodbury S Glos 36 F4
Chipping Warden Northants 52 E2
Chipstable Som 10 B5
Chipstead Kent 29 D5
Chipstead Sur 28 D3
Chirbury Shrops 60 E2
Chirk = Y Waun Wrex 73 F6
Chirk Bank Shrops 73 F6
Chirmorrie S Ayrs 105 B6
Chirnside Borders 122 D4
Chirnsidebridge Borders 122 D4
Chirton Wilts 25 D5
Chisbury Wilts 25 C7
Chiselborough Som 12 C2
Chiseldon Swindon 25 B6
Chiserley W Yorks 87 B8
Chislehampton Oxon 39 E5
Chislehurst London 28 B5
Chislet Kent 31 C6
Chiswell Green Herts 40 D4
Chiswick London 28 B3
Chiswick End Cambs 54 E4
Chisworth Derbys 87 E7
Chithurst W Sus 16 B2
Chittering Cambs 55 B5
Chitterne Wilts 24 E4
Chittlehamholt Devon 9 B8
Chittlehampton Devon 9 B8
Chittoe Wilts 24 C4
Chivenor Devon 20 F4
Chobham Sur 27 C7
Choicelee Borders 122 D3
Cholderton Wilts 25 E7
Cholesbury Bucks 40 D2
Chollerford Northumb 110 B2
Chollerton Northumb 110 B2
Cholmondeston Ches E 74 C3
Cholsey Oxon 39 F5
Cholstrey Hereford 49 D6
Chop Gate N Yorks 102 E3
Choppington Northumb 117 F8
Chopwell T&W 110 D4
Chorley Ches E 74 D2
Chorley Lancs 86 C3
Chorley Shrops 61 F6
Chorley Staffs 62 C4
Chorleywood Herts 40 E3
Chorlton cum Hardy Gtr Man 87 E6
Chorlton Lane Ches W 73 E8
Choulton Shrops 60 F3
Chowdene T&W 111 D5
Chowley Ches W 73 D8
Chrishall Essex 54 F5
Christchurch Cambs 66 E4
Christchurch Dorset 14 E2
Christchurch Glos 36 C2
Christchurch Newport 35 F7
Christian Malford Wilts 24 B4
Christleton Ches W 73 C8
Christmas Common Oxon 39 E7
Christon N Som 23 D5
Christon Bank Northumb 117 B8
Christow Devon 10 F3
Chryston N Lanark 119 B6
Chudleigh Devon 7 B6
Chudleigh Knighton Devon 7 B6
Chulmleigh Devon 9 C8
Chunal Derbys 87 E8
Church Lancs 86 B5
Church Aston Telford 61 C7
Church Brampton Northants 52 C5
Church Broughton Derbys 76 F2
Church Crookham Hants 27 D6
Church Eaton Staffs 62 C2
Church End C Beds 40 B2
Church End C Beds 53 F7
Church End C Beds 54 F2
Church End Cambs 66 D3
Church End Cambs 66 F2
Church End E Yorks 97 D6
Church End Essex 42 B3
Church End Essex 55 E6
Church End Hants 26 D4
Church End Lincs 78 F5
Church End Warks 63 E6
Church End Warks 63 E6
Church End Wilts 24 B5
Church Enstone Oxon 38 B3
Church Fenton N Yorks 95 F8
Church Green Devon 11 E6
Church Green Norf 68 E3
Church Gresley Derbys 63 C6
Church Hanborough Oxon 38 C4
Church Hill Ches W 74 C3
Church Houses N Yorks 102 E4
Church Knowle Dorset 13 F7
Church Laneham Notts 77 B8
Church Langton Leics 64 E4
Church Lawford Warks 52 B2
Church Lawton Ches E 74 D5
Church Leigh Staffs 75 F7
Church Lench Worcs 50 D5
Church Mayfield Staffs 75 E8
Church Minshull Ches E 74 C3
Church Norton W Sus 16 E2
Church Preen Shrops 60 E5
Church Pulverbatch Shrops 60 D4
Church Stoke Powys 60 E2
Church Stowe Northants 52 D4
Church Street Kent 29 B8
Church Stretton Shrops 60 E4
Church Town N Lincs 89 D8
Church Town Sur 28 D4
Church Village Rhondda 34 F4
Church Warsop Notts 77 C5
Churcham Glos 36 C4
Churchbank Shrops 48 B4
Churchbridge Staffs 62 D3
Churchdown Glos 37 C5
Churchend Essex 42 B2
Churchend Essex 43 E6
Churchend S Glos 36 E4
Churchfield W Mid 62 E4
Churchgate Street Essex 41 C7
Churchill Devon 11 D8
Churchill Devon 20 E4
Churchill N Som 23 D6
Churchill Oxon 38 B2
Churchill Worcs 50 B3
Churchill Worcs 50 D4
Churchinford Som 11 C7
Churchover Warks 64 F2
Churchstanton Som 11 C6
Churchstow Devon 6 E5
Churchtown Derbys 76 C2
Churchtown IoM 84 C4
Churchtown Lancs 92 E4

Churchtown Mers 85 C4
Churnsike Lodge Northumb 109 B6
Churston Ferrers Torbay 7 D7
Churt Sur 27 F6
Churton Ches W 73 D8
Churwell W Yorks 88 B3
Chute Standen Wilts 25 D8
Chwilog Gwyn 70 D5
Chyandour Corn 2 C3
Cilan Uchaf Gwyn 70 E3
Cilcain Flint 73 C5
Cilcennin Ceredig 46 C4
Cilfor Gwyn 71 D7
Cilfrew Neath 34 D1
Cilfynydd Rhondda 34 E4
Cilgerran Pembs 45 E3
Cilgwyn Carms 33 B8
Cilgwyn Gwyn 82 F4
Cilgwyn Pembs 45 F2
Ciliau Aeron Ceredig 46 D3
Cill Donnain W Isles 148 F2
Cille Bhrighde W Isles 148 G2
Cille Pheadair W Isles 148 G2
Cilmery Powys 48 D2
Cilsan Carms 33 B6
Ciltalgarth Gwyn 72 E2
Cilwendeg Pembs 45 F4
Cilybebyll Neath 33 D8
Cilycwm Carms 47 F6
Cimla Neath 34 E1
Cinderford Glos 36 C3
Cippyn Pembs 45 E3
Circebost W Isles 154 D6
Cirencester Glos 37 D7
Ciribhig W Isles 154 C6
City London 41 F6
City Powys 60 F2
City Dulas Anglesey 82 C4
Clachaig Argyll 145 E10
Clachan Argyll 124 D3
Clachan Argyll 125 D7
Clachan Argyll 130 E2
Clachan Argyll 144 H6
Clachan Highld 149 E10
Clachan W Isles 148 D2
Clachan na Luib W Isles 148 B3
Clachan of Campsie E Dunb 119 B6
Clachan of Glendaruel Argyll 145 E8
Clachan-Seil Argyll 124 D3
Clachan Strachur Argyll 125 E6
Clachaneasy Dumfries 105 B7
Clachanmore Dumfries 104 E4
Clachbreck Argyll 144 F6
Clachnabrain Angus 134 C3
Clachtoll Highld 156 G3
Clackmannan Clack 127 E8
Clacton-on-Sea Essex 43 C7
Cladach Chireboist W Isles 148 B2
Claddach-knockline W Isles 148 B2
Cladich Argyll 125 C6
Claggan Highld 131 B5
Claggan Highld 147 G9
Claigan Highld 148 C7
Claines Worcs 50 D3
Clandown Bath 23 D8
Clanfield Hants 15 C7
Clanfield Oxon 38 D2
Clanville Hants 25 E8
Claonaig Argyll 145 H7
Claonel Highld 157 J8
Clap Hill Kent 19 B7
Clapgate Dorset 13 D8
Clapgate Herts 41 B7
Clapham Bedford 53 D8
Clapham London 28 B3
Clapham N Yorks 93 C7
Clapham W Sus 16 D4
Clappers Borders 122 D5
Clappersgate Cumb 99 D5
Clapton Som 12 D2
Clapton-in-Gordano N Som 23 B6
Clapton-on-the-Hill Glos 38 C1
Clapworthy Devon 9 B8
Clara Vale T&W 110 C4
Clarach Ceredig 58 F3
Clarbeston Pembs 32 B1
Clarbeston Road Pembs 32 B1
Clarborough Notts 89 F8
Clardon Highld 158 D3
Clare Suff 55 E8
Clarebrand Dumfries 106 C4
Clarencefield Dumfries 107 C7
Clarilaw Borders 115 C8
Clark's Green Sur 28 F2
Clarkston E Renf 119 D5
Clashandorran Highld 151 G8
Clashcoig Highld 151 B9
Clashindarroch Aberds 152 E4
Clashmore Highld 151 C10
Clashmore Highld 156 F3
Clashnessie Highld 156 F3
Clashnoir Moray 139 B8
Clate Shetland 160 G7
Clathy Perth 127 C8
Clatt Aberds 140 B4
Clatter Powys 59 E6
Clatterford IoW 15 F5
Clatterin Bridge Aberds 135 B6
Clatworthy Som 22 F2
Claughton Lancs 92 E5
Claughton Lancs 93 C5
Claughton Mers 85 F4
Claverdon Warks 51 C6
Claverham N Som 23 C6
Clavering Essex 55 F5
Claverley Shrops 61 E7
Claverton Bath 24 C2
Clawdd-newydd Denb 72 D4
Clawthorpe Cumb 92 B5
Clawton Devon 9 E5
Claxby Lincs 79 B7
Claxby Lincs 90 E5
Claxton N Yorks 96 C2
Claxton Norf 69 D6
Clay Common Suff 69 F7
Clay Coton Northants 52 B3
Clay Cross Derbys 76 C3
Clay Hill W Berks 26 B3
Clay Lake Lincs 66 B2
Claybokie Aberds 139 E6
Claybrooke Magna Leics 63 F8
Claybrooke Parva Leics 63 F8
Claydon Oxon 52 D2
Claydon Suff 56 D5
Claygate Dumfries 108 B3
Claygate Kent 29 E8
Claygate Sur 28 C2
Claygate Cross Kent 29 D7
Clayhanger Devon 10 B5
Clayhanger W Mid 62 D4
Clayhidon Devon 11 C6
Clayhill E Sus 18 C5
Clayhill Hants 14 D4
Clayock Highld 158 E3
Claypole Lincs 77 E8
Clayton S Yorks 89 D5
Clayton Staffs 75 E5
Clayton W Sus 17 C6
Clayton W Yorks 94 F4
Clayton Green Lancs 86 B3
Clayton-le-Moors Lancs 93 F7
Clayton-le-Woods Lancs 86 B3
Clayton West W Yorks 88 C3
Clayworth Notts 89 F8
Cleadale Highld 146 C7
Cleadon T&W 111 C6
Clearbrook Devon 6 C3
Clearwell Glos 36 D2
Cleasby N Yorks 101 C7
Cleat Orkney 159 K5
Cleatlam Durham 101 C6
Cleator Cumb 98 C2
Cleator Moor Cumb 98 C2
Clebrig Highld 157 F8
Cleckheaton W Yorks 88 B2
Clee St Margaret Shrops 61 F5
Cleedownton Shrops 61 F5
Cleehill Shrops 49 B7
Cleethorpes NE Lincs 91 D7
Cleeton St Mary Shrops 49 B8
Cleeve N Som 23 C6
Cleeve Hill Glos 37 B6
Cleeve Prior Worcs 51 E5
Clegyrnant Powys 59 D6
Clehonger Hereford 49 F6
Cleish Perth 128 E2
Cleland N Lanark 119 D8
Clench Common Wilts 25 C6
Clenchwarton Norf 67 B5
Clent Worcs 50 B4
Cleobury Mortimer Shrops 49 B8
Cleobury North Shrops 61 F6
Cleongart Argyll 143 E7
Clephanton Highld 151 F11
Clerklands Borders 115 B8
Clestrain Orkney 159 H4
Cleuch Head Borders 115 C8
Cleughbrae Dumfries 107 B7
Clevancy Wilts 25 B5
Clevedon N Som 23 B6
Cleveley Oxon 38 B3
Cleveleys Lancs 92 E3
Cleverton Wilts 37 F6
Clevis Bridgend 21 B7
Clewer Som 23 D6
Cley next the Sea Norf 81 C6
Cliaid W Isles 148 H1
Cliasmol W Isles 154 G5
Cliburn Cumb 99 B7
Click Mill Orkney 159 F4
Cliddesden Hants 26 E4
Cliff End E Sus 19 D5
Cliffburn Angus 135 E6
Cliffe Medway 29 B8
Cliffe N Yorks 96 F2
Cliffe Woods Medway 29 B8
Clifford Hereford 48 E4
Clifford W Yorks 95 E7
Clifford Chambers Warks 51 D6
Clifford's Mesne Glos 36 B4
Cliffsend Kent 31 C7
Clifton Bristol 23 B7
Clifton C Beds 54 F2
Clifton Cumb 99 B7
Clifton Derbys 75 E8
Clifton Lancs 92 F4
Clifton N Yorks 94 E4
Clifton Northumb 117 F8
Clifton Nottingham 77 F5
Clifton Oxon 52 F2
Clifton S Yorks 89 E6
Clifton Stirling 131 F7
Clifton Worcs 50 E3
Clifton York 95 D8
Clifton Campville Staffs 63 C6
Clifton Green Gtr Man 87 D5
Clifton Hampden Oxon 39 E5
Clifton Reynes M Keynes 53 D7
Clifton upon Dunsmore Warks 52 B3
Clifton upon Teme Worcs 50 C2
Cliftoncote Borders 116 B4
Cliftonville Kent 31 B7
Climaen gwyn Neath 33 D8
Climping W Sus 16 D4
Climpy S Lanark 120 D2
Clink Som 24 E2
Clint N Yorks 95 D5
Clint Green Norf 68 C3
Clintmains Borders 122 F2
Cliobh W Isles 154 D5
Clippesby Norf 69 C7
Clipsham Rutland 65 C6
Clipston Northants 64 F4
Clipstone Notts 77 C5
Clitheroe Lancs 93 E7
Cliuthar W Isles 154 H6
Clive Shrops 60 B5
Clivocast Shetland 160 C8
Clixby Lincs 90 D5
Clocaenog Denb 72 D4
Clochan Moray 152 B4
Clock Face Mers 86 E3
Clockmill Borders 122 D3
Cloddiau Powys 60 D2
Clodock Hereford 35 B7
Clola Aberds 153 D10
Clophill C Beds 53 F8
Clopton Northants 65 F7
Clopton Suff 57 D6
Clopton Corner Suff 57 D6
Clopton Green Suff 55 D8
Close Clark IoM 84 E2
Closeburn Dumfries 113 E8
Closworth Som 12 C3
Clothall Herts 54 F3
Clotton Ches W 74 C2
Clough Foot W Yorks 87 B7
Cloughton N Yorks 103 E8
Cloughton Newlands N Yorks 103 E8
Clousta Shetland 160 H5
Clouston Orkney 159 G3
Clova Aberds 140 B3
Clova Angus 134 B3
Clove Lodge Durham 100 C4
Clovelly Devon 8 B5
Clovenfords Borders 121 F7
Clovenstone Aberds 141 C6
Clovullin Highld 130 C4
Clow Bridge Lancs 87 B6
Clowne Derbys 76 B4
Clows Top Worcs 50 B2
Cloy Wrex 73 E7
Cluanie Inn Highld 136 C3
Cluanie Lodge Highld 136 C3
Clun Shrops 60 F3
Clunbury Shrops 60 F3
Clunderwen Carms 32 C2
Clune Highld 138 B3
Clunes Highld 136 F5
Clungunford Shrops 49 B5
Clunie Aberds 153 C6
Clunie Perth 133 E8
Clunton Shrops 60 F3
Cluny Fife 128 E4
Cluny Castle Highld 138 E2
Clutton Bath 23 D8
Clutton Ches W 73 D8
Clwt-grugoer Conwy 72 C3
Clwt-y-bont Gwyn 83 E5
Clydach Mon 35 C6
Clydach Swansea 33 D7
Clydach Vale Rhondda 34 E3
Clydebank W Dunb 118 B4
Clydey Pembs 45 F4
Clyffe Pypard Wilts 25 B5
Clynder Argyll 145 E11
Clyne Neath 34 D2
Clynelish Highld 157 J11
Clynnog-fawr Gwyn 82 F4
Clyro Powys 48 E4
Clyst Honiton Devon 10 E4
Clyst Hydon Devon 10 D5
Clyst St George Devon 10 F4
Clyst St Lawrence Devon 10 D5
Clyst St Mary Devon 10 E4
Cnoc Amhlaigh W Isles 155 D10
Cnwch-coch Ceredig 47 B5
Coachford Aberds 152 D4
Coad's Green Corn 5 B7
Coal Aston Derbys 76 B3
Coalbrookdale Telford 61 D6
Coalbrookvale Bl Gwent 35 D5
Coalburn S Lanark 119 F8
Coalburns T&W 110 C4
Coalcleugh Northumb 109 E8
Coaley Glos 36 D4
Coalhall E Ayrs 112 C4
Coalhill Essex 42 E3
Coalpit Heath S Glos 36 F3
Coalport Telford 61 D6
Coalsnaughton Clack 127 E8
Coaltown of Balgonie Fife 128 E4
Coaltown of Wemyss Fife 128 E5
Coalville Leics 63 C8
Coalway Glos 36 C2
Coat Som 12 B2
Coatbridge N Lanark 119 C7
Coatdyke N Lanark 119 C7
Coate Swindon 38 F1
Coate Wilts 24 C5
Coates Cambs 66 E3
Coates Glos 37 D6
Coates Lancs 93 E8
Coates Notts 90 F2
Coates W Sus 16 C3
Coatham Redcar 102 B3
Coatham Mundeville Darl 101 B7
Coatsgate Dumfries 114 D3
Cobbaton Devon 9 B8
Cobbler's Green Norf 69 E5
Coberley Glos 37 C6
Cobham Kent 29 C7
Cobham Sur 28 C2
Cobholm Island Norf 69 D8
Cobleland Stirling 126 E4
Cobnash Hereford 49 C6
Coburty Aberds 153 B9
Cock Bank Wrex 73 E7
Cock Bridge Aberds 139 D8
Cock Clarks Essex 42 D4
Cockayne N Yorks 102 E4
Cockayne Hatley Cambs 54 E3
Cockburnspath Borders 122 B3
Cockenzie and Port Seton E Loth 121 B7
Cockerham Lancs 92 D4
Cockermouth Cumb 107 F8
Cockernhoe Green Herts 40 B4
Cockfield Durham 101 B6
Cockfield Suff 56 D3
Cockfosters London 41 E5
Cocking W Sus 16 C2
Cockington Torbay 7 C6
Cocklake Som 23 E6
Cockley Beck Cumb 98 D4
Cockley Cley Norf 67 D7
Cockshutt Shrops 60 B4
Cockthorpe Norf 81 C5
Cockwood Devon 10 F4
Cockyard Hereford 49 F6
Codda Corn 5 B6
Coddenham Suff 56 D5
Coddington Ches W 73 D8
Coddington Hereford 50 E2
Coddington Notts 77 D8
Codford St Mary Wilts 24 F4
Codford St Peter Wilts 24 F4
Codicote Herts 41 C5
Codmore Hill W Sus 16 B4
Codnor Derbys 76 E4
Codrington S Glos 24 B2
Codsall Staffs 62 D2
Codsall Wood Staffs 62 D2
Coed Duon = Blackwood Caerph 35 E5
Coed Mawr Gwyn 83 D5
Coed Morgan Mon 35 C7
Coed-Talon Flint 73 D6
Coed-y-bryn Ceredig 46 E2
Coed-y-paen Mon 35 E7
Coed-yr-ynys Powys 35 B5
Coed Ystumgwern Gwyn 71 E6
Coedely Rhondda 34 F4
Coedkernew Newport 35 F6
Coedpoeth Wrex 73 D6
Coedway Powys 60 C3
Coelbren Powys 34 C2
Coffinswell Devon 7 C6
Cofton Hackett Worcs 50 B5
Cogan V Glam 22 B3
Cogenhoe Northants 53 C6
Cogges Oxon 38 D3
Coggeshall Essex 42 B4
Coggeshall Hamlet Essex 42 B4
Coggins Mill E Sus 18 C2
Coig Peighinnean W Isles 155 A10
Coig Peighinnean Bhuirgh W Isles 155 B9
Coignafearn Lodge Highld 138 C2
Coilacriech Aberds 140 E2
Coilantogle Stirling 126 D4
Coilleag W Isles 148 G2
Coillore Highld 149 E8
Coity Bridgend 34 F3
Col W Isles 155 C9
Col Uarach W Isles 155 D9
Colaboll Highld 157 H8
Colan Corn 4 C3
Colaton Raleigh Devon 11 F5
Colbost Highld 148 D7
Colburn N Yorks 101 E6
Colby Cumb 100 B1
Colby IoM 84 E2
Colby Norf 81 D8
Colchester Essex 43 B6
Colcot V Glam 22 C3
Cold Ash W Berks 26 C3
Cold Ashby Northants 52 B4
Cold Ashton S Glos 24 B2
Cold Aston Glos 37 C8
Cold Blow Pembs 32 C2
Cold Brayfield M Keynes 53 D7
Cold Hanworth Lincs 90 F4
Cold Harbour Lincs 78 F2
Cold Hatton Telford 61 B6
Cold Hesledon Durham 111 E7
Cold Higham Northants 52 D4
Cold Kirby N Yorks 102 F3
Cold Newton Leics 64 D4
Cold Northcott Corn 8 F4
Cold Norton Essex 42 D4
Cold Overton Leics 64 C5
Coldbackie Highld 157 D9
Coldbeck Cumb 100 D2
Coldblow London 29 B6
Coldean Brighton 17 D7
Coldeast Devon 7 B6
Colden W Yorks 87 B7
Colden Common Hants 15 B5
Coldfair Green Suff 57 C8
Coldham Cambs 66 D4
Coldharbour Glos 36 D2
Coldharbour Kent 29 D6
Coldharbour Sur 28 E2
Coldingham Borders 122 C5
Coldrain Perth 128 D2
Coldred Kent 31 E6
Coldridge Devon 9 D8
Coldstream Angus 134 F3
Coldstream Borders 122 F4
Coldwaltham W Sus 16 C4
Coldwells Aberds 153 D11
Coldwells Croft Aberds 140 B4
Coldyeld Shrops 60 E3
Cole Som 23 F8
Cole Green Herts 41 C5
Cole Henley Hants 26 D2
Colebatch Shrops 60 F3
Colebrook Devon 10 D5
Colebrooke Devon 10 E2
Coleby Lincs 78 C2
Coleby N Lincs 90 C2
Coleford Devon 10 D2
Coleford Glos 36 C2
Coleford Som 23 E8
Colehill Dorset 13 D8
Coleman's Hatch E Sus 29 F5
Colemere Shrops 73 F8
Colemore Hants 26 F5
Coleorton Leics 63 C8
Colerne Wilts 24 B3
Cole's Green Suff 57 C6
Coles Green Suff 56 E4
Colesbourne Glos 37 C6
Colesden Bedford 54 D2
Coleshill Bucks 40 E2
Coleshill Oxon 38 E2
Coleshill Warks 63 F6
Colestocks Devon 11 D5
Colgate W Sus 28 F3
Colgrain Argyll 126 F2
Colinsburgh Fife 129 D6
Colinton Edin 120 C5
Colintraive Argyll 145 F9
Colkirk Norf 80 E5
Collace Perth 134 F2
Collafirth Shetland 160 G6
Collaton St Mary Torbay 7 D6
College Milton S Lanark 119 D6
Collessie Fife 128 C4
Collier Row London 41 E8
Collier Street Kent 29 E8
Collier's End Herts 41 B6
Collier's Green Kent 18 B4
Colliery Row T&W 111 E6
Collieston Aberds 141 B9
Collin Dumfries 107 B7
Collingbourne Ducis Wilts 25 D7
Collingbourne Kingston Wilts 25 D7
Collingham Notts 77 C8
Collingham W Yorks 95 E6
Collington Hereford 49 C8
Collingtree Northants 53 D5
Collins Green Warr 86 E3
Colliston Angus 135 E6
Collycroft Warks 63 F7
Collynie Aberds 153 E8
Collyweston Northants 65 D6
Colmonell S Ayrs 104 A5
Colmworth Bedford 54 D2
Coln Rogers Glos 37 D7
Coln St Aldwyn's Glos 37 D8
Coln St Dennis Glos 37 C7
Colnabaichin Aberds 139 D8
Colnbrook Slough 27 B8
Colne Cambs 54 B4
Colne Lancs 93 E8
Colne Edge Lancs 93 E8
Colne Engaine Essex 56 F2
Colney Norf 68 D4
Colney Heath Herts 41 D5
Colney Street Herts 40 D4
Colpy Aberds 153 E6
Colquhar Borders 121 E6
Colsterdale N Yorks 101 F6
Colsterworth Lincs 65 B6
Colston Bassett Notts 77 F6
Coltfield Moray 152 B1
Colthouse Cumb 99 E5
Coltishall Norf 69 C5
Coltness N Lanark 119 D8
Colton Cumb 99 F5
Colton N Yorks 95 E8
Colton Norf 68 D4
Colton Staffs 62 B4
Colton W Yorks 95 F6
Colva Powys 48 D4
Colvend Dumfries 107 D5
Colvister Shetland 160 D7
Colwall Green Hereford 50 E2
Colwall Stone Hereford 50 E2
Colwell Northumb 110 B2
Colwich Staffs 62 B4
Colwick Notts 77 E6
Colwinston V Glam 21 B8
Colworth W Sus 16 D3
Colwyn Bay = Bae Colwyn Conwy 83 D8
Colyford Devon 11 E7
Colyton Devon 11 E7
Combe Hereford 48 C5
Combe Oxon 38 C4
Combe W Berks 25 C8
Combe Common Sur 27 F7
Combe Down Bath 24 C2
Combe Florey Som 22 F3
Combe Hay Bath 24 D2
Combe Martin Devon 20 E4
Combe Moor Hereford 49 C5
Combe Raleigh Devon 11 D6
Combe St Nicholas Som 11 C8
Combeinteignhead Devon 7 B7
Comberbach Ches W 74 B3
Comberton Cambs 54 D4
Comberton Hereford 49 C6
Combpyne Devon 11 E7
Combridge Staffs 75 F7
Combrook Warks 51 D8
Combs Derbys 75 B7
Combs Suff 56 D4
Combs Ford Suff 56 D4
Combwich Som 22 E4
Comers Aberds 141 D5
Comins Coch Ceredig 58 F3
Commercial End Cambs 55 C6
Commins Capel Betws Ceredig 46 D5
Commins Coch Powys 58 D5
Common Edge Blackpool 92 F3
Common Side Derbys 76 B3
Commondale N Yorks 102 C4
Commonmoor Corn 5 C7
Commonside Ches W 74 B2
Compstall Gtr Man 87 E7
Compton Devon 7 C6
Compton Hants 15 B5
Compton Sur 27 E6
Compton Sur 27 E7
Compton W Berks 26 B3
Compton W Sus 15 C8
Compton Wilts 25 D6
Compton Abbas Dorset 13 C6
Compton Abdale Glos 37 C7
Compton Bassett Wilts 24 B5
Compton Beauchamp Oxon 38 F2
Compton Bishop Som 23 D5
Compton Chamberlayne Wilts 13 B8
Compton Dando Bath 23 C8
Compton Dundon Som 23 F6
Compton Martin Bath 23 D7
Compton Pauncefoot Som 12 B4
Compton Valence Dorset 12 E3
Comrie Fife 128 F2
Comrie Perth 127 B6
Conaglen House Highld 130 C4
Conchra Argyll 145 E9
Concraigie Perth 133 E8
Conder Green Lancs 92 D4
Conderton Worcs 50 F4
Condicote Glos 38 B1
Condorrat N Lanark 119 B7
Condover Shrops 60 D4
Coney Weston Suff 56 B3
Coneyhurst W Sus 16 B5
Coneysthorpe N Yorks 96 B3
Coneythorpe N Yorks 95 D6
Conford Hants 27 F6
Congash Highld 139 B6
Congdon's Shop Corn 5 B7
Congerstone Leics 63 D7
Congham Norf 80 E3
Congl-y-wal Gwyn 71 C8
Congleton Ches E 75 C5
Congresbury N Som 23 C6
Congreve Staffs 62 C3
Conicavel Moray 151 F12
Coningsby Lincs 78 D5
Conington Cambs 54 C4
Conington Cambs 65 F8
Conisbrough S Yorks 89 E6
Conisby Argyll 142 B3
Conisholme Lincs 91 E8
Coniston Cumb 99 E5
Coniston E Yorks 97 F7
Coniston Cold N Yorks 94 D2
Conistone N Yorks 94 C2
Connah's Quay Flint 73 C6
Connel Argyll 124 B5
Connel Park E Ayrs 113 C6
Connor Downs Corn 2 C4
Conon Bridge Highld 151 F8
Conon House Highld 151 F8
Cononley N Yorks 94 E2
Conordan Highld 149 E10
Consall Staffs 75 E6
Consett Durham 110 D4
Constable Burton N Yorks 101 E6
Constantine Corn 3 D6
Constantine Bay Corn 4 B3
Contin Highld 150 F7
Contlaw Aberdeen 141 D7
Conwy Conwy 83 D7
Conyer Kent 30 C3
Conyers Green Suff 56 C2
Cooden E Sus 18 E4
Cooil IoM 84 E3
Cookbury Devon 9 D6
Cookham Windsor 40 F1
Cookham Dean Windsor 40 F1
Cookham Rise Windsor 40 F1
Cookhill Worcs 51 D5
Cookley Suff 57 B7
Cookley Worcs 62 F2
Cookley Green Oxon 39 E6
Cookney Aberds 141 E7
Cookridge W Yorks 95 E5
Cooksbridge E Sus 17 C8
Cooksmill Green Essex 42 D2
Coolham W Sus 16 B5
Cooling Medway 29 B8
Coombe Corn 4 D4
Coombe Corn 8 C4
Coombe Hants 15 B7
Coombe Wilts 25 D6
Coombe Bissett Wilts 14 B2
Coombe Hill Glos 37 B5
Coombe Keynes Dorset 13 F6
Coombes W Sus 17 D5
Coopersale Common Essex 41 D7
Cootham W Sus 16 C4
Copdock Suff 56 E5
Copford Green Essex 43 B5
Copgrove N Yorks 95 C6
Copister Shetland 160 F6
Cople Bedford 54 E2
Copley Durham 101 B5
Coplow Dale Derbys 75 B8
Copmanthorpe York 95 E8
Coppathorne Corn 8 D4
Coppenhall Staffs 62 C3
Coppenhall Moss Ches E 74 D4
Copperhouse Corn 2 C4
Coppingford Cambs 65 F8
Copplestone Devon 10 D2
Coppull Lancs 86 C3
Coppull Moor Lancs 86 C3
Copsale W Sus 17 B5
Copster Green Lancs 93 F6
Copston Magna Warks 63 F8
Copt Heath W Mid 51 B6
Copt Hewick N Yorks 95 B6
Copt Oak Leics 63 C8
Copthorne Shrops 60 C4
Copthorne Sur 28 F4
Copy's Green Norf 80 D5
Copythorne Hants 14 C4
Corbets Tey London 42 F1
Corbridge Northumb 110 C2
Corby Northants 65 F5
Corby Glen Lincs 65 B6
Cordon N Ayrs 143 E11
Coreley Shrops 49 B8
Cores End Bucks 40 F2
Corfe Som 11 C7
Corfe Castle Dorset 13 F7
Corfe Mullen Dorset 13 E7
Corfton Shrops 60 F4
Corgarff Aberds 139 D8
Corhampton Hants 15 B7
Corlae Dumfries 113 E6
Corley Warks 63 F7
Corley Ash Warks 63 F6
Corley Moor Warks 63 F6
Cornaa IoM 84 D4
Cornabus Argyll 142 D4
Cornel Conwy 83 E7
Corner Row Lancs 92 F4
Corney Cumb 98 E3
Cornforth Durham 111 F6
Cornhill Aberds 152 C5
Cornhill-on-Tweed Northumb 122 F4
Cornholme W Yorks 87 B7
Cornish Hall End Essex 55 F7
Cornquoy Orkney 159 J6
Cornsay Durham 110 E4
Cornsay Colliery Durham 110 E4
Corntown Highld 151 F8
Corntown V Glam 21 B8
Cornwell Oxon 38 B2
Cornwood Devon 6 D4
Cornworthy Devon 7 D6
Corpach Highld 130 B4
Corpusty Norf 81 D7
Corran Highld 130 C4
Corran Highld 149 H13
Corranbuie Argyll 145 G7
Corrany IoM 84 D4
Corrie N Ayrs 143 D11
Corrie Common Dumfries 114 F5
Corriecravie N Ayrs 143 F10
Corriemoillie Highld 150 E6
Corriemulzie Lodge Highld 150 B6
Corrievarkie Lodge Perth 132 B2
Corrievorrie Highld 138 B3
Corrimony Highld 150 H6
Corringham Lincs 90 E2
Corringham Thurrock 42 F3
Corris Gwyn 58 D4
Corris Uchaf Gwyn 58 D4
Corrour Shooting Lodge Highld 131 C8
Corrow Argyll 125 E7
Corry Highld 149 F11
Corry of Ardnagrask Highld 151 G8
Corrykinloch Highld 156 G6
Corrymuckloch Perth 133 F5
Corrynachenchy Argyll 147 G9
Cors-y-Gedol Gwyn 71 E6
Corsback Highld 158 C4
Corscombe Dorset 12 D3
Corse Aberds 152 D6
Corse Glos 36 B4
Corse Lawn Worcs 50 F3
Corse of Kinnoir Aberds 152 D5
Corsewall Dumfries 104 C4
Corsham Wilts 24 B3
Corsindae Aberds 141 D5
Corsley Wilts 24 E3
Corsley Heath Wilts 24 E3
Corsock Dumfries 106 B4
Corston Bath 23 C8
Corston Wilts 37 F6
Corstorphine Edin 120 B4
Cortachy Angus 134 D3
Corton Suff 69 E8
Corton Wilts 24 E4
Corton Denham Som 12 B4
Coruanan Lodge Highld 130 C4
Corunna W Isles 148 B3
Corwen Denb 72 E4
Coryton Devon 9 F6
Coryton Thurrock 42 F3
Cosby Leics 64 E2
Coseley W Mid 62 E3
Cosgrove Northants 53 E5
Cosham Ptsmth 15 D7
Cosheston Pembs 32 D1
Cossall Notts 76 E4
Cossington Leics 64 C3
Cossington Som 23 E5
Costa Orkney 159 F4
Costessey Norf 68 C4
Costock Notts 64 B2
Coston Leics 64 B5
Cote Oxon 38 D3
Cotebrook Ches W 74 C2
Cotehill Cumb 108 D4
Cotes Cumb 99 F6
Cotes Leics 64 B2
Cotes Staffs 74 F5
Cotesbach Leics 64 F2
Cotgrave Notts 77 F6
Cothall Aberds 141 C7
Cotham Notts 77 E7
Cothelstone Som 22 F3
Cotherstone Durham 101 C5
Cothill Oxon 38 E4
Cotleigh Devon 11 D7
Cotmanhay Derbys 76 E4
Cotmaton Devon 11 F6
Coton Cambs 54 D5
Coton Northants 52 B4
Coton Staffs 62 B2
Coton Staffs 75 F6
Coton Clanford Staffs 62 B2
Coton Hill Shrops 60 C4
Coton Hill Staffs 75 F6
Coton in the Elms Derbys 63 C6
Cott Devon 7 C5
Cottam E Yorks 97 C5
Cottam Lancs 92 F5
Cottam Notts 77 B8
Cottartown Highld 151 H13
Cottenham Cambs 54 C5
Cotterdale N Yorks 100 E3
Cottered Herts 41 B6
Cotteridge W Mid 50 B5
Cotterstock Northants 65 E7
Cottesbrooke Northants 52 B5
Cottesmore Rutland 65 C6
Cotteylands Devon 10 C4
Cottingham E Yorks 97 F6
Cottingham Northants 64 E5
Cottingley W Yorks 94 F4
Cottisford Oxon 52 F3
Cotton Staffs 75 E7
Cotton Suff 56 C4
Cotton End Bedford 53 E8
Cottown Aberds 140 B4
Cottown Aberds 141 C6
Cottown Aberds 153 D8
Cotwalton Staffs 75 F6
Couch's Mill Corn 5 D6
Coughton Hereford 36 B2
Coughton Warks 51 C5
Coulaghailtro Argyll 144 G6
Coulags Highld 150 G2
Coulby Newham Mbro 102 C3
Coulderton Cumb 98 D1
Coulin Highld 150 F3
Coull Aberds 140 D4
Coull Argyll 142 B3
Coulport Argyll 145 E11
Coulsdon London 28 D3
Coulston Wilts 24 D4
Coulter S Lanark 120 F3
Coulton N Yorks 96 B2
Cound Shrops 61 D5
Coundon Durham 101 B7
Coundon W Mid 63 F7
Coundon Grange Durham 101 B7
Countersett N Yorks 100 F4
Countess Wilts 25 E6
Countess Wear Devon 10 F4
Countesthorpe Leics 64 E2
Countisbury Devon 21 E6
County Oak W Sus 28 F3
Coup Green Lancs 86 B3
Coupar Angus Perth 134 E2
Coupland Northumb 122 F5
Cour Argyll 143 D9
Courance Dumfries 114 E3
Court-at-Street Kent 19 B7
Court Henry Carms 33 B6
Courteenhall Northants 53 D5
Courtsend Essex 43 E6
Courtway Som 22 F4
Cousland Midloth 121 C6
Cousley Wood E Sus 18 B3
Cove Argyll 145 E11
Cove Borders 122 B3
Cove Devon 10 C4
Cove Hants 27 D6
Cove Highld 155 H13
Cove Bay Aberdeen 141 D8
Cove Bottom Suff 57 B8
Covehithe Suff 69 F8
Coven Staffs 62 D3
Coveney Cambs 66 F4
Covenham St Bartholomew Lincs 91 E7
Covenham St Mary Lincs 91 E7
Coventry W Mid 51 B8
Coverack Corn 3 E6
Coverham N Yorks 101 F5
Covesea Moray 152 A1
Covington Cambs 53 B8
Covington S Lanark 120 F2
Cow Ark Lancs 93 E6
Cowan Bridge Lancs 93 B6
Cowbeech E Sus 18 D3
Cowbit Lincs 66 C2
Cowbridge Lincs 79 E6
Cowbridge Som 21 E8
Cowbridge = Y Bont-Faen V Glam 21 B8
Cowdale Derbys 75 B7
Cowden Kent 29 E5
Cowdenbeath Fife 128 E3
Cowdenburn Borders 120 D5
Cowers Lane Derbys 76 E3
Cowes IoW 15 E5
Cowesby N Yorks 102 F2
Cowfold W Sus 17 B6
Cowgill Cumb 100 F2
Cowie Aberds 141 F7
Cowie Stirling 127 F7
Cowley Devon 10 E4
Cowley Glos 37 C6
Cowley London 40 F3
Cowley Oxon 39 D5
Cowleymoor Devon 10 C4
Cowling Lancs 86 C3
Cowling N Yorks 94 E2
Cowling N Yorks 101 F7
Cowlinge Suff 55 D8
Cowpe Lancs 87 B6
Cowpen Northumb 117 F8
Cowpen Bewley Stockton 102 B2
Cowplain Hants 15 C7
Cowshill Durham 109 E8
Cowslip Green N Som 23 C6
Cowstrandburn Fife 128 E2
Cowthorpe N Yorks 95 D7
Cox Common Suff 69 F6
Cox Green Windsor 27 B6
Cox Moor Notts 76 D5
Coxbank Ches E 74 E3
Coxbench Derbys 76 E3
Coxford Norf 80 E4
Coxford Soton 14 C4
Coxheath Kent 29 D8
Coxhill Kent 31 E6
Coxhoe Durham 111 F6
Coxley Som 23 E7
Coxwold N Yorks 95 B8
Coychurch Bridgend 21 B8
Coylton S Ayrs 112 B4
Coylumbridge Highld 138 C5
Coynach Aberds 140 D3
Coynachie Aberds 152 E4
Coytrahen Bridgend 34 F2
Crabadon Devon 7 D5
Crabbs Cross Worcs 50 C5
Crabtree W Sus 17 B6
Crackenthorpe Cumb 100 B1
Crackington Haven Corn 8 E3
Crackley Warks 51 B7
Crackleybank Shrops 61 C7
Crackpot N Yorks 100 E4
Cracoe N Yorks 94 C2
Craddock Devon 11 C5
Cradhlastadh W Isles 154 D5
Cradley Hereford 50 E2
Cradley Heath W Mid 62 F3
Crafthole Corn 5 D8
Cragg Vale W Yorks 87 B8
Craggan Highld 139 B6
Craggie Highld 151 H10
Craggie Highld 157 H11
Craghead Durham 110 D5
Crai Powys 34 B2
Craibstone Moray 152 C4
Craichie Angus 135 E5
Craig Dumfries 106 B3
Craig Dumfries 106 C3
Craig Highld 150 G3
Craig Castle Aberds 140 B3
Craig-cefn-parc Swansea 33 D7
Craig Penllyn V Glam 21 B8
Craig-y-don Conwy 83 C7
Craig-y-nos Powys 34 C2
Craiganor Lodge Perth 132 D3
Craigdam Aberds 153 E8
Craigdarroch Dumfries 113 E7
Craigdarroch Highld 150 F7
Craigdhu Highld 150 G7
Craigearn Aberds 141 C6
Craigellachie Moray 152 D2
Craigencross Dumfries 104 C4
Craigend Perth 128 B3
Craigend Stirling 127 F6
Craigendive Argyll 145 E9
Craigendoran Argyll 126 F2
Craigends Renfs 118 C4
Craigens Argyll 142 B3
Craigens E Ayrs 113 C5
Craighat Stirling 126 F3
Craighead Fife 129 D8
Craighlaw Mains Dumfries 105 C7
Craighouse Argyll 144 G4
Craigie Aberds 141 C8
Craigie Dundee 134 F4
Craigie Perth 128 B3
Craigie Perth 133 E8
Craigie S Ayrs 118 F4
Craigiefield Orkney 159 G5
Craigielaw E Loth 121 B7
Craiglockhart Edin 120 B5
Craigmalloch E Ayrs 112 E4
Craigmaud Aberds 153 C8
Craigmillar Edin 121 B5
Craigmore Argyll 145 G10
Craignant Shrops 73 F6
Craigneuk N Lanark 119 C7
Craigneuk N Lanark 119 D7
Craignure Argyll 124 B3
Craigo Angus 135 C6
Craigow Perth 128 D2
Craigrothie Fife 129 C5
Craigroy Moray 151 F14
Craigruie Stirling 126 B3
Craigston Castle Aberds 153 C7
Craigton Aberdeen 141 D7
Craigton Angus 134 D3
Craigton Angus 135 F5
Craigton Highld 151 B9
Craigtown Highld 157 D11
Craik Borders 115 D6
Crail Fife 129 D8
Crailing Borders 116 B2
Crailinghall Borders 116 B2
Craiselound N Lincs 89 E8
Crakehill N Yorks 95 B7
Crakemarsh Staffs 75 F7
Crambe N Yorks 96 C3
Cramlington Northumb 111 B5
Cramond Edin 120 B4
Cramond Bridge Edin 120 B4
Cranage Ches E 74 C4
Cranberry Staffs 74 F5
Cranborne Dorset 13 C8
Cranbourne Brack 27 B7
Cranbrook, Devon 10 E5
Cranbrook Kent 18 B4
Cranbrook Common Kent 18 B4
Crane Moor S Yorks 88 D4
Crane's Corner Norf 68 C2
Cranfield C Beds 53 E7
Cranford London 28 B2
Cranford St Andrew Northants 53 B7
Cranford St John Northants 53 B7
Cranham Glos 37 C5
Cranham London 42 F1
Crank Mers 86 E3
Crank Wood Gtr Man 86 D4
Cranleigh Sur 27 F8
Cranley Suff 57 B5
Cranmer Green Suff 56 B4
Cranmore IoW 14 F4
Cranna Aberds 153 C6
Crannich Argyll 147 G8
Crannoch Moray 152 C4
Cranoe Leics 64 E4
Cransford Suff 57 C7
Cranshaws Borders 122 C2
Cranstal IoM 84 B4
Crantock Corn 4 C2
Cranwell Lincs 78 E3
Cranwich Norf 67 E7
Cranworth Norf 68 D2
Craobh Haven Argyll 124 E3
Crapstone Devon 6 C3
Crarae Argyll 125 F5
Crask Inn Highld 157 G8
Crask of Aigas Highld 150 G7
Craskins Aberds 140 D4
Craster Northumb 117 C8
Craswall Hereford 48 F4
Cratfield Suff 57 B7
Crathes Aberds 141 E6
Crathie Aberds 139 E8
Crathie Highld 137 E8
Crathorne N Yorks 102 D2
Craven Arms Shrops 60 F4
Crawcrook T&W 110 C4
Crawford Lancs 86 D2
Crawford S Lanark 114 B2
Crawfordjohn S Lanark 113 B8
Crawick Dumfries 113 C7
Crawley Hants 26 F2
Crawley Oxon 38 C3
Crawley W Sus 28 F3
Crawley Down W Sus 28 F4
Crawleyside Durham 110 E2
Crawshawbooth Lancs 87 B6
Crawton Aberds 135 B8
Cray N Yorks 94 B2
Cray Perth 133 C8
Crayford London 29 B6
Crayke N Yorks 95 B8
Crays Hill Essex 42 E3
Cray's Pond Oxon 39 F6
Creacombe Devon 10 C3
Creag Ghoraidh W Isles 148 D2
Creagan Argyll 130 E3
Creaguaineach Lodge Highld 131 C7
Creaksea Essex 43 E5
Creaton Northants 52 B5
Creca Dumfries 108 B2
Credenhill Hereford 49 E6
Crediton Devon 10 D3
Creebridge Dumfries 105 C8
Creech Heathfield Som 11 B7
Creech St Michael Som 11 B7
Creed Corn 3 B8
Creekmouth London 41 F7
Creeting Bottoms Suff 56 D5
Creeting St Mary Suff 56 D4
Creeton Lincs 65 B7
Creetown Dumfries 105 D8
Creg-ny-Baa IoM 84 D3
Creggans Argyll 125 E6
Cregneash IoM 84 F1
Cregrina Powys 48 D3
Creich Fife 128 B5
Creigiau Cardiff 34 F4
Cremyll Corn 6 D2
Creslow Bucks 39 B8
Cressage Shrops 61 D5
Cressbrook Derbys 75 B8
Cresselly Pembs 32 D1
Cressing Essex 42 B3
Cresswell Northumb 117 E8
Cresswell Staffs 75 F6
Cresswell Quay Pembs 32 D1
Creswell Derbys 76 B5
Cretingham Suff 57 C6
Cretshengan Argyll 144 G6
Crewe Ches E 74 D4
Crewe Ches W 73 D8
Crewgreen Powys 60 C3
Crewkerne Som 12 D2
Crianlarich Stirling 126 B2
Cribyn Ceredig 46 D4
Criccieth Gwyn 71 D5
Crich Derbys 76 D3
Crichie Aberds 153 D9
Crichton Midloth 121 C6
Crick Mon 36 E1
Crick Northants 52 B3
Crickadarn Powys 48 E2
Cricket Malherbie Som 11 C8
Cricket St Thomas Som 11 D8
Crickheath Shrops 60 B2
Crickhowell Powys 35 C6
Cricklade Wilts 37 E8
Cricklewood London 41 F5
Cridling Stubbs N Yorks 89 B6
Crieff Perth 127 B7
Criggion Powys 60 C2
Crigglestone W Yorks 88 C4
Crimond Aberds 153 C10
Crimonmogate Aberds 153 C10
Crimplesham Norf 67 D6
Crinan Argyll 144 D6
Cringleford Norf 68 D4
Cringles W Yorks 94 E3
Crinow Pembs 32 C2
Cripplesease Corn 2 C4
Cripplestyle Dorset 13 C8
Cripp's Corner E Sus 18 C4
Croasdale Cumb 98 C2
Crock Street Som 11 C8
Crockenhill Kent 29 C6
Crockernwell Devon 10 E2
Crockerton Wilts 24 E3
Crocketford or Ninemile Bar Dumfries 106 B5
Crockey Hill York 96 E2
Crockham Hill Kent 28 D5
Crockleford Heath Essex 43 B6
Crockness Orkney 159 J4
Croes-goch Pembs 44 B3
Croes-lan Ceredig 46 E2
Croes-y-mwyalch Torf 35 E7
Croeserw Neath 34 E2
Croesor Gwyn 71 C7
Croesyceiliog Carms 33 C5
Croesyceiliog Torf 35 E7
Croesywaun Gwyn 82 F5
Croft Leics 64 E2
Croft Lincs 79 C8
Croft Pembs 45 E3
Croft Warr 86 E4
Croft-on-Tees N Yorks 101 D7
Croftamie Stirling 126 F3
Croftmalloch W Loth 120 C2
Crofton W Yorks 88 C4

Crofton Wilts 25 C7
Crofts of Benachielt Highld 158 G3
Crofts of Haddo Aberds 153 E8
Crofts of Inverthernie Aberds 153 D7
Crofts of Meikle Ardo Aberds 153 D8
Crofty Swansea 33 E6
Croggan Argyll 124 C3
Croglin Cumb 109 E5
Croich Highld 150 B7
Crois Dughaill W Isles 148 F2
Cromarty Highld 151 E10
Cromblet Aberds 153 E7
Cromdale Highld 139 B6
Cromer Herts 41 B5
Cromer Norf 81 C8
Cromford Derbys 76 D2
Cromhall S Glos 36 E3
Cromhall Common S Glos 36 F3
Cromor W Isles 155 E9
Cromra Highld 137 E8
Cromwell Notts 77 C7
Cronberry E Ayrs 113 B6
Crondall Hants 27 E5
Cronk-y-Voddy IoM 84 D3
Cronton Mers 86 F2
Crook Cumb 99 E6
Crook Durham 110 F4
Crook of Devon Perth 128 D2
Crookedholm E Ayrs 118 F4
Crookes S Yorks 88 F4
Crookham Northumb 122 F5
Crookham W Berks 26 C3
Crookham Village Hants 27 D5
Crookhaugh Borders 114 B4
Crookhouse Borders 116 B3
Crooklands Cumb 99 F7
Cropredy Oxon 52 E2
Cropston Leics 64 C2
Cropthorne Worcs 50 E4
Cropton N Yorks 103 F5
Cropwell Bishop Notts 77 F6
Cropwell Butler Notts 77 F6
Cros W Isles 155 A10
Crosbost W Isles 155 E8
Crosby Cumb 107 F7
Crosby IoM 84 E3
Crosby N Lincs 90 C2
Crosby Garrett Cumb 100 D2
Crosby Ravensworth Cumb 99 C8
Crosby Villa Cumb 107 F7
Croscombe Som 23 E7
Cross Som 23 D6
Cross Ash Mon 35 C8
Cross-at-Hand Kent 29 E8
Cross Green Devon 9 F5
Cross Green Suff 56 D2
Cross Green Suff 56 D3
Cross Green Warks 51 D8
Cross-hands Carms 32 B2
Cross Hands Carms 33 C6
Cross Hands Pembs 32 C1
Cross Hill Derbys 76 E4
Cross Houses Shrops 60 D5
Cross in Hand E Sus 18 C2
Cross in Hand Leics 64 F2
Cross Inn Ceredig 46 C4
Cross Inn Ceredig 46 D2
Cross Inn Rhondda 34 F4
Cross Keys Kent 29 D6
Cross Lane Head Shrops 61 E7
Cross Lanes Corn 3 D5
Cross Lanes N Yorks 95 C8
Cross Lanes Wrex 73 E7
Cross Oak Powys 35 B5
Cross of Jackston Aberds 153 E7
Cross o'th'hands Derbys 76 E2
Cross Street Suff 57 B5
Crossaig Argyll 143 C9
Crossal Highld 149 E9
Crossapol Argyll 146 G2
Crossburn Falk 119 B8
Crossbush W Sus 16 D4
Crosscanonby Cumb 107 F7
Crossdale Street Norf 81 D8
Crossens Mers 85 C4
Crossflatts W Yorks 94 E4
Crossford Fife 128 F2
Crossford S Lanark 119 E8
Crossgate Lincs 66 B2
Crossgatehall E Loth 121 C6
Crossgates Fife 128 F3
Crossgates Powys 48 C2
Crossgill Lancs 93 C5
Crosshill E Ayrs 112 B4
Crosshill Fife 128 E3
Crosshill S Ayrs 112 D3
Crosshouse E Ayrs 118 F3
Crossings Cumb 108 B5
Crosskeys Caerph 35 E6
Crosskirk Highld 157 B13
Crosslanes Shrops 60 C3
Crosslee Borders 115 C6
Crosslee Renfs 118 C4
Crossmichael Dumfries 106 C4
Crossmoor Lancs 92 F4
Crossroads Aberds 141 E6
Crossroads E Ayrs 118 F4
Crossway Hereford 49 F8
Crossway Mon 35 C8
Crossway Powys 48 D2
Crossway Green Worcs 50 C3
Crossways Dorset 13 F5
Crosswell Pembs 45 F3
Crosswood Ceredig 47 B5
Crosthwaite Cumb 99 E6
Croston Lancs 86 C2
Crostwick Norf 69 C5
Crostwight Norf 69 B6
Crothair W Isles 154 D6
Crouch Kent 29 D7
Crouch Hill Dorset 12 C5
Crouch House Green Kent 28 E5
Croucheston Wilts 13 B8
Croughton Northants 52 F3
Crovie Aberds 153 B8
Crow Edge S Yorks 88 D2
Crow Hill Hereford 36 B3
Crowan Corn 2 C5
Crowborough E Sus 18 B2
Crowcombe Som 22 F3
Crowdecote Derbys 75 C8
Crowden Derbys 87 E8
Crowell Oxon 39 E7
Crowfield Northants 52 E4
Crowfield Suff 56 D5
Crowhurst E Sus 18 D4
Crowhurst Sur 28 E4
Crowhurst Lane End Sur 28 E4
Crowland Lincs 66 C2
Crowlas Corn 2 C4
Crowle N Lincs 89 C8
Crowle Worcs 50 D4
Crowmarsh Gifford Oxon 39 F6
Crown Corner Suff 57 B6
Crownhill Plym 6 D2
Crownland Suff 56 C4
Crownthorpe Norf 68 D3
Crowntown Corn 2 C5
Crows-an-wra Corn 2 D2
Crowshill Norf 68 D2
Crowsnest Shrops 60 D3
Crowthorne Brack 27 C6
Crowton Ches W 74 B2
Croxall Staffs 63 C5
Croxby Lincs 91 E5
Croxdale Durham 111 F5
Croxden Staffs 75 F7
Croxley Green Herts 40 E3
Croxton Cambs 54 C3
Croxton N Lincs 90 C4
Croxton Norf 67 F8
Croxton Staffs 74 F4
Croxton Kerrial Leics 64 B5
Croxtonbank Staffs 74 F4
Croy Highld 151 G10
Croy N Lanark 119 B7
Croyde Devon 20 F3
Croydon Cambs 54 E4
Croydon London 28 C4
Crubenmore Lodge Highld 138 E2
Cruckmeole Shrops 60 D4
Cruckton Shrops 60 C4
Cruden Bay Aberds 153 E10
Crudgington Telford 61 C6
Crudwell Wilts 37 E6
Crug Powys 48 B3
Crugmeer Corn 4 B4
Crugybar Carms 47 F5
Crulabhig W Isles 154 D6
Crumlin = Crymlyn Caerph 35 E6
Crumpsall Gtr Man 87 D6
Crundale Kent 30 E4
Crundale Pembs 44 D4
Cruwys Morchard Devon 10 C3
Crux Easton Hants 26 D2
Crwbin Carms 33 C5
Crya Orkney 159 H4
Cryers Hill Bucks 40 E1
Crymlyn = Crumlin Caerph 35 E6
Crymlyn Gwyn 83 D6
Crymych Pembs 45 F3
Crynant Neath 34 D1
Crynfryn Ceredig 46 C4
Cuaig Highld 149 C12
Cuan Argyll 124 D3
Cubbington Warks 51 C8
Cubeck N Yorks 100 F4
Cubert Corn 4 D2
Cubley S Yorks 88 D3
Cubley Common Derbys 75 F8
Cublington Bucks 39 B8
Cublington Hereford 49 F6
Cuckfield W Sus 17 B7
Cucklington Som 13 B5
Cuckney Notts 77 B5
Cuckoo Hill Notts 89 E8
Cuddesdon Oxon 39 D6
Cuddington Bucks 39 C7
Cuddington Ches W 74 B3
Cuddington Heath Ches W 73 E8
Cuddy Hill Lancs 92 F4
Cudham London 28 D5
Cudliptown Devon 6 B3
Cudworth S Yorks 88 D4
Cudworth Som 11 C8
Cuffley Herts 41 D6
Cuiashader W Isles 155 B10
Cuidhir W Isles 148 H1
Cuidhtinis W Isles 154 J5
Culbo Highld 151 E9
Culbokie Highld 151 F9
Culburnie Highld 150 G7
Culcabock Highld 151 G9
Culcairn Highld 151 E9
Culcharry Highld 151 F11
Culcheth Warr 86 E4
Culdrain Aberds 152 E5
Culduie Highld 149 D12
Culford Suff 56 B2
Culgaith Cumb 99 B8
Culham Oxon 39 E5
Culkein Highld 156 F3
Culkein Drumbeg Highld 156 F4
Culkerton Glos 37 E6
Cullachie Highld 139 B5
Cullen Moray 152 B5
Cullercoats T&W 111 B6
Cullicudden Highld 151 E9
Cullingworth W Yorks 94 F3
Cullipool Argyll 124 D3
Cullivoe Shetland 160 C7
Culloch Perth 127 C6
Culloden Highld 151 G10
Cullompton Devon 10 D5
Culmaily Highld 151 B11
Culmazie Dumfries 105 D7
Culmington Shrops 60 F4
Culmstock Devon 11 C6
Culnacraig Highld 156 J3
Culnaknock Highld 149 B10
Culpho Suff 57 E6
Culrain Highld 151 B8
Culross Fife 127 F8
Culroy S Ayrs 112 C3
Culsh Aberds 140 E2
Culsh Aberds 153 D8
Culshabbin Dumfries 105 D7
Culswick Shetland 160 J4
Cultercullen Aberds 141 B8
Cults Aberdeen 141 D7
Cults Aberds 152 E5
Cults Dumfries 105 E8
Culverstone Green Kent 29 C7
Culverthorpe Lincs 78 E3
Culworth Northants 52 E3
Culzie Lodge Highld 151 D8
Cumbernauld N Lanark 119 B7
Cumbernauld Village N Lanark 119 B7
Cumberworth Lincs 79 B8
Cuminestown Aberds 153 C8
Cumlewick Shetland 160 L6
Cummersdale Cumb 108 D3
Cummertrees Dumfries 107 C8
Cummingston Moray 152 B1
Cumnock E Ayrs 113 B5
Cumnor Oxon 38 D4
Cumrew Cumb 108 D5
Cumwhinton Cumb 108 D4
Cumwhitton Cumb 108 D5
Cundall N Yorks 95 B7
Cunninghamhead N Ayrs 118 E3
Cunnister Shetland 160 D7
Cupar Fife 129 C5
Cupar Muir Fife 129 C5
Cupernham Hants 14 B4
Curbar Derbys 76 B2
Curbridge Hants 15 C6
Curbridge Oxon 38 D3
Curdridge Hants 15 C6
Curdworth Warks 63 E5
Curland Som 11 C7
Curlew Green Suff 57 C7
Currarie S Ayrs 112 E1
Curridge W Berks 26 B2
Currie Edin 120 C4
Curry Mallet Som 11 B8
Curry Rivel Som 11 B8
Curtisden Green Kent 29 E8
Curtisknowle Devon 6 D5
Cury Corn 3 D5
Cushnie Aberds 153 B7
Cushuish Som 22 F3
Cusop Hereford 48 E4
Cutcloy Dumfries 105 F8
Cutcombe Som 21 F8
Cutgate Gtr Man 87 C6
Cutiau Gwyn 58 C3
Cutlers Green Essex 55 F6
Cutnall Green Worcs 50 C3
Cutsdean Glos 51 F5
Cutthorpe Derbys 76 B3
Cutts Shetland 160 K6
Cuxham Oxon 39 E6
Cuxton Medway 29 C8
Cuxwold Lincs 91 D5
Cwm Bl Gwent 35 D5
Cwm Denb 72 B4
Cwm Swansea 33 E7
Cwm-byr Carms 46 F5
Cwm-Cewydd Gwyn 59 C5
Cwm-cou Ceredig 45 E4
Cwm-Dulais Swansea 33 D7
Cwm-felin-fach Caerph 35 E5
Cwm Ffrwd-oer Torf 35 D6
Cwm-hesgen Gwyn 71 E8
Cwm-hwnt Rhondda 34 D3
Cwm Irfon Powys 47 E7
Cwm-Llinau Powys 58 D5
Cwm-mawr Carms 33 C6
Cwm-parc Rhondda 34 E3
Cwm Penmachno Conwy 71 C8
Cwm-y-glo Carms 33 C6
Cwm-y-glo Gwyn 82 E5
Cwmafan Neath 34 E1
Cwmaman Rhondda 34 E4
Cwmann Carms 46 E4
Cwmavon Torf 35 D6
Cwmbâch Rhondda 34 D4
Cwmbach Carms 32 B3
Cwmbach Carms 33 D5
Cwmbach Powys 48 D2
Cwmbach Powys 48 F3
Cwmbelan Powys 59 F6
Cwmbrân = Cwmbran Torf 35 E6
Cwmbran = Cwmbrân Torf 35 E6
Cwmbrwyno Ceredig 58 F4
Cwmcarn Caerph 35 E6
Cwmcarvan Mon 36 D1
Cwmcych Carms 45 F4
Cwmdare Rhondda 34 D3
Cwmderwen Powys 59 D6
Cwmdu Carms 46 F5
Cwmdu Powys 35 B5
Cwmdu Swansea 33 E7
Cwmduad Carms 46 F2
Cwmdwr Carms 47 F6
Cwmfelin Bridgend 34 F2
Cwmfelin M Tydf 34 D4
Cwmfelin Boeth Carms 32 C2
Cwmfelin Mynach Carms 32 B3
Cwmffrwd Carms 33 C5
Cwmgiedd Powys 34 C1
Cwmgors Neath 33 C8
Cwmgwili Carms 33 C6
Cwmgwrach Neath 34 D2
Cwmhiraeth Carms 46 F2
Cwmifor Carms 33 B7
Cwmisfael Carms 33 C5
Cwmllynfell Neath 33 C8
Cwmorgan Pembs 45 F4
Cwmpengraig Carms 46 F2
Cwmrhos Powys 35 B5
Cwmsychpant Ceredig 46 E3
Cwmtillery Bl Gwent 35 D6
Cwmwysg Powys 34 B2
Cwmyoy Mon 35 B6
Cwmystwyth Ceredig 47 B6
Cwrt Gwyn 58 D3
Cwrt-newydd Ceredig 46 E3
Cwrt-y-cadno Carms 47 E5
Cwrt-y-gollen Powys 35 C6
Cydweli = Kidwelly Carms 33 D5
Cyffordd Llandudno = Llandudno Junction Conwy 83 D7
Cyffylliog Denb 72 D4
Cyfronydd Powys 59 D8
Cymer Neath 34 E2
Cyncoed Cardiff 35 F5
Cynghordy Carms 47 E7
Cynheidre Carms 33 D5
Cynwyd Denb 72 E4
Cynwyl Elfed Carms 32 B4
Cywarch Gwyn 59 C5

D

Dacre Cumb 99 B6
Dacre N Yorks 94 C4
Dacre Banks N Yorks 94 C4
Daddry Shield Durham 109 F8
Dadford Bucks 52 F4
Dadlington Leics 63 E8
Dafarn Faig Gwyn 71 C5
Dafen Carms 33 D6
Daffy Green Norf 68 D2
Dagenham London 41 F7
Daglingworth Glos 37 D6
Dagnall Bucks 40 C2
Dail Beag W Isles 154 C7
Dail bho Dheas W Isles 155 A9
Dail bho Thuath W Isles 155 A9
Dail Mor W Isles 154 C7
Daill Argyll 142 B4
Dailly S Ayrs 112 D2
Dairsie or Osnaburgh Fife 129 C6
Daisy Hill Gtr Man 86 D4
Dalabrog W Isles 148 F2
Dalavich Argyll 125 D5
Dalbeattie Dumfries 106 C5
Dalblair E Ayrs 113 C6
Dalbog Angus 135 B5
Dalbury Derbys 76 F2
Dalby IoM 84 E2
Dalby N Yorks 96 B2
Dalchalloch Perth 132 C4
Dalchalm Highld 157 J12
Dalchenna Argyll 125 E6
Dalchirach Moray 152 E1
Dalchork Highld 157 H8
Dalchreichart Highld 137 C5
Dalchruin Perth 127 C6
Dalderby Lincs 78 C5
Dale Pembs 44 E3
Dale Abbey Derbys 76 F4
Dale Head Cumb 99 C6
Dale of Walls Shetland 160 H3
Dalelia Highld 147 E10
Daless Highld 151 H11
Dalfaber Highld 138 C5
Dalgarven N Ayrs 118 E2
Dalgety Bay Fife 128 F3
Dalginross Perth 127 B6
Dalguise Perth 133 E6
Dalhalvaig Highld 157 D11
Dalham Suff 55 C8
Dalinlongart Argyll 145 E10
Dalkeith Midloth 121 C6
Dallam Warr 86 E3
Dallas Moray 151 F14
Dalleagles E Ayrs 113 C5
Dallinghoo Suff 57 D6
Dallington E Sus 18 D3
Dallington Northants 52 C5
Dallow N Yorks 94 B4
Dalmadilly Aberds 141 C6
Dalmally Argyll 125 C7
Dalmarnock Glasgow 119 C6
Dalmary Stirling 126 E4
Dalmellington E Ayrs 112 D4
Dalmeny Edin 120 B4
Dalmigavie Highld 138 C3
Dalmigavie Lodge Highld 138 B3
Dalmore Highld 151 E9
Dalmuir W Dunb 118 B4
Dalnabreck Highld 147 E9
Dalnacardoch Lodge Perth 132 B4
Dalnacroich Highld 150 F6
Dalnaglar Castle Perth 133 C8
Dalnahaitnach Highld 138 B4
Dalnaspidal Lodge Perth 132 B3
Dalnavaid Perth 133 C7
Dalnavie Highld 151 D9
Dalnawillan Lodge Highld 157 E13
Dalness Highld 131 D5
Dalnessie Highld 157 H9
Dalqueich Perth 128 D2
Dalreavoch Highld 157 J10
Dalry N Ayrs 118 E2
Dalrymple E Ayrs 112 C3
Dalserf S Lanark 119 D8
Dalston Cumb 108 D3
Dalswinton Dumfries 114 F2
Dalton Dumfries 107 B8
Dalton Lancs 86 D2
Dalton N Yorks 95 B7
Dalton N Yorks 101 D6
Dalton Northumb 110 B4
Dalton Northumb 110 D2
Dalton S Yorks 89 E5
Dalton-in-Furness Cumb 92 B2
Dalton-le-Dale Durham 111 E7
Dalton-on-Tees N Yorks 101 D7
Dalton Piercy Hrtlpl 111 F7
Dalveich Stirling 126 B5
Dalvina Lodge Highld 157 E9
Dalwhinnie Highld 138 F2
Dalwood Devon 11 D7
Dalwyne S Ayrs 112 E3
Dam Green Norf 68 F3
Dam Side Lancs 92 E4
Damerham Hants 14 C2
Damgate Norf 69 D7
Damnaglaur Dumfries 104 F5
Damside Borders 120 E4
Danbury Essex 42 D3
Danby N Yorks 103 D5
Danby Wiske N Yorks 101 E8
Dandaleith Moray 152 D2
Danderhall Midloth 121 C6
Dane End Herts 41 B6
Danebridge Ches E 75 C6
Danehill E Sus 17 B8
Danemoor Green Norf 68 D3
Danesford Shrops 61 E7
Daneshill Hants 26 D4
Dangerous Corner Lancs 86 C3
Danskine E Loth 121 C8
Darcy Lever Gtr Man 86 D5
Darenth Kent 29 B6
Daresbury Halton 86 F3
Darfield S Yorks 88 D5
Darfoulds Notts 77 B5
Dargate Kent 30 C4
Darite Corn 5 C7
Darlaston W Mid 62 E3
Darley N Yorks 94 D5
Darley Bridge Derbys 76 C2
Darley Head N Yorks 94 D4
Darlingscott Warks 51 E7
Darlington Darl 101 C7
Darliston Shrops 74 F2
Darlton Notts 77 B7
Darnall S Yorks 88 F4
Darnick Borders 121 F8
Darowen Powys 58 D5
Darra Aberds 153 D7
Darracott Devon 20 F3
Darras Hall Northumb 110 B4
Darrington W Yorks 89 B5
Darsham Suff 57 C8
Dartford Kent 29 B6
Dartford Crossing Kent 29 B6
Dartington Devon 7 C5
Dartmeet Devon 6 B4
Dartmouth Devon 7 D6
Darton S Yorks 88 D4
Darvel E Ayrs 119 F5
Darwell Hole E Sus 18 D3
Darwen Blackburn 86 B4
Datchet Windsor 27 B7
Datchworth Herts 41 C5
Datchworth Green Herts 41 C5
Daubhill Gtr Man 86 D5
Daugh of Kinermony Moray 152 D2
Dauntsey Wilts 37 F6
Dava Moray 151 H13
Davenham Ches W 74 B3
Davenport Green Ches E 74 B5
Daventry Northants 52 C3
David's Well Powys 48 B2
Davidson's Mains Edin 120 B5
Davidstow Corn 8 F3
Davington Dumfries 115 D5
Daviot Aberds 141 B6
Daviot Highld 151 H10
Davoch of Grange Moray 152 C4
Davyhulme Gtr Man 87 E5
Daw's House Corn 8 F5
Dawley Telford 61 D6
Dawlish Devon 7 B7
Dawlish Warren Devon 7 B7
Dawn Conwy 83 D8
Daws Heath Essex 42 F4
Daw's House Corn 8 F5
Dawsmere Lincs 79 F7
Dayhills Staffs 75 F6
Daylesford Glos 38 B2
Ddôl-Cownwy Powys 59 C7
Ddrydwy Anglesey 82 D3
Deadwater Northumb 116 E2
Deaf Hill Durham 111 F6
Deal Kent 31 D7
Deal Hall Essex 43 E6
Dean Cumb 98 B2
Dean Devon 6 C5
Dean Devon 20 E4
Dean Dorset 13 C7
Dean Hants 15 C6
Dean Som 23 E8
Dean Prior Devon 6 C5
Dean Row Ches E 87 F6
Deanburnhaugh Borders 115 C6
Deane Gtr Man 86 D4
Deane Hants 26 D3
Deanich Lodge Highld 150 C6
Deanland Dorset 13 C7
Deans W Loth 120 C3
Deanscales Cumb 98 B2
Deanshanger Northants 53 F5
Deanston Stirling 127 D6
Dearham Cumb 107 F7
Debach Suff 57 D6
Debden Essex 41 E7
Debden Essex 55 F6
Debden Cross Essex 55 F6
Debenham Suff 57 C5
Dechmont W Loth 120 B3
Deddington Oxon 52 F2
Dedham Essex 56 F4
Dedham Heath Essex 56 F4
Deebank Aberds 141 E5
Deene Northants 65 E6
Deenethorpe Northants 65 E6
Deepcar S Yorks 88 E3
Deepcut Sur 27 D7
Deepdale Cumb 100 F2
Deeping Gate Lincs 65 D8
Deeping St James Lincs 65 D8
Deeping St Nicholas Lincs 66 C2
Deerhill Moray 152 C4
Deerhurst Glos 37 B5
Deerness Orkney 159 H6
Defford Worcs 50 E4
Defynnog Powys 34 B3
Deganwy Conwy 83 D7
Deighton N Yorks 102 D1
Deighton W Yorks 88 C2
Deighton York 96 E2
Deiniolen Gwyn 83 E5
Delabole Corn 8 F2
Delamere Ches W 74 C2
Delfrigs Aberds 141 B8
Dell Lodge Highld 139 C6
Delliefure Highld 151 H13
Delnabo Moray 139 C7
Delnadamph Aberds 139 D8
Delph Gtr Man 87 D7
Delves Durham 110 E4
Delvine Perth 133 E8
Dembleby Lincs 78 F3
Denaby Main S Yorks 89 E5
Denbigh = Dinbych Denb 72 C4
Denbury Devon 7 C6
Denby Derbys 76 E3
Denby Dale W Yorks 88 D3
Denchworth Oxon 38 E3
Dendron Cumb 92 B2
Denel End C Beds 53 F8
Denend Aberds 152 E6
Denford Northants 53 B7
Dengie Essex 43 D5
Denham Bucks 40 F3
Denham Suff 55 C8
Denham Suff 57 B5
Denham Street Suff 57 B5
Denhead Aberds 153 C9
Denhead Fife 129 C6
Denhead of Arbilot Angus 135 E5
Denhead of Gray Dundee 134 F3
Denholm Borders 115 C8
Denholme W Yorks 94 F3
Denholme Clough W Yorks 94 F3
Denio Gwyn 70 D4
Denmead Hants 15 C7
Denmore Aberdeen 141 C8
Denmoss Aberds 153 D6
Dennington Suff 57 C6
Denny Falk 127 F7
Denny Lodge Hants 14 D4
Dennyloanhead Falk 127 F7
Denshaw Gtr Man 87 C7
Denside Aberds 141 E7
Densole Kent 31 E6
Denston Suff 55 D8
Denstone Staffs 75 E8
Dent Cumb 100 F2
Denton Cambs 65 F8
Denton Darl 101 C7
Denton E Sus 17 D8
Denton Gtr Man 87 E7
Denton Kent 31 E6
Denton Lincs 77 F8
Denton N Yorks 94 E4
Denton Norf 69 F5
Denton Northants 53 D6
Denton Oxon 39 D5
Denton's Green Mers 86 E2
Denver Norf 67 D6
Denwick Northumb 117 C8
Deopham Norf 68 D3
Deopham Green Norf 68 E3
Depden Suff 55 D8
Depden Green Suff 55 D8
Deptford London 28 B4
Deptford Wilts 24 F5
Derby Derby 76 F3
Derbyhaven IoM 84 F2
Dereham Norf 68 C2
Deri Caerph 35 D5
Derril Devon 8 D5
Derringstone Kent 31 E6
Derrington Staffs 62 B2
Derriton Devon 8 D5
Derry Hill Wilts 24 B4
Derryguaig Argyll 146 H7
Derrythorpe N Lincs 90 D2
Dersingham Norf 80 D2
Dervaig Argyll 146 F7
Derwen Denb 72 D4
Derwenlas Powys 58 E4
Desborough Northants 64 F5
Desford Leics 63 D8
Detchant Northumb 123 F6
Detling Kent 29 D8
Deuddwr Powys 60 C2
Devauden Mon 36 E1
Devil's Bridge Ceredig 47 B6
Devizes Wilts 24 C5
Devol Invclyd 118 B3
Devonport Plym 6 D2
Devonside Clack 127 E8
Devoran Corn 3 C6
Dewar Borders 121 E6
Dewlish Dorset 13 E5
Dewsbury W Yorks 88 B3
Dewsbury Moor W Yorks 88 B3
Dewshall Court Hereford 49 F6
Dhoon IoM 84 D4
Dhoor IoM 84 C4
Dhowin IoM 84 B4
Dial Post W Sus 17 C5
Dibden Hants 14 D5
Dibden Purlieu Hants 14 D5
Dickleburgh Norf 68 F4
Didbrook Glos 51 F5
Didcot Oxon 39 F5
Diddington Cambs 54 C2
Diddlebury Shrops 60 F5
Didley Hereford 49 F6
Didling W Sus 16 C2
Didmarton Glos 37 F5
Didsbury Gtr Man 87 E6
Didworthy Devon 6 C4
Digby Lincs 78 D3
Digg Highld 149 B9
Diggle Gtr Man 87 D8
Digmoor Lancs 86 D2
Digswell Park Herts 41 C5
Dihewyd Ceredig 46 D3
Dilham Norf 69 B6
Dilhorne Staffs 75 E6
Dillarburn S Lanark 119 E8
Dillington Cambs 54 C2
Dilston Northumb 110 C2
Dilton Marsh Wilts 24 E3
Dilwyn Hereford 49 D6
Dinas Carms 45 F4
Dinas Gwyn 70 D3
Dinas Cross Pembs 45 F2
Dinas Dinlle Gwyn 82 F4
Dinas-Mawddwy Gwyn 59 C5
Dinas Powys V Glam 22 B3
Dinbych = Denbigh Denb 72 C4
Dinbych-Y-Pysgod = Tenby Pembs 32 D2
Dinder Som 23 E7
Dinedor Hereford 49 F7
Dingestow Mon 36 C1
Dingle Mers 85 F4
Dingleden Kent 18 B5
Dingley Northants 64 F4
Dingwall Highld 151 F8
Dinlabyre Borders 115 E8
Dinmael Conwy 72 E4
Dinnet Aberds 140 E3
Dinnington S Yorks 89 F6
Dinnington Som 12 C2
Dinnington T&W 110 B5
Dinorwic Gwyn 83 E5
Dinton Bucks 39 C7
Dinton Wilts 24 F5
Dinwoodie Mains Dumfries 114 E4
Dinworthy Devon 8 C5
Dippen N Ayrs 143 F11
Dippenhall Sur 27 E6
Dipple Moray 152 C3
Dipple S Ayrs 112 D2
Diptford Devon 6 D5
Dipton Durham 110 D4
Dirdhu Highld 139 B6
Dirleton E Loth 129 F7
Dirt Pot Northumb 109 E8
Discoed Powys 48 C4
Diseworth Leics 63 B8
Dishes Orkney 159 F7
Dishforth N Yorks 95 B6
Disley Ches E 87 F7
Diss Norf 56 B5
Disserth Powys 48 D2
Distington Cumb 98 B2
Ditchampton Wilts 25 F5
Ditcheat Som 23 F8
Ditchingham Norf 69 E6
Ditchling E Sus 17 C7
Ditherington Shrops 60 C5
Dittisham Devon 7 D6
Ditton Halton 86 F2
Ditton Kent 29 D8
Ditton Green Cambs 55 D7
Ditton Priors Shrops 61 F6
Divach Highld 137 B7
Divlyn Carms 47 F6
Dixton Glos 50 F4
Dixton Mon 36 C2
Dobcross Gtr Man 87 D7
Dobwalls Corn 5 C7
Doc Penfro = Pembroke Dock Pembs 44 E4
Doccombe Devon 10 F2
Dochfour Ho. Highld 151 H9
Dochgarroch Highld 151 G9
Docking Norf 80 D3
Docklow Hereford 49 D7
Dockray Cumb 99 B5
Dockroyd W Yorks 94 F3
Dodburn Borders 115 D7
Doddinghurst Essex 42 E1
Doddington Cambs 66 E3
Doddington Kent 30 D3
Doddington Lincs 78 B2
Doddington Northumb 123 F5
Doddington Shrops 49 B8
Doddiscombsleigh Devon 10 F3
Dodford Northants 52 C4
Dodford Worcs 50 B4
Dodington S Glos 24 A2
Dodleston Ches W 73 C7
Dods Leigh Staffs 75 F7
Dodworth S Yorks 88 D4
Doe Green Warr 86 F3
Doe Lea Derbys 76 C4
Dog Village Devon 10 E4
Dogdyke Lincs 78 D5
Dogmersfield Hants 27 D5
Dogridge Wilts 37 F7
Dogsthorpe Pboro 65 D8
Dol-fôr Powys 58 D5
Dôl-y-Bont Ceredig 58 F3
Dol-y-cannau Powys 48 E4
Dolanog Powys 59 C7
Dolau Powys 48 C3
Dolau Rhondda 34 F3
Dolbenmaen Gwyn 71 C6
Dolfach Powys 59 D6
Dolfor Powys 59 F8
Dolgarrog Conwy 83 E7
Dolgellau Gwyn 58 C4
Dolgran Carms 46 F3
Dolhendre Gwyn 72 F2
Doll Highld 157 J11
Dollar Clack 127 E8
Dolley Green Powys 48 C4
Dollwen Ceredig 58 F3
Dolphin Flint 73 B5
Dolphinholme Lancs 92 D5
Dolphinton S Lanark 120 E4
Dolton Devon 9 C7
Dolwen Conwy 83 D8
Dolwen Powys 59 D6
Dolwyd Conwy 83 D8
Dolwyddelan Conwy 83 F7
Dolyhir Powys 48 D4
Doncaster S Yorks 89 D6
Dones Green Ches W 74 B3
Donhead St Andrew Wilts 13 B7
Donhead St Mary Wilts 13 B7
Donibristle Fife 128 F3
Donington Lincs 78 F5
Donington on Bain Lincs 91 F6
Donington South Ing Lincs 78 F5
Donisthorpe Leics 63 C7
Donkey Town Sur 27 C7
Donnington Glos 38 B1
Donnington Hereford 50 F2
Donnington Shrops 61 D5
Donnington Telford 61 C7
Donnington W Berks 26 C2
Donnington W Sus 16 D2
Donnington Wood Telford 61 C7
Donyatt Som 11 C8
Doonfoot S Ayrs 112 C3
Dorback Lodge Highld 139 C6
Dorchester Dorset 12 E4
Dorchester Oxon 39 E5
Dordon Warks 63 D6
Dore S Yorks 88 F4
Dores Highld 151 H8
Dorking Sur 28 E2
Dormansland Sur 28 E5
Dormanstown Redcar 102 B3
Dormington Hereford 49 E7
Dormston Worcs 50 D4
Dornal S Ayrs 105 B6
Dorney Bucks 27 B7
Dornie Highld 149 F13
Dornoch Highld 151 C10
Dornock Dumfries 108 C2
Dorrery Highld 158 E2
Dorridge W Mid 51 B6
Dorrington Lincs 78 D3
Dorrington Shrops 60 D4
Dorsington Warks 51 E6
Dorstone Hereford 48 E5
Dorton Bucks 39 C6
Dorusduain Highld 136 B2
Dosthill Staffs 63 E6
Dottery Dorset 12 E2
Doublebois Corn 5 C6
Dougarie N Ayrs 143 E9
Doughton Glos 37 E5
Douglas IoM 84 E3
Douglas S Lanark 119 F8
Douglas & Angus Dundee 134 F4
Douglas Water S Lanark 119 F8
Douglas West S Lanark 119 F8
Douglastown Angus 134 E4
Doulting Som 23 E8
Dounby Orkney 159 F3
Doune Highld 156 J7
Doune Stirling 127 D6
Doune Park Aberds 153 B7
Douneside Aberds 140 D3
Dounie Highld 151 B8
Dounreay Highld 157 C12
Dousland Devon 6 C3
Dovaston Shrops 60 B3
Dove Holes Derbys 75 B7
Dovenby Cumb 107 F7
Dover Kent 31 E7
Dovercourt Essex 57 F6
Doverdale Worcs 50 C3
Doveridge Derbys 75 F8
Doversgreen Sur 28 E3
Dowally Perth 133 E7
Dowbridge Lancs 92 F4
Dowdeswell Glos 37 C6
Dowlais M Tydf 34 D4
Dowland Devon 9 C7
Dowlish Wake Som 11 C8
Down Ampney Glos 37 E8
Down Hatherley Glos 37 B5
Down St Mary Devon 10 D2
Down Thomas Devon 6 D3
Downcraig Ferry N Ayrs 145 H10
Downderry Corn 5 D8
Downe London 28 C5
Downend IoW 15 F6
Downend S Glos 23 B8
Downend W Berks 26 B2
Downfield Dundee 134 F3
Downgate Corn 5 B8
Downham Essex 42 E3
Downham Lancs 93 E7
Downham Northumb 122 F4
Downham Market Norf 67 D6
Downhead Som 23 E8
Downhill Perth 133 F7
Downhill T&W 111 D6
Downholland Cross Lancs 85 D4
Downholme N Yorks 101 E6
Downies Aberds 141 E8
Downley Bucks 39 E8
Downside Som 23 E8
Downside Sur 28 D2
Downton Hants 14 E3
Downton Wilts 14 B2
Downton on the Rock Hereford 49 B6
Dowsby Lincs 65 B8
Dowsdale Lincs 66 C2
Dowthwaitehead Cumb 99 B5
Doxey Staffs 62 B3
Doxford Northumb 117 B7
Doxford Park T&W 111 D6
Doynton S Glos 24 B2
Draffan S Lanark 119 E7
Dragonby N Lincs 90 C3
Drakeland Corner Devon 6 D3
Drakemyre N Ayrs 118 D2
Drake's Broughton Worcs 50 E4
Drakes Cross Worcs 51 B5
Drakewalls Corn 6 B2
Draughton N Yorks 94 D3
Draughton Northants 53 B5
Drax N Yorks 89 B7
Draycote Warks 52 B2
Draycott Derbys 76 F4
Draycott Glos 51 F6
Draycott Som 23 D6
Draycott in the Clay Staffs 63 B5
Draycott in the Moors Staffs 75 E6
Drayford Devon 10 C2
Drayton Leics 64 E5
Drayton Lincs 78 F5
Drayton Norf 68 C4
Drayton Oxon 38 E4
Drayton Oxon 52 E2
Drayton Ptsmth 15 D7
Drayton Som 12 B2
Drayton Worcs 50 B4
Drayton Bassett Staffs 63 D5
Drayton Beauchamp Bucks 40 C2
Drayton Parslow Bucks 39 B8
Drayton St Leonard Oxon 39 E5
Dre-fach Carms 33 C7
Dre-fach Ceredig 46 E4
Drebley N Yorks 94 D3
Dreemskerry IoM 84 C4
Dreenhill Pembs 44 D4
Drefach Carms 33 C6
Drefach Carms 46 F2
Drefelin Carms 46 F2
Dreghorn N Ayrs 118 F3
Drellingore Kent 31 E6
Drem E Loth 121 B8
Dresden Stoke 75 E6
Dreumasdal W Isles 148 E2
Drewsteignton Devon 10 E2
Driby Lincs 79 B6
Driffield E Yorks 97 D6
Driffield Glos 37 E7
Drigg Cumb 98 E2
Drighlington W Yorks 88 B3
Drimnin Highld 147 F8
Drimpton Dorset 12 D2
Drimsynie Argyll 125 E7
Drinisiadar W Isles 154 H6
Drinkstone Suff 56 C3
Drinkstone Green Suff 56 C3
Drishaig Argyll 125 D7
Drissaig Argyll 124 D5
Drochil Borders 120 E4
Drointon Staffs 62 B4
Droitwich Spa Worcs 50 C3
Droman Highld 156 D4
Dron Perth 128 C3
Dronfield Derbys 76 B3
Dronfield Woodhouse Derbys 76 B3
Drongan E Ayrs 112 C4
Dronley Angus 134 F3
Droxford Hants 15 C7
Droylsden Gtr Man 87 E7
Druid Denb 72 E4
Druidston Pembs 44 D3
Druimarbin Highld 130 B4
Druimavuic Argyll 130 E4
Druimdrishaig Argyll 144 F6
Druimindarroch Highld 147 C9
Druimyeon More Argyll 143 C7
Drum Argyll 145 F8
Drum Perth 128 D2
Drumbeg Highld 156 F4
Drumblade Aberds 152 D5
Drumblair Aberds 153 D6
Drumbuie Dumfries 113 F5
Drumbuie Highld 149 E12
Drumburgh Cumb 108 D2
Drumburn Dumfries 107 C6
Drumchapel Glasgow 118 B5
Drumchardine Highld 151 G8
Drumchork Highld 155 J13
Drumclog S Lanark 119 F6
Drumderfit Highld 151 F9
Drumeldrie Fife 129 D6
Drumelzier Borders 120 F4
Drumfearn Highld 149 G11
Drumgask Highld 138 E2
Drumgley Angus 134 D4
Drumguish Highld 138 E3
Drumin Moray 152 E1
Drumlasie Aberds 140 D5
Drumlemble Argyll 143 G7
Drumligair Aberds 141 C8
Drumlithie Aberds 141 F6
Drummoddie Dumfries 105 E7
Drummond Highld 151 E9
Drummore Dumfries 104 F5
Drummuir Moray 152 D3
Drummuir Castle Moray 152 D3
Drumnadrochit Highld 137 B8
Drumnagorrach Moray 152 C5
Drumoak Aberds 141 E6
Drumpark Dumfries 107 A5
Drumphail Dumfries 105 C6
Drumrash Dumfries 106 B3
Drumrunie Highld 156 J4
Drums Aberds 141 B8
Drumsallie Highld 130 B3
Drumstinchall Dumfries 107 D5
Drumsturdy Angus 134 F4
Drumtochty Castle Aberds 135 B6
Drumtroddan Dumfries 105 E7
Drumuie Highld 149 D9
Drumuillie Highld 138 B5
Drumvaich Stirling 127 D5
Drumwhindle Aberds 153 E9
Drunkendub Angus 135 E6
Drury Flint 73 C6
Drury Square Norf 68 C2
Dry Doddington Lincs 77 E8
Dry Drayton Cambs 54 C4
Drybeck Cumb 100 C1
Drybridge Moray 152 B4
Drybridge N Ayrs 118 F3
Drybrook Glos 36 C3
Dryburgh Borders 121 F8
Dryhope Borders 115 B5
Drylaw Edin 120 B5
Drym Corn 2 C5
Drymen Stirling 126 F3
Drymuir Aberds 153 D9
Drynoch Highld 149 E9
Dryslwyn Carms 33 B6
Dryton Shrops 61 D5
Dubford Aberds 153 B8
Dubton Angus 135 D5
Duchally Highld 156 H6
Duchlage Argyll 126 F2
Duck Corner Suff 57 E7
Duckington Ches W 73 D8
Ducklington Oxon 38 D3
Duckmanton Derbys 76 B4
Duck's Cross Bedford 54 D2
Duddenhoe End Essex 55 F5
Duddingston Edin 121 B5
Duddington Northants 65 D6
Duddleswell E Sus 17 B8
Duddo Northumb 122 E5
Duddon Ches W 74 C2
Duddon Bridge Cumb 98 F4
Dudleston Shrops 73 F7
Dudleston Heath Shrops 73 F7
Dudley T&W 111 B5
Dudley W Mid 62 E3
Dudley Port W Mid 62 E3
Duffield Derbys 76 E3
Duffryn Neath 34 E2
Duffryn Newport 35 F6
Dufftown Moray 152 E3
Duffus Moray 152 B1
Dufton Cumb 100 B1
Duggleby N Yorks 96 C4
Duirinish Highld 149 E12
Duisdalemore Highld 149 G12
Duisky Highld 130 B4
Dukestown Bl Gwent 35 C5
Dukinfield Gtr Man 87 E7
Dulas Anglesey 82 C4
Dulcote Som 23 E7
Dulford Devon 11 D5
Dull Perth 133 E5
Dullatur N Lanark 119 B7
Dullingham Cambs 55 D7
Dulnain Bridge Highld 139 B5
Duloe Bedford 54 C2
Duloe Corn 5 D7
Dulsie Highld 151 G12
Dulverton Som 10 B4
Dulwich London 28 B4
Dumbarton W Dunb 118 B3
Dumbleton Glos 50 F5
Dumcrieff Dumfries 114 D4
Dumfries Dumfries 107 B6
Dumgoyne Stirling 126 F4
Dummer Hants 26 E3
Dumpford W Sus 16 B2
Dumpton Kent 31 C7
Dun Angus 135 D6
Dun Charlabhaigh W Isles 154 C6
Dunain Ho. Highld 151 G9
Dunalastair Perth 132 D4
Dunan Highld 149 F10
Dunans Argyll 145 D9
Dunball Som 22 E5
Dunbar E Loth 122 B2
Dunbeath Highld 158 H3
Dunbeg Argyll 124 B4
Dunblane Stirling 127 D6
Dunbog Fife 128 C4
Duncanston Highld 151 F8
Duncanstone Aberds 140 B4
Dunchurch Warks 52 B2
Duncote Northants 52 D4
Duncow Dumfries 114 F2
Duncraggan Stirling 126 D4
Duncrievie Perth 128 D3
Duncton W Sus 16 C3
Dundas Ho. Orkney 159 K5
Dundee Dundee 134 F4
Dundeugh Dumfries 113 F5
Dundon Som 23 F6
Dundonald S Ayrs 118 F3
Dundonnell Highld 150 C3
Dundonnell Hotel Highld 150 C3
Dundonnell House Highld 150 C4
Dundraw Cumb 108 E2
Dundreggan Highld 137 C6
Dundreggan Lodge Highld 137 C6
Dundrennan Dumfries 106 E4
Dundry N Som 23 C7
Dunecht Aberds 141 D6
Dunfermline Fife 128 F2
Dunfield Glos 37 E8
Dunford Bridge S Yorks 88 D2
Dungworth S Yorks 88 F3
Dunham Notts 77 B8
Dunham-on-the-Hill Ches W 73 B8

Dunham Town Gtr Man 86 F5
Dunhampton Worcs 50 C3
Dunholme Lincs 78 B3
Dunino Fife 129 C7
Dunipace Falk 127 F7
Dunira Perth 127 B6
Dunkeld Perth 133 E7
Dunkerton Bath 24 D2
Dunkeswell Devon 11 D6
Dunkeswick N Yorks 95 E6
Dunkirk Kent 30 D4
Dunkirk Norf 81 E8
Dunk's Green Kent 29 D7
Dunlappie Angus 135 C5
Dunley Hants 26 D2
Dunley Worcs 50 C2
Dunlichity Lodge Highld 151 H9
Dunlop E Ayrs 118 E4
Dunmaglass Lodge Highld 137 B8
Dunmore Argyll 144 G6
Dunmore Falk 127 F7
Dunnet Highld 158 C4
Dunnichen Angus 135 E5
Dunninald Angus 135 D7
Dunning Perth 128 C2
Dunnington E Yorks 97 D7
Dunnington Warks 51 D5
Dunnington York 96 D2
Dunnockshaw Lancs 87 B6
Dunollie Argyll 124 B4
Dunoon Argyll 145 F10
Dunragit Dumfries 105 D5
Dunrostan Argyll 144 E6
Duns Borders 122 D3
Duns Tew Oxon 38 B4
Dunsby Lincs 65 B8
Dunscore Dumfries 113 F8
Dunscroft S Yorks 89 D7
Dunsdale Redcar 102 C4
Dunsden Green Oxon 26 B5
Dunsfold Sur 27 F8
Dunsford Devon 10 F3
Dunshalt Fife 128 C4
Dunshillock Aberds 153 D9
Dunskey Ho. Dumfries 104 D4
Dunsley N Yorks 103 C6
Dunsmore Bucks 40 D1
Dunsop Bridge Lancs 93 D6
Dunstable C Beds 40 B3
Dunstall Staffs 63 B5
Dunstall Common Worcs 50 E3
Dunstall Green Suff 55 C8
Dunstan Northumb 117 C8
Dunstan Steads Northumb 117 B8
Dunster Som 21 E8
Duns Lincs 78 C3
Dunston Norf 68 D5
Dunston Staffs 62 C3
Dunston T&W 110 C5
Dunsville S Yorks 89 D7
Dunswell E Yorks 97 F6
Dunsyre S Lanark 120 E3
Dunterton Devon 5 B8
Duntisbourne Abbots Glos 37 D6
Duntisbourne Leer Glos 37 D6
Duntisbourne Rouse Glos 37 D6
Duntish Dorset 12 D4
Duntocher W Dunb 118 B4
Dunton Bucks 39 B8
Dunton C Beds 54 E3
Dunton Norf 80 D4
Dunton Bassett Leics 64 E2
Dunton Green Kent 29 D6
Dunton Wayletts Essex 42 E2
Duntulm Highld 149 A9
Dunure S Ayrs 112 C2
Dunvant Swansea 33 E6
Dunvegan Highld 148 D7
Dunwich Suff 57 B8
Dunwood Staffs 75 D6
Dupplin Castle Perth 128 C2
Durdar Cumb 108 D4
Durgates E Sus 18 B3
Durham Durham 111 E5
Durisdeer Dumfries 113 D8
Durisdeermill Dumfries 113 D8
Durkar W Yorks 88 C4
Durleigh Som 22 F4
Durley Hants 15 C6
Durley Wilts 25 C7
Durnamuck Highld 150 B3
Durness Highld 156 C7
Durno Aberds 141 B6
Duror Highld 130 D3
Durran Argyll 125 E5
Durran Highld 158 D3
Durrington W Sus 16 D5
Durrington Wilts 25 E6
Dursley Glos 36 E4
Durston Som 11 B7
Durweston Dorset 13 D6
Dury Shetland 160 G6
Duston Northants 52 C5
Duthil Highld 138 B5
Dutlas Powys 48 B4
Duton Hill Essex 42 B2
Dutson Corn 8 F5
Dutton Ches W 74 B2
Duxford Cambs 55 E5
Duxford Oxon 38 E3
Dwygyfylchi Conwy 83 D7
Dwyran Anglesey 82 E4
Dyce Aberdeen 141 C7
Dye House Northumb 110 D2
Dyffryn Bridgend 34 E2
Dyffryn Carms 32 B4
Dyffryn Pembs 44 B4
Dyffryn Ardudwy Gwyn 71 E6
Dyffryn Castell Ceredig 58 F4
Dyffryn Ceidrych Carms 33 B8
Dyffryn Cellwen Neath 34 D2
Dyke Lincs 65 B8
Dyke Moray 151 F12
Dykehead Angus 134 C3
Dykehead N Lanark 119 D8
Dykehead Stirling 126 E4
Dykelands Aberds 135 C7
Dykends Angus 134 D2
Dykeside Aberds 153 D7
Dykesmains N Ayrs 118 E2
Dylife Powys 59 E5
Dymchurch Kent 19 C7
Dymock Glos 50 F2
Dyrham S Glos 24 B2
Dysart Fife 128 E5
Dyserth Denb 72 B4

E

Eachwick Northumb 110 B4
Eadar Dha Fhadhail W Isles 154 D5
Eagland Hill Lancs 92 E4
Eagle Lincs 77 C8
Eagle Barnsdale Lincs 77 C8
Eagle Moor Lincs 77 C8
Eaglescliffe Stockton 102 C2
Eaglesfield Cumb 98 B2
Eaglesfield Dumfries 108 B2
Eaglesham E Renf 119 D5
Eaglethorpe Northants 65 E7
Eairy IoM 84 E2
Eakley Lanes M Keynes 53 D6
Eakring Notts 77 C6
Ealand N Lincs 89 C8
Ealing London 40 F4
Eals Northumb 109 D6
Eamont Bridge Cumb 99 B7
Earby Lancs 94 E2
Earcroft Blackburn 86 B4
Eardington Shrops 61 E7
Eardisland Hereford 49 D6
Eardisley Hereford 48 E5
Eardiston Shrops 60 B3
Eardiston Worcs 49 C8
Earith Cambs 54 B4
Earl Shilton Leics 63 E8
Earl Soham Suff 57 C6
Earl Sterndale Derbys 75 C7
Earl Stonham Suff 56 D5
Earle Northumb 117 B5
Earley Wokingham 27 B5
Earlham Norf 68 D5
Earlish Highld 149 B8
Earls Barton Northants 53 C6
Earls Colne Essex 42 B4
Earl's Croome Worcs 50 E3
Earl's Green Suff 56 C4
Earlsdon W Mid 51 B8
Earlsferry Fife 129 E6
Earlsfield Lincs 78 F2
Earlsford Aberds 153 E8
Earlsheaton W Yorks 88 B3
Earlsmill Moray 151 F12
Earlston Borders 121 F8
Earlston E Ayrs 118 F4
Earlswood Mon 36 E1
Earlswood Sur 28 E3
Earlswood Warks 51 B6
Earnley W Sus 16 E2
Earsairidh W Isles 148 J2
Earsdon T&W 111 B6
Earsham Norf 69 F6
Earswick York 96 D2
Eartham W Sus 16 D3
Easby N Yorks 101 D6
Easby N Yorks 102 D3
Easdale Argyll 124 D3
Easebourne W Sus 16 B2
Easenhall Warks 52 B2
Eashing Sur 27 E7
Easington Bucks 39 C6
Easington Durham 111 E7
Easington E Yorks 91 C7
Easington Northumb 123 F7
Easington Oxon 39 E6
Easington Oxon 52 F2
Easington Redcar 103 C5
Easington Colliery Durham 111 E7
Easington Lane T&W 111 E6
Easingwold N Yorks 95 C8
Easole Street Kent 31 D6
Eassie Angus 134 E3
East Aberthaw V Glam 22 C2
East Adderbury Oxon 52 F2
East Allington Devon 7 E5
East Anstey Devon 10 B3
East Appleton N Yorks 101 E7
East Ardsley W Yorks 88 B4
East Ashling W Sus 16 D2
East Auchronie Aberds 141 D7
East Ayton N Yorks 103 F7
East Bank Bl Gwent 35 D6
East Barkwith Lincs 91 F5
East Barming Kent 29 D8
East Barnby N Yorks 103 C6
East Barnet London 41 E5
East Barns E Loth 122 B3
East Barsham Norf 80 D5
East Beckham Norf 81 D7
East Bedfont London 27 B8
East Bergholt Suff 56 F4
East Bilney Norf 68 C2
East Blatchington E Sus 17 D8
East Boldre Hants 14 D4
East Brent Som 22 D5
East Bridgford Notts 77 E6
East Buckland Devon 21 F5
East Budleigh Devon 11 F5
East Burrafirth Shetland 160 H5
East Burton Dorset 13 F6
East Butsfield Durham 110 E4
East Butterwick N Lincs 90 D2
East Cairnbeg Aberds 135 B7
East Calder W Loth 120 C3
East Carleton Norf 68 D4
East Carlton Northants 64 F5
East Carlton W Yorks 94 E5
East Chaldon Dorset 13 F5
East Challow Oxon 38 F3
East Chiltington E Sus 17 C7
East Chinnock Som 12 C2
East Chisenbury Wilts 25 D6
East Clandon Sur 27 D8
East Claydon Bucks 39 B7
East Clyne Highld 157 J12
East Coker Som 12 C3
East Combe Som 22 F3
East Common N Yorks 96 F2
East Compton Som 23 E8
East Cottingwith E Yorks 96 E3
East Cowes IoW 15 E6
East Cowick E Yorks 89 B7
East Cowton N Yorks 101 D8
East Cramlington Northumb 111 B5
East Cranmore Som 23 E8
East Creech Dorset 13 F7
East Croachy Highld 138 B2
East Croftmore Highld 139 C5
East Curthwaite Cumb 108 E3
East Dean E Sus 18 F2
East Dean Hants 14 B3
East Dean W Sus 16 C3
East Down Devon 20 E5
East Drayton Notts 77 B7
East Ella Hull 90 B4
East End Dorset 13 E7
East End E Yorks 91 B6
East End Hants 14 E4
East End Hants 15 B7
East End Hants 26 C2
East End Herts 41 B7
East End Kent 18 B5
East End N Som 23 B6
East End Oxon 38 C3
East Farleigh Kent 29 D8
East Farndon Northants 64 F4
East Ferry Lincs 90 E2
East Fortune E Loth 121 B8
East Garston W Berks 25 B8
East Ginge Oxon 38 F4
East Goscote Leics 64 C3
East Grafton Wilts 25 C7
East Grimstead Wilts 14 B3
East Grinstead W Sus 28 F4
East Guldeford E Sus 19 C6
East Haddon Northants 52 C4
East Hagbourne Oxon 39 F5
East Halton N Lincs 90 C5
East Ham London 41 F7
East Hanney Oxon 38 E4
East Hanningfield Essex 42 D3
East Hardwick W Yorks 89 C5
East Harling Norf 68 F2
East Harlsey N Yorks 102 E2
East Harnham Wilts 14 B2
East Harptree Bath 23 D7
East Hartford Northumb 111 B5
East Harting W Sus 15 C8
East Hatley Cambs 54 D3
East Hauxwell N Yorks 101 E6
East Haven Angus 135 F5
East Heckington Lincs 78 E4
East Hedleyhope Durham 110 E4
East Hendred Oxon 38 F4
East Herrington T&W 111 D6
East Heslerton N Yorks 96 B5
East Hoathly E Sus 18 D2
East Horrington Som 23 E7
East Horsley Sur 27 D8
East Horton Northumb 123 F6
East Huntspill Som 22 E5
East Hyde C Beds 40 C4
East Ilkerton Devon 21 E6
East Ilsley W Berks 38 F4
East Keal Lincs 79 C6
East Kennett Wilts 25 C6
East Keswick W Yorks 95 E6
East Kilbride S Lanark 119 D6
East Kirkby Lincs 79 C6
East Knapton N Yorks 96 B4
East Knighton Dorset 13 F6
East Knoyle Wilts 24 F3
East Kyloe Northumb 123 F6
East Lambrook Som 12 C2
East Lamington Highld 151 D10
East Langdon Kent 31 E7
East Langton Leics 64 E4
East Langwell Highld 157 J10
East Lavant W Sus 16 D2
East Lavington W Sus 16 C3
East Layton N Yorks 101 D6
East Leake Notts 64 B2
East Learmouth Northumb 122 F4
East Leigh Devon 9 D8
East Lexham Norf 67 C8
East Lilburn Northumb 117 B6
East Linton E Loth 121 B8
East Liss Hants 15 B8
East Looe Corn 5 D7
East Lound N Lincs 89 E8
East Lulworth Dorset 13 F6
East Lutton N Yorks 96 C5
East Lydford Som 23 F7
East Mains Aberds 141 E5
East Malling Kent 29 D8
East March Angus 134 F4
East Marden W Sus 16 C2
East Markham Notts 77 B7
East Marton N Yorks 94 D2
East Meon Hants 15 B7
East Mere Devon 10 C4
East Mersea Essex 43 C6
East Mey Highld 158 C5
East Molesey Sur 28 C2
East Morden Dorset 13 E7
East Morton W Yorks 94 E3
East Ness N Yorks 96 B2
East Newton E Yorks 97 F8
East Norton Leics 64 D4
East Nynehead Som 11 B6
East Oakley Hants 26 D3
East Ogwell Devon 7 B6
East Orchard Dorset 13 C6
East Ord Northumb 123 D5
East Panson Devon 9 E5
East Peckham Kent 29 E7
East Pennard Som 23 F7
East Perry Cambs 54 C2
East Portlemouth Devon 6 F5
East Prawle Devon 7 F5
East Preston W Sus 16 D4
East Putford Devon 9 C5
East Quantoxhead Som 22 E3
East Rainton T&W 111 E6
East Ravendale NE Lincs 91 E6
East Raynham Norf 80 E4
East Rhidorroch Lodge Highld 150 B5
East Rigton W Yorks 95 E6
East Rounton N Yorks 102 D2
East Row N Yorks 103 C6
East Rudham Norf 80 E4
East Runton Norf 81 C7
East Ruston Norf 69 B6
East Saltoun E Loth 121 C7
East Sleekburn Northumb 117 F8
East Somerton Norf 69 C7
East Stockwith Lincs 89 E8
East Stoke Dorset 13 F6
East Stoke Notts 77 E7
East Stour Dorset 13 B6
East Stourmouth Kent 31 C6
East Stowford Devon 9 B8
East Stratton Hants 26 F3
East Studdal Kent 31 E7
East Suisnish Highld 149 E10
East Taphouse Corn 5 C6
East-the-Water Devon 9 B6
East Thirston Northumb 117 E7
East Tilbury Thurrock 29 B7
East Tisted Hants 26 F5
East Torrington Lincs 90 F5
East Tuddenham Norf 68 C3
East Tytherley Hants 14 B3
East Tytherton Wilts 24 B4
East Village Devon 10 D3
East Wall Shrops 60 E5
East Walton Norf 67 C7
East Wellow Hants 14 B4
East Wemyss Fife 128 E5
East Whitburn W Loth 120 C2
East Williamston Pembs 32 D1
East Winch Norf 67 C6
East Winterslow Wilts 25 F7
East Wittering W Sus 15 E8
East Witton N Yorks 101 F6
East Woodburn Northumb 116 F5
East Woodhay Hants 26 C2
East Worldham Hants 26 F5
East Worlington Devon 10 C2
East Worthing W Sus 17 D5
Eastbourne E Sus 18 F3
Eastbridge Suff 57 C8
Eastburn W Yorks 94 E3
Eastbury London 40 E3
Eastbury W Berks 25 B8
Eastby N Yorks 94 D3
Eastchurch Kent 30 B3
Eastcombe Glos 37 D5
Eastcote London 40 F4
Eastcote Northants 52 D4
Eastcote W Mid 51 B6
Eastcott Corn 8 C4
Eastcott Wilts 24 D5
Eastcourt Wilts 25 C7
Eastcourt Wilts 37 E6
Easter Ardross Highld 151 D9
Easter Balmoral Aberds 139 E8
Easter Boleskine Highld 137 B8
Easter Compton S Glos 36 F2
Easter Cringate Stirling 127 F6
Easter Davoch Aberds 140 D3
Easter Earshaig Dumfries 114 D3
Easter Fearn Highld 151 C9
Easter Galcantray Highld 151 G11
Easter Howgate Midloth 120 C5
Easter Howlaws Borders 122 E3
Easter Kinkell Highld 151 F8
Easter Lednathie Angus 134 C3
Easter Milton Highld 151 F12
Easter Moniack Highld 151 G8
Easter Ord Aberdeen 141 D7
Easter Quarff Shetland 160 K6
Easter Rhynd Perth 128 C3
Easter Row Stirling 127 E6
Easter Silverford Aberds 153 B7
Easter Skeld Shetland 160 J5
Easter Whyntie Aberds 152 B6
Eastergate W Sus 16 D3
Easterhouse Glasgow 119 C6
Eastern Green W Mid 63 F6
Easterton Wilts 24 D5
Eastertown Som 22 D5
Eastertown of Auchleuchries Aberds 153 E10
Eastfield N Lanark 119 C8
Eastfield N Yorks 103 F8
Eastfield Hall Northumb 117 D8
Eastgate Durham 110 F2
Eastgate Norf 81 E7
Eastham Mers 85 F4
Eastham Ferry Mers 85 F4
Easthampstead Brack 27 C6
Easthaugh Norf 68 C3
Eastheath Wokingham 27 C6
Easthope Shrops 61 E5
Easthorpe Essex 43 B5
Easthorpe Leics 77 F8
Easthorpe Notts 77 D7
Easthouses Midloth 121 C6
Eastington Devon 10 D2
Eastington Glos 36 D4
Eastington Glos 37 C8
Eastleach Martin Glos 38 D2
Eastleach Turville Glos 38 D1
Eastleigh Devon 9 B6
Eastleigh Hants 14 C5
Eastling Kent 30 D3
Eastmoor Derbys 76 B3
Eastmoor Norf 67 D7
Eastney Ptsmth 15 E7
Eastnor Hereford 50 F2
Eastoft N Lincs 90 C2
Eastoke Hants 15 E8
Easton Cambs 54 B2
Easton Cumb 108 B4
Easton Cumb 108 D2
Easton Devon 10 F2
Easton Dorset 12 G4
Easton Hants 26 F3
Easton Lincs 65 B6
Easton Norf 68 C4
Easton Som 23 E7
Easton Suff 57 D6
Easton Wilts 24 B3
Easton Grey Wilts 37 F5
Easton-in-Gordano N Som 23 B7
Easton Maudit Northants 53 D6
Easton on the Hill Northants 65 D7
Easton Royal Wilts 25 C7
Eastpark Dumfries 107 C7
Eastrea Cambs 66 E2
Eastriggs Dumfries 108 C2
Eastrington E Yorks 89 B8
Eastry Kent 31 D7
Eastville Bristol 23 B8
Eastville Lincs 79 D7
Eastwell Leics 64 B4
Eastwick Herts 41 C7
Eastwick Shetland 160 F5
Eastwood Notts 76 E4
Eastwood Southend 42 F4
Eastwood W Yorks 87 B7
Eathorpe Warks 51 C8
Eaton Ches E 75 C5
Eaton Ches W 74 C2
Eaton Leics 64 B4
Eaton Norf 68 D5
Eaton Notts 77 B7
Eaton Oxon 38 D4
Eaton Shrops 60 F3
Eaton Shrops 60 F5
Eaton Bishop Hereford 49 F6
Eaton Bray C Beds 40 B2
Eaton Constantine Shrops 61 D5
Eaton Green C Beds 40 B2
Eaton Hastings Oxon 38 E2
Eaton on Tern Shrops 61 B6
Eaton Socon Cambs 54 D2
Eavestone N Yorks 94 C5
Ebberston N Yorks 103 F6
Ebbesbourne Wake Wilts 13 B7
Ebbw Vale = Glyn Ebwy Bl Gwent 35 D5
Ebchester Durham 110 D4
Ebford Devon 10 F4
Ebley Glos 37 D5
Ebnal Ches W 73 E8
Ebrington Glos 51 E6
Ecchinswell Hants 26 D2
Ecclaw Borders 122 C3
Ecclefechan Dumfries 107 B8
Eccles Borders 122 E3
Eccles Gtr Man 87 E5
Eccles Kent 29 C8
Eccles on Sea Norf 69 B7
Eccles Road Norf 68 E3
Ecclesall S Yorks 88 F4
Ecclesfield S Yorks 88 E4
Ecclesgreig Aberds 135 C7
Eccleshall Staffs 62 B2
Eccleshill W Yorks 94 F4
Ecclesmachan W Loth 120 B3
Eccleston Ches W 73 C8
Eccleston Lancs 86 C3
Eccleston Mers 86 E2
Eccleston Park Mers 86 E2
Eccup W Yorks 95 E5
Echt Aberds 141 D6
Eckford Borders 116 B3
Eckington Derbys 76 B4
Eckington Worcs 50 E4
Ecton Northants 53 C6
Edale Derbys 88 F2
Edburton W Sus 17 C6
Edderside Cumb 107 E7
Edderton Highld 151 C10
Eddistone Devon 8 B4
Eddleston Borders 120 E5
Eden Park London 28 C4
Edenbridge Kent 28 E5
Edenfield Lancs 87 C5
Edenhall Cumb 109 F5
Edenham Lincs 65 B7
Edensor Derbys 76 C2
Edentaggart Argyll 126 E2
Edenthorpe S Yorks 89 D7
Edentown Cumb 108 D3
Ederline Argyll 124 E4
Edern Gwyn 70 D3
Edgarley Som 23 F7
Edgbaston W Mid 62 F4
Edgcott Bucks 39 B6
Edgcott Som 21 F7
Edge Shrops 60 D3
Edge End Glos 36 C2
Edge Green Ches W 73 D8
Edge Hill Mers 85 F4
Edgebolton Shrops 61 B5
Edgefield Norf 81 D6
Edgefield Street Norf 81 D6
Edgeside Lancs 87 B6
Edgeworth Glos 37 D6
Edgmond Telford 61 C7
Edgmond Marsh Telford 61 B7
Edgton Shrops 60 F3
Edgware London 40 E4
Edgworth Blackburn 86 C5
Edinample Stirling 126 B4
Edinbane Highld 149 C8
Edinburgh Edin 121 B5
Edingale Staffs 63 C6
Edingight Ho. Moray 152 C5
Edingley Notts 77 D6
Edingthorpe Norf 69 A6
Edingthorpe Green Norf 69 A6
Edington Som 23 F5
Edington Wilts 24 D4
Edintore Moray 152 D4
Edith Weston Rutland 65 D6
Edithmead Som 22 E5
Edlesborough Bucks 40 C2
Edlingham Northumb 117 D7
Edlington Lincs 78 B5
Edmondsham Dorset 13 C8
Edmondsley Durham 110 E5
Edmondthorpe Leics 65 C5
Edmonstone Orkney 159 F6
Edmonton London 41 E6
Edmundbyers Durham 110 D3
Ednam Borders 122 F3
Ednaston Derbys 76 E2
Edradynate Perth 133 D5
Edrom Borders 122 D4
Edstaston Shrops 74 F2
Edstone Warks 51 C6
Edvin Loach Hereford 49 D8
Edwalton Notts 77 F5
Edwardstone Suff 56 E3
Edwinsford Carms 46 F5
Edwinstowe Notts 77 C6
Edworth C Beds 54 E3
Edwyn Ralph Hereford 49 D8
Edzell Angus 135 C5
Efail Isaf Rhondda 34 F4
Efailnewydd Gwyn 70 D4
Efailwen Carms 32 B2
Efenechtyd Denb 72 D5
Effingham Sur 28 D2
Effirth Shetland 160 H5
Efford Devon 10 D3
Egdon Worcs 50 D4
Egerton Gtr Man 86 C5
Egerton Kent 30 E3
Egerton Forstal Kent 30 E2
Eggborough N Yorks 89 B6
Eggbuckland Plym 6 D3
Eggington C Beds 40 B2
Egginton Derbys 63 B6
Egglescliffe Stockton 102 C2
Eggleston Durham 100 B4
Egham Sur 27 B8
Egleton Rutland 65 D5
Eglingham Northumb 117 C7
Egloshayle Corn 4 B5
Egloskerry Corn 8 F4
Eglwys-Brewis V Glam 22 C2
Eglwys Cross Wrex 73 E8
Eglwys Fach Ceredig 58 E3
Eglwysbach Conwy 83 D8
Eglwyswen Pembs 45 F3
Eglwyswrw Pembs 45 F3
Egmanton Notts 77 C7
Egremont Cumb 98 C2
Egremont Mers 85 E4
Egton N Yorks 103 D6
Egton Bridge N Yorks 103 D6
Eight Ash Green Essex 43 B5
Eignaig Highld 130 E1
Eil Highld 138 C4
Eilanreach Highld 149 G13
Eilean Darach Highld 150 C4
Eileanach Lodge Highld 151 E8
Einacleite W Isles 154 E6
Eisgean W Isles 155 F8
Eisingrug Gwyn 71 D7
Elan Village Powys 47 C8
Elberton S Glos 36 F3
Elburton Plym 6 D3
Elcho Perth 128 B3
Elcombe Swindon 37 F8
Eldernell Cambs 66 E3
Eldersfield Worcs 50 F3
Elderslie Renfs 118 C4
Eldon Durham 101 B7
Eldrick S Ayrs 112 F2
Eldroth N Yorks 93 C7
Eldwick W Yorks 94 E4
Elfhowe Cumb 99 E6
Elford Northumb 123 F7
Elford Staffs 63 C5
Elgin Moray 152 B2
Elgol Highld 149 G10
Elham Kent 31 E5
Elie Fife 129 D6
Elim Anglesey 82 C3
Eling Hants 14 C4
Elishader Highld 149 B10
Elishaw Northumb 116 E4
Elkesley Notts 77 B6
Elkstone Glos 37 C6
Ellan Highld 138 B4
Elland W Yorks 88 B2
Ellary Argyll 144 F6
Ellastone Staffs 75 E8
Ellemford Borders 122 C3
Ellenbrook IoM 84 E3
Ellenhall Staffs 62 B2
Ellen's Green Sur 27 F8
Ellerbeck N Yorks 102 E2
Ellerburn N Yorks 103 F6
Ellerby N Yorks 103 C5
Ellerdine Heath Telford 61 B6
Ellerhayes Devon 10 D4
Elleric Argyll 130 E4
Ellerker E Yorks 90 B3
Ellerton E Yorks 96 F3
Ellerton Shrops 61 B7
Ellesborough Bucks 39 D8
Ellesmere Shrops 73 F8
Ellesmere Port Ches W 73 B8
Ellingham Norf 69 E6
Ellingham Northumb 117 B7
Ellingstring N Yorks 101 F6
Ellington Cambs 54 B2
Ellington Northumb 117 E8
Elliot Angus 135 F6
Ellisfield Hants 26 E4
Ellistown Leics 63 C8
Ellon Aberds 153 E9
Ellonby Cumb 108 F4
Ellough Suff 69 F7
Elloughton E Yorks 90 B3
Ellwood Glos 36 D2
Elm Cambs 66 D4
Elm Hill Dorset 13 B6
Elm Park London 41 F8
Elmbridge Worcs 50 C4
Elmdon Essex 55 F5
Elmdon W Mid 63 F5
Elmdon Heath W Mid 63 F5
Elmers End London 28 C4
Elmesthorpe Leics 63 E8
Elmfield IoW 15 E7
Elmhurst Staffs 62 C5
Elmley Castle Worcs 50 E4
Elmley Lovett Worcs 50 C3
Elmore Glos 36 C4
Elmore Back Glos 36 C4
Elmscott Devon 8 B4
Elmsett Suff 56 E4
Elmstead Market Essex 43 B6
Elmsted Kent 30 E5
Elmstone Kent 31 C6
Elmstone Hardwicke Glos 37 B6
Elmswell E Yorks 97 D5
Elmswell Suff 56 C3
Elmton Derbys 76 B5
Elphin Highld 156 H5
Elphinstone E Loth 121 B6
Elrick Aberds 141 D7
Elrig Dumfries 105 E7
Elsdon Northumb 117 E5
Elsecar S Yorks 88 E4
Elsenham Essex 41 B8
Elsfield Oxon 39 C5
Elsham N Lincs 90 C4
Elsing Norf 68 C3
Elslack N Yorks 94 E2
Elson Shrops 73 F7
Elsrickle S Lanark 120 E3
Elstead Sur 27 E7
Elsted W Sus 16 C2
Elsthorpe Lincs 65 B7
Elstob Durham 101 B8
Elston Notts 77 E7
Elston Wilts 25 E5
Elstone Devon 9 C8
Elstow Bedford 53 E8
Elstree Herts 40 E4
Elstronwick E Yorks 97 F8
Elswick Lancs 92 F4
Elsworth Cambs 54 C4
Elterwater Cumb 99 D5
Eltham London 28 B5
Eltisley Cambs 54 D3
Elton Cambs 65 E7
Elton Ches W 73 B8
Elton Derbys 76 C2
Elton Glos 36 C4
Elton Hereford 49 B6
Elton Notts 77 F7
Elton Stockton 102 C2
Elton Green Ches W 73 B8
Elvanfoot S Lanark 114 C2
Elvaston Derbys 76 F4
Elveden Suff 56 B2
Elvingston E Loth 121 B7
Elvington Kent 31 D6
Elvington York 96 E2
Elwick Hrtlpl 111 F7
Elwick Northumb 123 F7
Elworth Ches E 74 C4
Elworthy Som 22 F2
Ely Cambs 66 F5
Ely Cardiff 22 B3
Emberton M Keynes 53 E6
Embleton Cumb 107 F8
Embleton Northumb 117 B8
Embo Highld 151 B11
Embo Street Highld 151 B11
Emborough Som 23 D8
Embsay N Yorks 94 D3
Emery Down Hants 14 D3
Emersons Green S Glos 23 B8
Emley W Yorks 88 C3
Emmbrook Wokingham 27 C5
Emmer Green Reading 26 B5
Emmington Oxon 39 D7
Emneth Norf 66 D4
Emneth Hungate Norf 66 D5
Empingham Rutland 65 D6
Empshott Hants 27 F5
Emstrey Shrops 60 C5
Emsworth Hants 15 D8
Enborne W Berks 26 C2
Enchmarsh Shrops 60 E5
Enderby Leics 64 E2
Endmoor Cumb 99 F7
Endon Staffs 75 D6
Endon Bank Staffs 75 D6
Enfield London 41 E6
Enfield Wash London 41 E6
Enford Wilts 25 D6
Engamoor Shetland 160 H4
Engine Common S Glos 36 F3
Englefield W Berks 26 B4
Englefield Green Sur 27 B7
Englesea-brook Ches E 74 D4
English Bicknor Glos 36 C2
English Frankton Shrops 60 B4
Englishcombe Bath 24 C2
Enham Alamein Hants 25 E8
Enmore Som 22 F4
Ennerdale Bridge Cumb 98 C2
Enoch Dumfries 113 D8
Enochdhu Perth 133 C7
Ensay Argyll 146 G6
Ensbury Bmouth 13 E8
Ensdon Shrops 60 C4
Ensis Devon 9 B7
Enstone Oxon 38 B3
Enterkinfoot Dumfries 113 D8
Enterpen N Yorks 102 D2
Enville Staffs 62 F2
Eolaigearraidh W Isles 148 H2
Eorabus Argyll 146 J6
Eòropaidh W Isles 155 A10
Epperstone Notts 77 E6
Epping Essex 41 D7
Epping Green Essex 41 D7
Epping Green Herts 41 D5
Epping Upland Essex 41 D7
Eppleby N Yorks 101 C6
Eppleworth E Yorks 97 F6
Epsom Sur 28 C3
Epwell Oxon 51 E8
Epworth N Lincs 89 D8
Epworth Turbary N Lincs 89 D8
Erbistock Wrex 73 E7
Erbusaig Highld 149 F12
Erchless Castle Highld 150 G7
Erdington W Mid 62 E5
Eredine Argyll 125 E5
Eriboll Highld 156 D7
Ericstane Dumfries 114 C3
Eridge Green E Sus 18 B2
Erines Argyll 145 F7
Eriswell Suff 55 B8
Erith London 29 B6
Erlestoke Wilts 24 D4
Ermine Lincs 78 B2
Ermington Devon 6 D4
Erpingham Norf 81 D7
Errogie Highld 137 B8
Errol Perth 128 B4
Erskine Renfs 118 B4
Erskine Bridge Renfs 118 B4
Ervie Dumfries 104 C4
Erwarton Suff 57 F6
Erwood Powys 48 E2
Eryholme N Yorks 101 D8
Eryrys Denb 73 D6
Escomb Durham 101 B6
Escrick N Yorks 96 E2
Esgairdawe Carms 46 E5
Esgairgeiliog Powys 58 D4
Esh Durham 110 E4
Esh Winning Durham 110 E4
Esher Sur 28 C2
Esholt W Yorks 94 E4
Eshott Northumb 117 E8
Eshton N Yorks 94 D2
Esk Valley N Yorks 103 D6
Eskadale Highld 150 H7
Eskbank Midloth 121 C6
Eskdale Green Cumb 98 D3
Eskdalemuir Dumfries 115 E5
Eske E Yorks 97 E6
Eskham Lincs 91 E7
Esprick Lancs 92 F4
Essendine Rutland 65 C7
Essendon Herts 41 D5
Essich Highld 151 H9
Essington Staffs 62 D3
Esslemont Aberds 141 B8
Eston Redcar 102 C3
Eswick Shetland 160 H6
Etal Northumb 122 F5
Etchilhampton Wilts 24 C5
Etchingham E Sus 18 C4
Etchinghill Kent 19 B8
Etchinghill Staffs 62 C4
Ethie Castle Angus 135 E6
Ethie Mains Angus 135 E6
Etling Green Norf 68 C3
Eton Windsor 27 B7
Eton Wick Windsor 27 B7
Etteridge Highld 138 E2
Ettersgill Durham 100 B3
Ettingshall W Mid 62 E3
Ettington Warks 51 E7
Etton E Yorks 97 E5
Etton Pboro 65 D8
Ettrick Borders 115 C5
Ettrickbridge Borders 115 B6
Ettrickhill Borders 115 C5
Etwall Derbys 76 F2
Euston Suff 56 B2
Euximoor Drove Cambs 66 E4
Euxton Lancs 86 C3
Evanstown Bridgend 34 F3
Evanton Highld 151 E9
Evedon Lincs 78 E3
Evelix Highld 151 B10
Evenjobb Powys 48 C4
Evenley Northants 52 F3
Evenlode Glos 38 B2
Evenwood Durham 101 B6
Evenwood Gate Durham 101 B6
Everbay Orkney 159 F7
Evercreech Som 23 F8
Everdon Northants 52 D3
Everingham E Yorks 96 E4
Everleigh Wilts 25 D7
Everley N Yorks 103 F7
Eversholt C Beds 53 F7
Evershot Dorset 12 D3
Eversley Hants 27 C5
Eversley Cross Hants 27 C5
Everthorpe E Yorks 96 F5
Everton C Beds 54 D3
Everton Hants 14 E3
Everton Mers 85 E4
Everton Notts 89 E7
Evertown Dumfries 108 B3
Evesbatch Hereford 49 E8
Evesham Worcs 50 E5
Evington Leicester 64 D3
Ewden Village S Yorks 88 E3
Ewell Sur 28 C3
Ewell Minnis Kent 31 E6
Ewelme Oxon 39 E6
Ewen Glos 37 E7
Ewenny V Glam 21 B8
Ewerby Lincs 78 E3
Ewerby Thorpe Lincs 78 E4
Ewes Dumfries 115 E6
Ewesley Northumb 117 E6
Ewhurst Sur 27 E8
Ewhurst Green E Sus 18 C4
Ewhurst Green Sur 27 F8
Ewloe Flint 73 C7
Ewloe Green Flint 73 C6
Ewood Blackburn 86 B4
Eworthy Devon 9 E6
Ewshot Hants 27 E6
Ewyas Harold Hereford 35 B7
Exbourne Devon 9 D8
Exbury Hants 14 E5
Exebridge Devon 10 B4
Exelby N Yorks 101 F7
Exeter Devon 10 E4
Exford Som 21 F7
Exhall Warks 51 D6
Exley Head W Yorks 94 F3
Exminster Devon 10 F4
Exmouth Devon 10 F5
Exnaboe Shetland 160 M5
Exning Suff 55 C7
Exton Devon 10 F4
Exton Hants 15 B7
Exton Rutland 65 C6
Exton Som 21 F8
Exwick Devon 10 E4
Eyam Derbys 76 B2
Eydon Northants 52 D3
Eye Hereford 49 C6
Eye Pboro 66 D2
Eye Suff 56 B5
Eye Green Pboro 66 D2
Eyemouth Borders 122 C5
Eyeworth C Beds 54 E3
Eyhorne Street Kent 30 D2
Eyke Suff 57 D7
Eynesbury Cambs 54 D2
Eynort Highld 149 F8
Eynsford Kent 29 C6
Eynsham Oxon 38 D4
Eype Dorset 12 E2
Eyre Highld 149 C9
Eyre Highld 149 E10
Eythorne Kent 31 E6
Eyton Hereford 49 C6
Eyton Shrops 60 F3
Eyton Wrex 73 E7
Eyton upon the Weald Moors Telford 61 C6

F

Faccombe Hants 25 D8
Faceby N Yorks 102 D2
Facit Lancs 87 C6
Faddiley Ches E 74 D2
Fadmoor N Yorks 102 F4
Faerdre Swansea 33 D7
Failand N Som 23 B7
Failford S Ayrs 112 B4
Failsworth Gtr Man 87 D6
Fain Highld 150 D4
Fair Green Norf 67 C6
Fair Hill Cumb 108 F5
Fair Oak Hants 15 C5
Fair Oak Green Hants 26 C4
Fairbourne Gwyn 58 C3
Fairburn N Yorks 89 B5
Fairfield Derbys 75 B7
Fairfield Stockton 102 C2
Fairfield Worcs 50 B4
Fairfield Worcs 50 E5
Fairford Glos 38 D1
Fairhaven Lancs 85 B4
Fairlie N Ayrs 118 D2
Fairlight E Sus 19 D5
Fairlight Cove E Sus 19 D5
Fairmile Devon 11 E5
Fairmilehead Edin 120 C5
Fairoak Staffs 74 F4
Fairseat Kent 29 C7
Fairstead Essex 42 C3
Fairstead Norf 67 C6
Fairwarp E Sus 17 B8
Fairy Cottage IoM 84 D4
Fairy Cross Devon 9 B6
Fakenham Norf 80 E5
Fakenham Magna Suff 56 B3
Fala Midloth 121 C7
Fala Dam Midloth 121 C7
Falahill Borders 121 D6
Falcon Hereford 49 F8
Faldingworth Lincs 90 F4
Falfield S Glos 36 E3
Falkenham Suff 57 F6
Falkirk Falk 119 B8
Falkland Fife 128 D4
Falla Borders 116 C3
Fallgate Derbys 76 C3
Fallin Stirling 127 E7
Fallowfield Gtr Man 87 E6
Fallsidehill Borders 122 E2
Falmer E Sus 17 D7
Falmouth Corn 3 C7
Falsgrave N Yorks 103 F8
Falstone Northumb 116 F3
Fanagmore Highld 156 E4
Fangdale Beck N Yorks 102 E3
Fangfoss E Yorks 96 D3
Fankerton Falk 127 F6
Fanmore Argyll 146 G7
Fannich Lodge Highld 150 E5
Fans Borders 122 E2
Far Bank S Yorks 89 C7
Far Bletchley M Keynes 53 F6
Far Cotton Northants 52 D5
Far Forest Worcs 50 B2
Far Laund Derbys 76 E3
Far Sawrey Cumb 99 E5
Farcet Cambs 66 E2
Farden Shrops 49 B7
Fareham Hants 15 D6
Farewell Staffs 62 C4
Farforth Lincs 79 B6
Faringdon Oxon 38 E2
Farington Lancs 86 B3
Farlam Cumb 109 D5
Farlary Highld 157 J10
Farleigh N Som 23 C6
Farleigh Sur 28 C4
Farleigh Hungerford Som 24 D3
Farleigh Wallop Hants 26 E4
Farlesthorpe Lincs 79 B7
Farleton Cumb 99 F7
Farleton Lancs 93 C5
Farley Shrops 60 D3
Farley Staffs 75 E7
Farley Wilts 14 B3
Farley Green Sur 27 E8
Farley Hill Luton 40 B3
Farley Hill Wokingham 26 C5
Farleys End Glos 36 C4
Farlington N Yorks 96 C2
Farlow Shrops 61 F6
Farmborough Bath 23 C8
Farmcote Glos 37 B7
Farmcote Shrops 61 E7
Farmington Glos 37 C8
Farmoor Oxon 38 D4
Farmtown Moray 152 C5
Farnborough Hants 27 D6
Farnborough London 28 C5
Farnborough W Berks 38 F4
Farnborough Warks 52 E2
Farnborough Green Hants 27 D6
Farncombe Sur 27 E7
Farndish Bedford 53 C7
Farndon Ches W 73 D8
Farndon Notts 77 D7
Farnell Angus 135 D6
Farnham Dorset 13 C7
Farnham Essex 41 B7
Farnham N Yorks 95 C6
Farnham Suff 57 C7
Farnham Sur 27 E6
Farnham Common Bucks 40 F2
Farnham Green Essex 41 B7
Farnham Royal Bucks 40 F2
Farnhill N Yorks 94 E3
Farningham Kent 29 C6
Farnley N Yorks 94 E5
Farnley W Yorks 95 F5
Farnley Tyas W Yorks 88 C2
Farnsfield Notts 77 D6
Farnworth Gtr Man 86 D5
Farnworth Halton 86 F3
Farr Highld 138 D4
Farr Highld 151 H9
Farr Highld 157 C10
Farr House Highld 151 H9
Farringdon Devon 10 E5
Farrington Gurney Bath 23 D8
Farsley W Yorks 94 F5
Farthinghoe Northants 52 F3
Farthingloe Kent 31 E6
Farthingstone Northants 52 D4
Fartown W Yorks 88 C2
Farway Devon 11 E6
Fasag Highld 149 C13
Fascadale Highld 147 D8
Faslane Port Argyll 145 E11
Fasnacloich Argyll 130 E4
Fasnakyle Ho Highld 137 B6
Fassfern Highld 130 B4
Fatfield T&W 111 D6
Fattahead Aberds 153 C6
Faugh Cumb 108 D5
Fauldhouse W Loth 120 C2
Faulkbourne Essex 42 C3
Faulkland Som 24 D2
Fauls Shrops 74 F2
Faversham Kent 30 C4
Favillar Moray 152 E2
Fawdington N Yorks 95 B7
Fawfieldhead Staffs 75 C7
Fawkham Green Kent 29 C6
Fawler Oxon 38 C3
Fawley Bucks 39 F7
Fawley Hants 15 D5
Fawley W Berks 38 F3
Fawley Chapel Hereford 36 B2
Faxfleet E Yorks 90 B2
Faygate W Sus 28 F3
Fazakerley Mers 85 E4
Fazeley Staffs 63 D6
Fearby N Yorks 101 F6
Fearn Highld 151 D11
Fearn Lodge Highld 151 C9
Fearn Station Highld 151 D11
Fearnan Perth 132 E4
Fearnbeg Highld 149 C12
Fearnhead Warr 86 E4
Fearnmore Highld 149 B12
Featherstone Staffs 62 D3
Featherstone W Yorks 88 B5
Featherwood Northumb 116 D4
Feckenham Worcs 50 C5
Feering Essex 42 B4
Feetham N Yorks 100 E4
Feizor N Yorks 93 C7
Felbridge Sur 28 F4
Felbrigg Norf 81 D8
Felcourt Sur 28 E4
Felden Herts 40 D3
Felin-Crai Powys 34 B2
Felindre Carms 33 B6
Felindre Carms 33 B8
Felindre Carms 46 F2
Felindre Carms 47 F5
Felindre Ceredig 46 D4
Felindre Powys 59 F8
Felindre Swansea 33 D7
Felindre Farchog Pembs 45 F3
Felinfach Ceredig 46 D4
Felinfach Powys 48 F2
Felinfoel Carms 33 D6
Felingwm isaf Carms 33 B6

Felingwm uchaf Carms 33 B6
Felinwynt Ceredig 45 D4
Felixkirk N Yorks 102 F2
Felixstowe Suff 57 F6
Felixstowe Ferry Suff 57 F7
Felkington Northumb 122 E5
Felkirk W Yorks 88 C4
Fell Side Cumb 108 F3
Felling T&W 111 C5
Felmersham Bedford 53 D7
Felmingham Norf 81 E8
Felpham W Sus 16 E3
Felsham Suff 56 D3
Felsted Essex 42 B2
Feltham London 28 B2
Felthorpe Norf 68 C4
Felton Hereford 49 E7
Felton N Som 23 C7
Felton Northumb 117 D7
Felton Butler Shrops 60 C3
Feltwell Norf 67 E7
Fen Ditton Cambs 55 C5
Fen Drayton Cambs 54 C4
Fen End W Mid 51 B7
Fen Side Lincs 79 D6
Fenay Bridge W Yorks 88 C2
Fence Lancs 93 F8
Fence Houses T&W 111 D6
Fengate Norf 81 E7
Fengate Pboro 66 E2
Fenham Northumb 123 E6
Fenhouses Lincs 79 E5
Feniscliffe Blackburn 86 B4
Feniscowles Blackburn 86 B4
Feniton Devon 11 E6
Fenlake Bedford 53 E8
Fenny Bentley Derbys 75 D8
Fenny Bridges Devon 11 E6
Fenny Compton Warks 52 D2
Fenny Drayton Leics 63 E7
Fenny Stratford M Keynes 53 F6
Fenrother Northumb 117 E7
Fenstanton Cambs 54 C4
Fenton Cambs 54 B4
Fenton Lincs 77 B8
Fenton Lincs 77 D8
Fenton Stoke 75 E5
Fenton Barns E Loth 129 F7
Fenton Town Northumb 123 F5
Fenwick E Ayrs 118 E4
Fenwick Northumb 110 B3
Fenwick Northumb 123 E6
Fenwick S Yorks 89 C6
Feochaig Argyll 143 G8
Feock Corn 3 C7
Feolin Ferry Argyll 144 G3
Ferindonald Highld 149 H11
Feriniquarrie Highld 148 C6
Ferlochan Argyll 130 E3
Fern Angus 134 C4
Ferndale Rhondda 34 E4
Ferndown Dorset 13 D8
Ferness Highld 151 G12
Ferney Green Cumb 99 E6
Fernham Oxon 38 E2
Fernhill Heath Worcs 50 D3
Fernhurst W Sus 16 B2
Fernie Fife 128 C5
Ferniegair S Lanark 119 D7
Fernilea Highld 149 E8
Fernilee Derbys 75 B7
Ferrensby N Yorks 95 C6
Ferring W Sus 16 D4
Ferry Hill Cambs 66 F3
Ferry Point Highld 151 C10
Ferrybridge W Yorks 89 B5
Ferryden Angus 135 D7
Ferryhill Aberdeen 141 D8
Ferryhill Durham 111 F5
Ferryhill Station Durham 111 F6
Ferryside Carms 32 C4
Fersfield Norf 68 F3
Fersit Highld 131 B7
Ferwig Ceredig 45 E3
Feshiebridge Highld 138 D4
Fetcham Sur 28 D2
Fetterangus Aberds 153 C9
Fettercairn Aberds 135 B6
Fettes Highld 151 F8
Fewcott Oxon 39 B5
Fewston N Yorks 94 D4
Ffair-Rhos Ceredig 47 C6
Ffairfach Carms 33 B7
Ffaldybrenin Carms 46 E5
Ffarmers Carms 47 E5
Ffawyddog Powys 35 C6
Fforest Carms 33 D6
Fforest-fâch Swansea 33 E7
Ffos-y-ffin Ceredig 46 C3
Ffostrasol Ceredig 46 E2
Ffridd-Uchaf Gwyn 83 F5
Ffrith Wrex 73 D6
Ffrwd Gwyn 82 F4
Ffynnon ddrain Carms 33 B5
Ffynnon-oer Ceredig 46 D4
Ffynnongroyw Flint 85 F2
Fidden Argyll 146 J6
Fiddes Aberds 141 F7
Fiddington Glos 50 F4
Fiddington Som 22 E4
Fiddleford Dorset 13 C6
Fiddlers Hamlet Essex 41 D7
Field Staffs 75 F7
Field Broughton Cumb 99 F5
Field Dalling Norf 81 D6
Field Head Leics 63 D8
Fifehead Magdalen Dorset 13 B5
Fifehead Neville Dorset 13 C5
Fifield Oxon 38 C2
Fifield Wilts 25 D6
Fifield Windsor 27 B7
Fifield Bavant Wilts 13 B8
Figheldean Wilts 25 E6
Filands Wilts 37 F6
Filby Norf 69 C7
Filey N Yorks 97 A7
Filgrave M Keynes 53 E6
Filkins Oxon 38 D2
Filleigh Devon 9 B8
Filleigh Devon 10 C2
Fillingham Lincs 90 F3
Fillongley Warks 63 F6
Filton S Glos 23 B8
Fimber E Yorks 96 C4
Finavon Angus 134 D4
Finchairn Argyll 124 E5
Fincham Norf 67 D6
Finchampstead Wokingham 27 C5
Finchdean Hants 15 C8
Finchingfield Essex 55 F7
Finchley London 41 E5
Findern Derbys 76 F3
Findhorn Moray 151 E13
Findhorn Bridge Highld 138 B4
Findo Gask Perth 128 B2
Findochty Moray 152 B4
Findon Aberds 141 E8
Findon W Sus 16 D5
Findon Mains Highld 151 E9
Findrack Ho. Aberds 140 D5
Finedon Northants 53 B7
Fingal Street Suff 57 C6
Fingask Aberds 141 B6
Fingerpost Worcs 50 B2
Fingest Bucks 39 E7
Finghall N Yorks 101 F6
Fingland Cumb 108 D2
Fingland Dumfries 113 C7
Finglesham Kent 31 D7
Fingringhoe Essex 43 B6
Finlarig Stirling 132 F2
Finmere Oxon 52 F4
Finnart Perth 132 D2
Finningham Suff 56 C4
Finningley S Yorks 89 E7
Finnygaud Aberds 152 C5
Finsbury London 41 F6
Finstall Worcs 50 C4
Finsthwaite Cumb 99 F5
Finstock Oxon 38 C3
Finstown Orkney 159 G4
Fintry Aberds 153 C7
Fintry Dundee 134 F4
Fintry Stirling 126 F5
Finzean Aberds 140 E5
Fionnphort Argyll 146 J6
Fionnsbhagh W Isles 154 J5
Fir Tree Durham 110 F4
Firbeck S Yorks 89 F6
Firby N Yorks 96 C3
Firby N Yorks 101 F7
Firgrove Gtr Man 87 C7
Firsby Lincs 79 C7
Firsdown Wilts 25 F7
First Coast Highld 150 B2
Fishbourne IoW 15 E6
Fishbourne W Sus 16 D2
Fishburn Durham 111 F6
Fishcross Clack 127 E7
Fisher Place Cumb 99 C5
Fisherford Aberds 153 E6
Fisher's Pond Hants 15 B5
Fisherstreet W Sus 27 F7
Fisherton Highld 151 F10
Fisherton S Ayrs 112 C2
Fishguard = Abergwaun Pembs 44 B4
Fishlake S Yorks 89 C7
Fishleigh Barton Devon 9 B7
Fishponds Bristol 23 B8
Fishpool Glos 36 B3
Fishtoft Lincs 79 E6
Fishtoft Drove Lincs 79 E6
Fishtown of Usan Angus 135 D7
Fishwick Borders 122 D5
Fiskavaig Highld 149 E8
Fiskerton Lincs 78 B3
Fiskerton Notts 77 D7
Fitling E Yorks 97 F8
Fittleton Wilts 25 E6
Fittleworth W Sus 16 C4
Fitton End Cambs 66 C4
Fitz Shrops 60 C4
Fitzhead Som 11 B6
Fitzwilliam W Yorks 88 C5
Fiunary Highld 147 G9
Five Acres Glos 36 C2
Five Ashes E Sus 18 C2
Five Oak Green Kent 29 E7
Five Oaks Jersey 17
Five Oaks W Sus 16 B4
Five Roads Carms 33 D5
Fivecrosses Ches W 74 B2
Fivehead Som 11 B8
Flack's Green Essex 42 C3
Flackwell Heath Bucks 40 F1
Fladbury Worcs 50 E4
Fladdabister Shetland 160 K6
Flagg Derbys 75 C8
Flamborough E Yorks 97 B8
Flamstead Herts 40 C3
Flamstead End Herts 41 D6
Flansham W Sus 16 D3
Flanshaw W Yorks 88 B4
Flasby N Yorks 94 D2
Flash Staffs 75 C7
Flashader Highld 149 C8
Flask Inn N Yorks 103 D7
Flaunden Herts 40 D3
Flawborough Notts 77 E7
Flawith N Yorks 95 C7
Flax Bourton N Som 23 C7
Flaxby N Yorks 95 D6
Flaxholme Derbys 76 E3
Flaxley Glos 36 C3
Flaxpool Som 22 F3
Flaxton N Yorks 96 C2
Fleckney Leics 64 E3
Flecknoe Warks 52 C3
Fledborough Notts 77 B8
Fleet Hants 15 D8
Fleet Hants 27 D6
Fleet Lincs 66 B3
Fleet Hargate Lincs 66 B3
Fleetham Northumb 117 B7
Fleetlands Hants 15 D6
Fleetville Herts 40 D4
Fleetwood Lancs 92 E3
Flemingston V Glam 22 B2
Flemington S Lanark 119 D6
Flempton Suff 56 C2
Fleoideabhagh W Isles 154 J5
Fletchertown Cumb 108 E2
Fletching E Sus 17 B8
Flexbury Corn 8 D4
Flexford Sur 27 E7
Flimby Cumb 107 F7
Flimwell E Sus 18 B4
Flint = Y Fflint Flint 73 B6
Flint Mountain Flint 73 B6
Flintham Notts 77 E7
Flinton E Yorks 97 F8
Flintsham Hereford 48 D5
Flitcham Norf 80 E3
Flitton C Beds 53 F8
Flitwick C Beds 53 F8
Flixborough N Lincs 90 C2
Flixborough Stather N Lincs 90 C2
Flixton Gtr Man 86 E5
Flixton N Yorks 97 B6
Flixton Suff 69 F6
Flockton W Yorks 88 C3
Flodaigh W Isles 148 C3
Flodden Northumb 122 F5
Flodigarry Highld 149 A9
Flood's Ferry Cambs 66 E3
Flookburgh Cumb 92 B3
Florden Norf 68 E4
Flore Northants 52 C4
Flotterton Northumb 117 D5
Flowton Suff 56 E4
Flush House W Yorks 88 D2
Flushing Aberds 153 D10
Flushing Corn 3 C7
Flyford Flavell Worcs 50 D4
Foals Green Suff 57 B6
Fobbing Thurrock 42 F3
Fochabers Moray 152 C3
Fochriw Caerph 35 D5
Fockerby N Lincs 90 C2
Fodderletter Moray 139 B7
Fodderty Highld 151 F8
Foel Powys 59 C6
Foel-gastell Carms 33 C6
Foffarty Angus 134 E4
Foggathorpe E Yorks 96 F3
Fogo Borders 122 E3
Fogorig Borders 122 E3
Foindle Highld 156 E4
Folda Angus 134 C1
Fole Staffs 75 F7
Foleshill W Mid 63 F7
Folke Dorset 12 C4
Folkestone Kent 31 F6
Folkingham Lincs 78 F3
Folkington E Sus 18 E2
Folksworth Cambs 65 F8
Folkton N Yorks 97 B6
Folla Rule Aberds 153 E7
Follifoot N Yorks 95 D6
Folly Gate Devon 9 E7
Fonthill Bishop Wilts 24 F4
Fonthill Gifford Wilts 24 F4
Fontmell Magna Dorset 13 C6
Fontwell W Sus 16 D3
Foolow Derbys 75 B8
Foots Cray London 29 B5
Forbestown Aberds 140 C2
Force Mills Cumb 99 E5
Forcett N Yorks 101 C6
Ford Argyll 124 E4
Ford Bucks 39 D7
Ford Devon 9 B6
Ford Glos 37 B7
Ford Northumb 122 F5
Ford Shrops 60 C4
Ford Staffs 75 D7
Ford W Sus 16 D3
Ford Wilts 24 B3
Ford End Essex 42 C2
Ford Street Som 11 C6
Fordcombe Kent 29 E6
Fordell Fife 128 F3
Forden Powys 60 D2
Forder Green Devon 7 C5
Fordham Cambs 55 B7
Fordham Essex 43 B5
Fordham Norf 67 E6
Fordhouses W Mid 62 D3
Fordingbridge Hants 14 C2
Fordon E Yorks 97 B6
Fordoun Aberds 135 B7
Ford's Green Suff 56 C4
Fordstreet Essex 43 B5
Fordwells Oxon 38 C3
Fordwich Kent 31 D5
Fordyce Aberds 152 B5
Forebridge Staffs 62 B3
Forest Durham 109 F8
Forest Becks Lancs 93 D7
Forest Gate London 41 F7
Forest Green Sur 28 E2
Forest Hall Cumb 99 D7
Forest Head Cumb 109 D5
Forest Hill Oxon 39 D5
Forest Lane Head N Yorks 95 D6
Forest Lodge Argyll 131 E6
Forest Lodge Highld 139 C6
Forest Lodge Perth 133 B6
Forest Mill Clack 127 E8
Forest Row E Sus 28 F5
Forest Town Notts 77 C5
Forestburn Gate Northumb 117 E6
Foresterseat Moray 152 C1
Forestside W Sus 15 C8
Forfar Angus 134 D4
Forgandenny Perth 128 C2
Forge Powys 58 E4
Forge Side Torf 35 D6
Forgewood N Lanark 119 D7
Forgie Moray 152 C3
Forglen Ho. Aberds 153 C6
Formby Mers 85 D4
Forncett End Norf 68 E4
Forncett St Mary Norf 68 E4
Forncett St Peter Norf 68 E4
Forneth Perth 133 E7
Fornham All Saints Suff 56 C2
Fornham St Martin Suff 56 C2
Forres Moray 151 F13
Forrest Lodge Dumfries 113 F5
Forrestfield N Lanark 119 C8
Forsbrook Staffs 75 E6
Forse Highld 158 G4
Forse Ho. Highld 158 G4
Forsinain Highld 157 E12
Forsinard Highld 157 E11
Forsinard Station Highld 157 E11
Forston Dorset 12 E4
Fort Augustus Highld 137 D6
Fort George Guern 16
Fort George Highld 151 F10
Fort William Highld 131 B5
Forteviot Perth 128 C2
Forth S Lanark 120 D2
Forth Road Bridge Edin 120 B4
Forthampton Glos 50 F3
Fortingall Perth 132 E4
Forton Hants 26 E2
Forton Lancs 92 D4
Forton Shrops 60 C4
Forton Som 11 D8
Forton Staffs 61 B7
Forton Heath Shrops 60 C4
Fortrie Aberds 153 D6
Fortrose Highld 151 F10
Fortuneswell Dorset 12 G4
Forty Green Bucks 40 E2
Forty Hill London 41 E6
Forward Green Suff 56 D4
Fosbury Wilts 25 D8
Fosdyke Lincs 79 F6
Foss Perth 132 D4
Foss Cross Glos 37 D7
Fossebridge Glos 37 C7
Foster Street Essex 41 D7
Fosterhouses S Yorks 89 C7
Foston Derbys 75 F8
Foston Lincs 77 E8
Foston N Yorks 96 C2
Foston on the Wolds E Yorks 97 D7
Fotherby Lincs 91 E7
Fotheringhay Northants 65 E7
Foubister Orkney 159 H6
Foul Mile E Sus 18 D3
Foulby W Yorks 88 C4
Foulden Borders 122 D5
Foulden Norf 67 E7
Foulis Castle Highld 151 E8
Foulridge Lancs 93 E8
Foulsham Norf 81 E6
Fountainhall Borders 121 E7
Four Ashes Staffs 62 F2
Four Ashes Suff 56 B4
Four Crosses Powys 59 D7
Four Crosses Powys 60 C2
Four Crosses Wrex 73 D6
Four Elms Kent 29 E5
Four Forks Som 22 F4
Four Gotes Cambs 66 C4
Four Lane Ends Ches W 74 C2
Four Lanes Corn 3 C5
Four Marks Hants 26 F4
Four Mile Bridge Anglesey 82 D2
Four Oaks E Sus 19 C5
Four Oaks W Mid 62 E5
Four Oaks W Mid 63 F6
Four Roads Carms 33 D5
Four Roads IoM 84 F2
Four Throws Kent 18 C4
Fourlane Ends Derbys 76 D3
Fourlanes End Ches E 74 D5
Fourpenny Highld 151 B11
Fourstones Northumb 109 C8
Fovant Wilts 13 B8
Foveran Aberds 141 B8
Fowey Corn 5 D6
Fowley Common Warr 86 E4
Fowlis Angus 134 F3
Fowlis Wester Perth 127 B8
Fowlmere Cambs 54 E5
Fownhope Hereford 49 F7
Fox Corner Sur 27 D7
Fox Lane Hants 27 D6
Fox Street Essex 43 B6
Foxbar Renfs 118 C4
Foxcombe Hill Oxon 38 D4
Foxdale IoM 84 E2
Foxearth Essex 56 E2
Foxfield Cumb 98 F4
Foxham Wilts 24 B4
Foxhole Corn 4 D4
Foxhole Swansea 33 E7
Foxholes N Yorks 97 B6
Foxhunt Green E Sus 18 D2
Foxley Norf 81 E6
Foxley Wilts 37 F5
Foxt Staffs 75 E7
Foxton Cambs 54 E5
Foxton Durham 102 B1
Foxton Leics 64 E4
Foxup N Yorks 93 B8
Foxwist Green Ches W 74 C3
Foxwood Shrops 49 B8
Foy Hereford 36 B2
Foyers Highld 137 B7
Fraddam Corn 2 C4
Fraddon Corn 4 D4
Fradley Staffs 63 C5
Fradswell Staffs 75 F6
Fraisthorpe E Yorks 97 C7
Framfield E Sus 17 B8
Framingham Earl Norf 69 D5
Framingham Pigot Norf 69 D5
Framlingham Suff 57 C6
Frampton Dorset 12 E4
Frampton Lincs 79 F6
Frampton Cotterell S Glos 36 F3
Frampton Mansell Glos 37 D6
Frampton on Severn Glos 36 D4
Frampton West End Lincs 79 E5
Framsden Suff 57 D5
Framwellgate Moor Durham 111 E5
Franche Worcs 50 B3
Frankby Mers 85 F3
Frankley Worcs 62 F3
Frank's Bridge Powys 48 D3
Frankton Warks 52 B2
Frant E Sus 18 B2
Fraserburgh Aberds 153 B9
Frating Green Essex 43 B6
Fratton Ptsmth 15 E7
Freathy Corn 5 D8
Freckenham Suff 55 B7
Freckleton Lancs 86 B2
Freeby Leics 64 B5
Freehay Staffs 75 E7
Freeland Oxon 38 C4
Freester Shetland 160 H6
Freethorpe Norf 69 D7
Freiston Lincs 79 E6
Fremington Devon 20 F4
Fremington N Yorks 101 E5
Frenchay S Glos 23 B8
Frenchbeer Devon 9 F8
Frenich Stirling 126 D3
Frensham Sur 27 E6
Fresgoe Highld 157 C12
Freshfield Mers 85 D3
Freshford Bath 24 C2
Freshwater IoW 14 F4
Freshwater Bay IoW 14 F4
Freshwater East Pembs 32 E1
Fressingfield Suff 57 B6
Freston Suff 57 F5
Freswick Highld 158 D5
Fretherne Glos 36 D4
Frettenham Norf 68 C5
Freuchie Fife 128 D4
Freuchies Angus 134 C2
Freystrop Pembs 44 D4
Friar's Gate E Sus 29 F5
Friarton Perth 128 B3
Friday Bridge Cambs 66 D4
Friday Street E Sus 18 E3
Fridaythorpe E Yorks 96 D4
Friern Barnet London 41 E5
Friesland Argyll 146 F4
Friesthorpe Lincs 90 F4
Frieston Lincs 78 E2
Frieth Bucks 39 E7
Frilford Oxon 38 E4
Frilsham W Berks 26 B3
Frimley Sur 27 D6
Frimley Green Sur 27 D6
Frindsbury Medway 29 B8
Fring Norf 80 D3
Fringford Oxon 39 B6
Frinsted Kent 30 D2
Frinton-on-Sea Essex 43 B8
Friockheim Angus 135 E5
Friog Gwyn 58 C3
Frisby on the Wreake Leics 64 C3
Friskney Lincs 79 D7
Friskney Eaudike Lincs 79 D7
Friskney Tofts Lincs 79 D7
Friston E Sus 18 F2
Friston Suff 57 C8
Fritchley Derbys 76 D3
Frith Bank Lincs 79 E6
Frith Common Worcs 49 C8
Fritham Hants 14 C3
Frithelstock Devon 9 C6
Frithelstock Stone Devon 9 C6
Frithville Lincs 79 D6
Frittenden Kent 30 E2
Frittiscombe Devon 7 E6
Fritton Norf 68 E5
Fritton Norf 69 D7
Fritwell Oxon 39 B5
Frizinghall W Yorks 94 F4
Frizington Cumb 98 C2
Frocester Glos 36 D4
Frodesley Shrops 60 D5
Frodingham N Lincs 90 C2
Frodsham Ches W 74 B2
Frogden Borders 116 B3
Froggatt Derbys 76 B2
Froghall Staffs 75 E7
Frogmore Devon 7 E5
Frogmore Hants 27 D6
Frognall Lincs 65 C8
Frogshail Norf 81 D8
Frolesworth Leics 64 E2
Frome Som 24 E2
Frome St Quintin Dorset 12 D3
Fromes Hill Hereford 49 E8
Fron Denb 72 C4
Fron Gwyn 70 D4
Fron Gwyn 82 F5
Fron Powys 48 C2
Fron Powys 59 E8
Fron Powys 60 D2
Froncysyllte Wrex 73 E6
Frongoch Gwyn 72 F3
Frostenden Suff 69 F7
Frosterley Durham 110 F3
Frotoft Orkney 159 F5
Froxfield Wilts 25 C7
Froxfield Green Hants 15 B8
Froyle Hants 27 E5
Fryerning Essex 42 D2
Fryton N Yorks 96 B2
Fulbeck Lincs 78 D2
Fulbourn Cambs 55 D6
Fulbrook Oxon 38 C2
Fulford Som 11 B7
Fulford Staffs 75 F6
Fulford York 96 E2
Fulham London 28 B3
Fulking W Sus 17 C6
Full Sutton E Yorks 96 D3
Fullarton Glasgow 119 C6
Fullarton N Ayrs 118 F3
Fuller Street Essex 42 C3
Fuller's Moor Ches W 73 D8
Fullerton Hants 25 F8
Fulletby Lincs 79 B5
Fullwood E Ayrs 118 D4
Fulmer Bucks 40 F2
Fulmodestone Norf 81 D5
Fulnetby Lincs 78 B3
Fulstow Lincs 91 E7
Fulwell T&W 111 D6
Fulwood Lancs 92 F5
Fulwood S Yorks 88 F4
Fundenhall Norf 68 E4
Fundenhall Street Norf 68 E4
Funtington W Sus 15 D8
Funtley Hants 15 D6
Funtullich Perth 127 B6
Funzie Shetland 160 D8
Furley Devon 11 D7
Furnace Argyll 125 E6
Furnace Carms 33 D6
Furnace End Warks 63 E6
Furneaux Pelham Herts 41 B7
Furness Vale Derbys 87 F8
Furze Platt Windsor 40 F1
Furzehill Devon 21 E6
Fyfett Som 11 C7
Fyfield Essex 42 D1
Fyfield Glos 38 D2
Fyfield Hants 25 E7
Fyfield Oxon 38 E4
Fyfield Wilts 25 C6
Fylingthorpe N Yorks 103 D7
Fyvie Aberds 153 E7

G

Gabhsann bho Dheas W Isles 155 B9
Gabhsann bho Thuath W Isles 155 B9
Gablon Highld 151 B10
Gabroc Hill E Ayrs 118 D4
Gaddesby Leics 64 C3
Gadebridge Herts 40 D3
Gaer Powys 35 B5
Gaerllwyd Mon 35 E8
Gaerwen Anglesey 82 D4
Gagingwell Oxon 38 B4
Gaick Lodge Highld 138 F3
Gailey Staffs 62 C3
Gainford Durham 101 C6
Gainsborough Lincs 90 E2
Gainsborough Suff 57 E5
Gainsford End Essex 55 F8
Gairloch Highld 149 A13
Gairlochy Highld 136 F4
Gairney Bank Perth 128 E3
Gairnshiel Lodge Aberds 139 D8
Gaisgill Cumb 99 D8
Gaitsgill Cumb 108 E3
Galashiels Borders 121 F7
Galgate Lancs 92 D4
Galhampton Som 12 B4
Gallaberry Dumfries 114 F2
Gallachoille Argyll 144 E6
Gallanach Argyll 124 C4
Gallanach Argyll 146 E5
Gallantry Bank Ches E 74 D2
Gallatown Fife 128 E4
Galley Common Warks 63 E7
Galley Hill Cambs 54 C4
Galleyend Essex 42 D3
Galleywood Essex 42 D3
Gallin Perth 132 E2
Gallowfauld Angus 134 E4
Gallows Green Staffs 75 E7
Galltair Highld 149 F13
Galmisdale Highld 146 C7
Galmpton Devon 6 E4
Galmpton Torbay 7 D6
Galphay N Yorks 95 B5
Galston E Ayrs 118 F5
Galtrigill Highld 148 C6
Gamblesby Cumb 109 F6
Gamesley Derbys 87 E8
Gamlingay Cambs 54 D3
Gammersgill N Yorks 101 F5
Gamston Notts 77 B7
Ganarew Hereford 36 C2
Ganavan Argyll 124 B4
Gang Corn 5 C8
Ganllwyd Gwyn 71 E8
Gannochy Angus 135 B5
Gannochy Perth 128 B3
Gansclet Highld 158 F5
Ganstead E Yorks 97 F7
Ganthorpe N Yorks 96 B2
Ganton N Yorks 97 B5
Garbat Highld 150 E7
Garbhallt Argyll 125 F6
Garboldisham Norf 68 F3
Garden City Flint 73 C7
Garden Village W Yorks 95 F7
Garden Village Wrex 73 D7
Gardenstown Aberds 153 B7
Garderhouse Shetland 160 J5
Gardham E Yorks 97 E5
Gardin Shetland 160 G6
Gare Hill Som 24 E2
Garelochhead Argyll 145 D11
Garford Oxon 38 E4
Garforth W Yorks 95 F7
Gargrave N Yorks 94 D2
Gargunnock Stirling 127 E6
Garlic Street Norf 68 F5
Garlieston Dumfries 105 E8
Garlinge Green Kent 30 D5
Garlogie Aberds 141 D6
Garmond Aberds 153 C8
Garmony Argyll 147 G9
Garmouth Moray 152 B3
Garn-yr-erw Torf 35 C6
Garnant Carms 33 C7
Garndiffaith Torf 35 D6
Garndolbenmaen Gwyn 71 C5
Garnedd Conwy 83 F7
Garnett Bridge Cumb 99 E7
Garnfadryn Gwyn 70 D3
Garnkirk N Lanark 119 C6
Garnlydan Bl Gwent 35 C5
Garnswllt Swansea 33 D7
Garrabost W Isles 155 D10
Garraron Argyll 124 E4
Garras Corn 3 D6
Garreg Gwyn 71 C7
Garrick Perth 127 C7
Garrigill Cumb 109 E7
Garriston N Yorks 101 E6
Garroch Dumfries 113 F5
Garrogie Lodge Highld 137 C8
Garros Highld 149 B9
Garrow Perth 133 E5
Garryhorn Dumfries 113 E5
Garsdale Cumb 100 F2
Garsdale Head Cumb 100 E2
Garsdon Wilts 37 F6
Garshall Green Staffs 75 F6
Garsington Oxon 39 D5
Garstang Lancs 92 E4
Garston Mers 86 F2
Garswood Mers 86 E3
Gartcosh N Lanark 119 C6
Garth Bridgend 34 E2
Garth Gwyn 83 D5
Garth Powys 47 E8
Garth Shetland 160 H4
Garth Wrex 73 E6
Garth Row Cumb 99 E7
Garthamlock Glasgow 119 C6
Garthbrengy Powys 48 F2
Garthdee Aberdeen 141 D8
Gartheli Ceredig 46 D4
Garthmyl Powys 59 E8
Garthorpe Leics 64 B5
Garthorpe N Lincs 90 C2
Gartly Aberds 152 E5
Gartmore Stirling 126 E4
Gartnagrenach Argyll 144 H6
Gartness N Lanark 119 C7
Gartness Stirling 126 F4
Gartocharn W Dunb 126 F3
Garton E Yorks 97 F8
Garton-on-the-Wolds E Yorks 97 D5
Gartsherrie N Lanark 119 C7
Gartymore Highld 157 H13
Garvald E Loth 121 B8
Garvamore Highld 137 E8
Garvard Argyll 144 D2
Garvault Hotel Highld 157 F10
Garve Highld 150 E6
Garvestone Norf 68 D3
Garvock Aberds 135 B7
Garvock Invclyd 118 B2
Garway Hereford 36 B1
Garway Hill Hereford 35 B8
Gaskan Highld 130 B1
Gastard Wilts 24 C3
Gasthorpe Norf 68 F2
Gatcombe IoW 15 F5
Gate Burton Lincs 90 F2
Gate Helmsley N Yorks 96 D2
Gateacre Mers 86 F2
Gatebeck Cumb 99 F7
Gateford Notts 89 F6
Gateforth N Yorks 89 B6
Gatehead E Ayrs 118 F3
Gatehouse Northumb 116 F3
Gatehouse of Fleet Dumfries 106 D3
Gatelawbridge Dumfries 114 E2
Gateley Norf 81 E5
Gatenby N Yorks 101 F8
Gateshead T&W 111 C5
Gatesheath Ches W 73 C8
Gateside Aberds 140 C5
Gateside Angus 134 E4
Gateside E Renf 118 D4
Gateside Fife 128 D3
Gateside N Ayrs 118 D3
Gathurst Gtr Man 86 D3
Gatley Gtr Man 87 F6
Gattonside Borders 121 F8
Gatwick Airport W Sus 28 E3
Gaufron Powys 47 C8
Gaulby Leics 64 D3
Gauldry Fife 129 B5
Gaunt's Common Dorset 13 D8
Gautby Lincs 78 B4
Gavinton Borders 122 D3
Gawber S Yorks 88 D4
Gawcott Bucks 52 F4
Gawsworth Ches E 75 C5
Gawthorpe W Yorks 88 B3
Gawthrop Cumb 100 F1
Gawthwaite Cumb 98 F4
Gay Street W Sus 16 B4
Gaydon Warks 51 D8
Gayfield Orkney 159 C5
Gayhurst M Keynes 53 E6
Gayle N Yorks 100 F3
Gayles N Yorks 101 D6
Gayton Mers 85 F3
Gayton Norf 67 C7
Gayton Northants 52 D5
Gayton Staffs 62 B3
Gayton le Marsh Lincs 91 F8
Gayton le Wold Lincs 91 F6
Gayton Thorpe Norf 67 C7
Gaywood Norf 67 B6
Gazeley Suff 55 C8
Geanies House Highld 151 D11
Gearraidh Bhailteas W Isles 148 F2
Gearraidh Bhaird W Isles 155 E8
Gearraidh na h-Aibhne W Isles 154 D7
Gearraidh na Monadh W Isles 148 G2
Geary Highld 148 B7
Geddes House Highld 151 F11
Gedding Suff 56 D3
Geddington Northants 65 F5
Gedintailor Highld 149 E10
Gedling Notts 77 E6
Gedney Lincs 66 B4
Gedney Broadgate Lincs 66 B4
Gedney Drove End Lincs 66 B4
Gedney Dyke Lincs 66 B4
Gedney Hill Lincs 66 C3
Gee Cross Gtr Man 87 E7
Geilston Argyll 118 B3
Geirinis W Isles 148 D2
Geise Highld 158 D3
Geisiadar W Isles 154 D6
Geldeston Norf 69 E6
Gell Conwy 83 E8
Gelli Pembs 32 C1
Gelli Rhondda 34 E3
Gellideg M Tydf 34 D4
Gellifor Denb 72 C5
Gelligaer Caerph 35 E5
Gellilydan Gwyn 71 D7
Gellinudd Neath 33 D8
Gellyburn Perth 133 F7
Gellywen Carms 32 B3
Gelston Dumfries 106 D4
Gelston Lincs 78 E2
Gembling E Yorks 97 D7
Gentleshaw Staffs 62 C4
Geocrab W Isles 154 H6
George Green Bucks 40 F3
George Nympton Devon 10 B2
Georgefield Dumfries 115 E5
Georgeham Devon 20 F3
Georgetown Bl Gwent 35 D5
Gerlan Gwyn 83 E6
Germansweek Devon 9 E6
Germoe Corn 2 D4
Gerrans Corn 3 C7
Gerrards Cross Bucks 40 F3
Gestingthorpe Essex 56 F2
Geuffordd Powys 60 C2
Gib Hill Ches W 74 B3
Gibbet Hill Warks 64 F2
Gibbshill Dumfries 106 B4
Gidea Park London 41 F8
Gidleigh Devon 9 F8
Giffnock E Renf 119 D5
Gifford E Loth 121 C8
Giffordland N Ayrs 118 E2
Giffordtown Fife 128 C4
Giggleswick N Yorks 93 C8
Gilberdyke E Yorks 90 B2
Gilchriston E Loth 121 C7
Gilcrux Cumb 107 F8
Gildersome W Yorks 88 B3
Gildingwells S Yorks 89 F6
Gileston V Glam 22 C2
Gilfach Caerph 35 E5
Gilfach Goch Rhondda 34 F3
Gilfachrheda Ceredig 46 D3
Gillamoor N Yorks 102 F4
Gillar's Green Mers 86 E2
Gillen Highld 148 C7
Gilling East N Yorks 96 B2
Gilling West N Yorks 101 D6
Gillingham Dorset 13 B6
Gillingham Medway 29 C8
Gillingham Norf 69 E7
Gillock Highld 158 E4
Gillow Heath Staffs 75 D5
Gills Highld 158 C5
Gill's Green Kent 18 B4
Gilmanscleuch Borders 115 B6
Gilmerton Edin 121 C5
Gilmerton Perth 127 B7
Gilmonby Durham 100 C4
Gilmorton Leics 64 F2
Gilmourton S Lanark 119 E6
Gilsland Northumb 109 C6
Gilsland Spa Cumb 109 C6
Gilston Borders 121 D7
Gilston Herts 41 C7
Gilwern Mon 35 C6
Gimingham Norf 81 D8
Giosla W Isles 154 E6
Gipping Suff 56 C4
Gipsey Bridge Lincs 79 E5
Girdle Toll N Ayrs 118 E3
Girlsta Shetland 160 H6
Girsby N Yorks 102 D1
Girtford C Beds 54 D2
Girthon Dumfries 106 D3
Girton Cambs 54 C5
Girton Notts 77 C8
Girvan S Ayrs 112 E1
Gisburn Lancs 93 E8
Gisleham Suff 69 F8
Gislingham Suff 56 B4
Gissing Norf 68 F4
Gittisham Devon 11 E6
Gladestry Powys 48 D4
Gladsmuir E Loth 121 B7
Glais Swansea 33 D8
Glaisdale N Yorks 103 D5
Glame Highld 149 D10
Glamis Angus 134 E3
Glan Adda Gwyn 83 D5
Glan Conwy Conwy 83 D8
Glan-Conwy Conwy 83 F8
Glan-Duar Carms 46 E4
Glan-Dwyfach Gwyn 71 C5
Glan Gors Anglesey 82 D4
Glan-rhyd Gwyn 82 F4
Glan-traeth Anglesey 82 D2
Glan-y-don Flint 73 B5
Glan-y-nant Powys 59 F6
Glan-y-wern Gwyn 71 D7
Glan-yr-afon Anglesey 83 C6
Glan-yr-afon Gwyn 72 E3
Glan-yr-afon Gwyn 72 E4
Glanaman Carms 33 C7
Glandford Norf 81 C6
Glandwr Pembs 32 B2
Glandy Cross Carms 32 B2
Glandyfi Ceredig 58 E3
Glangrwyney Powys 35 C6
Glanmule Powys 59 E8
Glanrafon Ceredig 58 F3
Glanrhyd Gwyn 70 D3
Glanrhyd Pembs 45 E3
Glanton Northumb 117 C6
Glanton Pike Northumb 117 C6
Glanvilles Wootton Dorset 12 D4
Glapthorn Northants 65 E7
Glapwell Derbys 76 C4
Glas-allt Shiel Aberds 139 F8
Glasbury Powys 48 F3
Glaschoil Highld 151 H13
Glascoed Denb 72 B3
Glascoed Mon 35 D7
Glascoed Powys 59 C8
Glascorrie Aberds 140 E2
Glascote Staffs 63 D6
Glascwm Powys 48 D3
Glasdrum Argyll 130 E4
Glasfryn Conwy 72 D3
Glasgow Glasgow 119 C5
Glashvin Highld 149 B9
Glasinfryn Gwyn 83 E5
Glasnacardoch Highld 147 B9
Glasnakille Highld 149 G10
Glasphein Highld 148 D6
Glaspwll Powys 58 E4
Glassburn Highld 150 H6
Glasserton Dumfries 105 F8
Glassford S Lanark 119 E7
Glasshouse Hill Glos 36 B4
Glasshouses N Yorks 94 C4
Glasslie Fife 128 D4
Glasson Cumb 108 C2
Glasson Lancs 92 D4
Glassonby Cumb 109 F5
Glasterlaw Angus 135 D5
Glaston Rutland 65 D5
Glastonbury Som 23 F7
Glatton Cambs 65 F8
Glazebrook Warr 86 E4
Glazebury Warr 86 E4
Glazeley Shrops 61 F7
Gleadless S Yorks 88 F4
Gleadsmoss Ches E 74 C5
Gleann Tholàstaidh W Isles 155 C10
Gleaston Cumb 92 B2
Gleiniant Powys 59 E6
Glemsford Suff 56 E2
Glen Dumfries 106 B5
Glen Dumfries 106 D2
Glen Auldyn IoM 84 C4
Glen Bernisdale Highld 149 D9
Glen Ho Borders 121 F5
Glen Mona IoM 84 D4
Glen Nevis House Highld 131 B5
Glen Parva Leics 64 E2
Glen Sluain Argyll 125 F6
Glen Tanar House Aberds 140 E3
Glen Trool Lodge Dumfries 112 F4
Glen Village Falk 119 B8
Glen Vine IoM 84 E3
Glenamachrie Argyll 124 C5
Glenbarr Argyll 143 E7
Glenbeg Highld 139 B6
Glenbeg Highld 147 E8
Glenbervie Aberds 141 F6
Glenboig N Lanark 119 C7
Glenborrodale Highld 147 E9
Glenbranter Argyll 125 F7
Glenbreck Borders 114 B3
Glenbrein Lodge Highld 137 C7
Glenbrittle House Highld 149 F9
Glenbuchat Lodge Aberds 140 C2
Glenbuck E Ayrs 113 B7
Glenburn Renfs 118 C4
Glencalvie Lodge Highld 150 C7
Glencanisp Lodge Highld 156 G4
Glencaple Dumfries 107 C6
Glencarron Lodge Highld 150 F3
Glencarse Perth 128 B3
Glencassley Castle Highld 156 J7
Glenceitlein Highld 131 E5
Glencoe Highld 130 D4
Glencraig Fife 128 E3
Glencripesdale Highld 147 F9
Glencrosh Dumfries 113 F7
Glendavan Ho. Aberds 140 D3
Glendevon Perth 127 D8
Glendoe Lodge Highld 137 D7
Glendoebeg Highld 137 D7
Glendoick Perth 128 B4
Glendoll Lodge Angus 134 B2
Glendoune S Ayrs 112 E1
Glenduckie Fife 128 C4
Glendye Lodge Aberds 140 F5
Gleneagles Hotel Perth 127 C8
Gleneagles House Perth 127 D8
Glenegedale Argyll 142 C4
Glenelg Highld 149 G13
Glenernie Moray 151 G13
Glenfarg Perth 128 C3
Glenfarquhar Lodge Aberds 141 F6
Glenferness House Highld 151 G12
Glenfeshie Lodge Highld 138 E4
Glenfield Leics 64 D2
Glenfinnan Highld 147 C11
Glenfoot Perth 128 C3
Glenfyne Lodge Argyll 125 D8
Glengap Dumfries 106 D3
Glengarnock N Ayrs 118 D3
Glengorm Castle Argyll 146 F7
Glengrasco Highld 149 D9
Glenhead Farm Angus 134 C2
Glenhoul Dumfries 113 F6
Glenhurich Highld 130 C2
Glenkerry Borders 115 C5
Glenkiln Dumfries 106 B5
Glenkindie Aberds 140 C3
Glenlatterach Moray 152 C1
Glenlee Dumfries 113 F6
Glenlichorn Perth 127 C6
Glenlivet Moray 139 B7
Glenlochsie Perth 133 B7
Glenloig N Ayrs 143 E10
Glenluce Dumfries 105 D6
Glenmallan Argyll 125 F8
Glenmarksie Highld 150 F6
Glenmassan Argyll 145 E10
Glenmavis N Lanark 119 C7
Glenmaye IoM 84 E2
Glenmidge Dumfries 113 F8
Glenmore Argyll 124 D4
Glenmore Highld 149 D9
Glenmore Lodge Highld 139 D5
Glenmoy Angus 134 C4
Glenogil Angus 134 C4
Glenprosen Lodge Angus 134 C2
Glenprosen Village Angus 134 C3
Glenquiech Angus 134 C4
Glenreasdell Mains Argyll 145 H7
Glenree N Ayrs 143 F10
Glenridding Cumb 99 C5
Glenrossal Highld 156 J7
Glenrothes Fife 128 D4
Glensanda Highld 130 E2
Glensaugh Aberds 135 B6
Glenshero Lodge Highld 137 E8
Glenstockadale Dumfries 104 C4
Glenstriven Argyll 145 F9
Glentaggart S Lanark 113 B8
Glentham Lincs 90 E4
Glentirranmuir Stirling 127 E5
Glenton Aberds 140 B5
Glentress Borders 121 F5
Glentromie Lodge Highld 138 E3
Glentrool Village Dumfries 105 B7
Glentruan IoM 84 B4
Glentruim House Highld 138 E2
Glentworth Lincs 90 F3
Glenuig Highld 147 D9
Glenurquhart Highld 151 E10
Glespin S Lanark 113 B8
Gletness Shetland 160 H6
Glewstone Hereford 36 B2
Glinton Pboro 65 D8
Glooston Leics 64 E4
Glororum Northumb 123 F7
Glossop Derbys 87 E8
Gloster Hill Northumb 117 D8
Gloucester Glos 37 C5
Gloup Shetland 160 C7
Glusburn N Yorks 94 E3
Glutt Lodge Highld 157 F12
Glutton Bridge Staffs 75 C7
Glympton Oxon 38 B4
Glyn-Ceiriog Wrex 73 F6
Glyn-cywarch Gwyn 71 D7
Glyn Ebwy = Ebbw Vale Bl Gwent 35 D5
Glyn-neath = Glynedd Neath 34 D2
Glynarthen Ceredig 46 E2
Glynbrochan Powys 59 F6
Glyncoch Rhondda 34 E4
Glyncorrwg Neath 34 E2
Glynde E Sus 17 D8
Glyndebourne E Sus 17 C8
Glyndyfrdwy Denb 72 E5
Glynedd = Glyn-neath Neath 34 D2
Glynogwr Bridgend 34 F3
Glyntaff Rhondda 34 F4
Glyntawe Powys 34 C2
Gnosall Staffs 62 B2
Gnosall Heath Staffs 62 B2
Goadby Leics 64 E4
Goadby Marwood Leics 64 B4
Goat Lees Kent 30 E4
Goatacre Wilts 24 B5
Goathill Dorset 12 C4
Goathland N Yorks 103 D6
Goathurst Som 22 F4
Gobernuisgach Lodge Highld 156 E7
Gobhaig W Isles 154 G5
Gobowen Shrops 73 F7
Godalming Sur 27 E7
Godley Gtr Man 87 E7
Godmanchester Cambs 54 B3
Godmanstone Dorset 12 E4
Godmersham Kent 30 D4
Godney Som 23 E6
Godolphin Cross Corn 2 C5
Godre'r-graig Neath 34 D1
Godshill Hants 14 C2
Godshill IoW 15 F6
Godstone Sur 28 D4
Godwinscroft Hants 14 E2
Goetre Mon 35 D7
Goferydd Anglesey 82 C2
Goff's Oak Herts 41 D6
Gogar Edin 120 B4
Goginan Ceredig 58 F3
Golan Gwyn 71 C6
Golant Corn 5 D6
Golberdon Corn 5 B8
Golborne Gtr Man 86 E4
Golcar W Yorks 88 C2
Gold Hill Norf 66 E5
Goldcliff Newport 35 F7
Golden Cross E Sus 18 D2
Golden Green Kent 29 E7
Golden Grove Carms 33 C6

Golden Hill Hants 14 E3
Golden Pot Hants 26 E5
Golden Valley Glos 37 B6
Goldenhill Stoke 75 D5
Golders Green London 41 F5
Goldhanger Essex 43 D5
Golding Shrops 60 D5
Goldington Bedford 53 D8
Goldsborough N Yorks 95 D6
Goldsborough N Yorks 103 C6
Goldsithney Corn 2 C4
Goldsworthy Devon 9 B5
Goldthorpe S Yorks 89 D5
Gollanfield Highld 151 F11
Golspie Highld 157 J11
Golval Highld 157 C11
Gomeldon Wilts 25 F6
Gomersal W Yorks 88 B3
Gomshall Sur 27 E8
Gonalston Notts 77 E6
Gonfirth Shetland 160 G5
Good Easter Essex 42 C2
Gooderstone Norf 67 D7
Goodleigh Devon 20 F5
Goodmanham E Yorks 96 E4
Goodnestone Kent 30 C4
Goodnestone Kent 31 D6
Goodrich Hereford 36 C2
Goodrington Torbay 7 D6
Goodshaw Lancs 87 B6
Goodwick = Wdig Pembs 44 B4
Goodworth Clatford Hants 25 E8
Goole E Yorks 89 B8
Goonbell Corn 3 B6
Goonhavern Corn 4 D2
Goose Eye W Yorks 94 E3
Goose Green Gtr Man 86 D3
Goose Green Norf 68 F4
Goose Green W Sus 16 C5
Gooseham Corn 8 C4
Goosey Oxon 38 E3
Goosnargh Lancs 93 F5
Goostrey Ches E 74 B4
Gorcott Hill Warks 51 C5
Gord Shetland 160 L6
Gordon Borders 122 E2
Gordonbush Highld 157 J11
Gordonsburgh Moray 152 B4
Gordonstoun Moray 152 B1
Gordonstown Aberds 152 C5
Gordonstown Aberds 153 E7
Gore Kent 31 D7
Gore Cross Wilts 24 D5
Gore Pit Essex 42 C4
Gorebridge Midloth 121 C6
Gorefield Cambs 66 C4
Gorey Jersey 17
Gorgie Edin 120 B5
Goring Oxon 39 F6
Goring-by-Sea W Sus 16 D5
Goring Heath Oxon 26 B4
Gorleston-on-Sea Norf 69 D8
Gornalwood W Mid 62 E3
Gorrachie Aberds 153 C7
Gorran Churchtown Corn 3 B8
Gorran Haven Corn 3 B9
Gorrenberry Borders 115 E7
Gors Ceredig 46 B5
Gorse Hill Swindon 38 F1
Gorsedd Flint 73 B5
Gorseinon Swansea 33 E6
Gorseness Orkney 159 G5
Gorsgoch Ceredig 46 D3
Gorslas Carms 33 C6
Gorsley Glos 36 B3
Gorstan Highld 150 E6
Gorstanvorran Highld 130 B2
Gorsteyhill Staffs 74 D4
Gorsty Hill Staffs 62 B5
Gortantaoid Argyll 142 A4
Gorton Gtr Man 87 E6
Gosbeck Suff 57 D5
Gosberton Lincs 78 F5
Gosberton Clough Lincs 65 B8
Gosfield Essex 42 B3
Gosford Hereford 49 C7
Gosforth Cumb 98 D2
Gosforth T&W 110 C5
Gosmore Herts 40 B4
Gosport Hants 15 E7
Gossabrough Shetland 160 E7
Gossington Glos 36 D4
Goswick Northumb 123 E6
Gotham Notts 76 F5
Gotherington Glos 37 B6
Gott Shetland 160 J6
Goudhurst Kent 18 B4
Goulceby Lincs 79 B5
Gourdas Aberds 153 D7
Gourdon Aberds 135 B8
Gourock Invclyd 118 B2
Govan Glasgow 119 C5
Govanhill Glasgow 119 C5
Goveton Devon 7 E5
Govilon Mon 35 C6
Gowanhill Aberds 153 B10
Gowdall E Yorks 89 B7
Gowerton Swansea 33 E6
Gowkhall Fife 128 F2
Gowthorpe E Yorks 96 D3
Goxhill E Yorks 97 E7
Goxhill N Lincs 90 B5
Goxhill Haven N Lincs 90 B5
Goytre Neath 34 F1
Grabhair W Isles 155 F8
Graby Lincs 65 B7
Grade Corn 3 E6
Graffham W Sus 16 C3
Grafham Cambs 54 C2
Grafham Sur 27 E8
Grafton Hereford 49 F6
Grafton N Yorks 95 C7
Grafton Oxon 38 D2
Grafton Shrops 60 C4
Grafton Worcs 49 C7
Grafton Flyford Worcs 50 D4
Grafton Regis Northants 53 E5
Grafton Underwood Northants 65 F6
Grafty Green Kent 30 E2
Graianrhyd Denb 73 D6
Graig Conwy 83 D8
Graig Denb 72 B4
Graig-fechan Denb 72 D5
Grain Medway 30 B2
Grainsby Lincs 91 E6
Grainthorpe Lincs 91 E7
Grampound Corn 3 B8
Grampound Road Corn 4 D4
Gramsdal W Isles 148 C3
Granborough Bucks 39 B7
Granby Notts 77 F7
Grandborough Warks 52 C2
Grandtully Perth 133 D6
Grange Cumb 98 C4
Grange E Ayrs 118 F4
Grange Medway 29 C8
Grange Mers 85 F3
Grange Perth 128 B4
Grange Crossroads Moray 152 C4
Grange Hall Moray 151 E13
Grange Hill Essex 41 E7
Grange Moor W Yorks 88 C3
Grange of Lindores Fife 128 C4
Grange-over-Sands Cumb 92 B4
Grange Villa Durham 110 D5
Grangemill Derbys 76 D2
Grangemouth Falk 127 F8
Grangepans Falk 128 F2
Grangetown Cardiff 22 B3
Grangetown Redcar 102 B3
Granish Highld 138 C5
Gransmoor E Yorks 97 D7
Granston Pembs 44 B3
Grantchester Cambs 54 D5
Grantham Lincs 78 F2
Grantley N Yorks 94 C5
Grantlodge Aberds 141 C6
Granton Dumfries 114 D3
Granton Edin 120 B5
Grantown-on-Spey Highld 139 B6
Grantshouse Borders 122 C4
Grappenhall Warr 86 F4
Grasby Lincs 90 D4
Grasmere Cumb 99 D5
Grasscroft Gtr Man 87 D7
Grassendale Mers 85 F4
Grassholme Durham 100 B4
Grassington N Yorks 94 C3
Grassmoor Derbys 76 C4
Grassthorpe Notts 77 C7
Grateley Hants 25 E7
Gratwich Staffs 75 F7
Graveley Cambs 54 C3
Graveley Herts 41 B5
Gravelly Hill W Mid 62 E5
Gravels Shrops 60 D3
Graven Shetland 160 F6
Graveney Kent 30 C4
Gravesend Herts 41 B7
Gravesend Kent 29 B7
Grayingham Lincs 90 E3
Grayrigg Cumb 99 E7
Grays Thurrock 29 B7
Grayshott Hants 27 F6
Grayswood Sur 27 F7
Graythorp Hrtlpl 102 B3
Grazeley Wokingham 26 C4
Greasbrough S Yorks 88 E5
Greasby Mers 85 F3
Great Abington Cambs 55 E6
Great Addington Northants 53 B7
Great Alne Warks 51 D6
Great Altcar Lancs 85 D4
Great Amwell Herts 41 C6
Great Asby Cumb 100 C1
Great Ashfield Suff 56 C3
Great Ayton N Yorks 102 C3
Great Baddow Essex 42 D3
Great Bardfield Essex 55 F7
Great Barford Bedford 54 D2
Great Barr W Mid 62 E4
Great Barrington Glos 38 C2
Great Barrow Ches W 73 C8
Great Barton Suff 56 C2
Great Barugh N Yorks 96 B3
Great Bavington Northumb 117 F5
Great Bealings Suff 57 E6
Great Bedwyn Wilts 25 C7
Great Bentley Essex 43 B7
Great Billing Northants 53 C6
Great Bircham Norf 80 D3
Great Blakenham Suff 56 D5
Great Blencow Cumb 108 F4
Great Bolas Telford 61 B6
Great Bookham Sur 28 D2
Great Bourton Oxon 52 E2
Great Bowden Leics 64 F4
Great Bradley Suff 55 D7
Great Braxted Essex 42 C4
Great Bricett Suff 56 D4
Great Brickhill Bucks 53 F7
Great Bridge W Mid 62 E3
Great Bridgeford Staffs 62 B2
Great Brington Northants 52 C4
Great Bromley Essex 43 B6
Great Broughton Cumb 107 F7
Great Broughton N Yorks 102 D3
Great Budworth Ches W 74 B3
Great Burdon Darl 101 C8
Great Burgh Sur 28 D3
Great Burstead Essex 42 E2
Great Busby N Yorks 102 D3
Great Canfield Essex 42 C1
Great Carlton Lincs 91 F8
Great Casterton Rutland 65 D7
Great Chart Kent 30 E3
Great Chatwell Staffs 61 C7
Great Chesterford Essex 55 E6
Great Cheverell Wilts 24 D4
Great Chishill Cambs 54 F5
Great Clacton Essex 43 C7
Great Cliff W Yorks 88 C4
Great Clifton Cumb 98 B2
Great Coates NE Lincs 91 D6
Great Comberton Worcs 50 E4
Great Corby Cumb 108 D4
Great Cornard Suff 56 E2
Great Cowden E Yorks 97 E8
Great Coxwell Oxon 38 E2
Great Crakehall N Yorks 101 E7
Great Cransley Northants 53 B6
Great Cressingham Norf 67 D8
Great Crosby Mers 85 E4
Great Cubley Derbys 75 F8
Great Dalby Leics 64 C4
Great Denham Bedford 53 E8
Great Doddington Northants 53 C6
Great Dunham Norf 67 C8
Great Dunmow Essex 42 B2
Great Durnford Wilts 25 F6
Great Easton Essex 42 B2
Great Easton Leics 64 E5
Great Eccleston Lancs 92 E4
Great Edstone N Yorks 103 F5
Great Ellingham Norf 68 E3
Great Elm Som 24 E2
Great Eversden Cambs 54 D4
Great Fencote N Yorks 101 E7
Great Finborough Suff 56 D4
Great Fransham Norf 67 C8
Great Gaddesden Herts 40 C3
Great Gidding Cambs 65 F8
Great Givendale E Yorks 96 D4
Great Glemham Suff 57 C7
Great Glen Leics 64 E3
Great Gonerby Lincs 77 F8
Great Gransden Cambs 54 D3
Great Green Norf 69 F5
Great Green Suff 56 D3
Great Habton N Yorks 96 B3
Great Hale Lincs 78 E4
Great Hallingbury Essex 41 C8
Great Hampden Bucks 39 D8
Great Harrowden Northants 53 B6
Great Harwood Lancs 93 F7
Great Haseley Oxon 39 D6
Great Hatfield E Yorks 97 E7
Great Haywood Staffs 62 B4
Great Heath W Mid 63 F7
Great Heck N Yorks 89 B6
Great Henny Essex 56 F2
Great Hinton Wilts 24 D4
Great Hockham Norf 68 E2
Great Holland Essex 43 C8
Great Horkesley Essex 56 F3
Great Hormead Herts 41 B6
Great Horton W Yorks 94 F4
Great Horwood Bucks 53 F5
Great Houghton Northants 53 D5
Great Houghton S Yorks 88 D5
Great Hucklow Derbys 75 B8
Great Kelk E Yorks 97 D7
Great Kimble Bucks 39 D8
Great Kingshill Bucks 40 E1
Great Langton N Yorks 101 E7
Great Leighs Essex 42 C3
Great Lever Gtr Man 86 D5
Great Limber Lincs 90 D5
Great Linford M Keynes 53 E6
Great Livermere Suff 56 B2
Great Longstone Derbys 76 B2
Great Lumley Durham 111 E5
Great Lyth Shrops 60 D4
Great Malvern Worcs 50 E2
Great Maplestead Essex 56 F2
Great Marton Blackpool 92 F3
Great Massingham Norf 80 E3
Great Melton Norf 68 D4
Great Milton Oxon 39 D6
Great Missenden Bucks 40 D1
Great Mitton Lancs 93 F7
Great Mongeham Kent 31 D7
Great Moulton Norf 68 E4
Great Munden Herts 41 B6
Great Musgrave Cumb 100 C2
Great Ness Shrops 60 C3
Great Notley Essex 42 B3
Great Oakley Essex 43 B7
Great Oakley Northants 65 F5
Great Offley Herts 40 B4
Great Ormside Cumb 100 C2
Great Orton Cumb 108 D3
Great Ouseburn N Yorks 95 C7
Great Oxendon Northants 64 F4
Great Oxney Green Essex 42 D2
Great Palgrave Norf 67 C8
Great Parndon Essex 41 D7
Great Paxton Cambs 54 C3
Great Plumpton Lancs 92 F3
Great Plumstead Norf 69 C6
Great Ponton Lincs 78 F2
Great Preston W Yorks 88 B5
Great Raveley Cambs 66 F2
Great Rissington Glos 38 C1
Great Rollright Oxon 51 F8
Great Ryburgh Norf 81 E5
Great Ryle Northumb 117 C6
Great Ryton Shrops 60 D4
Great Saling Essex 42 B3
Great Salkeld Cumb 109 F5
Great Sampford Essex 55 F7
Great Sankey Warr 86 F3
Great Saxham Suff 55 C8
Great Shefford W Berks 25 B8
Great Shelford Cambs 55 D5
Great Smeaton N Yorks 101 D8
Great Snoring Norf 80 D5
Great Somerford Wilts 37 F6
Great Stainton Darl 101 B8
Great Stambridge Essex 42 E4
Great Staughton Cambs 54 C2
Great Steeping Lincs 79 C7
Great Stonar Kent 31 D7
Great Strickland Cumb 99 B7
Great Stukeley Cambs 54 B3
Great Sturton Lincs 78 B5
Great Sutton Ches W 73 B7
Great Sutton Shrops 60 F5
Great Swinburne Northumb 110 B2
Great Tew Oxon 38 B3
Great Tey Essex 42 B4
Great Thurkleby N Yorks 95 B7
Great Thurlow Suff 55 D7
Great Torrington Devon 9 C6
Great Tosson Northumb 117 D6
Great Totham Essex 42 C4
Great Totham Essex 42 C4
Great Tows Lincs 91 E6
Great Urswick Cumb 92 B2
Great Wakering Essex 43 F5
Great Waldingfield Suff 56 E3
Great Walsingham Norf 80 D5
Great Waltham Essex 42 C2
Great Warley Essex 42 E1
Great Washbourne Glos 50 F4
Great Weldon Northants 65 F6
Great Welnetham Suff 56 D2
Great Wenham Suff 56 F4
Great Whittington Northumb 110 B3
Great Wigborough Essex 43 C5
Great Wilbraham Cambs 55 D6
Great Wishford Wilts 25 F5
Great Witcombe Glos 37 C6
Great Witley Worcs 50 C2
Great Wolford Warks 51 F7
Great Wratting Suff 55 E7
Great Wymondley Herts 41 B5
Great Wyrley Staffs 62 D3
Great Wytheford Shrops 61 C5
Great Yarmouth Norf 69 D8
Great Yeldham Essex 55 F8
Greater Doward Hereford 36 C2
Greatford Lincs 65 C7
Greatgate Staffs 75 E7
Greatham Hants 27 F5
Greatham Hrtlpl 102 B2
Greatham W Sus 16 C4
Greatstone on Sea Kent 19 C7
Greatworth Northants 52 E3
Greave Lancs 87 B6
Greeba IoM 84 D3
Green Denb 72 C4
Green End Bedford 54 D2
Green Hammerton N Yorks 95 D7
Green Lane Powys 59 E8
Green Ore Som 23 D7
Green St Green London 29 C5
Green Street Herts 40 E4
Greenbank Shetland 160 C7
Greenburn W Loth 120 C2
Greendikes Northumb 117 B6
Greenfield C Beds 53 F8
Greenfield Flint 73 B5
Greenfield Gtr Man 87 D7
Greenfield Highld 136 D5
Greenfield Oxon 39 E7
Greenford London 40 F4
Greengairs N Lanark 119 B7
Greenham W Berks 26 C2
Greenhaugh Northumb 116 F3
Greenhead Northumb 109 C6
Greenhill Falk 119 B8
Greenhill Kent 31 C5
Greenhill Leics 63 C8
Greenhill London 40 F4
Greenhills N Ayrs 118 D3
Greenhithe Kent 29 B6
Greenholm E Ayrs 118 F5
Greenholme Cumb 99 D7
Greenhouse Borders 115 B8
Greenhow Hill N Yorks 94 C4
Greenigoe Orkney 159 H5
Greenland Highld 158 D4
Greenlands Bucks 39 F7
Greenlaw Aberds 153 C6
Greenlaw Borders 122 E3
Greenlea Dumfries 107 B7
Greenloaning Perth 127 D7
Greenmount Gtr Man 87 C5
Greenmow Shetland 160 L6
Greenock Invclyd 118 B2
Greenock West Invclyd 118 B2
Greenodd Cumb 99 F5
Greenrow Cumb 107 D8
Greens Norton Northants 52 E4
Greenside T&W 110 C4
Greensidehill Northumb 117 C5
Greenstead Green Essex 42 B4
Greensted Essex 41 D8
Greenwich London 28 B4
Greet Glos 50 F5
Greete Shrops 49 B7
Greetham Lincs 79 B6
Greetham Rutland 65 C6
Greetland W Yorks 87 B8
Gregg Hall Cumb 99 E6
Gregson Lane Lancs 86 B3
Greinetobht W Isles 148 A3
Greinton Som 23 F6
Gremista Shetland 160 J6
Grenaby IoM 84 E2
Grendon Northants 53 C6
Grendon Warks 63 D6
Grendon Common Warks 63 E6
Grendon Green Hereford 49 D7
Grendon Underwood Bucks 39 B6
Grenofen Devon 6 B2
Grenoside S Yorks 88 E4
Greosabhagh W Isles 154 H6
Gresford Wrex 73 D7
Gresham Norf 81 D7
Greshornish Highld 149 C8
Gressenhall Norf 68 C2
Gressingham Lancs 93 C5
Gresty Green Ches E 74 D4
Greta Bridge Durham 101 C5
Gretna Dumfries 108 C3
Gretna Green Dumfries 108 C3
Gretton Glos 50 F5
Gretton Northants 65 E5
Gretton Shrops 60 E5
Grewelthorpe N Yorks 94 B5
Grey Green N Lincs 89 D8
Greygarth N Yorks 94 B4
Greynor Carms 33 D6
Greysouthen Cumb 98 B2
Greystoke Cumb 108 F4
Greystone Angus 135 E5
Greystone Dumfries 107 B6
Greywell Hants 26 D5
Griais W Isles 155 C9
Grianan W Isles 155 D9
Gribthorpe E Yorks 96 F3
Gridley Corner Devon 9 E5
Griff Warks 63 F7
Griffithstown Torf 35 E6
Grimbister Orkney 159 G4
Grimblethorpe Lincs 91 F6
Grimeford Village Lancs 86 C4
Grimethorpe S Yorks 88 D5
Griminis W Isles 148 C2
Grimister Shetland 160 D6
Grimley Worcs 50 C3
Grimness Orkney 159 J5
Grimoldby Lincs 91 F7
Grimpo Shrops 60 B3
Grimsargh Lancs 93 F5
Grimsbury Oxon 52 E2
Grimsby NE Lincs 91 C6
Grimscote Northants 52 D4
Grimscott Corn 8 D4
Grimsthorpe Lincs 65 B7
Grimston E Yorks 97 F8
Grimston Leics 64 B3
Grimston Norf 80 E3
Grimston York 96 D2
Grimstone Dorset 12 E4
Grinacombe Moor Devon 9 E6
Grindale E Yorks 97 B7
Grindigar Orkney 159 H6
Grindiscol Shetland 160 K6
Grindle Shrops 61 D7
Grindleford Derbys 76 B2
Grindleton Lancs 93 E7
Grindley Staffs 62 B4
Grindley Brook Shrops 74 E2
Grindlow Derbys 75 B8
Grindon Northumb 122 E5
Grindon Staffs 75 D7
Grindonmoor Gate Staffs 75 D7
Gringley on the Hill Notts 89 E8
Grinsdale Cumb 108 D3
Grinshill Shrops 60 B5
Grinton N Yorks 101 E5
Griomsidar W Isles 155 E8
Grishipoll Argyll 146 F4
Grisling Common E Sus 17 B8
Gristhorpe N Yorks 103 F8
Griston Norf 68 E2
Gritley Orkney 159 H6
Grittenham Wilts 37 F7
Grittleton Wilts 37 F5
Grizebeck Cumb 98 F4
Grizedale Cumb 99 E5
Grobister Orkney 159 F7
Groby Leics 64 D2
Groes Conwy 72 C4
Groes Neath 34 F1
Groes-faen Rhondda 34 F4
Groes-lwyd Powys 60 C2
Groesffordd Marli Denb 72 B4
Groeslon Gwyn 82 E5
Groeslon Gwyn 82 F4
Grogport Argyll 143 D9
Gromford Suff 57 D7
Gronant Flint 72 A4
Groombridge E Sus 18 B2
Grosmont Mon 35 B8
Grosmont N Yorks 103 D6
Groton Suff 56 E3
Grougfoot Falk 120 B3
Grouville Jersey 17
Grove Dorset 12 G5
Grove Kent 31 C6
Grove Notts 77 B7
Grove Oxon 38 E4
Grove Park London 28 B5
Grove Vale W Mid 62 E4
Grovesend Swansea 33 D6
Grudie Highld 150 E6
Gruids Highld 157 J8
Gruinard House Highld 150 B2
Grula Highld 149 F8
Gruline Argyll 147 G8
Grunasound Shetland 160 K5
Grundisburgh Suff 57 D6
Grunsagill Lancs 93 D7
Gruting Shetland 160 J4
Grutness Shetland 160 N6
Gualachulain Highld 131 E5
Gualin Ho. Highld 156 D6
Guardbridge Fife 129 C6
Guarlford Worcs 50 E3
Guay Perth 133 E7
Guestling Green E Sus 19 D5
Guestling Thorn E Sus 18 D5
Guestwick Norf 81 E6
Guestwick Green Norf 81 E6
Guide Blackburn 86 B5
Guide Post Northumb 117 F8
Guilden Morden Cambs 54 E3
Guilden Sutton Ches W 73 C8
Guildford Sur 27 E7
Guildtown Perth 133 F8
Guilsborough Northants 52 B4
Guilsfield Powys 60 C2
Guilton Kent 31 D6
Guineaford Devon 20 F4
Guisborough Redcar 102 C4
Guiseley W Yorks 94 E4
Guist Norf 81 E5
Guith Orkney 159 E6
Guiting Power Glos 37 B7
Gulberwick Shetland 160 K6
Gullane E Loth 129 F6
Gulval Corn 2 C3
Gulworthy Devon 6 B2
Gumfreston Pembs 32 D2
Gumley Leics 64 E3
Gummow's Shop Corn 4 D3
Gun Hill E Sus 18 D2
Gunby E Yorks 96 F3
Gunby Lincs 65 B6
Gundleton Hants 26 F4
Gunn Devon 20 F5
Gunnerside N Yorks 100 E4
Gunnerton Northumb 110 B2
Gunness N Lincs 90 C2
Gunnislake Corn 6 B2
Gunnista Shetland 160 J7
Gunthorpe Norf 81 D6
Gunthorpe Notts 77 E6
Gunthorpe Pboro 65 D8
Gunville IoW 15 F5
Gunwalloe Corn 3 D5
Gurnard IoW 15 E5
Gurnett Ches E 75 B6
Gurney Slade Som 23 E8
Gurnos Powys 34 D1
Gussage All Saints Dorset 13 C8
Gussage St Michael Dorset 13 C7
Guston Kent 31 E7
Gutcher Shetland 160 D7
Guthrie Angus 135 D5
Guyhirn Cambs 66 D3
Guyhirn Gull Cambs 66 D3
Guy's Head Lincs 66 B4
Guy's Marsh Dorset 13 B6
Guyzance Northumb 117 D8
Gwaenysgor Flint 72 A4
Gwalchmai Anglesey 82 D3
Gwaun-Cae-Gurwen Neath 33 C8
Gwaun-Leision Neath 33 C8
Gwbert Ceredig 45 E3
Gweek Corn 3 D6
Gwehelog Mon 35 D7
Gwenddwr Powys 48 E2
Gwennap Corn 3 C6
Gwenter Corn 3 E6
Gwernaffield Flint 73 C6
Gwernesney Mon 35 D8
Gwernogle Carms 46 F4
Gwernymynydd Flint 73 C6
Gwersyllt Wrex 73 D7
Gwespyr Flint 85 F2
Gwithian Corn 2 B4
Gwredog Anglesey 82 C4
Gwyddelwern Denb 72 E4
Gwyddgrug Carms 46 F3
Gwydyr Uchaf Conwy 83 E7
Gwynfryn Wrex 73 D6
Gwystre Powys 48 C2
Gwytherin Conwy 83 E8
Gyfelia Wrex 73 E7
Gyffin Conwy 83 D7
Gyre Orkney 159 H4
Gyrn-goch Gwyn 70 C5

H

Habberley Shrops 60 D3
Habergham Lancs 93 F8
Habrough NE Lincs 90 C5
Haceby Lincs 78 F3
Hacheston Suff 57 D7
Hackbridge London 28 C3
Hackenthorpe S Yorks 88 F5
Hackford Norf 68 D3
Hackforth N Yorks 101 E7
Hackland Orkney 159 F4
Hackleton Northants 53 D6
Hackness N Yorks 103 E7
Hackness Orkney 159 J4
Hackney London 41 F6
Hackthorn Lincs 90 F3
Hackthorpe Cumb 99 B7
Haconby Lincs 65 B8
Hacton London 41 F8
Hadden Borders 122 F3
Haddenham Bucks 39 D7
Haddenham Cambs 55 B5
Haddington E Loth 121 B8
Haddington Lincs 78 C2
Haddiscoe Norf 69 E7
Haddon Cambs 65 E8
Haddon Ches E 75 C6
Hade Edge W Yorks 88 D2
Hademore Staffs 63 D5
Hadfield Derbys 87 E8
Hadham Cross Herts 41 C7
Hadham Ford Herts 41 B7
Hadleigh Essex 42 F4
Hadleigh Suff 56 E4
Hadley Telford 61 C6
Hadley End Staffs 62 B5
Hadlow Kent 29 E7
Hadlow Down E Sus 18 C2
Hadnall Shrops 60 C5
Hadstock Essex 55 E6
Hady Derbys 76 B3
Hadzor Worcs 50 C4
Haffenden Quarter Kent 30 E2
Hafod-Dinbych Conwy 83 F8
Hafod-lom Conwy 83 D8
Haggate Lancs 93 F8
Haggbeck Cumb 108 B4
Haggerston Northumb 123 E6
Haggrister Shetland 160 F5
Hagley Hereford 49 E7
Hagley Worcs 62 F3
Hagworthingham Lincs 79 C6
Haigh Gtr Man 86 D4
Haigh S Yorks 88 C3
Haigh Moor W Yorks 88 B3
Haighton Green Lancs 93 F5
Hail Weston Cambs 54 C2
Haile Cumb 98 D2
Hailes Glos 50 F5
Hailey Herts 41 C6
Hailey Oxon 38 C3
Hailsham E Sus 18 E2
Haimer Highld 158 D3
Hainault London 41 E7
Hainford Norf 68 C5
Hainton Lincs 91 F5
Hairmyres S Lanark 119 D6
Haisthorpe E Yorks 97 C7
Hakin Pembs 44 E3
Halam Notts 77 D6
Halbeath Fife 128 F3
Halberton Devon 10 C5
Halcro Highld 158 D4
Hale Gtr Man 87 F5
Hale Halton 86 F2
Hale Hants 14 C2
Hale Bank Halton 86 F2
Hale Street Kent 29 E7
Halebarns Gtr Man 87 F5
Hales Norf 69 E6
Hales Staffs 74 F4
Hales Place Kent 30 D5
Halesfield Telford 61 D7
Halesgate Lincs 66 B3
Halesowen W Mid 62 F3
Halesworth Suff 57 B7
Halewood Mers 86 F2
Halford Shrops 60 F4
Halford Warks 51 E7
Halfpenny Furze Carms 32 C3
Halfpenny Green Staffs 62 E2
Halfway Carms 46 F5
Halfway Carms 47 F7
Halfway W Berks 26 C2
Halfway Bridge W Sus 16 B3
Halfway House Shrops 60 C3
Halfway Houses Kent 30 B3
Halifax W Yorks 87 B8
Halket E Ayrs 118 D4
Halkirk Highld 158 E3
Halkyn Flint 73 B6
Hall Dunnerdale Cumb 98 E4
Hall Green W Mid 62 F5
Hall Green W Yorks 88 C4
Hall Grove Herts 41 C5
Hall of Tankerness Orkney 159 H6
Hall of the Forest Shrops 60 F2
Halland E Sus 18 D2
Hallaton Leics 64 E4
Hallatrow Bath 23 D8
Hallbankgate Cumb 109 D5
Hallen S Glos 36 F2
Halliburton Borders 122 E2
Hallin Highld 148 C7
Halling Medway 29 C8
Hallington Lincs 91 F7
Hallington Northumb 110 B2
Halliwell Gtr Man 86 C5
Halloughton Notts 77 D6
Hallow Worcs 50 D3
Hallrule Borders 115 C8
Halls E Loth 122 B2
Hall's Green Herts 41 B5
Hallsands Devon 7 F6
Hallthwaites Cumb 98 F3
Hallworthy Corn 8 F3
Hallyburton House Perth 134 F2
Hallyne Borders 120 E4
Halmer End Staffs 74 E4
Halmore Glos 36 D3
Halmyre Mains Borders 120 E4
Halnaker W Sus 16 D3
Halsall Lancs 85 C4
Halse Northants 52 E3
Halse Som 11 B6
Halsetown Corn 2 C4
Halsham E Yorks 91 B6
Halsinger Devon 20 F4
Halstead Essex 56 F2
Halstead Kent 29 C5
Halstead Leics 64 D4
Halstock Dorset 12 D3
Haltham Lincs 78 C5
Haltoft End Lincs 79 E6
Halton Bucks 40 C1
Halton Halton 86 F3
Halton Lancs 92 C5
Halton Northumb 110 C2
Halton W Yorks 95 F6
Halton Wrex 73 F7
Halton East N Yorks 94 D3
Halton Gill N Yorks 93 B8
Halton Holegate Lincs 79 C7
Halton Lea Gate Northumb 109 D6
Halton West N Yorks 93 D8
Haltwhistle Northumb 109 C7
Halvergate Norf 69 D7
Halwell Devon 7 D5
Halwill Devon 9 E6
Halwill Junction Devon 9 D6
Ham Devon 11 D7
Ham Glos 36 E3
Ham Highld 158 C4
Ham Kent 31 D7
Ham London 28 B2
Ham Shetland 160 K1
Ham Wilts 25 C8
Ham Common Dorset 13 B6
Ham Green Hereford 50 E2
Ham Green Kent 19 C5
Ham Green Kent 30 C2
Ham Green N Som 23 B7
Ham Green Worcs 50 C5
Ham Street Som 23 F7
Hamble-le-Rice Hants 15 D5
Hambleden Bucks 39 F7
Hambledon Hants 15 C7
Hambledon Sur 27 F7
Hambleton Lancs 92 E3
Hambleton N Yorks 95 F8
Hambridge Som 11 B8
Hambrook S Glos 23 B8
Hambrook W Sus 15 D8
Hameringham Lincs 79 C6
Hamerton Cambs 54 B2
Hametoun Shetland 160 K1
Hamilton S Lanark 119 D7
Hammer W Sus 27 F6
Hammerpot W Sus 16 D4
Hammersmith London 28 B3
Hammerwich Staffs 62 D4
Hammerwood E Sus 28 F5
Hammond Street Herts 41 D6
Hammoon Dorset 13 C6
Hamnavoe Shetland 160 E4
Hamnavoe Shetland 160 E6
Hamnavoe Shetland 160 F6
Hamnavoe Shetland 160 K5
Hampden Park E Sus 18 E3
Hamperden End Essex 55 F6
Hampnett Glos 37 C7
Hampole S Yorks 89 C6
Hampreston Dorset 13 E8
Hampstead London 41 F5
Hampstead Norreys W Berks 26 B3
Hampsthwaite N Yorks 95 D5
Hampton London 28 C2
Hampton Shrops 61 F7
Hampton Worcs 50 E5
Hampton Bishop Hereford 49 F7
Hampton Heath Ches W 73 E8
Hampton in Arden W Mid 63 F6
Hampton Loade Shrops 61 F7
Hampton Lovett Worcs 50 C3
Hampton Lucy Warks 51 D7
Hampton on the Hill Warks 51 C7
Hampton Poyle Oxon 39 C5
Hamrow Norf 80 E5
Hamsey E Sus 17 C8
Hamsey Green London 28 D4
Hamstall Ridware Staffs 62 C5
Hamstead IoW 14 E5
Hamstead W Mid 62 E4
Hamstead Marshall W Berks 26 C2
Hamsterley Durham 110 D4
Hamsterley Durham 110 F4
Hamstreet Kent 19 B7
Hamworthy Poole 13 E7
Hanbury Staffs 63 B5
Hanbury Worcs 50 C4
Hanbury Woodend Staffs 63 B5
Hanby Lincs 78 F3
Hanchurch Staffs 74 E5
Handbridge Ches W 73 C8
Handcross W Sus 17 B6
Handforth Ches E 87 F6
Handley Ches W 73 D8
Handsacre Staffs 62 C4
Handsworth S Yorks 88 F5
Handsworth W Mid 62 E4
Handy Cross Devon 9 B6
Hanford Stoke 75 E5
Hanging Langford Wilts 24 F5
Hangleton W Sus 16 D4
Hanham S Glos 23 B8
Hankelow Ches E 74 E3
Hankerton Wilts 37 E6
Hankham E Sus 18 E3
Hanley Stoke 75 E5
Hanley Castle Worcs 50 E3
Hanley Child Worcs 49 C8
Hanley Swan Worcs 50 E3
Hanley William Worcs 49 C8
Hanlith N Yorks 94 C2
Hanmer Wrex 73 F8
Hannah Lincs 79 B8
Hannington Hants 26 D3
Hannington Northants 53 B6
Hannington Swindon 38 E1
Hannington Wick Swindon 38 E1
Hansel Village S Ayrs 118 F3
Hanslope M Keynes 53 E6
Hanthorpe Lincs 65 B7
Hanwell London 40 F4
Hanwell Oxon 52 E2
Hanwood Shrops 60 D4
Hanworth London 28 B2
Hanworth Norf 81 D7
Happendon S Lanark 119 F8
Happisburgh Norf 69 A6
Happisburgh Common Norf 69 B6
Hapsford Ches W 73 B8
Hapton Lancs 93 F7
Hapton Norf 68 E4
Harberton Devon 7 D5
Harbertonford Devon 7 D5
Harbledown Kent 30 D5
Harborne W Mid 62 F4
Harborough Magna Warks 52 B2
Harbottle Northumb 117 D5
Harbury Warks 51 D8
Harby Leics 77 F7
Harby Notts 77 B8
Harcombe Devon 11 E6
Harden W Mid 62 D4
Harden W Yorks 94 F3
Hardenhuish Wilts 24 B4
Hardgate Aberds 141 D6
Hardham W Sus 16 C4
Hardingham Norf 68 D3
Hardingstone Northants 53 D5
Hardington Som 24 D2
Hardington Mandeville Som 12 C3
Hardington Marsh Som 12 D3
Hardley Hants 14 D5
Hardley Street Norf 69 D6
Hardmead M Keynes 53 E7
Hardrow N Yorks 100 E3
Hardstoft Derbys 76 C4
Hardway Hants 15 D7
Hardway Som 24 F2
Hardwick Bucks 39 C8
Hardwick Cambs 54 D4
Hardwick Norf 67 C6
Hardwick Norf 68 F5
Hardwick Northants 53 C6
Hardwick Notts 77 B6
Hardwick Oxon 38 D3
Hardwick Oxon 39 B5
Hardwick W Mid 62 E4
Hardwicke Glos 36 C4
Hardwicke Glos 37 B6
Hardwicke Hereford 48 E4
Hardy's Green Essex 43 B5
Hare Green Essex 43 B6
Hare Hatch Wokingham 27 B6
Hare Street Herts 41 B6
Hareby Lincs 79 C6
Hareden Lancs 93 D6
Harefield London 40 E3
Harehills W Yorks 95 F6
Harehope Northumb 117 B6
Haresceugh Cumb 109 E6
Harescombe Glos 37 C5
Haresfield Glos 37 C5
Hareshaw N Lanark 119 C8
Hareshaw Head Northumb 116 F4
Harewood W Yorks 95 E6
Harewood End Hereford 36 B2
Harford Carms 46 E5
Harford Devon 6 D4
Hargate Norf 68 E4
Hargatewall Derbys 75 B8
Hargrave Ches W 73 C8
Hargrave Northants 53 B8
Hargrave Suff 55 D8
Harker Cumb 108 C3
Harkland Shetland 160 E6
Harkstead Suff 57 F5
Harlaston Staffs 63 C6
Harlaw Ho. Aberds 141 B6
Harlaxton Lincs 77 F8
Harle Syke Lancs 93 F8
Harlech Gwyn 71 D6
Harlequin Notts 77 F6
Harlescott Shrops 60 C5
Harlesden London 41 F5
Harleston Devon 7 E5
Harleston Norf 68 F5
Harleston Suff 56 D4
Harlestone Northants 52 C5
Harley S Yorks 88 E4
Harley Shrops 61 D5
Harleyholm S Lanark 120 F2
Harlington C Beds 53 F8
Harlington London 27 B8
Harlington S Yorks 89 D5
Harlosh Highld 149 D7
Harlow Essex 41 C7
Harlow Hill N Yorks 95 D5
Harlow Hill Northumb 110 C3
Harlthorpe E Yorks 96 F3
Harlton Cambs 54 D4
Harman's Cross Dorset 13 F7
Harmby N Yorks 101 F6
Harmer Green Herts 41 C5
Harmer Hill Shrops 60 B4
Harmondsworth London 27 B8
Harmston Lincs 78 C2
Harnham Northumb 110 B3
Harnhill Glos 37 D7
Harold Hill London 41 E8
Harold Wood London 41 E8
Haroldston West Pembs 44 D3
Haroldswick Shetland 160 B8
Harome N Yorks 102 F4
Harpenden Herts 40 C4
Harpford Devon 11 E5
Harpham E Yorks 97 C6
Harpley Norf 80 E3
Harpley Worcs 49 C8
Harpole Northants 52 C4
Harpsdale Highld 158 E3
Harpsden Oxon 39 F7
Harpswell Lincs 90 F3
Harpur Hill Derbys 75 B7
Harpurhey Gtr Man 87 D6
Harraby Cumb 108 D4
Harrapool Highld 149 F11
Harrier Shetland 160 J1
Harrietfield Perth 127 B8
Harrietsham Kent 30 D2
Harrington Cumb 98 B1
Harrington Lincs 79 B6
Harrington Northants 64 F4
Harringworth Northants 65 E6
Harris Highld 146 B6
Harrogate N Yorks 95 D6
Harrold Bedford 53 D7
Harrow London 40 F4
Harrow on the Hill London 40 F4
Harrow Street Suff 56 F3
Harrow Weald London 40 E4
Harrowbarrow Corn 5 C8
Harrowden Bedford 53 E8
Harrowgate Hill Darl 101 C7
Harston Cambs 54 D5
Harston Leics 77 F8
Harswell E Yorks 96 E4
Hart Hrtlpl 111 F7
Hart Common Gtr Man 86 D4
Hart Hill Luton 40 B4
Hart Station Hrtlpl 111 F7
Hartburn Northumb 117 F6
Hartburn Stockton 102 C2
Hartest Suff 56 D2
Hartfield E Sus 29 F5
Hartford Cambs 54 B3
Hartford Ches W 74 B3
Hartford End Essex 42 C2
Hartfordbridge Hants 27 D5
Hartforth N Yorks 101 D6
Harthill Ches W 74 D2
Harthill N Lanark 120 C2
Harthill S Yorks 89 F5
Hartington Derbys 75 C8
Hartland Devon 8 B4
Hartlebury Worcs 50 B3
Hartlepool Hrtlpl 111 F8
Hartley Cumb 100 D2
Hartley Kent 18 B4
Hartley Kent 29 C7
Hartley Northumb 111 B6
Hartley Westpall Hants 26 D4
Hartley Wintney Hants 27 D5
Hartlip Kent 30 C2
Hartoft End N Yorks 103 E5
Harton N Yorks 96 C3
Harton Shrops 60 F4
Harton T&W 111 C6
Hartpury Glos 36 B4
Hartshead W Yorks 88 B2
Hartshill Warks 63 E7
Hartshorne Derbys 63 B7
Hartsop Cumb 99 C6
Hartwell Northants 53 D5
Hartwood N Lanark 119 D8
Harvieston Stirling 126 F4
Harvington Worcs 51 E5
Harvington Cross Worcs 51 E5
Harwell Oxon 38 F4
Harwich Essex 57 F6
Harwood Durham 109 F8
Harwood Gtr Man 86 C5
Harwood Dale N Yorks 103 E7
Harworth Notts 89 E7
Hasbury W Mid 62 F3
Hascombe Sur 27 E7
Haselbech Northants 52 B5
Haselbury Plucknett Som 12 C2
Haseley Warks 51 C7
Haselor Warks 51 D6
Hasfield Glos 37 B5
Hasguard Pembs 44 E3
Haskayne Lancs 85 D4
Hasketon Suff 57 D6
Hasland Derbys 76 C3
Haslemere Sur 27 F7
Haslingden Lancs 87 B5
Haslingfield Cambs 54 D5
Haslington Ches E 74 D4
Hassall Ches E 74 D4
Hassall Green Ches E 74 D4
Hassell Street Kent 30 E4
Hassendean Borders 115 B8
Hassingham Norf 69 D6
Hassocks W Sus 17 C6
Hassop Derbys 76 B2
Hastigrow Highld 158 D4
Hastingleigh Kent 30 E4
Hastings E Sus 18 E5
Hastingwood Essex 41 D7
Hastoe Herts 40 D2
Haswell Durham 111 E6
Haswell Plough Durham 111 E6
Hatch C Beds 54 E2
Hatch Hants 26 D4
Hatch Wilts 13 B7
Hatch Beauchamp Som 11 B8
Hatch End London 40 E4
Hatch Green Som 11 C8
Hatchet Gate Hants 14 D4
Hatching Green Herts 40 C4
Hatchmere Ches W 74 B2
Hatcliffe NE Lincs 91 D6
Hatfield Hereford 49 D7
Hatfield Herts 41 D5
Hatfield S Yorks 89 D7
Hatfield Worcs 50 D3
Hatfield Broad Oak Essex 41 C8
Hatfield Garden Village Herts 41 D5
Hatfield Heath Essex 41 C8
Hatfield Hyde Herts 41 C5
Hatfield Peverel Essex 42 C3
Hatfield Woodhouse S Yorks 89 D7
Hatford Oxon 38 E3
Hatherden Hants 25 D8
Hatherleigh Devon 9 D7
Hathern Leics 63 B8
Hatherop Glos 38 D1
Hathersage Derbys 88 F3
Hathershaw Gtr Man 87 D7

Hatherton Ches E 74 E3
Hatherton Staffs 62 C3
Hatley St George Cambs 54 D3
Hatt Corn 5 C8
Hattingley Hants 26 F4
Hatton Aberds 153 E10
Hatton Derbys 63 B6
Hatton Lincs 78 B4
Hatton Shrops 60 E4
Hatton Warks 51 C7
Hatton Warr 86 F3
Hatton Castle Aberds 153 D7
Hatton Heath Ches W 73 C8
Hatton of Fintray Aberds 141 C7
Hattoncrook Aberds 141 B7
Haugh E Ayrs 112 B4
Haugh Gtr Man 87 C7
Haugh Lincs 79 B7
Haugh Head Northumb 117 B6
Haugh of Glass Moray 152 E4
Haugh of Urr Dumfries 106 C5
Haugham Lincs 91 F7
Haughley Suff 56 C4
Haughley Green Suff 56 C4
Haughs of Clinterty Aberdeen 141 C7
Haughton Notts 77 B6
Haughton Shrops 60 B3
Haughton Shrops 61 C5
Haughton Shrops 61 D7
Haughton Shrops 61 E6
Haughton Staffs 62 B2
Haughton Castle Northumb 110 B2
Haughton Green Gtr Man 87 E7
Haughton Moss Ches E 74 D2
Haultwick Herts 41 B6
Haunn Argyll 146 G6
Haunn W Isles 148 G2
Haunton Staffs 63 C6
Hauxley Northumb 117 D8
Hauxton Cambs 54 D5
Havant Hants 15 D8
Haven Hereford 49 D6
Haven Bank Lincs 78 D5
Haven Side E Yorks 91 B5
Havenstreet IoW 15 E6
Havercroft W Yorks 88 C4
Haverfordwest = Hwlffordd Pembs 44 D4
Haverhill Suff 55 E7
Haverigg Cumb 92 B1
Havering-atte-Bower London 41 E8
Haveringland Norf 81 E7
Haversham M Keynes 53 E6
Haverthwaite Cumb 99 F5
Haverton Hill Stockton 102 B2
Hawarden = Penarlâg Flint 73 C7
Hawcoat Cumb 92 B2
Hawen Ceredig 46 E2
Hawes N Yorks 100 F3
Hawes' Green Norf 68 E5
Hawes Side Blackpool 92 F3
Hawford Worcs 50 C3
Hawick Borders 115 C8
Hawk Green Gtr Man 87 F7
Hawkchurch Devon 11 D8
Hawkedon Suff 55 D8
Hawkenbury Kent 18 B2
Hawkenbury Kent 30 E2
Hawkeridge Wilts 24 D3
Hawkerland Devon 11 F5
Hawkes End W Mid 63 F7
Hawkesbury S Glos 36 F4
Hawkesbury Warks 63 F7
Hawkesbury Upton S Glos 36 F4
Hawkhill Northumb 117 C8
Hawkhurst Kent 18 B4
Hawkinge Kent 31 F6
Hawkley Hants 15 B8
Hawkridge Som 21 F7
Hawkshead Cumb 99 E5
Hawkshead Hill Cumb 99 E5
Hawksland S Lanark 119 F8
Hawkswick N Yorks 94 B2
Hawksworth Notts 77 E7
Hawksworth W Yorks 94 E4
Hawksworth W Yorks 95 F5
Hawkwell Essex 42 E4
Hawley Hants 27 D6
Hawley Kent 29 B6
Hawling Glos 37 B7
Hawnby N Yorks 102 F3
Haworth W Yorks 94 F3
Hawstead Suff 56 D2
Hawthorn Durham 111 E7
Hawthorn Rhondda 35 F5
Hawthorn Wilts 24 C3
Hawthorn Hill Brack 27 B6
Hawthorn Hill Lincs 78 D5
Hawthorpe Lincs 65 B7
Hawton Notts 77 D7
Haxby York 96 D2
Haxey N Lincs 89 D8
Hay Green Norf 66 C5
Hay-on-Wye = Y Gelli Gandryll Powys 48 E4
Hay Street Herts 41 B6
Haydock Mers 86 E3
Haydon Dorset 12 C4
Haydon Bridge Northumb 109 C8
Haydon Wick Swindon 37 F8
Haye Corn 5 C8
Hayes London 28 C5
Hayes London 40 F4
Hayfield Derbys 87 F8
Hayfield Fife 128 E4
Hayhill E Ayrs 112 C4
Hayhillock Angus 135 E5
Hayle Corn 2 C4
Haynes C Beds 53 E8
Haynes Church End C Beds 53 E8
Hayscastle Pembs 44 C3
Hayscastle Cross Pembs 44 C4
Hayshead Angus 135 E6
Hayton Aberdeen 141 D8
Hayton Cumb 107 E8
Hayton Cumb 108 D5
Hayton E Yorks 96 E4
Hayton Notts 89 F8
Hayton's Bent Shrops 60 F5
Haytor Vale Devon 7 B5
Haywards Heath W Sus 17 B7
Haywood S Yorks 89 C6
Haywood Oaks Notts 77 D6
Hazel Grove Gtr Man 87 F7
Hazel Street Kent 18 B3
Hazelbank S Lanark 119 E8
Hazelbury Bryan Dorset 12 D5
Hazeley Hants 26 D5
Hazelhurst Gtr Man 87 D7
Hazelslade Staffs 62 C4
Hazelton Glos 37 C7
Hazelton Walls Fife 128 B5
Hazelwood Derbys 76 E3
Hazlemere Bucks 40 E1
Hazlerigg T&W 110 B5
Hazlewood N Yorks 94 D3
Hazon Northumb 117 D7
Heacham Norf 80 D2
Head of Muir Falk 127 F7
Headbourne Worthy Hants 26 F2
Headbrook Hereford 48 D5
Headcorn Kent 30 E2
Headingley W Yorks 95 F5
Headington Oxon 39 D5
Headlam Durham 101 C6
Headless Cross Worcs 50 C5
Headley Hants 26 C3
Headley Hants 27 F6
Headley Sur 28 D3
Headon Notts 77 B7
Heads S Lanark 119 E7
Heads Nook Cumb 108 D4
Heage Derbys 76 D3
Healaugh N Yorks 95 E7
Healaugh N Yorks 101 E5
Heald Green Gtr Man 87 F6
Heale Devon 20 E5
Heale Som 23 E8
Healey Gtr Man 87 C6
Healey N Yorks 101 F6
Healey Northumb 110 D3
Healing NE Lincs 91 C6
Heamoor Corn 2 C3
Heanish Argyll 146 G3
Heanor Derbys 76 E4
Heanton Punchardon Devon 20 F4
Heapham Lincs 90 F2
Hearthstane Borders 114 B4
Heasley Mill Devon 21 F6
Heast Highld 149 G11
Heath Cardiff 22 B3
Heath Derbys 76 C4
Heath and Reach C Beds 40 B2
Heath End Hants 26 C3
Heath End Sur 27 E6
Heath End Warks 51 C7
Heath Hayes Staffs 62 C4
Heath Hill Shrops 61 C7
Heath House Som 23 E6
Heath Town W Mid 62 E3
Heathcote Derbys 75 C8
Heather Leics 63 C7
Heatherfield Highld 149 D9
Heathfield Devon 7 B6
Heathfield E Sus 18 C2
Heathfield Som 11 B6
Heathhall Dumfries 107 B6
Heathrow Airport London 27 B8
Heathstock Devon 11 D7
Heathton Shrops 62 E2
Heatley Warr 86 F5
Heaton Lancs 92 C4
Heaton Staffs 75 C6
Heaton T&W 111 C5
Heaton W Yorks 94 F4
Heaton Moor Gtr Man 87 E6
Heaverham Kent 29 D6
Heaviley Gtr Man 87 F7
Heavitree Devon 10 E4
Hebburn T&W 111 C6
Hebden N Yorks 94 C3
Hebden Bridge W Yorks 87 B7
Hebron Anglesey 82 C4
Hebron Carms 32 B2
Hebron Northumb 117 F7
Heck Dumfries 114 F3
Heckfield Hants 26 C5
Heckfield Green Suff 57 B5
Heckfordbridge Essex 43 B5
Heckington Lincs 78 E4
Heckmondwike W Yorks 88 B3
Heddington Wilts 24 C4
Heddle Orkney 159 G4
Heddon-on-the-Wall Northumb 110 C4
Hedenham Norf 69 E6
Hedge End Hants 15 C5
Hedgerley Bucks 40 F2
Hedging Som 11 B8
Hedley on the Hill Northumb 110 D3
Hednesford Staffs 62 C4
Hedon E Yorks 91 B5
Hedsor Bucks 40 F2
Hedworth T&W 111 C6
Hegdon Hill Hereford 49 D7
Heggerscales Cumb 100 C3
Heglibister Shetland 160 H5
Heighington Darl 101 B7
Heighington Lincs 78 C3
Heights of Brae Highld 151 E8
Heights of Kinlochewe Highld 150 E3
Heilam Highld 156 C7
Heiton Borders 122 F3
Hele Devon 10 D4
Hele Devon 20 E4
Helensburgh Argyll 145 E11
Helford Corn 3 D6
Helford Passage Corn 3 D6
Helhoughton Norf 80 E4
Helions Bumpstead Essex 55 E7
Hellaby S Yorks 89 E6
Helland Corn 5 B5
Hellesdon Norf 68 C5
Hellidon Northants 52 D3
Hellifield N Yorks 93 D8
Hellingly E Sus 18 D2
Hellington Norf 69 D6
Hellister Shetland 160 J5
Helm Northumb 117 E7
Helmdon Northants 52 E3
Helmingham Suff 57 D5
Helmington Row Durham 110 F4
Helmsdale Highld 157 H13
Helmshore Lancs 87 B5
Helmsley N Yorks 102 F4
Helperby N Yorks 95 C7
Helperthorpe N Yorks 97 B5
Helpringham Lincs 78 E4
Helpston Pboro 65 D8
Helsby Ches W 73 B8
Helsey Lincs 79 B8
Helston Corn 3 D5
Helstone Corn 8 F2
Helton Cumb 99 B7
Helwith Bridge N Yorks 93 C8
Hemblington Norf 69 C6
Hemel Hempstead Herts 40 D3
Hemingbrough N Yorks 96 F2
Hemingby Lincs 78 B5
Hemingford Abbots Cambs 54 B3
Hemingford Grey Cambs 54 B3
Hemingstone Suff 57 D5
Hemington Leics 63 B8
Hemington Northants 65 F7
Hemington Som 24 D2
Hemley Suff 57 E6
Hemlington Mbro 102 C3
Hemp Green Suff 57 C7
Hempholme E Yorks 97 D6
Hempnall Norf 68 E5
Hempnall Green Norf 68 E5
Hempriggs House Highld 158 F5
Hempstead Essex 55 F7
Hempstead Medway 29 C8
Hempstead Norf 69 B7
Hempstead Norf 81 D7
Hempsted Glos 37 C5
Hempton Norf 80 E5
Hempton Oxon 52 F2
Hemsby Norf 69 C7
Hemswell Lincs 90 E3
Hemswell Cliff Lincs 90 F3
Hemsworth W Yorks 88 C5
Hemyock Devon 11 C6
Hen-feddau fawr Pembs 45 F4
Henbury Bristol 23 B7
Henbury Ches E 75 B5
Hendon London 41 F5
Hendon T&W 111 D7
Hendre Flint 73 C5
Hendre-ddu Conwy 83 E8
Hendreforgan Rhondda 34 F3
Hendy Carms 33 D6
Heneglwys Anglesey 82 D4
Henfield W Sus 17 C6
Henford Devon 9 E5
Henghurst Kent 19 B6
Hengoed Caerph 35 E5
Hengoed Powys 48 D4
Hengoed Shrops 73 F6
Hengrave Suff 56 C2
Henham Essex 41 B8
Heniarth Powys 59 D8
Henlade Som 11 B7
Henley Shrops 49 B7
Henley Som 23 F6
Henley Suff 57 D5
Henley W Sus 16 B2
Henley-in-Arden Warks 51 C6
Henley-on-Thames Oxon 39 F7
Henley's Down E Sus 18 D4
Henllan Ceredig 46 E2
Henllan Denb 72 C4
Henllan Amgoed Carms 32 B2
Henllys Torf 35 E6
Henlow C Beds 54 F2
Hennock Devon 10 F3
Henny Street Essex 56 F2
Henryd Conwy 83 D7
Henry's Moat Pembs 32 B1
Hensall N Yorks 89 B6
Henshaw Northumb 109 C7
Hensingham Cumb 98 C1
Henstead Suff 69 F7
Henstridge Som 12 C5
Henstridge Ash Som 12 B5
Henstridge Marsh Som 12 B5
Henton Oxon 39 D7
Henton Som 23 E6
Henwood Corn 5 B7
Heogan Shetland 160 J6
Heol-las Swansea 33 E7
Heol Senni Powys 34 B3
Heol-y-Cyw Bridgend 34 F3
Hepburn Northumb 117 B6
Hepple Northumb 117 D5
Hepscott Northumb 117 F8
Heptonstall W Yorks 87 B7
Hepworth Suff 56 B3
Hepworth W Yorks 88 D2
Herbrandston Pembs 44 E3
Hereford Hereford 49 E7
Heriot Borders 121 D6
Hermiston Edin 120 B4
Hermitage Borders 115 E8
Hermitage Dorset 12 D4
Hermitage W Berks 26 B3
Hermitage W Sus 15 D8
Hermon Anglesey 82 E3
Hermon Carms 33 B7
Hermon Carms 46 F2
Hermon Pembs 45 F4
Herne Kent 31 C5
Herne Bay Kent 31 C5
Herner Devon 9 B7
Hernhill Kent 30 C4
Herodsfoot Corn 5 C7
Herongate Essex 42 E2
Heronsford S Ayrs 104 A5
Herriard Hants 26 E4
Herringfleet Suff 69 E7
Herringswell Suff 55 B8
Hersden Kent 31 C6
Hersham Corn 8 D4
Hersham Sur 28 C2
Herstmonceux E Sus 18 D3
Herston Orkney 159 J5
Hertford Herts 41 C6
Hertford Heath Herts 41 C6
Hertingfordbury Herts 41 C6
Hesket Newmarket Cumb 108 F3
Hesketh Bank Lancs 86 B2
Hesketh Lane Lancs 93 E6
Heskin Green Lancs 86 C3
Hesleden Durham 111 F7
Hesleyside Northumb 116 F4
Heslington York 96 D2
Hessay York 95 D8
Hessenford Corn 5 D8
Hessett Suff 56 C3
Hessle E Yorks 90 B4
Hest Bank Lancs 92 C4
Heston London 28 B2
Hestwall Orkney 159 G3
Heswall Mers 85 F3
Hethe Oxon 39 B5
Hethersett Norf 68 D4
Hethersgill Cumb 108 C4
Hethpool Northumb 116 B4
Hett Durham 111 F5
Hetton N Yorks 94 D2
Hetton-le-Hole T&W 111 E6
Hetton Steads Northumb 123 F6
Heugh Northumb 110 B3
Heugh-head Aberds 140 C2
Heveningham Suff 57 B7
Hever Kent 29 E5
Heversham Cumb 99 F6
Hevingham Norf 81 E7
Hewas Water Corn 3 B8
Hewelsfield Glos 36 D2
Hewish N Som 23 C6
Hewish Som 12 D2
Heworth York 96 D2
Hexham Northumb 110 C2
Hextable Kent 29 B6
Hexton Herts 54 F2
Hexworthy Devon 6 B4
Hey Lancs 93 E8
Heybridge Essex 42 D4
Heybridge Essex 42 E2
Heybridge Basin Essex 42 D4
Heybrook Bay Devon 6 E3
Heydon Cambs 54 E5
Heydon Norf 81 E7
Heydour Lincs 78 F3
Heylipol Argyll 146 G2
Heylor Shetland 160 E4
Heysham Lancs 92 C4
Heyshott W Sus 16 C2
Heyside Gtr Man 87 D7
Heytesbury Wilts 24 E4
Heythrop Oxon 38 B3
Heywood Gtr Man 87 C6
Heywood Wilts 24 D3
Hibaldstow N Lincs 90 D3
Hickleton S Yorks 89 D5
Hickling Norf 69 B7
Hickling Notts 64 B3
Hickling Green Norf 69 B7
Hickling Heath Norf 69 B7
Hickstead W Sus 17 B6
Hidcote Boyce Glos 51 E6
High Ackworth W Yorks 88 C5
High Angerton Northumb 117 F6
High Bankhill Cumb 109 E5
High Barnes T&W 111 D6
High Beach Essex 41 E7
High Bentham N Yorks 93 C6
High Bickington Devon 9 B8
High Birkwith N Yorks 93 B7
High Blantyre S Lanark 119 D6
High Bonnybridge Falk 119 B8
High Bradfield S Yorks 88 E3
High Bray Devon 21 F5
High Brooms Kent 29 E6
High Bullen Devon 9 B7
High Buston Northumb 117 D8
High Callerton Northumb 110 B4
High Catton E Yorks 96 D3
High Cogges Oxon 38 D3
High Coniscliffe Darl 101 C7
High Cross Hants 15 B8
High Cross Herts 41 C6
High Easter Essex 42 C2
High Eggborough N Yorks 89 B6
High Ellington N Yorks 101 F6
High Ercall Telford 61 C5
High Etherley Durham 101 B6
High Garrett Essex 42 B3
High Grange Durham 110 F4
High Green Norf 68 D4
High Green S Yorks 88 E4
High Green Worcs 50 E3
High Halden Kent 19 B5
High Halstow Medway 29 B8
High Ham Som 23 F6
High Harrington Cumb 98 B2
High Hatton Shrops 61 B6
High Hawsker N Yorks 103 D7
High Hesket Cumb 108 E4
High Hesleden Durham 111 F7
High Hoyland S Yorks 88 C3
High Hunsley E Yorks 97 F5
High Hurstwood E Sus 17 B8
High Hutton N Yorks 96 C3
High Ireby Cumb 108 F2
High Kelling Norf 81 C7
High Kilburn N Yorks 95 B8
High Lands Durham 101 B6
High Lane Gtr Man 87 F7
High Lane Worcs 49 C8
High Laver Essex 41 D8
High Legh Ches E 86 F5
High Leven Stockton 102 C2
High Littleton Bath 23 D8
High Lorton Cumb 98 B3
High Marishes N Yorks 96 B4
High Marnham Notts 77 B8
High Melton S Yorks 89 D6
High Mickley Northumb 110 C3
High Mindork Dumfries 105 D7
High Newton Cumb 99 F6
High Newton-by-the-Sea Northumb 117 B8
High Nibthwaite Cumb 98 F4
High Offley Staffs 61 B7
High Ongar Essex 42 D1
High Onn Staffs 62 C2
High Roding Essex 42 C2
High Row Cumb 108 F3
High Salvington W Sus 16 D5
High Sellafield Cumb 98 D2
High Shaw N Yorks 100 E3
High Spen T&W 110 D4
High Stoop Durham 110 E4
High Street Corn 4 D4
High Street Kent 18 B4
High Street Suff 56 E2
High Street Suff 57 B8
High Street Suff 57 D8
High Street Green Suff 56 D4
High Throston Hrtlpl 111 F7
High Toynton Lincs 79 C5
High Trewhitt Northumb 117 D6
High Valleyfield Fife 128 F2
High Westwood Durham 110 D4
High Wray Cumb 99 E5
High Wych Herts 41 C7
High Wycombe Bucks 40 E1
Higham Derbys 76 D3
Higham Kent 29 B8
Higham Lancs 93 F8
Higham Suff 55 C8
Higham Suff 56 F4
Higham Dykes Northumb 110 B4
Higham Ferrers Northants 53 C7
Higham Gobion C Beds 54 F2
Higham on the Hill Leics 63 E7
Higham Wood Kent 29 E6
Highampton Devon 9 D6
Highbridge Highld 136 F4
Highbridge Som 22 E5
Highbrook W Sus 28 F4
Highburton W Yorks 88 C2
Highbury Som 23 E8
Highclere Hants 26 C2
Highcliffe Dorset 14 E3
Higher Ansty Dorset 13 D5
Higher Ashton Devon 10 F3
Higher Ballam Lancs 92 F3
Higher Bartle Lancs 92 F5
Higher Boscaswell Corn 2 C2
Higher Burwardsley Ches W 74 D2
Higher Clovelly Devon 8 B5
Higher End Gtr Man 86 D3
Higher Kinnerton Flint 73 C7
Higher Penwortham Lancs 86 B3
Higher Town Scilly 2 E4
Higher Walreddon Devon 6 B2
Higher Walton Lancs 86 B3
Higher Walton Warr 86 F3
Higher Wheelton Lancs 86 B4
Higher Whitley Ches W 86 F4
Higher Wincham Ches W 74 B3
Higher Wych Ches W 73 E8
Highfield E Yorks 96 F3
Highfield Gtr Man 86 D5
Highfield N Ayrs 118 D3
Highfield Oxon 39 B5
Highfield S Yorks 88 F4
Highfield T&W 110 D4
Highfields Cambs 54 D4
Highfields Northumb 123 D5
Highgate London 41 F5
Highlane Ches E 75 C5
Highlane Derbys 88 F5
Highlaws Cumb 107 E8
Highleadon Glos 36 B4
Highleigh W Sus 16 E2
Highley Shrops 61 F7
Highmoor Cross Oxon 39 F7
Highmoor Hill Mon 36 F1
Highnam Glos 36 C4
Highnam Green Glos 36 B4
Highsted Kent 30 C3
Highstreet Green Essex 55 F8
Hightae Dumfries 107 B7
Hightown Ches E 75 C5
Hightown Mers 85 D4
Hightown Green Suff 56 D3
Highway Wilts 24 B5
Highweek Devon 7 B6
Highworth Swindon 38 E2
Hilborough Norf 67 D8
Hilcote Derbys 76 D4
Hilcott Wilts 25 D6
Hilden Park Kent 29 E6
Hildenborough Kent 29 E6
Hildersham Cambs 55 E6
Hilderstone Staffs 75 F6
Hilderthorpe E Yorks 97 C7
Hilfield Dorset 12 D4
Hilgay Norf 67 E6
Hill Pembs 32 D2
Hill S Glos 36 E3
Hill W Mid 62 E5
Hill Brow W Sus 15 B8
Hill Dale Lancs 86 C2
Hill Dyke Lincs 79 E6
Hill End Durham 110 F3
Hill End Fife 128 E2
Hill End N Yorks 94 D3
Hill Head Hants 15 D6
Hill Head Northumb 110 C2
Hill Mountain Pembs 44 E4
Hill of Beath Fife 128 E3
Hill of Fearn Highld 151 D11
Hill of Mountblairy Aberds 153 C6
Hill Ridware Staffs 62 C4
Hill Top Durham 100 B4
Hill Top Hants 14 D5
Hill Top W Mid 62 E3
Hill Top W Yorks 88 C4
Hill View Dorset 13 E7
Hillam N Yorks 89 B6
Hillbeck Cumb 100 C2
Hillborough Kent 31 C6
Hillbrae Aberds 141 B6
Hillbrae Aberds 152 D6
Hillbrae Aberds 153 E7
Hillbutts Dorset 13 D7
Hillclifflane Derbys 76 E2
Hillcommon Som 11 B6
Hillend Fife 128 F3
Hillerton Devon 10 E2
Hillesden Bucks 39 B6
Hillesley Glos 36 F4
Hillfarance Som 11 B6
Hillhead Aberds 152 E5
Hillhead Devon 7 D7
Hillhead S Ayrs 112 C4
Hillhead of Auchentumb Aberds 153 C9
Hillhead of Cocklaw Aberds 153 D10
Hillhouse Borders 121 D8
Hilliclay Highld 158 D3
Hillingdon London 40 F3
Hillington Glasgow 118 C5
Hillington Norf 80 E3
Hillmorton Warks 52 B3
Hillockhead Aberds 140 C3
Hillockhead Aberds 140 D2
Hillside Aberds 141 E8
Hillside Angus 135 C7
Hillside Mers 85 C4
Hillside Orkney 159 J5
Hillside Shetland 160 G6
Hillswick Shetland 160 F4
Hillway IoW 15 F7
Hillwell Shetland 160 M5
Hilmarton Wilts 24 B5
Hilperton Wilts 24 D3
Hilsea Ptsmth 15 D7
Hilston E Yorks 97 F8
Hilton Aberds 153 E9
Hilton Cambs 54 C3
Hilton Cumb 100 B2
Hilton Derbys 76 F2
Hilton Dorset 13 D5
Hilton Durham 101 B6
Hilton Highld 151 C10
Hilton Shrops 61 E7
Hilton Stockton 102 C2
Hilton of Cadboll Highld 151 D11
Himbleton Worcs 50 D4
Himley Staffs 62 E2
Hincaster Cumb 99 F7
Hinckley Leics 63 E8
Hinderclay Suff 56 B4
Hinderton Ches W 73 B7
Hinderwell N Yorks 103 C5
Hindford Shrops 73 F7
Hindhead Sur 27 F6
Hindley Gtr Man 86 D4
Hindley Green Gtr Man 86 D4
Hindlip Worcs 50 D3
Hindolveston Norf 81 E6
Hindon Wilts 24 F4
Hindringham Norf 81 D5
Hingham Norf 68 D3
Hinstock Shrops 61 B6
Hintlesham Suff 56 E4
Hinton Hants 14 E3
Hinton Hereford 48 F5
Hinton Northants 52 D3
Hinton S Glos 24 B2
Hinton Shrops 60 D4
Hinton Ampner Hants 15 B6
Hinton Blewett Bath 23 D7
Hinton Charterhouse Bath 24 D2
Hinton-in-the-Hedges Northants 52 F3
Hinton Martell Dorset 13 D8
Hinton on the Green Worcs 50 E5
Hinton Parva Swindon 38 F2
Hinton St George Som 12 C2
Hinton St Mary Dorset 13 C5
Hinton Waldrist Oxon 38 E3
Hints Shrops 49 B8
Hints Staffs 63 D5
Hinwick Bedford 53 C7
Hinxhill Kent 30 E4
Hinxton Cambs 55 E5
Hinxworth Herts 54 E3
Hipperholme W Yorks 88 B2
Hipswell N Yorks 101 E6
Hirael Gwyn 83 D5
Hiraeth Carms 32 B2
Hirn Aberds 141 D6
Hirnant Powys 59 B7
Hirst N Lanark 119 C8
Hirst Northumb 117 F8
Hirst Courtney N Yorks 89 B7
Hirwaen Denb 72 C5
Hirwaun Rhondda 34 D3
Hiscott Devon 9 B7
Histon Cambs 54 C5
Hitcham Suff 56 D3
Hitchin Herts 40 B4
Hither Green London 28 B4
Hittisleigh Devon 10 E2
Hive E Yorks 96 F4
Hixon Staffs 62 B4
Hoaden Kent 31 D6
Hoaldalbert Mon 35 B7
Hoar Cross Staffs 62 B5
Hoarwithy Hereford 36 B2
Hoath Kent 31 C6
Hobarris Shrops 48 B5
Hobbister Orkney 159 H4
Hobkirk Borders 115 C8
Hobson Durham 110 D4
Hoby Leics 64 C3
Hockering Norf 68 C3
Hockerton Notts 77 D7
Hockley Essex 42 E4
Hockley Heath W Mid 51 B6
Hockliffe C Beds 40 B2
Hockwold cum Wilton Norf 67 F7
Hockworthy Devon 10 C5
Hoddesdon Herts 41 D6
Hoddlesden Blackburn 86 B5
Hoddom Mains Dumfries 107 B8
Hoddomcross Dumfries 107 B8
Hodgeston Pembs 32 E1
Hodley Powys 59 E8
Hodnet Shrops 61 B6
Hodthorpe Derbys 76 B5
Hoe Hants 15 C6
Hoe Norf 68 C2
Hoe Gate Hants 15 C7
Hoff Cumb 100 C1
Hog Patch Sur 27 E6
Hoggard's Green Suff 56 D2
Hoggeston Bucks 39 B8
Hogha Gearraidh W Isles 148 A2
Hoghton Lancs 86 B4
Hognaston Derbys 76 D2
Hogsthorpe Lincs 79 B8
Holbeach Lincs 66 B3
Holbeach Bank Lincs 66 B3
Holbeach Clough Lincs 66 B3
Holbeach Drove Lincs 66 C3
Holbeach Hurn Lincs 66 B3
Holbeach St Johns Lincs 66 C3
Holbeach St Marks Lincs 79 F6
Holbeach St Matthew Lincs 79 F7
Holbeck Notts 76 B5
Holbeck W Yorks 95 F5
Holbeck Woodhouse Notts 76 B5
Holberrow Green Worcs 50 D5
Holbeton Devon 6 D4
Holborn London 41 F6
Holbrook Derbys 76 E3
Holbrook S Yorks 88 F5
Holbrook Suff 57 F5
Holburn Northumb 123 F6
Holbury Hants 14 D5
Holcombe Devon 7 B7
Holcombe Som 23 E8
Holcombe Rogus Devon 11 C5
Holcot Northants 53 C5
Holden Lancs 93 E7
Holdenby Northants 52 C4
Holdenhurst Bmouth 14 E2
Holdgate Shrops 61 F5
Holdingham Lincs 78 E3
Holditch Dorset 11 D8
Hole-in-the-Wall Hereford 36 B3
Holefield Borders 122 F4
Holehouses Ches E 74 B4
Holemoor Devon 9 D6
Holestane Dumfries 113 E8
Holford Som 22 E3
Holgate York 95 D8
Holker Cumb 92 B3
Holkham Norf 80 C4
Hollacombe Devon 9 D5
Holland Orkney 159 C5
Holland Orkney 159 F7
Holland Fen Lincs 78 E5
Holland-on-Sea Essex 43 C8
Hollandstoun Orkney 159 C8
Hollee Dumfries 108 C2
Hollesley Suff 57 E7
Hollicombe Torbay 7 C6
Hollingbourne Kent 30 D2
Hollington Derbys 76 F2
Hollington E Sus 18 D4
Hollington Staffs 75 F7
Hollington Grove Derbys 76 F2
Hollingworth Gtr Man 87 E8
Hollins Gtr Man 87 D6
Hollins Green Warr 86 E4
Hollins Lane Lancs 92 D4
Hollinsclough Staffs 75 C7
Hollinwood Gtr Man 87 D7
Hollinwood Shrops 74 F2
Hollocombe Devon 9 C8
Hollow Meadows S Yorks 88 F3
Holloway Derbys 76 D3
Hollowell Northants 52 B4
Holly End Norf 66 D4
Holly Green Worcs 50 E3
Hollybush Caerph 35 D5
Hollybush E Ayrs 112 C3
Hollybush Worcs 50 F2
Hollym E Yorks 91 B7
Hollywood Worcs 51 B5
Holmbridge W Yorks 88 D2
Holmbury St Mary Sur 28 E2
Holmbush Corn 4 D5
Holmcroft Staffs 62 B3
Holme Cambs 65 F8
Holme Cumb 92 B5
Holme N Yorks 102 F1
Holme Notts 77 D8
Holme W Yorks 88 D2
Holme Chapel Lancs 87 B6
Holme Green N Yorks 95 E8
Holme Hale Norf 67 D8
Holme Lacy Hereford 49 F7
Holme Marsh Hereford 48 D5
Holme next the Sea Norf 80 C3
Holme-on-Spalding-Moor E Yorks 96 F4
Holme on the Wolds E Yorks 97 E5
Holme Pierrepont Notts 77 F6
Holme St Cuthbert Cumb 107 E8
Holme Wood W Yorks 94 F4
Holmer Hereford 49 E7
Holmer Green Bucks 40 E2
Holmes Chapel Ches E 74 C4
Holmesfield Derbys 76 B3
Holmeswood Lancs 86 C2
Holmewood Derbys 76 C4
Holmfirth W Yorks 88 D2
Holmhead Dumfries 113 F7
Holmhead E Ayrs 113 B5
Holmisdale Highld 148 D6
Holmpton E Yorks 91 B7
Holmrook Cumb 98 E2
Holmsgarth Shetland 160 J6
Holmwrangle Cumb 108 E5
Holne Devon 6 C5
Holnest Dorset 12 D4
Holsworthy Devon 8 D5
Holsworthy Beacon Devon 9 D5
Holt Dorset 13 D8
Holt Norf 81 D6
Holt Wilts 24 C3
Holt Worcs 50 C3
Holt Wrex 73 D8
Holt End Hants 26 F4
Holt End Worcs 51 C5
Holt Fleet Worcs 50 C3
Holt Heath Worcs 50 C3
Holt Park W Yorks 95 E5
Holtby York 96 D2
Holton Oxon 39 D6
Holton Som 12 B4
Holton Suff 57 B7
Holton cum Beckering Lincs 90 F5
Holton Heath Dorset 13 E7
Holton le Clay Lincs 91 D6
Holton le Moor Lincs 90 E4
Holton St Mary Suff 56 F4
Holwell Dorset 12 C5
Holwell Herts 54 F2
Holwell Leics 64 B4
Holwell Oxon 38 D2
Holwick Durham 100 B4
Holworth Dorset 13 F5
Holy Cross Worcs 50 B4
Holy Island Northumb 123 E7
Holybourne Hants 26 E5
Holyhead = Caergybi Anglesey 82 C2
Holymoorside Derbys 76 C3
Holyport Windsor 27 B6
Holystone Northumb 117 D5
Holytown N Lanark 119 C7
Holywell Cambs 54 B4
Holywell Corn 4 D2
Holywell Dorset 12 D3
Holywell E Sus 18 F2
Holywell = Treffynnon Flint 73 B5
Holywell Northumb 111 B6
Holywell Green W Yorks 87 C8
Holywell Lake Som 11 B6
Holywell Row Suff 55 B8
Holywood Dumfries 114 F2
Hom Green Hereford 36 B2
Homer Shrops 61 D6
Homersfield Suff 69 F5
Homington Wilts 14 B2
Honey Hill Kent 30 C5
Honey Street Wilts 25 C6
Honey Tye Suff 56 F3
Honeyborough Pembs 44 E4
Honeybourne Worcs 51 E6
Honeychurch Devon 9 D8
Honiley Warks 51 B7
Honing Norf 69 B6
Honingham Norf 68 C4
Honington Lincs 78 E2
Honington Suff 56 B3
Honington Warks 51 E7
Honiton Devon 11 D6
Honley W Yorks 88 C2
Hoo Green Ches E 86 F5
Hoo St Werburgh Medway 29 B8
Hood Green S Yorks 88 D4
Hooe E Sus 18 E3
Hooe Plym 6 D3
Hooe Common E Sus 18 D3
Hook E Yorks 89 B8
Hook Hants 26 D5
Hook London 28 C2
Hook Pembs 44 D4
Hook Wilts 37 F7
Hook Green Kent 18 B3
Hook Green Kent 29 C7
Hook Norton Oxon 51 F8
Hooke Dorset 12 E3
Hookgate Staffs 74 F4
Hookway Devon 10 E3
Hookwood Sur 28 E3
Hoole Ches W 73 C8
Hooley Sur 28 D3
Hoop Mon 36 D2
Hooton Ches W 73 B7
Hooton Levitt S Yorks 89 E6
Hooton Pagnell S Yorks 89 D5
Hooton Roberts S Yorks 89 E5
Hop Pole Lincs 65 C8
Hope Derbys 88 F2
Hope Devon 6 F4
Hope Highld 156 B7
Hope Powys 60 D2
Hope Shrops 60 D3
Hope Staffs 75 D8
Hope = Yr Hôb Flint 73 D7
Hope Bagot Shrops 49 B7
Hope Bowdler Shrops 60 E4
Hope End Green Essex 42 B1
Hope Green Ches E 87 F7
Hope Mansell Hereford 36 C3
Hope under Dinmore Hereford 49 D7
Hopeman Moray 152 B1
Hope's Green Essex 42 F3
Hopesay Shrops 60 F3
Hopley's Green Hereford 48 D5
Hopperton N Yorks 95 D7
Hopstone Shrops 61 E7
Hopton Shrops 60 B3
Hopton Shrops 61 B5
Hopton Staffs 62 B3
Hopton Suff 56 B3
Hopton Cangeford Shrops 60 F5
Hopton Castle Shrops 49 B5
Hopton on Sea Norf 69 D8
Hopton Wafers Shrops 49 B8
Hoptonheath Shrops 49 B5
Hopwas Staffs 63 D5
Hopwood Gtr Man 87 D6
Hopwood Worcs 50 B5
Horam E Sus 18 D2
Horbling Lincs 78 F4
Horbury W Yorks 88 C3
Horcott Glos 38 D1
Horden Durham 111 E7
Horderley Shrops 60 F4
Hordle Hants 14 E3
Hordley Shrops 73 F7
Horeb Carms 33 B6
Horeb Carms 33 D5
Horeb Ceredig 46 E2
Horfield Bristol 23 B8
Horham Suff 57 B6
Horkesley Heath Essex 43 B5
Horkstow N Lincs 90 C3
Horley Oxon 52 E2
Horley Sur 28 E3
Hornblotton Green Som 23 F7
Hornby Lancs 93 C5
Hornby N Yorks 101 E7
Hornby N Yorks 102 D1
Horncastle Lincs 79 C5
Hornchurch London 41 F8
Horncliffe Northumb 122 E5
Horndean Borders 122 E4
Horndean Hants 15 C8
Horndon Devon 6 B3
Horndon on the Hill Thurrock 42 F2
Horne Sur 28 E4
Horniehaugh Angus 134 C4
Horning Norf 69 C6
Horninghold Leics 64 E5
Horninglow Staffs 63 B6
Horningsea Cambs 55 C5
Horningsham Wilts 24 E3
Horningtoft Norf 80 E5
Hornsby Cumb 108 D5
Horns Corner Kent 18 C4
Horns Cross Devon 9 B5
Horns Cross E Sus 18 C5
Hornsea E Yorks 97 E8
Hornsea Bridge E Yorks 97 E8
Hornsey London 41 F6
Hornton Oxon 51 E8
Horrabridge Devon 6 C3
Horringer Suff 56 C2
Horringford IoW 15 F6
Horse Bridge Staffs 75 D6
Horsebridge Devon 6 B2
Horsebridge Hants 25 F8
Horsebrook Staffs 62 C2
Horsehay Telford 61 D6
Horseheath Cambs 55 E7
Horsehouse N Yorks 101 F5
Horsell Sur 27 D7
Horseman's Green Wrex 73 E8
Horseway Cambs 66 F4
Horsey Norf 69 B7
Horsford Norf 68 C4
Horsforth W Yorks 94 F5
Horsham W Sus 28 F2
Horsham Worcs 50 D2
Horsham St Faith Norf 68 C5
Horsington Lincs 78 C4
Horsington Som 12 B5
Horsley Derbys 76 E3
Horsley Glos 37 E5
Horsley Northumb 110 C3
Horsley Northumb 116 E4
Horsley Cross Essex 43 B7
Horsley Woodhouse Derbys 76 E3
Horsleycross Street Essex 43 B7
Horsleyhill Borders 115 C8
Horsleyhope Durham 110 E3
Horsmonden Kent 29 E7
Horspath Oxon 39 D5
Horstead Norf 69 C5
Horsted Keynes W Sus 17 B7
Horton Bucks 40 C2
Horton Dorset 13 D8
Horton Lancs 93 D8
Horton Northants 53 D6
Horton S Glos 36 F4
Horton Shrops 60 B4
Horton Som 11 C8
Horton Staffs 75 D6
Horton Swansea 33 F5
Horton Wilts 25 C5
Horton Windsor 27 B8
Horton-cum-Studley Oxon 39 C5
Horton Green Ches W 73 E8
Horton Heath Hants 15 C5
Horton in Ribblesdale N Yorks 93 B8
Horton Kirby Kent 29 C6
Hortonlane Shrops 60 C4
Horwich Gtr Man 86 C4
Horwich End Derbys 87 F8
Horwood Devon 9 B7
Hose Leics 64 B4
Hoselaw Borders 122 F4
Hoses Cumb 98 E4
Hosh Perth 127 B7
Hosta W Isles 148 A2
Hoswick Shetland 160 L6
Hotham E Yorks 96 F4
Hothfield Kent 30 E3
Hoton Leics 64 B2
Houbie Shetland 160 D8
Houdston S Ayrs 112 E1
Hough Ches E 74 D4
Hough Ches E 75 B5
Hough Green Halton 86 F2
Hough-on-the-Hill Lincs 78 E2
Hougham Lincs 77 E8
Houghton Cambs 54 B3
Houghton Cumb 108 D4
Houghton Hants 25 F8
Houghton Pembs 44 E4
Houghton W Sus 16 C4
Houghton Conquest C Beds 53 E8
Houghton Green E Sus 19 C6
Houghton Green Warr 86 E4
Houghton-le-Side Darl 101 B7
Houghton-Le-Spring T&W 111 E6
Houghton on the Hill Leics 64 D3
Houghton Regis C Beds 40 B3
Houghton St Giles Norf 80 D5
Houlland Shetland 160 F7
Houlland Shetland 160 H5
Houlsyke N Yorks 103 D5
Hound Hants 15 D5
Hound Green Hants 26 D5
Houndslow Borders 122 E2
Houndwood Borders 122 C4
Hounslow London 28 B2
Hounslow Green Essex 42 C2
Housay Shetland 160 F8
House of Daviot Highld 151 G10
House of Glenmuick Aberds 140 E2
Housetter Shetland 160 E5
Houss Shetland 160 K5
Houston Renfs 118 C4
Houstry Highld 158 G3
Houton Orkney 159 H4
Hove Brighton 17 D6
Hoveringham Notts 77 E6
Hoveton Norf 69 C6
Hovingham N Yorks 96 B2
How Cumb 108 D5
How Caple Hereford 49 F8
How End C Beds 53 E8
How Green Kent 29 E5
Howbrook S Yorks 88 E4
Howden Borders 116 B2
Howden E Yorks 89 B8
Howden-le-Wear Durham 110 F4
Howe Highld 158 D5
Howe N Yorks 101 F8
Howe Norf 69 D5
Howe Bridge Gtr Man 86 D4
Howe Green Essex 42 D3
Howe of Teuchar Aberds 153 D7
Howe Street Essex 42 C2
Howe Street Essex 55 F7
Howell Lincs 78 E4
Howey Powys 48 D2
Howgate Midloth 120 D5
Howick Northumb 117 C8
Howle Durham 101 B5
Howle Telford 61 B6
Howlett End Essex 55 F6
Howley Som 11 D7
Hownam Borders 116 C3
Hownam Mains Borders 116 B3
Howpasley Borders 115 D6
Howsham N Lincs 90 D4
Howsham N Yorks 96 C3
Howslack Dumfries 114 D3
Howtel Northumb 122 F4
Howton Hereford 35 B8
Howtown Cumb 99 C6
Howwood Renfs 118 C3
Hoxne Suff 57 B5
Hoy Orkney 159 H3
Hoylake Mers 85 F3
Hoyland S Yorks 88 D4
Hoylandswaine S Yorks 88 D3
Hubberholme N Yorks 94 B2
Hubbert's Bridge Lincs 79 E5
Huby N Yorks 95 C8
Huby N Yorks 95 E5
Hucclecote Glos 37 C5
Hucking Kent 30 D2
Hucknall Notts 76 E5
Huddersfield W Yorks 88 C2
Huddington Worcs 50 D4
Hudswell N Yorks 101 D6
Huggate E Yorks 96 D4
Hugglescote Leics 63 C8
Hugh Town Scilly 2 E4
Hughenden Valley Bucks 40 E1
Hughley Shrops 61 E5
Huish Devon 9 C7
Huish Wilts 25 C6
Huish Champflower Som 11 B5
Huish Episcopi Som 12 B2
Huisinis W Isles 154 F4
Hulcott Bucks 40 C1
Hulland Derbys 76 E2
Hulland Ward Derbys 76 E2
Hullavington Wilts 37 F5
Hullbridge Essex 42 E4
Hulme Gtr Man 87 E6

Hulme End Staffs 75 D8
Hulme Walfield Ches E 74 C5
Hulver Street Suff 69 F7
Hulverstone IoW 14 F4
Humber Hereford 49 D7
Humber Bridge N Lincs 90 B4
Humberston NE Lincs 91 D7
Humbie E Loth 121 C7
Humbleton E Yorks 97 F8
Humbleton Northumb 117 B5
Humby Lincs 78 F3
Hume Borders 122 E3
Humshaugh Northumb 110 B2
Huna Highld 158 C5
Huncoat Lancs 93 F7
Huncote Leics 64 E2
Hundalee Borders 116 C2
Hunderthwaite Durham 100 B4
Hundle Houses Lincs 79 D5
Hundleby Lincs 79 C6
Hundleton Pembs 44 E4
Hundon Suff 55 E8
Hundred Acres Hants 15 C6
Hundred End Lancs 86 B2
Hundred House Powys 48 D3
Hungarton Leics 64 D3
Hungerford Hants 14 C2
Hungerford W Berks 25 C8
Hungerford Newtown W Berks 25 B8
Hungerton Lincs 65 B5
Hungladder Highld 149 A8
Hunmanby N Yorks 97 B6
Hunmanby Moor N Yorks 97 B7
Hunningham Warks 51 C8
Hunny Hill IoW 15 F5
Hunsdon Herts 41 C7
Hunsingore N Yorks 95 D7
Hunslet W Yorks 95 F6
Hunsonby Cumb 109 F5
Hunspow Highld 158 C4
Hunstanton Norf 80 C2
Hunstanworth Durham 110 E2
Hunsterson Ches E 74 E3
Hunston Suff 56 C3
Hunston W Sus 16 D2
Hunstrete Bath 23 C8
Hunt End Worcs 50 C5
Hunter's Quay Argyll 145 F10
Hunthill Lodge Angus 134 B4
Hunting-tower Perth 128 B2
Huntingdon Cambs 54 B3
Huntingfield Suff 57 B7
Huntingford Dorset 24 F3
Huntington E Loth 121 B7
Huntington Hereford 48 D4
Huntington Staffs 62 C3
Huntington York 96 D2
Huntley Glos 36 C4
Huntly Aberds 152 E5
Huntlywood Borders 122 E2
Hunton Kent 29 E8
Hunton N Yorks 101 E6
Hunt's Corner Norf 68 F3
Hunt's Cross Mers 86 F2
Huntsham Devon 10 B5
Huntspill Som 22 E5
Huntworth Som 22 F5
Hunwick Durham 110 F4
Hunworth Norf 81 D6
Hurdsfield Ches E 75 B6
Hurley Warks 63 E6
Hurley Windsor 39 F8
Hurlford E Ayrs 118 F4
Hurliness Orkney 159 K3
Hurn Dorset 14 E2
Hurn's End Lincs 79 E7
Hursley Hants 14 B5
Hurst N Yorks 101 D5
Hurst Som 12 C2
Hurst Wokingham 27 B5
Hurst Green E Sus 18 C4
Hurst Green Lancs 93 F6
Hurst Wickham W Sus 17 C6
Hurstbourne Priors Hants 26 E2
Hurstbourne Tarrant Hants 25 D8
Hurstpierpoint W Sus 17 C6
Hurstwood Lancs 93 F8
Hurtmore Sur 27 E7
Hurworth Place Darl 101 D7
Hury Durham 100 C4
Husabost Highld 148 C7
Husbands Bosworth Leics 64 F3
Husborne Crawley C Beds 53 F7
Husthwaite N Yorks 95 B8
Hutchwns Bridgend 21 B7
Huthwaite Notts 76 D4
Huttoft Lincs 79 B8
Hutton Borders 122 D5
Hutton Cumb 99 B6
Hutton E Yorks 97 D6
Hutton Essex 42 E2
Hutton Lancs 86 B2
Hutton N Som 22 D5
Hutton Buscel N Yorks 103 F7
Hutton Conyers N Yorks 95 B6
Hutton Cranswick E Yorks 97 D6
Hutton End Cumb 108 F4
Hutton Gate Redcar 102 C3
Hutton Henry Durham 111 F7
Hutton-le-Hole N Yorks 103 E5
Hutton Magna Durham 101 C6
Hutton Roof Cumb 93 B5
Hutton Roof Cumb 108 F3
Hutton Rudby N Yorks 102 D2
Hutton Sessay N Yorks 95 B7
Hutton Village Redcar 102 C3
Hutton Wandesley N Yorks 95 D8
Huxley Ches W 74 C2
Huxter Shetland 160 G7
Huxter Shetland 160 H5
Huxton Borders 122 C4
Huyton Mers 86 E2
Hwlffordd = Haverfordwest Pembs 44 D4
Hycemoor Cumb 98 F2
Hyde Glos 37 D5
Hyde Gtr Man 87 E7
Hyde Hants 14 C2
Hyde Heath Bucks 40 D2
Hyde Park S Yorks 89 D6
Hydestile Sur 27 E7
Hylton Castle T&W 111 D6
Hyndford Bridge S Lanark 120 E2
Hynish Argyll 146 H2
Hyssington Powys 60 E3
Hythe Hants 14 D5
Hythe Kent 19 B8
Hythe End Windsor 27 B8
Hythie Aberds 153 C10

I

Ibberton Dorset 13 D5
Ible Derbys 76 D2
Ibsley Hants 14 D2
Ibstock Leics 63 C8
Ibstone Bucks 39 E7
Ibthorpe Hants 25 D8
Ibworth Hants 26 D3
Ichrachan Argyll 125 B6
Ickburgh Norf 67 E8
Ickenham London 40 F3
Ickford Bucks 39 D6
Ickham Kent 31 D6
Ickleford Herts 54 F2
Icklesham E Sus 19 D5
Ickleton Cambs 55 E5
Icklingham Suff 55 B8
Ickwell Green C Beds 54 E2
Icomb Glos 38 B2
Idbury Oxon 38 C2
Iddesleigh Devon 9 D7
Ide Devon 10 E3
Ide Hill Kent 29 D5
Ideford Devon 7 B6
Iden E Sus 19 C6
Iden Green Kent 18 B4
Iden Green Kent 18 B5
Idle W Yorks 94 F4
Idlicote Warks 51 E7
Idmiston Wilts 25 F6
Idole Carms 33 C5
Idridgehay Derbys 76 E2
Idrigill Highld 149 B8
Idstone Oxon 38 F2
Idvies Angus 135 E5
Iffley Oxon 39 D5
Ifield W Sus 28 F3
Ifold W Sus 27 F8
Iford E Sus 17 D8
Ifton Heath Shrops 73 F7
Ightfield Shrops 74 F2
Ightham Kent 29 D6
Iken Suff 57 D8
Ilam Staffs 75 D8
Ilchester Som 12 B3
Ilderton Northumb 117 B6
Ilford London 41 F7
Ilfracombe Devon 20 E4
Ilkeston Derbys 76 E4
Ilketshall St Andrew Suff 69 F6
Ilketshall St Lawrence Suff 69 F6
Ilketshall St Margaret Suff 69 F6
Ilkley W Yorks 94 E4
Illey W Mid 62 F3
Illingworth W Yorks 87 B8
Illogan Corn 3 B5
Illston on the Hill Leics 64 E4
Ilmer Bucks 39 D7
Ilmington Warks 51 E7
Ilminster Som 11 C8
Ilsington Devon 7 B5
Ilston Swansea 33 E6
Ilton N Yorks 94 B4
Ilton Som 11 C8
Imachar N Ayrs 143 D9
Imeraval Argyll 142 D4
Immingham NE Lincs 91 C5
Impington Cambs 54 C5
Ince Ches W 73 B8
Ince Blundell Mers 85 D4
Ince in Makerfield Gtr Man 86 D3
Inch of Arnhall Aberds 135 B6
Inchbare Angus 135 C6
Inchberry Moray 152 C3
Inchbraoch Angus 135 D7
Incheril Highld 150 E3
Inchgrundle Angus 134 B4
Inchina Highld 150 B2
Inchinnan Renfs 118 C4
Inchkinloch Highld 157 E8
Inchlaggan Highld 136 D4
Inchlumpie Highld 151 D8
Inchmore Highld 150 G6
Inchnacardoch Hotel Highld 137 C6
Inchnadamph Highld 156 G5
Inchree Highld 130 C4
Inchture Perth 128 B4
Inchyra Perth 128 B3
Indian Queens Corn 4 D4
Inerval Argyll 142 D4
Ingatestone Essex 42 E2
Ingbirchworth S Yorks 88 D3
Ingestre Staffs 62 B3
Ingham Lincs 90 F3
Ingham Norf 69 B6
Ingham Suff 56 B2
Ingham Corner Norf 69 B6
Ingleborough Norf 66 C4
Ingleby Derbys 63 B7
Ingleby Lincs 77 B8
Ingleby Arncliffe N Yorks 102 D2
Ingleby Barwick Stockton 102 C2
Ingleby Greenhow N Yorks 102 D3
Inglemire Hull 97 F6
Inglesbatch Bath 24 C2
Inglesham Swindon 38 E2
Ingleton Durham 101 B6
Ingleton N Yorks 93 B6
Inglewhite Lancs 92 E5
Ingliston Edin 120 B4
Ingoe Northumb 110 B3
Ingol Lancs 92 F5
Ingoldisthorpe Norf 80 D2
Ingoldmells Lincs 79 C8
Ingoldsby Lincs 78 F3
Ingon Warks 51 D7
Ingram Northumb 117 C6
Ingrow W Yorks 94 F3
Ings Cumb 99 E6
Ingst S Glos 36 F2
Ingworth Norf 81 E7
Inham's End Cambs 66 E2
Inkberrow Worcs 50 D5
Inkpen W Berks 25 C8
Inkstack Highld 158 C4
Inn Cumb 99 D6
Innellan Argyll 145 F10
Innerleithen Borders 121 F6
Innerleven Fife 129 D5
Innermessan Dumfries 104 C4
Innerwell E Loth 122 B3
Innerwick Perth 132 E2
Innis Chonain Argyll 125 C7
Insch Aberds 140 B5
Insh Highld 138 D4
Inshore Highld 156 C6
Inskip Lancs 92 F4
Instoneville S Yorks 89 C6
Instow Devon 20 F3
Intake S Yorks 89 D6
Inver Aberds 139 E8
Inver Highld 151 C11
Inver Perth 133 E7
Inver Mallie Highld 136 F4
Inverailort Highld 147 C10
Inveraldie Angus 134 F4
Inverallig in Highld 149 C13
Inverallochy Aberds 153 B10
Inveran Highld 151 B8
Inveraray Argyll 125 E6
Inverarish Highld 149 E10
Inverarity Angus 134 E4
Inverarnan Stirling 126 C2
Inverasdale Highld 155 J13
Inverbeg Argyll 126 E2
Inverbervie Aberds 135 B8
Inverboyndie Aberds 153 B6
Inverbroom Highld 150 C4
Invercassley Highld 156 J7
Invercauld House Aberds 139 E7
Inverchaolain Argyll 145 F9
Invercharnan Highld 131 E5
Inverchoran Highld 150 F5
Invercreran Argyll 130 E4
Inverdruie Highld 138 C5
Inverebrie Aberds 153 E9
Invereck Argyll 145 E10
Inverernan Ho. Aberds 140 C2
Invereshie House Highld 138 D4
Inveresk E Loth 121 B6
Inverey Aberds 139 F6
Inverfarigaig Highld 137 B8
Invergarry Highld 137 D6
Invergelder Aberds 139 E8
Invergeldie Perth 127 B6
Invergordon Highld 151 E10
Invergowrie Perth 134 F3
Inverguseran Highld 149 H12
Inverhadden Perth 132 D3
Inverharroch Moray 152 E3
Inverherive Stirling 126 B2
Inverie Highld 147 B10
Inverinan Argyll 125 D5
Inverinate Highld 136 B2
Inverkeilor Angus 135 E6
Inverkeithing Fife 128 F3
Inverkeithny Aberds 153 D6
Inverkip Invclyd 118 B2
Inverkirkaig Highld 156 H3
Inverlael Highld 150 C4
Inverlochlarig Stirling 126 C3
Inverlochy Argyll 125 C7
Inverlochy Highld 131 B5
Inverlussa Argyll 144 E5
Invermark Lodge Angus 140 F3
Invermoidart Highld 147 D9
Invermoriston Highld 137 C7
Invernaver Highld 157 C10
Inverneill Argyll 145 E7
Inverness Highld 151 G9
Invernettie Aberds 153 D11
Invernoaden Argyll 125 F7
Inveroran Hotel Argyll 131 E6
Inverpolly Lodge Highld 156 H3
Inverquharity Angus 134 D4
Inverquhomery Aberds 153 D10
Inverroy Highld 137 F5
Inversanda Highld 130 D3
Invershiel Highld 136 C2
Invershin Highld 151 B8
Inversnaid Hotel Stirling 126 D2
Inverugie Aberds 153 D11
Inveruglas Argyll 126 D2
Inveruglass Highld 138 D4
Inverurie Aberds 141 B6
Invervar Perth 132 E3
Inverythan Aberds 153 D7
Inwardleigh Devon 9 E7
Inworth Essex 42 C4
Iochdar W Isles 148 D2
Iping W Sus 16 B2
Ipplepen Devon 7 C6
Ipsden Oxon 39 F6
Ipsley Worcs 51 C5
Ipstones Staffs 75 D7
Ipswich Suff 57 E5
Irby Mers 85 F3
Irby in the Marsh Lincs 79 C7
Irby upon Humber NE Lincs 91 D5
Irchester Northants 53 C7
Ireby Cumb 108 F2
Ireby Lancs 93 B6
Ireland Orkney 159 H4
Ireland Shetland 160 L5
Ireland's Cross Shrops 74 E4
Ireleth Cumb 92 B2
Ireshopeburn Durham 109 F8
Irlam Gtr Man 86 E5
Irnham Lincs 65 B7
Iron Acton S Glos 36 F3
Iron Cross Warks 51 D5
Ironbridge Telford 61 D6
Irongray Dumfries 107 B6
Ironmacannie Dumfries 106 B3
Ironside Aberds 153 C8
Ironville Derbys 76 D4
Irstead Norf 69 B6
Irthington Cumb 108 C4
Irthlingborough Northants 53 B7
Irton N Yorks 103 F8
Irvine N Ayrs 118 F3
Isauld Highld 157 C12
Isbister Orkney 159 F3
Isbister Orkney 159 G4
Isbister Shetland 160 D5
Isbister Shetland 160 G7
Isfield E Sus 17 C8
Isham Northants 53 B6
Isle Abbotts Som 11 B8
Isle Brewers Som 11 B8
Isle of Whithorn Dumfries 105 F8
Isleham Cambs 55 B7
Isleornsay Highld 149 G12
Islesburgh Shetland 160 G5
Islesteps Dumfries 107 B6
Isleworth London 28 B2
Isley Walton Leics 63 B8
Islibhig W Isles 154 E4
Islington London 41 F6
Islip Northants 53 B7
Islip Oxon 39 C5
Istead Rise Kent 29 C7
Isycoed Wrex 73 D8
Itchen Soton 14 C5
Itchen Abbas Hants 26 F3
Itchen Stoke Hants 26 F3
Itchingfield W Sus 16 B5
Itchington S Glos 36 F3
Itteringham Norf 81 D7
Itton Devon 9 E8
Itton Common Mon 36 E1
Ivegill Cumb 108 E4
Iver Bucks 40 F3
Iver Heath Bucks 40 F3
Iveston Durham 110 D4
Ivinghoe Bucks 40 C2
Ivinghoe Aston Bucks 40 C2
Ivington Hereford 49 D6
Ivington Green Hereford 49 D6
Ivy Chimneys Essex 41 D7
Ivy Cross Dorset 13 B6
Ivy Hatch Kent 29 D6
Ivybridge Devon 6 D4
Ivychurch Kent 19 C7
Iwade Kent 30 C3
Iwerne Courtney or Shroton Dorset 13 C6
Iwerne Minster Dorset 13 C6
Ixworth Suff 56 B3
Ixworth Thorpe Suff 56 B3

J

Jack Hill N Yorks 94 D5
Jack in the Green Devon 10 E5
Jacksdale Notts 76 D4
Jackstown Aberds 153 E7
Jacobstow Corn 8 E3
Jacobstowe Devon 9 D7
Jameston Pembs 32 E1
Jamestown Dumfries 115 E6
Jamestown Highld 150 F7
Jamestown W Dunb 126 F2
Jarrow T&W 111 C6
Jarvis Brook E Sus 18 C2
Jasper's Green Essex 42 B3
Java Argyll 124 B3
Jawcraig Falk 119 B8
Jaywick Essex 43 C7
Jealott's Hill Brack 27 B6
Jedburgh Borders 116 B2
Jeffreyston Pembs 32 D1
Jellyhill E Dunb 119 B6
Jemimaville Highld 151 E10
Jersey Farm Herts 40 D4
Jesmond T&W 111 C5
Jevington E Sus 18 E2
Jockey End Herts 40 C3
John o'Groats Highld 158 C5
Johnby Cumb 108 F4
John's Cross E Sus 18 C4
Johnshaven Aberds 135 C7
Johnston Pembs 44 D4
Johnstone Renfs 118 C4
Johnstonebridge Dumfries 114 E3
Johnstown Carms 33 C5
Johnstown Wrex 73 E7
Joppa Edin 121 B6
Joppa S Ayrs 112 C4
Jordans Bucks 40 E2
Jordanthorpe S Yorks 88 F4
Jump S Yorks 88 D4
Jumpers Green Dorset 14 E2
Juniper Green Edin 120 C4
Jurby East IoM 84 C3
Jurby West IoM 84 C3

K

Kaber Cumb 100 C2
Kaimend S Lanark 120 E2
Kaimes Edin 121 C5
Kalemouth Borders 116 B3
Kames Argyll 124 D4
Kames Argyll 145 F8
Kames E Ayrs 113 B6
Kea Corn 3 B7
Keadby N Lincs 90 C2
Keal Cotes Lincs 79 C6
Kearsley Gtr Man 87 D5
Kearstwick Cumb 99 F8
Kearton N Yorks 100 E4
Kearvaig Highld 156 B5
Keasden N Yorks 93 C7
Keckwick Halton 86 F3
Keddington Lincs 91 F7
Kedington Suff 55 E8
Kedleston Derbys 76 E3
Keelby Lincs 91 C5
Keele Staffs 74 E5
Keeley Green Bedford 53 E8
Keeston Pembs 44 D4
Keevil Wilts 24 D4
Kegworth Leics 63 B8
Kehelland Corn 2 B5
Keig Aberds 140 C5
Keighley W Yorks 94 E3
Keil Highld 130 D3
Keilarsbrae Clack 127 E7
Keilhill Aberds 153 C7
Keillmore Argyll 144 E5
Keillor Perth 134 E2
Keillour Perth 127 B8
Keills Argyll 142 B5
Keils Argyll 144 G4
Keinton Mandeville Som 23 F7
Keir Mill Dumfries 113 E8
Keisby Lincs 65 B7
Keiss Highld 158 D5
Keith Moray 152 C4
Keith Inch Aberds 153 D11
Keithock Angus 135 C6
Kelbrook Lancs 94 E2
Kelby Lincs 78 E3
Keld Cumb 99 C7
Keld N Yorks 100 D3
Keldholme N Yorks 103 F5
Kelfield N Lincs 90 D2
Kelfield N Yorks 95 F8
Kelham Notts 77 D7
Kellan Argyll 147 G8
Kellas Angus 134 F4
Kellas Moray 152 C1
Kellaton Devon 7 F6
Kelleth Cumb 100 D1
Kelleythorpe E Yorks 97 D5
Kelling Norf 81 C6
Kellingley N Yorks 89 B6
Kellington N Yorks 89 B6
Kelloe Durham 111 F6
Kelloholm Dumfries 113 C7
Kelly Devon 9 F5
Kelly Bray Corn 5 B8
Kelmarsh Northants 52 B5
Kelmscot Oxon 38 E2
Kelsale Suff 57 C7
Kelsall Ches W 74 C2
Kelsall Hill Ches W 74 C2
Kelshall Herts 54 F4
Kelsick Cumb 107 D8
Kelso Borders 122 F3
Kelstedge Derbys 76 C3
Kelstern Lincs 91 E6
Kelston Bath 24 C2
Keltneyburn Perth 132 E4
Kelton Dumfries 107 B6
Kelty Fife 128 E3
Kelvedon Essex 42 C4
Kelvedon Hatch Essex 42 E1
Kelvin S Lanark 119 D6
Kelvinside Glasgow 119 C5
Kelynack Corn 2 C2
Kemback Fife 129 C6
Kemberton Shrops 61 D7
Kemble Glos 37 E6
Kemerton Worcs 50 F4
Kemeys Commander Mon 35 D7
Kemnay Aberds 141 C6
Kemp Town Brighton 17 D7
Kempley Glos 36 B3
Kemps Green Warks 51 B6
Kempsey Worcs 50 E3
Kempsford Glos 38 E1
Kempshott Hants 26 D4
Kempston Bedford 53 E8
Kempston Hardwick Bedford 53 E8
Kempton Shrops 60 F3
Kemsing Kent 29 D6
Kemsley Kent 30 C3
Kenardington Kent 19 B6
Kenchester Hereford 49 E6
Kencot Oxon 38 D2
Kendal Cumb 99 E7
Kendoon Dumfries 113 F6
Kendray S Yorks 88 D4
Kenfig Bridgend 34 F2
Kenfig Hill Bridgend 34 F2
Kenilworth Warks 51 B7
Kenknock Stirling 132 F1
Kenley London 28 D4
Kenley Shrops 61 D5
Kenmore Highld 149 C12
Kenmore Perth 132 E4
Kenn Devon 10 F4
Kenn N Som 23 C6
Kennacley W Isles 154 H6
Kennacraig Argyll 145 G7
Kennerleigh Devon 10 D3
Kennet Clack 127 E8
Kennethmont Aberds 140 B4
Kennett Cambs 55 C7
Kennford Devon 10 F4
Kenninghall Norf 68 F3
Kenninghall Heath Norf 68 F3
Kennington Kent 30 E4
Kennington Oxon 39 D5
Kennoway Fife 129 D5
Kenny Hill Suff 55 B7
Kennythorpe N Yorks 96 C3
Kenovay Argyll 146 G2
Kensaleyre Highld 149 C9
Kensington London 28 B3
Kensworth C Beds 40 C3
Kensworth Common C Beds 40 C3
Kent's Oak Hants 14 B4
Kent Street E Sus 18 D4
Kent Street Kent 29 D7
Kent Street W Sus 17 B6
Kentallen Highld 130 D4
Kentchurch Hereford 35 B8
Kentford Suff 55 C8
Kentisbeare Devon 11 D5
Kentisbury Devon 20 E5
Kentisbury Ford Devon 20 E5
Kentmere Cumb 99 D6
Kenton Devon 10 F4
Kenton Suff 57 C5
Kenton T&W 110 C5
Kenton Bankfoot T&W 110 C5
Kentra Highld 147 E9
Kents Bank Cumb 92 B3
Kent's Green Glos 36 B4
Kenwick Shrops 73 F8
Kenwyn Corn 3 B7
Keoldale Highld 156 C6
Keppanach Highld 130 C4
Keppoch Highld 136 B2
Keprigan Argyll 143 G7
Kepwick N Yorks 102 E2
Kerchesters Borders 122 F3
Keresley W Mid 63 F7
Kernborough Devon 7 E5
Kerne Bridge Hereford 36 C2
Kerris Corn 2 D3
Kerry Powys 59 F8
Kerrycroy Argyll 145 G10
Kerry's Gate Hereford 49 F5
Kerrysdale Highld 149 A13
Kersall Notts 77 C7
Kersey Suff 56 E4
Kershopefoot Cumb 115 F7
Kersoe Worcs 50 E4
Kerswell Devon 11 D5
Kerswell Green Worcs 50 E3
Kesgrave Suff 57 E6
Kessingland Suff 69 F8
Kessingland Beach Suff 69 F8
Kessington E Dunb 119 B5
Kestle Corn 3 B8
Kestle Mill Corn 4 D3
Keston London 28 C5
Keswick Cumb 98 B4
Keswick Norf 68 D5
Keswick Norf 81 D9
Ketley Telford 61 C6
Ketley Bank Telford 61 C6
Ketsby Lincs 79 B6
Kettering Northants 53 B6
Ketteringham Norf 68 D4
Kettins Perth 134 F2
Kettlebaston Suff 56 D3
Kettlebridge Fife 128 D5
Kettleburgh Suff 57 C6
Kettlehill Fife 128 D5
Kettleholm Dumfries 107 B8
Kettleness N Yorks 103 C6
Kettleshume Ches E 75 B6
Kettlesing Bottom N Yorks 94 D5
Kettlesing Head N Yorks 94 D5
Kettlestone Norf 81 D5
Kettlethorpe Lincs 77 B8
Kettletoft Orkney 159 E7
Kettlewell N Yorks 94 B2
Ketton Rutland 65 D6
Kew London 28 B2
Kew Br. London 28 B2
Kewstoke N Som 22 C5
Kexbrough S Yorks 88 D4
Kexby Lincs 90 F2
Kexby York 96 D3
Key Green Ches E 75 C5
Keyham Leics 64 D3
Keyhaven Hants 14 E4
Keyingham E Yorks 91 B6
Keymer W Sus 17 C7
Keynsham Bath 23 C8
Keysoe Bedford 53 C8
Keysoe Row Bedford 53 C8
Keyston Cambs 53 B8
Keyworth Notts 77 F6
Kibblesworth T&W 110 D5
Kibworth Beauchamp Leics 64 E3
Kibworth Harcourt Leics 64 E3
Kidbrooke London 28 B5
Kiddemore Green Staffs 62 D2
Kidderminster Worcs 50 B3
Kiddington Oxon 38 B4
Kidlington Oxon 38 C4
Kidmore End Oxon 26 B4
Kidsgrove Staffs 74 D5
Kidstones N Yorks 100 F4
Kidwelly = Cydweli Carms 33 D5
Kiel Crofts Argyll 124 B5
Kielder Northumb 116 E2
Kierfiold Ho Orkney 159 G3
Kilbagie Fife 127 F8
Kilbarchan Renfs 118 C4
Kilbeg Highld 149 H11
Kilberry Argyll 144 G6
Kilbirnie N Ayrs 118 D3
Kilbride Argyll 124 C4
Kilbride Argyll 124 C5
Kilbride Highld 149 F10
Kilburn Angus 134 C3
Kilburn Derbys 76 E3
Kilburn London 41 F5
Kilburn N Yorks 95 B8
Kilby Leics 64 E3
Kilchamaig Argyll 145 G7
Kilchattan Argyll 144 D2
Kilchattan Bay Argyll 145 H10
Kilchenzie Argyll 143 F7
Kilcheran Argyll 124 B4
Kilchiaran Argyll 142 B3
Kilchoan Argyll 124 D3
Kilchoan Highld 146 E7
Kilchoman Argyll 142 B3
Kilchrenan Argyll 125 C6
Kilconquhar Fife 129 D6
Kilcot Glos 36 B3
Kilcoy Highld 151 F8
Kilcreggan Argyll 145 E11
Kildale N Yorks 102 D4
Kildalloig Argyll 143 G8
Kildary Highld 151 D10
Kildermorie Lodge Highld 151 D8
Kildonan N Ayrs 143 F11
Kildonan Lodge Highld 157 G12
Kildonnan Highld 146 C7
Kildrummy Aberds 140 C3
Kildwick N Yorks 94 E3
Kilfinan Argyll 145 F8
Kilfinnan Highld 137 E5
Kilgetty Pembs 32 D2
Kilgwrrwg Common Mon 36 E1
Kilham E Yorks 97 C6
Kilham Northumb 122 F4
Kilkenneth Argyll 146 G2
Kilkerran Argyll 143 G8
Kilkhampton Corn 9 E6
Killamarsh Derbys 89 F5
Killay Swansea 33 E7
Killbeg Argyll 147 G9
Killean Argyll 143 D7
Killearn Stirling 126 F4
Killen Highld 151 F9
Killerby Darl 101 C6
Killichonan Perth 132 D2
Killiechonate Highld 136 F5
Killiechronan Argyll 147 G8
Killiecrankie Perth 133 C6
Killiemor Argyll 146 H7
Killiemore House Argyll 146 J7
Killilan Highld 150 H2
Killimster Highld 158 E5
Killin Stirling 132 F2
Killin Lodge Highld 137 D8
Killinallan Argyll 142 A4
Killinghall N Yorks 95 D5
Killington Cumb 99 F8
Killingworth T&W 111 B5
Killmahumaig Argyll 144 D6
Killochyett Borders 121 E7
Killocraw Argyll 143 E7
Killundine Highld 147 G8
Kilmacolm Invclyd 118 C3
Kilmaha Argyll 124 E5
Kilmahog Stirling 126 D5
Kilmalieu Highld 130 D2
Kilmaluag Highld 149 A9
Kilmany Fife 129 B5
Kilmarie Highld 149 G10
Kilmarnock E Ayrs 118 F4
Kilmaron Castle Fife 129 C5
Kilmartin Argyll 124 F4
Kilmaurs E Ayrs 118 E4
Kilmelford Argyll 124 D4
Kilmeny Argyll 142 B4
Kilmersdon Som 23 D8
Kilmeston Hants 15 B6
Kilmichael Argyll 143 F7
Kilmichael Glassary Argyll 145 D7
Kilmichael of Inverlussa Argyll 144 E6
Kilmington Devon 11 E7
Kilmington Wilts 24 F2
Kilmonivaig Highld 136 F4
Kilmorack Highld 150 G7
Kilmore Argyll 124 C4
Kilmore Highld 149 H11
Kilmory Argyll 144 F6
Kilmory Highld 147 D8
Kilmory Highld 149 H8
Kilmory N Ayrs 143 F10
Kilmuir Highld 148 D7
Kilmuir Highld 149 A8
Kilmuir Highld 151 D10
Kilmuir Highld 151 G9
Kilmun Argyll 124 D5
Kilmun Argyll 145 E10
Kiln Pit Hill Northumb 110 D3
Kilncadzow S Lanark 119 E8
Kilndown Kent 18 B4
Kilnhurst S Yorks 89 E5
Kilninian Argyll 146 G6
Kilninver Argyll 124 C4
Kilnsea E Yorks 91 C8
Kilnsey N Yorks 94 C2
Kilnwick E Yorks 97 E5
Kilnwick Percy E Yorks 96 D4
Kiloran Argyll 144 D2
Kilpatrick N Ayrs 143 F10
Kilpeck Hereford 49 F6
Kilphedir Highld 157 H12
Kilpin E Yorks 89 B8
Kilpin Pike E Yorks 89 B8
Kilrenny Fife 129 D7
Kilsby Northants 52 B3
Kilspindie Perth 128 B4
Kilsyth N Lanark 119 B7
Kiltarlity Highld 151 G8
Kilton Notts 77 B5
Kilton Som 22 E3
Kilton Thorpe Redcar 102 C4
Kilvaxter Highld 149 B8
Kilve Som 22 E3
Kilvington Notts 77 E7
Kilwinning N Ayrs 118 E3
Kimber worth S Yorks 88 E5
Kimberley Norf 68 D3
Kimberley Notts 76 E5
Kimble Wick Bucks 39 D8
Kimblesworth Durham 111 E5
Kimbolton Cambs 53 C8
Kimbolton Hereford 49 C7
Kimcote Leics 64 F2
Kimmeridge Dorset 13 G7
Kimmerston Northumb 123 F5
Kimpton Hants 25 E7
Kimpton Herts 40 C4
Kinbrace Highld 157 F11
Kinbuck Stirling 127 D6
Kincaple Fife 129 C6
Kincardine Fife 127 F8
Kincardine Highld 151 C9
Kincardine Bridge Falk 127 F8
Kincardine O'Neil Aberds 140 E4
Kinclaven Perth 134 F1
Kincorth Aberdeen 141 D8
Kincorth Ho. Moray 151 E13
Kincraig Highld 138 D4
Kincraigie Perth 133 E6
Kindallachan Perth 133 E6
Kineton Glos 37 B7
Kineton Warks 51 D8
Kinfauns Perth 128 B3
King Edward Aberds 153 C7
King Sterndale Derbys 75 B7
Kingairloch Highld 130 D2
Kingarth Argyll 145 H9
Kingcoed Mon 35 D8
Kingerby Lincs 90 E4
Kingham Oxon 38 B2
Kingholm Quay Dumfries 107 B6
Kinghorn Fife 128 F4
Kingie Highld 136 D4
Kinglassie Fife 128 E4
Kingoodie Perth 128 B5
King's Acre Hereford 49 E6
King's Bromley Staffs 62 C5
King's Caple Hereford 36 B2
King's Cliffe Northants 65 E7
King's Coughton Warks 51 D5
King's Heath W Mid 62 F4
Kings Hedges Cambs 55 C5
Kings Langley Herts 40 D3
King's Hill Kent 29 D7
King's Lynn Norf 67 B6
King's Meaburn Cumb 99 B8
King's Mills Wrex 73 E7
Kings Muir Borders 121 F5
King's Newnham Warks 52 B2
King's Newton Derbys 63 B7
King's Norton Leics 64 D3
King's Norton W Mid 51 B5
King's Nympton Devon 9 C8
King's Pyon Hereford 49 D6
King's Ripton Cambs 54 B3
King's Somborne Hants 25 F8
King's Stag Dorset 12 C5
King's Stanley Glos 37 D5
King's Sutton Northants 52 F2
King's Thorn Hereford 49 F7
King's Walden Herts 40 B4
Kings Worthy Hants 26 F2
Kingsand Corn 6 D2
Kingsbarns Fife 129 C7
Kingsbridge Devon 6 E5
Kingsbridge Som 21 F8
Kingsburgh Highld 149 C8
Kingsbury London 41 F5
Kingsbury Warks 63 E6
Kingsbury Episcopi Som 12 B2
Kingsclere Hants 26 D3
Kingscote Glos 37 E5
Kingscott Devon 9 C7
Kingscross N Ayrs 143 F11
Kingsdon Som 12 B3
Kingsdown Kent 31 E7
Kingseat Fife 128 E3
Kingsey Bucks 39 D7
Kingsfold W Sus 28 F2
Kingsford E Ayrs 118 E4
Kingsford Worcs 62 F2
Kingsforth N Lincs 90 C4
Kingsgate Kent 31 B7
Kingsheanton Devon 20 F4
Kingshouse Hotel Highld 131 D6
Kingside Hill Cumb 107 D8
Kingskerswell Devon 7 C6
Kingskettle Fife 128 D5
Kingsland Anglesey 82 C2
Kingsland Hereford 49 C6
Kingsley Ches W 74 B2
Kingsley Hants 27 F5
Kingsley Staffs 75 E7
Kingsley Green W Sus 27 F6
Kingsley Holt Staffs 75 E7
Kingsley Park Northants 53 C5
Kingsmuir Angus 134 E4
Kingsmuir Fife 129 D7
Kingsnorth Kent 19 B7
Kingstanding W Mid 62 E4
Kingsteignton Devon 7 B6
Kingsthorpe Northants 53 C5
Kingston Cambs 54 D4
Kingston Devon 6 E4
Kingston Dorset 13 D5
Kingston Dorset 13 G7
Kingston E Loth 129 F7
Kingston Hants 14 D2
Kingston IoW 15 F5
Kingston Kent 31 D5
Kingston Moray 152 B3
Kingston Bagpuize Oxon 38 E4
Kingston Blount Oxon 39 E7
Kingston by Sea W Sus 17 D6
Kingston Deverill Wilts 24 F3
Kingston Gorse W Sus 16 D4
Kingston Lisle Oxon 38 F3
Kingston Maurward Dorset 12 E5
Kingston near Lewes E Sus 17 D7
Kingston on Soar Notts 64 B2
Kingston Russell Dorset 12 E3
Kingston Seymour N Som 23 C6
Kingston St Mary Som 11 B7
Kingston Upon Hull Hull 90 B4
Kingston upon Thames London 28 C2
Kingston Vale London 28 B3
Kingstone Hereford 49 F6
Kingstone Som 11 C8
Kingstone Staffs 62 B4
Kingstown Cumb 108 D3
Kingswear Devon 7 D6
Kingswells Aberdeen 141 D7
Kingswinford W Mid 62 F2
Kingswood Bucks 39 C6
Kingswood Glos 36 E4
Kingswood Hereford 48 D4
Kingswood Kent 30 D2
Kingswood Powys 60 D2
Kingswood S Glos 23 B8
Kingswood Sur 28 D3
Kingswood Warks 51 B6
Kingthorpe Lincs 78 B4
Kington Hereford 48 D4
Kington Worcs 50 D4
Kington Langley Wilts 24 B4
Kington Magna Dorset 13 B5
Kington St Michael Wilts 24 B4
Kingussie Highld 138 D3
Kingweston Som 23 F7
Kininvie Ho. Moray 152 D3
Kinkell Bridge Perth 127 C8
Kinknockie Aberds 153 D10
Kinlet Shrops 61 F7
Kinloch Fife 128 C4
Kinloch Highld 146 B6
Kinloch Highld 149 G11
Kinloch Highld 156 F6
Kinloch Perth 133 E8
Kinloch Perth 134 E2
Kinloch Hourn Highld 136 D2
Kinloch Laggan Highld 137 F8
Kinloch Lodge Highld 157 D8
Kinloch Rannoch Perth 132 D3
Kinlochan Highld 130 C2
Kinlochard Stirling 126 D3
Kinlochbeoraid Highld 147 C11
Kinlochbervie Highld 156 D5
Kinlocheil Highld 130 B3
Kinlochewe Highld 150 E3
Kinlochleven Highld 131 C5
Kinlochmoidart Highld 147 D10
Kinlochmorar Highld 147 B11
Kinlochmore Highld 131 C5
Kinlochspelve Argyll 124 C2
Kinloid Highld 147 C9
Kinloss Moray 151 E13
Kinmel Bay Conwy 72 A3
Kinmuck Aberds 141 C7
Kinmundy Aberds 141 C7
Kinnadie Aberds 153 D9
Kinnaird Perth 128 B4
Kinnaird Castle Angus 135 D6
Kinneff Aberds 135 B8
Kinnelhead Dumfries 114 D3
Kinnell Angus 135 D6
Kinnerley Shrops 60 B3
Kinnersley Hereford 48 E5
Kinnersley Worcs 50 E3
Kinnerton Powys 48 C4
Kinnesswood Perth 128 D3
Kinninvie Durham 101 B5
Kinnordy Angus 134 D3
Kinoulton Notts 77 F6
Kinross Perth 128 D3
Kinrossie Perth 134 F1
Kinsbourne Green Herts 40 C4
Kinsey Heath Ches E 74 E3
Kinsham Hereford 49 C5
Kinsham Worcs 50 F4
Kinsley W Yorks 88 C5
Kinson Bmouth 13 E8
Kintbury W Berks 25 C8
Kintessack Moray 151 E12
Kintillo Perth 128 C3
Kintocher Aberds 140 D4
Kinton Hereford 49 B6
Kinton Shrops 60 C3
Kintore Aberds 141 C6
Kintour Argyll 142 C5
Kintra Argyll 142 D4
Kintra Argyll 146 J6
Kintraw Argyll 124 E4
Kinuachdrachd Argyll 124 F3
Kinveachy Highld 138 C5
Kinver Staffs 62 F2
Kippax W Yorks 95 F7
Kippen Stirling 127 E5
Kippen or Scaur Dumfries 106 D5
Kirbister Orkney 159 F7
Kirbister Orkney 159 H4
Kirbuster Orkney 159 F3
Kirby Bedon Norf 69 D5
Kirby Bellars Leics 64 C4
Kirby Cane Norf 69 E6
Kirby Cross Essex 43 B8
Kirby Grindalythe N Yorks 96 C5
Kirby Hill N Yorks 95 C6
Kirby Hill N Yorks 101 D6
Kirby Knowle N Yorks 102 F2
Kirby-le-Soken Essex 43 B8
Kirby Misperton N Yorks 96 B3
Kirby Muxloe Leics 64 D2
Kirby Row Norf 69 E6
Kirby Sigston N Yorks 102 E2
Kirby Underdale E Yorks 96 D4
Kirby Wiske N Yorks 102 F1
Kirdford W Sus 16 B4
Kirk Highld 158 E4
Kirk Bramwith S Yorks 89 C7
Kirk Deighton N Yorks 95 D6
Kirk Ella E Yorks 90 B4
Kirk Hallam Derbys 76 E4
Kirk Hammerton N Yorks 95 D7
Kirk Ireton Derbys 76 D2
Kirk Langley Derbys 76 F2
Kirk Merrington Durham 111 F5
Kirk Michael IoM 84 C3
Kirk of Shotts N Lanark 119 C8
Kirk Sandall S Yorks 89 D7
Kirk Smeaton N Yorks 89 C6
Kirk Yetholm Borders 116 B4
Kirkabister Shetland 160 K6
Kirkandrews Dumfries 106 E3
Kirkandrews upon Eden Cumb 108 D3
Kirkbampton Cumb 108 D3
Kirkbean Dumfries 107 D6
Kirkbride Cumb 108 D2
Kirkbuddo Angus 135 E5
Kirkburn Borders 121 F5
Kirkburn E Yorks 97 D5
Kirkburton W Yorks 88 C2
Kirkby Lincs 90 E4
Kirkby Mers 86 E2
Kirkby N Yorks 102 D3
Kirkby Fleetham N Yorks 101 E7
Kirkby Green Lincs 78 D3
Kirkby In Ashfield Notts 76 D5
Kirkby-in-Furness Cumb 98 F4
Kirkby la Thorpe Lincs 78 E3
Kirkby Lonsdale Cumb 93 B6
Kirkby Malham N Yorks 93 C8
Kirkby Mallory Leics 63 D8
Kirkby Malzeard N Yorks 94 B5
Kirkby Mills N Yorks 103 F5
Kirkby on Bain Lincs 78 C5
Kirkby Overflow N Yorks 95 E6
Kirkby Stephen Cumb 100 D2
Kirkby Thore Cumb 99 B8
Kirkby Underwood Lincs 65 B7
Kirkby Wharfe N Yorks 95 E8
Kirkbymoorside N Yorks 102 F4
Kirkcaldy Fife 128 E4
Kirkcambeck Cumb 108 C5
Kirkcarswell Dumfries 106 E4
Kirkcolm Dumfries 104 C4
Kirkconnel Dumfries 113 C7
Kirkconnell Dumfries 107 C6
Kirkcowan Dumfries 105 C7
Kirkcudbright Dumfries 106 D3
Kirkdale Mers 85 E4
Kirkfieldbank S Lanark 119 E8
Kirkgunzeon Dumfries 107 C5
Kirkham Lancs 92 F4
Kirkham N Yorks 96 C3
Kirkhamgate W Yorks 88 B3
Kirkharle Northumb 117 F6
Kirkheaton Northumb 110 B3
Kirkheaton W Yorks 88 C2
Kirkhill Angus 135 C6
Kirkhill Highld 151 G8
Kirkhill Midloth 120 C5
Kirkhill Moray 152 E2
Kirkhope Borders 115 B6
Kirkhouse Borders 121 F6
Kirkiboll Highld 157 D8
Kirkibost Highld 149 G10
Kirkinch Angus 134 E3
Kirkinner Dumfries 105 D8
Kirkintilloch E Dunb 119 B6
Kirkland Cumb 98 C2
Kirkland Cumb 109 F6
Kirkland Dumfries 113 C7
Kirkland Dumfries 113 E8
Kirkleatham Redcar 102 B3
Kirklevington Stockton 102 D2
Kirkley Suff 69 E8
Kirklington N Yorks 101 F8
Kirklington Notts 77 D6
Kirklinton Cumb 108 C4
Kirkliston Edin 120 B4
Kirkmaiden Dumfries 104 F5
Kirkmichael Perth 133 D7
Kirkmichael S Ayrs 112 D3
Kirkmuirhill S Lanark 119 E7
Kirknewton Northumb 122 F5
Kirknewton W Loth 120 C4
Kirkney Aberds 152 E5
Kirkoswald Cumb 109 E5
Kirkoswald S Ayrs 112 D2
Kirkpatrick Durham Dumfries 106 B4
Kirkpatrick-Fleming Dumfries 108 B2
Kirksanton Cumb 98 F3
Kirkstall W Yorks 95 F5
Kirkstead Lincs 78 C4
Kirkstile Aberds 152 E5
Kirkstyle Highld 158 C5
Kirkton Aberds 140 B5
Kirkton Aberds 153 D6
Kirkton Angus 134 E4
Kirkton Angus 134 F4
Kirkton Borders 115 C8
Kirkton Dumfries 114 F2
Kirkton Fife 129 B5
Kirkton Highld 149 F13
Kirkton Highld 150 G2
Kirkton Highld 151 B10
Kirkton Highld 151 F10
Kirkton Perth 127 C8
Kirkton S Lanark 114 B2
Kirkton Stirling 126 D4
Kirkton Manor Borders 120 F5
Kirkton of Airlie Angus 134 D3

Norwell Notts 77 C7
Norwell Woodhouse Notts 77 C7
Norwich Norf 68 D5
Norwick Shetland 160 B8
Norwood Derbys 89 F5
Norwood Hill Sur 28 E3
Norwoodside Cambs 66 E4
Noseley Leics 64 E4
Noss Shetland 160 M5
Noss Mayo Devon 6 E3
Nosterfield N Yorks 101 F7
Nostie Highld 149 F13
Notgrove Glos 37 B8
Nottage Bridgend 21 B7
Nottingham Nottingham 77 F5
Nottington Dorset 12 F4
Notton W Yorks 88 C4
Notton Wilts 24 C4
Nounsley Essex 42 C3
Noutard's Green Worcs 50 C2
Novar House Highld 151 E9
Nox Shrops 60 C4
Nuffield Oxon 39 F6
Nun Hills Lancs 87 B6
Nun Monkton N Yorks 95 D8
Nunburnholme E Yorks 96 E4
Nuncargate Notts 76 D5
Nuneaton Warks 63 E7
Nuneham Courtenay Oxon 39 E5
Nunney Som 24 E2
Nunnington N Yorks 96 B2
Nunnykirk Northumb 117 E6
Nunsthorpe NE Lincs 91 D6
Nunthorpe Mbro 102 C3
Nunthorpe York 96 D2
Nunton Wilts 14 B2
Nunwick N Yorks 95 B6
Nupend Glos 36 D4
Nursling Hants 14 C4
Nursted Hants 15 B8
Nutbourne W Sus 15 D8
Nutbourne W Sus 16 C4
Nutfield Sur 28 D4
Nuthall Notts 76 E5
Nuthampstead Herts 54 F5
Nuthurst W Sus 17 B5
Nutley E Sus 17 B8
Nutley Hants 26 E4
Nutwell S Yorks 89 D7
Nybster Highld 158 D5
Nyetimber W Sus 16 E2
Nyewood W Sus 16 B2
Nymet Rowland Devon 10 D2
Nymet Tracey Devon 10 D2
Nympsfield Glos 37 D5
Nynehead Som 11 B6
Nyton W Sus 16 D3

O

Oad Street Kent 30 C2
Oadby Leics 64 D3
Oak Cross Devon 9 E7
Oakamoor Staffs 75 E7
Oakbank W Loth 120 C3
Oakdale Caerph 35 E5
Oake Som 11 B6
Oaken Staffs 62 D2
Oakenclough Lancs 92 E5
Oakengates Telford 61 C7
Oakenholt Flint 73 B6
Oakenshaw Durham 110 F5
Oakenshaw W Yorks 88 B2
Oakerthorpe Derbys 76 D3
Oakes W Yorks 88 C2
Oakfield Torf 35 E7
Oakford Ceredig 46 D3
Oakford Devon 10 B4
Oakfordbridge Devon 10 B4
Oakgrove Ches E 75 C6
Oakham Rutland 65 D5
Oakhanger Hants 27 F5
Oakhill Som 23 E8
Oakhurst Kent 29 D6
Oakington Cambs 54 C5
Oaklands Herts 41 C5
Oaklands Powys 48 D2
Oakle Street Glos 36 C4
Oakley Bedford 53 D8
Oakley Bucks 39 C6
Oakley Fife 128 F2
Oakley Hants 26 D3
Oakley Oxon 39 D7
Oakley Poole 13 E8
Oakley Suff 57 B5
Oakley Green Windsor 27 B7
Oakley Park Powys 59 F6
Oakmere Ches W 74 C2
Oakridge Glos 37 D6
Oakridge Hants 26 D4
Oaks Shrops 60 D4
Oaks Green Derbys 75 F8
Oaksey Wilts 37 E6
Oakthorpe Leics 63 C7
Oakwoodhill Sur 28 F2
Oakworth W Yorks 94 F3
Oape Highld 156 J7
Oare Kent 30 C4
Oare Som 21 E7
Oare W Berks 26 B3
Oare Wilts 25 C6
Oasby Lincs 78 F3
Oathlaw Angus 134 D4
Oatlands N Yorks 95 D6
Oban Argyll 124 C4
Oban Highld 147 C11
Oborne Dorset 12 C4
Obthorpe Lincs 65 C7
Occlestone Green Ches W 74 C3
Occold Suff 57 B5
Ochiltree E Ayrs 112 B5
Ochtermuthill Perth 127 C7
Ochtertyre Perth 127 B7
Ockbrook Derbys 76 F4
Ockham Sur 27 D8
Ockle Highld 147 D8
Ockley Sur 28 F2
Ocle Pychard Hereford 49 E7
Octon E Yorks 97 C6
Octon Cross Roads E Yorks 97 C6
Odcombe Som 12 C3
Odd Down Bath 24 C2
Oddendale Cumb 99 C7
Odder Lincs 78 B2
Oddingley Worcs 50 D4
Oddington Glos 38 B2
Oddington Oxon 39 C5
Odell Bedford 53 D7
Odie Orkney 159 F7
Odiham Hants 26 D5
Odstock Wilts 14 B2
Odstone Leics 63 D7
Offchurch Warks 51 C8
Offenham Worcs 51 E5
Offham E Sus 17 C7
Offham Kent 29 D7
Offham W Sus 16 D4
Offord Cluny Cambs 54 C3
Offord Darcy Cambs 54 C3
Offton Suff 56 E4
Offwell Devon 11 E6
Ogbourne Maizey Wilts 25 B6
Ogbourne St Andrew Wilts 25 B6
Ogbourne St George Wilts 25 B7
Ogil Angus 134 C4
Ogle Northumb 110 B4
Ogmore V Glam 21 B7
Ogmore-by-Sea V Glam 21 B7
Ogmore Vale Bridgend 34 E3
Okeford Fitzpaine Dorset 13 C6
Okehampton Devon 9 E7
Okehampton Camp Devon 9 E7
Okraquoy Shetland 160 K6
Old Northants 53 B5
Old Aberdeen Aberdeen 141 D8
Old Alresford Hants 26 F3
Old Arley Warks 63 E6
Old Basford Nottingham 76 E5
Old Basing Hants 26 D4
Old Bewick Northumb 117 B6
Old Bolingbroke Lincs 79 C6
Old Bramhope W Yorks 94 E5
Old Brampton Derbys 76 B3
Old Bridge of Tilt Perth 133 C5
Old Bridge of Urr Dumfries 106 C4
Old Buckenham Norf 68 E3
Old Burghclere Hants 26 D2
Old Byland N Yorks 102 F3
Old Cassop Durham 111 F6
Old Castleton Borders 115 E8
Old Catton Norf 68 C5
Old Clee NE Lincs 91 D6
Old Cleeve Som 22 E2
Old Clipstone Notts 77 C6
Old Colwyn Conwy 83 D8
Old Coulsdon London 28 D4
Old Crombie Aberds 152 C5
Old Dailly S Ayrs 112 E2
Old Dalby Leics 64 B3
Old Deer Aberds 153 D9
Old Denaby S Yorks 89 E5
Old Edlington S Yorks 89 E6
Old Eldon Durham 101 B7
Old Ellerby E Yorks 97 F7
Old Felixstowe Suff 57 F7
Old Fletton Pboro 65 E8
Old Glossop Derbys 87 E8
Old Goole E Yorks 89 B8
Old Hall Powys 59 F6
Old Heath Essex 43 B6
Old Heathfield E Sus 18 C2
Old Hill W Mid 62 F3
Old Hunstanton Norf 80 C2
Old Hurst Cambs 54 B3
Old Hutton Cumb 99 F7
Old Kea Corn 3 B7
Old Kilpatrick W Dunb 118 B4
Old Kinnernie Aberds 141 D6
Old Knebworth Herts 41 B5
Old Langho Lancs 93 F7
Old Laxey IoM 84 D4
Old Leake Lincs 79 D7
Old Malton N Yorks 96 B3
Old Micklefield W Yorks 95 F7
Old Milton Hants 14 E3
Old Milverton Warks 51 C7
Old Monkland N Lanark 119 C7
Old Netley Hants 15 D5
Old Philpstoun W Loth 120 B3
Old Quarrington Durham 111 F6
Old Radnor Powys 48 D4
Old Rattray Aberds 153 C10
Old Rayne Aberds 141 B5
Old Romney Kent 19 C7
Old Sodbury S Glos 36 F4
Old Somerby Lincs 78 F2
Old Stratford Northants 53 E5
Old Thirsk N Yorks 102 F2
Old Town Cumb 99 F7
Old Town Cumb 108 E4
Old Town Northumb 116 E4
Old Town Scilly 2 E4
Old Trafford Gtr Man 87 E6
Old Tupton Derbys 76 C3
Old Warden C Beds 54 E2
Old Weston Cambs 53 B8
Old Whittington Derbys 76 B3
Old Wick Highld 158 E5
Old Windsor Windsor 27 B7
Old Wives Lees Kent 30 D4
Old Woking Sur 27 D8
Old Woodhall Lincs 78 C5
Oldany Highld 156 F4
Oldberrow Warks 51 C6
Oldborough Devon 10 D2
Oldbury Shrops 61 E7
Oldbury W Mid 62 F3
Oldbury Warks 63 E7
Oldbury-on-Severn S Glos 36 E3
Oldbury on the Hill Glos 37 F5
Oldcastle Bridgend 21 B8
Oldcastle Mon 35 B7
Oldcotes Notts 89 F6
Oldfallow Staffs 62 C3
Oldfield Worcs 50 C3
Oldford Som 24 D2
Oldham Gtr Man 87 D7
Oldhamstocks E Loth 122 B3
Oldland S Glos 23 B8
Oldmeldrum Aberds 141 B7
Oldshore Beg Highld 156 D4
Oldshoremore Highld 156 D5
Oldstead N Yorks 102 F3
Oldtown Aberds 140 B4
Oldtown of Ord Aberds 152 C6
Oldway Swansea 33 F6
Oldways End Devon 10 B3
Oldwhat Aberds 153 C8
Olgrinmore Highld 158 E2
Oliver's Battery Hants 15 B5
Ollaberry Shetland 160 E5
Ollerton Ches E 74 B4
Ollerton Notts 77 C6
Ollerton Shrops 61 B6
Olmarch Ceredig 46 D5
Olney M Keynes 53 D6
Olrig Ho. Highld 158 D3
Olton W Mid 62 F5
Olveston S Glos 36 F3
Olwen Ceredig 46 E4
Ombersley Worcs 50 C3
Ompton Notts 77 C6
Onchan IoM 84 E3
Onecote Staffs 75 D7
Onen Mon 35 C8
Ongar Hill Norf 67 B5
Ongar Street Hereford 49 C5
Onibury Shrops 49 B6
Onich Highld 130 C4
Onllwyn Neath 34 C2
Onneley Staffs 74 E4
Onslow Village Sur 27 E7
Onthank E Ayrs 118 E4
Openwoodgate Derbys 76 E3
Opinan Highld 149 A12
Opinan Highld 155 H13
Orange Lane Borders 122 E3
Orange Row Norf 66 B5
Orasaigh W Isles 155 F8
Orbliston Moray 152 C3
Orbost Highld 148 D7
Orby Lincs 79 C7
Orchard Hill Devon 9 B6
Orchard Portman Som 11 B7
Orcheston Wilts 25 E5
Orcop Hereford 36 B1
Orcop Hill Hereford 36 B1
Ord Highld 149 G11
Ordhead Aberds 141 C5
Ordie Aberds 140 D3
Ordiequish Moray 152 C3
Ordsall Notts 89 F7
Ore E Sus 18 D5
Oreton Shrops 61 F6
Orford Suff 57 E8
Orford Warr 86 E4
Orgreave Staffs 63 C5
Orlestone Kent 19 B6
Orleton Hereford 49 C6
Orleton Worcs 49 C8
Orlingbury Northants 53 B6
Ormesby Redcar 102 C3
Ormesby St Margaret Norf 69 C7
Ormesby St Michael Norf 69 C7
Ormiclate Castle W Isles 148 E2
Ormiscaig Highld 155 H13
Ormiston E Loth 121 C7
Ormsaigbeg Highld 146 E7
Ormsaigmore Highld 146 E7
Ormsary Argyll 144 F6
Ormsgill Cumb 92 B1
Ormskirk Lancs 86 D2
Orpington London 29 C5
Orrell Gtr Man 86 D3
Orrell Mers 85 E4
Orrisdale IoM 84 C3
Orroland Dumfries 106 E4
Orsett Thurrock 42 F2
Orslow Staffs 62 C2
Orston Notts 77 E7
Orthwaite Cumb 108 F2
Ortner Lancs 92 D5
Orton Cumb 99 D8
Orton Northants 53 B6
Orton Longueville Pboro 65 E8
Orton-on-the-Hill Leics 63 D7
Orton Waterville Pboro 65 E8
Orwell Cambs 54 D4
Osbaldeston Lancs 93 F6
Osbaldwick York 96 D2
Osbaston Shrops 60 B3
Osbournby Lincs 78 F3
Oscroft Ches W 74 C2
Ose Highld 149 D8
Osgathorpe Leics 63 C8
Osgodby Lincs 90 E4
Osgodby N Yorks 96 F2
Osgodby N Yorks 103 F8
Oskaig Highld 149 E10
Oskamull Argyll 146 G7
Osmaston Derby 76 F3
Osmaston Derbys 76 E2
Osmington Dorset 12 F5
Osmington Mills Dorset 12 F5
Osmotherley N Yorks 102 E2
Ospisdale Highld 151 C10
Ospringe Kent 30 C4
Ossett W Yorks 88 B3
Ossington Notts 77 C7
Ostend Essex 43 E5
Oswaldkirk N Yorks 96 B2
Oswaldtwistle Lancs 86 B5
Oswestry Shrops 60 B2
Otford Kent 29 D6
Otham Kent 29 D8
Othery Som 23 F5
Otley Suff 57 D6
Otley W Yorks 94 E5
Otter Ferry Argyll 145 E8
Otterbourne Hants 15 B5
Otterburn N Yorks 93 D8
Otterburn Northumb 116 E4
Otterburn Camp Northumb 116 E4
Otterham Corn 8 E3
Otterhampton Som 22 E4
Ottershaw Sur 27 C8
Otterswick Shetland 160 E7
Otterton Devon 11 F5
Ottery St Mary Devon 11 E6
Ottinge Kent 31 E5
Ottringham E Yorks 91 B6
Oughterby Cumb 108 D2
Oughtershaw N Yorks 100 F3
Oughterside Cumb 107 E8
Oughtibridge S Yorks 88 E4
Oughtrington Warr 86 F4
Oulston N Yorks 95 B8
Oulton Cumb 108 D2
Oulton Norf 81 E7
Oulton Staffs 75 F6
Oulton Suff 69 E8
Oulton W Yorks 88 B4
Oulton Broad Suff 69 E8
Oulton Street Norf 81 E7
Oundle Northants 65 F7
Ousby Cumb 109 F6
Ousdale Highld 158 H2
Ousden Suff 55 D8
Ousefleet E Yorks 90 B2
Ouston Durham 111 D5
Ouston Northumb 110 B3
Out Newton E Yorks 91 B7
Out Rawcliffe Lancs 92 E4
Outertown Orkney 159 G3
Outgate Cumb 99 E5
Outhgill Cumb 100 D2
Outlane W Yorks 87 C8
Outwell Norf 66 D5
Outwick Hants 14 C2
Outwood Sur 28 E4
Outwood W Yorks 88 B4
Outwoods Staffs 61 C7
Ovenden W Yorks 87 B8
Ovenscloss Borders 121 F7
Over Cambs 54 B4
Over Ches W 74 C3
Over S Glos 36 F2
Over Compton Dorset 12 C3
Over Green W Mid 63 E5
Over Haddon Derbys 76 C2
Over Hulton Gtr Man 86 D4
Over Kellet Lancs 92 B5
Over Kiddington Oxon 38 B4
Over Knutsford Ches E 74 B4
Over Monnow Mon 36 C2
Over Norton Oxon 38 B3
Over Peover Ches E 74 B4
Over Silton N Yorks 102 E2
Over Stowey Som 22 F3
Over Stratton Som 12 C2
Over Tabley Ches E 86 F5
Over Wallop Hants 25 F7
Over Whitacre Warks 63 E6
Over Worton Oxon 38 B4
Overbister Orkney 159 D7
Overbury Worcs 50 F4
Overcombe Dorset 12 F4
Overgreen Derbys 76 B3
Overleigh Som 23 F6
Overley Green Warks 51 D5
Overpool Ches W 73 B7
Overscaig Hotel Highld 156 G7
Overseal Derbys 63 C6
Oversland Kent 30 D4
Overstone Northants 53 C6
Overstrand Norf 81 C8
Overthorpe Northants 52 E2
Overton Aberdeen 141 C7
Overton Ches W 74 B2
Overton Dumfries 107 C6
Overton Hants 26 E3
Overton Lancs 92 D4
Overton N Yorks 95 D8
Overton Shrops 49 B7
Overton Swansea 33 F5
Overton W Yorks 88 C3
Overton = Owrtyn Wrex 73 E7
Overton Bridge Wrex 73 E7
Overtown N Lanark 119 D8
Oving Bucks 39 B7
Oving W Sus 16 D3
Ovingdean Brighton 17 D7
Ovingham Northumb 110 C3
Ovington Durham 101 C6
Ovington Essex 55 E8
Ovington Hants 26 F3
Ovington Norf 68 D2
Ovington Northumb 110 C3
Ower Hants 14 C4
Owermoigne Dorset 13 F5
Owlbury Shrops 60 E3
Owler Bar Derbys 76 B2
Owlerton S Yorks 88 F4
Owl's Green Suff 57 C6
Owlswick Bucks 39 D7
Owmby Lincs 90 D4
Owmby-by-Spital Lincs 90 F4
Owrtyn = Overton Wrex 73 E7
Owslebury Hants 15 B6
Owston Leics 64 D4
Owston S Yorks 89 C6
Owston Ferry N Lincs 90 D2
Owstwick E Yorks 97 F8
Owthorne E Yorks 91 B7
Owthorpe Notts 77 F6
Oxborough Norf 67 D7
Oxcombe Lincs 79 B6
Oxen Park Cumb 99 F5
Oxenholme Cumb 99 F7
Oxenhope W Yorks 94 F3
Oxenton Glos 50 F4
Oxenwood Wilts 25 D8
Oxford Oxon 39 D5
Oxhey Herts 40 E4
Oxhill Warks 51 E8
Oxley W Mid 62 D3
Oxley Green Essex 43 C5
Oxley's Green E Sus 18 C3
Oxnam Borders 116 C2
Oxshott Sur 28 C2
Oxspring S Yorks 88 D3
Oxted Sur 28 D4
Oxton Borders 121 D7
Oxton Notts 77 D6
Oxwich Swansea 33 F5
Oxwick Norf 80 E5
Oykel Bridge Highld 156 J6
Oyne Aberds 141 B5

P

Pabail Iarach W Isles 155 D10
Pabail Uarach W Isles 155 D10
Pace Gate N Yorks 94 D4
Packington Leics 63 C7
Padanaram Angus 134 D4
Padbury Bucks 52 F5
Paddington London 41 F5
Paddlesworth Kent 19 B8
Paddock Wood Kent 29 E7
Paddockhaugh Moray 152 C2
Paddockhole Dumfries 115 F5
Padfield Derbys 87 E8
Padiham Lancs 93 F7
Padog Conwy 83 F8
Padside N Yorks 94 D4
Padstow Corn 4 B4
Padworth W Berks 26 C4
Page Bank Durham 110 F5
Pagham W Sus 16 E2
Paglesham Churchend Essex 43 E5
Paglesham Eastend Essex 43 E5
Paibeil W Isles 148 B2
Paible W Isles 154 H5
Paignton Torbay 7 C6
Pailton Warks 63 F8
Painscastle Powys 48 E3
Painshawfield Northumb 110 C3
Painsthorpe E Yorks 96 D4
Painswick Glos 37 D5
Pairc Shiaboist W Isles 154 C7
Paisley Renfs 118 C4
Pakefield Suff 69 E8
Pakenham Suff 56 C3
Pale Gwyn 72 F3
Palestine Hants 25 E7
Paley Street Windsor 27 B6
Palfrey W Mid 62 E4
Palgowan Dumfries 112 F3
Palgrave Suff 56 B5
Pallion T&W 111 D6
Palmarsh Kent 19 B8
Palnackie Dumfries 106 D5
Palnure Dumfries 105 C8
Palterton Derbys 76 C4
Pamber End Hants 26 D4
Pamber Green Hants 26 D4
Pamber Heath Hants 26 C4
Pamphill Dorset 13 D7
Pampisford Cambs 55 E5
Pan Orkney 159 J4
Panbride Angus 135 F5
Pancrasweek Devon 8 D4
Pandy Gwyn 58 D3
Pandy Mon 35 B7
Pandy Powys 59 D6
Pandy Wrex 73 F5
Pandy Tudur Conwy 83 E8
Panfield Essex 42 B3
Pangbourne W Berks 26 B4
Pannal N Yorks 95 D6
Panshanger Herts 41 C5
Pant Shrops 60 B2
Pant-glâs Powys 58 E4
Pant-glas Carms 33 B6
Pant-glas Gwyn 71 C5
Pant-glas Shrops 73 F6
Pant-lasau Swansea 33 E7
Pant Mawr Powys 59 F5
Pant-teg Carms 33 B5
Pant-y-Caws Carms 32 B2
Pant-y-dwr Powys 47 B8
Pant-y-ffridd Powys 59 D8
Pant-y-Wacco Flint 72 B5
Pant-yr-awel Bridgend 34 F3
Pantgwyn Carms 33 B6
Pantgwyn Ceredig 45 E4
Panton Lincs 78 B4
Pantperthog Gwyn 58 D4
Pantyffynnon Carms 33 C7
Pantymwyn Flint 73 C5
Panxworth Norf 69 C6
Papcastle Cumb 107 F8
Papigoe Highld 158 E5
Papil Shetland 160 K5
Papley Orkney 159 J5
Papple E Loth 121 B8
Papplewick Notts 76 D5
Papworth Everard Cambs 54 C3
Papworth St Agnes Cambs 54 C3
Par Corn 5 D5
Parbold Lancs 86 C2
Parbrook Som 23 F7
Parbrook W Sus 16 B4
Parc Gwyn 72 F2
Parc-Seymour Newport 35 E8
Parc-y-rhôs Carms 46 E4
Parcllyn Ceredig 45 D4
Pardshaw Cumb 98 B2
Parham Suff 57 C7
Park Dumfries 114 E2
Park Corner Oxon 39 F6
Park Corner Windsor 40 F1
Park End Mbro 102 C3
Park End Northumb 109 B8
Park Gate Hants 15 D6
Park Hill N Yorks 95 C6
Park Hill Notts 77 D6
Park Street W Sus 28 F2
Parkend Glos 36 D3
Parkeston Essex 57 F6
Parkgate Ches W 73 B6
Parkgate Dumfries 114 F3
Parkgate Kent 19 B5
Parkgate Sur 28 E3
Parkham Devon 9 B5
Parkham Ash Devon 9 B5
Parkhill Ho. Aberds 141 C7
Parkhouse Mon 36 D1
Parkhouse Green Derbys 76 C4
Parkhurst IoW 15 E5
Parkmill Swansea 33 F6
Parkneuk Aberds 135 B7
Parkstone Poole 13 E8
Parley Cross Dorset 13 E8
Parracombe Devon 21 E5
Parrog Pembs 45 F2
Parsley Hay Derbys 75 C8
Parson Cross S Yorks 88 E4
Parson Drove Cambs 66 D3
Parsonage Green Essex 42 D3
Parsonby Cumb 107 F8
Parson's Heath Essex 43 B6
Partick Glasgow 119 C5
Partington Gtr Man 86 E5
Partney Lincs 79 C7
Parton Cumb 98 B1
Parton Dumfries 106 B3
Parton Glos 37 B5
Partridge Green W Sus 17 C5
Parwich Derbys 75 D8
Passenham Northants 53 F5
Paston Norf 81 D9
Patchacott Devon 9 E6
Patcham Brighton 17 D7
Patching W Sus 16 D4
Patchole Devon 20 E5
Pateley Bridge N Yorks 94 C4
Paternoster Heath Essex 43 C5
Path of Condie Perth 128 C2
Pathe Som 23 F5
Pathhead Aberds 135 C7
Pathhead E Ayrs 113 C6
Pathhead Fife 128 E4
Pathhead Midloth 121 C6
Pathstruie Perth 128 C2
Patna E Ayrs 112 C4
Patney Wilts 25 D5
Patrick IoM 84 D2
Patrick Brompton N Yorks 101 E7
Patrington E Yorks 91 B7
Patrixbourne Kent 31 D5
Patterdale Cumb 99 C5
Pattingham Staffs 62 E2
Pattishall Northants 52 D4
Pattiswick Green Essex 42 B4
Patton Bridge Cumb 99 E7
Paul Corn 2 D3
Paulerspury Northants 52 E5
Paull E Yorks 91 B5
Paulton Bath 23 D8
Pavenham Bedford 53 D7
Pawlett Som 22 E5
Pawston Northumb 122 F4
Paxford Glos 51 F6
Paxton Borders 122 D5
Payhembury Devon 11 D5
Paythorne Lancs 93 D8
Peacehaven E Sus 17 D8
Peak Dale Derbys 75 B7
Peak Forest Derbys 75 B8
Peakirk Pboro 65 D8
Pearsie Angus 134 D3
Pease Pottage W Sus 28 F3
Peasedown St John Bath 24 D2
Peasemore W Berks 26 B2
Peasenhall Suff 57 C7
Peaslake Sur 27 E8
Peasley Cross Mers 86 E3
Peasmarsh E Sus 19 C5
Peaston E Loth 121 C7
Peastonbank E Loth 121 C7
Peat Inn Fife 129 D6
Peathill Aberds 153 B9
Peatling Magna Leics 64 E2
Peatling Parva Leics 64 F2
Peaton Shrops 60 F5
Peats Corner Suff 57 C5
Pebmarsh Essex 56 F2
Pebworth Worcs 51 E6
Pecket Well W Yorks 87 B7
Peckforton Ches E 74 D2
Peckham London 28 B4
Peckleton Leics 63 D8
Pedlinge Kent 19 B8
Pedmore W Mid 62 F3
Pedwell Som 23 F6
Peebles Borders 121 E5
Peel IoM 84 D2
Peel Common Hants 15 D6
Peel Park S Lanark 119 D6
Peening Quarter Kent 19 C5
Pegsdon C Beds 54 F2
Pegswood Northumb 117 F8
Pegwell Kent 31 C7
Peinchorran Highld 149 E10
Peinlich Highld 149 C9
Pelaw T&W 111 C5
Pelcomb Bridge Pembs 44 D4
Pelcomb Cross Pembs 44 D4
Peldon Essex 43 C5
Pellon W Yorks 87 B8
Pelsall W Mid 62 D4
Pelton Durham 111 D5
Pelutho Cumb 107 E8
Pelynt Corn 5 D7
Pemberton Gtr Man 86 D3
Pembrey Carms 33 D5
Pembridge Hereford 49 D5
Pembroke = Penfro Pembs 44 E4
Pembroke Dock = Doc Penfro Pembs 44 E4
Pembury Kent 29 E7
Pen-bont Rhydybeddau Ceredig 58 F3
Pen-clawdd Swansea 33 E6
Pen-ffordd Pembs 32 B1
Pen-groes-oped Mon 35 D7
Pen-llyn Anglesey 82 C3
Pen-lon Anglesey 82 E4
Pen-sarn Gwyn 70 C5
Pen-sarn Gwyn 71 E6
Pen-twyn Mon 36 D2
Pen-y-banc Carms 33 B7
Pen-y-bont Carms 32 B4
Pen-y-bont Gwyn 58 D4
Pen-y-bont Gwyn 71 E7
Pen-y-bont Powys 60 B2
Pen-Y-Bont Ar Ogwr = Bridgend Bridgend 21 B8
Pen-y-bryn Gwyn 58 C3
Pen-y-bryn Pembs 45 E3
Pen-y-cae Powys 34 C2
Pen-y-cae-mawr Mon 35 E8
Pen-y-cefn Flint 72 B5
Pen-y-clawdd Mon 36 D1
Pen-y-coedcae Rhondda 34 F4
Pen-y-fai Bridgend 34 F2
Pen-y-garn Carms 46 F4
Pen-y-garn Ceredig 58 F3
Pen-y-garnedd Anglesey 82 D5
Pen-y-gop Conwy 72 E3
Pen-y-graig Gwyn 70 D2
Pen-y-groes Carms 33 C6
Pen-y-groeslon Gwyn 70 D3
Pen-y-Gwryd Hotel Gwyn 83 F6
Pen-y-stryt Denb 73 D5
Pen-yr-heol Mon 35 C8
Pen-yr-Heolgerrig M Tydf 34 D4
Penallt Mon 36 C2
Penally Pembs 32 E2
Penalt Hereford 36 B2
Penare Corn 3 B8
Penarlâg = Hawarden Flint 73 C7
Penarth V Glam 22 B3
Penbryn Ceredig 45 D4
Pencader Carms 46 F3
Pencaenewydd Gwyn 70 C5
Pencaitland E Loth 121 C7
Pencarnisiog Anglesey 82 D3
Pencarreg Carms 46 E4
Pencelli Powys 34 B4
Pencoed Bridgend 34 F3
Pencombe Hereford 49 D7
Pencoyd Hereford 36 B2
Pencraig Hereford 36 B2
Pencraig Powys 59 B7
Pendeen Corn 2 C2
Penderyn Rhondda 34 D3
Pendine Carms 32 D3
Pendlebury Gtr Man 87 D5
Pendleton Lancs 93 F7
Pendock Worcs 50 F2
Pendoggett Corn 4 B5
Pendomer Som 12 C3
Pendoylan V Glam 22 B2
Pendre Bridgend 34 F3
Penegoes Powys 58 D4
Penfro = Pembroke Pembs 44 E4
Pengam Caerph 35 E5
Penge London 28 B4
Pengenffordd Powys 48 F3
Pengorffwysfa Anglesey 82 B4
Pengover Green Corn 5 C7
Penhale Corn 3 E5
Penhale Corn 4 D4
Penhalvaen Corn 3 C6
Penhill Swindon 38 F1
Penhow Newport 35 E8
Penhurst E Sus 18 D3
Peniarth Gwyn 58 D3
Penicuik Midloth 120 C5
Peniel Carms 33 B5
Peniel Denb 72 C4
Penifiler Highld 149 D9
Peninver Argyll 143 F8
Penisarwaun Gwyn 83 E5
Penistone S Yorks 88 D3
Penjerrick Corn 3 C6
Penketh Warr 86 F3
Penkill S Ayrs 112 E2
Penkridge Staffs 62 C3
Penley Wrex 73 F8
Penllergaer Swansea 33 E7
Penllyn V Glam 21 B8
Penmachno Conwy 83 F7
Penmaen Swansea 33 F6
Penmaenan Conwy 83 D7
Penmaenmawr Conwy 83 D7
Penmaenpool Gwyn 58 C3
Penmark V Glam 22 C2
Penmarth Corn 3 C6
Penmon Anglesey 83 C6
Penmore Mill Argyll 146 F7
Penmorfa Ceredig 46 D2
Penmorfa Gwyn 71 C6
Penmynydd Anglesey 82 D5
Penn Bucks 40 E2
Penn W Mid 62 E2
Penn Street Bucks 40 E2
Pennal Gwyn 58 D4
Pennan Aberds 153 B8
Pennant Ceredig 46 C4
Pennant Denb 72 D4
Pennant Denb 72 F4
Pennant Powys 59 E5
Pennant Melangell Powys 59 B7
Pennar Pembs 44 E4
Pennard Swansea 33 F6
Pennerley Shrops 60 E3
Pennington Cumb 92 B2
Pennington Gtr Man 86 E4
Pennington Hants 14 E4
Penny Bridge Cumb 99 F5
Pennycross Argyll 147 J8
Pennygate Norf 69 B6
Pennygown Argyll 147 G8
Pennymoor Devon 10 C3
Pennywell T&W 111 D6
Penparc Ceredig 45 E4
Penparc Pembs 44 B3
Penparcau Ceredig 58 F2
Penperlleni Mon 35 D7
Penpillick Corn 5 D5
Penpol Corn 3 C7
Penpoll Corn 5 D6
Penpont Dumfries 113 E8
Penpont Powys 34 B3
Penrhôs Mon 35 C8
Penrherber Carms 45 F4
Penrhiw goch Carms 33 C6
Penrhiw-llan Ceredig 46 E2
Penrhiw-pâl Ceredig 46 E2
Penrhiwceiber Rhondda 34 E4
Penrhos Gwyn 70 D4
Penrhos Powys 34 C1
Penrhosfeilw Anglesey 82 C2
Penrhyn Bay Conwy 83 C8
Penrhyn-coch Ceredig 58 F3
Penrhyndeudraeth Gwyn 71 D7
Penrhynside Conwy 83 C8
Penrice Swansea 33 F5
Penrith Cumb 108 F5
Penrose Corn 4 B3
Penruddock Cumb 99 B6
Penryn Corn 3 C6
Pensarn Carms 33 C5
Pensarn Conwy 72 B3
Pensax Worcs 50 C2
Pensby Mers 85 F3
Penselwood Som 24 F2
Pensford Bath 23 C8
Penshaw T&W 111 D6
Penshurst Kent 29 E6
Pensilva Corn 5 C7
Penston E Loth 121 B7
Pentewan Corn 3 B9
Pentir Gwyn 83 E5
Pentire Corn 4 C2
Pentlow Essex 56 E2
Pentney Norf 67 C7
Penton Mewsey Hants 25 E8
Pentraeth Anglesey 82 D5
Pentre Carms 33 C6
Pentre Powys 59 F7
Pentre Powys 60 E2
Pentre Rhondda 34 E3
Pentre Shrops 60 C3
Pentre Wrex 72 F5
Pentre Wrex 73 E6
Pentre-bâch Ceredig 46 E4
Pentre-bach Powys 47 F8
Pentre Berw Anglesey 82 D4
Pentre-bont Conwy 83 F7
Pentre-celyn Denb 72 D5
Pentre-Celyn Powys 59 D5
Pentre-chwyth Swansea 33 E7
Pentre-cwrt Carms 46 F2
Pentre Dolau-Honddu Powys 47 E8
Pentre-dwr Swansea 33 E7
Pentre-galar Pembs 45 F3
Pentre-Gwenlais Carms 33 C7
Pentre Gwynfryn Gwyn 71 E6
Pentre Halkyn Flint 73 B6
Pentre-Isaf Conwy 83 E8
Pentre Llanrhaeadr Denb 72 C4
Pentre-llwyn-llŵyd Powys 47 D8
Pentre-llyn Ceredig 46 B5
Pentre-llyn cymmer Conwy 72 D3
Pentre Meyrick V Glam 21 B8
Pentre-poeth Newport 35 F6
Pentre-rhew Ceredig 47 D5
Pentre-tafarn-y-fedw Conwy 83 E8
Pentre-ty-gwyn Carms 47 F7
Pentrebach M Tydf 34 D4
Pentrebach Swansea 33 D7
Pentrebeirdd Powys 59 C8
Pentrecagal Carms 46 E2
Pentredwr Denb 73 E5
Pentrefelin Carms 33 B6
Pentrefelin Ceredig 46 E5
Pentrefelin Conwy 83 D8
Pentrefelin Gwyn 71 D6
Pentrefoelas Conwy 83 F8
Pentregat Ceredig 46 D2
Pentreheyling Shrops 60 E2
Pentre'r Felin Conwy 83 E8
Pentre'r-felin Powys 47 F8
Pentrich Derbys 76 D3
Pentridge Dorset 13 C8
Pentyrch Cardiff 35 F5
Penuchadre V Glam 21 B7
Penuwch Ceredig 46 C4
Penwithick Corn 4 D5
Penwyllt Powys 34 C2
Penybanc Carms 33 C7
Penybont Powys 48 C3
Penybontfawr Powys 59 B7
Penycae Wrex 73 E6
Penycwm Pembs 44 C3
Penyffordd Flint 73 C7
Penyffridd Gwyn 82 F5
Penygarnedd Powys 59 B8
Penygraig Rhondda 34 E3
Penygroes Gwyn 82 F4
Penygroes Pembs 45 F3
Penyrheol Caerph 35 F5
Penysarn Anglesey 82 B4
Penywaun Rhondda 34 D3
Penzance Corn 2 C3
Peopleton Worcs 50 D4
Peover Heath Ches E 74 B4
Peper Harow Sur 27 E7
Perceton N Ayrs 118 E3
Percie Aberds 140 E4
Percyhorner Aberds 153 B9
Periton Som 21 E8
Perivale London 40 F4
Perkinsville Durham 111 D5
Perlethorpe Notts 77 B6
Perranarworthal Corn 3 C6
Perranporth Corn 4 D2
Perranuthnoe Corn 2 D4
Perranzabuloe Corn 4 D2
Perry Barr W Mid 62 E4
Perry Green Herts 41 C7
Perry Green Wilts 37 F6
Perry Street Kent 29 B7
Perryfoot Derbys 88 F2
Pershall Staffs 74 F5
Pershore Worcs 50 E4
Pert Angus 135 C6
Pertenhall Bedford 53 C8
Perth Perth 128 B3
Perthy Shrops 73 F7
Perton Staffs 62 E2
Pertwood Wilts 24 F3
Peter Tavy Devon 6 B3
Peterborough Pboro 65 E8
Peterburn Highld 155 J12
Peterchurch Hereford 48 F5
Peterculter Aberdeen 141 D7
Peterhead Aberds 153 D11
Peterlee Durham 111 E7
Peter's Green Herts 40 C4
Peters Marland Devon 9 C6
Petersfield Hants 15 B8
Peterston super-Ely V Glam 22 B2
Peterstone Wentlooge Newport 35 F6
Peterstow Hereford 36 B2
Petertown Orkney 159 H4
Petham Kent 30 D5
Petrockstow Devon 9 D7
Pett E Sus 19 D5
Pettaugh Suff 57 D5
Petteridge Kent 29 E7
Pettinain S Lanark 120 E2
Pettistree Suff 57 D6
Petton Devon 10 B5
Petton Shrops 60 B4
Petts Wood London 28 C5
Petty Aberds 153 E7
Pettycur Fife 128 F4
Pettymuick Aberds 141 B8
Petworth W Sus 16 B3
Pevensey E Sus 18 E3
Pevensey Bay E Sus 18 E3
Pewsey Wilts 25 C6
Philham Devon 8 B4
Philiphaugh Borders 115 B7
Phillack Corn 2 C4
Philleigh Corn 3 C7
Philpstoun W Loth 120 B3
Phocle Green Hereford 36 B3
Phoenix Green Hants 27 D5
Pica Cumb 98 B2
Piccotts End Herts 40 D3
Pickering N Yorks 103 F5
Picket Piece Hants 25 E8
Picket Post Hants 14 D2
Pickhill N Yorks 101 F8
Picklescott Shrops 60 E4
Pickletillem Fife 129 B6
Pickmere Ches E 74 B3
Pickney Som 11 B6
Pickstock Telford 61 B7
Pickwell Devon 20 E3
Pickwell Leics 64 C4
Pickworth Lincs 78 F3
Pickworth Rutland 65 C6
Picton Ches W 73 B8
Picton Flint 85 F2
Picton N Yorks 102 D2
Piddinghoe E Sus 17 D8
Piddington Northants 53 D6
Piddington Oxon 39 C6
Piddlehinton Dorset 12 E5
Piddletrenthide Dorset 12 E5
Pidley Cambs 54 B4
Piercebridge Darl 101 C7
Pierowall Orkney 159 D5
Pigdon Northumb 117 F7
Pikehall Derbys 75 D8
Pilgrims Hatch Essex 42 E1
Pilham Lincs 90 E2
Pill N Som 23 B7
Pillaton Corn 5 C8
Pillerton Hersey Warks 51 E8
Pillerton Priors Warks 51 E7
Pilleth Powys 48 C4
Pilley Hants 14 E4
Pilley S Yorks 88 D4
Pilling Lancs 92 E4
Pilling Lane Lancs 92 E3
Pillowell Glos 36 D3
Pillwell Dorset 13 C5
Pilning S Glos 36 F2
Pilsbury Derbys 75 C8
Pilsdon Dorset 12 E2
Pilsgate Pboro 65 D7
Pilsley Derbys 76 B2
Pilsley Derbys 76 C4
Pilton Devon 20 F4
Pilton Northants 65 F7
Pilton Rutland 65 D6
Pilton Som 23 E7
Pilton Green Swansea 33 F5
Pimperne Dorset 13 D7
Pin Mill Suff 57 F6
Pinchbeck Lincs 66 B2
Pinchbeck Bars Lincs 65 B8
Pinchbeck West Lincs 66 B2
Pincheon Green S Yorks 89 C7
Pinehurst Swindon 38 F1
Pinfold Lancs 85 C4
Pinged Carms 33 D5
Pinhoe Devon 10 E4
Pinkneys Green Windsor 40 F1
Pinley W Mid 51 B8
Pinminnoch S Ayrs 112 E1
Pinmore S Ayrs 112 E2
Pinmore Mains S Ayrs 112 E2
Pinner London 40 F4
Pinvin Worcs 50 E4
Pinwherry S Ayrs 112 F1
Pinxton Derbys 76 D4
Pipe and Lyde Hereford 49 E7
Pipe Gate Shrops 74 E4
Piperhill Highld 151 F11
Piper's Pool Corn 8 F4
Pipewell Northants 64 F5
Pippacott Devon 20 F4
Pipton Powys 48 F3
Pirbright Sur 27 D7
Pirnmill N Ayrs 143 D9
Pirton Herts 54 F2
Pirton Worcs 50 E3
Pisgah Ceredig 47 B5
Pisgah Stirling 127 D6
Pishill Oxon 39 F7
Pistyll Gwyn 70 C4
Pitagowan Perth 133 C5
Pitblae Aberds 153 B9
Pitcairngreen Perth 128 B2
Pitcalnie Highld 151 D11
Pitcaple Aberds 141 B6
Pitch Green Bucks 39 D7
Pitch Place Sur 27 D7
Pitchcombe Glos 37 D5
Pitchcott Bucks 39 B7
Pitchford Shrops 60 D5
Pitcombe Som 23 F8
Pitcorthie Fife 129 D7
Pitcox E Loth 122 B2
Pitcur Perth 134 F2
Pitfichie Aberds 141 C5
Pitforthie Aberds 135 B8
Pitgrudy Highld 151 B10
Pitkennedy Angus 135 D5
Pitkevy Fife 128 D4
Pitkierie Fife 129 D7
Pitlessie Fife 128 D5
Pitlochry Perth 133 D6
Pitmachie Aberds 141 B5
Pitmain Highld 138 D3
Pitmedden Aberds 141 B7
Pitminster Som 11 C7
Pitmuies Angus 135 E5
Pitmunie Aberds 141 C5
Pitney Som 12 B2
Pitscottie Fife 129 C6
Pitsea Essex 42 F3
Pitsford Northants 53 C5
Pitsmoor S Yorks 88 F4
Pitstone Bucks 40 C2
Pitstone Green Bucks 40 C2
Pittendreich Moray 152 B1
Pittentrail Highld 157 J10
Pittenweem Fife 129 D7
Pittington Durham 111 E6
Pittodrie Aberds 141 B5
Pitton Wilts 25 F7
Pittswood Kent 29 E7
Pittulie Aberds 153 B9
Pity Me Durham 111 E5
Pityme Corn 4 B4
Pityoulish Highld 138 C5
Pixey Green Suff 57 B6
Pixham Sur 28 D2
Pixley Hereford 49 F8
Place Newton N Yorks 96 B4
Plaidy Aberds 153 C7
Plains N Lanark 119 C7
Plaish Shrops 60 E5
Plaistow W Sus 27 F8
Plaitford Wilts 14 C3
Plank Lane Gtr Man 86 E4
Plas-canol Gwyn 58 C2
Plas Gogerddan Ceredig 58 F3
Plas Llwyngwern Powys 58 D4
Plas Nantyr Wrex 73 F5
Plas-yn-Cefn Denb 72 B4
Plastow Green Hants 26 C3
Platt Kent 29 D7
Platt Bridge Gtr Man 86 D4
Platts Common S Yorks 88 D4
Plawsworth Durham 111 E5
Plaxtol Kent 29 D7
Play Hatch Oxon 26 B5
Playden E Sus 19 C6
Playford Suff 57 E6
Playing Place Corn 3 B7
Playley Green Glos 50 F2
Plealey Shrops 60 D4
Plean Stirling 127 F7
Pleasington Blackburn 86 B4
Pleasley Derbys 76 C5
Pleckgate Blackburn 93 F6
Plenmeller Northumb 109 C7
Pleshey Essex 42 C2
Plockton Highld 149 E13
Plocrapol W Isles 154 H6
Ploughfield Hereford 49 E5
Plowden Shrops 60 F3
Ploxgreen Shrops 60 D3
Pluckley Kent 30 E3
Pluckley Thorne Kent 30 E3
Plumbland Cumb 107 F8
Plumley Ches E 74 B4
Plumpton Cumb 108 F4
Plumpton E Sus 17 C7
Plumpton Green E Sus 17 C7
Plumpton Head Cumb 108 F5
Plumstead London 29 B5
Plumstead Norf 81 D7
Plumtree Notts 77 F6
Plungar Leics 77 F7
Plush Dorset 12 D5
Plwmp Ceredig 46 D2
Plymouth Plym 6 D2
Plympton Plym 6 D3

Ros–Shi 223

Rosehall Highld 156 J7
Rosehaugh Mains Highld 151 F9
Rosehearty Aberds 153 B9
Rosehill Shrops 74 F3
Roseisle Moray 152 B1
Roselands E Sus 18 E3
Rosemarket Pembs 44 E4
Rosemarkie Highld 151 F10
Rosemary Lane Devon 11 C6
Rosemount Perth 134 E1
Rosenannon Corn 4 C4
Rosewell Midloth 121 C5
Roseworth Stockton 102 B2
Roseworthy Corn 2 C5
Rosgill Cumb 99 C7
Roshven Highld 147 D10
Roskhill Highld 149 D7
Roskill House Highld 151 F9
Rosley Cumb 108 E3
Roslin Midloth 121 C5
Rosliston Derbys 63 C6
Rosneath Argyll 145 E11
Ross Dumfries 106 E3
Ross Northumb 123 F7
Ross Perth 127 B6
Ross-on-Wye Hereford 36 B3
Rossett Wrex 73 D7
Rossett Green N Yorks 95 D6
Rossie Ochill Perth 128 C2
Rossie Priory Perth 134 F2
Rossington S Yorks 89 E7
Rosskeen Highld 151 E9
Rossland Renfs 118 B4
Roster Highld 158 G4
Rostherne Ches E 86 F5
Rosthwaite Cumb 98 C4
Roston Derbys 75 E8
Rosyth Fife 128 F3
Rothbury Northumb 117 D6
Rotherby Leics 64 C3
Rotherfield E Sus 18 C2
Rotherfield Greys Oxon 39 F7
Rotherfield Peppard Oxon 39 F7
Rotherham S Yorks 88 E5
Rothersthorpe Northants 52 D5
Rotherwick Hants 26 D5
Rothes Moray 152 D2
Rothesay Argyll 145 G9
Rothiebrisbane Aberds 153 E7
Rothienorman Aberds 153 E7
Rothiesholm Orkney 159 F7
Rothley Leics 64 C2
Rothley Northumb 117 F6
Rothley Shield East Northumb 117 E6
Rothmaise Aberds 153 E6
Rothwell Lincs 91 E5
Rothwell Northants 64 F5
Rothwell W Yorks 88 B4
Rothwell Haigh W Yorks 88 B4
Rotsea E Yorks 97 D6
Rottal Angus 134 C3
Rotten End Suff 57 C7
Rottingdean Brighton 17 D7
Rottington Cumb 98 C1
Roud IoW 15 F6
Rough Close Staffs 75 F6
Rough Common Kent 30 D5
Rougham Norf 80 E4
Rougham Suff 56 C3
Rougham Green Suff 56 C3
Roughburn Highld 137 F6
Roughlee Lancs 93 E8
Roughley W Mid 62 E5
Roughsike Cumb 108 B5
Roughton Lincs 78 C5
Roughton Norf 81 D8
Roughton Shrops 61 E7
Roughton Moor Lincs 78 C5
Roundhay W Yorks 95 F6
Roundstonefoot Dumfries 114 D4
Roundstreet Common W Sus 16 B4
Roundway Wilts 24 C5
Rous Lench Worcs 50 D5
Rousdon Devon 11 E7
Routenburn N Ayrs 118 C1
Routh E Yorks 97 E6
Row Corn 5 B5
Row Cumb 99 F6
Row Heath Essex 43 C7
Rowanburn Dumfries 108 B4
Rowardennan Stirling 126 E2
Rowde Wilts 24 C4
Rowen Conwy 83 D7
Rowfoot Northumb 109 C6
Rowhedge Essex 43 B6
Rowhook W Sus 28 F2
Rowington Warks 51 C7
Rowland Derbys 76 B2
Rowlands Castle Hants 15 C8
Rowlands Gill T&W 110 D4
Rowledge Sur 27 E6
Rowlestone Hereford 35 B7
Rowley E Yorks 97 F5
Rowley Shrops 60 D3
Rowley Hill W Yorks 88 C2
Rowley Regis W Mid 62 F3
Rowly Sur 27 E8
Rowney Green Worcs 50 B5
Rownhams Hants 14 C4
Rowrah Cumb 98 C2
Rowsham Bucks 39 C8
Rowsley Derbys 76 C2
Rowstock Oxon 38 F4
Rowston Lincs 78 D3
Rowton Ches W 73 C8
Rowton Shrops 60 C3
Rowton Telford 61 C6
Roxburgh Borders 122 F3
Roxby N Lincs 90 C3
Roxby N Yorks 103 C5
Roxton Bedford 54 D2
Roxwell Essex 42 D2
Royal Leamington Spa Warks 51 C8
Royal Oak Darl 101 B7
Royal Oak Lancs 86 D2
Royal Tunbridge Wells Kent 18 B2
Royal Wootton Bassett Wilts 37 F7
Roybridge Highld 137 F5
Roydhouse W Yorks 88 C3
Roydon Essex 41 D7
Roydon Norf 68 F3
Roydon Norf 80 E3
Roydon Hamlet Essex 41 D7
Royston Herts 54 E4
Royston S Yorks 88 C4
Royton Gtr Man 87 D7
Rozel Jersey 17
Ruabon = Rhiwabon Wrex 73 E7
Ruaig Argyll 146 G3
Ruan Lanihorne Corn 3 B7
Ruan Minor Corn 3 E6
Ruarach Highld 136 B2
Ruardean Glos 36 C3
Ruardean Woodside Glos 36 C3
Rubery Worcs 50 B4
Ruckcroft Cumb 108 E5
Ruckhall Hereford 49 F6
Ruckinge Kent 19 B7
Ruckland Lincs 79 B6
Ruckley Shrops 60 D5
Rudbaxton Pembs 44 C4
Rudby N Yorks 102 D2
Ruddington Notts 77 F5
Rudford Glos 36 B4
Rudge Shrops 62 E2
Rudge Som 24 D3
Rudgeway S Glos 36 F3
Rudgwick W Sus 27 F8
Rudhall Hereford 36 B3
Rudheath Ches W 74 B3
Rudley Green Essex 42 D4
Rudry Caerph 35 F5
Rudston E Yorks 97 C6
Rudyard Staffs 75 D6
Rufford Lancs 86 C2
Rufforth York 95 D8
Rugby Warks 52 B3
Rugeley Staffs 62 C4
Ruglen S Ayrs 112 D2
Ruilick Highld 151 G8
Ruishton Som 11 B7
Ruisigearraidh W Isles 154 J4
Ruislip London 40 F3
Ruislip Common London 40 F3
Rumbling Bridge Perth 128 E2
Rumburgh Suff 69 F6
Rumford Corn 4 B3
Rumney Cardiff 22 B4
Runcorn Halton 86 F3
Runcton W Sus 16 D2
Runcton Holme Norf 67 D6
Rundlestone Devon 6 B3
Runfold Sur 27 E6
Runhall Norf 68 D3
Runham Norf 69 C7
Runham Norf 69 D8
Runnington Som 11 B6
Runsell Green Essex 42 D3
Runswick Bay N Yorks 103 C6
Runwell Essex 42 E3
Ruscombe Wokingham 27 B5
Rush Green London 41 F8
Rush-head Aberds 153 D8
Rushall Hereford 49 F8
Rushall Norf 68 F4
Rushall W Mid 62 D4
Rushall Wilts 25 D6
Rushbrooke Suff 56 C2
Rushbury Shrops 60 E5
Rushden Herts 54 F4
Rushden Northants 53 C7
Rushenden Kent 30 B3
Rushford Norf 68 F2
Rushlake Green E Sus 18 D3
Rushmere Suff 69 F7
Rushmere St Andrew Suff 57 E6
Rushmoor Sur 27 E6
Rushock Worcs 50 B3
Rusholme Gtr Man 87 E6
Rushton Ches W 74 C2
Rushton Northants 64 F5
Rushton Shrops 61 D6
Rushton Spencer Staffs 75 C6
Rushwick Worcs 50 D3
Rushyford Durham 101 B7
Ruskie Stirling 126 D5
Ruskington Lincs 78 D3
Rusland Cumb 99 F5
Rusper W Sus 28 F3
Ruspidge Glos 36 C3
Russell's Water Oxon 39 F7
Russel's Green Suff 57 B6
Rusthall Kent 18 B2
Rustington W Sus 16 D4
Ruston N Yorks 103 F7
Ruston Parva E Yorks 97 C6
Ruswarp N Yorks 103 D6
Rutherford Borders 122 F2
Rutherglen S Lanark 119 C6
Ruthernbridge Corn 4 C5
Ruthin = Rhuthun Denb 72 D5
Ruthrieston Aberdeen 141 D8
Ruthven Aberds 152 D5
Ruthven Angus 134 E2
Ruthven Highld 138 E3
Ruthven Highld 151 H11
Ruthven House Angus 134 E3
Ruthvoes Corn 4 C4
Ruthwell Dumfries 107 C7
Ruyton-XI-Towns Shrops 60 B3
Ryal Northumb 110 B3
Ryal Fold Blackburn 86 B4
Ryall Dorset 12 E2
Ryarsh Kent 29 D7
Rydal Cumb 99 D5
Ryde IoW 15 E6
Rye E Sus 19 C6
Rye Foreign E Sus 19 C5
Rye Harbour E Sus 19 D6
Rye Park Herts 41 C6
Rye Street Worcs 50 F2
Ryecroft Gate Staffs 75 C6
Ryehill E Yorks 91 B6
Ryhall Rutland 65 C7
Ryhill W Yorks 88 C4
Ryhope T&W 111 D7
Rylstone N Yorks 94 D2
Ryme Intrinseca Dorset 12 C3
Ryther N Yorks 95 F8
Ryton Glos 50 F2
Ryton N Yorks 96 B3
Ryton Shrops 61 D7
Ryton T&W 110 C4
Ryton-on-Dunsmore Warks 51 B8

S

Sabden Lancs 93 F7
Sacombe Herts 41 C6
Sacriston Durham 110 E5
Sadberge Darl 101 C8
Saddell Argyll 143 E8
Saddington Leics 64 E3
Saddle Bow Norf 67 C6
Saddlescombe W Sus 17 C6
Sadgill Cumb 99 D6
Saffron Walden Essex 55 F6
Sageston Pembs 32 D1
Saham Hills Norf 68 D2
Saham Toney Norf 68 D2
Saighdinis W Isles 148 B3
Saighton Ches W 73 C8
St Abbs Borders 122 C5
St Abb's Haven Borders 122 C5
St Agnes Corn 4 D2
St Agnes Scilly 2 F3
St Albans Herts 40 D4
St Allen Corn 4 D3
St Andrews Fife 129 C7
St Andrew's Major V Glam 22 B3
St Anne Ald 16
St Annes Lancs 85 B4
St Ann's Dumfries 114 E3
St Ann's Chapel Corn 6 B2
St Ann's Chapel Devon 6 E4
St Anthony-in-Meneage Corn 3 D6
St Anthony's Hill E Sus 18 E3
St Arvans Mon 36 E2
St Asaph = Llanelwy Denb 72 B4
St Athan V Glam 22 C2
St Aubin Jersey 17
St Austell Corn 4 D5
St Bees Cumb 98 C1
St Blazey Corn 5 D5
St Boswells Borders 121 F8
St Brelade Jersey 17
St Breock Corn 4 B4
St Breward Corn 5 B5
St Briavels Glos 36 D2
St Bride's Pembs 44 D3
St Brides Major V Glam 21 B7
St Bride's Netherwent Mon 35 F8
St Brides super Ely V Glam 22 B2
St Brides Wentlooge Newport 35 F6
St Budeaux Plym 6 D2
St Buryan Corn 2 D3
St Catherine Bath 24 B2
St Catherine's Argyll 125 E7
St Clears = Sanclêr Carms 32 C3
St Cleer Corn 5 C7
St Clement Corn 3 B7
St Clements Jersey 17
St Clether Corn 8 F4
St Colmac Argyll 145 G9
St Columb Major Corn 4 C4
St Columb Minor Corn 4 C3
St Columb Road Corn 4 D4
St Combs Aberds 153 B10
St Cross South Elmham Suff 69 F5
St Cyrus Aberds 135 C7
St David's Perth 127 B8
St David's = Tyddewi Pembs 44 C2
St Day Corn 3 B6
St Dennis Corn 4 D4
St Devereux Hereford 49 F6
St Dogmaels Pembs 45 E3
St Dogwells Pembs 44 C4
St Dominick Corn 6 C2
St Donat's V Glam 21 C8
St Edith's Wilts 24 C4
St Endellion Corn 4 B4
St Enoder Corn 4 D3
St Erme Corn 4 D3
St Erney Corn 5 D8
St Erth Corn 2 C4
St Ervan Corn 4 B3
St Eval Corn 4 C3
St Ewe Corn 3 B8
St Fagans Cardiff 22 B3
St Fergus Aberds 153 C10
St Fillans Perth 127 B5
St Florence Pembs 32 D1
St Genny's Corn 8 E3
St George Conwy 72 B3
St George's V Glam 22 B2
St Germans Corn 5 D8
St Giles Lincs 78 B2
St Giles in the Wood Devon 9 C7
St Giles on the Heath Devon 9 E5
St Harmon Powys 47 B8
St Helen Auckland Durham 101 B6
St Helena Warks 63 D6
St Helen's E Sus 18 D5
St Helens IoW 15 F7
St Helens Mers 86 E3
St Helier Jersey 17
St Helier London 28 C3
St Hilary Corn 2 C4
St Hilary V Glam 22 B2
Saint Hill W Sus 28 F4
St Illtyd Bl Gwent 35 D6
St Ippollytts Herts 40 B4
St Ishmael's Pembs 44 E3
St Issey Corn 4 B4
St Ive Corn 5 C8
St Ives Cambs 54 B4
St Ives Corn 2 B4
St Ives Dorset 14 D2
St James South Elmham Suff 69 F6
St Jidgey Corn 4 C4
St John Corn 6 D2
St John's IoM 84 D2
St John's Jersey 17
St John's Sur 27 D7
St John's Worcs 50 D3
St John's Chapel Durham 109 F8
St John's Fen End Norf 66 C5
St John's Highway Norf 66 C5
St John's Town of Dalry Dumfries 113 F6
St Judes IoM 84 C3
St Just Corn 2 C2
St Just in Roseland Corn 3 C7
St Katherine's Aberds 153 E7
St Keverne Corn 3 D6
St Kew Corn 4 B5
St Kew Highway Corn 4 B5
St Keyne Corn 5 C7
St Lawrence Corn 4 C5
St Lawrence Essex 43 D5
St Lawrence IoW 15 G6
St Leonard's Bucks 40 D2
St Leonards Dorset 14 D2
St Leonards E Sus 18 E4
Saint Leonards S Lanark 119 D6
St Levan Corn 2 D2
St Lythans V Glam 22 B3
St Mabyn Corn 4 B5
St Madoes Perth 128 B3
St Margaret's Hereford 49 F5
St Margarets Herts 41 C6
St Margaret's at Cliffe Kent 31 E7
St Margaret's Hope Orkney 159 J5
St Margaret South Elmham Suff 69 F6
St Mark's IoM 84 E2
St Martin Corn 5 D7
St Martins Corn 3 D6
St Martin's Jersey 17
St Martins Perth 134 F1
St Martin's Shrops 73 F7
St Mary Bourne Hants 26 D2
St Mary Church V Glam 22 B2
St Mary Cray London 29 C5
St Mary Hill V Glam 21 B8
St Mary Hoo Medway 30 B2
St Mary in the Marsh Kent 19 C7
St Mary's Jersey 17
St Mary's Orkney 159 H5
St Mary's Bay Kent 19 C7
St Maughans Mon 36 C1
St Mawes Corn 3 C7
St Mawgan Corn 4 C3
St Mellion Corn 5 C8
St Mellons Cardiff 35 F6
St Merryn Corn 4 B3
St Mewan Corn 4 D4
St Michael Caerhays Corn 3 B8
St Michael Penkevil Corn 3 B7
St Michael South Elmham Suff 69 F6
St Michael's Kent 19 B5
St Michaels Worcs 49 C7
St Michael's on Wyre Lancs 92 E4
St Minver Corn 4 B4
St Monans Fife 129 D7
St Neot Corn 5 C6
St Neots Cambs 54 C2
St Newlyn East Corn 4 D3
St Nicholas Pembs 44 B3
St Nicholas V Glam 22 B2
St Nicholas at Wade Kent 31 C6
St Ninians Stirling 127 E6
St Osyth Essex 43 C7
St Osyth Heath Essex 43 C7
St Ouens Jersey 17
St Owens Cross Hereford 36 B2
St Paul's Cray London 29 C5
St Paul's Walden Herts 40 B4
St Peter Port Guern 16
St Peter's Jersey 17
St Peter's Kent 31 C7
St Petrox Pembs 44 F4
St Pinnock Corn 5 C7
St Quivox S Ayrs 112 B3
St Ruan Corn 3 E6
St Sampson Guern 16
St Stephen Corn 4 D4
St Stephen's Corn 8 F5
St Stephens Corn 6 D2
St Stephens Herts 40 D4
St Teath Corn 8 F2
St Thomas Devon 10 E4
St Tudy Corn 5 B5
St Twynnells Pembs 44 F4
St Veep Corn 5 D6
St Vigeans Angus 135 E6
St Wenn Corn 4 C4
St Weonards Hereford 36 B1
Saintbury Glos 51 F6
Salcombe Devon 6 F5
Salcombe Regis Devon 11 F6
Salcott Essex 43 C5
Sale Gtr Man 87 E5
Sale Green Worcs 50 D4
Saleby Lincs 79 B7
Salehurst E Sus 18 C4
Salem Carms 33 B7
Salem Ceredig 58 F3
Salen Argyll 147 G8
Salen Highld 147 E9
Salesbury Lancs 93 F6
Salford C Beds 53 F7
Salford Gtr Man 87 E6
Salford Oxon 38 B2
Salford Priors Warks 51 D5
Salfords Sur 28 E3
Salhouse Norf 69 C6
Saline Fife 128 E2
Salisbury Wilts 14 B2
Sallachan Highld 130 C3
Sallachy Highld 150 H2
Sallachy Highld 157 J8
Salle Norf 81 E7
Salmonby Lincs 79 B6
Salmond's Muir Angus 135 F5
Salperton Glos 37 B7
Salph End Bedford 53 D8
Salsburgh N Lanark 119 C8
Salt Staffs 62 B3
Salt End E Yorks 91 B5
Saltaire W Yorks 94 F4
Saltash Corn 6 D2
Saltburn Highld 151 E10
Saltburn-by-the-Sea Redcar 102 B4
Saltby Leics 65 B5
Saltcoats Cumb 98 E2
Saltcoats N Ayrs 118 E2
Saltdean Brighton 17 D7
Salter Lancs 93 C6
Salterforth Lancs 93 E8
Salterswall Ches W 74 C3
Saltfleet Lincs 91 E8
Saltfleetby All Saints Lincs 91 E8
Saltfleetby St Clements Lincs 91 E8
Saltfleetby St Peter Lincs 91 F8
Saltford Bath 23 C8
Salthouse Norf 81 C6
Saltmarshe E Yorks 89 B8
Saltney Flint 73 C7
Salton N Yorks 96 B3
Saltwick Northumb 110 B4
Saltwood Kent 19 B8
Salum Argyll 146 G3
Salvington W Sus 16 D5
Salwarpe Worcs 50 C3
Salwayash Dorset 12 E2
Sambourne Warks 51 C5
Sambrook Telford 61 B7
Samhla W Isles 148 B2
Samlesbury Lancs 93 F5
Samlesbury Bottoms Lancs 86 B4
Sampford Arundel Som 11 C6
Sampford Brett Som 22 E2
Sampford Courtenay Devon 9 D8
Sampford Peverell Devon 10 C5
Sampford Spiney Devon 6 B3
Sampool Bridge Cumb 99 F6
Samuelston E Loth 121 B7
Sanachan Highld 149 D13
Sanaigmore Argyll 142 A3
Sanclêr = St Clears Carms 32 C3
Sancreed Corn 2 D3
Sancton E Yorks 96 F5
Sand Highld 150 B2
Sand Shetland 160 J5
Sand Hole E Yorks 96 F4
Sand Hutton N Yorks 96 D2
Sandaig Highld 149 H12
Sandal Magna W Yorks 88 C4
Sandale Cumb 108 E2
Sandbach Ches E 74 C4
Sandbank Argyll 145 E10
Sandbanks Poole 13 F8
Sandend Aberds 152 B5
Sanderstead London 28 C4
Sandfields Glos 37 B6
Sandford Cumb 100 C2
Sandford Devon 10 D3
Sandford Dorset 13 F7
Sandford IoW 15 F6
Sandford N Som 23 D6
Sandford S Lanark 119 E7
Sandford Shrops 74 F2
Sandford on Thames Oxon 39 D5
Sandford Orcas Dorset 12 B4
Sandford St Martin Oxon 38 B4
Sandfordhill Aberds 153 D11
Sandgate Kent 19 B8
Sandgreen Dumfries 106 D2
Sandhaven Aberds 153 B9
Sandhead Dumfries 104 E4
Sandhills Sur 27 F7
Sandhoe Northumb 110 C2
Sandholme E Yorks 96 F4
Sandholme Lincs 79 F6
Sandhurst Brack 27 C6
Sandhurst Glos 37 B5
Sandhurst Kent 18 C4
Sandhurst Cross Kent 18 C4
Sandhutton N Yorks 102 F1
Sandiacre Derbys 76 F4
Sandilands Lincs 91 F9
Sandilands S Lanark 119 F8
Sandiway Ches W 74 B3
Sandleheath Hants 14 C2
Sandling Kent 29 D8
Sandlow Green Ches E 74 C4
Sandness Shetland 160 H3
Sandon Essex 42 D3
Sandon Herts 54 F4
Sandon Staffs 75 F6
Sandown IoW 15 F6
Sandplace Corn 5 D7
Sandridge Herts 40 C4
Sandridge Wilts 24 C4
Sandringham Norf 67 B6
Sandsend N Yorks 103 C6
Sandside Ho. Highld 157 C12
Sandsound Shetland 160 J5
Sandtoft N Lincs 89 D8
Sandway Kent 30 D2
Sandwell W Mid 62 F4
Sandwich Kent 31 D7
Sandwick Cumb 99 C6
Sandwick Orkney 159 K5
Sandwick Shetland 160 L6
Sandwith Cumb 98 C1
Sandy C Beds 54 E2
Sandy Carms 33 D5
Sandy Bank Lincs 79 D5
Sandy Haven Pembs 44 E3
Sandy Lane Wilts 24 C4
Sandy Lane Wrex 73 E7
Sandycroft Flint 73 C7
Sandyford Dumfries 114 E5
Sandyford Stoke 75 D5
Sandygate IoM 84 C3
Sandyhills Dumfries 107 D5
Sandylands Lancs 92 C4
Sandypark Devon 10 F2
Sandysike Cumb 108 C3
Sangobeg Highld 156 C7
Sangomore Highld 156 C7
Sanna Highld 146 E7
Sanndabhaig W Isles 148 D3
Sanndabhaig W Isles 155 D9
Sannox N Ayrs 143 D11
Sanquhar Dumfries 113 D7
Santon N Lincs 90 C3
Santon Bridge Cumb 98 D3
Santon Downham Suff 67 F8
Sapcote Leics 63 E8
Sapey Common Hereford 50 C2
Sapiston Suff 56 B3
Sapley Cambs 54 B3
Sapperton Glos 37 D6
Sapperton Lincs 78 F3
Saracen's Head Lincs 66 B3
Sarclet Highld 158 F5
Sardis Carms 33 D6
Sarn Bridgend 34 F3
Sarn Powys 60 E2
Sarn Bach Gwyn 70 E4
Sarn Meyllteyrn Gwyn 70 D3
Sarnau Carms 32 C4
Sarnau Ceredig 46 D2
Sarnau Gwyn 72 F3
Sarnau Powys 48 F2
Sarnau Powys 60 C2
Sarnesfield Hereford 49 D5
Saron Carms 33 C7
Saron Carms 46 F2
Saron Denb 72 C4
Saron Gwyn 82 E5
Saron Gwyn 82 F4
Sarratt Herts 40 E3
Sarre Kent 31 C6
Sarsden Oxon 38 B2
Sarsgrum Highld 156 C6
Satley Durham 110 E4
Satron N Yorks 100 E4
Satterleigh Devon 9 B8
Satterthwaite Cumb 99 E5
Satwell Oxon 39 F7
Sauchen Aberds 141 C5
Saucher Perth 134 F1
Sauchie Clack 127 E7
Sauchieburn Aberds 135 C6
Saughall Ches W 73 B7
Saughtree Borders 115 E8
Saul Glos 36 D4
Saundby Notts 89 F8
Saundersfoot Pembs 32 D2
Saunderton Bucks 39 D7
Saunton Devon 20 F3
Sausthorpe Lincs 79 C6
Saval Highld 157 J8
Savary Highld 147 G9
Savile Park W Yorks 87 B8
Sawbridge Warks 52 C3
Sawbridgeworth Herts 41 C7
Sawdon N Yorks 103 F7
Sawley Derbys 76 F4
Sawley Lancs 93 E7
Sawley N Yorks 94 C5
Sawston Cambs 55 E5
Sawtry Cambs 65 F8
Saxby Leics 64 C5
Saxby Lincs 90 F4
Saxby All Saints N Lincs 90 C3
Saxelbye Leics 64 B4
Saxham Street Suff 56 C4
Saxilby Lincs 77 B8
Saxlingham Norf 81 D6
Saxlingham Green Norf 68 E5
Saxlingham Nethergate Norf 68 E5
Saxlingham Thorpe Norf 68 E5
Saxmundham Suff 57 C7
Saxon Street Cambs 55 D7
Saxondale Notts 77 F6
Saxtead Suff 57 C6
Saxtead Green Suff 57 C6
Saxthorpe Norf 81 D7
Saxton N Yorks 95 F7
Sayers Common W Sus 17 C6
Scackleton N Yorks 96 B2
Scadabhagh W Isles 154 H6
Scaftworth Notts 89 E7
Scagglethorpe N Yorks 96 B4
Scaitcliffe Lancs 87 B5
Scalasaig Argyll 144 D2
Scalby E Yorks 90 B2
Scalby N Yorks 103 E8
Scaldwell Northants 53 B5
Scale Houses Cumb 109 E5
Scaleby Cumb 108 C4
Scaleby Hill Cumb 108 C4
Scales Cumb 92 B2
Scales Cumb 99 B5
Scales Lancs 92 F4
Scalford Leics 64 B4
Scaling Redcar 103 C5
Scallastle Argyll 124 B2
Scalloway Shetland 160 K6
Scalpay W Isles 154 H7
Scalpay Ho. Highld 149 F11
Scalpsie Argyll 145 H9
Scamadale Highld 147 B10
Scamblesby Lincs 79 B5
Scamodale Highld 130 B2
Scampston N Yorks 96 B4
Scampton Lincs 78 B2
Scapa Orkney 159 H5
Scapegoat Hill W Yorks 87 C8
Scar Orkney 159 D7
Scarborough N Yorks 103 F8
Scarcliffe Derbys 76 C4
Scarcroft W Yorks 95 E6
Scarcroft Hill W Yorks 95 E6
Scardroy Highld 150 F5
Scarff Shetland 160 E4
Scarfskerry Highld 158 C4
Scargill Durham 101 C5
Scarinish Argyll 146 G3
Scarisbrick Lancs 85 C4
Scarning Norf 68 C2
Scarrington Notts 77 E7
Scartho NE Lincs 91 D6
Scarwell Orkney 159 F3
Scatness Shetland 160 M5
Scatraig Highld 151 H10
Scawby N Lincs 90 D3
Scawsby S Yorks 89 D6
Scawton N Yorks 102 F3
Scayne's Hill W Sus 17 B7
Scethrog Powys 35 B5
Scholar Green Ches E 74 D5
Scholes W Yorks 88 B2
Scholes W Yorks 88 D2
Scholes W Yorks 95 F6
School Green Ches W 74 C3
Scleddau Pembs 44 B4
Sco Ruston Norf 81 E8
Scofton Notts 89 F7
Scole Norf 56 B5
Scolpaig W Isles 148 A2
Scone Perth 128 B3
Sconser Highld 149 E10
Scoonie Fife 129 D5
Scoor Argyll 146 K7
Scopwick Lincs 78 D3
Scoraig Highld 150 B3
Scorborough E Yorks 97 E6
Scorrier Corn 3 B6
Scorton Lancs 92 E5
Scorton N Yorks 101 D7
Scotbheinn W Isles 148 C3
Scotby Cumb 108 D4
Scotch Corner N Yorks 101 D7
Scotforth Lancs 92 D4
Scothern Lincs 78 B3
Scotland Gate Northumb 117 F8
Scotlandwell Perth 128 D3
Scotsburn Highld 151 D10
Scotscalder Station Highld 158 E2
Scotscraig Fife 129 B6
Scots' Gap Northumb 117 F6
Scotston Aberds 135 B7
Scotston Perth 133 E6
Scotstoun Glasgow 118 C5
Scotstown Highld 130 C2
Scotswood T&W 110 C4
Scottas Highld 149 H12
Scotter Lincs 90 D2
Scotterthorpe Lincs 90 D2
Scottlethorpe Lincs 65 B7
Scotton Lincs 90 E2
Scotton N Yorks 95 D6
Scotton N Yorks 101 E6
Scottow Norf 81 E8
Scoughall E Loth 129 F8
Scoulag Argyll 145 H10
Scoulton Norf 68 D2
Scourie Highld 156 E4
Scourie More Highld 156 E4
Scousburgh Shetland 160 M5
Scrabster Highld 158 C2
Scrafield Lincs 79 C6
Scrainwood Northumb 117 D5
Scrane End Lincs 79 E6
Scraptoft Leics 64 D3
Scratby Norf 69 C8
Scrayingham N Yorks 96 C3
Scredington Lincs 78 E3
Scremby Lincs 79 C7
Scremerston Northumb 123 E6
Screveton Notts 77 E7
Scrivelsby Lincs 79 C5
Scriven N Yorks 95 D6
Scrooby Notts 89 E7
Scropton Derbys 75 F8
Scrub Hill Lincs 78 D5
Scruton N Yorks 101 E7
Sculcoates Hull 97 F6
Sculthorpe Norf 80 D4
Scunthorpe N Lincs 90 C2
Scurlage Swansea 33 F5
Sea Palling Norf 69 B7
Seaborough Dorset 12 D2
Seacombe Mers 85 E4
Seacroft Lincs 79 C8
Seacroft W Yorks 95 F6
Seadyke Lincs 79 F6
Seafield S Ayrs 112 B3
Seafield W Loth 120 C3
Seaford E Sus 17 E8
Seaforth Mers 85 E4
Seagrave Leics 64 C3
Seaham Durham 111 E7
Seahouses Northumb 123 F8
Seal Kent 29 D6
Sealand Flint 73 C7
Seale Sur 27 E6
Seamer N Yorks 102 C2
Seamer N Yorks 103 F8
Seamill N Ayrs 118 E2
Searby Lincs 90 D4
Seasalter Kent 30 C4
Seascale Cumb 98 D2
Seathorne Lincs 79 C8
Seathwaite Cumb 98 C4
Seathwaite Cumb 98 E4
Seatoller Cumb 98 C4
Seaton Corn 5 D8
Seaton Cumb 107 F7
Seaton Devon 11 F7
Seaton Durham 111 D6
Seaton E Yorks 97 E7
Seaton Northumb 111 B6
Seaton Rutland 65 E6
Seaton Burn T&W 110 B5
Seaton Carew Hrtlpl 102 B3
Seaton Delaval Northumb 111 B6
Seaton Ross E Yorks 96 E3
Seaton Sluice Northumb 111 B6
Seatown Aberds 152 B5
Seatown Dorset 12 E2
Seave Green N Yorks 102 D3
Seaview IoW 15 E7
Seaville Cumb 107 D8
Seavington St Mary Som 12 C2
Seavington St Michael Som 12 C2
Sebergham Cumb 108 E3
Seckington Warks 63 D6
Second Coast Highld 150 B2
Sedbergh Cumb 100 E1
Sedbury Glos 36 E2
Sedbusk N Yorks 100 E3
Sedgeberrow Worcs 50 F5
Sedgebrook Lincs 77 F8
Sedgefield Durham 102 B1
Sedgeford Norf 80 D3
Sedgehill Wilts 13 B6
Sedgley W Mid 62 E3
Sedgwick Cumb 99 F7
Sedlescombe E Sus 18 D4
Sedlescombe Street E Sus 18 D4
Seend Wilts 24 C4
Seend Cleeve Wilts 24 C4
Seer Green Bucks 40 E2
Seething Norf 69 E6
Sefton Mers 85 D4
Seghill Northumb 111 B5
Seifton Shrops 60 F4
Seighford Staffs 62 B2
Seilebost W Isles 154 H5
Seion Gwyn 82 E5
Seisdon Staffs 62 E2
Seisiadar W Isles 155 D10
Selattyn Shrops 73 F6
Selborne Hants 26 F5
Selby N Yorks 96 F2
Selham W Sus 16 B3
Selhurst London 28 C4
Selkirk Borders 115 B7
Sellack Hereford 36 B2
Sellafirth Shetland 160 D7
Sellibister Orkney 159 D8
Sellindge Kent 19 B7
Sellindge Lees Kent 19 B8
Selling Kent 30 D4
Sells Green Wilts 24 C4
Selly Oak W Mid 62 F4
Selmeston E Sus 18 E2
Selsdon London 28 C4
Selsey W Sus 16 E2
Selsfield Common W Sus 28 F4
Selsted Kent 31 E6
Selston Notts 76 D4
Selworthy Som 21 E8
Semblister Shetland 160 H5
Semer Suff 56 E3
Semington Wilts 24 C3
Semley Wilts 13 B6
Send Sur 27 D8
Send Marsh Sur 27 D8
Senghenydd Caerph 35 E5
Sennen Corn 2 D2
Sennen Cove Corn 2 D2
Sennybridge = Pont Senni Powys 34 B3
Serlby Notts 89 F7
Sessay N Yorks 95 B7
Setchey Norf 67 C6
Setley Hants 14 D4
Setter Shetland 160 E6
Setter Shetland 160 H5
Setter Shetland 160 J7
Settiscarth Orkney 159 G4
Settle N Yorks 93 C8
Settrington N Yorks 96 B4
Seven Kings London 41 F7
Seven Sisters Neath 34 D2
Sevenhampton Glos 37 B7
Sevenoaks Kent 29 D6
Sevenoaks Weald Kent 29 D6
Severn Beach S Glos 36 F2
Severn Stoke Worcs 50 E3
Severnhampton Swindon 38 E2
Sevington Kent 30 E4
Sewards End Essex 55 F6
Sewardstone Essex 41 E6
Sewardstonebury Essex 41 E6
Sewerby E Yorks 97 C7
Seworgan Corn 3 C6
Sewstern Leics 65 B5
Sezincote Glos 51 F6
Sgarasta Mhor W Isles 154 H5
Sgiogarstaigh W Isles 155 A10
Shabbington Bucks 39 D6
Shackerstone Leics 63 D7
Shackleford Sur 27 E7
Shade W Yorks 87 B7
Shadforth Durham 111 E6
Shadingfield Suff 69 F7
Shadoxhurst Kent 19 B6
Shadsworth Blackburn 86 B5
Shadwell Norf 68 F2
Shadwell W Yorks 95 F6
Shaftesbury Dorset 13 B6
Shafton S Yorks 88 C4
Shalbourne Wilts 25 C8
Shalcombe IoW 14 F4
Shalden Hants 26 E4
Shaldon Devon 7 B7
Shalfleet IoW 14 F5
Shalford Essex 42 B3
Shalford Sur 27 E8
Shalford Green Essex 42 B3
Shallowford Devon 21 E6
Shalmsford Street Kent 30 D4
Shalstone Bucks 52 F4
Shamley Green Sur 27 E8
Shandon Argyll 145 E11
Shandwick Highld 151 D11
Shangton Leics 64 E4
Shankhouse Northumb 111 B5
Shanklin IoW 15 F6
Shanquhar Aberds 152 E5
Shanzie Perth 134 D2
Shap Cumb 99 C7
Shapwick Dorset 13 D7
Shapwick Som 23 F6
Shardlow Derbys 76 F4
Shareshill Staffs 62 D3
Sharlston W Yorks 88 C4
Sharlston Common W Yorks 88 C4
Sharnbrook Bedford 53 D7
Sharnford Leics 63 E8
Sharoe Green Lancs 92 F5
Sharow N Yorks 95 B6
Sharp Street Norf 69 B6
Sharpenhoe C Beds 53 F8
Sharperton Northumb 117 D5
Sharpness Glos 36 D3
Sharpthorne W Sus 28 F4
Sharrington Norf 81 D6
Shatterford Worcs 61 F7
Shaugh Prior Devon 6 C3
Shavington Ches E 74 D4
Shaw Gtr Man 87 D7
Shaw W Berks 26 C2
Shaw Wilts 24 C3
Shaw Green Lancs 86 C3
Shaw Mills N Yorks 95 C5
Shawbury Shrops 61 B5
Shawdon Hall Northumb 117 C6
Shawell Leics 64 F2
Shawford Hants 15 B5
Shawforth Lancs 87 B6
Shawhead Dumfries 107 B5
Shawhill Dumfries 108 C2
Shawton S Lanark 119 E6
Shawtonhill S Lanark 119 E6
Shear Cross Wilts 24 E3
Shearington Dumfries 107 C7
Shearsby Leics 64 E3
Shebbear Devon 9 D6
Shebdon Staffs 61 B7
Shebster Highld 157 C13
Sheddens E Renf 119 D5
Shedfield Hants 15 C6
Sheen Staffs 75 C8
Sheepscar W Yorks 95 F6
Sheepscombe Glos 37 C5
Sheepstor Devon 6 C3
Sheepwash Devon 9 D6
Sheepway N Som 23 B6
Sheepy Magna Leics 63 D7
Sheepy Parva Leics 63 D7
Sheering Essex 41 C8
Sheerness Kent 30 B3
Sheet Hants 15 B8
Sheffield S Yorks 88 F4
Sheffield Bottom W Berks 26 C4
Sheffield Green E Sus 17 B8
Shefford C Beds 54 F2
Shefford Woodlands W Berks 25 B8
Sheigra Highld 156 C4
Sheinton Shrops 61 D6
Shelderton Shrops 49 B6
Sheldon Derbys 75 C8
Sheldon Devon 11 D6
Sheldon W Mid 63 F5
Sheldwich Kent 30 D4
Shelf W Yorks 88 B2
Shelfanger Norf 68 F4
Shelfield W Mid 62 D4
Shelfield Warks 51 C6
Shelford Notts 77 E6
Shellacres Northumb 122 E4
Shelley Essex 42 D1
Shelley Suff 56 F4
Shelley W Yorks 88 C3
Shellingford Oxon 38 E3
Shellow Bowells Essex 42 D2
Shelsley Beauchamp Worcs 50 C2
Shelsley Walsh Worcs 50 C2
Shelthorpe Leics 64 C2
Shelton Bedford 53 C8
Shelton Norf 68 E5
Shelton Notts 77 E7
Shelton Shrops 60 C4
Shelton Green Norf 68 E5
Shelve Shrops 60 E3
Shelwick Hereford 49 E7
Shenfield Essex 42 E2
Shenington Oxon 51 E8
Shenley Herts 40 D4
Shenley Brook End M Keynes 53 F6
Shenley Church End M Keynes 53 F6
Shenleybury Herts 40 D4
Shenmore Hereford 49 F5
Shennanton Dumfries 105 C7
Shenstone Staffs 62 D5
Shenstone Worcs 50 B3
Shenton Leics 63 D7
Shenval Highld 137 B7
Shenval Moray 139 B8
Shepeau Stow Lincs 66 C3
Shephall Herts 41 B5
Shepherd's Green Oxon 39 F7
Shepherd's Port Norf 80 D2
Shepherdswell Kent 31 E6
Shepley W Yorks 88 D2
Shepperdine S Glos 36 E3
Shepperton Sur 27 C8
Shepreth Cambs 54 E4
Shepshed Leics 63 C8
Shepton Beauchamp Som 12 C2
Shepton Mallet Som 23 E8
Shepton Montague Som 23 F8
Shepway Kent 29 D8
Sheraton Durham 111 F7
Sherborne Dorset 12 C4
Sherborne Glos 38 C1
Sherborne St John Hants 26 D4
Sherbourne Warks 51 C7
Sherburn Durham 111 E6
Sherburn N Yorks 97 B5
Sherburn Hill Durham 111 E6
Sherburn in Elmet N Yorks 95 F7
Shere Sur 27 E8
Shereford Norf 80 E4
Sherfield English Hants 14 B3
Sherfield on Loddon Hants 26 D4
Sherford Devon 7 E5
Sheriff Hutton N Yorks 96 C2
Sheriffhales Shrops 61 C7
Sheringham Norf 81 C7
Sherington M Keynes 53 E6
Shernal Green Worcs 50 C4
Shernborne Norf 80 D3
Sherrington Wilts 24 F4
Sherston Wilts 37 F5
Sherwood Green Devon 9 B7
Shettleston Glasgow 119 C6
Shevington Gtr Man 86 D3
Shevington Moor Gtr Man 86 C3
Shevington Vale Gtr Man 86 D3
Sheviock Corn 5 D8
Shide IoW 15 F5
Shiel Bridge Highld 136 C2
Shieldaig Highld 149 A13
Shieldaig Highld 149 C13
Shieldhill Dumfries 114 F3
Shieldhill Falk 119 B8
Shieldhill S Lanark 120 E3
Shielfoot Highld 147 E9
Shielhill Angus 134 D4
Shielhill Invclyd 118 B2
Shifford Oxon 38 D3
Shifnal Shrops 61 D7
Shilbottle Northumb 117 D7
Shildon Durham 101 B7
Shillingford Devon 10 B4
Shillingford Oxon 39 E5
Shillingford St George Devon 10 F4
Shillingstone Dorset 13 C6
Shillington C Beds 54 F2
Shillmoor Northumb 116 D4
Shilton Oxon 38 D2
Shilton Warks 63 F8
Shilvington Northumb 117 F7
Shimpling Norf 68 F4
Shimpling Suff 56 D2
Shimpling Street Suff 56 D2
Shincliffe Durham 111 E5
Shiney Row T&W 111 D6
Shinfield Wokingham 26 C5
Shingham Norf 67 D7
Shingle Street Suff 57 E7
Shinner's Bridge Devon 7 C5
Shinness Highld 157 H8
Shipbourne Kent 29 D6
Shipdham Norf 68 D2
Shipham Som 23 D6
Shiphay Torbay 7 C6
Shiplake Oxon 27 B5
Shipley Derbys 76 E4
Shipley Northumb 117 C7
Shipley Shrops 62 E2
Shipley W Sus 16 B5
Shipley W Yorks 94 F4
Shipley Shiels Northumb 116 E3
Shipmeadow Suff 69 F6
Shippea Hill Station Cambs 67 F6
Shippon Oxon 38 E4
Shipston-on-Stour Warks 51 E7
Shipton Glos 37 C7
Shipton N Yorks 95 D8
Shipton Shrops 61 E5
Shipton Bellinger Hants 25 E7
Shipton Gorge Dorset 12 E2
Shipton Green W Sus 16 D2
Shipton Moyne Glos 37 F5
Shipton on Cherwell Oxon 38 C4
Shipton Solers Glos 37 C7
Shipton-under-Wychwood Oxon 38 C2
Shiptonthorpe E Yorks 96 E4
Shirburn Oxon 39 E6
Shirdley Hill Lancs 85 C4
Shirebrook Derbys 76 C5

224 Shi–Sto

Shiregreen S Yorks 88 E4
Shirehampton Bristol 23 B7
Shiremoor T&W 111 B6
Shirenewton Mon 36 E1
Shireoaks Notts 89 F6
Shirkoak Kent 19 B6
Shirl Heath Hereford 49 D6
Shirland Derbys 76 D3
Shirley Derbys 76 E2
Shirley London 28 C4
Shirley Soton 14 C5
Shirley W Mid 51 B6
Shirrell Heath Hants 15 C6
Shirwell Devon 20 F4
Shirwell Cross Devon 20 F4
Shiskine N Ayrs 143 F10
Shobdon Hereford 49 C6
Shobnall Staffs 63 B6
Shobrooke Devon 10 D3
Shoby Leics 64 C3
Shocklach Ches W 73 E8
Shoeburyness Southend 43 F5
Sholden Kent 31 D7
Sholing Soton 14 C5
Shoot Hill Shrops 60 C4
Shop Corn 4 B3
Shop Corn 8 C4
Shop Corner Suff 57 F6
Shore Mill Highld 151 E10
Shoreditch London 41 F6
Shoreham Kent 29 C6
Shoreham-By-Sea W Sus 17 D6
Shoresdean Northumb 123 E5
Shoreswood Northumb 122 E5
Shoreton Highld 151 E9
Shorncote Glos 37 E7
Shorne Kent 29 B7
Short Heath W Mid 62 D3
Shortacombe Devon 9 F7
Shortgate E Sus 17 C8
Shortlanesend Corn 3 B7
Shortlees E Ayrs 118 F4
Shortstown Bedford 53 E8
Shorwell IoW 15 F5
Shoscombe Bath 24 D2
Shotatton Shrops 60 B3
Shotesham Norf 69 E5
Shotgate Essex 42 E3
Shotley Suff 57 F6
Shotley Bridge Durham 110 D3
Shotley Gate Suff 57 F6
Shotleyfield Northumb 110 D3
Shottenden Kent 30 D4
Shottermill Sur 27 F6
Shottery Warks 51 D6
Shotteswell Warks 52 E2
Shottisham Suff 57 E7
Shottle Derbys 76 E3
Shottlegate Derbys 76 E3
Shotton Durham 111 F7
Shotton Flint 73 C7
Shotton Northumb 122 F4
Shotton Colliery Durham 111 E6
Shotts N Lanark 119 C8
Shotwick Ches W 73 B7
Shouldham Norf 67 D6
Shouldham Thorpe Norf 67 D6
Shoulton Worcs 50 D3
Shover's Green E Sus 18 B3
Shrawardine Shrops 60 C4
Shrawley Worcs 50 C3
Shrewley Common Warks 51 C7
Shrewsbury Shrops 60 C4
Shrewton Wilts 25 E5
Shripney W Sus 16 D3
Shrivenham Oxon 38 F2
Shropham Norf 68 E2
Shrub End Essex 43 B5
Shucknall Hereford 49 E7
Shudy Camps Cambs 55 E7
Shulishadermor Highld 149 D9
Shurdington Glos 37 C6
Shurlock Row Windsor 27 B6
Shurrery Highld 157 D13
Shurrery Lodge Highld 157 D13
Shurton Som 22 E4
Shustoke Warks 63 E6
Shute Devon 10 D3
Shute Devon 11 E7
Shutford Oxon 51 E8
Shuthonger Glos 50 F3
Shutlanger Northants 52 D5
Shuttington Warks 63 D6
Shuttlewood Derbys 76 B4
Siabost bho Dheas W Isles 154 C7
Siabost bho Thuath W Isles 154 C7
Siadar W Isles 155 B8
Siadar Iarach W Isles 155 B8
Siadar Uarach W Isles 155 B8
Sibbaldbie Dumfries 114 F4
Sibbertoft Northants 64 F3
Sibdon Carwood Shrops 60 F4
Sibford Ferris Oxon 51 F8
Sibford Gower Oxon 51 F8
Sible Hedingham Essex 55 F8
Sibsey Lincs 79 D6
Sibson Cambs 65 E7
Sibson Leics 63 D7
Sibthorpe Notts 77 E7
Sibton Suff 57 C7
Sibton Green Suff 57 B7
Sicklesmere Suff 56 C2
Sicklinghall N Yorks 95 E6
Sid Devon 11 F6
Sidbury Devon 11 E6
Sidbury Shrops 61 F6
Sidcot N Som 23 D6
Sidcup London 29 B5
Siddick Cumb 107 F7
Siddington Ches E 74 B5
Siddington Glos 37 E7
Sidemoor Worcs 50 B4
Sidestrand Norf 81 D8
Sidford Devon 11 E6
Sidlesham W Sus 16 E2
Sidley E Sus 18 E4
Sidlow Sur 28 E3
Sidmouth Devon 11 F6
Sigford Devon 7 B5
Sigglesthorne E Yorks 97 E7
Sighthill Edin 120 B4
Sigingstone V Glam 21 B8
Signet Oxon 38 C2
Silchester Hants 26 C4
Sildinis W Isles 155 F7
Sileby Leics 64 C2
Silecroft Cumb 98 F3
Silfield Norf 68 E4
Silian Ceredig 46 D4
Silk Willoughby Lincs 78 E3
Silkstone S Yorks 88 D3
Silkstone Common S Yorks 88 D3
Silloth Cumb 107 D8
Sills Northumb 116 D4
Sillyearn Moray 152 C5
Siloh Carms 47 F6
Silpho N Yorks 103 E7
Silsden W Yorks 94 E3
Silsoe C Beds 53 F8
Silver End Essex 42 C4
Silverburn Midloth 120 C5
Silverdale Lancs 92 B4
Silverdale Staffs 74 E5
Silvergate Norf 81 E7
Silverhill E Sus 18 D4
Silverley's Green Suff 57 B6
Silverstone Northants 52 E4
Silverton Devon 10 D4
Silvington Shrops 49 B8
Silwick Shetland 160 J4
Simmondley Derbys 87 E8
Simonburn Northumb 109 B8
Simonsbath Som 21 F6
Simonstone Lancs 93 F7
Simprim Borders 122 E4
Simpson M Keynes 53 F6
Simpson Cross Pembs 44 D3
Sinclair's Hill Borders 122 D4
Sinclairston E Ayrs 112 C4
Sinderby N Yorks 101 F8
Sinderhope Northumb 109 D8
Sindlesham Wokingham 27 C5
Singdean Borders 115 D8
Singleborough Bucks 53 F5
Singleton Lancs 92 F3
Singleton W Sus 16 C2
Singlewell Kent 29 B7
Sinkhurst Green Kent 30 E2
Sinnahard Aberds 140 C3
Sinnington N Yorks 103 F5
Sinton Green Worcs 50 C3
Sipson London 27 B8
Sirhowy Bl Gwent 35 C5
Sisland Norf 69 E6
Sissinghurst Kent 18 B4
Sisterpath Borders 122 E3
Siston S Glos 23 B8
Sithney Corn 2 D5
Sittingbourne Kent 30 C2
Six Ashes Staffs 61 F7
Six Hills Leics 64 B3
Six Mile Bottom Cambs 55 D6
Sixhills Lincs 91 F5
Sixpenny Handley Dorset 13 C7
Sizewell Suff 57 C8
Skail Highld 157 E10
Skaill Orkney 159 E5
Skaill Orkney 159 G3
Skaill Orkney 159 H6
Skares E Ayrs 113 C5
Skateraw E Loth 122 B3
Skaw Shetland 160 G7
Skeabost Highld 149 D9
Skeabrae Orkney 159 F3
Skeeby N Yorks 101 D7
Skeffington Leics 64 D4
Skeffling E Yorks 91 C7
Skegby Notts 76 C4
Skegness Lincs 79 C8
Skelberry Shetland 160 M5
Skelbo Highld 151 B10
Skelbrooke S Yorks 89 C6
Skeldyke Lincs 79 F6
Skellingthorpe Lincs 78 B2
Skellister Shetland 160 H6
Skellow S Yorks 89 C6
Skelmanthorpe W Yorks 88 C3
Skelmersdale Lancs 86 D2
Skelmonae Aberds 153 E8
Skelmorlie N Ayrs 118 C1
Skelmuir Aberds 153 D9
Skelpick Highld 157 D10
Skelton Cumb 108 F4
Skelton E Yorks 89 B8
Skelton N Yorks 101 D5
Skelton Redcar 102 C4
Skelton York 95 D8
Skelton-on-Ure N Yorks 95 C6
Skelwick Orkney 159 D5
Skelwith Bridge Cumb 99 D5
Skendleby Lincs 79 C7
Skene Ho. Aberds 141 D6
Skenfrith Mon 36 B1
Skerne E Yorks 97 D6
Skeroblingarry Argyll 143 F8
Skerray Highld 157 C9
Skerton Lancs 92 C4
Sketchley Leics 63 E8
Sketty Swansea 33 E7
Skewen Neath 33 E8
Skewsby N Yorks 96 B2
Skeyton Norf 81 E8
Skiag Bridge Highld 156 G5
Skibo Castle Highld 151 C10
Skidbrooke Lincs 91 E8
Skidbrooke North End Lincs 91 E8
Skidby E Yorks 97 F6
Skilgate Som 10 B4
Skillington Lincs 65 B5
Skinburness Cumb 107 D8
Skinflats Falk 127 F8
Skinidin Highld 148 D7
Skinnet Highld 157 C8
Skinningrove Redcar 103 B5
Skipness Argyll 145 H7
Skippool Lancs 92 E3
Skipsea E Yorks 97 D7
Skipsea Brough E Yorks 97 D7
Skipton N Yorks 94 D2
Skipton-on-Swale N Yorks 95 B6
Skipwith N Yorks 96 F2
Skirbeck Lincs 79 E6
Skirbeck Quarter Lincs 79 E6
Skirlaugh E Yorks 97 F7
Skirling Borders 120 F3
Skirmett Bucks 39 F7
Skirpenbeck E Yorks 96 D3
Skirwith Cumb 109 F6
Skirza Highld 158 D5
Skulamus Highld 149 F11
Skullomie Highld 157 C9
Skyborry Green Shrops 48 B4
Skye of Curr Highld 139 B5
Skyreholme N Yorks 94 C3
Slackhall Derbys 87 F8
Slackhead Moray 152 B4
Slad Glos 37 D5
Slade Devon 20 E4
Slade Pembs 44 D4
Slade Green London 29 B6
Slaggyford Northumb 109 D6
Slaidburn Lancs 93 D7
Slaithwaite W Yorks 87 C8
Slaley Northumb 110 D2
Slamannan Falk 119 B8
Slapton Bucks 40 B2
Slapton Devon 7 E6
Slapton Northants 52 E4
Slatepit Dale Derbys 76 C3
Slattocks Gtr Man 87 D6
Slaugham W Sus 17 B6
Slaughterford Wilts 24 B3
Slawston Leics 64 E4
Sleaford Hants 27 F6
Sleaford Lincs 78 E3
Sleagill Cumb 99 C7
Sleapford Telford 61 C6
Sledge Green Worcs 50 F3
Sledmere E Yorks 96 C5
Sleightholme Durham 100 C4
Sleights N Yorks 103 D6
Slepe Dorset 13 E7
Slickly Highld 158 D4
Sliddery N Ayrs 143 F10
Sligachan Hotel Highld 149 F9
Slimbridge Glos 36 D4
Slindon Staffs 74 F5
Slindon W Sus 16 D3
Slinfold W Sus 28 F2
Sling Gwyn 83 E6
Slingsby N Yorks 96 B2
Slioch Aberds 152 E5
Slip End C Beds 40 C3
Slip End Herts 54 F3
Slipton Northants 53 B7
Slitting Mill Staffs 62 C4
Slochd Highld 138 B4
Slockavullin Argyll 124 F4
Sloley Norf 81 E8
Sloothby Lincs 79 B7
Slough Slough 27 B7
Slough Green W Sus 17 B6
Sluggan Highld 138 B4
Slumbay Highld 149 E13
Slyfield Sur 27 D7
Slyne Lancs 92 C4
Smailholm Borders 122 F2
Small Dole W Sus 17 C6
Small Hythe Kent 19 B5
Smallbridge Gtr Man 87 C7
Smallburgh Norf 69 B6
Smallburn Aberds 153 D10
Smallburn E Ayrs 113 B6
Smalley Derbys 76 E4
Smallfield Sur 28 E4
Smallridge Devon 11 D8
Smannell Hants 25 E8
Smardale Cumb 100 D2
Smarden Kent 30 E2
Smarden Bell Kent 30 E2
Smeatharpe Devon 11 C6
Smeeth Kent 19 B7
Smeeton Westerby Leics 64 E3
Smercleit W Isles 148 G2
Smerral Highld 158 G3
Smethwick W Mid 62 F4
Smirisary Highld 147 D9
Smisby Derbys 63 C7
Smith Green Lancs 92 D4
Smithfield Cumb 108 C4
Smithincott Devon 11 C5
Smith's Green Essex 42 B1
Smithstown Highld 149 A12
Smithton Highld 151 G10
Smithy Green Ches E 74 B4
Smockington Leics 63 F8
Smoogro Orkney 159 H4
Smythe's Green Essex 43 C5
Snaigow House Perth 133 E7
Snailbeach Shrops 60 D3
Snailwell Cambs 55 C7
Snainton N Yorks 103 F7
Snaith E Yorks 89 B7
Snape N Yorks 101 F7
Snape Suff 57 D7
Snape Green Lancs 85 C4
Snarestone Leics 63 D7
Snarford Lincs 90 F4
Snargate Kent 19 C6
Snave Kent 19 C7
Snead Powys 60 E3
Sneath Common Norf 68 F4
Sneaton N Yorks 103 D6
Sneatonthorpe N Yorks 103 D7
Snelland Lincs 90 F4
Snelston Derbys 75 E8
Snettisham Norf 80 D2
Sniseabhal W Isles 148 E2
Snitter Northumb 117 D6
Snitterby Lincs 90 E3
Snitterfield Warks 51 D7
Snitton Shrops 49 B7
Snodhill Hereford 48 E5
Snodland Kent 29 C7
Snowden Hill S Yorks 88 D3
Snowdown Kent 31 D6
Snowshill Glos 51 F5
Snydale W Yorks 88 C5
Soar Anglesey 82 D3
Soar Carms 33 B7
Soar Devon 6 F5
Soar-y-Mynydd Ceredig 47 D6
Soberton Hants 15 C7
Soberton Heath Hants 15 C7
Sockbridge Cumb 99 B7
Sockburn Darl 101 D8
Soham Cambs 55 B6
Soham Cotes Cambs 55 B6
Solas W Isles 148 A3
Soldon Cross Devon 8 C5
Soldridge Hants 26 F4
Sole Street Kent 29 C7
Sole Street Kent 30 E4
Solihull W Mid 51 B6
Sollers Dilwyn Hereford 49 D6
Sollers Hope Hereford 49 F8
Sollom Lancs 86 C2
Solva Pembs 44 C2
Somerby Leics 64 C4
Somerby Lincs 90 D4
Somercotes Derbys 76 D4
Somerford Dorset 14 E2
Somerford Keynes Glos 37 E7
Somerley W Sus 16 E2
Somerleyton Suff 69 E7
Somersal Herbert Derbys 75 F8
Somersby Lincs 79 B6
Somersham Cambs 54 B4
Somersham Suff 56 E4
Somerton Oxon 38 B4
Somerton Som 12 B2
Sompting W Sus 17 D5
Sonning Wokingham 27 B5
Sonning Common Oxon 39 F7
Sonning Eye Oxon 27 B5
Sontley Wrex 73 E7
Sopley Hants 14 E2
Sopwell Herts 40 D4
Sopworth Wilts 37 F5
Sorbie Dumfries 105 E8
Sordale Highld 158 D3
Sorisdale Argyll 146 E5
Sorn E Ayrs 113 B5
Sornhill E Ayrs 118 F5
Sortat Highld 158 D4
Sotby Lincs 78 B5
Sots Hole Lincs 78 C4
Sotterley Suff 69 F7
Soudley Shrops 61 B7
Soughton Flint 73 C6
Soulbury Bucks 40 B1
Soulby Cumb 100 C2
Souldern Oxon 52 F3
Souldrop Bedford 53 C7
Sound Ches E 74 E3
Sound Shetland 160 H5
Sound Shetland 160 J6
Sound Heath Ches E 74 E3
Soundwell S Glos 23 B8
Sourhope Borders 116 B4
Sourin Orkney 159 E5
Sourton Devon 9 E7
Soutergate Cumb 98 F4
South Acre Norf 67 C8
South Allington Devon 7 F5
South Alloa Falk 127 E7
South Ambersham W Sus 16 B3
South Anston S Yorks 89 F6
South Ascot Windsor 27 C7
South Ballachulish Highld 130 D4
South Balloch S Ayrs 112 E3
South Bank Redcar 102 B3
South Barrow Som 12 B4
South Beach Gwyn 70 D4
South Benfleet Essex 42 F3
South Bersted W Sus 16 D3
South Brent Devon 6 C4
South Brewham Som 24 F2
South Broomhill Northumb 117 E8
South Burlingham Norf 69 D6
South Cadbury Som 12 B4
South Cairn Dumfries 104 C3
South Carlton Lincs 78 B2
South Cave E Yorks 96 F5
South Cerney Glos 37 E7
South Chard Som 11 D8
South Charlton Northumb 117 B7
South Cheriton Som 12 B4
South Cliffe E Yorks 96 F4
South Clifton Notts 77 B8
South Cockerington Lincs 91 F7
South Cornelly Bridgend 34 F2
South Cove Suff 69 F7
South Creagan Argyll 130 E3
South Creake Norf 80 D4
South Croxton Leics 64 C3
South Croydon London 28 C4
South Dalton E Yorks 97 E5
South Darenth Kent 29 C6
South Duffield N Yorks 96 F2
South Elkington Lincs 91 F6
South Elmsall W Yorks 89 C5
South End Bucks 40 B1
South End Cumb 92 C2
South End N Lincs 90 B5
South Erradale Highld 149 A12
South Fambridge Essex 42 E4
South Fawley W Berks 38 F3
South Ferriby N Lincs 90 B3
South Garth Shetland 160 D7
South Garvan Highld 130 B3
South Glendale W Isles 148 G2
South Godstone Sur 28 E4
South Gorley Hants 14 C2
South Green Essex 42 E2
South Green Kent 30 C2
South-haa Shetland 160 E5
South Ham Hants 26 D4
South Hanningfield Essex 42 E3
South Harting W Sus 15 C8
South Hatfield Herts 41 D5
South Hayling Hants 15 E8
South Hazelrigg Northumb 123 F6
South Heath Bucks 40 D2
South Heighton E Sus 17 D8
South Hetton Durham 111 E6
South Hiendley W Yorks 88 C4
South Hill Corn 5 B8
South Hinksey Oxon 39 D5
South Hole Devon 8 B4
South Holme N Yorks 96 B2
South Holmwood Sur 28 E2
South Hornchurch London 41 F8
South Hykeham Lincs 78 C2
South Hylton T&W 111 D6
South Kelsey Lincs 90 E4
South Kessock Highld 151 G9
South Killingholme N Lincs 91 C5
South Kilvington N Yorks 102 F2
South Kilworth Leics 64 F3
South Kirkby W Yorks 88 C5
South Kirkton Aberds 141 D6
South Kiscadale N Ayrs 143 F11
South Kyme Lincs 78 E4
South Lancing W Sus 17 D5
South Leigh Oxon 38 D3
South Leverton Notts 89 F8
South Littleton Worcs 51 E5
South Lopham Norf 68 F3
South Luffenham Rutland 65 D6
South Malling E Sus 17 C8
South Marston Swindon 38 F1
South Middleton Northumb 117 B5
South Milford N Yorks 95 F7
South Millbrex Aberds 153 D8
South Milton Devon 6 E5
South Mimms Herts 41 D5
South Molton Devon 10 B2
South Moreton Oxon 39 F5
South Mundham W Sus 16 D2
South Muskham Notts 77 D7
South Newbald E Yorks 96 F5
South Newington Oxon 52 F2
South Newton Wilts 25 F5
South Normanton Derbys 76 D4
South Norwood London 28 C4
South Nutfield Sur 28 E4
South Ockendon Thurrock 42 F1
South Ormsby Lincs 79 B6
South Otterington N Yorks 102 F1
South Owersby Lincs 90 E4
South Oxhey Herts 40 E4
South Perrott Dorset 12 D2
South Petherton Som 12 C2
South Petherwin Corn 8 F5
South Pickenham Norf 67 D8
South Pool Devon 7 E5
South Port Argyll 125 C6
South Radworthy Devon 21 F6
South Rauceby Lincs 78 E3
South Raynham Norf 80 E4
South Reston Lincs 91 F8
South Runcton Norf 67 D6
South Scarle Notts 77 C8
South Shian Argyll 130 E3
South Shields T&W 111 C6
South Shore Blackpool 92 F3
South Somercotes Lincs 91 E8
South Stainley N Yorks 95 C6
South Stainmore Cumb 100 C3
South Stifford Thurrock 29 B7
South Stoke Oxon 39 F5
South Stoke W Sus 16 D4
South Street E Sus 17 C7
South Street Kent 30 C5
South Street Kent 30 D4
South Street London 28 D5
South Tawton Devon 9 E8
South Thoresby Lincs 79 B7
South Tidworth Wilts 25 E7
South Town Hants 26 F4
South View Hants 26 D4
South Walsham Norf 69 C6
South Warnborough Hants 26 E5
South Weald Essex 42 E1
South Weston Oxon 39 E7
South Wheatley Corn 8 E4
South Wheatley Notts 89 F8
South Whiteness Shetland 160 J5
South Widcombe Bath 23 D7
South Wigston Leics 64 E2
South Willingham Lincs 91 F5
South Wingfield Derbys 76 D3
South Witham Lincs 65 C6
South Wonston Hants 26 F2
South Woodham Ferrers Essex 42 E4
South Wootton Norf 67 B6
South Wraxall Wilts 24 C3
South Zeal Devon 9 E8
Southall London 40 F4
Southam Glos 37 B6
Southam Warks 52 C2
Southampton Soton 14 C5
Southborough Kent 29 E6
Southbourne Bmouth 14 E2
Southbourne W Sus 15 D8
Southburgh Norf 68 D2
Southburn E Yorks 97 D5
Southchurch Southend 43 F5
Southcott Wilts 25 D6
Southcourt Bucks 39 C8
Southdean Borders 116 D2
Southdene Mers 86 E2
Southease E Sus 17 D8
Southend Argyll 143 H7
Southend W Berks 26 B3
Southend Wilts 25 B6
Southend-on-Sea Southend 42 F4
Southernden Kent 30 E2
Southerndown V Glam 21 B7
Southerness Dumfries 107 D6
Southery Norf 67 E6
Southfield Northumb 111 B5
Southfleet Kent 29 B7
Southgate Ceredig 46 B4
Southgate London 41 E5
Southgate Norf 81 E7
Southgate Swansea 33 F6
Southill C Beds 54 E2
Southleigh Devon 11 E7
Southminster Essex 43 E5
Southmoor Oxon 38 E3
Southoe Cambs 54 C2
Southolt Suff 57 C5
Southorpe Pboro 65 D7
Southowram W Yorks 88 B2
Southport Mers 85 C4
Southpunds Shetland 160 L6
Southrepps Norf 81 D8
Southrey Lincs 78 C4
Southrop Glos 38 D1
Southrope Hants 26 E4
Southsea Ptsmth 15 E7
Southstoke Bath 24 C2
Southtown Norf 69 D8
Southtown Orkney 159 J5
Southwaite Cumb 108 E4
Southwark London 28 B4
Southwater W Sus 17 B5
Southwater Street W Sus 17 B5
Southway Som 23 E7
Southwell Dorset 12 G4
Southwell Notts 77 D6
Southwick Hants 15 D7
Southwick Northants 65 E7
Southwick T&W 111 D6
Southwick W Sus 17 D6
Southwick Wilts 24 D3
Southwold Suff 57 B9
Southwood Norf 69 D6
Southwood Som 23 F7
Soval Lodge W Isles 155 E8
Sowber Gate N Yorks 102 F1
Sowerby N Yorks 102 F2
Sowerby W Yorks 87 B8
Sowerby Bridge W Yorks 87 B8
Sowerby Row Cumb 108 F3
Sowood W Yorks 87 C8
Sowton Devon 10 E4
Soyal Highld 151 B8
Spa Common Norf 81 D8
Spacey Houses N Yorks 95 D6
Spadeadam Farm Cumb 109 B5
Spalding Lincs 66 B2
Spaldington E Yorks 96 F3
Spaldwick Cambs 54 B2
Spalford Notts 77 C8
Spanby Lincs 78 F3
Sparham Norf 68 C3
Spark Bridge Cumb 99 F5
Sparkford Som 12 B4
Sparkhill W Mid 62 F4
Sparkwell Devon 6 D3
Sparrow Green Norf 68 C2
Sparrowpit Derbys 87 F8
Sparsholt Hants 26 F2
Sparsholt Oxon 38 F3
Spartylea Northumb 109 E8
Spaunton N Yorks 103 F5
Spaxton Som 22 F4
Spean Bridge Highld 136 F5
Spear Hill W Sus 16 C5
Speen Bucks 39 E8
Speen W Berks 26 C2
Speeton N Yorks 97 B7
Speke Mers 86 F2
Speldhurst Kent 29 E6
Spellbrook Herts 41 C7
Spelsbury Oxon 38 B3
Spelter Bridgend 34 E2
Spencers Wood Wokingham 26 C5
Spennithorne N Yorks 101 F6
Spennymoor Durham 111 F5
Spetchley Worcs 50 D3
Spetisbury Dorset 13 D7
Spexhall Suff 69 F6
Spey Bay Moray 152 B3
Speybridge Highld 139 B6
Speyview Moray 152 D2
Spilsby Lincs 79 C7
Spindlestone Northumb 123 F7
Spinkhill Derbys 76 B4
Spinningdale Highld 151 C9
Spirthill Wilts 24 B4
Spital Hill S Yorks 89 E7
Spital in the Street Lincs 90 F3
Spithurst E Sus 17 C8
Spittal Dumfries 105 D7
Spittal E Loth 121 B7
Spittal Highld 158 E3
Spittal Northumb 123 D6
Spittal Pembs 44 C4
Spittal Stirling 126 F4
Spittal of Glenmuick Aberds 140 F2
Spittal of Glenshee Perth 133 B8
Spittalfield Perth 133 E8
Spixworth Norf 68 C5
Splayne's Green E Sus 17 B8
Spofforth N Yorks 95 D6
Spon End W Mid 51 B8
Spon Green Flint 73 C6
Spondon Derby 76 F4
Spooner Row Norf 68 E3
Sporle Norf 67 C8
Spott E Loth 122 B2
Spratton Northants 52 B5
Spreakley Sur 27 E6
Spreyton Devon 9 E8
Spridlington Lincs 90 F4
Spring Vale S Yorks 88 D3
Spring Valley IoM 84 E3
Springburn Glasgow 119 C6
Springfield Dumfries 108 C3
Springfield Essex 42 D3
Springfield Fife 128 C5
Springfield Moray 151 F13
Springfield W Mid 62 F4
Springhill Staffs 62 D3
Springholm Dumfries 106 C5
Springkell Dumfries 108 B2
Springside N Ayrs 118 F3
Springthorpe Lincs 90 F2
Springwell T&W 111 D5
Sproatley E Yorks 97 F7
Sproston Green Ches W 74 C4
Sprotbrough S Yorks 89 D6
Sproughton Suff 56 E5
Sprouston Borders 122 F3
Sprowston Norf 68 C5
Sproxton Leics 65 B5
Sproxton N Yorks 102 F4
Spurstow Ches E 74 D2
Spynie Moray 152 B2
Squires Gate Blackpool 92 F3
Srannda W Isles 154 J5
Sronphadruig Lodge Perth 132 B4
Stableford Shrops 61 E7
Stableford Staffs 74 F5
Stacey Bank S Yorks 88 E3
Stackhouse N Yorks 93 C8
Stackpole Pembs 44 F4
Staddiscombe Plym 6 D3
Staddlethorpe E Yorks 90 B2
Stadhampton Oxon 39 E6
Stadhlaigearraidh W Isles 148 E2
Staffield Cumb 108 E5
Staffin Highld 149 B9
Stafford Staffs 62 B3
Stagsden Bedford 53 E7
Stainburn Cumb 98 B2
Stainburn N Yorks 94 E5
Stainby Lincs 65 B6
Staincross S Yorks 88 C4
Staindrop Durham 101 B6
Staines-upon-Thames Sur 27 B8
Stainfield Lincs 65 B7
Stainfield Lincs 78 B4
Stainforth N Yorks 93 C8
Stainforth S Yorks 89 C7
Staining Lancs 92 F3
Stainland W Yorks 87 C8
Stainsacre N Yorks 103 D7
Stainsby Derbys 76 C4
Stainton Cumb 99 B6
Stainton Cumb 99 F7
Stainton Durham 101 C5
Stainton Mbro 102 C2
Stainton N Yorks 101 E6
Stainton S Yorks 89 E6
Stainton by Langworth Lincs 78 B3
Stainton le Vale Lincs 91 E5
Stainton with Adgarley Cumb 92 B2
Staintondale N Yorks 103 E7
Stair Cumb 98 B4
Stair E Ayrs 112 B4
Stairhaven Dumfries 105 D6
Staithes N Yorks 103 C5
Stake Pool Lancs 92 E4
Stakeford Northumb 117 F8
Stalbridge Dorset 12 C5
Stalbridge Weston Dorset 12 C5
Stalham Norf 69 B6
Stalham Green Norf 69 B6
Stalisfield Green Kent 30 D3
Stalling Busk N Yorks 100 F4
Stallingborough NE Lincs 91 C5
Stalmine Lancs 92 E3
Stalybridge Gtr Man 87 E7
Stambourne Essex 55 F8
Stambourne Green Essex 55 E8
Stamford Lincs 65 D7
Stamford Bridge Ches W 73 C8
Stamford Bridge E Yorks 96 D3
Stamfordham Northumb 110 B3
Stanah Cumb 99 C5
Stanborough Herts 41 C5
Stanbridge C Beds 40 B2
Stanbridge Dorset 13 D8
Stanbrook Worcs 50 E3
Stanbury W Yorks 94 F3
Stand Gtr Man 87 D5
Stand N Lanark 119 C7
Standburn Falk 120 B2
Standeford Staffs 62 D3
Standen Kent 30 E2
Standford Hants 27 F6
Standingstone Cumb 107 F7
Standish Gtr Man 86 C3
Standlake Oxon 38 D3
Standon Hants 14 B5
Standon Herts 41 B6
Standon Staffs 74 F5
Stane N Lanark 119 D8
Stanfield Norf 80 E5
Stanford C Beds 54 E2
Stanford Kent 19 B8
Stanford Bishop Hereford 49 D8
Stanford Bridge Worcs 50 C2
Stanford Dingley W Berks 26 B3
Stanford in the Vale Oxon 38 E3
Stanford-le-Hope Thurrock 42 F2
Stanford on Avon Northants 52 B3
Stanford on Soar Notts 64 B2
Stanford on Teme Worcs 50 C2
Stanford Rivers Essex 41 D8
Stanfree Derbys 76 B4
Stanghow Redcar 102 C4
Stanground Pboro 66 E2
Stanhoe Norf 80 D4
Stanhope Borders 114 B4
Stanhope Durham 110 F2
Stanion Northants 65 F6
Stanley Derbys 76 E4
Stanley Durham 110 D4
Stanley Lancs 86 D2
Stanley Perth 133 F8
Stanley Staffs 75 D6
Stanley W Yorks 88 B4
Stanley Common Derbys 76 E4
Stanley Gate Lancs 86 D2
Stanley Hill Hereford 49 E8
Stanlow Ches W 73 B8
Stanmer Brighton 17 D7
Stanmore Hants 15 B5
Stanmore London 40 E4
Stanmore W Berks 26 B2
Stannergate Dundee 134 F4
Stanningley W Yorks 94 F5
Stannington Northumb 110 B5
Stannington S Yorks 88 F4
Stansbatch Hereford 48 C5
Stansfield Suff 55 D8
Stanstead Suff 56 E2
Stanstead Abbotts Herts 41 C6
Stansted Kent 29 C7
Stansted Airport Essex 42 B1
Stansted Mountfitchet Essex 41 B8
Stanton Glos 51 F5
Stanton Mon 35 B7
Stanton Northumb 117 F7
Stanton Staffs 75 E8
Stanton Suff 56 B3
Stanton by Bridge Derbys 63 B7
Stanton-by-Dale Derbys 76 F4
Stanton Drew Bath 23 C7
Stanton Fitzwarren Swindon 38 E1
Stanton Harcourt Oxon 38 D4
Stanton Hill Notts 76 C4
Stanton in Peak Derbys 76 C2
Stanton Lacy Shrops 49 B6
Stanton Long Shrops 61 E5
Stanton-on-the-Wolds Notts 77 F6
Stanton Prior Bath 23 C8
Stanton St Bernard Wilts 25 C5
Stanton St John Oxon 39 D5
Stanton St Quintin Wilts 24 B4
Stanton Street Suff 56 C3
Stanton under Bardon Leics 63 C8
Stanton upon Hine Heath Shrops 61 B5
Stanton Wick Bath 23 C8
Stanwardine in the Fields Shrops 60 B4
Stanwardine in the Wood Shrops 60 B4
Stanway Essex 43 B5
Stanway Glos 51 F5
Stanway Green Suff 57 B6
Stanwell Sur 27 B8
Stanwell Moor Sur 27 B8
Stanwick Northants 53 B7
Stanwick-St-John N Yorks 101 C6
Stanwix Cumb 108 D4
Stanydale Shetland 160 H4
Staoinebrig W Isles 148 E2
Stape N Yorks 103 E5
Stapehill Dorset 13 D8
Stapeley Ches E 74 E3
Stapenhill Staffs 63 B6
Staple Kent 31 D6
Staple Som 22 E3
Staple Cross E Sus 18 C4
Staple Fitzpaine Som 11 C7
Staplefield W Sus 17 B6
Stapleford Cambs 55 D5
Stapleford Herts 41 C6
Stapleford Leics 64 C5
Stapleford Lincs 77 D8
Stapleford Notts 76 F4
Stapleford Wilts 25 F5
Stapleford Abbotts Essex 41 E8
Stapleford Tawney Essex 41 E8
Staplegrove Som 11 B7
Staplehay Som 11 B7
Staplehurst Kent 29 E8
Staplers IoW 15 F6
Stapleton Bristol 23 B8
Stapleton Cumb 108 B5
Stapleton Hereford 48 C5
Stapleton Leics 63 E8
Stapleton N Yorks 101 C7
Stapleton Shrops 60 D4
Stapleton Som 12 B2
Stapley Som 11 C6
Staploe Bedford 54 C2
Staplow Hereford 49 E8
Star Fife 128 D5
Star Pembs 45 F4
Star Som 23 D6
Stara Orkney 159 F3
Starbeck N Yorks 95 D6
Starbotton N Yorks 94 B2
Starcross Devon 10 F4
Stareton Warks 51 B8
Starkholmes Derbys 76 D3
Starlings Green Essex 55 F5
Starston Norf 68 F5
Startforth Durham 101 C5
Startley Wilts 37 F6
Stathe Som 11 B8
Stathern Leics 77 F7
Station Town Durham 111 F7
Staughton Green Cambs 54 C2
Staughton Highway Cambs 54 C2
Staunton Glos 36 B4
Staunton Glos 36 C2
Staunton in the Vale Notts 77 E8
Staunton on Arrow Hereford 49 C5
Staunton on Wye Hereford 49 E5
Staveley Cumb 99 E6
Staveley Cumb 99 F5
Staveley Derbys 76 B4
Staveley N Yorks 95 C6
Staverton Devon 7 C5
Staverton Glos 37 B5
Staverton Northants 52 C3
Staverton Wilts 24 C3
Staverton Bridge Glos 37 B5
Stawell Som 23 F5
Staxigoe Highld 158 E5
Staxton N Yorks 97 B6
Staylittle Powys 59 E5
Staynall Lancs 92 E3
Staythorpe Notts 77 D7
Stean N Yorks 94 B3
Stearsby N Yorks 96 B2
Steart Som 22 E4
Stebbing Essex 42 B2
Stebbing Green Essex 42 B2
Stedham W Sus 16 B2
Steele Road Borders 115 E8
Steen's Bridge Hereford 49 D7
Steep Hants 15 B8
Steep Marsh Hants 15 B8
Steeple Dorset 13 F7
Steeple Essex 43 D5
Steeple Ashton Wilts 24 D4
Steeple Aston Oxon 38 B4
Steeple Barton Oxon 38 B4
Steeple Bumpstead Essex 55 E7
Steeple Claydon Bucks 39 B6
Steeple Gidding Cambs 65 F8
Steeple Langford Wilts 24 F5
Steeple Morden Cambs 54 E3
Steeton W Yorks 94 E3
Stein Highld 148 C7
Steinmanhill Aberds 153 D7
Stelling Minnis Kent 30 E5
Stemster Highld 158 D3
Stemster Ho. Highld 158 D3
Stenalees Corn 4 D5
Stenhousemuir Falk 127 F7
Stenigot Lincs 91 F6
Stenness Shetland 160 F4
Stenscholl Highld 149 B9
Stenso Orkney 159 F4
Stenson Derbys 63 B7
Stenton E Loth 122 B2
Stenton Fife 128 E4
Stenwith Lincs 77 F8
Stepaside Pembs 32 D2
Stepping Hill Gtr Man 87 F7
Steppingley C Beds 53 F8
Stepps N Lanark 119 C6
Sterndale Moor Derbys 75 C8
Sternfield Suff 57 C7
Sterridge Devon 20 E4
Stert Wilts 24 D5
Stetchworth Cambs 55 D7
Stevenage Herts 41 B5
Stevenston N Ayrs 118 E2
Steventon Hants 26 E3
Steventon Oxon 38 E4
Stevington Bedford 53 D7
Stewartby Bedford 53 E8
Stewarton Argyll 143 G7
Stewarton E Ayrs 118 E4
Stewkley Bucks 40 B1
Stewton Lincs 91 F7
Steyne Cross IoW 15 F7
Steyning W Sus 17 C5
Steynton Pembs 44 E4
Stibb Corn 8 C4
Stibb Cross Devon 9 C6
Stibb Green Wilts 25 C7
Stibbard Norf 81 E5
Stibbington Cambs 65 E7
Stichill Borders 122 F3
Sticker Corn 4 D4
Stickford Lincs 79 D6
Sticklepath Devon 9 E8
Stickney Lincs 79 D6
Stiffkey Norf 81 C5
Stifford's Bridge Hereford 50 E2
Stillingfleet N Yorks 95 E8
Stillington N Yorks 95 C8
Stillington Stockton 102 B1
Stilton Cambs 65 F8
Stinchcombe Glos 36 E4
Stinsford Dorset 12 E5
Stirchley Telford 61 D7
Stirkoke Ho. Highld 158 E5
Stirling Aberds 153 D11
Stirling Stirling 127 E6
Stisted Essex 42 B3
Stithians Corn 3 C6
Stittenham Highld 151 D9
Stivichall W Mid 51 B8
Stixwould Lincs 78 C4
Stoak Ches W 73 B8
Stobieside S Lanark 119 F6
Stobo Borders 120 F4
Stoborough Dorset 13 F7
Stoborough Green Dorset 13 F7
Stobshiel E Loth 121 C7
Stobswood Northumb 117 E8
Stock Essex 42 E2
Stock Green Worcs 50 D4
Stock Wood Worcs 50 D5
Stockbridge Hants 25 F8
Stockbury Kent 30 C2
Stockcross W Berks 26 C2
Stockdalewath Cumb 108 E3
Stockerston Leics 64 E5
Stockheath Hants 15 D8
Stockiemuir Stirling 126 F4
Stocking Pelham Herts 41 B7
Stockingford Warks 63 E7
Stockland Devon 11 D7
Stockland Bristol Som 22 E4
Stockleigh English Devon 10 D3
Stockleigh Pomeroy Devon 10 D3
Stockley Wilts 24 C5
Stocklinch Som 11 C8
Stockport Gtr Man 87 E6
Stocksbridge S Yorks 88 E3
Stocksfield Northumb 110 C3
Stockton Hereford 49 C7
Stockton Norf 69 E6
Stockton Shrops 60 D2
Stockton Shrops 61 E7
Stockton Warks 52 C2
Stockton Wilts 24 F4
Stockton Heath Warr 86 F4
Stockton-on-Tees Stockton 102 C2
Stockton on Teme Worcs 50 C2
Stockton on the Forest York 96 D2
Stodmarsh Kent 31 C6
Stody Norf 81 D6
Stoer Highld 156 G3
Stoford Som 12 C3
Stoford Wilts 25 F5
Stogumber Som 22 F2
Stogursey Som 22 E4
Stoke Devon 8 B4
Stoke Hants 15 D8
Stoke Hants 26 D2
Stoke Medway 30 B2
Stoke Suff 57 E5
Stoke Abbott Dorset 12 D2
Stoke Albany Northants 64 F5
Stoke Ash Suff 56 B5
Stoke Bardolph Notts 77 E6
Stoke Bliss Worcs 49 C8
Stoke Bruerne Northants 52 E5
Stoke by Clare Suff 55 E8
Stoke-by-Nayland Suff 56 F3
Stoke Canon Devon 10 E4
Stoke Charity Hants 26 F2
Stoke Climsland Corn 5 B8
Stoke D'Abernon Sur 28 D2
Stoke Doyle Northants 65 F7
Stoke Dry Rutland 65 E5
Stoke Farthing Wilts 13 B8
Stoke Ferry Norf 67 E7
Stoke Fleming Devon 7 E6
Stoke Gabriel Devon 7 D6
Stoke Gifford S Glos 23 B8
Stoke Golding Leics 63 E7
Stoke Goldington M Keynes 53 E6
Stoke Green Bucks 40 F2
Stoke Hammond Bucks 40 B1
Stoke Heath Shrops 61 B6
Stoke Holy Cross Norf 68 D5
Stoke Lacy Hereford 49 E8
Stoke Lyne Oxon 39 B5
Stoke Mandeville Bucks 39 C8
Stoke Newington London 41 F6
Stoke on Tern Shrops 61 B6
Stoke-on-Trent Stoke 75 E5
Stoke Orchard Glos 37 B6
Stoke Poges Bucks 40 F2
Stoke Prior Hereford 49 D7
Stoke Prior Worcs 50 C4
Stoke Rivers Devon 20 F5
Stoke Rochford Lincs 65 B6
Stoke Row Oxon 39 F6
Stoke St Gregory Som 11 B8
Stoke St Mary Som 11 B7
Stoke St Michael Som 23 E8
Stoke St Milborough Shrops 61 F5

Stoke sub Hamdon Som 12 C2
Stoke Talmage Oxon 39 E6
Stoke Trister Som 12 B5
Stoke Wake Dorset 13 D5
Stokeford Dorset 13 F6
Stokeham Notts 77 B7
Stokeinteignhead Devon 7 B7
Stokenchurch Bucks 39 E7
Stokenham Devon 7 E6
Stokesay Shrops 60 F4
Stokesby Norf 69 C7
Stokesley N Yorks 102 D3
Stolford Som 22 E4
Ston Easton Som 23 D8
Stondon Massey Essex 42 D1
Stone Bucks 39 C7
Stone Glos 36 E3
Stone Kent 19 C6
Stone Kent 29 B6
Stone S Yorks 89 F6
Stone Staffs 75 F6
Stone Worcs 50 B3
Stone Allerton Som 23 D6
Stone Bridge Corner Pboro 66 D2
Stone Chair W Yorks 88 B2
Stone Cross E Sus 18 E3
Stone Cross Kent 31 D7
Stone-edge Batch N Som 23 B6
Stone House Cumb 100 F2
Stone Street Kent 29 D6
Stone Street Suff 56 F3
Stone Street Suff 69 F6
Stonebroom Derbys 76 D4
Stoneferry Hull 97 F7
Stonefield S Lanark 119 D6
Stonegate E Sus 18 C3
Stonegate N Yorks 103 D5
Stonegrave N Yorks 96 B2
Stonehaugh Northumb 109 B7
Stonehaven Aberds 141 F7
Stonehouse Glos 37 D5
Stonehouse Northumb 109 D6
Stonehouse S Lanark 119 E7
Stoneleigh Warks 51 B8
Stonely Cambs 54 C2
Stoner Hill Hants 15 B8
Stone's Green Essex 43 B7
Stonesby Leics 64 B5
Stonesfield Oxon 38 C3
Stonethwaite Cumb 98 C4
Stoney Cross Hants 14 C3
Stoney Middleton Derbys 76 B2
Stoney Stanton Leics 63 E8
Stoney Stoke Som 24 F2
Stoney Stratton Som 23 F8
Stoney Stretton Shrops 60 D3
Stoneybreck Shetland 160 N8
Stoneyburn W Loth 120 C2
Stoneygate Aberds 153 E10
Stoneygate Leicester 64 D3
Stoneyhills Essex 43 E5
Stoneykirk Dumfries 104 D4
Stoneywood Aberdeen 141 C7
Stoneywood Falk 127 F6
Stonganess Shetland 160 C7
Stonham Aspal Suff 56 D5
Stonnall Staffs 62 D4
Stonor Oxon 39 F7
Stonton Wyville Leics 64 E4
Stony Cross Hereford 50 E2
Stony Stratford M Keynes 53 E5
Stonyfield Highld 151 D9
Stoodleigh Devon 10 C4
Stopes S Yorks 88 F3
Stopham W Sus 16 C4
Stopsley Luton 40 B4
Stores Corner Suff 57 E7
Storeton Mers 85 F4
Stornoway W Isles 155 D9
Storridge Hereford 50 E2
Storrington W Sus 16 C4
Storrs Cumb 99 E5
Storth Cumb 99 F6
Storwood E Yorks 96 E3
Stotfield Moray 152 A2
Stotfold C Beds 54 F3
Stottesdon Shrops 61 F6
Stoughton Leics 64 D3
Stoughton Sur 27 D7
Stoughton W Sus 16 C2
Stoul Highld 147 B10
Stoulton Worcs 50 E4
Stour Provost Dorset 13 B5
Stour Row Dorset 13 B6
Stourbridge W Mid 62 F3
Stourpaine Dorset 13 D6
Stourport on Severn Worcs 50 B3
Stourton Staffs 62 F2
Stourton Warks 51 F7
Stourton Wilts 24 F2
Stourton Caundle Dorset 12 C5
Stove Orkney 159 E7
Stove Shetland 160 L6
Stoven Suff 69 F7
Stow Borders 121 E7
Stow Lincs 78 F3
Stow Lincs 90 F2
Stow Bardolph Norf 67 D6
Stow Bedon Norf 68 E2
Stow cum Quy Cambs 55 C6
Stow Longa Cambs 54 B2
Stow Maries Essex 42 E4
Stow-on-the-Wold Glos 38 B1
Stowbridge Norf 67 D6
Stowe Shrops 48 B5
Stowe-by-Chartley Staffs 62 B4
Stowe Green Glos 36 D2
Stowell Som 12 B4
Stowford Devon 9 F6
Stowlangtoft Suff 56 C3
Stowmarket Suff 56 D4
Stowting Kent 30 E5
Stowupland Suff 56 D4
Straad Argyll 145 G9
Strachan Aberds 141 E5
Stradbroke Suff 57 B6
Stradishall Suff 55 D8
Stradsett Norf 67 D6
Stragglethorpe Lincs 78 D2
Straid S Ayrs 112 E1
Straith Dumfries 113 F8
Straiton Edin 121 C5
Straiton S Ayrs 112 D3
Straloch Aberds 141 B7
Straloch Perth 133 C7
Stramshall Staffs 75 F7
Strang IoM 84 E3
Stranraer Dumfries 104 C4
Stratfield Mortimer W Berks 26 C4
Stratfield Saye Hants 26 C4
Stratfield Turgis Hants 26 D4
Stratford London 41 F6
Stratford St Andrew Suff 57 C7
Stratford St Mary Suff 56 F4
Stratford Sub Castle Wilts 25 F6
Stratford Tony Wilts 13 B8
Stratford-upon-Avon Warks 51 D6
Strath Highld 149 A12
Strath Highld 158 E4
Strathan Highld 136 E2
Strathan Highld 156 G3
Strathan Highld 157 C8
Strathaven S Lanark 119 E7
Strathblane Stirling 119 B5
Strathcanaird Highld 156 J4
Strathcarron Highld 150 G2
Strathcoil Argyll 124 B2
Strathdon Aberds 140 C2
Strathellie Aberds 153 B10
Strathkinness Fife 129 C6
Strathmashie House Highld 137 E8
Strathmiglo Fife 128 C4
Strathmore Lodge Highld 158 F3
Strathpeffer Highld 150 F7
Strathrannoch Highld 150 D6
Strathtay Perth 133 D6
Strathvaich Lodge Highld 150 D6
Strathwhillan N Ayrs 143 E11
Strathy Highld 157 C11
Strathyre Stirling 126 C4
Stratton Corn 8 D4
Stratton Dorset 12 E4
Stratton Glos 37 D7
Stratton Audley Oxon 39 B6
Stratton on the Fosse Som 23 D8
Stratton St Margaret Swindon 38 F1
Stratton St Michael Norf 68 E5
Stratton Strawless Norf 81 E8
Stravithie Fife 129 C7
Streat E Sus 17 C7
Streatham London 28 B4
Streatley C Beds 40 B3
Streatley W Berks 39 F5
Street Lancs 92 D5
Street N Yorks 103 D5
Street Som 23 F6
Street Dinas Shrops 73 F7
Street End Kent 30 D5
Street End W Sus 16 E2
Street Gate T&W 110 D5
Street Lydan Wrex 73 F8
Streethay Staffs 62 C5
Streetlam N Yorks 101 E8
Streetly W Mid 62 E4
Streetly End Cambs 55 E7
Strefford Shrops 60 F4
Strelley Notts 76 E5
Strensall York 96 C2
Stretcholt Som 22 E4
Strete Devon 7 E6
Stretford Gtr Man 87 E6
Strethall Essex 55 F5
Stretham Cambs 55 B6
Strettington W Sus 16 D2
Stretton Ches W 73 D8
Stretton Derbys 76 C3
Stretton Rutland 65 C6
Stretton Staffs 62 C2
Stretton Staffs 63 B6
Stretton Warr 86 F4
Stretton Grandison Hereford 49 E8
Stretton-on-Dunsmore Warks 52 B2
Stretton-on-Fosse Warks 51 F7
Stretton Sugwas Hereford 49 E6
Stretton under Fosse Warks 63 F8
Stretton Westwood Shrops 61 E5
Strichen Aberds 153 C9
Strines Gtr Man 87 F7
Stringston Som 22 E3
Strixton Northants 53 C7
Stroat Glos 36 E2
Stromeferry Highld 149 E13
Stromemore Highld 149 E13
Stromness Orkney 159 H3
Stronaba Highld 136 F5
Stronachlachar Stirling 126 C3
Stronchreggan Highld 130 B4
Stronchrubie Highld 156 H5
Strone Argyll 145 E10
Strone Highld 136 F4
Strone Highld 137 B8
Strone Invclyd 118 B2
Stronmilchan Argyll 125 C7
Strontian Highld 130 C2
Strood Medway 29 C8
Strood Green Sur 28 E3
Strood Green W Sus 16 B4
Strood Green W Sus 28 F2
Stroud Glos 37 D5
Stroud Hants 15 B8
Stroud Green Essex 42 E4
Stroxton Lincs 78 F2
Struan Highld 149 E8
Struan Perth 133 C5
Strubby Lincs 91 F8
Strumpshaw Norf 69 D6
Strutherhill S Lanark 119 E7
Struy Highld 150 H6
Stryt-issa Wrex 73 E6
Stuartfield Aberds 153 D9
Stub Place Cumb 98 E2
Stubbington Hants 15 D6
Stubbins Lancs 87 C5
Stubbs Cross Kent 19 B6
Stubb's Green Norf 69 E5
Stubbs Green Norf 69 E6
Stubhampton Dorset 13 C7
Stubton Lincs 77 E8
Stuckgowan Argyll 126 D2
Stuckton Hants 14 C2
Stud Green Windsor 27 B6
Studham C Beds 40 C3
Studland Dorset 13 F8
Studley Warks 51 C5
Studley Wilts 24 B4
Studley Roger N Yorks 95 B5
Stump Cross Essex 55 E6
Stuntney Cambs 55 B6
Sturbridge Staffs 74 F5
Sturmer Essex 55 E7
Sturminster Marshall Dorset 13 D7
Sturminster Newton Dorset 13 C5
Sturry Kent 31 C5
Sturton N Lincs 90 D3
Sturton by Stow Lincs 90 F2
Sturton le Steeple Notts 89 F8
Stuston Suff 56 B5
Stutton N Yorks 95 E7
Stutton Suff 57 F5
Styal Ches E 87 F6
Styrrup Notts 89 E7
Suainebost W Isles 155 A10
Suardail W Isles 155 D9
Succoth Aberds 152 E4
Succoth Argyll 125 E8
Suckley Worcs 50 D2
Suckquoy Orkney 159 K5
Sudborough Northants 65 F6
Sudbourne Suff 57 D8
Sudbrook Lincs 78 E2
Sudbrook Mon 36 F2
Sudbrooke Lincs 78 B3
Sudbury Derbys 75 F8
Sudbury London 40 F4
Sudbury Suff 56 E2
Suddie Highld 151 F9
Sudgrove Glos 37 D6
Suffield N Yorks 103 E7
Suffield Norf 81 D8
Sugnall Staffs 74 F4
Suladale Highld 149 C8
Sulaisiadar W Isles 155 D10
Sulby IoM 84 C3
Sulgrave Northants 52 E3
Sulham W Berks 26 B4
Sulhamstead W Berks 26 C4
Sulland Orkney 159 D6
Sullington W Sus 16 C4
Sullom Shetland 160 F5
Sullom Voe Oil Terminal Shetland 160 F5
Sully V Glam 22 C3
Sumburgh Shetland 160 N6
Summer Bridge N Yorks 94 C5
Summer-house Darl 101 C7
Summercourt Corn 4 D3
Summerfield Norf 80 D3
Summergangs Hull 97 F7
Summerleaze Mon 35 F8
Summersdale W Sus 16 D2
Summerseat Gtr Man 87 C5
Summertown Oxon 39 D5
Summit Gtr Man 87 D7
Sunbury-on-Thames Sur 28 C2
Sundaywell Dumfries 113 F8
Sunderland Argyll 142 B3
Sunderland Cumb 107 F8
Sunderland T&W 111 D6
Sunderland Bridge Durham 111 F5
Sundhope Borders 115 B6
Sundon Park Luton 40 B3
Sundridge Kent 29 D5
Sunipol Argyll 146 F6
Sunk Island E Yorks 91 C6
Sunningdale Windsor 27 C7
Sunninghill Windsor 27 C7
Sunningwell Oxon 38 D4
Sunniside Durham 110 F4
Sunniside T&W 110 D5
Sunnyhurst Blackburn 86 B4
Sunnylaw Stirling 127 E6
Sunnyside W Sus 28 F4
Sunton Wilts 25 D7
Surbiton London 28 C2
Surby IoM 84 E2
Surfleet Lincs 66 B2
Surfleet Seas End Lincs 66 B2
Surlingham Norf 69 D6
Sustead Norf 81 D7
Susworth Lincs 90 D2
Sutcombe Devon 8 C5
Suton Norf 68 E3
Sutors of Cromarty Highld 151 E11
Sutterby Lincs 79 B6
Sutterton Lincs 79 F5
Sutton C Beds 54 E3
Sutton Cambs 54 B5
Sutton Kent 31 E7
Sutton London 28 C3
Sutton Mers 86 E3
Sutton N Yorks 89 B5
Sutton Norf 69 B6
Sutton Notts 77 F7
Sutton Notts 89 F7
Sutton Oxon 38 D4
Sutton Pboro 65 E7
Sutton S Yorks 89 C6
Sutton Shrops 61 F7
Sutton Shrops 74 F3
Sutton Som 23 F8
Sutton Staffs 61 B7
Sutton Suff 57 E7
Sutton Sur 27 E8
Sutton W Sus 16 C3
Sutton at Hone Kent 29 B6
Sutton Bassett Northants 64 E4
Sutton Benger Wilts 24 B4
Sutton Bonington Notts 64 B2
Sutton Bridge Lincs 66 B4
Sutton Cheney Leics 63 D8
Sutton Coldfield W Mid 62 E5
Sutton Courtenay Oxon 39 E5
Sutton Crosses Lincs 66 B4
Sutton Grange N Yorks 95 B5
Sutton Green Sur 27 D8
Sutton Howgrave N Yorks 95 B6
Sutton In Ashfield Notts 76 D4
Sutton-in-Craven N Yorks 94 E3
Sutton in the Elms Leics 64 E2
Sutton Ings Hull 97 F7
Sutton Lane Ends Ches E 75 B6
Sutton Leach Mers 86 E3
Sutton Maddock Shrops 61 D7
Sutton Mallet Som 23 F5
Sutton Mandeville Wilts 13 B7
Sutton Manor Mers 86 E3
Sutton Montis Som 12 B4
Sutton on Hull Hull 97 F7
Sutton on Sea Lincs 91 F9
Sutton-on-the-Forest N Yorks 95 C8
Sutton on the Hill Derbys 76 F2
Sutton on Trent Notts 77 C7
Sutton Scarsdale Derbys 76 C4
Sutton Scotney Hants 26 F2
Sutton St Edmund Lincs 66 C3
Sutton St James Lincs 66 C3
Sutton St Nicholas Hereford 49 E7
Sutton under Brailes Warks 51 F8
Sutton-under-Whitestonecliffe N Yorks 102 F2
Sutton upon Derwent E Yorks 96 E3
Sutton Valence Kent 30 E2
Sutton Veny Wilts 24 E3
Sutton Waldron Dorset 13 C6
Sutton Weaver Ches W 74 B2
Sutton Wick Bath 23 D7
Swaby Lincs 79 B6
Swadlincote Derbys 63 C7
Swaffham Norf 67 D8
Swaffham Bulbeck Cambs 55 C6
Swaffham Prior Cambs 55 C6
Swafield Norf 81 D8
Swainby N Yorks 102 D2
Swainshill Hereford 49 E6
Swainsthorpe Norf 68 D5
Swainswick Bath 24 C2
Swalcliffe Oxon 51 F8
Swalecliffe Kent 30 C5
Swallow Lincs 91 D5
Swallowcliffe Wilts 13 B7
Swallowfield Wokingham 26 C5
Swallownest S Yorks 89 F5
Swallows Cross Essex 42 E2
Swan Green Ches W 74 B4
Swan Green Suff 57 B6
Swanage Dorset 13 G8
Swanbister Orkney 159 H4
Swanbourne Bucks 39 B8
Swanland E Yorks 90 B3
Swanley Kent 29 C6
Swanley Village Kent 29 C6
Swanmore Hants 15 C6
Swannington Leics 63 C8
Swannington Norf 68 C4
Swanscombe Kent 29 B7
Swansea = Abertawe Swansea 33 E7
Swanton Abbott Norf 81 E8
Swanton Morley Norf 68 C3
Swanton Novers Norf 81 D6
Swanton Street Kent 30 D2
Swanwick Derbys 76 D4
Swanwick Hants 15 D6
Swarby Lincs 78 E3
Swardeston Norf 68 D5
Swarister Shetland 160 E7
Swarkestone Derbys 63 B7
Swarland Northumb 117 D7
Swarland Estate Northumb 117 D7
Swarthmoor Cumb 92 B2
Swathwick Derbys 76 C3
Swaton Lincs 78 F4
Swavesey Cambs 54 C4
Sway Hants 14 E3
Swayfield Lincs 65 B6
Swaythling Soton 14 C5
Sweet Green Worcs 49 C8
Sweetham Devon 10 E3
Sweethouse Corn 5 C5
Sweffling Suff 57 C7
Swepstone Leics 63 C7
Swerford Oxon 51 F8
Swettenham Ches E 74 C5
Swetton N Yorks 94 B4
Swffryd Caerph 35 E6
Swiftsden E Sus 18 C4
Swilland Suff 57 D5
Swillington W Yorks 95 F6
Swimbridge Devon 9 B8
Swimbridge Newland Devon 20 F5
Swinbrook Oxon 38 C2
Swinderby Lincs 77 C8
Swindon Glos 37 B6
Swindon Staffs 62 E2
Swindon Swindon 38 F1
Swine E Yorks 97 F7
Swinefleet E Yorks 89 B8
Swineshead Bedford 53 C8
Swineshead Lincs 78 E5
Swineshead Bridge Lincs 78 E5
Swiney Highld 158 G4
Swinford Leics 52 B3
Swinford Oxon 38 D4
Swingate Notts 76 E5
Swingfield Minnis Kent 31 E6
Swingfield Street Kent 31 E6
Swinhoe Northumb 117 B8
Swinhope Lincs 91 E6
Swining Shetland 160 G6
Swinithwaite N Yorks 101 F5
Swinnow Moor W Yorks 94 F5
Swinscoe Staffs 75 E8
Swinside Hall Borders 116 C3
Swinstead Lincs 65 B7
Swinton Borders 122 E4
Swinton Gtr Man 87 D5
Swinton N Yorks 94 B5
Swinton N Yorks 96 B3
Swinton S Yorks 88 E5
Swintonmill Borders 122 E4
Swithland Leics 64 C2
Swordale Highld 151 E8
Swordland Highld 147 B10
Swordly Highld 157 C10
Sworton Heath Ches E 86 F4
Swydd-ffynnon Ceredig 47 C5
Swynnerton Staffs 75 F5
Swyre Dorset 12 F3
Sychtyn Powys 59 D6
Syde Glos 37 C6
Sydenham London 28 B4
Sydenham Oxon 39 D7
Sydenham Damerel Devon 6 B2
Syderstone Norf 80 D4
Sydling St Nicholas Dorset 12 E4
Sydmonton Hants 26 D2
Syerston Notts 77 E7
Syke Gtr Man 87 C6
Sykehouse S Yorks 89 C7
Sykes Lancs 93 D6
Syleham Suff 57 B6
Sylen Carms 33 D6
Symbister Shetland 160 G7
Symington S Ayrs 118 F3
Symington S Lanark 120 F2
Symonds Yat Hereford 36 C2
Symondsbury Dorset 12 E2
Synod Inn Ceredig 46 D3
Syre Highld 157 E9
Syreford Glos 37 B7
Syresham Northants 52 E4
Syston Leics 64 C3
Syston Lincs 78 E2
Sytchampton Worcs 50 C3
Sywell Northants 53 C6

T

Taagan Highld 150 E3
Tàbost W Isles 155 A10
Tabost W Isles 155 F8
Tackley Oxon 38 B4
Tacleit W Isles 154 D6
Tacolneston Norf 68 E4
Tadcaster N Yorks 95 E7
Taddington Derbys 75 B8
Taddiport Devon 9 C6
Tadley Hants 26 C4
Tadlow C Beds 54 E3
Tadmarton Oxon 51 F8
Tadworth Sur 28 D3
Tafarn-y-gelyn Denb 73 C5
Tafarnau-bach Bl Gwent 35 C5
Taff's Well Rhondda 35 F5
Tafolwern Powys 59 D5
Tai Conwy 83 E7
Tai-bach Powys 59 B8
Tai-mawr Conwy 72 E3
Tai-Ucha Denb 72 D4
Taibach Neath 34 F1
Taigh a Ghearraidh W Isles 148 A2
Tain Highld 151 C10
Tain Highld 158 D4
Tainant Wrex 73 E6
Tainlon Gwyn 82 F4
Tairbeart = Tarbert W Isles 154 G6
Tai'r-Bull Powys 34 B3
Tairgwaith Neath 33 C8
Takeley Essex 42 B1
Takeley Street Essex 41 B8
Tal-sarn Ceredig 46 D4
Tal-y-bont Ceredig 58 F3
Tal-y-Bont Conwy 83 E7
Tal-y-bont Gwyn 71 E6
Tal-y-bont Gwyn 83 D6
Tal-y-cafn Conwy 83 D7
Tal-y-llyn Gwyn 58 D4
Tal-y-wern Powys 58 D5
Talachddu Powys 48 F2
Talacre Flint 85 F2
Talardd Gwyn 59 B5
Talaton Devon 11 E5
Talbenny Pembs 44 D3
Talbot Green Rhondda 34 F4
Talbot Village Poole 13 E8
Tale Devon 11 D5
Talerddig Powys 59 D6
Talgarreg Ceredig 46 D3
Talgarth Powys 48 F3
Talisker Highld 149 E8
Talke Staffs 74 D5
Talkin Cumb 109 D5
Talla Linnfoots Borders 114 B4
Talladale Highld 150 D2
Tallarn Green Wrex 73 E8
Tallentire Cumb 107 F8
Talley Carms 46 F5
Tallington Lincs 65 D7
Talmine Highld 157 C8
Talog Carms 32 B4
Talsarn Carms 34 B1
Talsarnau Gwyn 71 D7
Talskiddy Corn 4 C4
Talwrn Anglesey 82 D4
Talwrn Wrex 73 E6
Talybont-on-Usk Powys 35 B5
Talygarn Rhondda 34 F4
Talyllyn Powys 35 B5
Talysarn Gwyn 82 F4
Talywain Torf 35 D6
Tame Bridge N Yorks 102 D3
Tamerton Foliot Plym 6 C2
Tamworth Staffs 63 D6
Tan Hinon Powys 59 F5
Tan-lan Conwy 83 E7
Tan-lan Gwyn 71 C7
Tan-y-bwlch Gwyn 71 C7
Tan-y-fron Conwy 72 C3
Tan-y-graig Anglesey 82 D5
Tan-y-graig Gwyn 70 D4
Tan-y-groes Ceredig 45 E4
Tan-y-pistyll Powys 59 B7
Tan-yr-allt Gwyn 82 F4
Tandem W Yorks 88 C2
Tanden Kent 19 B6
Tandridge Sur 28 D4
Tanerdy Carms 33 B5
Tanfield Durham 110 D4
Tanfield Lea Durham 110 D4
Tangasdal W Isles 148 J1
Tangiers Pembs 44 D4
Tangley Hants 25 D8
Tanglwst Carms 46 F2
Tangmere W Sus 16 D3
Tangwick Shetland 160 F4
Tankersley S Yorks 88 D4
Tankerton Kent 30 C5
Tannach Highld 158 F5
Tannachie Aberds 141 F6
Tannadice Angus 134 D4
Tannington Suff 57 C6
Tansley Derbys 76 D3
Tansley Knoll Derbys 76 C3
Tansor Northants 65 E7
Tantobie Durham 110 D4
Tanton N Yorks 102 C3
Tanworth-in-Arden Warks 51 B6
Tanygrisiau Gwyn 71 C7
Tanyrhydiau Ceredig 47 C6
Taobh a Chaolais W Isles 148 G2
Taobh a Thuath Loch Aineort W Isles 148 F2
Taobh a Tuath Loch Baghasdail W Isles 148 F2
Taobh a'Ghlinne W Isles 155 F8
Taobh Tuath W Isles 154 J4
Taplow Bucks 40 F2
Tapton Derbys 76 B3
Tarbat Ho. Highld 151 D10
Tarbert Argyll 143 C7
Tarbert Argyll 144 E5
Tarbert Argyll 145 G7
Tarbert = Tairbeart W Isles 154 G6
Tarbet Argyll 126 D2
Tarbet Highld 147 B10
Tarbet Highld 156 E4
Tarbock Green Mers 86 F2
Tarbolton S Ayrs 112 B4
Tarbrax S Lanark 120 D3
Tardebigge Worcs 50 C5
Tarfside Angus 134 B4
Tarland Aberds 140 D3
Tarleton Lancs 86 B2
Tarlogie Highld 151 C10
Tarlscough Lancs 86 C2
Tarlton Glos 37 E6
Tarnbrook Lancs 93 D5
Tarporley Ches W 74 C2
Tarr Som 22 F3
Tarrant Crawford Dorset 13 D7
Tarrant Gunville Dorset 13 C7
Tarrant Hinton Dorset 13 C7
Tarrant Keyneston Dorset 13 D7
Tarrant Launceston Dorset 13 D7
Tarrant Monkton Dorset 13 D7
Tarrant Rawston Dorset 13 D7
Tarrant Rushton Dorset 13 D7
Tarrel Highld 151 C11
Tarring Neville E Sus 17 D8
Tarrington Hereford 49 E8
Tarsappie Perth 128 B3
Tarskavaig Highld 149 H10
Tarves Aberds 153 E8
Tarvie Highld 150 F7
Tarvie Perth 133 C7
Tarvin Ches W 73 C8
Tasburgh Norf 68 E5
Tasley Shrops 61 E6
Taston Oxon 38 B3
Tatenhill Staffs 63 B6
Tathall End M Keynes 53 E6
Tatham Lancs 93 C6
Tathwell Lincs 91 F7
Tatling End Bucks 40 F3
Tatsfield Sur 28 D5
Tattenhall Ches W 73 D8
Tattenhoe M Keynes 53 F6
Tatterford Norf 80 E4
Tattersett Norf 80 D4
Tattershall Lincs 78 D5
Tattershall Bridge Lincs 78 D4
Tattershall Thorpe Lincs 78 D5
Tattingstone Suff 56 F5
Tatworth Som 11 D8
Taunton Som 11 B7
Taverham Norf 68 C4
Tavernspite Pembs 32 C2
Tavistock Devon 6 B2
Taw Green Devon 9 E8
Tawstock Devon 9 B7
Taxal Derbys 75 B7
Tay Bridge Dundee 129 B6
Tayinloan Argyll 143 D7
Taymouth Castle Perth 132 E4
Taynish Argyll 144 E6
Taynton Glos 36 B4
Taynton Oxon 38 C2
Taynuilt Argyll 125 B6
Tayport Fife 129 B6
Tayvallich Argyll 144 E6
Tealby Lincs 91 E5
Tealing Angus 134 F4
Teangue Highld 149 H11
Teanna Mhachair W Isles 148 B2
Tebay Cumb 99 D8
Tebworth C Beds 40 B2
Tedburn St Mary Devon 10 E3
Teddington Glos 50 F4
Teddington London 28 B2
Tedstone Delamere Hereford 49 D8
Tedstone Wafre Hereford 49 D8
Teeton Northants 52 B4
Teffont Evias Wilts 24 F4
Teffont Magna Wilts 24 F4
Tegryn Pembs 45 F4
Teigh Rutland 65 C5
Teigncombe Devon 9 F8
Teigngrace Devon 7 B6
Teignmouth Devon 7 B7
Telford Telford 61 D6
Telham E Sus 18 D4
Tellisford Som 24 D3
Telscombe E Sus 17 D8
Telscombe Cliffs E Sus 17 D7
Templand Dumfries 114 F3
Temple Corn 5 B6
Temple Glasgow 118 C5
Temple Midloth 121 D6
Temple Balsall W Mid 51 B7
Temple Bar Carms 33 C6
Temple Bar Ceredig 46 D4
Temple Cloud Bath 23 D8
Temple Combe Som 12 B5
Temple Ewell Kent 31 E6
Temple Grafton Warks 51 D6
Temple Guiting Glos 37 B7
Temple Herdewyke Warks 51 D8
Temple Hirst N Yorks 89 B7
Temple Normanton Derbys 76 C4
Temple Sowerby Cumb 99 B8
Templehall Fife 128 E4
Templeton Devon 10 C3
Templeton Pembs 32 C2
Templeton Bridge Devon 10 C3
Templetown Durham 110 D4
Tempsford C Beds 54 D2
Ten Mile Bank Norf 67 E6
Tenbury Wells Worcs 49 C7
Tenby = Dinbych-Y-Pysgod Pembs 32 D2
Tendring Essex 43 B7
Tendring Green Essex 43 B7
Tenston Orkney 159 G3
Tenterden Kent 19 B5
Terling Essex 42 C3
Ternhill Shrops 74 F3
Terregles Banks Dumfries 107 B6
Terrick Bucks 39 D8
Terrington N Yorks 96 B2
Terrington St Clement Norf 66 C5
Terrington St John Norf 66 C5
Teston Kent 29 D8
Testwood Hants 14 C4
Tetbury Glos 37 E5
Tetbury Upton Glos 37 E5
Tetchill Shrops 73 F7
Tetcott Devon 8 E5
Tetford Lincs 79 B6
Tetney Lincs 91 D7
Tetney Lock Lincs 91 D7
Tetsworth Oxon 39 D6
Tettenhall W Mid 62 E2
Teuchan Aberds 153 E10
Teversal Notts 76 C4
Teversham Cambs 55 D5
Teviothead Borders 115 D7
Tewel Aberds 141 F7
Tewin Herts 41 C5
Tewkesbury Glos 50 F3
Teynham Kent 30 C3
Thackthwaite Cumb 98 B3
Thainston Aberds 135 B6
Thakeham W Sus 16 C5
Thame Oxon 39 D7
Thames Ditton Sur 28 C2
Thames Haven Thurrock 42 F3
Thamesmead London 41 F7
Thanington Kent 30 D5
Thankerton S Lanark 120 F2
Tharston Norf 68 E4
Thatcham W Berks 26 C3
Thatto Heath Mers 86 E3
Thaxted Essex 55 F7
The Aird Highld 149 C9
The Arms Norf 67 E8
The Bage Hereford 48 E4
The Balloch Perth 127 C7
The Barony Orkney 159 F3
The Bog Shrops 60 E3
The Bourne Sur 27 E6
The Braes Highld 149 E10
The Broad Hereford 49 C6
The Butts Som 24 E2
The Camp Glos 37 D6
The Camp Herts 40 D4
The Chequer Wrex 73 E8
The City Bucks 39 E7
The Common Wilts 25 F7
The Craigs Highld 150 B7
The Cronk IoM 84 C3
The Dell Suff 69 E7
The Den N Ayrs 118 D3
The Eals Northumb 116 F3
The Eaves Glos 36 D3
The Flatt Cumb 109 B5
The Four Alls Shrops 74 F3
The Garths Shetland 160 B8
The Green Cumb 98 F3
The Green Wilts 24 F3
The Grove Dumfries 107 B6
The Hall Shetland 160 D8
The Haven W Sus 27 F8
The Heath Norf 81 E7
The Heath Suff 56 F5
The Hill Cumb 98 F3
The Howe Cumb 99 F6
The Howe IoM 84 F1
The Hundred Hereford 49 C7
The Lee Bucks 40 D2
The Lhen IoM 84 B3
The Marsh Powys 60 E3
The Marsh Wilts 37 F7
The Middles Durham 110 D5
The Moor Kent 18 C4
The Mumbles = Y Mwmbwls Swansea 33 F7
The Murray S Lanark 119 D6
The Neuk Aberds 141 E6
The Oval Bath 24 C2
The Pole of Itlaw Aberds 153 C6
The Quarry Glos 36 E4
The Rhos Pembs 32 C1
The Rock Telford 61 D6
The Ryde Herts 41 D5
The Sands Sur 27 E6
The Stocks Kent 19 C6
The Throat Wokingham 27 C6
The Vauld Hereford 49 E7
The Wyke Shrops 61 D7
Theakston N Yorks 101 F8
Thealby N Lincs 90 C2
Theale Som 23 E6
Theale W Berks 26 B4
Thearne E Yorks 97 F6
Theberton Suff 57 C8
Theddingworth Leics 64 F3
Theddlethorpe All Saints Lincs 91 F8
Theddlethorpe St Helen Lincs 91 F8
Thelbridge Barton Devon 10 C2
Thelnetham Suff 56 B4
Thelveton Norf 68 F4
Thelwall Warr 86 F4
Themelthorpe Norf 81 E6
Thenford Northants 52 E3
Therfield Herts 54 F4
Thetford Lincs 65 C8
Thetford Norf 67 F8
Theydon Bois Essex 41 E7
Thickwood Wilts 24 B3
Thimbleby Lincs 78 C5
Thimbleby N Yorks 102 E2
Thingwall Mers 85 F3
Thirdpart N Ayrs 118 E1
Thirlby N Yorks 102 F2
Thirlestane Borders 121 E8
Thirn N Yorks 101 F7
Thirsk N Yorks 102 F2
Thirtleby E Yorks 97 F7
Thistleton Lancs 92 F4
Thistleton Rutland 65 C6
Thistley Green Suff 55 B7
Thixendale N Yorks 96 C4
Thockrington Northumb 110 B2
Tholomas Drove Cambs 66 D3
Tholthorpe N Yorks 95 C7
Thomas Chapel Pembs 32 D2
Thomas Close Cumb 108 E4
Thomastown Aberds 152 E5
Thompson Norf 68 E2
Thomshill Moray 152 C2
Thong Kent 29 B7
Thongsbridge W Yorks 88 D2
Thoralby N Yorks 101 F5
Thoresway Lincs 91 E5
Thorganby Lincs 91 E6
Thorganby N Yorks 96 E2
Thorgill N Yorks 103 E5
Thorington Suff 57 B8
Thorington Street Suff 56 F4
Thorlby N Yorks 94 D2
Thorley Herts 41 C7
Thorley Street Herts 41 C7
Thorley Street IoW 14 F4
Thormanby N Yorks 95 B7
Thornaby-on-Tees Stockton 102 C2
Thornage Norf 81 D6
Thornborough Bucks 52 F5
Thornborough N Yorks 95 B5
Thornbury Devon 9 D6
Thornbury Hereford 49 D8
Thornbury S Glos 36 E3
Thornbury W Yorks 94 F4
Thornby Northants 52 B4
Thorncliffe Staffs 75 D7
Thorncombe Dorset 11 D8
Thorncombe Dorset 13 D6
Thorncombe Street Sur 27 E8
Thorncote Green C Beds 54 E2
Thorncross IoW 14 F5
Thorndon Suff 56 C5
Thorndon Cross Devon 9 E7
Thorne S Yorks 89 C7
Thorne St Margaret Som 11 B5
Thorner W Yorks 95 E6
Thorney Notts 77 B8
Thorney Pboro 66 D2
Thorney Crofts E Yorks 91 B6
Thorney Green Suff 56 C4
Thorney Hill Hants 14 E2
Thorney Toll Pboro 66 D3
Thornfalcon Som 11 B7
Thornford Dorset 12 C4
Thorngumbald E Yorks 91 B6
Thornham Norf 80 C3
Thornham Magna Suff 56 B5
Thornham Parva Suff 56 B5
Thornhaugh Pboro 65 D7
Thornhill Cardiff 35 F5
Thornhill Cumb 98 D2
Thornhill Derbys 88 F2
Thornhill Dumfries 113 E8
Thornhill Soton 15 C5
Thornhill Stirling 127 E5
Thornhill W Yorks 88 C3
Thornhill Edge W Yorks 88 C3
Thornhill Lees W Yorks 88 C3
Thornholme E Yorks 97 C7
Thornley Durham 110 F4
Thornley Durham 111 F6
Thornliebank E Renf 118 D5
Thorns Suff 55 D8
Thorns Green Ches E 87 F5
Thornsett Derbys 87 F8
Thornthwaite Cumb 98 B4
Thornthwaite N Yorks 94 D4
Thornton Angus 134 E3
Thornton Bucks 53 F5
Thornton E Yorks 96 E3
Thornton Fife 128 E4
Thornton Lancs 92 E3
Thornton Leics 63 D8
Thornton Lincs 78 C5
Thornton Mbro 102 C2
Thornton Mers 85 D4
Thornton Northumb 123 E5
Thornton Pembs 44 E4
Thornton W Yorks 94 F4
Thornton Curtis N Lincs 90 C4
Thornton Heath London 28 C4
Thornton Hough Mers 85 F4
Thornton in Craven N Yorks 94 E2
Thornton-le-Beans N Yorks 102 E1
Thornton-le-Clay N Yorks 96 C2
Thornton-le-Dale N Yorks 103 F6
Thornton le Moor Lincs 90 E4
Thornton-le-Moor N Yorks 102 F1
Thornton-le-Moors Ches W 73 B8
Thornton-le-Street N Yorks 102 F2
Thornton Rust N Yorks 100 F4
Thornton Steward N Yorks 101 F6
Thornton Watlass N Yorks 101 F7
Thorntonhall S Lanark 119 D5
Thorntonloch E Loth 122 B3
Thorntonpark Northumb 122 E5
Thornwood Common Essex 41 D7
Thornydykes Borders 122 E2
Thoroton Notts 77 E7
Thorp Arch W Yorks 95 E7
Thorpe Derbys 75 D8
Thorpe E Yorks 97 E5
Thorpe Lincs 91 F8
Thorpe N Yorks 94 C3
Thorpe Norf 69 E7
Thorpe Notts 77 E7
Thorpe Sur 27 C8
Thorpe Abbotts Norf 57 B5
Thorpe Acre Leics 64 B2
Thorpe Arnold Leics 64 B4
Thorpe Audlin W Yorks 89 C5
Thorpe Bassett N Yorks 96 B4
Thorpe Bay Southend 43 F5
Thorpe by Water Rutland 65 E5
Thorpe Common Suff 57 F6
Thorpe Constantine Staffs 63 D6
Thorpe Culvert Lincs 79 C7
Thorpe End Norf 69 C5
Thorpe Fendykes Lincs 79 C7
Thorpe Green Essex 43 B7
Thorpe Green Suff 56 D3
Thorpe Hesley S Yorks 88 E4
Thorpe in Balne S Yorks 89 C6
Thorpe in the Fallows Lincs 90 F3
Thorpe Langton Leics 64 E4
Thorpe Larches Durham 102 B1
Thorpe-le-Soken Essex 43 B7
Thorpe le Street E Yorks 96 E4
Thorpe Malsor Northants 53 B6
Thorpe Mandeville Northants 52 E3
Thorpe Market Norf 81 D8
Thorpe Marriot Norf 68 C4
Thorpe Morieux Suff 56 D3
Thorpe on the Hill Lincs 78 C2
Thorpe Salvin S Yorks 89 F6
Thorpe Satchville Leics 64 C4
Thorpe St Andrew Norf 69 D5
Thorpe St Peter Lincs 79 C7
Thorpe Thewles Stockton 102 B2
Thorpe Tilney Lincs 78 D4
Thorpe Underwood N Yorks 95 D7
Thorpe Waterville Northants 65 F7
Thorpe Willoughby N Yorks 95 F8
Thorpeness Suff 57 D8
Thorrington Essex 43 C6
Thorverton Devon 10 D4
Thrandeston Suff 56 B5
Thrapston Northants 53 B7
Thrashbush N Lanark 119 C7
Threapland Cumb 107 F8
Threapland N Yorks 94 C2
Threapwood Ches W 73 E8
Threapwood Staffs 75 E7
Three Ashes Hereford 36 B2
Three Bridges W Sus 28 F3
Three Burrows Corn 3 B6
Three Chimneys Kent 18 B5
Three Cocks Powys 48 F3
Three Crosses Swansea 33 E6
Three Cups Corner E Sus 18 C3
Three Holes Norf 66 D5
Three Leg Cross E Sus 18 B3
Three Legged Cross Dorset 13 D8
Three Oaks E Sus 18 D5
Threehammer Common Norf 69 C6
Threekingham Lincs 78 F3
Threemile Cross Wokingham 26 C5
Threemilestone Corn 3 B6
Threemiletown W Loth 120 B3
Threlkeld Cumb 99 B5
Threshfield N Yorks 94 C2
Thrigby Norf 69 C7
Thringarth Durham 100 B4
Thringstone Leics 63 C8
Thrintoft N Yorks 101 E8
Thriplow Cambs 54 E5
Throckenholt Lincs 66 D3
Throcking Herts 54 F4
Throckley T&W 110 C4
Throckmorton Worcs 50 E4
Throphill Northumb 117 F7
Thropton Northumb 117 D6
Throsk Stirling 127 E7
Throwleigh Devon 9 E8
Throwley Kent 30 D3
Thrumpton Notts 76 F5
Thrumster Highld 158 F5
Thrunton Northumb 117 C6
Thrupp Glos 37 D5
Thrupp Oxon 38 C4
Thrushelton Devon 9 F6
Thrussington Leics 64 C3
Thruxton Hants 25 E7
Thruxton Hereford 49 F6
Thrybergh S Yorks 89 E5
Thulston Derbys 76 F4
Thundergay N Ayrs 143 D9
Thundersley Essex 42 F3
Thundridge Herts 41 C6
Thurcaston Leics 64 C2
Thurcroft S Yorks 89 F5
Thurgarton Norf 81 D7
Thurgarton Notts 77 E6
Thurgoland S Yorks 88 D3
Thurlaston Leics 64 E2
Thurlaston Warks 52 B2
Thurlbear Som 11 B7
Thurlby Lincs 65 C8
Thurlby Lincs 78 C2
Thurleigh Bedford 53 D8
Thurlestone Devon 6 E4
Thurloxton Som 22 F4
Thurlstone S Yorks 88 D3
Thurlton Norf 69 E7
Thurlwood Ches E 74 D5
Thurmaston Leics 64 D3
Thurnby Leics 64 D3
Thurne Norf 69 C7
Thurnham Kent 30 D2
Thurnham Lancs 92 D4
Thurning Norf 81 E6
Thurning Northants 65 F7
Thurnscoe S Yorks 89 D5
Thurnscoe East S Yorks 89 D5
Thursby Cumb 108 D3
Thursford Norf 81 D5
Thursley Sur 27 F7
Thurso Highld 158 D3
Thurso East Highld 158 D3
Thurstaston Mers 85 F3
Thurston Suff 56 C3
Thurstonfield Cumb 108 D3
Thurstonland W Yorks 88 C2
Thurton Norf 69 D6
Thurvaston Derbys 76 F2
Thuxton Norf 68 D3
Thwaite N Yorks 100 E3

Thwaite Suff 56 C5
Thwaite St Mary Norf 69 E6
Thwaites W Yorks 94 E3
Thwaites Brow W Yorks 94 E3
Thwing E Yorks 97 B6
Tibbermore Perth 128 B2
Tibberton Glos 36 B4
Tibberton Telford 61 B6
Tibberton Worcs 50 D4
Tibenham Norf 68 F4
Tibshelf Derbys 76 C4
Tibthorpe E Yorks 97 D5
Ticehurst E Sus 18 B3
Tichborne Hants 26 F3
Tickencote Rutland 65 D6
Tickenham N Som 23 B6
Tickhill S Yorks 89 E6
Ticklerton Shrops 60 E4
Ticknall Derbys 63 B7
Tickton E Yorks 97 E6
Tidcombe Wilts 25 D7
Tiddington Oxon 39 D6
Tiddington Warks 51 D7
Tidebrook E Sus 18 C3
Tideford Corn 5 D8
Tideford Cross Corn 5 C8
Tidenham Glos 36 E2
Tideswell Derbys 75 B8
Tidmarsh W Berks 26 B4
Tidmington Warks 51 F7
Tidpit Hants 13 C8
Tidworth Wilts 25 E7
Tiers Cross Pembs 44 D4
Tiffield Northants 52 D4
Tifty Aberds 153 D7
Tigerton Angus 135 C5
Tigh-na-Blair Perth 127 C6
Tighnabruaich Argyll 145 F8
Tighnafiline Highld 155 J13
Tigley Devon 7 C5
Tilbrook Cambs 53 C8
Tilbury Thurrock 29 B7
Tilbury Juxta Clare Essex 55 E8
Tile Cross W Mid 63 F5
Tile Hill W Mid 51 B7
Tilehurst Reading 26 B4
Tilford Sur 27 E6
Tilgate W Sus 28 F3
Tilgate Forest Row W Sus 28 F3
Tillathrowie Aberds 152 E4
Tilley Shrops 60 B5
Tillicoultry Clack 127 E8
Tillingham Essex 43 D5
Tillington Hereford 49 E6
Tillington W Sus 16 B3
Tillington Common Hereford 49 E6
Tillyarblet Angus 135 C5
Tillybirloch Aberds 141 D5
Tillycorthie Aberds 141 B8
Tillydrine Aberds 140 E5
Tillyfour Aberds 140 C4
Tillyfourie Aberds 140 C5
Tillygarmond Aberds 140 E5
Tillygreig Aberds 141 B7
Tillykerrie Aberds 141 B7
Tilmanstone Kent 31 D7
Tilney All Saints Norf 67 C5
Tilney High End Norf 67 C5
Tilney St Lawrence Norf 66 C5
Tilshead Wilts 24 E5
Tilstock Shrops 74 F2
Tilston Ches W 73 D8
Tilstone Fearnall Ches W 74 C2
Tilsworth C Beds 40 B2
Tilton on the Hill Leics 64 D4
Timberland Lincs 78 D4
Timbersbrook Ches E 75 C5
Timberscombe Som 21 E8
Timble N Yorks 94 D4
Timperley Gtr Man 87 F5
Timsbury Bath 23 D8
Timsbury Hants 14 B4
Timsgearraidh W Isles 154 D5
Timworth Green Suff 56 C2
Tincleton Dorset 13 E5
Tindale Cumb 109 D6
Tingewick Bucks 52 F4
Tingley W Yorks 88 B3
Tingrith C Beds 53 F8
Tingwall Orkney 159 F4
Tinhay Devon 9 F5
Tinshill W Yorks 95 F5
Tinsley S Yorks 88 E5
Tintagel Corn 8 F2
Tintern Parva Mon 36 D2
Tintinhull Som 12 C3
Tintwistle Derbys 87 E8
Tinwald Dumfries 114 F3
Tinwell Rutland 65 D7
Tipperty Aberds 141 B8
Tipsend Norf 66 E5
Tipton W Mid 62 E3
Tipton St John Devon 11 E5
Tiptree Essex 42 C4
Tir-y-dail Carms 33 C7
Tirabad Powys 47 E7
Tiraghoil Argyll 146 J6
Tirley Glos 37 B5
Tirphil Caerph 35 D5
Tirril Cumb 99 B7
Tisbury Wilts 13 B7
Tisman's Common W Sus 27 F8
Tissington Derbys 75 D8
Titchberry Devon 8 B4
Titchfield Hants 15 D6
Titchmarsh Northants 53 B8
Titchwell Norf 80 C3
Tithby Notts 77 F6
Titley Hereford 48 C5
Titlington Northumb 117 C7
Titsey Sur 28 D5
Tittensor Staffs 75 F5
Tittleshall Norf 80 E4
Tiverton Ches W 74 C2
Tiverton Devon 10 C4
Tivetshall St Margaret Norf 68 F4
Tivetshall St Mary Norf 68 F4
Tividale W Mid 62 E3
Tivy Dale S Yorks 88 D3
Tixall Staffs 62 B3
Tixover Rutland 65 D6
Toab Orkney 159 H6
Toab Shetland 160 M5
Toadmoor Derbys 76 D3
Tobermory Argyll 147 F8
Toberonochy Argyll 124 E3
Tobha Mor W Isles 148 E2
Tobhtarol W Isles 154 D6
Tobson W Isles 154 D6
Tocher Aberds 153 E6
Tockenham Wilts 24 B5
Tockenham Wick Wilts 37 F7
Tockholes Blackburn 86 B4
Tockington S Glos 36 F3
Tockwith N Yorks 95 D7
Todber Dorset 13 B6
Todding Hereford 49 B6
Toddington C Beds 40 B3
Toddington Glos 50 F5
Todenham Glos 51 F7
Todhills Cumb 108 C3
Todlachie Aberds 141 C5
Todmorden W Yorks 87 B7
Todrig Borders 115 C7
Todwick S Yorks 89 F5
Toft Cambs 54 D4
Toft Lincs 65 C7
Toft Hill Durham 101 B6
Toft Hill Lincs 78 C5
Toft Monks Norf 69 E7
Toft next Newton Lincs 90 F4
Toftrees Norf 80 E4
Tofts Highld 158 D5
Toftwood Norf 68 C2
Togston Northumb 117 D8
Tokavaig Highld 149 G11
Tokers Green Oxon 26 B5
Tolastadh a Chaolais W Isles 154 D6
Tolastadh bho Thuath W Isles 155 C10
Toll Bar S Yorks 89 D6
Toll End W Mid 62 E3
Toll of Birness Aberds 153 E10
Tolland Som 22 F3
Tollard Royal Wilts 13 C7
Tollbar End W Mid 51 B8
Toller Fratrum Dorset 12 E3
Toller Porcorum Dorset 12 E3
Tollerton N Yorks 95 C8
Tollerton Notts 77 F6
Tollesbury Essex 43 C5
Tolleshunt D'Arcy Essex 43 C5
Tolleshunt Major Essex 43 C5
Tolm W Isles 155 D9
Tolpuddle Dorset 13 E5
Tolvah Highld 138 E4
Tolworth London 28 C2
Tomatin Highld 138 B4
Tombreck Highld 151 H9
Tomchrasky Highld 137 C5
Tomdoun Highld 136 D4
Tomich Highld 137 B6
Tomich Highld 151 D9
Tomich House Highld 151 G8
Tomintoul Aberds 139 E7
Tomintoul Moray 139 C7
Tomnaven Moray 152 E4
Tomnavoulin Moray 139 B8
Ton-Pentre Rhondda 34 E3
Tonbridge Kent 29 E6
Tondu Bridgend 34 F2
Tonfanau Gwyn 58 D2
Tong Shrops 61 D7
Tong W Yorks 94 F5
Tong Norton Shrops 61 D7
Tonge Leics 63 B8
Tongham Sur 27 E6
Tongland Dumfries 106 D3
Tongue Highld 157 D8
Tongue End Lincs 65 C8
Tongwynlais Cardiff 35 F5
Tonna Neath 34 E1
Tonwell Herts 41 C6
Tonypandy Rhondda 34 E3
Tonyrefail Rhondda 34 F4
Toot Baldon Oxon 39 D5
Toot Hill Essex 41 D8
Toothill Hants 14 C4
Top of Hebers Gtr Man 87 D6
Topcliffe N Yorks 95 B7
Topcroft Norf 69 E5
Topcroft Street Norf 69 E5
Toppesfield Essex 55 F8
Toppings Gtr Man 86 C5
Topsham Devon 10 F4
Torbay Torbay 7 D7
Torbeg N Ayrs 143 F10
Torboll Farm Highld 151 B10
Torbrex Stirling 127 E6
Torbryan Devon 7 C6
Torcross Devon 7 E6
Tore Highld 151 F9
Torinturk Argyll 145 G7
Torksey Lincs 77 B8
Torlum W Isles 148 C2
Torlundy Highld 131 B5
Tormarton S Glos 24 B2
Tormisdale Argyll 142 C2
Tormitchell S Ayrs 112 E2
Tormore N Ayrs 143 E9
Tornagrain Highld 151 G10
Tornahaish Aberds 139 D8
Tornaveen Aberds 140 D5
Torness Highld 137 B8
Toronto Durham 110 F4
Torpenhow Cumb 108 F2
Torphichen W Loth 120 B2
Torphins Aberds 140 D5
Torpoint Corn 6 D2
Torquay Torbay 7 C7
Torquhan Borders 121 E7
Torran Argyll 124 E4
Torran Highld 149 D10
Torran Highld 151 D10
Torrance E Dunb 119 B6
Torrans Argyll 146 J7
Torranyard N Ayrs 118 E3
Torre Torbay 7 C7
Torridon Highld 150 F2
Torridon Ho. Highld 149 C13
Torrin Highld 149 F10
Torrisdale Highld 157 C9
Torrisdale-Square Argyll 143 E8
Torrish Highld 157 H12
Torrisholme Lancs 92 C4
Torroble Highld 157 J8
Torry Aberdeen 141 D8
Torry Aberds 152 E4
Torryburn Fife 128 F2
Torterston Aberds 153 D10
Torthorwald Dumfries 107 B7
Tortington W Sus 16 D4
Tortworth S Glos 36 E4
Torvaig Highld 149 D9
Torver Cumb 98 E4
Torwood Falk 127 F7
Torworth Notts 89 F7
Tosberry Devon 8 B4
Toscaig Highld 149 E12
Toseland Cambs 54 C3
Tosside N Yorks 93 D7
Tostock Suff 56 C3
Totaig Highld 148 C7
Totaig Highld 149 F13
Tote Highld 149 D9
Totegan Highld 157 C11
Tothill Lincs 91 F8
Totland IoW 14 F4
Totnes Devon 7 C6
Toton Notts 76 F5
Totronald Argyll 146 F4
Totscore Highld 149 B8
Tottenham London 41 E6
Tottenhill Norf 67 C6
Tottenhill Row Norf 67 C6
Totteridge London 41 E5
Totternhoe C Beds 40 B2
Tottington Gtr Man 87 C5
Totton Hants 14 C4
Touchen End Windsor 27 B6
Tournaig Highld 155 J13
Toux Aberds 153 C9
Tovil Kent 29 D8
Tow Law Durham 110 F4
Toward Argyll 145 G10
Towcester Northants 52 E4
Towednack Corn 2 C3
Tower End Norf 67 C6
Towersey Oxon 39 D7
Towie Aberds 140 C3
Towie Aberds 153 B8
Towiemore Moray 152 D3
Town End Cambs 66 E4
Town End Cumb 99 F6
Town Row E Sus 18 B2
Town Yetholm Borders 116 B4
Townend W Dunb 118 B4
Towngate Lincs 65 C8
Townhead Cumb 108 F5
Townhead Dumfries 106 E3
Townhead S Ayrs 112 D2
Townhead S Yorks 88 D2
Townhead of Greenlaw Dumfries 106 C4
Townhill Fife 128 F3
Townsend Bucks 39 D7
Townsend Herts 40 D4
Townshend Corn 2 C4
Towthorpe York 96 D2
Towton N Yorks 95 F7
Towyn Conwy 72 B3
Toxteth Mers 85 F4
Toynton All Saints Lincs 79 C6
Toynton Fen Side Lincs 79 C6
Toynton St Peter Lincs 79 C7
Toy's Hill Kent 29 D5
Trabboch E Ayrs 112 B4
Traboe Corn 3 D6
Tradespark Highld 151 F11
Tradespark Orkney 159 H5
Trafford Park Gtr Man 87 E5
Trallong Powys 34 B3
Tranent E Loth 121 B7
Tranmere Mers 85 F4
Trantlebeg Highld 157 D11
Trantlemore Highld 157 D11
Tranwell Northumb 117 F7
Trapp Carms 33 C7
Traprain E Loth 121 B8
Traquair Borders 121 F6
Trawden Lancs 94 F2
Trawsfynydd Gwyn 71 D8
Tre-Gibbon Rhondda 34 D3
Tre-Taliesin Ceredig 58 E3
Tre-vaughan Carms 32 B4
Tre-wyn Mon 35 B7
Trealaw Rhondda 34 E4
Treales Lancs 92 F4
Trearddur Anglesey 82 D2
Treaslane Highld 149 C8
Trebanog Rhondda 34 E4
Trebanos Neath 33 D8
Trebartha Corn 5 B7
Trebarwith Corn 8 F2
Trebetherick Corn 4 B4
Treborough Som 22 F2
Trebudannon Corn 4 C3
Trebullett Corn 5 B8
Treburley Corn 5 B8
Trebyan Corn 5 C5
Trecastle Powys 34 B2
Trecenydd Caerph 35 F5
Trecwn Pembs 44 B4
Trecynon Rhondda 34 D3
Tredavoe Corn 2 D3
Treddiog Pembs 44 C3
Tredegar Bl Gwent 35 D5
Tredegar = Newydd New Tredegar Caerph 35 D5
Tredington Glos 37 B6
Tredington Warks 51 E7
Tredinnick Corn 4 B4
Tredomen Powys 48 F3
Tredunnock Mon 35 E7
Tredustan Powys 48 F3
Treen Corn 2 D2
Treeton S Yorks 88 F5
Tref-Y-Clawdd = Knighton Powys 48 B4
Trefaldwyn = Montgomery Powys 60 E2
Trefasser Pembs 44 B3
Trefdraeth Anglesey 82 D4
Trefdraeth = Newport Pembs 45 F2
Trefecca Powys 48 F3
Trefechan Ceredig 58 F2
Trefeglwys Powys 59 E6
Trefenter Ceredig 46 C5
Treffgarne Pembs 44 C4
Treffynnon = Holywell Flint 73 B5
Treffynnon Pembs 44 C3
Trefgarn Owen Pembs 44 C3
Trefil Bl Gwent 35 C5
Trefilan Ceredig 46 D4
Trefin Pembs 44 B3
Treflach Shrops 60 B2
Trefnanney Powys 60 C2
Trefnant Denb 72 B4
Trefonen Shrops 60 B2
Trefor Anglesey 82 C3
Trefor Gwyn 70 C4
Treforest Rhondda 34 F4
Trefriw Conwy 83 E7
Trefynwy = Monmouth Mon 36 C2
Tregadillett Corn 8 F4
Tregaian Anglesey 82 D4
Tregare Mon 35 C8
Tregaron Ceredig 47 D5
Tregarth Gwyn 83 E6
Tregeare Corn 8 F4
Tregeiriog Wrex 73 F5
Tregele Anglesey 82 B3
Tregidden Corn 3 D6
Treglemais Pembs 44 C3
Tregole Corn 8 E3
Tregonetha Corn 4 C4
Tregony Corn 3 B8
Tregoss Corn 4 C4
Tregoyd Powys 48 F4
Tregroes Ceredig 46 E3
Tregurrian Corn 4 C3
Tregynon Powys 59 E7
Trehafod Rhondda 34 E4
Treharris M Tydf 34 E4
Treherbert Rhondda 34 E3
Trekenner Corn 5 B8
Treknow Corn 8 F2
Trelan Corn 3 E6
Trelash Corn 8 E3
Trelassick Corn 4 D3
Trelawnyd Flint 72 B4
Trelech Carms 45 F4
Treleddyd-fawr Pembs 44 C2
Trelewis M Tydf 35 E5
Treligga Corn 8 F2
Trelights Corn 4 B4
Trelill Corn 4 B5
Trelissick Corn 3 C7
Trellech Mon 36 D2
Trelleck Grange Mon 36 D1
Trelogan Flint 85 F2
Trelystan Powys 60 D2
Tremadog Gwyn 71 C6
Tremail Corn 8 F3
Tremain Ceredig 45 E4
Tremaine Corn 8 F4
Tremar Corn 5 C7
Trematon Corn 5 D8
Tremeirchion Denb 72 B4
Trenance Corn 4 C3
Trenarren Corn 3 B9
Trench Telford 61 C6
Treneglos Corn 8 F4
Trenewan Corn 5 D6
Trent Dorset 12 C3
Trent Vale Stoke 75 E5
Trentham Stoke 75 E5
Trentishoe Devon 20 E5
Treoes V Glam 21 B8
Treorchy = Treorci Rhondda 34 E3
Treorci = Treorchy Rhondda 34 E3
Tre'r-ddôl Ceredig 58 E3
Trerulefoot Corn 5 D8
Tresaith Ceredig 45 D4
Tresawle Corn 3 B7
Trescott Staffs 62 E2
Trescowe Corn 2 C4
Tresham Glos 36 E4
Tresillian Corn 3 B7
Tresinwen Pembs 44 A4
Treskinnick Cross Corn 8 E4
Tresmeer Corn 8 F4
Tresparrett Corn 8 E3
Tresparrett Posts Corn 8 E3
Tressait Perth 133 C5
Tresta Shetland 160 D8
Tresta Shetland 160 H5
Treswell Notts 77 B7
Trethosa Corn 4 D4
Trethurgy Corn 4 D5
Tretio Pembs 44 C2
Tretire Hereford 36 B2
Tretower Powys 35 B5
Treuddyn Flint 73 D6
Trevalga Corn 8 F2
Trevalyn Wrex 73 D7
Trevanson Corn 4 B4
Trevarren Corn 4 C4
Trevarrian Corn 4 C3
Trevarrick Corn 3 B8
Trevaughan Carms 32 C2
Treveighan Corn 5 B5
Trevellas Corn 4 D2
Treverva Corn 3 C6
Trevethin Torf 35 D6
Trevigro Corn 5 C8
Treviscoe Corn 4 D4
Trevone Corn 4 B3
Trewarmett Corn 8 F2
Trewassa Corn 8 F3
Trewellard Corn 2 C2
Trewen Corn 8 F4
Trewennack Corn 3 D5
Trewern Powys 60 C2
Trewethern Corn 4 B5
Trewidland Corn 5 D7
Trewint Corn 8 E3
Trewint Corn 8 F4
Trewithian Corn 3 C7
Trewoofe Corn 2 D3
Trewoon Corn 4 D4
Treworga Corn 3 B7
Treworlas Corn 3 C7
Treyarnon Corn 4 B3
Treyford W Sus 16 C2
Trezaise Corn 4 D4
Triangle W Yorks 87 B8
Trickett's Cross Dorset 13 D8
Triffleton Pembs 44 C4
Trimdon Durham 111 F6
Trimdon Colliery Durham 111 F6
Trimdon Grange Durham 111 F6
Trimingham Norf 81 D8
Trimley Lower Street Suff 57 F6
Trimley St Martin Suff 57 F6
Trimley St Mary Suff 57 F6
Trimpley Worcs 50 B2
Trimsaran Carms 33 D5
Trimstone Devon 20 E3
Trinafour Perth 132 C4
Trinant Caerph 35 D6
Tring Herts 40 C2
Tring Wharf Herts 40 C2
Trinity Angus 135 C6
Trinity Jersey 17
Trisant Ceredig 47 B6
Trislaig Highld 130 B4
Trispen Corn 4 D3
Tritlington Northumb 117 E8
Trochry Perth 133 E6
Trodigal Argyll 143 F7
Troed-rhiwdalar Powys 47 D8
Troedyraur Ceredig 46 E2
Troedyrhiw M Tydf 34 D4
Tromode IoM 84 E3
Trondavoe Shetland 160 F5
Troon Corn 3 C5
Troon S Ayrs 118 F3
Trosaraidh W Isles 148 G2
Trossachs Hotel Stirling 126 D4
Troston Suff 56 B2
Trottiscliffe Kent 29 C7
Trotton W Sus 16 B2
Troutbeck Cumb 99 B5
Troutbeck Cumb 99 D6
Troutbeck Bridge Cumb 99 D6
Trow Green Glos 36 D2
Trowbridge Wilts 24 D3
Trowell Notts 76 F4
Trowle Common Wilts 24 D3
Trowley Bottom Herts 40 C3
Trows Borders 122 F2
Trowse Newton Norf 68 D5
Trudoxhill Som 24 E2
Trull Som 11 B7
Trumaisgearraidh W Isles 148 A3
Trumpan Highld 148 B7
Trumpet Hereford 49 F8
Trumpington Cambs 54 D5
Trunch Norf 81 D8
Trunnah Lancs 92 E3
Truro Corn 3 B7
Trusham Devon 10 F3
Trusley Derbys 76 F2
Trusthorpe Lincs 91 F9
Trysull Staffs 62 E2
Tubney Oxon 38 E4
Tuckenhay Devon 7 D6
Tuckhill Shrops 61 F7
Tuckingmill Corn 3 B5
Tuddenham Suff 55 B8
Tuddenham St Martin Suff 57 E5
Tudeley Kent 29 E7
Tudhoe Durham 111 F5
Tudorville Hereford 36 B2
Tudweiliog Gwyn 70 D3
Tuesley Sur 27 E7
Tuffley Glos 37 C5
Tufton Hants 26 E2
Tufton Pembs 32 B1
Tugby Leics 64 D4
Tugford Shrops 61 F5
Tullibardine Perth 127 C8
Tullibody Clack 127 E7
Tullich Argyll 125 D6
Tullich Highld 138 B2
Tullich Muir Highld 151 D10
Tulliemet Perth 133 D6
Tulloch Aberds 135 B7
Tulloch Aberds 153 E8
Tulloch Perth 128 B2
Tulloch Castle Highld 151 E8
Tullochgorm Argyll 125 F5
Tulloes Angus 135 E5
Tullybannocher Perth 127 B6
Tullybelton Perth 133 F7
Tullyfergus Perth 134 E2
Tullymurdoch Perth 134 D1
Tullynessle Aberds 140 C4
Tumble Carms 33 C6
Tumby Woodside Lincs 79 D5
Tummel Bridge Perth 132 D4
Tunga W Isles 155 D9
Tunstall E Yorks 97 F9
Tunstall Kent 30 C2
Tunstall Lancs 93 B6
Tunstall N Yorks 101 E7
Tunstall Norf 69 D7
Tunstall Stoke 75 D5
Tunstall Suff 57 D7
Tunstall T&W 111 D6
Tunstead Derbys 75 B8
Tunstead Gtr Man 87 D8
Tunstead Norf 81 E8
Tunworth Hants 26 E4
Tupsley Hereford 49 E7
Tupton Derbys 76 C3
Tur Langton Leics 64 E4
Turgis Green Hants 26 D4
Turin Angus 135 D5
Turkdean Glos 37 C8
Turleigh Wilts 24 C3
Turn Lancs 87 C6
Turnastone Hereford 49 F5
Turnberry S Ayrs 112 D2
Turnditch Derbys 76 E2
Turners Hill W Sus 28 F4
Turners Puddle Dorset 13 E6
Turnford Herts 41 D6
Turnhouse Edin 120 B4
Turnworth Dorset 13 D6
Turriff Aberds 153 C7
Turton Bottoms Blackburn 86 C5
Turves Cambs 66 E3
Turvey Bedford 53 D7
Turville Bucks 39 E7
Turville Heath Bucks 39 E7
Turweston Bucks 52 F4
Tushielaw Borders 115 C6
Tutbury Staffs 63 B6
Tutnall Worcs 50 B4
Tutshill Glos 36 E2
Tuttington Norf 81 E8
Tutts Clump W Berks 26 B3
Tuxford Notts 77 B7
Twatt Orkney 159 F3
Twatt Shetland 160 H5
Twechar E Dunb 119 B7
Tweedmouth Northumb 123 D5
Tweedsmuir Borders 114 B3
Twelve Heads Corn 3 B6
Twemlow Green Ches E 74 C4
Twenty Lincs 65 B8
Twerton Bath 24 C2
Twickenham London 28 B2
Twigworth Glos 37 B5
Twineham W Sus 17 C6
Twinhoe Bath 24 D2
Twinstead Essex 56 F2
Twinstead Green Essex 56 F2
Twiss Green Warr 86 E4
Twiston Lancs 93 E8
Twitchen Devon 21 F6
Twitchen Shrops 49 B5
Two Bridges Devon 6 B4
Two Dales Derbys 76 C2
Two Mills Ches W 73 B7
Twycross Leics 63 D7
Twyford Bucks 39 B6
Twyford Derbys 63 B7
Twyford Hants 15 B5
Twyford Leics 64 C4
Twyford Lincs 65 B6
Twyford Norf 81 E6
Twyford Wokingham 27 B5
Twyford Common Hereford 49 F7
Twyn-y-Sheriff Mon 35 D8
Twynholm Dumfries 106 D3
Twyning Glos 50 F3
Twyning Green Glos 50 F4
Twynllanan Carms 34 B1
Twynmynydd Carms 33 C7
Twywell Northants 53 B7
Ty-draw Conwy 83 F8
Ty-hen Carms 32 B4
Ty-hen Gwyn 70 D2
Ty-mawr Anglesey 82 C4
Ty Mawr Carms 46 E4
Ty Mawr Cwm Conwy 72 E3
Ty-nant Conwy 72 E3
Ty-nant Gwyn 59 B6
Ty-uchaf Powys 59 B7
Tyberton Hereford 49 F5
Tyburn W Mid 62 E5
Tycroes Carms 33 C7
Tycrwyn Powys 59 C8
Tydd Gote Lincs 66 C4
Tydd St Giles Cambs 66 C4
Tydd St Mary Lincs 66 C4
Tyddewi = St David's Pembs 44 C2
Tyddyn-mawr Gwyn 71 C6
Tye Green Essex 41 D7
Tye Green Essex 42 B3
Tye Green Essex 55 F6
Tyldesley Gtr Man 86 D4
Tyler Hill Kent 30 C5
Tylers Green Bucks 40 E2
Tylorstown Rhondda 34 E4
Tylwch Powys 59 F6
Tyn-y-celyn Wrex 73 F5
Tyn-y-coed Shrops 60 B2
Tyn-y-fedwen Powys 72 F5
Tyn-y-ffridd Powys 72 F5
Tyn-y-graig Powys 48 D2
Ty'n-y-groes Conwy 83 D7
Ty'n-y-maes Gwyn 83 E6
Tyn-y-pwll Anglesey 82 C4
Ty'n-yr-eithin Ceredig 47 C5
Tyncelyn Ceredig 46 C5
Tyndrum Stirling 131 F7
Tyne Tunnel T&W 111 C6
Tyneham Dorset 13 F6
Tynehead Midloth 121 D6
Tynemouth T&W 111 C6
Tynewydd Rhondda 34 E3
Tyninghame E Loth 122 B2
Tynron Dumfries 113 E8
Tynygongl Anglesey 82 C5
Tynygraig Ceredig 47 C5
Tŷ'r-felin-isaf Conwy 83 E8
Tyrie Aberds 153 B9
Tyringham M Keynes 53 E6
Tythecott Devon 9 C6
Tythegston Bridgend 21 B7
Tytherington Ches E 75 B6
Tytherington S Glos 36 F3
Tytherington Som 24 E2
Tytherington Wilts 24 E4
Tytherleigh Devon 11 D8
Tywardreath Corn 5 D5
Tywyn Conwy 83 D7
Tywyn Gwyn 58 D2

U

Uachdar W Isles 148 C2
Uags Highld 149 E12
Ubbeston Green Suff 57 B7
Ubley Bath 23 D7
Uckerby N Yorks 101 D7
Uckfield E Sus 17 B8
Uckington Glos 37 B6
Uddingston S Lanark 119 C6
Uddington S Lanark 119 F8
Udimore E Sus 19 D5
Udny Green Aberds 141 B7
Udny Station Aberds 141 B8
Udston S Lanark 119 D6
Udstonhead S Lanark 119 E7
Uffcott Wilts 25 B6
Uffculme Devon 11 C5
Uffington Lincs 65 D7
Uffington Oxon 38 F3
Uffington Shrops 60 C5
Ufford Pboro 65 D7
Ufford Suff 57 D6
Ufton Warks 51 C8
Ufton Nervet W Berks 26 C4
Ugadale Argyll 143 F8
Ugborough Devon 6 D4
Uggeshall Suff 69 F7
Ugglebarnby N Yorks 103 D6
Ughill S Yorks 88 E3
Ugley Essex 41 B8
Ugley Green Essex 41 B8
Ugthorpe N Yorks 103 C5
Uidh W Isles 148 J1
Uig Argyll 145 E10
Uig Highld 148 C6
Uig Highld 149 B8
Uigen W Isles 154 D5
Uigshader Highld 149 D9
Uisken Argyll 146 K6
Ulbster Highld 158 F5
Ulceby Lincs 79 B7
Ulceby N Lincs 90 C5
Ulceby Skitter N Lincs 90 C5
Ulcombe Kent 30 E2
Uldale Cumb 108 F2
Uley Glos 36 E4
Ulgham Northumb 117 E8
Ullapool Highld 150 B4
Ullenhall Warks 51 C6
Ullenwood Glos 37 C6
Ulleskelf N Yorks 95 E8
Ullesthorpe Leics 64 F2
Ulley S Yorks 89 F5
Ullingswick Hereford 49 E7
Ullinish Highld 149 E8
Ullock Cumb 98 B2
Ulnes Walton Lancs 86 C3
Ulpha Cumb 98 E3
Ulrome E Yorks 97 D7
Ulsta Shetland 160 E6
Ulva House Argyll 146 H7
Ulverston Cumb 92 B2
Ulwell Dorset 13 F8
Umberleigh Devon 9 B8
Unapool Highld 156 F5
Unasary W Isles 148 F2
Underbarrow Cumb 99 E6
Undercliffe W Yorks 94 F4
Underhoull Shetland 160 C7
Underriver Kent 29 D6
Underwood Notts 76 D4
Undy Mon 35 F8
Unifirth Shetland 160 H4
Union Cottage Aberds 141 E7
Union Mills IoM 84 E3
Union Street E Sus 18 B4
Unstone Derbys 76 B3
Unstone Green Derbys 76 B3
Unthank Cumb 108 F4
Unthank Cumb 109 E6
Unthank End Cumb 108 F4
Up Cerne Dorset 12 D4
Up Exe Devon 10 D4
Up Hatherley Glos 37 B6
Up Holland Lancs 86 D3
Up Marden W Sus 15 C8
Up Nately Hants 26 D4
Up Somborne Hants 25 F8
Up Sydling Dorset 12 D4
Upavon Wilts 25 D6
Upchurch Kent 30 C2
Upcott Hereford 48 D5
Upend Cambs 55 D7
Upgate Norf 68 C4
Uphall W Loth 120 B3
Uphall Station W Loth 120 B3
Upham Devon 10 D3
Upham Hants 15 B6
Uphampton Worcs 50 C3
Uphill N Som 22 D5
Uplawmoor E Renf 118 D4
Upleadon Glos 36 B4
Upleatham Redcar 102 C4
Uplees Kent 30 C3
Uploders Dorset 12 E3
Uplowman Devon 10 C5
Uplyme Devon 11 E8
Upminster London 42 F1
Upnor Medway 29 B8
Upottery Devon 11 D7
Upper Affcot Shrops 60 F4
Upper Ardchronie Highld 151 C9
Upper Arley Worcs 61 F7
Upper Arncott Oxon 39 C6
Upper Astrop Northants 52 F3
Upper Badcall Highld 156 E4
Upper Basildon W Berks 26 B3
Upper Beeding W Sus 17 C5
Upper Benefield Northants 65 F6
Upper Bighouse Highld 157 D11
Upper Boddington Northants 52 D2
Upper Borth Ceredig 58 F3
Upper Boyndlie Aberds 153 B9
Upper Brailes Warks 51 F8
Upper Breakish Highld 149 F11
Upper Breinton Hereford 49 E6
Upper Broadheath Worcs 50 D3
Upper Broughton Notts 64 B3
Upper Bucklebury W Berks 26 C3
Upper Burnhaugh Aberds 141 E7
Upper Caldecote C Beds 54 E2
Upper Catesby Northants 52 D3
Upper Chapel Powys 48 E2
Upper Church Village Rhondda 34 F4
Upper Chute Wilts 25 D7
Upper Clatford Hants 25 E8
Upper Clynnog Gwyn 71 C5
Upper Cumberworth W Yorks 88 D3
Upper Cwm-twrch Powys 34 C1
Upper Cwmbran Torf 35 E6
Upper Dallachy Moray 152 B3
Upper Dean Bedford 53 C8
Upper Denby W Yorks 88 D3
Upper Denton Cumb 109 C6
Upper Derraid Highld 151 H13
Upper Dicker E Sus 18 E2
Upper Dovercourt Essex 57 F6
Upper Druimfin Argyll 147 F8
Upper Dunsforth N Yorks 95 C7
Upper Eathie Highld 151 E10
Upper Elkstone Staffs 75 D7
Upper End Derbys 75 B7
Upper Farringdon Hants 26 F5
Upper Framilode Glos 36 C4
Upper Glenfintaig Highld 137 F5
Upper Gornal W Mid 62 E3
Upper Gravenhurst C Beds 54 F2
Upper Green Mon 35 C7
Upper Green W Berks 25 C8
Upper Grove Common Hereford 36 B2
Upper Hackney Derbys 76 C2
Upper Hale Sur 27 E6
Upper Halistra Highld 148 C7
Upper Halling Medway 29 C7
Upper Hambleton Rutland 65 D6
Upper Hardres Court Kent 31 D5
Upper Hartfield E Sus 29 F5
Upper Haugh S Yorks 88 E5
Upper Heath Shrops 61 F5
Upper Hellesdon Norf 68 C5
Upper Helmsley N Yorks 96 D2
Upper Hergest Hereford 48 D4
Upper Heyford Northants 52 D4
Upper Heyford Oxon 38 B4
Upper Hill Hereford 49 D6
Upper Hopton W Yorks 88 C2
Upper Horsebridge E Sus 18 D2
Upper Hulme Staffs 75 C7
Upper Inglesham Swindon 38 E2
Upper Inverbrough Highld 151 H11
Upper Killay Swansea 33 E6
Upper Knockando Moray 152 D1
Upper Lambourn W Berks 38 F3
Upper Leigh Staffs 75 F7
Upper Lenie Highld 137 B8
Upper Lochton Aberds 141 E5
Upper Longdon Staffs 62 C4
Upper Lybster Highld 158 G4
Upper Lydbrook Glos 36 C3
Upper Maes-coed Hereford 48 F5
Upper Midway Derbys 63 B6
Upper Milovaig Highld 148 D6
Upper Minety Wilts 37 E7
Upper Mitton Worcs 50 B3
Upper North Dean Bucks 39 E8
Upper Obney Perth 133 F7
Upper Ollach Highld 149 E10
Upper Padley Derbys 76 B2
Upper Pollicott Bucks 39 C7
Upper Poppleton York 95 D8
Upper Quinton Warks 51 E6
Upper Ratley Hants 14 B4
Upper Rissington Glos 38 C2
Upper Rochford Worcs 49 C8
Upper Sandaig Highld 149 G12
Upper Sanday Orkney 159 H6
Upper Sapey Hereford 49 C8
Upper Saxondale Notts 77 F6
Upper Seagry Wilts 37 F6
Upper Shelton C Beds 53 E7
Upper Sheringham Norf 81 C7
Upper Skelmorlie N Ayrs 118 C2
Upper Slaughter Glos 38 B1
Upper Soudley Glos 36 C3
Upper Stondon C Beds 54 F2
Upper Stowe Northants 52 D4
Upper Stratton Swindon 38 F1
Upper Street Hants 14 C2
Upper Street Norf 69 C6
Upper Street Norf 69 C6
Upper Street Suff 56 F5
Upper Strensham Worcs 50 F4
Upper Sundon C Beds 40 B3
Upper Swell Glos 38 B1
Upper Tean Staffs 75 F7
Upper Tillyrie Perth 128 D3
Upper Tooting London 28 B3
Upper Tote Highld 149 C10
Upper Town N Som 23 C7
Upper Treverward Shrops 48 B4
Upper Tysoe Warks 51 E8
Upper Upham Wilts 25 B7
Upper Wardington Oxon 52 E2
Upper Weald M Keynes 53 F5
Upper Weedon Northants 52 D4
Upper Wield Hants 26 F4
Upper Winchendon Bucks 39 C7
Upper Witton W Mid 62 E4
Upper Woodend Aberds 141 C5
Upper Woodford Wilts 25 F6
Upper Wootton Hants 26 D3
Upper Wyche Hereford 50 E2
Upperby Cumb 108 D4
Uppermill Gtr Man 87 D7
Uppersound Shetland 160 J6
Upperthong W Yorks 88 D2
Upperthorpe N Lincs 89 D8
Upperton W Sus 16 B3
Uppertown Derbys 76 C3
Uppertown Highld 158 C5
Uppertown Orkney 159 J5
Uppingham Rutland 65 E5
Uppington Shrops 61 D6
Upsall N Yorks 102 F2
Upshire Essex 41 D7
Upstreet Kent 31 C6
Upthorpe Suff 56 B3
Upton Cambs 54 B2
Upton Ches W 73 C8
Upton Corn 8 D4
Upton Dorset 12 F5
Upton Dorset 13 E7
Upton Hants 14 C4
Upton Hants 25 D8
Upton Leics 63 E7
Upton Lincs 90 F2
Upton Mers 85 F3
Upton Norf 69 C6
Upton Northants 52 C5
Upton Notts 77 B7
Upton Notts 77 D7
Upton Oxon 39 F5
Upton Pboro 65 D8
Upton Slough 27 B7
Upton Som 10 B4
Upton W Yorks 89 C5
Upton Bishop Hereford 36 B3
Upton Cheyney S Glos 23 C8
Upton Cressett Shrops 61 E6
Upton Cross Corn 5 B7
Upton Grey Hants 26 E4
Upton Hellions Devon 10 D3
Upton Lovell Wilts 24 E4
Upton Magna Shrops 61 C5
Upton Noble Som 24 F2
Upton Pyne Devon 10 E4
Upton Scudamore Wilts 24 E3
Upton St Leonard's Glos 37 C5
Upton Snodsbury Worcs 50 D4
Upton upon Severn Worcs 50 E3
Upton Warren Worcs 50 C4
Upwaltham W Sus 16 C3
Upware Cambs 55 B6
Upwell Norf 66 D4
Upwey Dorset 12 F4
Upwood Cambs 66 F2
Uradale Shetland 160 K6
Urafirth Shetland 160 F5
Urchfont Wilts 24 D5
Urdimarsh Hereford 49 E7
Ure Shetland 160 F4
Ure Bank N Yorks 95 B6
Urgha W Isles 154 H6
Urishay Common Hereford 48 F5
Urlay Nook Stockton 102 C1
Urmston Gtr Man 87 E5
Urpeth Durham 110 D5
Urquhart Highld 151 F8
Urquhart Moray 152 B2
Urra N Yorks 102 D3
Urray Highld 151 F8
Ushaw Moor Durham 110 E5
Usk = Brynbuga Mon 35 D7
Usselby Lincs 90 E4
Usworth T&W 111 D6
Utkinton Ches W 74 C2
Utley W Yorks 94 E3
Uton Devon 10 E3
Utterby Lincs 91 E7
Uttoxeter Staffs 75 F7
Uwchmynydd Gwyn 70 E2
Uxbridge London 40 F3
Uyeasound Shetland 160 C7
Uzmaston Pembs 44 D4

V

Valley Anglesey 82 D2
Valley Truckle Corn 8 F2
Valleyfield Dumfries 106 D3
Valsgarth Shetland 160 B8
Valtos Highld 149 B10
Van Powys 59 F6
Vange Essex 42 F3
Varteg Torf 35 D6
Vatten Highld 149 D7
Vaul Argyll 146 G3
Vaynor M Tydf 34 C4
Veensgarth Shetland 160 J6
Velindre Powys 48 F3
Vellow Som 22 F2
Veness Orkney 159 F6
Venn Green Devon 9 C5
Venn Ottery Devon 11 E5
Vennington Shrops 60 D3
Venny Tedburn Devon 10 E3
Ventnor IoW 15 G6
Vernham Dean Hants 25 D8
Vernham Street Hants 25 D8
Vernolds Common Shrops 60 F4
Verwood Dorset 13 D8
Veryan Corn 3 C8
Vicarage Devon 11 F7
Vickerstown Cumb 92 C1
Victoria Corn 4 C4
Victoria S Yorks 88 D2
Vidlin Shetland 160 G6
Viewpark N Lanark 119 C7
Vigo Village Kent 29 C7
Vinehall Street E Sus 18 C4
Vine's Cross E Sus 18 D2
Viney Hill Glos 36 D3
Virginia Water Sur 27 C8
Virginstow Devon 9 E5
Vobster Som 24 E2
Voe Shetland 160 E5
Voe Shetland 160 G6
Vowchurch Hereford 49 F5
Voxter Shetland 160 F5
Voy Orkney 159 G3

W

Wackerfield Durham 101 B6
Wacton Norf 68 E4
Wadbister Shetland 160 J6
Wadborough Worcs 50 E4
Waddesdon Bucks 39 C7
Waddingham Lincs 90 E3
Waddington Lancs 93 E7
Waddington Lincs 78 C2
Wadebridge Corn 4 B4
Wadeford Som 11 C8
Wadenhoe Northants 65 F7
Wadesmill Herts 41 C6
Wadhurst E Sus 18 B3
Wadshelf Derbys 76 B3
Wadsley S Yorks 88 E4
Wadsley Bridge S Yorks 88 E4
Wadworth S Yorks 89 E6
Waen Denb 72 C3
Waen Denb 72 C5
Waen Fach Powys 60 C2
Waen Goleugoed Denb 72 B4
Wag Highld 157 G13
Wainfleet All Saints Lincs 79 D7
Wainfleet Bank Lincs 79 D7
Wainfleet St Mary Lincs 79 D8
Wainfleet Tofts Lincs 79 D7
Wainhouse Corner Corn 8 E3
Wainscott Medway 29 B8
Wainstalls W Yorks 87 B8
Waitby Cumb 100 D2
Waithe Lincs 91 D6
Wake Lady Green N Yorks 102 E4
Wakefield W Yorks 88 B4
Wakerley Northants 65 E6
Wakes Colne Essex 42 B4
Walberswick Suff 57 B8
Walberton W Sus 16 D3
Walbottle T&W 110 C4
Walcot Lincs 78 F3
Walcot N Lincs 90 B2
Walcot Shrops 60 F3
Walcot Swindon 38 F1
Walcot Telford 61 C5
Walcot Green Norf 68 F4
Walcote Leics 64 F2
Walcote Warks 51 D6
Walcott Lincs 78 D4
Walcott Norf 69 A6
Walden N Yorks 101 F5
Walden Head N Yorks 100 F4
Walden Stubbs N Yorks 89 C6
Waldersey Cambs 66 D4
Walderslade Medway 29 C8
Walderton W Sus 15 C8
Walditch Dorset 12 E2
Waldley Derbys 75 F8
Waldridge Durham 111 D5
Waldringfield Suff 57 E6
Waldringfield Heath Suff 57 E6
Waldron E Sus 18 D2
Wales S Yorks 89 F5
Walesby Lincs 90 E5
Walesby Notts 77 B6
Walford Hereford 36 B2
Walford Hereford 49 B5
Walford Shrops 60 B4

Walford Heath Shrops 60 C4
Walgherton Ches E 74 E3
Walgrave Northants 53 B6
Walhampton Hants 14 E4
Walk Mill Lancs 93 F8
Walkden Gtr Man 86 D5
Walker T&W 111 C5
Walker Barn Ches E 75 B6
Walker Fold Lancs 93 E6
Walkerburn Borders 121 F6
Walkeringham Notts 89 E8
Walkerith Lincs 89 E8
Walkern Herts 41 B5
Walker's Green Hereford 49 E7
Walkerville N Yorks 101 E7
Walkford Dorset 14 E3
Walkhampton Devon 6 C3
Walkington E Yorks 97 F5
Walkley S Yorks 88 F4
Wall Northumb 110 C2
Wall Staffs 62 D5
Wall Bank Shrops 60 E5
Wall Heath W Mid 62 F2
Wall under Heywood Shrops 60 E5
Wallaceton Dumfries 113 F8
Wallacetown S Ayrs 112 B3
Wallacetown S Ayrs 112 D2
Wallands Park E Sus 17 C8
Wallasey Mers 85 E4
Wallcrouch E Sus 18 B3
Wallingford Oxon 39 F6
Wallington Hants 15 D6
Wallington Herts 54 F3
Wallington London 28 C3
Wallis Pembs 32 B1
Walliswood Sur 28 F2
Walls Shetland 160 J4
Wallsend T&W 111 C5
Wallston V Glam 22 B3
Wallyford E Loth 121 B6
Walmer Kent 31 D7
Walmer Bridge Lancs 86 B2
Walmersley Gtr Man 87 C6
Walmley W Mid 62 E5
Walpole Suff 57 B7
Walpole Cross Keys Norf 66 C5
Walpole Highway Norf 66 C5
Walpole Marsh Norf 66 C4
Walpole St Andrew Norf 66 C5
Walpole St Peter Norf 66 C5
Walsall W Mid 62 E4
Walsall Wood W Mid 62 D4
Walsden W Yorks 87 B7
Walsgrave on Sowe W Mid 63 F7
Walsham le Willows Suff 56 B3
Walshaw Gtr Man 87 C5
Walshford N Yorks 95 D7
Walsoken Cambs 66 C4
Walston S Lanark 120 E3
Walsworth Herts 54 F3
Walters Ash Bucks 39 E8
Walterston V Glam 22 B2
Walterstone Hereford 35 B7
Waltham Kent 30 E5
Waltham NE Lincs 91 D6
Waltham Abbey Essex 41 D6
Waltham Chase Hants 15 C6
Waltham Cross Herts 41 D6
Waltham on the Wolds Leics 64 B5
Waltham St Lawrence Windsor 27 B6
Walthamstow London 41 F6
Walton Cumb 108 C5
Walton Derbys 76 C3
Walton Leics 64 F2
Walton M Keynes 53 F6
Walton Mers 85 E4
Walton Pboro 65 D8
Walton Powys 48 D4
Walton Som 23 F6
Walton Staffs 75 F5
Walton Suff 57 F6
Walton Telford 61 C5
Walton W Yorks 88 C4
Walton W Yorks 95 E7
Walton Warks 51 D7
Walton Cardiff Glos 50 F4
Walton East Pembs 32 B1
Walton-in-Gordano N Som 23 B6
Walton-le-Dale Lancs 86 B3
Walton-on-Thames Sur 28 C2
Walton on the Hill Staffs 62 B3
Walton on the Hill Sur 28 D3
Walton-on-the-Naze Essex 43 B8
Walton on the Wolds Leics 64 C2
Walton-on-Trent Derbys 63 C6
Walton West Pembs 44 D3
Walwen Flint 73 B6
Walwick Northumb 110 B2
Walworth Darl 101 C7
Walworth Gate Darl 101 B7
Walwyn's Castle Pembs 44 D3
Wambrook Som 11 D7
Wanborough Sur 27 E7
Wanborough Swindon 38 F2
Wandsworth London 28 B3
Wangford Suff 57 B8
Wanlockhead Dumfries 113 C8
Wansford E Yorks 97 D6
Wansford Pboro 65 E7
Wanstead London 41 F7
Wanstrow Som 24 E2
Wanswell Glos 36 D3
Wantage Oxon 38 F3
Wapley S Glos 24 B2
Wappenbury Warks 51 C8
Wappenham Northants 52 E4
Warbleton E Sus 18 D3
Warblington Hants 15 D8
Warborough Oxon 39 E5
Warboys Cambs 66 F3
Warbreck Blackpool 92 F3
Warbstow Corn 8 E4
Warburton Gtr Man 86 F5
Warcop Cumb 100 C2
Ward End W Mid 62 F5
Ward Green Suff 56 C4
Warden Kent 30 B4
Warden Northumb 110 C2
Wardhill Orkney 159 F7
Wardington Oxon 52 E2
Wardlaw Borders 115 C5
Wardle Ches E 74 D3
Wardle Gtr Man 87 C7
Wardley Rutland 64 D5
Wardlow Derbys 75 B8
Wardy Hill Cambs 66 F4
Ware Herts 41 C6
Ware Kent 31 C6
Wareham Dorset 13 F7
Warehorne Kent 19 B6
Waren Mill Northumb 123 F7
Warenford Northumb 117 B7
Warenton Northumb 123 F7
Wareside Herts 41 C6
Waresley Cambs 54 D3
Waresley Worcs 50 B3
Warfield Brack 27 B6
Warfleet Devon 7 D6
Wargrave Wokingham 27 B5
Warham Norf 80 C5
Warhill Gtr Man 87 E7
Wark Northumb 109 B8
Wark Northumb 122 F4
Warkleigh Devon 9 B8
Warkton Northants 53 B6
Warkworth Northants 52 E2
Warkworth Northumb 117 D8
Warlaby N Yorks 101 E8
Warland W Yorks 87 B7
Warleggan Corn 5 C6
Warlingham Sur 28 D4
Warmfield W Yorks 88 B4
Warmingham Ches E 74 C4
Warmington Northants 65 E7
Warmington Warks 52 E2
Warminster Wilts 24 E3
Warmlake Kent 30 D2
Warmley S Glos 23 B8
Warmley Tower S Glos 23 B8
Warmonds Hill Northants 53 C7
Warmsworth S Yorks 89 D6
Warmwell Dorset 13 F5
Warndon Worcs 50 D3
Warnford Hants 15 B7
Warnham W Sus 28 F2
Warninglid W Sus 17 B6
Warren Ches E 75 B5
Warren Pembs 44 F4
Warren Heath Suff 57 E6
Warren Row Windsor 39 F8
Warren Street Kent 30 D3
Warrington M Keynes 53 D6
Warrington Warr 86 F4
Warsash Hants 15 D5
Warslow Staffs 75 D7
Warter E Yorks 96 D4
Warthermarske N Yorks 94 B5
Warthill N Yorks 96 D2
Wartling E Sus 18 E3
Wartnaby Leics 64 B4
Warton Lancs 86 B2
Warton Lancs 92 B4
Warton Northumb 117 D6
Warton Warks 63 D6
Warwick Warks 51 C7
Warwick Bridge Cumb 108 D4
Warwick on Eden Cumb 108 D4
Wasbister Orkney 159 E4
Wasdale Head Cumb 98 D3
Wash Common W Berks 26 C2
Washaway Corn 4 C5
Washbourne Devon 7 D5
Washfield Devon 10 C4
Washfold N Yorks 101 D5
Washford Som 22 E2
Washford Pyne Devon 10 C3
Washingborough Lincs 78 B3
Washington T&W 111 D6
Washington W Sus 16 C5
Wasing W Berks 26 C3
Waskerley Durham 110 E3
Wasperton Warks 51 D7
Wasps Nest Lincs 78 C3
Wass N Yorks 95 B8
Watchet Som 22 E2
Watchfield Oxon 38 E2
Watchfield Som 22 E5
Watchgate Cumb 99 E7
Watchhill Cumb 107 E8
Watcombe Torbay 7 C7
Watendlath Cumb 98 C4
Water Devon 10 F2
Water Lancs 87 B6
Water End E Yorks 96 F3
Water End Herts 40 C3
Water End Herts 41 D5
Water Newton Cambs 65 E8
Water Orton Warks 63 E5
Water Stratford Bucks 52 F4
Water Yeat Cumb 98 F4
Waterbeach Cambs 55 C5
Waterbeck Dumfries 108 B2
Waterden Norf 80 D4
Waterfall Staffs 75 D7
Waterfoot E Renf 119 D5
Waterfoot Lancs 87 B6
Waterford Hants 14 E4
Waterford Herts 41 C6
Waterhead Cumb 99 D5
Waterhead Dumfries 114 E4
Waterheads Borders 120 D5
Waterhouses Durham 110 E4
Waterhouses Staffs 75 D7
Wateringbury Kent 29 D7
Waterloo Gtr Man 87 D7
Waterloo Highld 149 F11
Waterloo Mers 85 E4
Waterloo N Lanark 119 D8
Waterloo Norf 68 C5
Waterloo Perth 133 F7
Waterloo Poole 13 E8
Waterloo Shrops 74 F2
Waterloo Port Gwyn 82 E4
Waterlooville Hants 15 D7
Watermeetings S Lanark 114 C2
Watermillock Cumb 99 B6
Waterperry Oxon 39 D6
Waterrow Som 11 B5
Water's Nook Gtr Man 86 D4
Waters Upton Telford 61 C6
Watersfield W Sus 16 C4
Waterside Aberds 141 B9
Waterside Blackburn 86 B5
Waterside Cumb 108 E2
Waterside E Ayrs 112 D4
Waterside E Ayrs 118 E4
Waterside E Dunb 119 B6
Waterside E Renf 118 D5
Waterstock Oxon 39 D6
Waterston Pembs 44 E4
Watford Herts 40 E4
Watford Northants 52 C4
Watford Gap Staffs 62 D5
Wath N Yorks 94 C4
Wath N Yorks 95 B6
Wath N Yorks 96 B2
Wath Brow Cumb 98 C2
Wath upon Dearne S Yorks 88 D5
Watlington Norf 67 C6
Watlington Oxon 39 E6
Watnall Notts 76 E5
Watten Highld 158 E4
Wattisfield Suff 56 B4
Wattisham Suff 56 D4
Wattlesborough Heath Shrops 60 C3
Watton E Yorks 97 D6
Watton Norf 68 D2
Watton at Stone Herts 41 C6
Wattston N Lanark 119 B7
Wattstown Rhondda 34 E4
Wauchan Highld 136 F2
Waulkmill Lodge Orkney 159 H4
Waun Powys 59 D5
Waun-y-clyn Carms 33 D5
Waunarlwydd Swansea 33 E7
Waunclunda Carms 47 F5
Waunfawr Gwyn 82 F5
Waungron Swansea 33 D6
Waunlwyd Bl Gwent 35 D5
Wavendon M Keynes 53 F7
Waverbridge Cumb 108 E2
Waverton Ches W 73 C8
Waverton Cumb 108 E2
Wavertree Mers 85 F4
Wawne E Yorks 97 F6
Waxham Norf 69 B7
Waxholme E Yorks 91 B7
Way Kent 31 C7
Way Village Devon 10 C3
Wayfield Medway 29 C8
Wayford Som 12 D2
Waymills Shrops 74 E2
Wayne Green Mon 35 C8
Wdig = Goodwick Pembs 44 B4
Weachyburn Aberds 153 C6
Weald Oxon 38 D3
Wealdstone London 40 F4
Weardley W Yorks 95 E5
Weare Som 23 D6
Weare Giffard Devon 9 B6
Wearhead Durham 109 F8
Weasdale Cumb 100 D1
Weasenham All Saints Norf 80 E4
Weasenham St Peter Norf 80 E4
Weatherhill Sur 28 E4
Weaverham Ches W 74 B3
Weaverthorpe N Yorks 97 B5
Webheath Worcs 50 C5
Wedderlairs Aberds 153 E8
Wedderlie Borders 122 D2
Weddington Warks 63 E7
Wedhampton Wilts 25 D5
Wedmore Som 23 E6
Wednesbury W Mid 62 E3
Wednesfield W Mid 62 D3
Weedon Bucks 39 C8
Weedon Bec Northants 52 D4
Weedon Lois Northants 52 E4
Weeford Staffs 62 D5
Week Devon 10 C2
Week St Mary Corn 8 E4
Weeke Hants 26 F2
Weekley Northants 65 F5
Weel E Yorks 97 F6
Weeley Essex 43 B7
Weeley Heath Essex 43 B7
Weem Perth 133 E5
Weeping Cross Staffs 62 B3
Weethley Gate Warks 51 D5
Weeting Norf 67 F7
Weeton E Yorks 91 B7
Weeton Lancs 92 F3
Weeton N Yorks 95 E5
Weetwood Hall Northumb 117 B6
Weir Lancs 87 B6
Weir Quay Devon 6 C2
Welborne Norf 68 D3
Welbourn Lincs 78 D2
Welburn N Yorks 96 C3
Welburn N Yorks 102 F4
Welbury N Yorks 102 D1
Welby Lincs 78 F2
Welches Dam Cambs 66 F4
Welcombe Devon 8 C4
Weld Bank Lancs 86 C3
Weldon Northumb 117 E7
Welford Northants 64 F3
Welford W Berks 26 B2
Welford-on-Avon Warks 51 D6
Welham Leics 64 E4
Welham Notts 89 F8
Welham Green Herts 41 D5
Well Hants 27 E5
Well Lincs 79 B7
Well N Yorks 101 F7
Well End Bucks 40 F1
Well Heads W Yorks 94 F3
Well Hill Kent 29 C5
Well Town Devon 10 D4
Welland Worcs 50 E2
Wellbank Angus 134 F4
Welldale Dumfries 107 C8
Wellesbourne Warks 51 D7
Welling London 29 B5
Wellingborough Northants 53 C6
Wellingham Norf 80 E4
Wellingore Lincs 78 D2
Wellington Cumb 98 D2
Wellington Hereford 49 E6
Wellington Som 11 B6
Wellington Telford 61 C6
Wellington Heath Hereford 50 E2
Wellington Hill W Yorks 95 F6
Wellow Bath 24 D2
Wellow IoW 14 F4
Wellow Notts 77 C6
Wellpond Green Herts 41 B7
Wells Som 23 E7
Wells Green Ches E 74 D3
Wells-Next-The-Sea Norf 80 C5
Wellsborough Leics 63 D7
Wellswood Torbay 7 C7
Wellwood Fife 128 F2
Welney Norf 66 E5
Welsh Bicknor Hereford 36 C2
Welsh End Shrops 74 F2
Welsh Frankton Shrops 73 F7
Welsh Hook Pembs 44 C4
Welsh Newton Hereford 36 C1
Welsh St Donats V Glam 22 B2
Welshampton Shrops 73 F8
Welshpool = Y Trallwng Powys 60 D2
Welton Cumb 108 E3
Welton E Yorks 90 B3
Welton Lincs 78 B3
Welton Northants 52 C3
Welton Hill Lincs 90 F4
Welton le Marsh Lincs 79 C7
Welton le Wold Lincs 91 F6
Welwick E Yorks 91 B7
Welwyn Herts 41 C5
Welwyn Garden City Herts 41 C5
Wem Shrops 60 B5
Wembdon Som 22 F4
Wembley London 40 F4
Wembury Devon 6 E3
Wembworthy Devon 9 D8
Wemyss Bay Involyd 118 C1
Wenallt Ceredig 47 B5
Wenallt Gwyn 72 E3
Wendens Ambo Essex 55 F6
Wendlebury Oxon 39 C5
Wendling Norf 68 C2
Wendover Bucks 40 D1
Wendron Corn 3 C5
Wendy Cambs 54 E4
Wenfordbridge Corn 5 B5
Wenhaston Suff 57 B8
Wennington Cambs 54 B3
Wennington Lancs 93 B6
Wennington London 41 F8
Wensley Derbys 76 C2
Wensley N Yorks 101 F5
Wentbridge W Yorks 89 C5
Wentnor Shrops 60 E3
Wentworth Cambs 55 B5
Wentworth S Yorks 88 E4
Wenvoe V Glam 22 B3
Weobley Hereford 49 D6
Weobley Marsh Hereford 49 D6
Wereham Norf 67 D6
Wergs W Mid 62 D2
Wern Powys 59 C6
Wern Powys 60 C2
Wernffrwd Swansea 33 E6
Wernyrheolydd Mon 35 C7
Werrington Corn 8 F5
Werrington Pboro 65 D8
Werrington Staffs 75 E6
Wervin Ches W 73 B8
Wesham Lancs 92 F4
Wessington Derbys 76 D3
West Acre Norf 67 C7
West Adderbury Oxon 52 F2
West Allerdean Northumb 123 E5
West Alvington Devon 6 E5
West Amesbury Wilts 25 E6
West Anstey Devon 10 B3
West Ashby Lincs 79 B5
West Ashling W Sus 16 D2
West Ashton Wilts 24 D3
West Auckland Durham 101 B6
West Ayton N Yorks 103 F7
West Bagborough Som 22 F3
West Barkwith Lincs 91 F5
West Barnby N Yorks 103 C6
West Barns E Loth 122 B2
West Barsham Norf 80 D5
West Bay Dorset 12 E2
West Beckham Norf 81 D7
West Bedfont Sur 27 B8
West Benhar N Lanark 119 C8
West Bergholt Essex 43 B5
West Bexington Dorset 12 F3
West Bilney Norf 67 C7
West Blatchington Brighton 17 D6
West Bowling W Yorks 94 F4
West Bradford Lancs 93 E7
West Bradley Som 23 F7
West Bretton W Yorks 88 C3
West Bridgford Notts 77 F5
West Bromwich W Mid 62 E4
West Buckland Devon 21 F5
West Buckland Som 11 B6
West Burrafirth Shetland 160 H4
West Burton N Yorks 101 F5
West Burton W Sus 16 C3
West Butterwick N Lincs 90 D2
West Byfleet Sur 27 C8
West Caister Norf 69 C8
West Calder W Loth 120 C3
West Camel Som 12 B3
West Challow Oxon 38 F3
West Chelborough Dorset 12 D3
West Chevington Northumb 117 E8
West Chiltington W Sus 16 C4
West Chiltington Common W Sus 16 C4
West Chinnock Som 12 C2
West Chisenbury Wilts 25 D6
West Clandon Sur 27 D8
West Cliffe Kent 31 E7
West Clyne Highld 157 J11
West Clyth Highld 158 G4
West Coker Som 12 C3
West Compton Dorset 12 E3
West Compton Som 23 E7
West Cowick E Yorks 89 B7
West Cranmore Som 23 E8
West Cross Swansea 33 F7
West Cullery Aberds 141 D6
West Curry Corn 8 E4
West Curthwaite Cumb 108 E3
West Darlochan Argyll 143 F7
West Dean W Sus 16 C2
West Dean Wilts 14 B3
West Deeping Lincs 65 D8
West Derby Mers 85 E4
West Dereham Norf 67 D6
West Didsbury Gtr Man 87 E6
West Ditchburn Northumb 117 B7
West Down Devon 20 E4
West Drayton London 27 B8
West Drayton Notts 77 B7
West Ella E Yorks 90 B4
West End Bedford 53 D7
West End E Yorks 96 F5
West End E Yorks 97 F7
West End Hants 15 C5
West End Lancs 86 B5
West End N Som 23 C6
West End N Yorks 94 D4
West End Norf 68 D2
West End Norf 69 C8
West End Oxon 38 D4
West End S Lanark 120 E2
West End S Yorks 89 D7
West End Suff 69 F7
West End Sur 27 C7
West End W Sus 17 C6
West End Wilts 13 B7
West End Wilts 24 B4
West End Green Hants 26 C4
West Farleigh Kent 29 D8
West Felton Shrops 60 B3
West Fenton E Loth 129 F6
West Ferry Dundee 134 F4
West Firle E Sus 17 D8
West Ginge Oxon 38 F4
West Grafton Wilts 25 C7
West Green Hants 26 D5
West Greenskares Aberds 153 B7
West Grimstead Wilts 14 B3
West Grinstead W Sus 17 B5
West Haddlesey N Yorks 89 B6
West Haddon Northants 52 B4
West Hagbourne Oxon 39 F5
West Hagley Worcs 62 F3
West Hall Cumb 109 C5
West Hallam Derbys 76 E4
West Halton N Lincs 90 B3
West Ham London 41 F7
West Handley Derbys 76 B3
West Hanney Oxon 38 E4
West Hanningfield Essex 42 E3
West Hardwick W Yorks 88 C5
West Harnham Wilts 14 B2
West Harptree Bath 23 D7
West Hatch Som 11 B7
West Head Norf 67 D5
West Heath Ches E 74 C5
West Heath Hants 26 D3
West Heath Hants 27 D6
West Helmsdale Highld 157 H13
West Hendred Oxon 38 F4
West Heslerton N Yorks 96 B5
West Hill Devon 11 E5
West Hill E Yorks 97 C7
West Hill N Som 23 B6
West Hoathly W Sus 28 F4
West Holme Dorset 13 F6
West Horndon Essex 42 F2
West Horrington Som 23 E7
West Horsley Sur 27 D8
West Horton Northumb 123 F6
West Hougham Kent 31 E6
West Houlland Shetland 160 H4
West-houses Derbys 76 D4
West Huntington York 96 D2
West Hythe Kent 19 B8
West Ilsley W Berks 38 F4
West Itchenor W Sus 15 D8
West Keal Lincs 79 C6
West Kennett Wilts 25 C6
West Kilbride N Ayrs 118 E2
West Kingsdown Kent 29 C6
West Kington Wilts 24 B3
West Kinharrachie Aberds 153 E9
West Kirby Mers 85 F3
West Knapton N Yorks 96 B4
West Knighton Dorset 12 F5
West Knoyle Wilts 24 F3
West Kyloe Northumb 123 E6
West Lambrook Som 12 C2
West Langdon Kent 31 E7
West Langwell Highld 157 J9
West Lavington W Sus 16 B2
West Lavington Wilts 24 D5
West Layton N Yorks 101 D6
West Lea Durham 111 E7
West Leake Notts 64 B2
West Learmouth Northumb 122 F4
West Leigh Devon 9 D8
West Lexham Norf 67 C8
West Lilling N Yorks 96 C2
West Linton Borders 120 D4
West Liss Hants 15 B8
West Littleton S Glos 24 B2
West Looe Corn 5 D7
West Luccombe Som 21 E7
West Lulworth Dorset 13 F6
West Lutton N Yorks 96 C5
West Lydford Som 23 F7
West Lyng Som 11 B8
West Lynn Norf 67 B6
West Malling Kent 29 D7
West Malvern Worcs 50 E2
West Marden W Sus 15 C8
West Marina E Sus 18 E4
West Markham Notts 77 B7
West Marsh NE Lincs 91 C6
West Marton N Yorks 93 D8
West Meon Hants 15 B7
West Mersea Essex 43 C6
West Milton Dorset 12 E3
West Minster Kent 30 B3
West Molesey Sur 28 C2
West Monkton Som 11 B7
West Moors Dorset 13 D8
West Morriston Borders 122 E2
West Muir Angus 135 C5
West Ness N Yorks 96 B2
West Newham Northumb 110 B3
West Newton E Yorks 97 F7
West Newton Norf 67 B6
West Norwood London 28 B4
West Ogwell Devon 7 B6
West Orchard Dorset 13 C6
West Overton Wilts 25 C6
West Park Hrtlpl 111 F7
West Parley Dorset 13 E8
West Peckham Kent 29 D7
West Pelton Durham 110 D5
West Pennard Som 23 F7
West Pentire Corn 4 C2
West Perry Cambs 54 C2
West Putford Devon 9 C5
West Quantoxhead Som 22 E3
West Rainton Durham 111 E6
West Rasen Lincs 90 F4
West Raynham Norf 80 E4
West Retford Notts 89 F7
West Rounton N Yorks 102 D2
West Row Suff 55 B7
West Rudham Norf 80 E4
West Runton Norf 81 C7
West Saltoun E Loth 121 C7
West Sandwick Shetland 160 E6
West Scrafton N Yorks 101 F5
West Sleekburn Northumb 117 F8
West Somerton Norf 69 C7
West Stafford Dorset 12 F5
West Stockwith Notts 89 E8
West Stoke W Sus 16 D2
West Stonesdale N Yorks 100 D3
West Stoughton Som 23 E6
West Stour Dorset 13 B5
West Stourmouth Kent 31 C6
West Stow Suff 56 B2
West Stowell Wilts 25 C6
West Strathan Highld 157 C8
West Stratton Hants 26 E3
West Street Kent 30 D3
West Tanfield N Yorks 95 B5
West Taphouse Corn 5 C6
West Tarbert Argyll 145 G7
West Thirston Northumb 117 E7
West Thorney W Sus 15 D8
West Thurrock Thurrock 29 B6
West Tilbury Thurrock 29 B7
West Tisted Hants 15 B7
West Tofts Norf 67 E8
West Tofts Perth 133 F8
West Torrington Lincs 90 F5
West Town Hants 15 E8
West Town N Som 23 C6
West Tytherley Hants 14 B3
West Tytherton Wilts 24 B4
West Walton Norf 66 C4
West Walton Highway Norf 66 C4
West Wellow Hants 14 C3
West Wemyss Fife 128 E5
West Wick N Som 23 C5
West Wickham Cambs 55 E7
West Wickham London 28 C4
West Williamston Pembs 32 D1
West Willoughby Lincs 78 E2
West Winch Norf 67 C6
West Winterslow Wilts 25 F7
West Wittering W Sus 15 E8
West Witton N Yorks 101 F5
West Woodburn Northumb 116 F4
West Woodhay W Berks 25 C8
West Woodlands Som 24 E2
West Worldham Hants 26 F5
West Worlington Devon 10 C2
West Worthing W Sus 16 D5
West Wratting Cambs 55 D7
West Wycombe Bucks 39 E8
West Wylam Northumb 110 C4
West Yell Shetland 160 E6
Westacott Devon 20 F4
Westbere Kent 31 C5
Westborough Lincs 77 E8
Westbourne Bmouth 13 E8
Westbourne Suff 56 E5
Westbourne W Sus 15 D8
Westbrook W Berks 26 B2
Westbury Bucks 52 F4
Westbury Shrops 60 D3
Westbury Wilts 24 D3
Westbury Leigh Wilts 24 D3
Westbury-on-Severn Glos 36 C4
Westbury on Trym Bristol 23 B7
Westbury-sub-Mendip Som 23 E7
Westby Lancs 92 F3
Westcliff-on-Sea Southend 42 F4
Westcombe Som 23 F8
Westcote Glos 38 B2
Westcott Bucks 39 C7
Westcott Devon 10 D5
Westcott Sur 28 E2
Westcott Barton Oxon 38 B4
Westdean E Sus 18 F2
Westdene Brighton 17 D6
Wester Aberchalder Highld 137 B8
Wester Balgedie Perth 128 D3
Wester Culbeuchly Aberds 153 B6
Wester Dechmont W Loth 120 C3
Wester Denoon Angus 134 E3
Wester Fintray Aberds 141 C7
Wester Gruinards Highld 151 B8
Wester Lealty Highld 151 D9
Wester Milton Highld 151 F12
Wester Newburn Fife 129 D6
Wester Quarff Shetland 160 K6
Wester Skeld Shetland 160 J4
Westerdale Highld 158 E3
Westerdale N Yorks 102 D4
Westerfield Shetland 160 H5
Westerfield Suff 57 E5
Westergate W Sus 16 D3
Westerham Kent 28 D5
Westerhope T&W 110 C4
Westerleigh S Glos 23 B9
Westerton Angus 135 D6
Westerton Durham 110 F5
Westerton W Sus 16 D2
Westerwick Shetland 160 J4
Westfield Cumb 98 B1
Westfield E Sus 18 D5
Westfield Hereford 50 E2
Westfield Highld 158 D2
Westfield N Lanark 119 B7
Westfield Norf 68 D2
Westfield W Loth 120 B2
Westfields Dorset 12 D5
Westfields of Rattray Perth 134 E1
Westgate Durham 110 F2
Westgate N Lincs 89 D8
Westgate Norf 80 C4
Westgate Norf 81 C5
Westgate on Sea Kent 31 B7
Westhall Aberds 141 B5
Westhall Suff 69 F7
Westham Dorset 12 G4
Westham E Sus 18 E3
Westham Som 23 E6
Westhampnett W Sus 16 D2
Westhay Som 23 E6
Westhead Lancs 86 D2
Westhide Hereford 49 E7
Westhill Aberds 141 D7
Westhill Highld 151 G10
Westhope Hereford 49 D6
Westhope Shrops 60 F4
Westhorpe Lincs 78 F5
Westhorpe Suff 56 C4
Westhoughton Gtr Man 86 D4
Westhouse N Yorks 93 B6
Westhumble Sur 28 D2
Westing Shetland 160 C7
Westlake Devon 6 D4
Westleigh Devon 9 B6
Westleigh Devon 11 C5
Westleigh Gtr Man 86 D4
Westleton Suff 57 C8
Westley Shrops 60 D3
Westley Suff 56 C2
Westley Waterless Cambs 55 D7
Westlington Bucks 39 C7
Westlinton Cumb 108 C3
Westmarsh Kent 31 C6
Westmeston E Sus 17 C7
Westmill Herts 41 B6
Westminster London 28 B4
Westmuir Angus 134 D3
Westness Orkney 159 F4
Westnewton Cumb 107 E8
Westnewton Northumb 122 F5
Westoe T&W 111 C6
Weston Bath 24 C2
Weston Ches E 74 D4
Weston Devon 11 F6
Weston Dorset 12 G4
Weston Halton 86 F3
Weston Hants 15 B8
Weston Herts 54 F3
Weston Lincs 66 B2
Weston N Yorks 94 E4
Weston Northants 52 E3
Weston Notts 77 C7
Weston Shrops 61 B5
Weston Shrops 61 E5
Weston Staffs 62 B3
Weston W Berks 25 B8
Weston Beggard Hereford 49 E7
Weston by Welland Northants 64 E4
Weston Colville Cambs 55 D7
Weston Coyney Stoke 75 E6
Weston Favell Northants 53 C5
Weston Green Cambs 55 D7
Weston Green Norf 68 C4
Weston Heath Shrops 61 C7
Weston Hills Lincs 66 B2
Weston-in-Gordano N Som 23 B6
Weston Jones Staffs 61 B7
Weston Longville Norf 68 C4
Weston Lullingfields Shrops 60 B4
Weston-on-the-Green Oxon 39 C5
Weston-on-Trent Derbys 63 B8
Weston Patrick Hants 26 E4
Weston Rhyn Shrops 73 F6
Weston-Sub-Edge Glos 51 E6
Weston-super-Mare N Som 22 C5
Weston Turville Bucks 40 C1
Weston under Lizard Staffs 62 C2
Weston under Penyard Hereford 36 B3
Weston under Wetherley Warks 51 C8
Weston Underwood Derbys 76 E2
Weston Underwood M Keynes 53 D6
Westonbirt Glos 37 F5
Westoncommon Shrops 60 B4
Westoning C Beds 53 F8
Westonzoyland Som 23 F5
Westow N Yorks 96 C3
Westport Argyll 143 F7
Westport Som 11 C8
Westrigg W Loth 120 C2
Westruther Borders 122 E2
Westry Cambs 66 E3
Westville Notts 76 E5
Westward Cumb 108 E2
Westward Ho! Devon 9 B6
Westwell Kent 30 E3
Westwell Oxon 38 D2
Westwell Leacon Kent 30 E3
Westwick Cambs 54 C5
Westwick Durham 101 C5
Westwick Norf 81 E8
Westwood Devon 10 E5
Westwood Wilts 24 D3
Westwoodside N Lincs 89 E8
Wetheral Cumb 108 D4
Wetherby W Yorks 95 E7
Wetherden Suff 56 C4
Wetheringsett Suff 56 C5
Wethersfield Essex 55 F8
Wethersta Shetland 160 G5
Wetherup Street Suff 56 C5
Wetley Rocks Staffs 75 E6
Wettenhall Ches E 74 C3
Wetton Staffs 75 D8
Wetwang E Yorks 96 D5
Wetwood Staffs 74 F4
Wexcombe Wilts 25 D7
Wexham Street Bucks 40 F2
Weybourne Norf 81 C7
Weybread Suff 68 F5
Weybridge Sur 27 C8
Weycroft Devon 11 E8
Weydale Highld 158 D3
Weyhill Hants 25 E8
Weymouth Dorset 12 G4
Whaddon Bucks 53 F6
Whaddon Cambs 54 E4
Whaddon Glos 37 C5
Whaddon Wilts 14 B2
Whale Cumb 99 B7
Whaley Derbys 76 B5
Whaley Bridge Derbys 87 F8
Whaley Thorns Derbys 76 B5
Whaligoe Highld 158 F5
Whalley Lancs 93 F7
Whalton Northumb 117 F7
Wham N Yorks 93 C7
Whaplode Lincs 66 B3
Whaplode Drove Lincs 66 C3
Whaplode St Catherine Lincs 66 B3
Wharfe N Yorks 93 C7
Wharles Lancs 92 F4
Wharncliffe Side S Yorks 88 E3
Wharram le Street N Yorks 96 C4
Wharton Ches W 74 C3
Wharton Green Ches W 74 C3
Whashton N Yorks 101 D6
Whatcombe Dorset 13 D6
Whatcote Warks 51 E8
Whatfield Suff 56 E4
Whatley Som 11 D8
Whatley Som 24 E2
Whatlington E Sus 18 D4
Whatstandwell Derbys 76 D3
Whatton Notts 77 F7
Whauphill Dumfries 105 E8
Whaw N Yorks 100 D4
Wheatacre Norf 69 E7
Wheatcroft Derbys 76 D3
Wheathampstead Herts 40 C4
Wheathill Shrops 61 F6
Wheatley Devon 10 E4
Wheatley Hants 27 E5
Wheatley Oxon 39 D5
Wheatley S Yorks 89 D6
Wheatley W Yorks 87 B8
Wheatley Hill Durham 111 F6
Wheaton Aston Staffs 62 C2
Wheddon Cross Som 21 F8
Wheedlemont Aberds 140 B3
Wheelerstreet Sur 27 E7
Wheelock Ches E 74 D4
Wheelock Heath Ches E 74 D4
Wheelton Lancs 86 B4
Wheen Angus 134 B3
Wheldrake York 96 E2
Whelford Glos 38 E1
Whelpley Hill Herts 40 D2
Whempstead Herts 41 B6
Whenby N Yorks 96 C2
Whepstead Suff 56 D2
Wherstead Suff 57 E5
Wherwell Hants 25 E8
Wheston Derbys 75 B8
Whetsted Kent 29 E7
Whetstone Leics 64 E2
Whicham Cumb 98 F3
Whichford Warks 51 F8
Whickham T&W 110 C5
Whiddon Down Devon 9 E8
Whigstreet Angus 134 E4
Whilton Northants 52 C4
Whim Farm Borders 120 D5
Whimble Devon 9 D5
Whimple Devon 10 E5
Whimpwell Green Norf 69 B6
Whinburgh Norf 68 D3
Whinnieliggate Dumfries 106 D4
Whinnyfold Aberds 153 E10
Whippingham IoW 15 E6
Whipsnade C Beds 40 C3
Whipton Devon 10 E4
Whirlow S Yorks 88 F4
Whisby Lincs 78 C2
Whissendine Rutland 64 C5
Whissonsett Norf 80 E5
Whistlefield Argyll 145 D10
Whistlefield Argyll 145 D11
Whistley Green Wokingham 27 B5
Whiston Mers 86 E2
Whiston Northants 53 C6
Whiston S Yorks 88 F5
Whiston Staffs 62 C2
Whiston Staffs 75 E7
Whitbeck Cumb 98 F3
Whitbourne Hereford 50 D2
Whitburn T&W 111 C7
Whitburn W Loth 120 C2
Whitburn Colliery T&W 111 C7
Whitby Ches W 73 B7
Whitby N Yorks 103 C6
Whitbyheath Ches W 73 B7
Whitchurch Bath 23 C8
Whitchurch Bucks 39 B7
Whitchurch Cardiff 35 F5
Whitchurch Devon 6 B2
Whitchurch Hants 26 E2
Whitchurch Hereford 36 C2
Whitchurch Oxon 26 B4
Whitchurch Pembs 44 C2
Whitchurch Shrops 74 E2
Whitchurch Canonicorum Dorset 11 E8
Whitchurch Hill Oxon 26 B4
Whitcombe Dorset 12 F5
Whitcott Keysett Shrops 60 F2
White Coppice Lancs 86 C4
White Lackington Dorset 12 E5
White Ladies Aston Worcs 50 D4
White Lund Lancs 92 C4
White Mill Carms 33 B5
White Ness Shetland 160 J5
White Notley Essex 42 C3
White Pit Lincs 79 B6
White Post Notts 77 D6
White Rocks Hereford 35 B8
White Roding Essex 42 C1
White Waltham Windsor 27 B6
Whiteacen Moray 152 D2
Whiteacre Heath Warks 63 E6
Whitebridge Highld 137 C7
Whitebrook Mon 36 D2
Whiteburn Borders 121 E8
Whitecairn Dumfries 105 D6
Whitecairns Aberds 141 C8
Whitecastle S Lanark 120 E3
Whitechapel Lancs 93 E5
Whitecleat Orkney 159 H6
Whitecraig E Loth 121 B6
Whitecroft Glos 36 D3
Whitecross Corn 4 B4
Whitecross Falk 120 B2
Whitecross Staffs 62 B2
Whiteface Highld 151 C10
Whitefarland N Ayrs 143 D9
Whitefaulds S Ayrs 112 D2
Whitefield Gtr Man 87 D6
Whitefield Perth 134 F1
Whiteford Aberds 141 B6
Whitegate Ches W 74 C3
Whitehall Blackburn 86 B4
Whitehall W Sus 16 B5
Whitehall Village Orkney 159 F7
Whitehaven Cumb 98 C1
Whitehill Hants 27 F5
Whitehills Aberds 153 B6
Whitehills S Lanark 119 D6
Whitehough Derbys 87 F8
Whitehouse Aberds 140 C5
Whitehouse Argyll 145 G7
Whiteinch Glasgow 118 C5
Whitekirk E Loth 129 F7
Whitelaw S Lanark 119 E6
Whiteleas T&W 111 C6
Whiteley Bank IoW 15 F6
Whiteley Green Ches E 75 B6
Whiteley Village Sur 27 C8
Whitemans Green W Sus 17 B7
Whitemire Moray 151 F12
Whitemoor Corn 4 D4
Whitemore Staffs 75 C5
Whitenap Hants 14 B4
Whiteoak Green Oxon 38 C3
Whiteparish Wilts 14 B3
Whiterashes Aberds 141 B7
Whiterow Highld 158 F5
Whiteshill Glos 37 D5
Whiteside Northumb 109 C7
Whiteside W Loth 120 C2
Whitesmith E Sus 18 D2
Whitestaunton Som 11 C7
Whitestone Devon 10 E3
Whitestone Devon 20 E3
Whitestone Warks 63 F7
Whitestones Aberds 153 C8
Whitestreet Green Suff 56 F3
Whitewall Corner N Yorks 96 B3
Whiteway Glos 37 C6
Whiteway Glos 37 E5
Whitewell Aberds 153 B9
Whitewell Lancs 93 E6
Whitewell Bottom Lancs 87 B6
Whiteworks Devon 6 B4
Whitfield Kent 31 E7
Whitfield Northants 52 F4
Whitfield Northumb 109 D7
Whitfield S Glos 36 E3
Whitford Devon 11 E7
Whitford Flint 72 B5
Whitgift E Yorks 90 B2
Whitgreave Staffs 62 B2
Whithorn Dumfries 105 E8
Whiting Bay N Ayrs 143 F11
Whitkirk W Yorks 95 F6
Whitland Carms 32 C2
Whitletts S Ayrs 112 B3
Whitley N Yorks 89 B6
Whitley Reading 26 B5
Whitley Wilts 24 C3
Whitley Bay T&W 111 B6
Whitley Chapel Northumb 110 D2
Whitley Lower W Yorks 88 C3
Whitley Row Kent 29 D5
Whitlock's End W Mid 51 B6
Whitminster Glos 36 D4
Whitmore Staffs 74 E5
Whitnage Devon 10 C5
Whitnash Warks 51 C8
Whitney-on-Wye Hereford 48 E4
Whitrigg Cumb 108 D2
Whitrigg Cumb 108 F2
Whitsbury Hants 14 C2
Whitsome Borders 122 D4
Whitson Newport 35 F7
Whitstable Kent 30 C5
Whitstone Corn 8 E4
Whittingham Northumb 117 C6
Whittingslow Shrops 60 F4
Whittington Glos 37 B7
Whittington Lancs 93 B6
Whittington Norf 67 E7
Whittington Shrops 73 F7
Whittington Staffs 62 F2
Whittington Staffs 63 D5
Whittington Worcs 50 D3
Whittle-le-Woods Lancs 86 B3
Whittlebury Northants 52 E4
Whittlesey Cambs 66 E2
Whittlesford Cambs 55 E5
Whittlestone Head Blackburn 86 C5
Whitton Borders 116 B3
Whitton N Lincs 90 B3
Whitton Northumb 117 D6
Whitton Powys 48 C4
Whitton Shrops 49 B7
Whitton Stockton 102 B1
Whitton Suff 56 E5
Whittonditch Wilts 25 B7
Whittonstall Northumb 110 D3
Whitway Hants 26 D2
Whitwell Derbys 76 B5
Whitwell Herts 40 B4
Whitwell IoW 15 G6
Whitwell N Yorks 101 E7